Alternative Dispute Resolution

The International Library of Essays in Law and Legal Theory
Series Editor: Tom D. Campbell

Schools

Natural Law, Vols I & II *John Finnis*
Justice *Thomas Morawetz*
Law and Economics, Vols I & II *Jules Coleman and Jeffrey Lange*
Critical Legal Studies *James Boyle*
Marxian Legal Theory *Csaba Varga*
Legal Reasoning, Vols I & II *Aulis Aarnio and D. Neil MacCormick*
Legal Positivism *Mario Jori*
American Legal Theory *Robert Samuel Summers*
Postmodernism and Law *Dennis Patterson*
Law and History *David Sugarman*
Law and Language *Fred Schauer*
Sociological Theories of Law *Kahei Rokumoto*
Rights *Carlos Nino*
Law and Psychology *Martin Lyon Levine*
Feminist Legal Theory, Vols I & II *Frances Olsen*
Law and Society *Roger Cotterrell*
Contemporary Criminological Theory *Francis T. Cullen and Velmer S. Burton Jr.*

Areas

Criminal Law *Thomas Morawetz*
Tort Law *Ernest J. Weinrib*
Contract Law, Vols I & II *Larry Alexander*
Anti-Discrimination Law *Christopher McCrudden*
Consumer Law *Iain Ramsay*
International Law *Martti Koskenniemi*
Property Law, Vols I & II *Elizabeth Mensch and Alan Freeman*
Constitutional Law *Mark V. Tushnet*
Procedure *D.J. Galligan*
Evidence and Proof *William Twining and Alex Stein*
Company Law *Sally Wheeler*
Privacy, Vols I & II *Raymond Wacks*
Lawyers' Ethics *David J. Luban*
Administrative Law *D.J. Galligan*
Child Law *Harry D. Krause*
Family Law, Vols I & II *Harry D. Krause*
Welfare Law *Peter Robson*
Medicine and the Law *Bernard M. Dickens*
Commercial Law *Ross Cranston*
Environmental Law *Michael C. Blumm*
Conflict of Laws *Richard Fentiman*
Law and Religion *Wojciech Sadurski*
Human Rights Law *Philip Alston*
European Community Law, Vols I & II *Francis Snyder*
Tax Law, Vols I & II *Patricia D. White*
Media Law *Eric Barendt*
Labour Law *David L. Gregory*
Alternative Dispute Resolution *Michael D.A. Freeman*

Legal Cultures

Comparative Legal Cultures *Csaba Varga*
Law and Anthropology *Peter Sack*
Hindu Law and Legal Theory *Ved Nanda*
Islamic Law and Legal Theory *Ian Edge*
Chinese Law and Legal Theory *Michael Palmer*
Russian Legal Theory *W. Butler*
Common Law *Michael Arnheim*
Japanese Law and Legal Theory *Koichiro Fujikura*
Law and Development *Anthony Carty*
Jewish Law and Legal Theory *Martin P. Golding*
Legal Education *Martin Lyon Levine*
Civil Law *Ralf Rogowski*
African Law and Legal Theory *Gordon Woodman and Akintunde Obilade*

Future Volume
Cumulative index

Alternative Dispute Resolution

Edited by

Michael Freeman

University College London

NEW YORK UNIVERSITY PRESS
REFERENCE COLLECTION

First published in the U.S.A. in 1995 by
NEW YORK UNIVERSITY PRESS
Washington Square
New York NY 10003

Library of Congress Cataloging-in-Publication Data
Alternative dispute resolution / edited by Michael Freeman.
p. cm. — (International library of essays in law and legal theory. Areas ; 26)
Includes bibliographical references.
ISBN 0-8147-2636-4
1. Dispute resolution (Law) 2. Mediation. 3. Compromise (Law)
I. Freeman, Michael D. A. II. Series.
K2390.A84 1995
347'.09—dc20
[342.79] 95–7994
CIP

Contents

PART IV LEGAL SCHOLARSHIP AND ALTERNATIVE DISPUTE RESOLUTION

PART V THE QUALITY OF ALTERNATIVE DISPUTE RESOLUTION

Acknowledgements

The editor and publishers wish to thank the following for permission to use copyright material.

Blackwell Publishers for the essay: William Twining (1993), 'Alternative to What? Theories of Litigation, Procedure and Dispute Settlement in Anglo-American Jurisprudence: Some Neglected Classics', *Modern Law Review*, **56**, pp. 380–92.

Denver University Law Review for the essays: Susan Silbey and Austin Sarat (1989), 'Dispute Processing in Law and Legal Scholarship: From Institutional Critique to the Reconstruction of the Juridical Subject', *Denver University Law Review*, **66**, pp. 437–98; John P. Esser (1989), 'Evaluations of Dispute Processing: We Do Not Know What We Think and We Do Not Think What We Know', *Denver University Law Review*, **66**, pp. 499–543.

J.M. Eekelaar and S.N. Katz for the essay: Michael D.A. Freeman (1984), 'Questioning the Delegalization Movement in Family Law: Do We Really Want a Family Court?' in *The Resolution of Family Conflict*, pp. 7–25. Copyright © J.M. Eekelaar and S.N. Katz.

Harvard Law Review Association for the essay: Lon L. Fuller (1978), 'The Forms and Limits of Adjudication', *Harvard Law Review*, **92**, pp. 353–409.

Journal of Conflict Resolution for the essays: Vilhelm Aubert (1967), 'Courts and Conflict Resolution', *Journal of Conflict Resolution*, **11**, pp. 40–51; Vilhelm Aubert (1963), 'Competition and Dissensus: Two Types of Conflict and of Conflict Resolution', *Journal of Conflict Resolution*, **7**, pp. 26–42.

Sweet & Maxwell Limited for the essay: Ross Cranston (1986), 'What Do Courts Do?', *Civil Justice Quarterly*, **5**, pp. 123–43.

University of California Los Angeles Law Review and Fred B. Rothman & Co. for the essay: Carrie Menkel-Meadow (1984), 'Toward Another View of Legal Negotiation: The Structure of Problem Solving', *UCLA Law Review*, **31**, pp. 754–842. Copyright © 1984, The Regents of the University of California. All Rights Reserved.

University of Florida for the essay: Frank E.A. Sander (1985), 'Alternative Methods of Dispute Resolution: An Overview', *University of Florida Law Review*, **37**, pp. 1–18.

University of Southern California for the essay: Lon L. Fuller (1971), 'Mediation – Its Forms and Functions', *Southern California Law Review*, **44**, pp. 305–39. Reprinted with the permission of the Southern California Law Review.

The Yale Law Journal and Fred B. Rothman & Company for the essays: Laura Nader (1979), 'Disputing Without the Force of Law', *The Yale Law Journal*, **88**, pp. 998–1021; Owen M. Fiss (1984), 'Against Settlement', *The Yale Law Journal*, **93**, pp. 1073–90; Trina Grillo (1991), 'The Mediation Alternative: Process Dangers for Women', *The Yale Law Journal*, **100**, pp. 1545–1610.

Every effort has been made to trace all the copyright holders, but if any have been inadvertently overlooked the publishers will be pleased to make the necessary arrangement at the first opportunity.

Series Preface

The International Library of Law and Legal Theory is designed to provide important research materials in an accessible form. Each volume contains essays of central theoretical importance in its subject area. The series as a whole makes available an extensive range of valuable material which will be of considerable interest to those involved in the research, teaching and study of law.

The series has been divided into three sections. The Schools section is intended to represent the main distinctive approaches and topics of special concern to groups of scholars. The Areas section takes in the main branches of law with an emphasis on essays which present analytical and theoretical insights of broad application. The section on Legal Cultures makes available the distinctive legal theories of different legal traditions and takes up topics of general comparative and developmental concern.

I have been delighted and impressed by the way in which the editors of the individual volumes have set about the difficult task of selecting, ordering and presenting essays from the immense quantity of academic legal writing published in journals throughout the world. Editors were asked to pick out those essays from law, philosophy and social science journals which they consider to be fundamental for the understanding of law, as seen from the perspective of a particular approach or sphere of legal interest. This is not an easy task and many difficult decisions have had to be made in order to ensure that a representative sample of the best journal essays available takes account of the scope of each topic or school.

I should like to express my thanks to all the volume editors for their willing participation and scholarly judgement. The interest and enthusiasm which the project has generated is well illustrated by the fact that an original projection of 12 volumes drawn up in 1989 has now become a list of some 60 volumes. I must also acknowledge the vision, persistence and constant cheerfulness of John Irwin and the marvellous work done by Mrs Margaret O'Reilly and Sonia Hubbard.

TOM D. CAMPBELL
Series Editor
The Faculty of Law
The Australian National University

Introduction

Lawyers' interest in conflict and in conflict resolution was awakened by the Realist movement in the United States[1] and by anthropology.[2] Using the concept of 'dispute', or what Llewellyn and Hoebel called the 'trouble case',[3] scholars were able to shift their focus from the analysis of law as a system of rules[4] to the study of law as a process for handling trouble cases. But it was sociologists like Vilhelm Aubert[5] who provided the sort of analysis of conflict itself which made an understanding of different types of conflict resolution meaningful and, in particular, which related mediation and adjudication to different forms of conflict. His dichotomy between conflict of interests and conflict of values remains a key distinction.

There was a move away from the courts, though not necessarily from adjudication, in the early part of the century. This was seen in the development of tribunals[6] and arbitration[7]: it was also to some extent reflected in the development of the 'commercial court'[8] and the juvenile court.[9] But it is only really in the 1980s that the alternative dispute resolution movement has taken off.[10] That it has done so can be related to court congestion, what Galanter[11] has called a 'litigation explosion', to too much law or 'hyperlexis'[12] on the one hand, and to anti-professionalism on the other. As Silbey and Sarat explain: 'ADR is part of a continuing contest over the dominance of courts in the apparatus of state law'.[13] De Sousa Santos relates it to the promise to extend the realm of self-government and 'real' community.[14]

There is no generally accepted abstract or theoretical definition of ADR as such. A convenient starting point, however, is that posited by Lieberman and Henry. It is, they suggest, 'a set of practices and techniques that aim (1) to permit legal disputes to be resolved outside the courts for the benefit of all disputants; (2) to reduce the cost of conventional litigation and the delays to which it is ordinarily subject; or (3) to prevent legal disputes that would otherwise likely be brought to the courts'.[15] Of course, it is true that courts do not decide most disputes anyway. So, as Sander acknowledges in Chapter 4, the argument for 'alternatives' is not based on the need to find a substitute for court adjudication. 'Rather, it is based on the need to gain a better understanding of the functioning of these alternative mechanisms and processes.'

It is therefore important, as Galanter argues, not to be 'distracted by the fiction of a radical split between ADR and "traditional adjudication"'.[16] For '[m]ost ADR is not located in autonomous institutions that operate independently of the norms and sanctions of the legal system. Instead, ADR is typically situated near legal institutions and dependent upon legal norms and sanctions.'[17] It is far too easy to assume that ADR and adjudication are located in their own distinct and discrete normative worlds. Perhaps this is, as Galanter points out, part of the 'mythology' of the partisans of each, but the truth is closer to one of 'pervasive' continuity.[18]

There are, nevertheless, real distinctions between different processes of conflict resolution, as the appended tables usefully illustrate. Ury, Brett and Goldberg distinguish among the different processes in terms of whether the aim is to reconcile the disputants' underlying interests, determine who is right, or determine who is more powerful.[19] Reconciling interests typically occurs during negotiation processes, including those involved where the dyad has become a triad[20] (mediation). It involves 'probing for deep-seated concerns, devising creative solutions and making trade-offs'.[21] The paradigmatic rights-focused procedure is adjudication. Some negotiation is power-based, where there is 'an exchange of threats'.[22] Strikes and war are other examples of power procedures. As Ury, Brett and Goldberg point out, 'reconciling interests is less costly than determining who is right'[23] but, as they also acknowledge, determining who is more powerful may cost even less.

This draws attention to one aspect of the differences only. Mediation and adjudication may also be distinguished in terms of the control the disputants exercise over the process of resolution. Where there is negotiation, the parties can control both the process and the solution. If they bring in a third party, a mediator, they lose some control over the process but they may retain some power over the solution. The mediator assists disputants to arrive at their own solution. The adjudicator, by contrast, imposes a solution on the parties. S/he may be a judge – in which case it is abnormal for the disputants to have any choice in who that person will be – or an arbitrator. Arbitrators, like many but not all mediators, are likely to have specialized subject expertise: judges do not always have this.

It is an acknowledged virtue of mediation that it is forward-looking, that it looks to the future and to resolutions which promote relationships in trouble. It is perhaps for this reason that cultures which put a premium upon community (Japan[24] or the Lozi[25]) have emphasized processes of dispute resolution that promote cohesion. Equally, it is not surprising that ADR should first appear prominently in areas where adjudication is prone to disrupt or distort continuing relationships – the family,[26] labour relations[27] and long-standing business transactions.[28] Adjudication which, as Aubert points out in Chapter 6, metamorphises simple conflicts of interest into conflicts of value, is backward-looking: actions and events are measured against a normative standard, with one disputant held to be in the right, the other in the wrong. Relationships as such are no business of adjudication and rarely perhaps survive it. Think of the difference between a divorce mediation, which at the least may preserve parent-child relationships and at best ensure a civilized untangling of bonds, with the stereotypical adversarial adjudication which judges and destroys. Adjudication can apportion responsibility (it can work with a modern concept like contributory negligence), but it usually operates on a mini-max principle. And if, as in England, the system of adjudication operates on the basis that the loser of the litigation pays the winner's costs, this problem is accentuated.[29]

It may be said, then, that mediation and adjudication have different goals and certainly they can have different effects. An adjudication leaves its mark on the legal and social order. It results in a reasoned judgment, in most cases given in public and often published. It constitutes a precedent which of course is a consideration of greater importance in common law countries than elsewhere. It has an immediate impact upon the parties and a longer-term effect upon the public. Mediation, by contrast, is a private affair. Even if bargaining takes place in the 'shadow' of the law,[30] mediators are less likely to be distracted by the shadow which the law casts over the dispute.[31] They can look at the complete picture, unconstrained by the narrow parameters imposed by legal doctrine (see Chapter 8). Adjudicators are limited in the type of solutions which they can reach: mediators are not necessarily so constrained and can search for creative solutions that no court or arbitrator could impose – for example, a re-negotiation of a contract.

The context within which adjudication takes place is also very different from the mediation setting. Adjudication tends to be formalized and highly structured, with strict procedural stages and steps. What evidence can be put to the courts is controlled. Mediation, by contrast, is informal and unstructured. There are no constraints on the presentation of evidence or argument. Adjudicators have the power of the state behind them: their judgments can be enforced. The results of a mediation can only be enforced if they can be conceptualized as an agreement and therefore enforced as a contract.

It is easy to enthuse over ADR processes like mediation. Indeed, some have wondered why people still go to court and have come up with answers like 'verification demands lawsuits' (see Chapter 3 by Aubert, p. 89). But ADR has its critics too. Owen Fiss, for example, argues that by diverting cases from courts, society loses the benefit of court-sanctioned judgments. Thus he writes:

> [The courts'] job is not to maximize the ends of private parties, nor simply to secure the peace, but to explicate and give force to the values embodied in authoritative texts such as the Constitution and statutes: to interpret those values and to bring reality into accord with them. This duty is not discharged when the parties settle (Chapter 9, p. 297).

Fiss also argues that ADR is used to prevent an activist state from meddling with private economic interests, and he maintains that resolution of disputes out of court lacks the legitimacy of cases which are fully adjudicated to judgment. But, of course, not even the most enthusiastic advocate of ADR believes that every dispute has an ADR solution: in countries such as the United States where the courts are guardians of the Constitution, they have a role which ADR cannot possibly usurp. No one[32] would have wanted *Brown* v *Board of Education*[33] to have been resolved by mediation. Nor is ADR the prerogative or privilege only of powerful economic interests. Whether, as Lieberman and Henry say in their riposte to Fiss, an 'open society needs the tension of open questions'[34] (in other words that not all questions need to be answered) is more politically contentious.

Mediation has attracted criticism from feminists as well. Grillo[35] in Chapter 10, Bryan,[36] Lerman,[37] Astor[38] and others[39] are concerned about the impact on women, in particular but not exclusively, where mediation is used to resolve problems which have arisen out of an abusive relationship. With mediation – in practice, possibly compulsory mediation – set to feature prominently in the divorce process of England,[40] the issue is an important one. A US Civil Rights Commission report on legal responses to domestic violence encapsulated the problem as follows:

> Mediation and arbitration place the parties on equal footing and ask them to negotiate an agreement for future behaviour. Beyond failing to punish assailants for their crimes, this process implies that victims share responsibility for the illegal conduct and requires them to modify their own behaviour in exchange for the assailants' promises not to commit further crimes.[41]

Many structural aspects of mediation have been criticized as ill-suited to the problems presented within the context of domestic violence. Lerman summarizes these as 'the summary nature of mediation, the lack of accountability, the failure to account for the parties' vastly unequal bargaining power, and the use of mediation to bar women from access to courts for enforceable protection from future violence or punishment of the abuser for past violence'.[42] It is uncontentious that violence (but, of course, not only violence) does create an extreme imbalance of power between the parties. Astor makes the point cogently:

> People do not simply come to mediation as independent units, the bearers of more or less of any of the sources of power. They come to mediation (perhaps most particularly to family mediation) in the context of a relationship which has its own history, habits and patterns, including patterns of the exercise of power and control. ... A relationship where there has been violence is very far from a relationship of equals. It is a relationship where the perpetrator has used violence to ensure compliance by the target of his violence. This relationship, with its habits of coercion and compliance, is brought to mediation.[43]

Mediation is often portrayed as having the capacity to remove conflict and reconstitute at least some of the functions of the ideal family. Martha Fineman notes the way in which mediators describe divorce, not as the termination of a marital relationship, but 'as a process which, through mediation, restructures and reformulates the spouses' relationship'.[44] Mediation is claimed to have the capacity to preserve the family unit for the children. Thus proponents can argue that, 'as mediation continues to develop, integrative work is being done that is blending family therapy objectives with family mediation'.[45] And this, we are told, leads to the awareness that 'both parents from broken marriages continue to function in important ways in the lives of their children...'[45] But, as Geffner and Pagelow note:

> [W]omen in general, and battered women in particular, are typically the primary caretakers of the children before and after divorce, and they have great fear of losing custody, while the batterer has nothing to lose by requesting custody as a bargaining and power tactic. Batterers have already demonstrated their willingness to use violence as a response to anger, stress or frustration, and to control the behaviour of others. ... Thus, the children in these cases are at risk of being abused after divorce even if they have not been abused before.[47]

It is therefore not surprising that statutes in some American states (Minnesota,[48] Massachusetts,[49] Maine,[50] North Dakota[51]) prohibit mediation for child custody and visitation cases involving alleged spousal violence.[52]

A premise of the ADR is that it is better than traditional adjudicative processes, that the results of ADR are often superior to court judgments. Properly designed ADR processes make it more likely, so it is said, that settlement decisions will be based on the merits of the dispute. If the impetus for ADR comes variously from a desire to reduce costs and delay, to provide accessibility for people with disputes, to encourage resolutions suited to parties' needs, to improve the public's satisfaction with the justice system or to strengthen neighbourhood ties and community values – and all of these feature in commonly-set objectives – how successful is ADR? Can we measure success in such terms and, if so, how?

Some of these hypotheses have begun to be tested. The work of Merry and Milner is particularly interesting.[53] In 1976 the San Francisco Community Boards programme was launched to strengthen urban neighbourhood ties and to find an alternative to the public justice system. Turning its back on courts, lawyers and the adversarial process, it developed a mediation programme and instituted a well-respected training programme for volunteer mediators. But Merry and Milner's research found no evidence that the programme achieved the desired neighbourhood changes. Indeed, with a half-million dollar annual budget, the boards still mediated only about 100 cases a year.

Debates about quality are inevitable. As Esser notes in Chapter 14, 'published evaluations of dispute processing programs are now so numerous that it is difficult for the average scholar, policy-maker or practitioner to locate, read or digest them all' (p. 470). But, as Esser demonstrates, evaluation is even more difficult than it might first seem. For a start, those involved in ADR programmes have different agendas (compare, for example, court administrators concerned with issues like time and cost with practitioners whose concern is that traditional adjudication constitutes an institutional barrier to the provision of equal access to justice). It would be easier to evaluate ADR and its programmes if there were a general consensus about what those programmes were supposed to achieve and, indeed, the alternatives to which they should be compared. But no such consensus exists. Measurement problems are a reflection of differences in values.

Whilst acknowledging then that the findings which emerge lack the status of fully-fledged 'facts', some conclusions, tentative perhaps, can be drawn. Tyler puts it this way:

> First, alternative resolution programs can be implemented in ways that will lower costs to disputants and to the court system. Such gains, when found, however, are small. Of central importance to the cost question is the desire of those in positions of authority to cut costs. If there is such a desire, many approaches can be taken to achieving that objective. Alternative dispute resolution procedures are one such approach.
>
> The timeliness of dispute resolution can also be enhanced by the use of alternative dispute resolution procedures and through changes in adjudication procedures. It is not clear whether one of these approaches is intrinsically better than another. In addition, such gains will not occur automatically. Rather, whether such gains occur depends on the effective implementation of innovative programs.
>
> Perhaps the most striking aspect of alternative dispute resolution programs which emerges from evaluations is the general popularity of ADR programs. People typically seem satisfied with informal dispute resolution efforts, often more so than with traditional adjudication, and generally feel committed to the decisions reached in them. Compliance is also as high or higher with decisions following such sessions, as with decisions reached in adjudications. Having the opportunity to present one's complaints and work towards a solution in an informal setting is clearly highly valued by disputants and leads to positive feelings.[54]

Conclusions such as these can at best be tentative. The danger is that any reservations will be overlooked by policy-makers whose agendas include jettisoning traditional procedures. Those too have their value, though assessing such impenetrables as the 'rule of law' may be even more difficult. The debate is set to continue for some considerable time yet.

Notes

1 In particular by the writings of Karl Llewellyn. See William Twining (1973), *Karl Llewellyn and the Realist Movement*, London: Weidenfeld and Nicolson (see particularly the discussion of his 'law-jobs' theory at pp. 175–94).

2 See Simon Roberts (1979), *Order and Dispute*, Harmondsworth: Penguin; Laura Nader (1969), *Law in Culture and Society*, Chicago: Aldine Press.

3 K. Llewellyn and E.A. Hoebel (1941), *The Cheyenne Way*, Norman: University of Oklahoma Press; E.A. Hoebel (1954), *The Law of Primitive Man*, Cambridge, Mass: Harvard University Press; K. Llewellyn (1940), 'The Normative, the Legal and the Law – Jobs: The Problem of Juristic

Method', *Yale Law Journal*, **49**, 1355–1400.
4 The paradigm has not, of course, entirely shifted. See H.L.A. Hart (1961), *The Concept of Law*, Oxford: Clarendon Press (revised edition, 1994).
5 See Chapters 6 and 3 in this volume.
6 Sir William Wade and Christopher Forsyth (1994), *Administrative Law*, Oxford: Clarendon Press (7th ed.), ch. 23.
7 See Robert B. Ferguson (1980), 'The Adjudication of Commercial Disputes and the Legal System in Modern England', *British Journal of Law and Society*, **7**, 141–57.
8 See A.D. Colman (1986), *The Practice and Procedure of the Commercial Court* (2nd ed.), London: Butterworths, ch. 1.
9 Anthony Platt (1977), *The Child Savers: The Invention of Delinquency*, Chicago: University of Chicago Press.
10 See Richard Abel (1982), *The Politics of Informal Justice*, New York: Academic Press (2 vols). For an historical perspective, see Jerold S. Auerbach (1983), *Justice without Law?*, New York: Oxford University Press. Marc Galanter (1983), 'Reading the Landscape of Disputes', *UCLA Law Review*, **31**, 4–71.
11 Marc Galanter (1986), 'The Day After the Litigation Explosion', *Maryland Law Review*, **36**, 3–39; also Marc Galanter (1983), op cit, note 10.
12 See Chapter 13, at p. 409.
13 *Ibid*, p. 408.
14 Boaventura de Sousa Santos (1982), 'Law and Community: The Changing Nature of State Power in Late Capitalism' in Richard Abel (ed.), *The Politics of Informal Justice*, New York: Academic Press, 249 at 265 (vol. 1).
15 Jethro K. Lieberman and James F. Henry (1986), 'Lessons from the Alternative Dispute Resolution Movement', *University of Chicago Law Review*, **53**, 424–39 at pp. 425–26.
16 Marc Galanter (1986), 'Compared to What? Assessing the Quality of Disputes Processing', *Denver University Law Review*, **66**, xi–xiv, at p. xiii.
17 *Idem*.
18 *Idem*.
19 William Ury, Jeanne Brett and Stephen Goldberg (1988), *Getting Disputes Resolved: Designing the System to Cut the Costs of Conflict*, San Francisco: Josey-Bass.
20 See Chapter 6.
21 Ury, Brett and Goldberg, p. 6.
22 *Ibid*, p. 8.
23 *Ibid*, p. 15.
24 See Takeyoshi Kawashima (1964), 'Dispute Resolution in Contemporary Japan' in Arthur Taylor von Mehren (ed.), *Law in Japan: The Legal Order of a Changing Society*, Tokyo: Charles F. Tuttle, 41–52.
25 See Max Gluckman (1955), *The Judicial Process among the Barotse of Northern Rhodesia*, Manchester: Manchester University Press.
26 See Lon Fuller's comment in Chapter 5 that the continuing relationship aspect of family controversies often necessitates 'person-oriented' rather than 'act-oriented' interventions.
27 See Lord Amulee (1929), *Industrial Arbitration in Great Britain*, London: Oxford University Press. See also Paul Davies and Mark Freedland (1983), *Kahn-Freund's Labour and the Law*, London: Stevens, pp. 128–40, and Julius G. Getman (1979), 'Labour Arbitration and Dispute Resolution', *Yale Law Journal*, **88**, 916–49.
28 See Stewart Macaulay (1963), 'Non-Contractual Relations in Business: A Preliminary Study', *American Sociological Review*, **28**, 55–67.
29 Some of the problems of this were pointed out by the Law Society (of England and Wales) as long ago as 1963: see (1963–1964), 'The Indemnity Rule in Litigation' in *Law Society Annual Report*, 73.
30 In the memorable phrase of Robert Mnookin and Lewis Kornhauser (1979), 'Bargaining in the Shadow of the Law: The Case of Divorce', *Yale Law Journal*, **88**, 950–97. But cf. Herbert Jacob (1992), 'The Elusive Shadow of the Law', *Law and Society Review*, **26**, 565–90.

31 Robert Cooter, Stephen Marks and Robert Mnookin (1982), 'Bargaining in the Shadow of the Law: A Testable Model of Strategic Behaviour', *Journal of Legal Studies*, **11**, 225–51.
32 Though it is the fact that a similar dispute in the UK would employ, at least initially, a mediation-type model.
33 347 US 483 (1954). See also Lauren B. Edelman, Howard S. Erlanger and John Lande (1993), 'Internal Dispute Resolution: The Transformation of Civil Rights in the Workplace', *Law and Society Review*, **27**, 497–534 where ADR is shown to undermine legal rights by de-emphasizing and depoliticizing workplace discrimination.
34 Lieberman and Henry (1986), note 15 above, p. 434.
35 For a reply to Grillo, see Joshua D. Rosenberg (1991), 'In Defense of Mediation', *Arizona Law Review*, **33**, 467–507.
36 Penelope Bryan (1992), 'Killing Us Softly: Divorce Mediation and the Politics of Power', *Buffalo Law Review*, **40**, 441–523. See also her article (1994), 'Reclaiming Professionalism: The Lawyer's Role in Divorce Mediation', *Family Law Quarterly*, **28**, 177–222.
37 Lisa Lerman (1984), 'Mediation of Wife Abuse Cases: The Adverse Impact of Informal Dispute Resolution on Women', *Harvard Women's Law Journal*, **7**, 57–113.
38 Hilary Astor (1990), 'Domestic Violence and Mediation', *Australian Dispute Resolution Journal*, **1**, 143–66.
39 Martha Fineman (1988), 'Dominant Discourse, Professional Language and Legal Change in Child Custody Decision Making', *Harvard Law Review*, **101**, 727–74. Karla Fischer, Neil Vidmar and René Ellis (1993), 'The Culture of Battering and the Role of Mediation in Domestic Violence Cases', *Southern Methodist University Law Review*, **46**, 2117–2174.
40 Lord Chancellor's Office (1993), *Looking to the Future: Mediation and the Ground for Divorce* (Cm. 2424), London: HMSO.
41 Quoted in Lerman (1984), note 37 above, p. 71.
42 *Ibid*, p. 72.
43 Hilary Astor (1994), 'Swimming Against the Tide: Keeping Violent Men out of Mediation' in Julie Stubbs (ed.), *Women, Male Violence and the Law*, Sydney: Federation Press, 147–73, at p. 151.
44 Fineman (1988), note 39 above, p. 732.
45 Barbara Landau, Mario Bartoletti and Ruth Mesbur (1987), *Family Mediation Handbook*, Toronto: Butterworths, p. 183.
46 Idem.
47 Robert Geffner and Mildred Pagelow (1990), 'Mediation and Child Custody in Abusive Relationships', *Behavioral Science and the Law*, **8**, at pp. 152–53.
48 Minn. Stat. Ann. §518, 619.
49 Mass. Gen. Laws, ch. 209A, §2.
50 Me. Rev. Stat. Ann. tit 19, §768. On Maine more generally, see Craig A. McEwen, Richard J. Maiman and Lynn Mather (1994), 'Lawyers, Mediation and the Management of Divorce Practice', *Law and Society Review*, **28**, 149–86.
51 N.D. Cent. Cod §14 09.1–02.
52 Others impose restrictions. For instance, California does not require the parties to attend sessions together, and the alleged victim can be assigned a court-paid advocate. See Cal. Civil Code §§4351.6, 4607.2.
53 Sally Engle Merry and Neal Milner (1993), *Popular Justice, Social Transformation and the Ideology of Community: Perspectives on Community Mediation*, Ann Arbor: University of Michigan Press.
54 Tom R. Tyler (1989), 'The Quality of Dispute Resolution Procedure and Outcomes: Measurement Problems and Possibilities', *Denver University Law Review*, **66**, 419–36, at pp. 435–36.

Appendix

Table A.1 'Primary' Dispute Resolution Processes

Characteristics	*Adjudication*	*Arbitration**	*Mediation*	*Negotiation*
Voluntary/ Involuntary	Involuntary	Voluntary	Voluntary	Voluntary
Binding/ Nonbinding	Binding: subject to appeal	Binding, subject to review on limited grounds	If agreement, enforceable as contract	If agreement, enforceable as contract
Third party	Imposed, third-party neutral decisionmaker, generally with no specialized expertise in dispute subject	Party-selected third-party decisionmaker, often with specialized subject expertise	Party-selected outside facilitator	No third-party facilitator
Degree of formality	Formalized and highly structured by predetermined, rigid rules	Procedurally less formal; procedural rules and substantive law may be set by parties	Usually informal, unstructured	Usually informal, unstructured
Nature of proceeding	Opportunity for each party to present proofs and arguments	Opportunity for each party to present proofs and arguments	Unbounded presentation of evidence, arguments and interests	Unbounded presentation of evidence, arguments and interests
Outcome	Principled decision, supported by reasoned opinion	Sometimes principled decision supported by reasoned opinion; sometimes compromise without opinion	Mutually acceptable agreement sought	Mutually acceptable agreement sought
Private/ Public	Public	Private, unless judicial review sought	Private	Private

*Court-annexed arbitration is involuntary, nonbinding, and public.

Source: Stephen B. Goldberg, Frank E.A. Sander, Nancy H. Rogers (eds) (1992), *Dispute Resolution: Negotiation, Mediation and Other Processes*, 2nd edn, Boston: Little Brown, pp. 4–5.

Table A.2 'Hybrid' Dispute Resolution Processes

Characteristics	*Private Judging*	*Neutral Expert Fact-Finding*	*MiniTrial*	*Ombudsman*	*Summary Jury Trial*
Voluntary/ Involuntary	Voluntary	Voluntary or involuntary under FRE 706	Voluntary	Voluntary	Voluntary or involuntary;
Binding/ Nonbinding	Binding, subject to appeal	Nonbinding, but results may be admissible	If agreement, enforceable as contract	Nonbinding	Nonbinding
Third party	Party-selected third-party decisionmaker, may have to be former judge or lawyer	Third-party neutral with specialized subject matter expertise; may be selected by the parties or the court	Party-selected neutral advisor, sometimes with specialized subject expertise	Third-party selected by institution	Mock jury impaneled by court
Degree of formality	Statutory procedure but highly flexible as to timing, place and procedures	Informal	Less formal than adjudication; procedural rules may be set by parties	Informal	Procedural rules fixed; less formal than adjudication
Nature of proceeding	Opportunity for each party to present proofs and arguments	Investigatory	Opportunity and responsibility to present summary proofs and arguments	Investigatory	Opportunity for each side to present summary proofs and arguments
Outcome	Principled decision, sometimes supported by findings of fact and conclusions of law	Report or testimony	Mutually acceptable agreement sought	Report	Advisory verdict
Private/ Public	Private, unless judicial enforcement sought	Private, unless disclosed in court	Private	Private	Usually public;

Source: See Table A.1.

Part I
The Courts and Dispute Resolution

[1]

THE FORMS AND LIMITS OF ADJUDICATION

*Lon L. Fuller**

Special Editor's Note

The initial version of The Forms and Limits of Adjudication *was circulated to the members of the Legal Philosophy Discussion Group at Harvard Law School in 1957. A revised and expanded version was prepared in 1959 for use in Mr. Fuller's course in Jurisprudence and for discussion at the Round Table on Jurisprudence at the 1959 meeting of the Association of American Law Schools. Further refinements resulted in a third version for classroom use in 1961; I have followed that version here.*

The editing has consisted principally of minor grammatical corrections and changes of punctuation; the addition of several paragraphs in Part VI, section 2 (see note 22); and the identification, where possible, of important references and sources, which are inserted in brackets. I am deeply grateful to Mrs. Marjorie Fuller, who made it possible for me to examine the library and private papers of her late husband.

The complete essay has never before been published, but portions of it were included in two articles by Mr. Fuller: Adjudication and the Rule of Law, 54 PROC. AM. SOC'Y INT'L L. 1 (1960) *and* Collective Bargaining and the Arbitrator, 1963 WIS. L. REV. 3. *Mr. Fuller also granted permission for the printing of a substantial part of the essay in* AMERICAN COURT SYSTEMS: READINGS IN JUDICIAL PROCESS AND BEHAVIOR (S. Goldman & A. Sarat eds. 1978). *That Mr. Fuller never published the entire essay is due, I believe, to a plan he formulated in 1958 or 1959 to expand it into a book of the same title. By 1960 the projected volume had become* The Principles of Social Order, *an essay in eunomics — that is, in Mr. Fuller's words, "the theory of good order and workable arrangements." Though Mr. Fuller was subsequently diverted from this project, it embodied what one can see retrospectively was the central preoccupation of his writings during the 1960's and early 1970's.*

Kenneth I Winston **

I. THE PROBLEMS TOWARD WHICH THIS ESSAY IS ADDRESSED

THE subject matter of this essay is adjudication in the very broadest sense. As the term is used here it includes a father attempting to assume the role of judge in a dispute between his children over possession of a toy. At the other extreme it embraces the most formal and even awesome exercises of adjudicative power: a Senate trying the impeachment of a President, a Supreme Court sitting in judgment on the powers of the govern-

* Late Carter Professor of General Jurisprudence, Harvard Law School. A.B., Stanford 1924; J.D., 1926.

** Associate Professor of Philosophy, Wheaton College (Mass.); Lecturer on Education, Harvard University.

ment of which it is a part, an international tribunal deciding a dispute between nations, a faculty of law — in former centuries — undertaking to judge the rival claims of kings and popes, the Congregation of Rites of the Roman Catholic Church hearing the arguments pro and con in a procedure for canonization.

As the term adjudication is used here its application is not restricted to tribunals functioning as part of an established government. It includes adjudicative bodies which owe their powers to the consent of the litigants expressed in an agreement of submission, as in labor relations and in international law. It also includes tribunals that assume adjudicative powers without the sanction either of consent or of superior governmental power, the most notable example being the court that sat in the Nuremberg Trials.

The problems that are the concern of this paper are those suggested by the two terms of the title, the *forms* and *limits* of adjudication. By speaking of the *limits* of adjudication I mean to raise such questions as the following: What kinds of social tasks can properly be assigned to courts and other adjudicative agencies? What are the lines of division that separate such tasks from those that require an exercise of executive power or that must be entrusted to planning boards or public corporations? What tacit assumptions underlie the conviction that certain problems are inherently unsuited for adjudicative disposition and should be left to the legislature? More generally, to borrow the title of a famous article by Roscoe Pound, what are the limits of effective legal action? [1] — bearing in mind that legislative determinations often can only become effective if they are of such a nature that they are suited for judicial interpretation and enforcement.

By the *forms* of adjudication I refer to the ways in which adjudication may be organized and conducted. For example, in labor relations and in international law we encounter a hybrid form called "tripartite arbitration" in which a "public" or "impartial" arbitrator sits flanked by arbitrators appointed by the interested parties. Such a deviation from the ordinary organization of adjudication presents such questions as: What, if any, are its proper uses? What are its peculiar limits and dangers? Other deviational forms present less subtle questions, such as Judge Bridlegoose's decisions by a throw of the dice.[2] In general the questions posed for consideration are: What are the permissible variations in the forms of adjudication? When has its nature

[1] [Pound, *The Limits of Effective Legal Action*, 3 A.B.A.J. 55 (1917).]

[2] [3 F. Rabelais, The Histories of Gargantua and Pantagruel ch. 39 (J.M. Cohen trans. 1955).]

been so altered that we are compelled to speak of an "abuse" or a "perversion" of the adjudicative process?

Questions of the permissible forms and the proper limits of adjudication have probably been under discussion ever since something equivalent to a judicial power first emerged in primitive society. In our own history the Supreme Court at an early date excluded from its jurisdiction certain issues designated as "political." This exclusion could hardly be said to rest on any principle made explicit in the Constitution; it was grounded rather in a conviction that certain problems by their intrinsic nature fall beyond the proper limits of adjudication, though how these problems are to be defined remains even today a subject for debate. In international law one of the most significant issues lies in the concept of "justiciability." Similar problems recur in labor relations, where the proper role of the arbitrator has always been a matter in active dispute.

It is in the field of administrative law that the issues dealt with in this paper become most acute. An official charged with allocating television channels wants to know of one applicant "what kind of fellow he really is" and accepts an invitation to a leisurely chat over the luncheon table. The fact of this meeting is disclosed by a crusading legislator. The official is accused of an abuse of judicial office. Charges and countercharges fill the air and before the debate is over it appears that nearly everyone concerned with the agency's functioning has in some measure violated the proprieties that attach to a discharge of judicial functions. In the midst of this murky argument few are curious enough to ask whether the tasks assigned to such agencies as the Federal Communications Commission (FCC) and the Civil Aeronautics Board (CAB) are really suited for adjudicative determination, whether, in other words, they fall within the proper limits of adjudication. No one seems inclined to take up the line of thought suggested by a remark of James M. Landis to the effect that the CAB is charged with what is essentially a managerial job, unsuited to adjudicative determination or to judicial review.[3]

The purpose of this Article is to offer an analysis that may be helpful in answering questions like those posed in the preceding paragraphs. Now it is apparent that any analysis of this sort, transcending as it does so many conventional boundaries, will be meaningless if it does not rest on some concept equivalent to "true adjudication." For if there is no such thing as "true adjudica-

---

[3] [*See* J.M. Landis, Report on Regulatory Agencies to the President-Elect 41–45 (December 1960), *reprinted in* SUBCOMM. ON ADMINISTRATIVE PRACTICE AND PROCEDURE, SENATE COMM. ON THE JUDICIARY, 81ST CONG., 2D SESS., REPORT ON REGULATORY AGENCIES TO THE PRESIDENT-ELECT 41–45 (Comm. Print 1960).]

tion," then it becomes impossible to distinguish the uses and abuses of adjudication. Yet it is unfortunately also true that any suggestion of a notion like "true adjudication" goes heavily against the grain of modern thought. Today it is a mark of intellectual liberation to realize that there is and can be no such thing as "true science," "true religion," "true education," or "true adjudication." "It is all a matter of definition." The modern professional university philosopher is particularly allergic to anything suggesting the doctrine of essence and takes it as a sure sign of philosophic illiteracy when a writer speaks of "the essence of art" or "the essence of democracy."

Yet we must examine critically the implications of this rejection. Does it imply, for example, that international lawyers are talking nonsense when they discuss the question of what kinds of disputes between nations are suited to decision by a tribunal? Are students of labor relations engaged in mere verbal shadow-boxing when they ask how an arbitration should be conducted and what sorts of questions arbitrators are fitted to decide? Do those engaged in discussions of this sort deceive themselves in believing that they are engaged in a rational inquiry? Surely if adjudication is subject to a reasoned analysis in a particular context, there is no a priori reason for supposing that the context cannot be expanded so that adjudication becomes the object of a more general analysis.

A.D. Lindsay once observed that it is scarcely possible to talk intelligently about social institutions without recognizing that they exist *because* and *insofar as* men pursue certain goals or ideals.[4] The ideals that keep a social institution alive and functioning are never perceived with complete clarity, so that even if there is no failure of good intentions, the existent institution will never be quite what it might have been had it been supported by a clearer insight into its guiding principles. As Lindsay remarks, quoting Charley Lomax in Shaw's *Major Barbara*, there is a certain amount of tosh about the Salvation Army. Surely there is a good deal of tosh — that is, superfluous rituals, rules of procedure without clear purpose, needless precautions preserved through habit — in the adjudicative process as we observe it in this country. Our task is to separate the tosh from the essential. If in undertaking that task we go counter to a deeply held modern belief that there is nothing about society or about man's relations to his fellows that is essential and that all is in effect tosh, this is a price we shall have to pay to accomplish our objective. Certainly there is nothing commendable in a procedure that avoids having to pay that price by keeping the discussion on a speciously

[4] [A.D. LINDSAY, 1 THE MODERN DEMOCRATIC STATE 42 (1943).]

ad hoc plane, where its broader implications raise no questions because they are not perceived.

Accordingly I shall have to begin our inquiry with an attempt to define "true adjudication," or adjudication as it might be if the ideals that support it were fully realized. In doing so I shall of necessity be describing something that never fully exists. Yet it is only with the aid of this nonexistent model that we can pass intelligent judgment on the accomplishments of adjudication as it actually is. Indeed, it is only with the aid of that model that we can distinguish adjudication as an existent institution from other social institutions and procedures by which decisions may be reached.

II. The Two Basic Forms of Social Ordering

It is customary to think of adjudication as a means of settling disputes or controversies. This is, of course, its most obvious aspect. The normal occasion for a resort to adjudication is when parties are at odds with one another, often to such a degree that a breach of social order is threatened.

More fundamentally, however, adjudication should be viewed as a form of social ordering, as a way in which the relations of men to one another are governed and regulated. Even in the absence of any formalized doctrine of stare decisis or res judicata, an adjudicative determination will normally enter in some degree into the litigants' future relations and into the future relations of other parties who see themselves as possible litigants before the same tribunal. Even if there is no statement by the tribunal of the reasons for its decision, some reason will be perceived or guessed at, and the parties will tend to govern their conduct accordingly.

If, then, adjudication is a form of social ordering, to understand it fully we must view it in its relation to other forms of social ordering. It is submitted that there are two basic forms of social ordering: *organization by common aims* and *organization by reciprocity*. Without one or the other of these nothing resembling a society can exist.

These two forms of ordering represent the two basic ways in which men may, by coming together, secure an advantage for all participants. We may illustrate these forms very simply by assuming, first, that two men share an objective which neither could achieve without the aid of the other or could not achieve so easily without that aid. A roadway connects two farms with a highway; it becomes blocked by a boulder. Neither farmer is strong enough to remove the boulder by himself. When the two join forces to remove the boulder we have, obviously, organization or association by common aims. Now let us suppose that our two farmers are to a considerable extent engaged in "subsistence" farming. One of them has a large crop of onions, the other an abundance of potatoes. A trade of a portion of their respective crops may make each richer; to the potato-raising farmer the "last" potato is not so valuable as the "first" onion, and, of course, a surfeit of onions will put the other farmer in the reverse position. Here we have illustrated in its crassest and most obvious form organization or association by reciprocity.

It should be noticed that the conditions which make these two principles of ordering effective are directly opposite to one another. To make organization by reciprocity effective the participants must want different things; organization by common aims requires that the participants want the same thing or things.

In order to bring these forms of ordering into closer relation with adjudication let us now consider briefly *their forms* and *limits*. With respect to reciprocity the form of the relationship may run all the way from a tacit perception of the advantages of an association, scarcely rising to consciousness, to a highly formalized written contract or treaty. Two men find pleasure in one another's company without realizing that the source of that pleasure lies in the fact that they have complementary qualities, so that each needs what the other has to give. There are probably few marriages in which the relations of the spouses are not to some degree organized or directed by the principle of reciprocity. There may, however, be an understandable reluctance to give explicit recognition to this principle, and the acknowledged basis of the relationship may be something closer to a fiction that all aims are shared aims. This may, indeed, be a beneficent fiction; not all the tosh in human relations is harmful. At any rate, whatever reciprocity may underlie any particular marriage, it illustrates the principle of reciprocity in one of its most tacit and informal expressions. At the other end of the scale we might instance a collective labor agreement, every sentence of which was the result of prolonged and explicit bargaining.

Association by common aims also varies over a wide range in the degree of its formality. At the one end of the spectrum, we have the small group, its members all actively sharing and all understanding the same objectives. Such is the case of our farmers uniting to remove a roadblock. At an intermediate point on the scale of formality, we have the voluntary association, the political party, the labor union, and the benevolent society. Here some general aims will commonly be shared actively by most intelligent members; other aims will be promulgated by the leaders which will not in any real sense be shared or even understood by most members; finally, some aims will be pursued by the leaders in the name of the association that will not even be known outside a small circle. In considering this constellation of objectives, it should not be forgotten that it is, in the long run, the actively shared and at least vaguely understood aims that give the association its motive power. Ascending farther along the scale of increasing formality, we finally encounter the nation or the state. Here we have what may be truly called an involuntary association, in the sense that there is no readily available procedure by which the member may resign or effectively disclaim his membership. At the same time he is bound by rules enacted to secure certain objectives whether or not he approves of these objectives or even understands them. The extent to which he and other citizens actively share the objectives pursued by their government is something that varies from nation to nation and over time within a given nation. In times of war the area of actively shared aims normally expands greatly. At other times the area of shared aims may shrink to the point where it embraces merely the negative object of avoiding the disruptions of revolution, of preserving an unsatisfactory status quo. It is possible, in extreme cases, that even this impoverished objective may be shared only by a minority of the citizens, sufficiently organized to impose their will on the majority. At the same time, it is important to recall that without some actual sharing of aims affirmatively entertained, however impoverished the aims and however restricted the sharing, no government is possible. It is for that reason that a government is here considered as a highly formalized variety of organization by common aims.

With respect to the *limits* or the proper provinces of the two basic forms of social ordering, what has just been said sufficiently disposes of organization by common aims. In the case of organization by reciprocity it is obvious that it properly comes into play where an exchange, or something equivalent to it, may enrich both parties. Its proper province lies in that area where divergent human objectives exist. This simple truth is obscured in our complex society, where men and organizations deliberately specialize in order to prepare themselves to enter into relations of reciprocity, as in the case of a factory that expands its earnings and restricts its market by making a highly specialized component part. It may seem silly to say that the sale of a loaf of bread presents a case of "divergent objectives" in the sense that I want the bread more than the twenty cents I pay for it, while the grocer wants my twenty cents more than he wants the bread. Yet the transaction makes no sense in any other terms. Any paradox involved is simply the general one that we cannot truly understand routinized and habitual actions in terms of the actual psychological states that accompany their performance.

The last observation suggests a more general criticism that may be directed against the whole analysis being presented here, namely that it grossly overstates the role of rational calculation in human affairs. It forgets that men often act in blind conformity to custom, in passive acquiescence to authority, and — sometimes at least — in response to inarticulate impulses of altruism. But there is no intention here to deny that the springs of human actions are diverse and often obscure.

What is being assumed in this analysis is not that human beings at all times behave rationally but that it is the rational core of human institutions that is alone capable of keeping those institutions viable and sound, that can preserve them from deterioration, that can get them back on course after they have temporarily lost their bearings. In general what I have called the tosh is something that must be gauged and identified on an ad hoc basis. It is usually determined by some local context, some particular conjunction of historical forces, some special accommodation of opposing interests. If we wish to judge truly any social institution in its particular setting, we must take this accretion of tosh into account. Many well-intentioned reforms have failed because they neglected to do this. But to elevate the tosh to the point of treating it as the basic source of social order is to abandon any hope of fruitful analysis.

I have spoken of the tosh that accumulates about institutions as something that develops out of some local and nonrecurring combination of circumstances — as a phenomenon, in other words, that follows no general laws. It may be that this is an overstatement. It may be possible to predict within given limits that under certain circumstances, or at a given stage of development, an institution will acquire a particular kind of tosh. If this is so, then the thesis of this paper may require some modification. But the possibility that some such modification may turn out to be necessary is surely not of itself a reason for abandoning all effort to analyze the rational elements that inhere in social organization.

In attempting to extract the "rational core" that gives direction and constancy to our institutions, we should be on the lookout for a tacit assumption that equates rational behavior with the calculating advancement of self and views all that is noble in human nature as essentially irrational. This assumption is apt to become particularly operative when a comparison is made between what I have called the two basic forms of social ordering. The principle of reciprocity — as symbolized in its crassest form, the economic trade or "deal" — is considered as a manifestation of human nature in its most selfish, calculating mood. Man is seen as being wholly good when he ceases to calculate, when he surrenders to aims larger than himself which he does not wholly understand — when, in other words, his relations with his fellows are wholly dominated by the principle of common or "social" aims.

This is, I think, a dangerous view of human nature and of the principles that determine a sound organization of man's relations with his fellows. In the first place, a relation of reciprocity may be entered for altruistic reasons. For example, two men enter a contract for the construction of an orphan asylum. The man for whom the asylum is being built is a man of means who desires to put all of his wealth into a home for orphaned children. The contractor enters the same agreement in order to secure funds to put a gifted nephew through college. Both view themselves, surely with some reason, as acting to advance the interests of others, though their relation is one of reciprocity.

Second, no social organization can be good that is grossly inefficient. At the present time in the communist countries, particularly in Poland and Russia, there is an active interest in "rationalizing" the pricing of goods and the computation of costs. It is plain that this requires a type of economic organization that embraces the market principle, in which the units of industry organize their relations with one another by the principle of reciprocity. It may sometimes be convenient to a dictator to have at his command compliant subjects who have lost the habit of calculation. But if he wishes to express his own benevolence (or even his malevolence) toward society effectively, he has to know what he is doing and that he cannot do without some method of measuring economic costs. This means in turn that at least the higher echelons of those concerned with economic activity must organize their relations by the principle of reciprocity.

Third — and this is the most fundamental point — we must look more closely to see just what facets of human nature the two basic forms of ordering do in fact bring to the fore. It is, of course, true that in a relation of reciprocity each party is expected to stand up for himself; indeed, this is required if the full advantages of this form of association are to be obtained. At the same time, it must be realized that this relationship requires of each party that he understand as fully as he possibly can what the other party is like and what his wants are. In an organization dominated by the principle of common ends, nothing is easier than to slip into the assumption that the other fellow wants what we want, or that he will want the same thing when his perception has developed to the level of our own. There is no automatic corrective for this kind of error, which is probably as common as any that men are subject to.

In a relation of reciprocity, however, we must know, if we are to obtain what we want, what the other fellow wants. It is true that, like Tom Sawyer when he got himself out of a fence-painting job, we may persuade the other fellow he wants something that he really does not, or like the modern advertiser we may elevate this persuasion to the level of a skillful manipulation of mass opinion. But even in this manipulation there is latent a certain regard for human dignity; we at least try to make the fellow over so that *he* will want what we have to give him. We do not merely thrust something on him and say, "Here it is." The now-repudiated Soviet legal philosopher Pashukanis discerned the quintessence of capitalist morality in the ethical principle proclaimed by Kant, that we should treat our fellow man as an end-in-himself and never as a mere means. Pashukanis argued that it is only in a society dominated by the principle of exchange that such a precept could be attractive or even workable.[5] In a society shaped by the principle of common aims all men would be means for society and for one another; no man would be treated as an end-in-himself. In terms of Pashukanis' analysis the relationship of reciprocity may in fact be defined as one in which each participant is treated by the other as an end-in-himself.

In judging the relative faults and virtues of the two basic forms of social ordering — for each has both faults and virtues — it would be well to recall Jeremy Bentham's wry comment that if Eve's every act had been for Adam, and his for her, they would both have starved to death.[6] It should also be recalled that the two modern forms of totalitarianism have shared a contempt for "trading morality" and have pretended to direct every individual activity "for the good of all." Finally, it may be well to point out that the principle of reciprocity is implicit in the "golden rule."

These remarks may seem something of a digression from adjudication. But since the analysis presented in this paper discerns an intimate connection between adjudication and what I have called the two basic forms of social ordering, it was thought wise to forestall at the outset at least the more obvious misunderstandings that may be engendered in the course of the discussion. It is now time, however, to place adjudication in its proper relation to the two basic forms of social organization.

---

[5] [*See* Fuller, *Pashukanis and Vyshinsky: A Study in the Development of Marxian Legal Theory*, 47 MICH. L. REV. 1157 (1949).]

[6] [*See* L. STEPHEN, 1 THE ENGLISH UTILITARIANS 312 (1900).]

III. Adjudication As a Form of Social Ordering

In discussing reciprocity and organization by common aims, I pointed out that these two forms of social ordering present themselves along a scale of varying formal explicitness. To some extent the same thing is true of adjudication. We talk, for example, of "taking our case to the forum of public opinion." Or two men may argue in the presence of a third with a kind of tacit hope that he will decide which is right, but without any explicit submission of their dispute to his arbitrament.

On the very informal level, however, forms of social ordering are too mixed and ambiguous to make comparisons fruitful. It is only when a particular form of ordering explicitly controls a relationship that it can be set off clearly against alternative forms of ordering. For this reason, therefore, I am here employing contract to represent reciprocity in its formal and explicit expression. I shall take elections as the most familiar formalization of organization by common aims.

Adjudication, contract, and elections are three ways of reaching decisions, of settling disputes, of defining men's relations to one another. Now I submit that the characteristic feature of each of these forms of social ordering lies in the manner in which the affected party participates in the decision reached. This may be presented graphically as follows:

Form of Social Ordering	*Mode of Participation by the Affected Party*
Contract	Negotiation
Elections	Voting
Adjudication	Presentation of proofs and reasoned arguments

It is characteristic of these three ways of ordering men's relations that though they are subject to variation — they present themselves in different "forms" — each contains certain intrinsic demands that must be met if it is to function properly. We may distinguish roughly between "optimum conditions," which would lift a particular form of order to its highest expression, and "essential conditions," without which the form of order ceases to function in any significant sense at all.

With respect to the principle of contract an analysis of optimum and essential conditions would be exceedingly complex and would require an analysis of the requirements of a market economy, of the peculiar qualities of bargaining in situations of oligopoly, etc. We can observe, however, that a regime of contract presupposes the absence of certain kinds of coercion; a contract signed at the point of a gun is hardly in any significant sense a contract at all. However, it will be simpler if we confine our attention here to a comparison of elections with adjudication.

Elections present themselves in many forms, varying from the town meeting to the "ja-nein" plebiscite. Voting can be organized in many ways: simple majority vote, PR [proportional representation], STV [single transferable voting], and various complicated mixed forms.[7] At the same time all of these expressions of political democracy have in common that they afford the person affected by the decision which emerges a peculiar form of participation in that decision, namely, some form of voting. The optimum conditions that would give fullest meaning to this participation include an intelligent and fully informed electorate, an active interest by the electorate in the issues, candor in discussing those issues by those participating in public debate — conditions, it is needless to say, that are scarcely ever realized in practice. On the other hand, there are certain essential conditions without which the participation of the voter loses its meaning altogether. These would include that the votes be honestly counted, that the ballot boxes not be "stuffed," that certain types of intimidation be absent, etc.

Now much of this paper will be concerned in carrying through with a similiar analysis of the optimum and essential conditions for the functioning of adjudication. This whole analysis will derive from one simple proposition, namely, that the distinguishing characteristic of adjudication lies in the fact that it confers on the affected party a peculiar form of participation in the decision, that of presenting proofs and reasoned arguments for a decision in his favor. Whatever heightens the significance of this participation lifts adjudication toward its optimum expression. Whatever destroys the meaning of that participation destroys the integrity of adjudication itself. Thus, participation through reasoned argument loses its meaning if the arbiter of the dispute is inaccessible to reason because he is insane, has been bribed, or is hopelessly prejudiced. The purpose of this paper is to trace out the somewhat less obvious implications of the proposition that the distinguishing feature of adjudication lies in the mode of participation which it accords to the party affected by the decision.

But first it will be necessary to deal with certain objections that may be raised against my starting point, namely against the

---

[7] [*See* W.J.M. MACKENZIE, FREE ELECTIONS: AN ELEMENTARY TEXTBOOK (1958).]

proposition that the "essence" of adjudication lies in the mode of participation it accords to the affected party.

IV. Adjudication and Rationality

It may be said that the essence of adjudication lies not in the manner in which the affected party participates in the decision but in the office of judge. If there is a judge and a chance to appear before him, it is a matter of indifference whether the litigant chooses to present proofs or reasoned arguments. He may, if he sees fit, offer no argument at all, or pitch his appeal entirely on an emotional level, or even indicate his willingness that the judge decide the case by a throw of the dice. It might seem, then, that our analysis should take as its point of departure the office of judge. From this office certain requirements might be deduced, for example, that of impartiality, since a judge to be "truly" such must be impartial. Then, as the next step, if he is to be impartial he must be willing to hear both sides, etc.

The trouble with this is that there are people who are called "judges" holding official positions and expected to be impartial who nevertheless do not participate in an adjudication in any sense directly relevant to the subject of this paper. Judges at an agricultural fair or an art exhibition may serve as examples. Again, a baseball umpire, though he is not called a judge, is expected to make impartial rulings. What distinguishes these functionaries is not that they do not hold governmental office, for the duties of a judge at a livestock fair would scarcely be changed if he were an official of the Department of Agriculture. What distinguishes them from courts, administrative tribunals, and boards of arbitration is that their decisions are not reached within an institutional framework that is intended to assure to the disputants an opportunity for the presentation of proofs and reasoned arguments. The judge of livestock may or may not permit such a presentation; it is not an integral part of his office to permit and to attend to it.

If, on the other hand, we start with the notion of a process of decision in which the affected party's participation consists in an opportunity to present proofs and reasoned arguments, the office of judge or arbitrator and the requirement of impartiality follow as necessary implications. The logician Frege once took the expression "I accuse" as exemplifying the complex implications contained in the most ordinary language. We may say that the verb "to accuse" presupposes five elements: (1) an accuser, (2) a person accused, (3) a person before whom the accusation is presented, (4) an act charged against the accused, and (5) a principle by which the act may be condemned.[8] The similarity to the analysis here presented is apparent; the fifth element, it should be noted, corresponds to the notion of a *reasoned* argument. Of course, Frege was concerned merely to spell out the implications contained in a phrase, not, as we are here, with the problem of creating and maintaining a social institution that will give effect to those implications.

It may be objected at this point that "reasoned argument" is, after all, not a monopoly of forensic proceedings. A political speech may take the form of a reasoned appeal to the electorate; to be sure, it often takes other forms, but the same thing may be said of speeches in court. This objection fails to take account of a conception that underlies the whole analysis being presented here, the conception, namely, of a form of participating in a decision that is institutionally defined and assured.

When I am entering a contract with another person I may present proofs and arguments to him, but there is generally no formal assurance that I will be given this opportunity or that he will listen to my arguments if I make them. (Perhaps the only exception to this generalization lies in the somewhat anomalous legal obligation "to bargain in good faith" in labor relations.) During an election I may actively campaign for one side and may present what I consider to be "reasoned arguments" to the electorate. If I am an effective campaigner this participation in the decision ultimately reached may greatly outweigh in importance the casting of my own single vote. At the same time, it is only the latter form of participation that is the subject of an affirmative institutional guarantee. The protection accorded my right to present arguments to the electorate is almost entirely indirect and negative. The way will be held clear for me, but I shall have to pave it myself. Even if I am given an affirmative right (for example, under the "equal time" rule of the FCC) I am given no formal assurance that anyone will listen to my appeal. The voter who goes to sleep before his television set is surely not subject to the same condemnation as the judge who sleeps through the arguments of counsel.

Adjudication is, then, a device which gives formal and institutional expression to the influence of reasoned argument in human affairs. As such it assumes a burden of rationality not borne by any other form of social ordering. A decision which is the product of reasoned argument must be prepared itself to meet the test of

[8] [This analysis is taken from an anonymous review of TRANSLATIONS FROM THE PHILOSOPHICAL WRITINGS OF GOTTLOB FREGE (P. Geach & M. Black eds. 1952) in 1952 THE TIMES (London) LITERARY SUPPLEMENT 553, col. 1. The reviewer offers the analysis to illustrate the notion of "functional expression." The fifth element has been added by Mr. Fuller.]

reason. We demand of an adjudicative decision a kind of rationality we do not expect of the results of contract or of voting. This higher responsibility toward rationality is at once the strength *and the weakness* of adjudication as a form of social ordering.

In entering contracts, men are of course in some measure guided by rational considerations. The subsistence farmer who has a surfeit of potatoes and only a handful of onions acts reasonably when he trades potatoes for onions. But there is no test of rationality that can be applied to the result of the trade considered in abstraction from the interests of the parties. Indeed, the trade of potatoes for onions, which is a rational act by one trader, might be considered irrational if indulged in by his opposite number, who has a storehouse full of onions and only a bushel of potatoes. If we asked one party to the contract, "Can you defend that contract?" he might answer, "Why, yes. It was good for me and it was good for him." If we then said, "But that is not what we meant. We meant, can you defend it on general grounds?" he might well reply that he did not know what we were talking about. Yet this is precisely the kind of question we normally direct toward the decision of a judge or arbitrator. The results that emerge from adjudication are subject, then, to a standard of rationality that is different from that imposed on the results of an exchange.

I believe that the same observation holds true when adjudication is compared with elections. The key to the difference lies again in the mode in which the affected party participates in a decision. If, as in adjudication, the only mode of participation consists in the opportunity to present proofs and arguments, the purpose of this participation is frustrated, and the whole proceeding becomes a farce, should the decision that emerges make no pretense whatever to rationality. The same cannot be said of the mode of participation called voting. We may assume that the preferences of voters are ultimately emotional, inarticulate, and not subject to rational defense. At the same time there is a need for social order, and it may be assumed that this need is best met when order rests on the broadest possible base of popular support. On this ground, a negative defense of democracy is possible; the will of the majority controls, not because it is right, but— well, because it *is* the will of the majority. This is surely an impoverished conception of democracy, but it expresses at least one ingredient of any philosophy of democracy, and it suggests a reason why we demand of adjudication a kind of rationality that we do not expect of elections.

This problem can be approached somewhat obliquely from a different direction by asking what is implied by "a right" or by "a claim of right." If I say to someone, "Give me that!" I do not necessarily assert a right. I may be begging for an act of charity, or I may be threatening to take by force something to which I admittedly have no right. On the other hand, if I say, "Give that to me, I have a right to it," I necessarily assert the existence of some principle or standard by which my "right" can be tested.

To be sure, this principle or standard may not have antedated my claim. If one boy says to another, "Give me that catcher's mitt," and answers the question, "Why?" by saying, "Because I am the best catcher on the team," he asserts a principle by which the equipment of the team ought to be apportioned in accordance with the ability to use it. He necessarily implies that, were the respective abilities of the two boys reversed, the mitt should remain where it is. But he does not, by necessary implication, assert that the principle by which he supports his claim is an established one. Indeed, up to the time this claim is made, the right to be catcher might depend not on ability but on ownership of the catcher's mitt. In that event the claim based upon the new principle of ability might, in effect, propose a revolution in the organization of the team. At the same time, this claim does necessarily imply *a* principle which can give meaning to the demand that like cases be given like treatment.

Now if we ask ourselves what kinds of questions are commonly decided by judges and arbitrators, the answer may well be, "Claims of right." Indeed, in the older literature (including notably John Chipman Gray's *The Nature and Sources of the Law*) courts were often distinguished from administrative or executive agencies on the ground that it is the function of courts to "declare rights." [9] If, then, we seek to define "the limits of adjudication," a tempting answer would be that the proper province of courts is limited to cases where rights are asserted. On reflection we might enlarge this to include cases where fault or guilt is charged (broadly, "the trial of accusations"), since in many cases it is artificial to treat the accuser (who may be the district attorney) as claiming a right. Though it is not particularly artificial to view the lawbreaker as violating "a right" of the state, to say that when the state indicts the lawbreaker it is claiming a remedial "right" against him does seem to reflect a misguided impulse toward forcing a symmetry between civil and criminal remedies. To avoid any such manipulations of natural modes of thought, let us then amend the suggested criterion to read as follows: The proper province of adjudication is to make an authoritative determination of questions raised by claims of right and accusations of guilt.

[9] [J.C. GRAY, THE NATURE AND SOURCES OF THE LAW 115 (2d ed. 1921).]

Is this a significant way of describing "the limits of adjudication"? I do not think so. In fact, what purports here to be a distinct assertion is merely an implication of the fact that adjudication is a form of decision that defines the affected party's participation as that of offering proofs and reasoned arguments. It is not so much that adjudicators decide only issues presented by claims of right or accusations. The point is rather that *whatever* they decide, or *whatever* is submitted to them for decision, tends to be converted into a claim of right or an accusation of fault or guilt. This conversion is effected by the institutional framework within which both the litigant and the adjudicator function.

Let me spell out rather painstakingly the steps of an argument that will show why this should be so. (1) Adjudication is a process of decision that grants to the affected party a form of participation that consists in the opportunity to present proofs and reasoned arguments. (2) The litigant must therefore, if his participation is to be meaningful, assert some principle or principles by which his arguments are sound and his proofs relevant. (3) A naked demand is distinguished from a claim of right by the fact that the latter is a demand supported by a principle; likewise, a mere expression of displeasure or resentment is distinguished from an accusation by the fact that the latter rests upon some principle. Hence, (4) issues tried before an adjudicator tend to become claims of right or accusations of fault.

We may see this process of conversion in the case of an employee who desires an increase in pay. If he asks his boss for a raise, he may, of course, claim "a right" to the raise. He may argue the fairness of the principle of equal treatment and call attention to the fact that Joe, who is no better than he, recently got a raise. But he does not have to rest his plea on any ground of this sort. He may merely beg for generosity, urging the needs of his family. Or he may propose an exchange, offering to take on extra duties if he gets the raise. If, however, he takes his case to an arbitrator he cannot, explicitly at least, support his case by an appeal to charity or by proposing a bargain. He will have to support his demand by a principle of some kind, and a demand supported by principle is the same thing as a claim of right. So, when he asks his boss for a raise, he may or may not make a claim of right; when he presents his demand to an arbitrator he *must* make a claim of right. (I do not overlook the possibility of the arbitrator's proposing to the parties a "deal" by which the employee would get the raise but take on extra duties. But it is obvious that in such a case the arbitrator steps out of the role of adjudicator and assumes that of mediator. This kind of case presents the problem of "mixed forms" of ordering, which will be discussed later at some length. It may be observed that the American Arbitration Association strives to keep its arbitrators from assuming the role of mediators. Whatever the wisdom of this policy, it is apparent that it rests on some conception of the proper limits of adjudication and presents the sort of question toward which this paper is addressed.)

If the analysis presented here is correct, three aspects of adjudication that seem to present distinct qualities are in fact all expressions of a single quality: (1) the peculiar mode by which the affected party participates in the decision; (2) the peculiarly urgent demand of rationality that the adjudicative process must be prepared to meet; and (3) the fact that adjudication finds its normal and "natural" province in judging claims of right and accusations of fault. So, when we say that a party entering a contract, or voting in an election, has no "right" to any particular outcome, we are describing the same fundamental fact that we allude to when we say that adjudication has to meet a test of rationality or of "principle" that is not applied to contracts and elections.

In this connection it is interesting to recall that Langdell once argued that, although there are rights at law, there is no such thing as "a right in equity."[10] This is because, he contended, courts of law are bound by rules, while courts of equity proceed by discretion. A similiar issue is presented by the question whether the regulations of administrative agencies create "rights" and by the common argument whether some dispensation resting within an agency's power is a matter of "right" or of "privilege." When it is said, for example, that entry into the legal profession is a matter of privilege and not of right, it is important to see that all that is really asserted is that a decision denying admission to the bar need not be supported by any general principle.

I have suggested that it is not a significant description of the limits of adjudication to say that its proper province lies where rights are asserted or accusations of fault are made, for such a statement involves a circle of reasoning. If, however, we regard a formal definition of rights and wrongs as a nearly inevitable product of the adjudicative process, we can arrive at what is perhaps the most significant of all limitations on the proper province of adjudication. Adjudication is not a proper form of

[10] [Langdell, *Classifications of Rights and Wrongs* (pt. II), 13 HARV. L. REV. 659, 670–71 (1900), *reprinted in* C.C. LANGDELL, A BRIEF SURVEY OF EQUITY JURISDICTION 239, 251–52 (1905).]

social ordering in those areas where the effectiveness of human association would be destroyed if it were organized about formally defined "rights" and "wrongs." Courts have, for example, rather regularly refused to enforce agreements between husband and wife affecting the internal organization of family life. There are other and wider areas where the intrusion of "the machinery of the law" is equally inappropriate. An adjudicative board might well undertake to allocate one thousand tons of coal among three claimants; it could hardly conduct even the simplest coal-mining enterprise by the forms of adjudication. Wherever successful human association depends upon spontaneous and informal collaboration, shifting its forms with the task at hand, there adjudication is out of place except as it may declare certain ground rules applicable to a wide variety of activities.

These are vague and perhaps trite observations. I shall attempt to bring them into sharper focus in a later part of this paper, particularly in a discussion of the relative incapacity of adjudication to solve "polycentric" problems. Meanwhile, the point I should like to stress is that the incapacity of a given area of human activity to endure a pervasive delimitation of rights and wrongs is also a measure of its incapacity to respond to a too exigent rationality, a rationality that demands an immediate and explicit reason for every step taken. Back of both of these incapacities lies the fundamental truth that certain kinds of human relations are not appropriate raw material for a process of decision that is institutionally committed to acting on the basis of reasoned argument.

(It may be well here to deal parenthetically with one or two small points capable of giving difficulty. When we speak of adjudication as implying an institutional guarantee of participation in the decision by presenting proofs and arguments, we do not imply that the litigant must always avail himself of his right to this participation. The facts may be stipulated by agreement of the parties, thus dispensing with the necessity for proof in court. Again, one or both parties may waive argument. There is no real point of difficulty here, any more than there is in the fact that an election affords an opportunity for participation of which many qualified to vote do not avail themselves. A slightly more sticky point is this: there are exceptional instances of decisions between disputants where no argument is ever contemplated because it is superfluous. An example is where a dispute about "conformity to sample" arises between a seller and a buyer of textiles and the parties agree to abide by the decision of a laboratory. Whether such a process of decision should be called "adjudication" is not a matter of real importance because its simplicity excludes the problems that are the subject of analysis in this essay.)

V. Adjudication and the Rule of Law

So far a point of crucial importance and difficulty has not been reached in this discussion. It has been repeatedly asserted that adjudication is institutionally committed to a "reasoned" decision, to a decision based on "principle." But what is the source of the "principle" on the basis of which the case is to be argued and decided? Where do the parties and the adjudicator get their respective "reasons"?

Recent discussions of "the rule of law" reveal — or I should perhaps say, largely conceal — a very fundamental difference of opinion on this question of the source of principle. There is at present a very active movement aimed at extending the rule of law to international relations and at assisting peoples who have never known stable and constitutional government to achieve internally a condition known as the rule of law. Much of the discussion engendered is on an inspirational and rhetorical level that does not permit underlying difficulties to come to the surface. When, however, those difficulties are candidly faced a serious issue emerges that may be somewhat too simply stated as: Which comes first, courts or rules?

All are agreed that courts are essential to "the rule of law." The object of the rule of law is to substitute for violence peaceful ways of settling disputes. Obviously peace cannot be assured simply by treaties, agreements, and legislative enactment. There must be some agency capable of determining the rights of parties in concrete situations of controversy. Beyond this point, however, disagreement begins.

On the one side the advocates of the view "first courts, then rules" see adjudication as the primary source of peaceful order. The essence of the rule of law consists in being assured of your day in court. Courts can be counted on to make a reasoned disposition of controversies, either by the application of statutes or treaties, or in the absence of these sources, by the development of rules appropriate to the cases before them and derived from general principles of fairness and equity.

Critics of this view assert that it does a disservice to a great and valid ideal. It dodges the whole issue of "justiciability" and assumes there can be no problem or controversy that lies beyond the limits of adjudication. It substitutes for critical judgment a naive trust in good intentions. It forgets that you cannot be fair in a moral and legal vacuum. It ignores the fact that adjudication cannot function without some standard of decision, either imposed by superior authority or willingly accepted by the disputants. Without some standard of decision the requirement that the judge be impartial becomes meaningless. Similarly, without such a standard the litigants' participation through reasoned argument loses its meaning. Communication and persuasion presuppose some shared context of principle.

Furthermore, say these critics, it is futile to assume that the void can be filled by contracts and treaties. Where the words of an agreement have a plain and obvious meaning, public opinion will ordinarily supply a sufficient sanction to ensure its performance. The necessity of a resort to adjudication will arise precisely in those cases where the proper meaning of the contract is in dispute. International treaties are often filled with purposeful ambiguities; some issues are simply too touchy to be resolved by agreement. When a dispute later develops around such issues, the agreement offers no guidance. To demand of a court that it simply resolve such issues "fairly" is to ask the court to decide something about which the parties themselves could not agree and for the determination of which no standard exists. Furthermore, the most troublesome issues arising out of treaties often involve cases where the original situation, on the basis of which the parties contracted, has been overtaken by events, so that the factual underpinnings of the agreement have been removed. In such a case, the court either has to declare the agreement no longer in force, thus leaving itself and the parties without any standard of decision, or it has to engage in a drastic revision of the contract, again without the guidance of any clear standard.

To all this argument the opposing party enters a rejoinder along these lines: The views just expressed are founded on a gross ignorance of history. The two great systems of law that dominate the world today — the common law and the civil law — took their origins in a case-by-case evolution of doctrine. Even today when developments occur in the common law it is usually only at the end of a series of cases that the governing principle becomes clear. In the civil law countries the codes from which courts purport to derive their principles often provide little beyond a vocabulary for stating legal results. They are filled with clauses referring to "good faith," "equity," "fair practice," and the like — standards that any court could apply without the aid of a code. One of the best of modern codes, the Swiss Code of Obligations, lays down very few rules and contents itself largely with charting the range of judicial discretion and with setting forth what might be called checklists for the judge to consult to make certain that he has overlooked no factor properly bearing on the exercise of his discretion.

To this argument the final reply would probably run somewhat as follows: The views just expressed themselves betray a deep ignorance of history. The developments related have occurred in situations where there was already outside the law a strong sense of community, where there were generally shared conceptions of right and wrong that could gradually be crystallized into legal doctrine. In a community of traders, apparently vague phrases like "fair practice" have a definiteness of meaning that they cannot have in international relations or among people just emerging from primitive feudalism. Where legal rules have evolved out of the process of adjudication, law has in effect been built on community. Uncritical proponents of extending the rule of law propose to build community on law. It cannot be done.

A less compromising reply would be given by Friedrich A. Hayek, a true stalwart of the "law first, then courts" school of thought. In his lectures *The Political Ideal of the Rule of Law*, he declares his conviction that the case-by-case methods of the common law are inconsistent with the ideal of the rule of law.[11] The startling conclusion seems to follow that precisely those nations that have most often been held up as ideals of a peaceful and just internal order themselves violate the rule of law by their systems of adjudication. Hayek further connects the decline of the liberal state in Europe and the rise of totalitarian philosophies with the increasing use of vague provisions in codes, such as those requiring "good faith" and "fair practice" without further specification of the kind of behavior intended.[12]

Now it seems to me clear that, if we exclude such extreme views as that of Hayek, there is much to be said for both sides. We need, I believe, to keep two important truths before us: (1) It is sometimes possible to initiate adjudication effectively without definite rules; in this situation a case-by-case evolution of legal principle does often take place. (2) This evolution does not always occur, and we need to analyze more clearly than we generally have what conditions foster or hinder it.

A good many of our regulatory agencies were initiated in the hope that as knowledge was gained case by case a body of principle would emerge that would be understandable by all concerned and that would bring their adjudicative decisions within the rule of law. In some cases this hope has been at least partially vindicated; in others it has been almost completely disappointed. Here is a pool of experience that has been inadequately tapped.

---

[11] [F.A. Hayek, The Political Ideal of the Rule of Law 19 (1955).]

[12] [*Id.* at 35, 39–42.]

It may be suggested, parenthetically, that the often remarked tendency of regulatory agencies to identify themselves with the interests of the industry they regulate may proceed from a deeper cause than mere familiar rubbing of elbows or a desire on the part of the regulator to curry favor with an industry that may some day put him on its payroll. I suggest that the cause may lie in a desire to escape the frustration of trying to act as a judge in a situation affording no standard of decision. To escape from a moral vacuum one has to identify oneself with something, and the most obvious object of identification lies in the regulated industry.

It will be useful at this point to consider a kind of paradigm instance of a case-by-case growth of legal doctrine. The model or example I am about to present has been borrowed from an earlier article of mine.[13] The cases are of course schematic and hypothetical. They are given in the order of their assumed chronology. The parties in each case are different persons, but to facilitate comparisons the symbols used to designate the parties will be the same throughout and will indicate the role played by the particular party; thus in all five cases *O* will designate the original owner of the horse which came by theft or fraud into the hands of *T*.

Case No. 1. *T* steals *O*'s horse and sells it to *G*, who pays full value for it and has no reason to know it had been stolen from *O*. *O* brings suit against *G* to recover the horse. *Held*, for *O*. One of the deterrents to thievery is the difficulty of disposing of stolen goods. If a purchaser like *G* were able to take goods free of the claim of the true owner, a market for stolen goods would be created and thus an incentive to theft. In any event, it was impossible for *T*, a thief who had no rightful title to the horse, to pass any title to *G*; he who has nothing can give nothing.

Case No. 2. *T* buys a horse from *O* giving as payment a forged note purporting to be that of *X*. *T* knew that the note was forged. After delivering the horse to *T*, *O* discovers that he has been defrauded. He brings suit against *T* to recover the horse. It is argued on behalf of *T* that *O* delivered the horse to him with the intent to confer title; the horse is now *T*'s and *O*'s only remedy is to sue for the price. *Held*, for *O*. The passage of title was vitiated by the fraud of *T*; title throughout remained in *O*.

Case No. 3. The case is similar to Case No. 2, except that after receiving possession of the horse, *T* sold it to *G*, who knew *T* had bought it from *O* but had no reason to know that *T* had worked any fraud on *O*. *O* brings suit against *G* to recover the

[13] [Fuller, *A Rejoinder to Professor Nagel,*] 3 NAT. L.F. 83, 96–98 (1958).

horse. It is argued on behalf of *O* that title remained in him in accordance with the principle laid down in Case No. 2. Since *T* had no title, he could pass none to *G*. *Held*, for *G*. It would be an intolerable burden on commerce if purchasers of property were compelled to scrutinize the details of a transaction by which the former owner voluntarily delivered it into the hands of the person now offering it for sale. Fraud takes many and subtle forms; if the victim could not recognize it, it is unreasonable to ask of a stranger to the transaction that he ascertain whether it was present. With respect to Case No. 2, all that was said there was with reference to the legal relations between the owner and the defrauder; the court's mind was not directed toward the possibility that a subsequent purchaser, like *G*, might intervene. The principle we are here applying is that if the horse is in the hands of *T* or of someone who knew of his fraud, it may be recovered by *O*. In the hands of an innocent purchaser like *G*, the horse may not be recovered by *O*, for reasons we have already indicated.

Case No. 4. The case is like Case No. 3, except that after buying the horse from *T*, *G* sold it to *K*, who, before he bought the horse from *G*, had been informed of the fraud worked by *T* on *O*. *O* sues *K* to recover the horse. It is argued on behalf of *O* that *K* was not an innocent purchaser, since he knew of *T*'s fraud when he bought the horse. In accordance with the principle laid down in Case No. 3, *O* became entitled to the horse when it came into the hands of *K*. *Held*, for *K*. If the argument made by *O* were accepted, it would be possible for a person in the position of *O* to destroy the value of the title acquired by *G* simply by giving general publicity to the fact that *T* had induced the sale by fraud. Thus the objective of protecting the bona fide purchaser *G* would be defeated, for his property would become unsalable. When the court in Case No. 3 said that *O* could recover the horse from anyone who knew of the fraud of *T*, it did not have in mind the possibility that the horse might have passed previously through the hands of a bona fide purchaser like *G*. When the horse was bought from *T* by *G*, title to it was perfected and was no longer vulnerable to attack by *O*. *G* was then free to sell it to anyone he saw fit.

Case No. 5. This case is like Case No. 4, except that *K* not only knew of *T*'s fraud but had participated in it by forging *X*'s name on the note used by *T* to pay *O* for the horse. *O* sues *K* to recover the horse. *K* rests his defense on the reasoning of Case No. 4; *G* had title to the horse and was free to sell it to anyone he saw fit. If *K* was guilty of any misconduct, that is a question for the criminal law; it ought not to affect his property rights. *Held*? . . . perhaps it would be well to suspend the series at this point and leave to the reader the burden of decision and the more onerous burden of explanation.

Although the development here traced is considerably neater than anything likely to be encountered in legal history, I assume that lawyers would generally agree that this sort of thing does occur. I assume also it will be agreed that, despite the zigzag pattern which the decisions seem to present, the process illustrated is a "rational" one, falling within the limits of meaningful adjudication. What is the source of this "rational" quality? It seems clear that it derives from the fact that the courts engaged in this development are drawing out the necessary, or at least the reasonable, implications of a regime of private property and exchange.

I suggest more generally that where adjudication appears to operate meaningfully without the support of rules formally declared or accepted in advance, it does so because it draws its intellectual sustenance from the two basic forms of social ordering I have already described. It has done this historically with most notable success in the field where the accepted objective is to develop a regime of reciprocity or exchange. Students of comparative law are often struck by the fact that in the area of commercial transactions courts operating in entirely different environments of legal doctrine will often reach identical or similar results in the decision of actual cases.

But the possibility of a case-by-case development of principle is by no means confined to the field of commercial transactions. For example, the demands of a viable system of federalism are by no means immediately obvious. In gradually discovering and articulating the principles that will make federalism work, the courts may exemplify the process Mansfield had in mind when he spoke of the law "working itself pure."[14] Indeed, just such a development was envisaged by Hamilton in No. 82 of the *Federalist Papers*, where he wrote:

> The erection of a new government, whatever care or wisdom may distinguish the work, cannot fail to originate questions of intricacy and nicety; and these may, in a particular manner, be expected to flow from the establishment of a constitution founded upon the total or partial incorporation of a number of distinct sovereignties. 'Tis time only that can mature and perfect so compound a system, can liquidate the meaning of all the parts, and can adjust them to each other in a harmonious and consistent *whole*.[15]

Obviously this kind of development — this gradual tracing out of the full implications of a system already established — can

[14] [*See* 12 W. Holdsworth, A History of English Law 551 (1938).]

[15] [The Federalist No. 82 vol. 2, at 130 (A. Hamilton) (Tudor ed. 1947).]

take place only in an atmosphere dominated by the shared desire to make federalism work.

It should be made clear that the view expressed here is radically different from one which it superficially resembles that threatens to become commonplace in sociology. I refer to the conception that in a sufficiently homogeneous society certain "values" will develop automatically and without anyone intending or directing their development. In such a society it is assumed that the legal rules developed and enforced by courts will reflect these prevailing "values." In our own discussion, however, we are not talking about disembodied "values" but about human purposes actively, if often tacitly, held and given intelligent direction at critical junctures. In working out the implications of federalism or of a regime of exchange, a court is not an inert mirror reflecting current mores but an active participant in the enterprise of articulating the implications of shared purposes.

If the conception here advanced is sound, it follows that in extending "the rule of law" to international relations, law and community of purpose must develop together. It is also apparent that a community of purpose which consists simply in a shared desire to avoid reciprocal destruction is too impoverished to furnish a proper basis for meaningful adjudication. Where the only shared objective is the negative one of preventing a holocaust, there is nothing that can make meaningful a process of decision that depends upon proofs and reasoned argument. It is of course conceivable that, moved by a desire to prevent such a holocaust, two nations (say, Russia and the United States) might submit a dispute to arbitration, but they would do so in much the same spirit that they might resort to a throw of the dice — unless there were perceived by both some body of principle, however vague, that might control and give rationality to the decision. Such a body of emergent principle would have to derive from one of the two basic principles of order. In practice this would mean that it would have to derive from relationships of reciprocity. Hence a desideratum of overriding importance in the relations of Russia and the United States is the development of every possible bond of reciprocity, every kind of useful exchange, between the two countries. This is essential not merely to promote "understanding" and an atmosphere of good will but to create a community of interest from which adjudication can draw intellectual sustenance.

In this connection a development has occurred that, from one point of view, seems to leave no hope for the rule of law in international relations, but seen from a different vantage point will appear as a most encouraging portent. In agreements with foreign traders Soviet industry has insisted on the inclusion of a clause subjecting all disputes arising out of the agreement to arbitration before a specially constituted Soviet board of arbitration. On its face, one of the most fundamental principles of the rule of law — that no man shall be judge in his own cause — seems to be violated. (On a purely formal level, it should be noted, the rule is equally violated by the United States Court of Claims.) Soviet lawyers seem genuinely eager that this Soviet tribunal shall establish a reputation for impartiality and fairness. Its decisions so far seem generally to merit for it such a reputation.[16] Where does this tribunal get its standards of decision? Essentially they are those of a bourgeois trading community. Where else could one go for standards of fair dealings between traders? (The situation is reminiscent of certain communities in Delaware dedicated to the principles of the single tax as taught by Henry George.[17] In disputes between these communities and their members concerning the rate to be paid for the use of land, arbitrators have been compelled to turn to the hated and rejected land market as offering the only meaningful standard of decision.)

When the Soviet commercial tribunals have to take their standards of fairness from a system their philosophy condemns, the way has been paved for wider understanding, and with it an atmosphere in which there is a real basis for the hope that nations may yet be subjected to the rule of law.

There remains one further point of capital importance, though of a somewhat abstruse nature. This relates to a possible obstacle to the development of the rule of law that may be presented by the prevailing temper of Western philosophy. I am speaking chiefly of professional philosophy, and particularly of the philosophy taught in British and American universities. Though the direct influence of this philosophy in practical affairs is slight, its indirect influence may be of enormous significance. Generations of students have been raised in a university atmosphere strongly imbued with the tenets of the philosophers' philosophy of which I speak.

There is a line of thought going back to David Hume according to which there are two areas, and two areas only, for the operation of human reason. These are the areas of empirical fact and of logical implication.[18] Stated in another way, the human mind can occupy itself either by observing facts and testing hypotheses about these facts or by tracing out the logical implica-

---

[16] *See* Pisar, *The Communist System of Foreign-Trade Adjudication*, 72 HARV. L. REV. 1409 (1959).

[17] [H. GEORGE, PROGRESS AND POVERTY (75th ed. 1955).]

[18] [D. HUME, A TREATISE OF HUMAN NATURE 463 (L. Selby-Bigge ed. 1888).]

tions of agreed premises. There is no *tertium quid*. If in any process of human decision there enters any element that is not traceable to empirical fact or logical entailment, it is not and cannot be a "rational" element; its origin must be in "sentiment," not in "reason."

Now in Hume's time the implications of this philosophy were perceived clearly enough, but they were not really taken seriously. Men went right on discussing and arguing issues of morality, law, and politics, assuming all the while that they were engaged in rational discourse, though it was apparent that very little of what they said — and that generally the least important — had to do with empirical fact or logical deduction. But as the decades passed the exclusions implied in the Humean view came to be taken more seriously and applied more rigorously. More important, these exclusions passed over into the general climate of our times.[19]

The view taken in this paper is that adjudication is a form of social ordering institutionally committed to "rational" decision. This follows from the only mode of participation it accords to the affected party, the litigant. If we combine this view with the Humean philosophy, what is the result? It is apparent that adjudicators seldom rest their decisions directly on matters of empirical fact. When they seem to do this the "facts" they find are not the kind contemplated by Hume, since they are generally human faults or shortcomings. To "find" such a "fact" is to express a condemnation — something remote from Hume's "matters of fact." This leaves logical deduction. Now it is apparent that when adjudication proceeds by previously established rules, at least one aspect of the tribunal's task involves something akin to logical deduction. If this is the only significant area of rationality permitted to adjudication, then it can act rationally only insofar as it applies previously established rules. This seems to be the basis on which Hayek reaches his startling conclusion that the whole system of the common law is violative of the rule of law.[20]

Let us apply the Humean test of reason to the paradigm or model of a case-by-case evolution of legal doctrine previously given, that involving a series of cases having to do with the buying and stealing of horses. Now there is little in these cases exemplifying anything like a discovery of empirical fact. In the early cases the courts did not have imagination enough to foresee the situations of fact that did later arise, but when those situations arose they contained nothing not accessible to the minds of the judges

[19] *See* J.W. SMITH, THEME FOR REASON [145–46, 176–77] (1957).

[20] [F.A. HAYEK, *supra* note 11, at 34–36.]

from the beginning. Nor is there much that can be called deduction from explicit premises. Indeed, the premises seem to be shaped by the conclusions, and clarity of premise comes at the end of the development, not at the beginning. Are we justified in calling the process that is exemplified a "rational" one? By the Humean test, the answer would have to be, "No," and the appearance of rationality would have to rest on some self-deception. This is, in fact, the conclusion apparently reached apropos of the model presented here by a leading American logician.[21]

There is, I submit, a third area of rational discourse, not embraced by empirical fact or logical implication. This is the area where men seek to trace out and articulate the implications of shared purposes. The intellectual activity that takes place in this area resembles logical deduction, but it also differs in important respects from it. In logical deduction, the greater the clarity of the premise, the more secure will be the deduction. In the process I have in mind the discussion often proceeds most helpfully when the purposes, which serve as "premises" or starting points, are stated generally and are held in intellectual contact with other related or competing purposes. The end result is not a mere demonstration of what follows from a given purpose but a reorganization and clarification of the purposes that constituted the starting point of inquiry.

However we may define this third area, a rigid adherence to the Humean view is, I believe, destructive of any understanding of the problems of adjudication. It not only falsifies the conditions essential for the effective operation of adjudication but distorts the meaning of any adjudicative process that is functioning successfully.

VI. The Forms of Adjudication

1. *Introduction*

The remainder of this paper will be divided into three main sections: The Forms of Adjudication, The Limits of Adjudication, and Mixed, Parasitic, and Perverted Forms of Adjudication. Of course, all of these topics stand in close relation to one another and some degree of anticipation will be unavoidable.

For example, the limits of adjudication are affected by its forms. Reference has already been made to so-called "tripartite" arbitration. This special and deviant form of adjudication sometimes makes it possible to undertake through an adjudicative process tasks that could not otherwise be handled satisfactorily

[21] *See* Nagel, *Fact, Value and Human Purpose*, 4 Nat. L.F. 26 (1959).

through adjudication at all. At the same time, this form may impair the effectiveness of adjudication in its more usual employments.

The joining of "mixed, parasitic, and perverted" forms of adjudication in one title should not mislead the reader into thinking that this paper condemns all departures of adjudication from a state of pristine purity. Certain mixed forms are valuable and almost indispensable, though their use is often attended by certain dangers.

In determining whether a deviant or mixed form impairs the integrity of adjudication the test throughout will be that already stressed repeatedly: Does it affect adversely the meaning of the affected party's participation in the decision by proofs and reasoned arguments?

2. *Is an Adversary Presentation Necessary to Adjudication?* [22]

The Lawyer's Role as Advocate in Open Court

The lawyer appearing as an advocate before a tribunal presents, as persuasively as he can, the facts and the law of the case as seen from the standpoint of his client's interest. It is essential that both the lawyer and the public understand clearly the nature of the rôle thus discharged. Such an understanding is required not only to appreciate the need for an adversary presentation of issues, but also in order to perceive truly the limits partisan advocacy must impose on itself if it is to remain wholesome and useful.

In a very real sense it may be said that the integrity of the adjudicative process itself depends upon the participation of the advocate. This becomes apparent when we contemplate the nature of the task assumed by any arbiter who attempts to decide a dispute without the aid of partisan advocacy.

Such an arbiter must undertake, not only the role of judge, but that of representative for both of the litigants. Each of these roles must be played to the full without being muted by qualifications derived from the others. When he is developing for each side the most effective statement of its case, the arbiter must put aside his neutrality and permit himself to be moved by a sympathetic identification sufficiently intense to draw from his mind all that it is capable of giving, — in analysis, patience and creative power. When he resumes his neutral position, he must

[22] [Under this heading in the original text, Mr. Fuller simply referred the reader to a statement coauthored with John D. Randall entitled *Professional Responsibility: Report of the Joint Conference*. The Joint Conference on Professional Responsibility was established in 1952 by the American Bar Association and the Association of American Law Schools. The *Report* appeared in 44 A.B.A.J. 1159 (1958). A few excerpts from the *Report*, *id.* at 1160–61, 1162, 1216, have been inserted into the text.]

be able to view with distrust the fruits of this identification and be ready to reject the products of his own best mental efforts. The difficulties of this undertaking are obvious. If it is true that a man in his time must play many parts, it is scarcely given to him to play them all at once.

It is small wonder, then, that failure generally attends the attempt to dispense with the distinct roles traditionally implied in adjudication. What generally occurs in practice is that at some early point a familiar pattern will seem to emerge from the evidence; an accustomed label is wanting for the case and, without awaiting further proofs, this label is promptly assigned to it. It is a mistake to suppose that this premature cataloguing must necessarily result from impatience, prejudice or mental sloth. Often it proceeds from a very understandable desire to bring the hearing into some order and coherence, for without some tentative theory of the case there is no standard of relevance by which testimony may be measured. But what starts as a preliminary diagnosis designed to direct the inquiry tends, quickly and imperceptibly, to become a fixed conclusion, as all that confirms the diagnosis makes a strong imprint on the mind, while all that runs counter to it is received with diverted attention.

An adversary presentation seems the only effective means for combatting this natural human tendency to judge too swiftly in terms of the familiar that which is not yet fully known. The arguments of counsel hold the case, as it were, in suspension between two opposing interpretations of it. While the proper classification of the case is thus kept unresolved, there is time to explore all of its peculiarities and nuances.

These are the contributions made by partisan advocacy during the public hearing of the cause. When we take into account the preparations that must precede the hearing, the essential quality of the advocate's contribution becomes even more apparent. Preceding the hearing, inquiries must be instituted to determine what facts can be proved or seem sufficiently established to warrant a formal test of their truth during the hearing. There must also be a preliminary analysis of the issues, so that the hearing may have form and direction. These preparatory measures are indispensable whether or not the parties involved in the controversy are represented by advocates.

Where that representation is present there is an obvious advantage in the fact that the area of dispute may be greatly reduced by an exchange of written pleadings or by stipulations of counsel. Without the participation of someone who can act responsibly for each of the parties, this essential narrowing of the issues becomes impossible. But here again the true significance of partisan advocacy lies deeper, touching once more the integrity of the adjudicative process itself. It is only through the advocate's participation that the hearing may remain in fact what it purports to be in theory: a public trial of the facts and issues.

Each advocate comes to the hearing prepared to present his proofs and arguments, knowing at the same time that his arguments may fail to persuade and that his proofs may be rejected as inadequate. It is a part of his role to absorb these possible disappointments. The deciding tribunal, on the other hand, comes to the hearing uncommitted. It has not represented to the public that any fact can be proved, that any argument is sound, or that any particular way of stating a litigant's case is the most effective expression of its merits.

. . . .

These, then, are the reasons for believing that partisan advocacy plays a vital and essential role in one of the most fundamental procedures of a democratic society. But if we were to put all of these detailed considerations to one side, we should still be confronted by the fact that, in whatever form adjudication may appear, the experienced judge or arbitrator desires and actively seeks to obtain an adversary presentation of the issues. Only when he has had the benefit of intelligent and vigorous advocacy on both sides can he feel fully confident of his decision.

Viewed in this light, the role of the lawyer as a partisan advocate appears not as a regrettable necessity, but as an indispensable part of a larger ordering of affairs. The institution of advocacy is not a concession to the frailties of human nature, but an expression of human insight in the design of a social framework within which man's capacity for impartial judgment can attain its fullest realization.

When advocacy is thus viewed, it becomes clear by what principle limits must be set to partisanship. The advocate plays his role well when zeal for his client's cause promotes a wise and informed decision of the case. He plays his role badly, and trespasses against the obligations of professional responsibility, when his desire to win leads him to muddy the headwaters of decision, when, instead of lending a needed perspective to the controversy, he distorts and obscures its true nature.

. . . .

The Lawyer as a Guardian of Due Process

The lawyer's highest loyalty is at the same time the most intangible. It is a loyalty that runs, not to persons, but to procedures and institutions. The lawyer's role imposes on him a trusteeship for the integrity of those fundamental processes of government and self-government upon which the successful functioning of our society depends.

. . . Everywhere democratic and constitutional government is tragically dependent on voluntary and understanding co-operation in the maintenance of its fundamental processes and forms.

It is the lawyer's duty to preserve and advance this indispensable co-operation by keeping alive the willingness to engage in it and by imparting the understanding necessary to give it direction and effectiveness. This is a duty that attaches not only to his private practice, but to his relations with the public. In this matter he is not entitled to take public opinion as a datum by which to orient and justify his actions. He has an affirmative duty to help shape the growth and development of public attitudes toward fair procedures and due process.

3. *May the Arbiter Act on His Own Motion in Initiating the Case?*

In his *The Nature and Sources of the Law*, John Chipman Gray wrote:

> A judge of an organized body is a man appointed by that body to determine duties and the corresponding rights *upon the application of persons claiming those rights*. It is the fact that such application must be made to him, which distinguishes a judge from an administrative officer. The essence of a judge's office is that he shall be impartial, that he is to sit apart, is not to interfere voluntarily in affairs . . . but is to determine cases which are presented to him. To use the phrase of the English Ecclesiastical courts, the office of the judge must be promoted by some one.[23]

A German socialist critic of "bourgeois law" once caricatured this view by saying that courts are like defective clocks; they have to be shaken to set them going. He, of course, added the point that shaking costs money.

Certainly it is true that in most of the practical manifestations of adjudication the arbiter's function has to be "promoted" by the litigant and is not initiated by itself. But is this coy quality of waiting to be asked an essential part of adjudication?

It would seem that it is not. Suppose, for example, the collision of two ships under circumstances that suggest that one or both masters were at fault. Suppose a board is given authority to initiate hearings in such a case and to make a determination of fault. Such a board might conduct its hearings after the pattern of court proceedings. Both masters might be accorded counsel and a full opportunity for cross-examination. There would be no impairment of the affected parties' full participation by proofs and reasoned argument; the integrity of adjudication seems to be preserved.

Yet I think that most of us would consider such a case exceptional and would not be deterred by it from persisting in the belief that the adjudicative process should normally not be initiated by the tribunal itself. There are, I believe, sound reasons for adhering to that belief.

Certainly it is clear that the integrity of adjudication is im-

[23] [J.C. GRAY, *supra* note 9, at 114–15.]

paired if the arbiter not only initiates the proceedings but also, in advance of the public hearing, forms theories about what happened and conducts his own factual inquiries. In such a case the arbiter cannot bring to the public hearing an uncommitted mind; the effectiveness of participation through proofs and reasoned arguments is accordingly reduced. Now it is probably true that under most circumstances the mere initiation of proceedings carries with it a certain commitment and often a theory of what occurred. The case of the collision at sea is exceptional because there the facts themselves speak eloquently for the need of some kind of inquiry, so that the initiation of the proceedings implies nothing more than a recognition of this need. In most situations the initiation of proceedings could not have the same neutral quality, as, for example, where the occasion consists simply in the fact that a corporation had gone two years without declaring a dividend.

There is another reason which justifies the common conception that it is not normal for the adjudicative process to be initiated by the deciding tribunal. If we view adjudication in its widest extension, as including not only the work of courts but also that of arbitrators in labor, commerce, and international relations, it is apparent that the overwhelming majority of cases submitted to adjudication involve the assertion of claims founded directly or indirectly on *contract* or *agreement*. It seems clear that a regime of contract (more broadly, a regime of reciprocity) implies that the determination whether to assert a claim must be left to the interested party.

A contrary suggestion is advanced by Karl Llewellyn in *The Cheyenne Way*. In answer to the question "Why do we leave it to the affected party whether to assert his claim for breach of contract?" he gives the startling explanation that this is because as a matter of actual experience the motive of self-interest has proved sufficient to maintain a regime of contract.[24] He suggests that if in the future this motive were to suffer a serious decline, then the state might find itself compelled to intervene to strengthen the regime of contract. This curious conception is symptomatic of a general tendency of our times to obscure the role of reciprocity as an organizing principle and to convert everything into "social policy," which is another way of saying that all organization is by common aims (or by the aims that in the mind of the "policy-maker" ought to be common).

Any individual contract serves "society" only insofar as society is interested in the individual enrichment made possible by a regime of reciprocity. (Naturally, "individual" here has to be given an extended meaning to include groups and formal entities

[24] [K.N. Llewellyn & E.A. Hoebel, The Cheyenne Way 48 (1941).]

like the corporation.) If two men discover that by an agreement each can profit by giving up something he values less than the thing he receives in exchange for it, the individuals are enriched by virtue of their own evaluations of the objects of the exchange. If ten days after the agreement is entered there is a change in those evaluations, so that neither party has any further interest in the performance of the agreement, this is as much their affair as was the original agreement. To enforce a contract for a party who is willing to leave it unenforced is just as absurd as making the contract for him in the first place. (I realize, of course, that there are contracts required by law, but this is obviously a derivative phenomenon which would lose all meaning if every human relation were imposed by the state and were called a "contract.")

The belief that it is not normal for the arbiter himself to initiate the adjudicative process has, then, a twofold basis. *First*, it is generally impossible to keep even the bare initiation of proceedings untainted by preconceptions about what happened and what its consequences should be. In this sense, initiation of the proceedings by the arbiter impairs the integrity of adjudication by reducing the effectiveness of the litigant's participation through proofs and arguments. *Second*, the great bulk of claims submitted to adjudication are founded directly or indirectly on relationships of reciprocity. In this case, unless the affected party is deceived or ignorant of his rights, the very foundations of the claim asserted dictate that the processes of adjudication must be invoked by the claimant.

4. Must the Decision Be Accompanied by a Statement of the Reasons for It?

We tend to think of the judge or arbitrator as one who decides and who gives reasons for his decision. Does the integrity of adjudication require that reasons be given for the decision rendered? I think the answer is, not necessarily. In some fields of labor arbitration (chiefly, I believe, where arbitration is a facility made available without charge by the state) it is the practice to render "blind" awards. The reasons for this practice probably include a belief that reasoned awards are often misinterpreted and "stir up trouble," as well as the circumstance that the arbitrator is so busy he has no time to write opinions. Under the procedures of the American Arbitration Association awards in commercial cases are rendered usually without opinion. (Written opinions are, however, usual in *labor* cases.) Perhaps the special practice in commercial cases has arisen because arbitrators in such cases normally serve without fee and writing opinions is hard work. Perhaps also there is a fear that explanations ineptly phrased by lay arbitrators might open too wide a door to judicial review.

By and large it seems clear that the fairness and effectiveness of adjudication are promoted by reasoned opinions. Without such opinions the parties have to take it on faith that their participation in the decision has been real, that the arbiter has in fact understood and taken into account their proofs and arguments. A less obvious point is that, where a decision enters into some continuing relationship, if no reasons are given the parties will almost inevitably guess at reasons and act accordingly. Here the effectiveness of adjudication is impaired, not only because the results achieved may not be those intended by the arbiter, but also because his freedom of decision in future cases may be curtailed by the growth of practices based on a misinterpretation of decisions previously rendered.

5. *May the Arbiter Rest His Decision on Grounds Not Argued by the Parties?*

Obviously the bond of participation by the litigant is most secure when the arbiter rests his decision wholly on the proofs and argument actually presented to him by the parties. In practice, however, it is not always possible to realize this ideal. Even where all of the considerations on which the decision rests were touched on by the parties' arguments, the emphasis may be very different. An issue dealt with only in passing by one of the parties, or perhaps by both, may become the headstone of the arbiter's decision. This may mean not only that, had they foreseen this outcome, the parties would have presented different arguments, but that they might also have introduced evidence on very different factual issues.

If the ideal of a perfect congruence between the arbiter's view of the issues and that of the parties is unattainable, this is no excuse for a failure to work toward an achievement of the closest approximation of it. We need to remind ourselves that if this congruence is utterly absent — if the grounds for the decision fall completely outside the framework of the argument, making all that was discussed or proved at the hearing irrelevant — then the adjudicative process has become a sham, for the parties' participation in the decision has lost all meaning. We need to analyze what factors influence the desired congruence and what measures may be taken to promote it.

One circumstance of capital importance is the extent to which a particular process of adjudication takes place in a context of established rules. In branches of the law where the rules have become fairly settled and certain, it may be possible for lawyers to reach agreement easily in defining the crucial issues presented by a particular case. In such an area the risk is slight that the decision will fall outside the frame of reference set by the proofs and arguments. On the other hand, in areas of uncertainty, this risk is greatly increased. There are, to be sure, dangers in a premature crystallization of standards. On the other hand, one of the less obvious dangers of a too long delayed formulation of doctrine lies in the inevitable impairment of the integrity of adjudication that is entailed, for the reality of the parties' participation is reduced when it is impossible to foretell what issues will become relevant in the ultimate disposition of the case.

These are considerations often overlooked in criticisms of the conduct of administrative agencies and labor arbitrators. Ex parte posthearing conferences with the parties are often motivated by a well-intentioned desire to preserve the reality of the parties' participation in the decision. Where the standards of decision are vague and fluctuating, when the time comes for final disposition of the case it may be apparent that most of what was argued and proved at the public hearing has become irrelevant. A desire to give a litigant a meaningful "day in court" may, paradoxically, lead to giving him a lunchhour out of court. In many cases this conduct should be characterized as inept, rather than wicked.

Those inexperienced in legal procedures often do not know of devices which have been developed by courts that will eliminate much of the need for such practices. In particular, requests for a reargument and the device of the tentative decree, with something like an order to show cause why it should not be made final, could often be used with advantage by labor arbitrators and administrative tribunals. This is not to say that these expedients will solve all problems. An arbitrator paid on a per diem basis by the parties may hesitate to run up his bill by requesting a second argument. In some situations a tentative decree may arouse expectations of such an intensity that a later modification becomes very difficult. The fundamental point made here, however, is that before we demand of lay arbiters that they act like judges, we must place them in a context, and arm them with procedures, that will make it possible for them to do their job properly and still act throughout like judges. It is distressing to see Congress assign to administrative agencies tasks that plainly lie beyond the limits of adjudication and yet demand of those agencies that they act as if their tasks fell within those limits. Even more distressing is it when they are compelled to announce "standards" and "policies" which they consider they cannot conscientiously follow in the discharge of their duties.

In this rather messy situation the influence of the individual practicing lawyer can be a most wholesome one. If he is an expert in a particular field of administrative law, he can often judge accurately in a particular case what issues will ultimately become crucial. This means that he will be able to present at the public hearing all that will be needed for a proper decision; thus the temptation of posthearing conferences may be removed. Generally the professional advocate can play an important role in preserving the integrity of adjudication. It is painful for a lawyer to attend the hearings of a board where most of the representation is by laymen, say, a board of appeals hearing applications for variances from zoning laws. The hearing is customarily devoted to irrelevancies, and the issues really pertinent to decision may be scarcely touched on in the arguments presented. This would be the situation in all fields of adjudication were we to remove from the scene the professional advocate. His presence is usually essential for adjudication to be in fact what it pretends to be.

I have mentioned two devices that can help to prevent a lack of fit between the case as argued and the case as decided — the request for a reargument and the tentative decree. Oral argument is also of the greatest importance in this connection, for a written submission is often truly a shot in the dark. In appellate cases it is also important that the judges have studied the record before oral argument, for without this preparation the virtue of the oral argument in defining the crucial issues may be lost.

So far I have been discussing precautionary measures that will reduce the risk that the arbiter will have to rest his decision on considerations not argued before him. I have assumed that the area of adjudication in question is such that these precautionary measures can have some measure of success. The matter stands quite differently when cases are assigned to a process called "adjudication" under circumstances such that the best informed advocate could not possibly present to the tribunal the grounds that must be taken into account in the decision. For example, G. D. H. Cole in his *Socialist Economics* proposes that under socialism wages should be set by "arbitrators" who would be "guided by common sense."[25] Presumably there would be public hearings and the affected employees would be permitted to present arguments in favor of an increase of their remuneration. However, Professor Cole recognizes that his "arbitrators" cannot be guided solely by what is argued before them. In fact, he recommends that they meet together from time to time to see to it that the combined effect of their awards will produce a proper flow of labor. Here, plainly, the bond of the affected party's participation has largely been destroyed. He is given the appearance of a hearing,

[25] [G.D.H. COLE, SOCIALIST ECONOMICS 96 (1950).]

presumably because this will make him happier, but the grounds of decision are largely unrelated to what occurred at the hearing. Professor Cole's "arbitrators" are in fact business managers who from time to time put on a show by going through the motions of adjudication. This is the kind of case I have in mind in speaking of problems that fall beyond the limits of adjudication.

6. *Qualifications and Disqualifications of the Arbiter*

A full discussion of the questions suggested by this title would lead too far afield for the purposes of this paper. Even a consideration of the comparative efficacy of the various devices intended to guarantee impartiality would require a long chapter.

I shall merely suggest that the problem of securing a properly qualified and impartial arbiter be tried by the same touchstone that has been used throughout — what will preserve the efficacy and meaning of the affected party's participation through proofs and arguments? Obviously, a strong emotional attachment by the arbiter to one of the interests involved in the dispute is destructive of that participation. In practice, however, another kind of "partiality" is much more dangerous. I refer to the situation where the arbiter's experience of life has not embraced the area of the dispute, or, worse still, where he has always viewed that area from some single vantage point. Here a blind spot of which he is quite unconscious may prevent him from getting the point of testimony or argument. By and large I think the decisions of our courts in commercial cases do not represent adjudication at its highest level. The reason is a lack of judicial "feel" for the problems involved.

A sailor was once brought before a three-judge German court for violation of a provision of the criminal code which made it a serious offense to threaten another with bodily harm. Uncontradicted testimony proved that the prisoner had been heard to say, "I'll stick a knife in your guts and turn it around three times." Two judges, who had spent their lives in genteel surroundings far from the waterfront, were with great difficulty persuaded by the third to acquit.

7. *Must the Decision Be Retrospective?*

In practice both the decisions of courts and the awards of arbitrators are retrospective, both as to their effect on the litigants' rights and their effect as precedents for the decisions of other cases. A paradox is sometimes squeezed from this traditional way of acting, to the effect that courts, in order to avoid the appearance of legislating, cast their legislative enactments in the harshest possible form, making them ex post facto.

The philosophy underlying the retrospective effect of the judicial decision can be stated somewhat as follows: It is not the function of courts to create new aims for society or to impose on society new basic directives. The courts for various reasons analyzed previously are unsuited for this sort of task. Perhaps the most compelling objection to an assumption of any such function lies in the limited participation in the decision by the litigants who (1) represent generally only themselves and (2) participate in the decision only by proofs and arguments addressed to the arbiter. On the other hand, with respect to the generally shared aims and the authoritative directives of a society, the courts do have an important function to perform, that of developing (or even "discovering") case by case what these aims or directives demand for their realization in particular situations of fact. In the discharge of this function, at times the result is so obvious that no one thinks of a "retroactive effect." Theoretically, a court might distinguish between such decisions and those which announce a rule or standard that seems "new," even though it may represent a reasoned conclusion from familiar premises. But if an attempt were made to apply such a distinction pervasively, so that some decisions would be retrospective, some prospective only, the resulting confusion might be much less bearable than the situation that now obtains.

Generally the same considerations apply also to arbitration awards. It is not a matter of "concealing" the legislative nature of the arbitrator's award which makes him give it a retrospective effect. It is rather a conservative philosophy about the proper functions of adjudication, a philosophy which seeks to keep meaningful the adversary presentation, the participation of litigants only through appeals to reason, etc.

8. *Moot Cases and Declaratory Judgments*

There has not been time to consider seriously the problems presented by this title. It is believed, however, that the general analysis of this paper might be helpful in dealing with those problems.

9. *How Is Adjudication Affected by the Source of the Arbiter's Power?*

The power to adjudicate may represent a delegated power of government, as in the case of a judge, or it may derive from the consent of the litigants, as in most forms of arbitration. Are these two basically different "forms" of adjudication? Obviously it has been a tacit assumption of this paper that they are not.

On the other hand, this does not mean that the discharge of the arbiter's function is wholly unaffected by the source of his power. In a summary way we may say that the possible advantages of adjudication supported by governmental authority are: (1) The judge is under less temptation to "compromise" than is the contractually appointed arbitrator. (2) The acceptability of the judge's decision may be enhanced by the fact that he seems to play a subservient role, as one who merely applies rules which he himself did not make.

Among the possible advantages of adjudication which derives its power from a contract of the parties are the following: (1) Being unbacked by state power (or insufficiently backed by it in the case of an ineffective legal sanction), the arbitrator must concern himself directly with the acceptability of his award. He may be at greater pains than a judge to get his facts straight, to state accurately the arguments of the parties, and generally to display in his award a full understanding of the case. (2) Being relatively free from technical rules of procedure, the wise and conscientious arbitrator can shape his procedures upon what he perceives to be the intrinsic demands of effective adjudication. Thus, the "due process" which animates his conduct of the hearing may appear to the parties as something real and not something that has to be taken on faith, as allegedly inhering in technical rules that seem quite arbitrary to the layman.

As a special quality of contractually authorized arbitration, which cannot unequivocally be called either an "advantage" or "disadvantage," we may note that the contract to arbitrate may contain explicit or implicit limits upon the adjudicative process itself. The arbitrator often comes to the hearing with a feeling that he must conduct himself in a way that conforms generally to the expectations of the parties and that this restriction is implicit in the contract of submission. Thus, if both parties desire and expect a more "literal" interpretation than the arbitrator himself would prefer, he may feel obligated to adopt an attitude of interpretation that he finds intellectually uncongenial.

VII. The Limits of Adjudication

1. Introduction

Attention is now directed to the question, What kinds of tasks are inherently unsuited to adjudication? The test here will be that used throughout. If a given task is assigned to adjudicative treatment, will it be possible to preserve the meaning of the affected party's participation through proofs and arguments?

2. *Polycentric Tasks and Adjudication*

This section introduces a concept — that of the "polycentric" task — which has been derived from Michael Polanyi's book *The Logic of Liberty*.[26] In approaching that concept it will be well to begin with a few examples.

Some months ago a wealthy lady by the name of Timken died in New York leaving a valuable, but somewhat miscellaneous, collection of paintings to the Metropolitan Museum and the National Gallery "in equal shares," her will indicating no particular apportionment.[27] When the will was probated the judge remarked something to the effect that the parties seemed to be confronted with a real problem. The attorney for one of the museums spoke up and said, "We are good friends. We will work it out somehow or other." What makes this problem of effecting an equal division of the paintings a polycentric task? It lies in the fact that the disposition of any single painting has implications for the proper disposition of every other painting. If it gets the Renoir, the Gallery may be less eager for the Cezanne but all the more eager for the Bellows, etc. If the proper apportionment were set for argument, there would be no clear issue to which either side could direct its proofs and contentions. Any judge assigned to hear such an argument would be tempted to assume the role of mediator or to adopt the classical solution: Let the older brother (here the Metropolitan) divide the estate into what he regards as equal shares, let the younger brother (the National Gallery) take his pick.

As a second illustration suppose in a socialist regime it were decided to have all wages and prices set by courts which would proceed after the usual forms of adjudication. It is, I assume, obvious that here is a task that could not successfully be undertaken by the adjudicative method. The point that comes first to mind is that courts move too slowly to keep up with a rapidly changing economic scene. The more fundamental point is that the forms of adjudication cannot encompass and take into account the complex repercussions that may result from any change in prices or wages. A rise in the price of aluminum may affect in varying degrees the demand for, and therefore the proper price of, thirty kinds of steel, twenty kinds of plastics, an infinitude of woods, other metals, etc. Each of these separate effects may have its own complex repercussions in the economy. In such a case it is simply impossible to afford each affected party a meaningful

---

[26] [M. Polanyi, The Logic of Liberty: Reflections and Rejoinders 171 (1951).]

[27] [*See* N.Y. Times, May 15, 1960, at 77, col. 1.]

participation through proofs and arguments. It is a matter of capital importance to note that it is not merely a question of the huge number of possibly affected parties, significant as that aspect of the thing may be. A more fundamental point is that each of the various forms that award might take (say, a three-cent increase per pound, a four-cent increase, a five-cent increase, etc.) would have a different set of repercussions and might require in each instance a redefinition of the "parties affected."

We may visualize this kind of situation by thinking of a spider web. A pull on one strand will distribute tensions after a complicated pattern throughout the web as a whole. Doubling the original pull will, in all likelihood, not simply double each of the resulting tensions but will rather create a different complicated pattern of tensions. This would certainly occur, for example, if the doubled pull caused one or more of the weaker strands to snap. This is a "polycentric" situation because it is "many centered" — each crossing of strands is a distinct center for distributing tensions.

Suppose, again, it were decided to assign players on a football team to their positions by a process of adjudication. I assume that we would agree that this is also an unwise application of adjudication. It is not merely a matter of eleven different men being possibly affected; each shift of any one player might have a different set of repercussions on the remaining players: putting Jones in as quarterback would have one set of carryover effects, putting him in as left end, another. Here, again, we are dealing with a situation of interacting points of influence and therefore with a polycentric problem beyond the proper limits of adjudication.

Let me now mention a polycentric problem that would be difficult to handle by adjudication as usually conducted, where the form of adjudication is sometimes modified to accomodate it to the nature of the problem. A textile mill is in agreement with a labor union that its internal wage scale is out of balance; over the years the payments made for certain kinds of jobs have "got out of line" and are now too high or too low in comparison with what is paid for other jobs. The company and the union agree that a fund equal to five cents an hour for the whole payroll shall be employed to create a proper balance. If the parties are unable to agree on the adjustments that should be made, the question shall go to arbitration.

Here we have a problem with strong polycentric features. If the weavers are raised, say, more than three cents an hour, it will be necessary to raise the spinners; the spinners' wages are, however, locked in a traditional relationship with those of the spinning doffers, etc. If there are thirty different classifications involved, it is obvious how many different forms the arbitration award might take; each pattern of the award could produce its own peculiar pattern of repercussions. If such a problem is presented to a single arbitrator, he will be under strong temptation to "try out" various forms of award in private conversations with the parties. Irregular and improper as such conversations may appear when judged by the usual standards of adjudication, it should be noted that the motive for them may be the arbitrator's desire to preserve the reality of the parties' participation in the decision — to preserve, in other words, the very core of adjudication.

Now it is in cases like this that the "tripartite" arbitration board finds its most useful application. The "impartial chairman" is flanked by two fellow arbitrators, one selected by the company, the other by the union. After the hearings the three consult together, the impartial chairman at some point proposing to the other members of the board various wage scales. He will in the process learn such things as that an increase for a particular occupation that seemed to him both proper and feasible will have repercussions in the bleachery of which he was unaware.

This is what I have called a "mixed" form of adjudication. In fact the device as I have stated it amounts to a mixture of adjudication and negotiation. All mixed forms have their dangers, and tripartite arbitration is no exception. The danger lies in the difficult role to be played by the flanking arbitrators. They can be neither wholly advocates nor wholly judges. They cannot perform their role adequately if they are completely impartial; it is their task during the deliberations to represent an interest, a point of view. It may be that they will wish to communicate with the parties they represent to inform themselves of the implications of some step proposed — though whether they should feel free to indulge in such consultations, and if so, to what extent, is one of the ambiguities that plague this form of arbitration. If, on the one hand, each of the flanking arbitrators must represent the party who appointed him, he must at the same time observe some of the restraints that go with a judicial position. If he runs back and forth between those he represents and the meetings of the arbitration board, reporting freely everything that happens during those meetings, the adjudicative process breaks down and there is substituted for it an awkward form of bargaining — in a situation, be it remembered, where negotiation has already failed to produce a solution.

As a prophylaxis against the arbitration's deteriorating into a mere continuation of bargaining — in an inept form — a variation on the tripartite pattern is now written into a good many labor contracts. It is provided that a unanimous decision of the three arbitrators shall control, but if such a decision cannot be obtained, the chairman shall determine the rights of the parties. Where there is from the beginning no real hope of a unanimous decision, this arrangement comes close to being little more than a contractual legitimation of the practice of holding posthearing conferences, though it has the advantage of officially designating the representatives who may take part in these conferences. On the other hand, where there is some genuine prospect of a unanimous agreement, the arrangement preserves for the flanking arbitrators a role that retains some of the functions, and with them some of the restraints, that go with judicial office.

The description just given is of tripartite arbitration when it is employed intelligently and with some appreciation of its advantages and dangers. In practice it is often used uncritically and tends to deteriorate, on the one hand, into a kind of continuation of bargaining behind closed doors, or, on the other, into an empty form, whereby it is understood from the beginning that the chairman is the "real" arbitrator.

It should be carefully noted that a multiplicity of affected persons is not an invariable characteristic of polycentric problems. This is sufficiently illustrated in the case of Mrs. Timken's will. That case also illustrated the fact that rapid changes with time are not an invariable characteristic of such problems. On the other hand, in practice polycentric problems of possible concern to adjudication will normally involve many affected parties and a somewhat fluid state of affairs. Indeed, the last characteristic follows from the simple fact that the more interacting centers there are, the more the likelihood that one of them will be affected by a change in circumstances, and, if the situation is polycentric, this change will communicate itself after a complex pattern to other centers. This insistence on a clear conception of polycentricity may seem to be laboring a point, but clarity of analysis is essential if confusion is to be avoided. For example, if a reward of $1000 is offered for the capture of a criminal and six claimants assert a right to the award, hearing the six-sided controversy may be an awkward affair. The problem does not, however, present any significant polycentric element as that term is here used.

Now, if it is important to see clearly what a polycentric problem is, it is equally important to realize that the distinction involved is often a matter of degree. There are polycentric elements in almost all problems submitted to adjudication. A decision may act as a precedent, often an awkward one, in some situation not foreseen by the arbiter. Again, suppose a court in a suit between one litigant and a railway holds that it is an act of negligence for the railway not to construct an underpass at a particular crossing. There may be nothing to distinguish this crossing from other crossings on the line. As a matter of statistical probability it may be clear that constructing underpasses along the whole line would cost more lives (through accidents in blasting, for example) than would be lost if the only safety measure were the familiar "Stop, Look & Listen" sign. If so, then what seems to be a decision simply declaring the rights and duties of two parties is in fact an inept solution for a polycentric problem, some elements of which cannot be brought before the court in a simple suit by one injured party against a defendant railway. In lesser measure, concealed polycentric elements are probably present in almost all problems resolved by adjudication. It is not, then, a question of distinguishing black from white. It is a question of knowing when the polycentric elements have become so significant and predominant that the proper limits of adjudication have been reached.

In speaking of the covert polycentric elements almost always present in even the most simple-appearing cases, it should be noted that the efficacy of adjudication as a whole is strongly affected by the manner in which the doctrine of stare decisis is applied. If judicial precedents are liberally interpreted and are subject to reformulation and clarification as problems not originally foreseen arise, the judicial process as a whole is enabled to absorb these covert polycentric elements. By considering the process of decision as a collaborative one projected through time, an accommodation of legal doctrine to the complex aspects of a problem can be made as these aspects reveal themselves in successive cases. On the other hand, if a strict or "literal" interpretation is made of precedents, the limits of adjudication must perforce be more strictly drawn, for its power of accommodation has been reduced.

If problems sufficiently polycentric are unsuited to solution by adjudication, how may they in fact be solved? So far as I can see, there are only two suitable methods: *managerial direction* and *contract* (or reciprocity).

The manner in which managerial direction solves polycentric problems is exemplified by the baseball manager who assigns his players to their positions, decides when to take a pitcher out, when and whom to pinch-hit, when and how far to shift the infield and outfield for a particular batter, etc. The relationships potentially affected by these decisions are in formal mathematical terms of great complexity — and in the practical solution of them a good deal of "intuition" is indispensable.

Many problems of economic management are of a similar nature. Substitution of plastic for aluminum in a component part may produce a paper saving of twenty cents on each unit produced but involve the disruption of a longstanding relation with a supplier, the possibility of a strike over the necessary changes in piece rates, though the strike might turn out in the long run to be a good thing, etc., etc. In the solution of some economic polycentric problems, recently developed mathematical methods, like those of Leontief, may reduce the necessity to rely on intuition, though they can never eliminate the element of human judgment.[28]

The other method by which polycentric problems are solved is that of contract or a reciprocal adjustment of each center of interest with those with which it interacts. Thus, an economic market can solve the extremely complex problems of allocating resources, "costing" production, and pricing goods. Whenever the literature of socialism actually deals seriously with those problems the only solution found is the establishment of something akin to a market among the various state enterprises.[29] It is interesting that the best solution even for problems of engineering calculation is often found by deriving an answer from a series of approximations, first from one center of stress, and then from another.[30]

Recently a branch of mathematics known as game theory has been proposed as a method of adjusting adjudication to the solution of what are here called polycentric problems.[31] In essence these proposals convert adjudication into a kind of contractual game, in principle much like the classical solution already mentioned for dividing an estate equally between two sons. Each party draws up a priority list indicating his order of preference for the various possible solutions of the controversy; mathematical methods are then used to produce the "optimum" solution. The fault of this procedure is that it solves a polycentric problem only by grossly simplifying and distorting it. The priority list, for example, indicates one party's preferences as *A, D, E, B*; it does not indicate that if he gets one tenth of *A* he might be willing to move *E* ahead of *D*, etc.

It is important to note that the majority principle is quite incapable of solving polycentric problems. A baseball manager surveying in his mind all the possible ways of deploying the talent

---

[28] [*See* Leontief, *Input-Output Economics*, SCIENTIFIC AM., Oct. 1951, at 15. *See also* W. LEONTIEF, H.B. CHENERY, P.G. CLARK, J.S. DUSENBERRY, A.R. FERGUSON, A.P. GROSSE, R.N. GROSSE, M. HOLZMAN, W. IZARD & H. KISTIN, STUDIES IN THE STRUCTURE OF THE AMERICAN ECONOMY (1953).]

[29] *See* O. LANGE & F.M. TAYLOR, ON THE ECONOMIC THEORY OF SOCIALISM ([B. Lippincott ed.] 1938).

[30] [*See* M. POLANYI, *supra* note 26, at 173-74].

[31] *See* R.B. BRAITHWAITE, THEORY OF GAMES AS A TOOL FOR THE MORAL PHILOSOPHER [53-54 (1955)].

at his disposal may come up with the optimum solution; it would only be by accident that such a solution could result from a vote of the players or fans. Indeed, where voting is by the majority principle, the choice must be limited to two alternatives, say, Solution *X* or *Y*, and most of the problems would have to be solved before a vote could be taken. But even when voting methods are modified, polycentric problems remain beyond the reach of anything like an election. Even if the choices are limited to three and voters are asked to list Solutions *X*, *Y*, and *Z* in the order of their preference, the vote may result in a circle of priorities and thus yield no solution at all, either good or bad.

On the other hand, polycentric problems can often be solved, at least after a measure, by parliamentary methods which include an element of contract in the form of the political "deal." The parties in interest — or, more realistically, the parties most obviously concerned — are called together at a legislative hearing or in a conference with legislative leaders and "an accommodation of interests" is worked out. I suggest that we need a philosophy of the "political deal" that will discern its proper uses from its abuses. I believe the concept of the polycentric problem could help in drawing the line.

If we survey the whole field of adjudication and ask ourselves where the solution of polycentric problems by adjudication has most often been attempted, the answer is: in the field of administrative law. The instinct for giving the affected citizen his "day in court" pulls powerfully toward casting exercises of governmental power in the mold of adjudication, however inappropriate that mold may turn out to be. It is interesting to observe, however, that during World War II the agencies charged with allocative tasks did not attempt to follow the forms of adjudication. The War Labor Board proceeded after the pattern of tripartite arbitration, but it was theoretically barred from raising wages to influence the flow of labor, the allocative function in this case being assigned to the War Manpower Commission, which was not an adjudicative body. The Office of Price Administration and the War Production Board, vast as their powers were, did not pretend to act adjudicatively, except in trying alleged violations.

Generally speaking, it may be said that problems in the allocation of economic resources present too strong a polycentric aspect to be suitable for adjudication. Thus, a proposal made in England after World War II that scarce newspaper print be allocated by jury verdict could hardly have been the product of serious reflection. In a somewhat different category is the proposal by James B. Conant that a "quasi-judicial" procedure be used in allocating government funds among competing projects of scientific research. Obviously Dr. Conant has given serious thought to this question, and he seeks some procedure which will avoid the compromises that so often result in no project's getting enough money to make it effective. His desire to preserve the integrity of adjudication is shown by the fact that he suggests, "If there is no [competing project], some technical expert should be appointed to speak on behalf of the taxpayer *against* the proposed research . . . ."[32] Yet when one considers the nature of the problem of allocation, one wonders whether the "adjudication" here proposed could be that in anything but name. In allocating $100 million for scientific research it is never a case of Project *A* v. Project *B*, but rather of Project *A* v. Project *B* v. Project *C* v. Project *D* . . . . bearing in mind that Project *Q* may be an alternative to Project *B*, while Project *M* supplements it, and that Project *R* may seek the same objective as Project *C* by a cheaper method, though one less certain to succeed, etc.

The final question to be addressed is this: When an attempt is made to deal by adjudicative forms with a problem that is essentially polycentric, what happens? As I see it, three things can happen, sometimes all at once. *First*, the adjudicative solution may fail. Unexpected repercussions make the decision unworkable; it is ignored, withdrawn, or modified, sometimes repeatedly. *Second*, the purported arbiter ignores judicial proprieties — he "tries out" various solutions in posthearing conferences, consults parties not represented at the hearings, guesses at facts not proved and not properly matters for anything like judicial notice. *Third*, instead of accommodating his procedures to the nature of the problem he confronts, he may reformulate the problem so as to make it amenable to solution through adjudicative procedures.

Only the last of these needs illustration. Suppose it is agreed that an employer's control over promotions shall be subject to review through arbitration. Now obviously an arbitrator cannot decide whether when Jones was made a Machinist Class A there was someone else more deserving in the plant, or whether, in view of Jones' age, it would have been better to put him in another job with comparable pay. This is the kind of allocative problem for which adjudication is utterly unsuited. There are, however, two ways of obtaining a workable control over promotions through arbitration. One of these is through the posting of jobs; when a job is vacant, interested parties may apply for promotion into it.

[32] [J.B. Conant, Science and Common Sense 337 (1951). The sentence in the text is a slight misquotation; the original reads, "If there are no contrary arguments, some technical expert . . . ."]

At the hearing, only those who have made application are entitled to be considered, and of course only the posted job is in issue. Here the problem is simplified in advance to the point where it can be arbitrated, though not without difficulty, particularly in the form of endless arguments as to whether there was in fact a vacancy that ought to have been posted, and whether a claimant filed his application on time and in the proper form, etc. The other way of accommodating the problem to arbitration is for the arbitrator to determine not who should be promoted but who *has* been promoted. That is, the contract contains certain "job descriptions" with the appropriate rate for each; the claimant asserts that he is in fact doing the work of a Machinist A, though he is still assigned the pay and title of a Machinist B. The controversy has two parties — the company and the claimant as represented by the union — and a single factual issue, Is the claimant in fact doing the work of a Machinist A?

In practice the procedure of applying for appointment to posted jobs will normally be prescribed in the contract itself, so that the terms of the agreement keep the arbitrator's function with respect to promotions within manageable limits. The other method of making feasible a control of promotions through arbitration will normally result from the arbitrator's own perception of the limitations of his role. The contract may simply contain a schedule of job rates and job classifications and a general clause stating that "discharges, promotions, and layoffs shall be subject to the grievance procedure." If the arbitrator were to construe such a contract to give him a general supervision over promotions, he would embark himself upon managerial tasks wholly unsuited to solution by any arbitrative procedure. An instinct toward preserving the integrity of his role will move him, therefore, to construe the contract in the manner already indicated, so that he avoids any responsibility with respect to the assignment of duties and merely decides whether the duties actually assigned make appropriate the classification assigned by the company to the complaining employee.

Let me take another example, where my interpretation of what has occurred may or may not be correct. The FCC early established the policy that generally applicants for radio or television channels must propose a well-rounded, general program. In rural areas, where only one or two channels are available for local receivers, this policy can be justified on grounds having nothing to do with the inappropriateness of using adjudication for allocative purposes. But in many areas there are available five to ten television channels and many more radio channels. What one would expect here would be the development of specialized markets: one station catering to the sports fan, another to the opera lover, etc. In England the BBC has three kinds of programs, ranging from lowbrow, to middlebrow, to highbrow. In this country some development of specialization has occurred — despite the FCC — in a general distinction in the appeal of AM and FM radio. Yet contests for television channels today are still competitions among applicants each of whom promises the most inclusive, "well-rounded" program, each undertaking to satisfy more incompatible tastes than his rivals. Is not this phenomenon to be explained by the fact that it is sensed by all, the FCC and the applicants alike, that the whole adjudicative procedure would break down if one applicant promised to satisfy one market, another a different market? In such a case, the meaning of the applicant's participation through proofs and arguments would be destroyed because (1) there would be no real joinder of issues and (2) the FCC would have to consider whether parties not present at the hearings were not already satisfying one or more of the markets proposed to be opened. To preserve some substance for the form of adjudication you have to judge pumpkins against pumpkins, not pumpkins against cucumbers, especially when there are some relevant cucumbers not entered in the show.

In closing this discussion of polycentricity, it will be well to caution against two possible misunderstandings. The suggestion that polycentric problems are often solved by a kind of "managerial intuition" should not be taken to imply that it is an invariable characteristic of polycentric problems that they resist rational solution. There are rational principles for building bridges of structural steel. But there is no rational principle which states, for example, that the angle between girder *A* and girder *B* must always be 45 degrees. This depends on the bridge as a whole. One cannot construct a bridge by conducting successive separate arguments concerning the proper angle for every pair of intersecting girders. One must deal with the whole structure.

Finally, the fact that an adjudicative decision affects and enters into a polycentric relationship does not of itself mean that the adjudicative tribunal is moving out of its proper sphere. On the contrary, there is no better illustration of a polycentric relationship than an economic market, and yet the laying down of rules that will make a market function properly is one for which adjudication is generally well suited. The working out of our common law of contracts case by case has proceeded through adjudication, yet the basic principle underlying the rules thus developed is that they should promote the free exchange of goods in a polycentric market. The court gets into difficulty, not when it lays down rules about contracting, but when it attempts to write contracts.

3. Is the Proper Province of Adjudication Limited to the Declaration of Rights and Duties?

I have already pointed out that an attempt is often made to distinguish adjudication by saying that the decisions of courts declare or create rights and duties, while the decisions of executives and administrators do not. Does this formulation state a distinct limit of adjudication, different from those just discussed? I do not believe so, or rather, I believe this formulation of the limits of adjudication derives from considerations very closely allied to those analyzed in the discussion of polycentric tasks.

A right is a demand founded on a principle — a principle regarded as appropriately controlling the relations of two parties. Now it is characteristic of a polycentric relationship that the relations of individual members to one another are not controlled by principles peculiar to those relations, just as it is impossible to build a bridge by establishing distinct principles governing the angle of every pair of girders. So in a baseball team, no one has a "right" to left field, or at least, no one ought to.

The transformation by which economic relations that ought to remain flexible tend to crystallize into "rights" is, in effect, the same process I attempted to describe when I spoke of cases where adjudication, instead of accommodating its forms to a polycentric problem, has accommodated the problem to its forms. Our railways are taken as a prime example of a field of human relations penetrated by inappropriate "rights" that interfere with efficiency. It is said by the railways themselves that this development began during World War I when a government, then unused to managerial tasks, undertook to run the railways after its accustomed forms and converted every managerial problem into something suitable for decision by adjudication.[33]

4. Is It a Significant Statement of the Proper Province of Adjudication To Say That Courts Cannot By and Large Undertake an "Affirmative" Direction of Affairs?

It is often said that courts cannot undertake the responsibility for an affirmative direction of affairs. Miss Johanna Wagner can be restrained from singing for Mr. Gye; she cannot be compelled to sing for Mr. Lumley — the British courts cannot go into the theatre business.[34]

[33] *See* [Executive Committee, Bureau of Information of the Eastern Railways,] Wages and Labor Relations in the Railway Industry 1900–1941, at 55–60 [(n.d.)].

[34] [Lumley v. Wagner, 1 DeG. M. & G. 604, 42 Eng. Rep. 687 (Ch. 1852),

Once again, I believe that this is merely a reformulation of the limitations discussed in connection with polycentric problems. What we call "affirmative" direction involves a summoning and ordering of individual and collective human energies. Polanyi reminds us that it is a characteristic of living creatures that they can deal with polycentric problems, indeed, this is the nature of all "creative" actions.[35] This is apparent when we think of the artist, the architect, the painter. But on the lowest level we see life struggling to survive by solving polycentric problems when the ameba restlessly readjusts its pseudopods in the manner most appropriate to its changing liquid environment.

It has often been remarked that rights in rem (that is, rights against the world generally, such as the right not to be struck) are invariably "negative." What this means is that the law can clear the way for creative acts by restraining certain obviously destructive ones; it cannot effect the reordering that is involved in acts of creation.

Before leaving this problem of the distinction between the "negative" and the "affirmative," I should like to record my conviction that one of the most unsatisfactory chapters in legal analysis is that dealing with this distinction, as, for example, in the well-known distinction between malfeasance and nonfeasance and in assertions to the effect that "an affirmative is easier to prove" and that the party seeking to establish an affirmative proposition therefore bears the burden of proof. Discussions of problems like these often proceed as if reality presented itself to us already bearing the labels *plus* or *minus*. That this is not the case can readily be seen if we remember that we can always convert a negative into an affirmative by adding another "not" — Miss Wagner can be ordered to cease not singing. The distinction between what we think of as affirmative and negative conduct is something deeper than a grammatical sign.

VIII. Mixed, Parasitic, and Perverted Forms of Social Order Involving Adjudication

1. Introduction

This concluding section will be sketchy and suggestive, without any pretense to dealing exhaustively with the problems it raises.

It may be well to warn again against the assumption that every mixed or "impure" form of adjudication is here condemned. In

reprinted in L.L. Fuller & M.A. Eisenberg, Basic Contract Law 783 (3d ed. 1972).]

[35] [M. Polanyi, *supra* note 26, at 176.]

the previous discussion of tripartite arbitration, I tried to show how useful this form might be, at the same time calling attention to the dangers contained in it and to the possibilities of its abuse.

When I speak of a form of order as being parasitic, I mean merely that, although it seems to possess an original strength of its own, it in fact draws its moral sustenance from another form of order. In labeling it "parasitic," I intend no more condemnation than when a botanist calls a certain fungus "parasitic." Just as, from the standpoint of human interest, there are good and bad fungi, so parasitic forms of order may be good or bad.

2. *Mixed Forms of Social Ordering Involving Adjudication and Contract*

a. Adjudication and Mediation. — During World War II the War Labor Board undertook to revise the internal structure of wages in a number of industries. This polycentric task could not have been accomplished by adjudication in its usual forms. Instead, following the hearing, a member of the Board met alternately with representatives first of industry, then of the union, and sounded them out on various changes in the wage scale. The result was a mediated contract negotiated under the threat of an exercise of adjudicative functions. For rather obvious reasons, this is a dangerous procedure, requiring the skill of a George Taylor and the capacity to make a rather uninhibited use of public power that characterizes a war economy.[36] In peacetimes functions of this sort are usually exercised by a kind of industrial "czar." The fact that persons occupying this sort of role normally start as arbitrators has produced a very dangerous confusion. It has misled many uninformed persons into believing that "good arbitration" involves the formless exercise of a kind of wisdom-directed personal power. The fact is that these "czars" gradually drift into a kind of charismatic leadership, the peculiar magic of which is valid only within a limited context. Even within that context the business of "playing god" can be very dangerous, as experience has often demonstrated.

b. Tripartite Arbitration. — This mixed form has already been discussed at considerable length in other connections.

c. Obligations to Negotiate Under the Threat of an Exercise of Adjudicative Powers. — A complex long term supply contract provides for a renegotiation of the price from time to time and, failing agreement, for a determination of the price through arbitration. Here adjudication and contract reciprocally support one another. Parties desirous of entering a contract would hardly stipulate

[36] [*See* G.W. Taylor, Effectuating the Labor Contract Through Arbitration, Address Before the National Academy of Arbitrators (January 14, 1949).]

that on their failure to agree the whole contract should be written by an arbitrator. The function assigned to the arbitrator has to take place within the framework of an agreement, most of the terms of which are fixed. On the other hand, without the threat of arbitration it might be difficult for the parties to reach agreement on the terms left for periodic renegotiation.

In practice the arbitration clause in such a contract is included in the fervent hope that it will not have to be used; it is intended as a spur toward a negotiated agreement. On the other hand, the substance of the negotiations can scarcely escape being influenced by the parties' conceptions of what a resort to arbitration would probably produce. Expectations as to the way in which an arbitrator would view the case affect the relative bargaining power of the parties, and hence the outcome of the negotiations. This influence may detract from a full realization of the gains of reciprocity. On the other hand, if the arbitrator's powers are invoked he may try to decide the case by asking how the negotiations would have come out had the parties been more reasonable toward each other. Thus, each side of the arrangement — that is, the arbitrator on one side, the parties on the other — is likely to borrow its standards from the other, something generally undesirable and working against a fully effective use of either form of order, contract or adjudication.

This defect in the arrangement may become more serious when the parties have left for negotiated settlement something more complex than price, say, a seniority or vacation clause. Here the parties will realize that if the arbitrator's powers are invoked he will in all likelihood base his decision on "standard" or "typical" practice, simply because there is no other way of giving it a semblance of rationality. This anticipation of the results of arbitration strengthens the hand of that party who has the most to gain from an adoption of "standard" procedure, even though the needs of both parties might be better met by some deviation from that procedure.

3. Parasitic and Perverted Forms of Adjudication

a. Adjudication Parasitic on Contract. — Since the participation of litigants in adjudication is limited to making an appeal to the arbiter's reason, it is of the essence that adjudication be based on "rational" standards in the senses previously discussed. Arbitrations to set wages and prices can under some circumstances derive their "rationality" from a market, as in the following cases: (1) In times of emergency, where the task of the arbitrator is to preserve normal relationships that threaten to be disturbed by the temporary crisis. Here the arbitrator's task becomes increasingly "irrational" as the normal pattern recedes in time and becomes increasingly inappropriate. (2) For a segment of industry, where the arbitrator's task is to preserve the "normal" relationship of this segment to industry as a whole. (3) For a single nation which is strongly dependent upon the world market.

The relative success of such adjudicative ventures has led to much confusion. We are told to follow the "middle way of Sweden," or to outlaw the strike by making all wages subject to arbitration, or to carry into peacetimes the controls that were so successful in time of war, etc. These well-intentioned proposals can only arise because those who make them do not see that the adjudicative process they praise is parasitic upon a regime of contract.

b. Contract Parasitic on Adjudication. — The leaders of a union privately agree with an employer on a five-cent-an-hour increase for the members of the union. Though the union leaders know the company's financial condition will not permit it to absorb a greater increase, they are doubtful of their ability to "sell" the five-cent settlement to their membership. Accordingly, an "arbitration" is arranged. The arbitrator is told that he is to render an award of five cents. Extended hearings are held during which the unsuspecting union members have the satisfaction of hearing their representatives argue vigorously that they are entitled to at least twenty cents an hour. The arbitrator "deliberates" for a month and renders an award of five cents an hour. The members of the union reluctantly acquiesce in the advice of their leaders that this is the most they could get with the aid of the best legal talent in town.

Here one form of order, contract, has not the strength to stand on its own feet; it has to be given an infusion from a phony arbitration. It seems to me that the term "parasitic" is here wholly apt, and I would not hesitate to add the designation "perverted." Plainly, if *all* awards were "fixed," casting a contract in the form of an adjudication would accomplish nothing. Those who take advantage of the phony arbitration are able to do so only because their example is not generally followed. One is reminded of Schopenhauer's remark that the prostitute owes her bargaining power to the restraint of virtuous women.

It should be noted that the case I am speaking of (and such cases do in fact occur) involves an arbitrator who derives his power from an agreement of the litigants. The moot or "fixed" case before a court presents a different set of problems. Historically court procedure has often been employed to assure the legal effect of an agreement. "Fines" and "recoveries," two modes for conveying land in England, were based upon an innocently "collusive" suit. Developments of this sort seem in retrospect quite unobjectionable and even wholesome. The procedure now available in Reno and other places for converting an agreement into a legally effective divorce has not yet acquired the same shielding patina of history. In an interesting little book by a Soviet judge, the author tells of discovering that there were an extraordinary number of suits brought before him by consignees against railways claiming shortages.[37] In all of these cases the judgment was for the railway, on the ground that the alleged "shortage" was simply the shrinkage that would naturally occur in certain products in course of shipment. When the judge asked the plaintiffs why they persisted in bringing such suits, the answer was, "Well, in case any questions were raised about the amount we put into inventory, we thought we ought to have the protection of a court decree." I find in this little incident an eloquent though indirect tribute to commercial adjudication in Russia. If the commercial courts were not by and large "on the level," this mild abuse of judicial procedure would not have served any purpose.

Happily, the "fixed" labor award in the crass form I related is a rarity. In fairness, we must recognize further that the admixture of contractual elements in an adjudicative process is a matter of degree. Even in the most formal and adversary presentation an arbiter can often discern some indication of what the parties would regard as an acceptable settlement simply from the relative emphasis placed on the various issues and arguments. This discreet reading between the lines, far from being a perversion of adjudication, serves to enhance its efficacy. But the fact that all human relations are tinctured with a slight element of dissimulation is no reason to elevate dissimulation to the level of principle.

[37] G. Ivanov, Notes of a People's Judge 55–56 (1950).

[2]

What Do Courts Do?

By Ross Cranston*

In as much as writers on jurisprudence are concerned with what the civil courts do, their focus is on adjudication and law-making—matters such as the exercise of discretion in judicial decision-making, resolving trouble or hard cases, and the role of morality and policy arguments.[1] Another strand of writing, influenced by legal anthropology, places disputes centre stage: disputes or controversies which cannot be settled between the parties or their friends may be referred to a court. In one view the civil courts deal with disputes by the application of doctrine, a method of operation which distinguishes them from mediation and arbitration.[2] Influenced by the Lasswellian notion of politics as who gets what, when and how, a number of American commentators have regarded the civil courts as part of the political process. This third approach focuses, for example, on how interest groups use the courts to attain their goals, just as they might use the legislature or the executive.[3] More radical writers see the civil courts as agencies of the state, reinforcing the position of commercial and property interests in society. One study, for instance, concludes: "Effectively what the court is doing is continually re-stating the rules, re-stating those entitlements and obligations which constitute the legal basis of use rights ("property") in our society."[4] Finally, lawyer-economists see the civil courts as performing allocative functions, as does the market, and examine matters such as the efficiency of the procedure used and the rules made.[5]

None of these approaches necessarily provides an answer, in broad terms, to the question, what do the civil courts do? Each may provide a persuasive account of particular aspects, and each may focus on critical or intellectually difficult parts of their operation. But none paints the whole

* Australian National University.

[1] The literature is vast: see, in particular, R. Dworkin, *Taking Rights Seriously* (1977) esp. pp. 81–149; N. MacCormick, *Legal Reasoning and Legal Theory* (1978); J. Bell, *Policy Arguments in Judicial Decisions* (1983); Waluchow "Strong Discretion" (1983) 33 Phil. Q. 133.

[2] Again, there is an academic industry: Abel, "A Comparative Theory of Dispute Institutions in Society" (1973) 8 L. & Soc. R. 217; L. Nader & H. Todd (eds.), *The Disputing Process* (1978); are examples.

[3] W. Murphy, *Congress and the Court* (1962) and G. Schubert, *The Judicial Mind* (1965) are representative of the different approaches within this tradition. Studies at the local level are K. Dolbeare, *Trial Courts in Urban Politics* (1967); M. Levin, *Urban Politics and the Criminal Courts* (1977).

[4] Cain, "Where Are the Disputes? A Study of a First Instance Civil Court in the U.K.," in M. Cain and K. Kulcsar (eds.), *Disputes and the Law* (1983), p. 130 *cf.* Blankenburg, "Some Conditions Restricting Innovativeness of Legal Services in Germany," in E. Blankenburg (ed.), *Innovations in the Legal Services* (1980), pp. 202–3.

[5] *e.g.* Priest, "Regulating the Content and Volume of Litigation: An Economic Analysis" (1982) 1 Sup. Court Econ. R. 163; N. Mercuro & T. Ryan, *Law, Economics and Public Policy* (1984), p. 119 ff; G. Tullock, *Trials on Trial* (New York, Columbia U.P. 1980).

picture; the matters going to civil courts, how they are handled, and with what result. The obvious retort is that none purports to do this, that they are formulating answers to different questions. Even if this is accepted, I want to suggest that the approach taken below throws some light on the questions which the other approaches address, for example, the nature of rights, how legal rules are applied, and the functions of law in society.[6] Moreover, it provides a perspective on the whole system, and as well identifies important areas in the operation of civil courts of which there is presently a significant ignorance.

As institutions of the state, courts make authoritative decisions about certain matters presented to them. The social, political and economic environment influence, possibly indirectly, the nature of these matters. Granted this truism, the issues which arise include how this environment produces particular "inputs" for courts, and the nature of these and the character of those advancing them. Comparisons can then be made with the inputs of, say, the political system or the market. What happens to these inputs? First, they are converted into legal issues in accordance with procedural and substantive rules of law. Secondly, they are disposed of at different points and in different ways in the process of litigation. Whereas jurists concentrate on complex adjudication, courts dispose of the majority of matters in a routine, mundane manner, or the parties settle a matter before, often well before, exhausting the legal process. The decisions of civil courts are not automatically implemented; enforcement may be necessary. In addition, there is a larger issue of the impact that decisions may have on other than those directly involved. Consideration of these aspects of court "output" throw light on whether courts are central to state decision-making.

I. Inputs

Courts operate within a particular social environment. Across societies, what are called courts do not necessarily handle the same matters.[7] Within the one society, changes in the social environment may affect the civil courts.[8] Over recent decades, for example, changing social values have been at least partly responsible for the increasing number of applications for divorce. It is well-known that depression in the economy produces an upsurge in insolvency work. Even political change can produce a not inconsiderable volume of litigation. For convenience, this part eschews cross-

[6] *Cf.* the systems analysis of political science, notably, D. Easton, *A Framework for Political Analysis* (1979). The approach adopted here does not fit into the models identified in Jacob, "Trial Courts in the United States" (1983) 17 L. & Soc. R. 407; Krislov, "Theoretical Perspectives on Case Load Studies" in K. Boyum & L. Mather (eds.), *Empirical Theories About Courts* (1983), pp. 180–2.

[7] See, *e.g.*, Abel, "Western Courts in Non-Western Settings," in S. Burman & B. Harrell-Bond (eds.), *The Imposition of Law* (1979).

[8] Daniels, "Ladders and Bushes: The Problem of Caseloads and Studying Court Activities over Time" [1984] A.B.F. Res. J. 751; Engel, "The Oven Bird's Song: Insiders, Outsiders, and Personal Injuries in an American Community" (1984) 18 L. & Soc. R. 551; Friedman, "Courts Over Time" in K. Boyum & L. Mather (eds.), op. cit.; Friedman & Percival, "A Tale of Two Courts: Litigation in Alameda and San Benito Counties" (1976) 10 L. & Soc. R. 267; F. Laurent, *The Business of a Trial Court* (1959); Lempert, "More Tales of Two Courts: Exploring Changes in the 'Dispute Settlement Function' of Trial Courts" (1978) 13 L. & Soc. R. 91; McIntosh, "150 Years of Litigation and Dispute Settlement" (1980–81) 15 L. & Soc. R. 823.

cultural and historical analyses to concentrate on the present-day inputs of civil courts. The focus is on litigation, although courts perform a range of other functions from issuing warrants and subpoenas, though granting probate on wills, to keeping records. In particular, how do social and economic problems become grievances which in turn are taken to courts as legal proceedings? And who litigates what types of issues?

The sources of litigation

Ostensibly, the courts operate on the assumption that people know their rights and will take the initiative to enforce them if they expect to be successful. In this sense the courts parallel the free market, which assumes that self-interest will motivate rational activity. In fact, social and economic factors mediate legal action; for example consciousness of rights, community and group norms, capability, the nature of the relationship between the parties, the desirability of publicity, the type of problem (what is at stake, its complexity, its legal dimensions) and the perception of, and access to, legal assistance. The result is that many problems are not regarded as someone else's responsibility, many are "lumped," many claims abandoned, and many disputes compromised or avoided by the parties without outside assistance (let alone legal assistance).[9] For example, residents of an area affected by environmental decay might not conceptualise this as a grievance but regard it as an aspect of life which must be tolerated. Consumers might not realise that a transaction has not satisfied legal requirements (*e.g.* to be in writing) or not think it worthwhile, given the cost of an item, to do anything about it. A retailer might not want to engage in legal action against its suppliers because it thinks that this will disturb the harmonious nature of continuing relations with them, and so it might prefer to settle disputes by steps such as appropriate adjustments to price.

First, then, the issue of whether problems are perceived of as grievances, that is, as being the responsibility of someone else. There are several recent studies which have tapped the nature and extent of personal grievances in the community.[10] In them members of households in the United States and Australia were asked if anyone residing in the household had experienced one of a range of possible problems entailing injury, harm or loss within the previous three years. Both studies uncovered a similarity in the respective ranking of grievances, with tort and landlord-tenant problems being the most reported. Debt problems and those related to schools and voluntary associations were relatively unusual. The figures are subject to important qualifications. The method of survey required almost instant memory recall, persons might not have revealed certain problems (*e.g.* debt), and certain of the grievances were admittedly minor (*e.g.* neigh-

[9] R. Cotterrell, *The Sociology of Law* (1984), p. 267; Felstiner, "Avoidance as Dispute Processing" (1975) 9 L. & Soc. R. 695. Felstiner, Abel & Sarat, "The Emergence and Transformation of Disputes" (1980–81) 15 L. & Soc. R. 631. *Cf.* Baumgartner, "Social Control in Surburbia," in D. Black (ed.), *Toward a General Theory of Social Control* (1984).

[10] Miller & Sarat, "Grievances, Claims and Disputes" (1981) 15 L. & Soc. R. 525; FitzGerald, "Grievances, Disputes and Outcomes" (1983) 1 Law in Context 15. The terminology "problem," "grievance," "claim" and "dispute" is as used in these studies.

bourhood disputes). Moreover, the surveys were confined to personal rather than organisational grievances. Nonetheless, the findings show the relative significance of grievances about certain matters, which rarely make an appearance in the courts, in particular about discrimination and relating to government and neighbours. Interestingly, there was an apparent lack of association between income and education, but not age, and the number of grievances experienced.

Now many such grievances would have been quite trivial and better forgotten or resolved informally. However, it seems fair to say that there were a substantial number of grievances, objectively significant, which were not pursued to litigation. The studies showed that only a proportion of respondents made a claim against the person perceived of as being responsible. Claims in turn did not always give rise to disputes; in some cases the other party provided satisfaction. Nor did all disputes lead people to seek legal assistance, and even fewer instituted legal action. Graphically, the results of the studies can be presented as a pyramid, showing the number of claims, disputes, times that lawyers were used, and court cases instituted per 1,000 grievances. Not all litigation would progress step by step through such a pyramid. The person who challenges a prosecution on the basis of an administrative law or constitutional law doctrine would proceed directly from a grievance to civil litigation. More detailed analysis for the studies showed a variation with the type of matter; for example, in both countries grievances about divorce gave rise to most litigation, grievances about tort gave rise to the next most litigation, whereas grievances about discrimination led to the least litigation.

Motives are one factor underlying such patterns. Take litigation. Towards one end of the spectrum of litigation are relatively mundane motives such as the collection of debt, the pursuit of compensation, inducing compliance with the terms of a contract, and preventing further dissemination of a publication (by issuing a "stop writ" alleging defamation). At the other end of the spectrum a business or government defeated in the political arena might turn to the courts for a remedy. Along the spectrum are many motives, such as delaying the other party, seeking a decision in the forum not overtly affected by political considerations, threatening the other party, revenge, vindicating a principle, gaining a tactical advantage in a continuing relationship, and obtaining a competitive advantage.

In addition to motives, various social and economic influences underlie whether grievances are pursued through to the courts.[11] Another aspect is that some sections of society might fail to take the initiative over matters capable of legal resolution because they are intimidated by what law is usually associated with or fear that if they do their employer, their insurance company, the social welfare department and so on will in some way retaliate.[12] While the law tends to assume that granting rights to weaker parties neutralises differences in power, many people will regard acquiescence, avoidance or tolerating a situation as a more rational response than

[11] D. Black, *The Behaviour of Law* (1976), pp. 27–8. R. Cranston, *Legal Foundations of the Welfare State* (1985) pp. 51–62, 77–8, 131–2; J. Jowell, *Law and Bureaucracy* (1975) p. 4; R. Hunting & G. Neuwirth, *Who Sues in New York City?* (1962), pp. 11, 98.

[12] A not always unjustified fear: A. Best, *When Consumers Complain* (1981) pp. 40–2.

asserting legal rights. There is little empirical evidence about the extent to which group and community norms affect legal action. One aspect is whether the propensity to litigate varies between jurisdictions; there is no strong empirical support for the popular view that the United States is more litigation minded than all other societies.[13]

The tendency to take legal action also turns on institutional factors. Commercial and property interests may have a different propensity to litigate compared with individuals, not least because of the different transactions entered and interests to be protected. Then there is the capacity of the courts to handle litigation: the more resources available to the courts, the more likely that if other things are equal claims will go there rather than be abandoned or channelled into alternative venues. Indeed, other institutions might offer acceptable avenues for the resolution of a matter.[14] For example, private arbitration occurs in commercial and building disputes, and governments have established a range of tribunals and bodies to handle certain matters. Many of the matters which the latter bodies deal with could go to the courts, although in some cases government has attempted to give these other bodies exclusive jurisdiction, but the cost of litigation acts as a deterrent, quite apart from perceptions about the quality of adjudication offered. The courts still act as a long stop for such disputes, for parties dissatisfied with these bodies might begin afresh in the courts or seek judicial review of a decision, if there is no privative clause preventing it. However, the vast majority of such matters are handled without resort to the courts.

Finally, there are the gatekeepers to litigation. For example, lawyers identify avenues for litigation of which laypersons are ignorant. On the other hand, even if individuals seek legal assistance, lawyers might inhibit litigation by screening out particular types of claim. An American study found that lawyers did not regard litigation in relation to consumer claims as being worthwhile or in some cases worthy, had little or no knowledge of the applicable substantive law, but attempted to mediate some claims informally with the relevant retailer, manufacturer or finance house.[15] These findings are likely to be replicated elsewhere and would probably extend to other matters such as disputes with neighbours. Then there are the courts, for what they say influences perceptions about what are grievances, claims and disputes. Courts might discourage litigation through developments in procedural and substantive law.[16] Examples of the courts explicitly encouraging litigation are rare, but courts can indirectly foment litigation by doctrinal developments which make it worthwhile to pursue a claim.[17] Finally, legislation can affect litigation. The introduction of new

[13] Galanter, "Reading the Landscape of Disputes" (1983) 31 U.C.L.A. L.R. 4, 51–61. But a distinction must be made between the amount of litigation instituted and the amount carried through to a hearing.

[14] See generally R. Abel (ed.), *The Politics of Informal Justice* (1982), v. 1–2.

[15] Macaulay, "Lawyers and Consumer Protection Law" (1979) 14 L. & Soc. R. 115.

[16] Explicitly recognised in the floodgates" argument; *e.g. Winterbottom* v. *Wright* (1842) 10 M. & W. 109; 152 E.R. 402.

[17] *e.g.* the litigation following *Anns* v. *Merton B.C.* [1978] A.C. 728. The High Court of Australia has refused to follow *Anns: Sutherland Shire Council* v. *Heyman* (1985) 59 A.L.J.R. 564.

legislation might multiply the occasions for disputed interpretations, but it might also resolve points of legal contention and so discourage litigation.

Who uses the Courts?

The nature of those involved in litigation has a profound influence on the issues courts address, the involvement of lawyers, the development of doctrine and outcomes. To take an example: if a particular type of litigant constantly brings claims against another type of litigant, and the latter typically does not defend or does not obtain legal representation, it would not be surprising if outcomes tended to favour the first type of litigant. Without any conscious bias on their part, judges would simply be more exposed to the arguments favouring the first type of litigant so that these attained a more "natural" quality. Beyond any impact on the courts, the nature of litigants might have ramifications for society. For example, if plaintiffs were typically commercial and property interests claiming against individual defendants, the courts would be functioning to reinforce other institutional outcomes in society rather than acting as an avenue for redressing the balance. By contrast, there is a widely accepted notion in the United States that minority groups ought to look to the courts for social reform if the legislatures are unsympathetic.

There is scattered evidence of the types of parties using the civil courts. Data from the civil litigation research project in the United States indicates that in four of the five state courts studied, plaintiffs were individuals in about three-quarters of the cases terminated in 1978. In the fifth state court, there was more balance between individuals and organisations. The largest category of organisational plaintiffs consisted of financial institutions. Government rarely brought actions in any of the state courts. In the five federal courts studied, there were generally fewer individual plaintiffs, more organisational plaintiffs, and a significant number of cases instituted by government, compared with the state courts. As for defendants, individuals were the largest category in the state courts, while governments appeared infrequently. In the federal courts, the number of organisational defendants was somewhat higher than in the state courts, with the number of cases in which government was a defendant being substantially higher. It is important to note that these figures exclude uncontested collection cases and family matters. Personal injury claims were the largest single category of court actions in the state courts.[18] Similarly, in a survey of a representative sample of cases commenced in three Australian state supreme courts, about one half of the cases had individuals as both plaintiffs and defendants. Analysis of the cases with individuals as plaintiffs reveals that one half were personal injury claims. The proportion of cases with individuals as plaintiffs increased, but the proportion of those with individuals as defendants fell, as matters progressed through the courts, since almost all mortgage default, and many money owing cases, were quickly settled or went to default judgment.[19] By contrast with these studies in the United States and

[18] Grossman, *et al.*, "Dimensions of Institutional Participation: Who Uses the Courts, and How?" (1982) 44 J. of Politics 86.

[19] These results (unpublished) are derived from R. Cranston, P. Haynes, J. Pullen & I. Scott, *Delays and Efficiency in Civil Litigation* (1985).

Australia, a study of one London County Court in 1980–81 found that private plaintiffs were only a small minority of plaintiffs (10·9%), whereas they formed the vast majority of defendants (83·9%).[20]

It is clear that the civil courts cannot be characterised universally as a forum where commercial and property institutions successfully claim against individuals. Different civil courts have different jurisdictions. Individual plaintiffs constitute an important, indeed sometimes the largest, category of users of some civil courts. Admittedly, this is partly attributable to the importance of personal injury litigation before these courts. In addition, there are many proceedings before the civil courts which involve businesses instituting debt or property claims against individuals. A great number of these proceedings are undefended, and many are disposed of by way of default judgment. Many, indeed most, of such cases might be legally unanswerable, for example, the defendant has failed to pay the debt or rent or has fallen into arrears with a mortgage. In other words, the courts might be simply perfecting what the law permits, so that attention needs to be given primarily to the substantive law rather than to the role of the courts.

Moreover, the high proportion of plaintiffs and defendants who were individuals in the United States and Australian studies says nothing about the many individuals with legal problems who do not get to court. Nor does it lead to the conclusion that the individuals who sue are representative of the population. Groups may stand behind some of the individuals who sue or are sued. It is difficult to uncover in a systematic way the extent to which this occurs. It is probably little on the plaintiff's side, although in theory the derivative suit is possible in the commercial context and individuals claiming on behalf of groups are not unknown in administrative law.[21] More significantly, with regard to defendants, although individuals appear as such in personal injury motor vehicle cases, in practice the third party insurers conduct the defence, often without any assistance from those against whom the action is nominally being brought.

What might be surprising is that the United States and Australian surveys suggest that commercial and property interests use the courts little, comparatively speaking, for dispute settlement amongst themselves. One answer may be that other institutions provide a more convenient forum for commercial matters: for example, they may be referred to arbitration. Perhaps more importantly, the relative absence of disputes between commercial and property interests might testify to planning, with legal help, to avoid their arising in the first place, and to the desire to maintain long-

[20] Cain, *op. cit.*, p. 122. Similar results were obtained in another recent study of a lower court. In the Melbourne magistrates court in 1982, 96 per cent. of summons issued were default summons. Only 3·7 per cent. of these were instituted by individuals; some 75·8 per cent. of defendants were individuals. J. Pullen, N. Young, S. Geddes, *Court Surveys and Studies* 1978–1984 (1985) pp. 239–41. *Cf.* Wanner, "The Public Ordering of Private Relations" (1974) 8 L. & Soc. R. 421 (courts of first instance in three U.S. cities—plaintiffs were 49 per cent. organisations, 42 per cent. individuals, 9 per cent. government); C. McKie & P. Reed, *Civil Justice in Canada* (1979), p. 72 (Canadian civil courts—a single organisation suing a single individual accounted for forty per cent. of cases sampled).

[21] *e.g. Bushell* v. *Secretary of State for the Environment* [1981] A.C. 75, 100. In another area: *Helby* v. *Matthews* [1895] A.C. 471 was funded by the Hire Purchase Trade Association.

term, continuing relations between those such as suppliers, customers and financiers.[22]

II. The Conversion Process

Procedure has long been recognised as playing a central role in the administration of civil justice. Jeremy Bentham's concern about "the burthens of judicial procedure" takes form in current interests such as widening access to the courts and reducing delay and expense. Substantive law, too, channels civil litigation. Of primary interest here is the extent to which the substantive law means that social issues can be converted into legal problems so that the courts can deal with them. To put it another way, only if there is a cause of action is it worth suing. A further aspect of what can be termed the conversion process in courts is the extent to which the majority of cases commenced never go to trial. Mention has been made of the many debt and property claims going to default judgment, but in addition substantial numbers of cases settle, often as late as at the door of the court and sometimes during trial.

Court procedures

Procedural law has an influence on those resorting to the courts, the matters litigated and the results obtained. Technicalities, anomalies and complexities in procedural rules discourage claims, delay them unnecessarily, or distort outcomes by preventing meritorious defences being heard.[23] Consider, for example, how court procedures facilitate delay in cases in which the outcome is reasonably clear-cut. Certain parties have an obvious motive to delay: activity in violation of the law, for example, can be continued up to the hearing, unless interlocutory relief can be obtained. Similarly, a person might be induced to abandon a claim, or a case might be weakened with time because witnesses are no longer available. The rules of evidence also throw up barriers to establishing a case. Statistical evidence is not admissible to show, say, that a surgeon has a much higher wound infection rate than average.[24] Yet if only one case is examined, it will be much easier for the surgeon to argue chance and to have any inference of negligence rejected.

Transformation of issues

Categories for the subject-matter of litigation, such as the description "personal injury claims" used above, coincide roughly with an everyday understanding of cases. If cases were to be categorised by the relief requested (damages, possession, injunction, declaration, etc.), there would be some move away from that everyday understanding. And if cases were to be analysed according to legal categories, the transformation of social issues might be even starker. At one level this transformation is relatively straightforward and recognised as a motor vehicle accident becomes a

[22] Macaulay, "Non-Contractual Relations in Business: A Preliminary Study" (1963) 28 Am. Soc. Rev. 55; Beale & Dugdale, "Contracts between Businessmen: Planning and the Use of Contractual Remedies" (1975) 2 Brit. J.L. & S. 45. For arbitration see Mann, "Private Arbitration and Public Policy" (1985) 4 Civil Justice Quarterly 257.

[23] J. Jacob, The Reform of Civil Procedural Law and Other Essays in Civil Procedure (1982), pp. 193–4.

[24] *Cf. Hales* v. *Kerr* [1908] 2 K.B. 601; *Phipson on Evidence* (13th ed., 1982), p. 230.

claim in negligence for money damages, a quarrel between two neighbours changes into a dispute over planning approval, and a marital contest takes form as a child custody case.[25] At least on the surface, certain standards in civil law, notably that of the "reasonable person," draw on community notions of proper behaviour.

But the transformation might be more fundamental as regards the number of parties involved or the issues addressed. Thus conflicts over economic resources, political principles, the exercise of government power or use of the environment become conflicts over the meaning and application of legal doctrine. *Johnston* v. *Kent*[26] involved the issue of whether the Australian government could build a multipurpose tower on the top of Black Mountain, in the Australian Capital Territory, without Parliamentary approval. Objection was taken to the tower on environmental grounds, but before the High Court of Australia the issue was disposed of on the grounds that the Commonwealth had executive power in relation to activity on its land, that the Post and Telegraph Act 1901 empowered the Postmaster-General to erect structures for telegraphic, telephonics and other like services, and that this Act did not limit the exercise of the Commonwealth prerogative power in the Australian Capital Territory. As Jacobs J. commented in his judgment:

> [W]hat was at base a dispute involving community attitudes and purposes, a political dispute in the broad sense, had perforce when it was brought before the Court to turn itself largely into a technical legal dispute on the question whether there was legal authority to erect the structure.[27]

The transformation of social into legal issues is facilitated by the advent of detailed, regulatory legislation. In addition to relying on broad common law and equitable principles, a party might be able to invoke a range of statutory law relevant to a particular issue. The meaning of statutory language being in many cases arguable, the potential for legal action is considerable in the modern state. The upshot is that cases are often formulated in legal terms far removed from the underlying social or economic reality and might even be reformulated in the course of their progress. Lawyers handling a case are clearly important in this transformation process. The focus might be narrowed to one legally relevant issue or widened from a private dispute into one involving issues of public importance. A significant development in the law might result from a strategy adopted in relation to a client's case.[28] In rare cases, it might even emerge from a court's decision on an issue not raised by the person's lawyers. Is it any wonder that many clients do not understand why they succeed, or more importantly, fail in court when the matter has been transformed beyond their recognition? Moreover, if the legal process is dealing with legal conceptualisations, it might not be addressing the underlying social issue. Neither point is necess-

[25] Yngresson & Mather, "Courts, Moots and the Disputing Process" in Keith O. Boyum & Lynn Mather, *op. cit.*, p. 64.

[26] (1975) 132 C.L.R. 164. See Howard, "Public Law and Common Law," in D. Galligan (ed.), Essays in Legal Theory (1984), pp. 8–13.

[27] At. p. 173.

[28] A. Paterson, *The Law Lords* (1982), pp. 38–45.

arily objectionable: many individuals approach lawyers precisely so that the legal implications of their problems can be used to their advantage (or to the disadvantage of their opponents), and avoiding the underlying social issue may well be functional for society. In addition, the outcome of many cases is dictated, as will be seen, by non-legal considerations, as cases are disposed of in a routine way or are settled.

Attrition of Cases

At the centre of thinking about civil courts is the model of formal adjudication—parties present their cases to a court, the adversary process operates and a matter is disposed of by formal adjudication. Despite this popular picture, relatively few of the cases which are begun in court are adjudicated.[29] Instead, the great majority are discontinued, disposed of by default judgment or settled. For example, in one study of a United States civil court, only one defendant in four made any formal move to oppose the plaintiff at any point (*e.g.* by filing an answer to the complaint), in only a tenth of cases was there a trial, and only one case in every 180 cases commenced was appealed.[30] A study of cases commenced in three Australian state supreme courts found that in only about one half did at least one defendant formally enter an appearance, fewer cases still entered a court list, and less than eight in 100 in one jurisdiction and about three in 100 in the other jurisdictions, were adjudicated by way of a full hearing.[31]

Overall, then, the passage of cases through the courts can be characterised as a continuation of the pyramidal structure already drawn in relation to grievances. Not all cases pass through each stage of the process, with many dropping out along the way and being dealt with other than by the intervention of judges; they are discontinued, an outcome is rubber-stamped as with a default judgment, or they are settled. Much depends on the type of matter; whereas many personal injury cases enter a court list, few debt or mortgage default matters reach this point.

III. Decision Making

Formal adjudication of civil law cases is atypical. Although a number of cases are disposed of in this way, the civil courts dispose of the bulk of cases by routine administration or by providing a forum in which cases are settled. Characterised in this way, the civil courts parallel other organisations in society to a greater extent than if the focus were to be, as it often is, on adjudication alone. Whether handling cases by routine administration or by facilitating settlement is desirable is a separate issue from that of describing the manner in which courts actually work in practice. However, the normative question inevitably arises, just as it does in the criminal courts, where the counterparts of routine administration and settlement

[29] Engel & Steele, "Civil Cases and Society" [1979] A.B.F. Res. J. 295, 300; D. Harris *et al.*, *Compensation and Support for Illness and Injury* (1984) pp. 112–3, *Report of the Royal Commission on Civil Liability and Compensation for Personal Injury*, Cmnd. 7054, 1978, v. 2, pp. 154–5.

[30] Engel, "Legal Pluralism in an American Community: Perspectives on a Civil Trial Court" [1980] A.B.F. Res. J. 425, 433.

[31] R. Cranston et al., *op. cit.* p. 23. Other findings are gathered by Zemans, "Framework for Analysis of Legal Mobilisation" [1982] A.B.F. Res. J. 989, 1062–3.

are the sentencing of those pleading guilty in lower courts on the one hand, and plea bargaining on the other.

Routine administration

Much of what the courts do in disposing of cases involves routine administration; approving outcomes agreed elsewhere or determined by structural factors. A court order might be desired to guarantee compliance with those outcomes or because it is a precondition to further action. One aspect of routine administration is the consent judgment, where parties have settled a case and simply enter judgment.[32] Another aspect is the default judgment, whereby a plaintiff can obtain judgment in default of any moves to defend the case.[33] With routine processing, court officials undertake a limited inquiry to ensure that an application fits established categories (often, this only involves checking that documents are correctly completed) and then give their imprimatur by entering judgment. There are no contested issues, as where both parties want a divorce and have agreed on custody and property, yet still need formal court approval. (Divorce is an example of a court order being a legal prerequisite to persons taking certain action, in the particular case, remarrying). As with divorce, a court might order an individual's bankruptcy or the winding up of a company in a routine manner when there are no disputed matters. Nonetheless, such orders have profound consequences; a change in a person's status in the case of bankruptcy (similarly, with divorce) and the dissolution of a company in the case of a winding up.

Debt collection and mortgage default are well recognised as areas where the civil courts frequently engage in the routine processing of cases. As noted, such claims typically result from institutions such as business, banks and building societies taking action against individuals. While not legally necessary, a judgment might be valuable in a creditor or mortgagee taking further action such as seeking the insolvency of a debtor or writing off the debt to tax. Although individuals might have a defence or cross-claim in relation to debt or mortgage claims, these are not always raised because of the cost (the very fact of a debt or possession action indicates a lack of financial resources) or because of social factors such as ignorance. The extent to which a particular civil court becomes involved in debt and mortgage claims depends, in part, on the jurisdiction of the court immediately lower in the hierarchy. The higher its upper monetary limit, the less the default work which should occur in the higher court since plaintiffs will not obtain their full costs if they could have taken action in the lower court.

Greater procedural safeguards ought to be introduced in relation to the routine processing of cases, especially default work, since there is some evidence that plaintiffs' cases are not always unassailable.[34] One approach would be to require a plaintiff to establish a *prima facie* case as a precondition to obtaining a default judgment. At present plaintiffs who obtain a default judgment are in a strong position, because of the difficulties of having it set aside. The costs of legal action can be added to the original claim, and if judgment is entered an order for costs can be obtained. Even if there

[32] *e.g.* R.S.C. O.42, r. 5A.

[33] *e.g.* R.S.C. O.13, r. 1; O.19, r. 2.

[34] Empirical studies from the United States are referred to in Cavanagh & Sarat, "Thinking about Courts" (1980) 14 L. & Soc. R. 371, 390.

is no defence to a claim for debt or for possession, a procedure is desirable whereby the possibility is always properly explored of assisting individuals to repay by instalments and over a longer period.

Settlement

The conventional legal wisdom is that civil litigation is wasteful and disruptive, and that strong efforts ought to be made to settle cases out of court. The law facilitates settlement in various ways, such as the protection given to "without prejudice" communications.[35] Clearly what courts do has an influence on settlements; as some writers put it, settlements occur in the "shadow of law."[36] Courts do this through their decisions, which are used in bargaining and which shape expectations as to what is acceptable and as to what would occur if a matter went to a hearing. An obvious example is that the amounts awarded in personal injury cases are taken into account in settling similar claims. Also, the cost of litigation, in particular the rule that costs follow the event, induces settlements.

In addition, the civil courts might facilitate settlement more directly through certain of their rules and procedures. For instance, the date from which interest rates are calculated on judgments might provide an incentive for plaintiffs to have a case disposed of quickly.[37] However, the interest payable on judgments is probably not high enough to constitute any real incentive to settle, especially in the commercial area where it is often economically rational behaviour to postpone payment as long as possible. An example of court rules being designed to facilitate settlements are those for payment into court.[38] These might induce settlements by providing for a cost penalty if plaintiffs obtain less than the amount a defendant pays in. The cost penalty is that they might have to bear the defendant's costs as from the date of payment in. It has been said that discovery furthers settlement, by enabling parties to make a more accurate evaluation of the strengths and weaknesses of a case. There is little, if any, evidence to support the theory.[39] If discovery does encourage settlements it might be because it makes the cost of litigation unacceptably high for one of the parties, not because they are better informed as a result of it.

Settlement practices, and the potential for settlement, vary with a range of factors including the parties involved, the existing or future relationship between them, the type of case, legal costs, certainty of outcome,[40] and the attitude and reputation of the lawyers involved.[41] Some cases are more difficult to settle than normal because of the personal animosity of the parties, because they are test cases, or because of what is at stake. A continuing

[35] *D.* v. *N.S.P.C.C.* [1978] A.V. 171, at 232.

[36] Mnookin & Kornhauser, "Bargaining in the Shadow of the Law: The Case of Divorce" (1979) 88 Yale L.J. 950.

[37] *e.g.* Supreme Court Act 1981, s.35A.

[38] *e.g.* R.S.C. O.22.

[39] W. Glaser, *Pretrial Discovery and the Adversary System* (1968) cited in J. Levine, *Discovery* (1982) pp. 3–4.

[40] The decision to settle is reciprocal in character: the plaintiff with a high probability of success is usually matched by a defendant with a low probability. Priest, "Re-examining the Selection Hypothesis" (1985) 14 J. Leg. Stud. 215, 219.

[41] For an attempt to theorise settlement: Black, "Social Control as a Dependent Variable," in D. Black, *Toward a General Theory of Social Control* (1984), pp. 22–3. See also D. Harris, *et al.*, *op. cit.*, pp. 93–112; H. Ross, *Settled Out of Court* (1970).

relationship between the parties, on the other hand, is conducive to settlement because a range of informal sanctions push in that direction. On the basis of reputation and experience lawyers evaluate whether their opponents genuinely want settlement. Lawyers might not rush into settlement negotiations for fear of giving the impression that their case is shaky. Clients sometimes determine the pace of settlement negotiations; for example, financial necessity might make them interested in a quick settlement. Lawyers sometimes delay matters deliberately in the interests of clients, for example, if they are representing a defendant debtor, a person who wishes a particular custody arrangement to continue, or a target company in a takeover battle. In commercial litigation, where large sums of money are at stake, it is possible by excessive discovery, procedural manoeuvres and appeals to frustrate the other side and possibly to force it to a settlement. The practices of institutional litigants regarding settlements is also an important factor, for instance, the approach of insurance companies in personal injury litigation.

An undesirable aspect of settlements at the door of the court might be that a litigant has to make within minutes a decision which might affect his or her whole life.[42] However, lawyers defend late settlements as being necessary if they are to perform their duties to their clients. This view is put strongly by lawyers who believe that it is only at the door of the court that realistic offers are made. However, another explanation for settlements at the door of the court is that where late briefing occurs it is only on the eve of the hearing that the barristers can properly and realistically appraise a case. Yet another explanation, given by practitioners, is that settlements often eventuate at the door of the court because only then do the parties appreciate what a court hearing involves. Practitioners' perceptions of the particular judge allocated to hear a case might also affect whether or not they try to settle it.

Traditionally, the civil courts facilitated settlement indirectly, through the "radiating" effects of their decisions and the existence of rules such as those relating to interest payable on judgments and payments into court. Following the introduction of pre-trial conferences in the United States, Canada and Australia, civil courts now play a more active role in the settlement of cases.[43] The way in which pre-trial conferences are conducted varies in practice between different jurisdictions and different courts in the same jurisdiction. While the rules might be designed ostensibly to formulate the issues to be tried, courts sometimes use the opportunity of the conferences to encourage negotiation and settlement. It seems that even if settlement conferences have not increased the rate of settlement, they have at least led to earlier settlements as cases settle there rather than at the door of the court. Any assessment of the benefits overall would have to take the costs of pre-trial conferences into account.

Adjudication

The attrition of cases means that in relation to cases commenced it is relatively rare that the courts give authoritative rulings after a completed

[42] *Royal Commission on Legal Services*. Cmnd. 7648, 1979, p. 300.

[43] Galanter, ". . . A Settlement Judge, not a Trial Judge: Judicial Mediation in the United States" (1985) 12 J.L. & Soc. 1. *Cf.* Fiss, "Against Settlement" (1984) 93 Yale L.J. 1073.

adjudication.[44] Even cases which obtain a date for hearing might have settled by the hearing. As noted already, there is a high incidence of settlement at the door of the court. In addition, cases sometimes settle after the hearing has commenced, which might occur because the weaknesses of a party's case are exposed or because the partial hearing resolves important issues, with the result that the parties are able to agree on the others.

Cases where there is a completed adjudication do not always match the adversary model of the conventional wisdom. It might be that there is only an applicant, and no defendant, as where a party obtains an *ex parte* injunction, an executor seeks an authoritative construction of a will, a company applies for its winding up, or a liquidator wants a ruling on how he (or she) ought to proceed. Moreover, adjudications do not necessarily involve a judge. Masters now perform work which in the past was the responsibility of judges.

A further qualification is that where there is a jury trial, a completed adjudication will obviously not involve a final ruling on the case by the trial judge, although he or she rules on the evidence, instructs the jury on the relevant law and makes observations to them on the facts. Although jury trial for civil cases is infrequent or non-existent in, say England, it is still firmly entrenched in jurisdictions in the United States and Australia. Jury trial is said to have advantages such as enabling community participation in the administration of justice, providing a means by which community values are taken into account, acting as a check on judges and reducing appeals. By contrast it is said that juries are costly, cause inconvenience and possibly monetary loss to jurors, require the retention of rigid, technical rules of evidence, and introduce irrationality into decision-making which cannot readily be appealed.[45]

Even if these qualifications are taken into account, adjudication is still far removed from the world of most jurists. Delays, expense, and tactics all distort the ideal model. Outcomes may reflect the nature, interests and representation of the parties, rather than the legal merits. Llewellyn described the position neatly in relation to the right to sue for damages for breach of contract:

> "[T]he right could rather more accurately be phrased somewhat as follows: if the other party does not perform as agreed, you can sue, and *if* you have a fair lawyer, and nothing goes wrong with your witnesses or the jury, *and* you give up four or five days of time and some ten to thirty percent of the proceeds, and wait two to twenty months, you will *probably* get judgment for a sum considerably less than what the performance would have been worth—which, if the other party is sol-

[44] On adjudication: R. Cover & O. Fiss, *The Structure of Procedure* (1979) Part II; Eisenberg, "Participation, Responsiveness, and the Consultative Process" (1978) 92 Harv. L.R. 410. L. Fuller, The Principles of Social Order (1981) pp. 86–124; H. Hart & A. Sacks, The Legal Process (1958) pp. 662–9; J. Pennock & J. Chapman (eds.), Due Process (1977); Simon "The Ideology of Advocacy" [1978] Wisc. L.R. 29. *Cf.* Abel, "Theories of Litigation in Society" (1980) 6 *Jahrbuch fur Rechtssoziologie und Rechtstheorie* 165, 171–7; J. Mashaw, *Bureaucratic Justice* (1983); Rapoport, "Theories of Conflict Resolution and the Law" in Martin L. Friedland (ed.), *Courts and Trials* (1975), pp. 27–9.

[45] Twining, "Identification and Misidentification in Legal Processes," in S. Lloyd-Bostock and B. Clifford (eds.), *Evaluating Witness Evidence* (1983), pp. 260–1.

vent, and has not secreted his assets, you can, in further due course, collect with six percent interest delay."[46]

At the end the process, after the parties present their positions, courts do give authoritative rulings on matters, possible in some cases those which cannot be dealt with by other institutions in society. But if there is an underlying dispute, adjudication will not necessarily lead to its resolution. Obvious examples are provided by a family court, whose decision might exacerbate, rather than resolve, the underlying dispute between the parties. As will be seen, in all areas where an adjudication has occurred, the parties might do nothing, might refuse to accept the outcome, or might pursue non-legal avenues for redress of the matter.

Rules are central to adjudication, although not determinative. They are supplemented by norms, such as those falling under the rubric of legal ethics, which influence the behaviour of lawyers and judges involved in the process. The basis of the rules and norms is to ensure that decisions accord with the relevant law and facts. But they also affect matters such as participation of the parties in the decision, public support for the courts, procedural fairness, rationality and finality.

Adjectival rules (procedural and evidentiary) must address matters such as the definition of issues, the identity of the adjudicator and whether he (or she) ought to be disqualified in the particular case, the hearing of the matter (for example, requiring the adjudicator to give all parties an opportunity to present their case, determining how matters are to be proved), the method of decision-making (for example, allocating responsibility for decisions between judge and jury, confining a decision to evidence and arguments presented by the parties at the hearing with all present), the nature of the decision (for example, whether it is to be announced in open court, whether reasons are needed in support), and the extent of any appeals (for example, time limits, whether confined to issues of law).[47]

Under the common law adversary system, procedural rules confine adjudication, in the main, to the issues raised by the pleadings. Courts are reluctant to force a party not to pursue what they think are trivial or spurious issues, just as they do not interfere by calling witnesses without the consent of the parties. While courts are now under a duty to suggest amendments to pleadings to ensure justice there are cases where, through ignorance or incompetence, matters are not pleaded or raised on which a party might succeed or the court might come to a different conclusion.[48] Evidentary rules and norms are designed to elicit relevant evidence and to minimise distortions resulting from practices such as coaching witnesses and fraud. There is still the problem that evidence might be inaccurate for reasons such as honest mistake and lapses of memory. However, under the common law system courts make definitive findings of fact and use them as

[46] Llewellyn, "A Realistic Jurisprudence—The Next Step" (1930) 30 Colum. L.R. 431, 437–8. Twining notes the variety of perspectives on trials: "[T]rials are referred to as forensic lotteries or degradation ceremonies or licensed battles or conveyor belts": "Evidence and Legal Theory" (1984) 47 M.L.R. 261, 274. See, also, Weinberg, "Evidence Scholarship and Theories of Adjudication," in D. Galligan (ed.), *op. cit.*

[47] Summers, "Law, Adjudicative Processes and Civil Justice," in Graham Hughes (ed.), *Law, Reason, and Justice* (New York, N.Y.U. Press, 1969), pp. 176–8.

[48] See Law Commission, *Civil Procedure Seminar* (1984), v. 1, pp. 47–8.

a basis for judgment, even though they have only been established on the preponderance of evidence.[49] Overall, the adversary system is based on the assumption that the judge should play a relatively passive role during the trial, relying on the parties to present their side of the matter to the best advantage.[50] The stance is said to aid neutrality, since the judge need not make any premature decisions about a matter.

A variety of issues arise in considering substantive rules. Which rules of law are relevant? What do they mandate, if anything, in the particular case? How are they to be applied consistently with what has occurred in prior similar cases? What if they do not clearly cover the issue in dispute: is reference made, or should it be, to analogous rules, to underlying principles of law, to the public interest, to morality, to justice, or to yet other factors? Do the results the rules produce accord with community notions of morality and justice? To what extent do and should courts develop new rules? Such issues are the meat of the jurisprudential literature on adjudication and beyond the scope of the present inquiry.

IV. Outputs

Llewellyn's point that legal maxims hunt in pairs is neatly illustrated in relation to remedies: *ubi jus ibi remedium* (where there is a right, there is a remedy), as opposed to *ubi remedium ibi jus* (where there is a remedy, there is right).[51] Whatever the truth of the matter historically, it is certainly the case that the law relating to remedies has a profound influence on what the civil courts can do. Two issues are discussed here: first, the outcome of cases for the parties involved, and secondly, whether those outcomes have an impact on wider social behaviour.

Outcomes

Various outcomes of civil cases have already been alluded to—settlements, discontinuances, consent orders, default judgments, summary judgments and judgments after trial. The remedies granted by civil courts range from declarations as to what the law is, through money awards (liquidated and unliquidated damages), to specific orders such as injunctions, specific performance, company liquidation and custody orders. The grant of specific orders such as injunctions is hedged with limitations, however, and overall the range of court orders is more limited than what can be done through legislation. Typically, the civil courts have only a limited concern with the parties before them unlike, say, some children's courts or the courts in totalitarian societies, where a case provides an avenue for the examination of a person's whole personality and behaviour.

Court orders typically decide that one party is legally right and the other legally wrong. Compromise is not acceptable, even though it might be in keeping with community views of doing justice or conducive to resolving the social disputes underlying litigation. The issue arises in an acute form when two parties are adversely affected by the fraud of a third party, who disappears or is unable to pay compensation to the person suffering the

[49] Alternative approaches, such as the use of presumptions, are discussed in M. Shapiro, *Courts* (1981), pp. 11–12.

[50] See P. Devlin, *The Judge* (1979), pp. 55–6, 60–4.

[51] F. Lawson, *Remedies of English Law* (2nd ed., 1980), p. 1.

loss. Both parties might be innocent or both might share some responsibility for the fraud having occurred. Yet the courts do not formally divide the loss according to the justice of the case but decide the issue in black and white terms.[52] Legislation has provided for a formal apportionment of loss in some cases, most notably with contributory negligence.[53] Similar adjustments might occur in some small claims courts, which are empowered to decide according to what is just and equitable in the circumstances.[54]

The civil courts might be characterised as plaintiffs' courts, in that generally the majority of parties instituting action are successful. Perhaps this should not be surprising when so many matters proceed to default judgment. Moreover, it seems a reasonable assumption that most plaintiffs act rationally and have calculated that they are likely to succeed, before they institute legal action. However, just because a plaintiff succeeds does not mean that the defendant has lost. Typically, for the purposes of settlement negotiations, plaintiffs claim for more than they know they will obtain, and defendants deny liability whatever their real views. In other words a final result, where the plaintiff succeeds, might be closer to what the defendant, rather than the plaintiff, really wanted all along. Because plaintiffs are very successful overall in obtaining relief, courts authorise the transfer of considerable sums of money. However, individual parties do not necessarily recover substantial amounts when money awards are obtained through settlement or judgment. There are substantial recoveries, but these are atypical.[55] Moreover, significant numbers of recoveries seem to fall below the upper jurisdictional limit of the lower courts. Cost penalties in the rules of court are supposed to deter parties from commencing actions in higher courts if the amount sought falls within the monetary limit of the lower court.[56] But parties might think other factors more important, such as the form of relief, the need to impress the other side with the seriousness of a case, what they perceive to be the quality of the judges, and the nature of enforcement procedures. This is especially the case since most matters are settled, and the issue of costs does not loom as large when cases are settled as when they are tried. In any event, lawyers might obtain an indemnity from their clients to cover the cost of proceeding in the higher court.

The coercive quality of court decisions derives partly from the standing which courts have in society. Many parties obey the decision of a court, whether or not they agree with it, because it issues from an institution with such authority, and there is no need for enforcement action.[57] However, the binding quality of court decisions might involve an element of coercion. In some cases parties might seek to have judgment executed by obtaining the appropriate order, for example, a writ of possession, a levy of property, an attachment of wages, or a charging order. Often, an order for

[52] *Ingram* v. *Little* [1961] 1 Q.B. 31, 73–4 *per* Devlin L.J.

[53] *Ibid.* at p. 74.

[54] *e.g.* Consumer Claims Tribunals Act 1974 (New South Wales) s.23(2).

[55] D. Harris *et al.*, *op. cit.*, pp. 86–91 (not all these cases involved court proceedings: see p. 112); R. Cranston *et al.*, *op. cit.*, p. 32. In 1983, judgments in the High Court, Queen's Bench division, divided as follows: up to £1,000, 150; £1,000–2,500, 520; £2,500–5,000, 730; £5,000–7,500, 660; £7,500–10,000, 470; over £10,000, 2,640; non-money judgments, 1890. *Judicial Statistics*, Cmnd. 9370, 1984, p. 37.

[56] *e.g.* County Courts Act 1984, ss.19–20.

[57] Lloyd-Bostock, "Explaining Compliance with Imposed Law," in S. Burman & B. Harrell-Bond (eds.), *The Imposition of Law* (1979).

execution is obtained *in terrorem*, so that court officials need never implement it, since subsequently the property is transferred, the sum of money paid, or other appropriate action taken. Sometimes coercion is necessary, however, because of evasion or defiance of a court order. Well publicised is the family law area, where non-compliance with orders relating to maintenance is high. Enforcing judgment generally requires a party to approach the court afresh and might even involve him in further litigation. This creates problems in areas such as domestic violence. A woman might obtain an injunction which supposedly restrains a man from assaulting her, but if he breaches it she must negotiate the hurdles of seeking an order against him for contempt of court. Legislation in some jurisdictions attempts to overcome this problem by providing that breach of such an order is an arrestable offence.[58] Even if a party succeeds in a particular case, that success might be undermined because of some other action by the other party.[59]

Impact

There are many conceptual problems in assessing the social impact of judicial decisions, as opposed to the outcomes of particular litigants. The intended law-making effects of a decision might be ambiguous or conflicting; the actual effects might prove beneficial to a losing party, or at least to the group of which it is a representative; and even partial implementation might be a considerable success in terms of the difficulties of achieving the intended law making effects. A real difficulty in assessing the impact of courts is in isolating the relevant causal factors.[60] Judge-made law is one among a number of instruments of social control, and it might be impossible to isolate its impact on behaviour from that produced in other ways. Individuals or institutions might comply with the terms of a decision because of factors independent of the court such as political and community pressures. Moreover, there is the problem of identifying effects. For example, a judicial decision might not have any visible impact because key actors ignore it, because it is technically impossible for them to change their behaviour beyond a certain point, or because its effect is simply to adopt a practice which they intended to introduce in any event. Finally, there are the independent and unintended effects of a decision. With these qualifications in mind, it is possible to advance some tentative assessments of the impact of courts.

There are a relatively small number of the cases decided in the civil courts which can have a significant impact on public policy. They touch important areas of the political process, determine major civil liberties issues, result in the delay or abandonment of major developments, or dispose of economic prizes or burdens. Constitutional decisions of courts interpreting a written constitution provide the clearest examples. In other

[58] Australian Law Reform Commission, *Community Law Reform: Domestic Violence in the A.C.T.* (1984), pp. 42–3.

[59] See some of the case-studies in R. Danzig, *The Capability Problem in Contract Law* (1978).

[60] M. Feeley, "Power, Impact, and the Supreme Court," in T. Becker & M. Feeley (eds.), *The Impact of Supreme Court Decisions* (2nd ed., 1973), pp. 222–4; R. Tomasic, *The Sociology of Law* (1985), pp. 108–9.

areas of public law the influence of judicial decisions is usually less dramatic and pervasive. Judicial review of administrative action provides an example. There are relatively few applications for judicial review to begin with. Many of these are unsuccessful thus upholding, possibly reinforcing, government policy. Even if successful, the particular applicants might not succeed when the matter is administratively redetermined, and other applicants in a similar position might be thwarted by changes in procedure.[61] Nonetheless, decisions sometimes have effects beyond their particular circumstances. A simple example of public law affecting behaviour in the private sector is the response to decisions of the courts on taxation. Once particular tax avoidance measures have been sanctioned, many taxpayers have structured their affairs to reap the advantage (if they have not do so previously).

It is difficult to identify a large number of single private law decisions which have had a significant impact on social behaviour. Despite the attention lavished on private law decisions by lawyers, they do not have the same dramatic social consequences as much legislation, even though the latter might be rarely, if ever, litigated.[62] For example, it is arguable that the establishment of small claims courts has been of far greater social importance than particular cases on contract. Similarly, town planning legislation has been more influential than decisions on the law of nuisance, and consumer credit legislation than decisions on the sale of goods. Perhaps this limited impact is not surprising when the implications of particular private law cases are not obvious to most members of the community.[63] Moreover, case law is generally not a powerful factor in constituting economic and social relation when compared with other factors, notably the drive for profits and community mores.[64] This is not to deny that some single private law decisions might have an effect on behaviour in the wider community. For instance, after decisions such as *Somma* v. *Hazlehurst*,[65] landlords are likely to redraft their standard form leases so as to increase the chance of claims for possession being upheld. Another example is that *Paris* v. *Stepney Borough Council*[66] is said to have inhibited the recruitment of persons with monocular vision, to have severely retarded the employment of other disabled persons, and to have involved industry in considerable expense in evaluating its ramifications.[67]

A cluster of cases, or repeated litigation, in an area of private law might have greater social significance. The whole complex of contract law, say, has had an effect on the way contracts are negotiated and implemented. A

[61] C. Harlow & R. Rawlings, *Law and Administration* (1984), pp. 257–63; A. Hutchinson, "The Rise and Ruse of Administrative Law and Scholarship" (1985) 48 M.L.R. 293, 316.

[62] The conclusion of authors working from quite different standpoints: Epstein, "The Social Consequences of Common Law Rules" (1982) 95 Harv. L.R. 1717, 1744–51; Hurst, "The Functions of Courts in the United States, 1950–1980" (1980–81) 15 L. & Soc. R. 401, 448–9; Unger, "The Critical Legal Studies Movement" (1983) 96 Harv. L.R. 561, 581.

[63] See Galanter, "Justice in Many Rooms: Courts, Private Ordering, and Indigenous Law" (1981) 19 J. Leg. Pluralism 1, 11–15.

[64] W. Muir, *Law and Attitude Change* (1973) examines the role of social mores in the impact of a "school prayer" decision of the United States Supreme Court in one city.

[65] [1978] 2 All E.R. 1011; [1978] 1 W.L.R. 1014.

[66] [1951] A.C. 367.

[67] Wigglesworth, "Legislation and Injury Control" (1978) 18 Med. Sci. Law 191, 193.

series of tort cases "opened the floodgates" to persons injured in motor vehicle and industrial accidents obtaining compensation through litigation. As a result, what is effectively a social welfare function is performed by the courts, rather than a government agency, because of favourable doctrinal developments and the growth of private insurance. However, it is extremely doubtful whether liability rules have had any deterrent effect on the way people drive or work, compared with the influences of road traffic penalties and health and safety at work legislation.[68] On the other hand, the way damages are assessed in such cases, generously or otherwise, might affect the level of premiums payable by motorists and employers to insure against liability. Still in the area of tort law, it is said that the corpus of defamation law outside the United States greatly inhibits investigative journalism. The proposition is dubious when many areas, ripe for investigative journalism, where defamation is irrelevant, go unexplored. And there are whole areas of economic and social life, education, transport, the arts, and so on, where the private law is largely irrelevant.

As well as social factors, courts might have little impact because of their own institutional limitations. For example, courts rely on the executive to enforce judgments and to punish those in contempt of its orders.[69] They might also have a limited impact because their decisions are undermined, either directly or indirectly. There have been some blatant examples of administrative action of this character. A more dramatic factor is that the decisions of courts might be reversed by legislation.[70] Where the financial consequences of their decisions are significant, for example damages for personal injury claims, the legislature might act relatively quickly to overturn them. Legislative reversal might be especially swift if government revenue is directly threatened. Without such financial incentives spurring them to action, however, governments are usually more dilatory about introducing legislation to reverse the effect of judicial decisions. Much depends on whether the government or a relevant minister is sympathetic to changing the law. Liberal and Labour governments in Britain acted relatively quickly and exempted trade unions from the ambit of some of the economic tort doctrines developed by the courts. The time which elapses before the effect of a decision, or body of decisions, is reversed might be compounded if a matter is referred to a law reform body for comment and recommendation. It might be that some governments have taken this course with a view to delaying controversial legislation. A final point to make in this regard is that the courts might be able to limit legislative reversal of their decisions by their interpretation of the relevant legislation or the application of other common law doctrines. In other words, judicial decisions and legislation might be part of a continuing process, adjusted by the judges or by government as a response to each other.

[68] See P. Atiyah, *Accidents, Compensation and the Law* (3rd ed., 1980), pp. 606–7; Cranston, "Consumer Protection and Economic Theory" in A. Duggan & L. Darvall (eds.), *Consumer Protection Law and Theory* (1980), pp. 244–5; D. Harris *et al.*, *op. cit.*, pp. 20, 145–6; New South Wales Law Reform Commission, *Accident Compensation* (1984), v. 1, paras. 3.7–3.10; 3.37–3.39. See also Rabin "Impact Analysis and Tort Law: A Comment" (1979) 13 L. & Soc. R. 987.

[69] R. Cranston, Legal Foundations of the Welfare State, *op. cit.*, pp. 305–10.

[70] There are examples in D. Miers & A. Page, *Legislation* (1982), pp. 3, 198; Zellick, "Government Beyond Law" [1985] P.L. 283, 288–92.

V. Conclusion

Concentrating on trouble or hard cases misses much of the process of the civil courts. In many respects, the courts are functioning as administrative agencies or as facilitators of compromises rather than directly resolving contested issues of law and fact. Even if the concern is hard or trouble cases, it would seem crucial to understand how they come before the relevant court for decision. The use of disputes as an organising category for understanding courts overlooks important aspects such as their role in law-making, and the assertion of public values. In addition, there are the many occasions when parties approach courts to obtain the imprimatur of the state in relation to a matter, without any suggestion that there is a dispute, or even a potential dispute, about a matter. While civil courts are part of the political process, most litigation is oriented to the claim of individuals and organisations far removed from what is ordinarily obtainable, under existing arrangements, through the political process. So long as individuals continue to advance so many claims through the courts, in particular with accident litigation, it is difficult to argue that the courts are predominantly concerned with ratifying the legal claims of dominant groups in society. And given the limited impact of liability rules on behaviour, it seems beside the point to concentrate attention on the efficiency of those rules.

The approach to the courts outlined above provided an overall framework for understanding their internal operation, as well as their relationship with society. It lays a tentative basis for formulating middle range theories about matters such as how legal procedures operate and the functions of law. Take just a few of the issues touched on above. First, there is the uneven use of the courts in terms of who brings cases and over what issues. How else are grievances dealt with in society, how is conflict channelled, and how are challenges to basic structures filtered so that the courts rarely deal with them? Secondly, there are many cases before the civil courts where commercial and property interests obtain default against individuals. How is it possible to talk about the latter having legal rights if those rights do not govern what actually happens? Thirdly, the transformation of issues, and the identification of the legally relevant, raise questions about power, in particular about how the understanding and interpretation of events takes place legally. Finally, there is the role of the courts as an instrument of social control. Compared with the legislation which can work through the executive arm of the state, it seems that courts are marginal in this regard, although the outcomes in particular cases might affect individual behaviour.

[3]

Courts and conflict resolution

VILHELM AUBERT
University of Oslo and Institute for Social Research, Oslo

Law seems to have two basic and intimately connected tasks: to solve conflicts and to foster conformity to legal rules. The conflict-solving function has left the most distinctive marks upon the structure of legal thinking and upon the occupational role of the professional jurist. In this paper I shall deal only with a few selected aspects of the relationship between the task of conflict resolution and the structure of law. I shall discuss how this particular task has influenced the structure of the judiciary and the courts, by making some comparisons with other decision-making bodies. I shall then discuss some implications for the development of international machinery for conflict resolution.

Underlying the following analysis is a thesis that the task of conflict resolution demands and creates structures of thinking and decision-making which are, on important points, in sharp contrast with scientific thinking (see Aubert, 1963a). If this is true, it raises an important issue on the international level. Many bits of evidence suggest that modern science has furnished a better basis for consensus on the world level than has the embryonic international law. To put it crudely, scientists in all countries, by and large, accept the operation of the same natural laws, and are willing to proceed on these common assumptions. Man-made laws are wholly dependent upon a comprehensive social system, whose members may reach consensus based upon law, but whose relationships to nonmembers will not be governed to any large extent by a consensus based upon law.

The world is a natural system but not a social system. International bargaining, as well as the use of force or the threat of force, are governed by utilitarian considerations, schemes of thought shaped on the means-end model. Insofar as such considerations coalesce, conflicts may be resolved, tensions eased, and stability achieved. The history and sociology of domestic law, however, suggest that other types of decision-making, based upon a man-made structure emanating from the power of a comprehensive social system, are a necessary precondition of stable peace. The promise of the world consensus of scientists, when confronted with the reliance upon nonscientific structures of conflict resolution on the national level, suggests one approach to a deeper understanding of the structure of an emerging social system on a world scale and of the conditions of peace. The following comments, however, must be considered as mere preliminaries to such an understanding, as they are based exclusively upon certain aspects of conflict resolution within the framework of one state.

The Judge as Decision-Maker

Decision-making is the task around which the legal profession has developed. Lawyers have traditionally been the experts on the use of power. That is not to say that lawyers have always been among the most powerful groups in society. But insofar as they have exerted power, or served those who wielded power, they have done so in a professional capacity, as a duty towards the abstract ideals of law, and on the basis of a theoretical and technical mastery of the field.

"Power over clients" may appear to be a contradiction in terms, since a client is a person who buys services from a professional, and is free to take or leave these services at will. The term is used to suggest the ambivalence which attaches to the role of the judge, due to his dual function of settling disputes and enforcing rules. Like the private lawyer, the judge waits for somebody to take the initiative and ask for his professional opinion. A large proportion of the parties who appear before a court of law could have stayed away if they had strongly preferred to do so. In this sense they are recruited to their role in court on the basis of a choice, as is the case when an individual becomes the client of an attorney. Once they are in court, however, barring an agreement between the litigants, they have to abide by the decisions made by the judge. The decisions are binding upon these "clients." The will of the judge will be made to prevail over the will of the "clients," if necessary by the use of force.

There are other aspects of judicial decision-making to which we shall soon return. It seems appropriate, however, to emphasize the service function of the judge, since the settlement of conflicts between private individuals has played such a dominant part in shaping the law—its theory as well as the techniques of decision-making. It is inherent in the situation of the judge *vis-à-vis* his clients that his service must be different in kind from that contributed by a doctor, an architect, or an engineer. His service is a contribution, not to an individual, but to a dyadic system in conflict. The fact that a plaintiff has asked the judge for a decision establishes no particularistic relationship between plaintiff and judge. Any attempt on the part of one of the litigants to reward the judge, or any willingness on the part of the judge to receive remuneration from the winning party, would be considered wrong and a grave breach of the obligations incumbent upon him.

Not everybody who appears before a court of law has chosen to do so, or has even had the chance of opting against doing so, given that certain actions have taken place. The criminal is normally brought before the court on the intiative of the state, represented by the prosecution. In criminal cases the function of settling conflicts recedes at the expense of the task of upholding conformity with the laws. Historically, criminal law has developed from a less differentiated system with strong elements of private litigation between two parties. Even today, criminal procedure is heavily influenced by the fact that it takes place before a tribunal which is also, and predominantly, concerned with the settlement of disputes between private parties in civilian suits. This notwithstanding, the power relationship between the judge and the defendant must be classified as power over citizens, meaning a power from which there is no escape for the individual.

Whether the judge exerts power over "clients" or over "citizens," he plays a passive role. The difference between those decision-makers whose function depends upon outside initiative and those who can take the initiative themselves is an important one. It is probably one of the determinants of public attitudes toward decision-makers, which tend to be more favorable with regard to those, like judges, who wait for others to make them decide.

Those authorities who need outside initiative to make decisions seem to work primarily with the task of reducing or solving conflicts between individuals or groups. Civil servants who take independent initiative to make decisions, e.g., through legislation, are more concerned with the other basic task of law: to create conformity to rules, whether these rules increase or decrease the amount of conflict in society. Judges, and other decision-makers who need the initiative of others to function, can be viewed as contributing a general service to the group within which they work. They do so by an institutionalized readiness to intervene in conflicts where the parties themselves seem unable to reach a solution. Under such circumstances it has not been uncommon for groups or communities to call in an outsider, a supposedly neutral person, to make the decision. The quality for which these people have been sought after was precisely their distance from the parties. It is a primitive, mechanical way of achieving "objectivity." Or, to put it the other way around, the rules governing the modern judiciary are a sophisticated way of making full-blown members of the community into "professional strangers." The nature of the particular "service" which judges contribute, its origin in a conflict between two parties, implies that the service can only be contributed when an atmosphere of objectivity prevails. The point of departure prevents particularistic norms from gaining any foothold in the role of the judge (Aubert, 1963b).

The meaning of the service functions of the judge becomes clearer if we study the way in which he has been recruited to his position, and his relationship to resources and sanctions. Judges are appointed by the government on the basis of a law degree, achievements in a different branch of law, and seniority.[1] They are paid by the state for rendering their services to the judiciary, and they cannot be fired without due process of law, which occurs very rarely. In these respects the judges are typical bureaucrats, but they do not work within hierarchical organizations as the civil servants do. They receive no instructions from superiors, although superior courts may review and possibly reverse their decisions. There is an intimate relationship between the service function of the judiciary, the emphasis upon conflict resolution, and the relatively independent position of the judge. It may be doubted that a government department would be capable of rendering justice as a service to the population.

The resources available to the judge consist of his own knowledge and skills and his ability to call upon the compulsory force of the state. He is in no position to reward clients, except insofar as the loss suffered by one of the parties to a civil suit represents the gain of the adversary. The judge's lack of positive resources severely limits his capacity to shape the course of events on the basis of means-ends schemes. He is not a planner or an executor of plans. We can here see a close relationship between the nature of legal thinking, relatively unconcerned with utilitarian planning for the future (cf. Aubert, 1963a), and the type of decision-making delegated to the judiciary. There is a close correspondence between his way of thinking and the fact that he is without command of the resources which other decision-makers, who shape the future according to scientific plans, must control.

[1] This is the situation in Norway. But on these particular points there are wide international variations.

The judge is in control of negative sanctions. He, and only he, can release the sanction of legal punishment. But he can do so only when a criminal case is brought before his court by the prosecution. Thus he is strictly limited in his choice of strategy for achieving general ends of the kind which can be achieved by penalties and deterrence. Bound by the choice of cases made by other agencies, and by the demands for concrete justice, he may on occasion feel obligated to render a verdict contrary to what he believes would be best suited to foster a development which he considers desirable. Whether dealing with clients or with citizens, the judge will play a much more passive part with respect to the execution of plans for the future than do other legal decision-makers. His plans will be limited to influencing the interests of the parties on a short run basis.

Why Do Clients Go to Court?

It has been emphasized that the kind of legal decision-making which takes place in courts has, in part, the character of a service. A private demand is regularly required for the decision-making machinery to be set in operation. This raises the question of why there is such a demand, or under what conditions it will be released. When a conflict passes from the stage of private bargaining to litigation before a court of law, this involves the risk of total loss for one of the parties (cf. Aubert, 1963b). Although it may be rational for one of the parties to incur this risk in marginal cases, where the stakes are overwhelmingly on his side, it cannot normally be in the interests of both to have a judicial tribunal deal with the case. This is especially so if we take the legal costs into consideration. As a system the contestants always stand to lose by litigation due to the legal costs. And one of them courts maximal loss plus legal costs, although it may be uncertain which one of the two is most likely to be the loser. By going to court, neither of the adversaries buys the same kind of service as he does when he hires a private lawyer. The judge does not become *his* judge in the same way as the lawyer became *his* counsel. Why is the "service" of the courts nevertheless sought after? Why doesn't one of the parties always try to buy himself out of the situation where intransigence might lead to total loss? Why is the minimax principle, at least apparently, set aside?

In criminal cases it is not a question of service, not of power over clients. It is a case of power over citizens, and it is established by law that a judicial decision is needed in order to inflict penalities upon offenders. The parties are not free to bargain. Let it just be mentioned that this does not exclude all elements of bargaining from criminal cases. It may not be unusual after certain kinds of offenses for the victim to agree to abstain from making charges against the offender, if he promises compensation; or the offender will abstain from delinquencies in the future, and can make such promises credible. Such bargains may be very common in cases of embezzlement and betrayal of economic trust, but also in other areas of criminal law. Bargains of a sort may also be struck between the offender and the police or the prosecution. Thus even the prospective defendant may face a choice between intransigence, leading possibly to maximally severe treatment by a court of law, or some kind of compromise whereby he avoids this alternative. He may voluntarily make a lesser sacrifice, e.g., by pleading guilty to a less serious crime than the one for which he would otherwise be indicted. What needs to be answered here, however, is not why some criminal cases come before a court of law, but why the other category of court cases, the civil suits, are not settled out of court.

Possibly the most general reason why two conflicting parties deviate from "rational" behavior and permit a case to be settled in a court of law, with greatly increased chances of total loss for one, is the tendency to overestimate one's chances of winning. Only in a borderline case are the chances of winning 100 per cent for one of the parties.

There are some rather general reasons why people should tend to overestimate their chances to win legal suits. For one thing, the arguments favoring one's own case are much more readily available than those favoring the other party. Cognitively speaking, full insight into all the aspects of the case is lacking. The positive aspects will easily be perceptually overrepresented.

Legal suits have a moral tinge. To predict loss in a courtroom would normally imply doubt concerning one's own moral right. The personal defense erected against such moral doubt will therefore tend to render factual predictions unreliable. There may even exist a need to retain one's moral aggression against the other party. Legal suits represent an area of life where it is hard for people to be completely rational, in the sense of attempting an unbiased prediction of the future based on available empirical grounds. It is, in addition—and for other reasons—an area where predictions are often "technically" difficult to make.

In view of the preceding argument it is surprising how few legal suits are brought before the courts. This is no doubt partly due to the attorneys. As legal counsel, standing outside the conflict, they may furnish the objectivity and coolness which the client lacks, but which he needs in order to act rationally. Thus many conflicts are settled out of court, through a compromise. Another factor, counteracting the general psychological force in the direction of overestimating one's own chances of success, is the discomfort and cost involved in lawsuits. Even if a party relies on obtaining compensation for legal costs, it is a future and somewhat uncertain gain to be measured against a certain and immediate economic obligation. The judiciary also instills a certain discomfort, or even fear, in many people, notwithstanding their good faith. Even if the one party has the right on his side, it must be expected that the opponent's legal counsel will utilize all points of doubt, every reason to distrust his right. It may even be that such a negative, or at least ambivalent, attitude to the law and to lawyers is a functional necessity if legal administration is to avoid overwork and breakdown.

When confronting the possible gains and losses involved in bargaining and lawsuits respectively, it must be observed that the choice of procedure as such may imply a taste for, or dislike of, the procedure itself. The litigants may be so agitated and aggressive that to meet and negotiate and agree will be full of unpleasantness, irrespective of the outcome.

Other desiderata come into play. To demonstrate a "firm attitude" may take on independent value, for the enactment of which one, or both, of the parties is willing to pay. But of course this attitude will often be combined with a tendency to overestimate the probability of success in the courtroom, thus bringing into operation the mechanisms of distortion outlined above.

In some litigation one of the parties may have interests which transcend the individual case. It may then be rational to behave differently from what would have been indicated were the case to be viewed in isolation. Thus an insurance company or the state may have an interest in testing a case before the courts, even if it would have been more profitable in the individual case to settle out of court on the basis of a compromise. But the insurance company may be primarily interested in obtaining certainty with regard to its rights and duties.

A lawsuit which is representative of other and similar suits may also be viewed from a somewhat different angle. To test a case before the courts is not merely a way of discovering what the law is. A legal suit may also be viewed as an attempt to create new law, to change and modify the existing law, thereby establishing different conditions for what may become rational behavior in the future.

Generally speaking there will often be asymmetry between the parties, insofar as the suit is a regular, calculable element in business operations for one of them, and a unique event for the other. It means that the former will be much more concerned with obtaining predictability, and will be less deterred by the likelihood of losing individual cases, provided he can transfer the loss to a group of customers or clients.

In this context it must also be observed that the attorneys in each individual case have interests transcending the case. In their conduct of any one case they will be concerned with their general standing as attorneys. They will also be somewhat influenced by their own personal legal opinions, and by an "idealistic" interest in furthering law and justice. Most lawyers have a professional interest in finding out what the law is, independent of other considerations. To the extent that this motive prevails, legal counsel may have reason to instigate a lawsuit even in some cases where it would be more rational from his client's point of view to work towards a compromise settlement out of court.

A lawyer may obtain various kinds of occupational rewards, such as economic success and the consciousness of having aided his client. But a significant source of satisfaction must lie in the sense of mastering the legal tools in a purely professional sense, akin to the pleasure of an artist in a star performance. A lawyer can most reliably verify his skill in two ways: by predicting the outcome of court cases, and by influencing the verdict of the court. This verification demands lawsuits.

It may well be that when lawyers deviate from strict utilitarian caution, from the client's point of view, they further wider social interests. The legal system would in the long run become unable to draw the finer distinctions between right and wrong if there were no attorneys who dared to bring even dubious cases before a court of law, but always preferred compromises. It is also in the interest of the legal system and its general functions that lawyers should not unswervingly attempt to adjust to probable court decisions, like meteorologists adjusting to the weather. The law is continuously moulded through attempts to change the status quo, although this may in the individual case be irrational from a strict minimax point of view.

There may be conflicts in which one of the parties assumes that he is going to lose a lawsuit, and knows that he might obtain a more advantageous result through bargaining and compromise. Nevertheless, he may choose to let himself be forced to pay in full rather than agree voluntarily to a partial payment. Voluntary fulfillment of a demand from the opponent will often be interpreted as an admission of moral weakness, even of guilt. Since peoples's ability to think in terms of probabilities about problems with moral overtones is limited, an admission of probable loss may be perceived as an admission of total normative weakness on the particular point under dispute. Because of the normative inferences which may be drawn from such admissions, although they are based upon purely descriptive predictions, some litigants may choose to court total loss rather than expose themselves to suspicions of a guilty conscience. This attitude may imperceptibly blend with a more genuine moral stubborness, an unwillingness to bargain about one's moral rights. It may be considered morally wrong, even, to yield without a command from the court.

These considerations may take on additional strength if the issue of the conflict concerns others than the two directly involved in litigation: family, heirs, partners, colleagues. If the legal or *de facto* position of these outsiders depends in some measure upon the solution of the individual conflict, it may appear advantageous for the parties to delegate the decision and the final responsibility to the courts. In case of an adverse decision, the party cannot be blamed for not having done his utmost to defend the interest of the others. The outcome of a bargain will in no small measure be viewed as a symptom of the skill and loyalty of the parties. The court's verdict will more often be perceived as an authoritative expression of what the legal situation of all concerned "really" is.

In some conflicts the object of the dispute may be indivisible, thus precluding compromise. The famous story of Solomon and the two mothers illustrates this type of situation. In many divorce cases there is only one child, and the child is indivisible. Only one of the parents can normally keep it, while the spouse will be restricted to visits and vacation get-togethers. Thus normal motivation for a compromise settlement out of court may disappear, since the situation brooks no alternatives anyway. The situation may sometimes be similar in inheritance disputes over material objects, if these are considered to have emotional values which cannot be translated into money. Under such conditions the factual calculations of success chances are often intermingled with moral comparisons (e.g., concerning the relationships between the deceased and the various heirs), thus making bargains and compromise irrelevant. Such conflicts remain in the realm of dichotomous rights and duties, the proper sphere of legal decisions.

One final motive for wanting a lawsuit lies precisely in the risk involved. It is to some extent a game of chance, the parties being at the mercy of rules over which they have no control, unlike the bargaining situation where rules and facts can be modified according to the will of the parties. I have in other contexts argued that men seek the uncertain and unpredictable frequently, and for profound reasons (cf. Aubert, 1965, especially ch. 5). Getting an unpredictable answer from the law may, to the legally naive individual, mean a verification or falsification of important assumptions about his moral worth and standing in the social realm. It may even take on religious overtones, law being in some measure perceived as a manifestation of divine justice. Thus a court proceeding may take on the character of a moral test case for the individual, which the settlement out of court could not have. This element of more or less unpredictable verification or falsification through a verdict may of course also exert some attraction on the lawyer. To the lawyer the uncertainty of the case may be exciting, like games and sports, thus adding pleasure to his work.

Implications for the Development of International Law

Out of the preceding analysis arise a number of questions which relate to the functioning of law as a way of resolving conflicts on the international level. The most obvious and probably also the most profound reason why the international legal order is such a rudimentary means for solving conflicts is that there exists no world society, no world government, and no psychologically internalized supranational authority. The intellectual tools for solving international conflicts are available, and so are the formal organs needed. The world is not, however, a social system in a sense which often makes it pay, emotionally and materially, to accept the authority of available conflict-solvers.

This problem has another aspect. Insofar as international law deals with the relationship between states, the legal subjects have an entirely different motivational structure from human organisms. Nations do not behave as individuals do. They are units of a different order. Many of the points discussed above refer to psychological mechanisms characteristic of human beings. These may or may not have application also to nations. But it does not follow from a legal definition of a state as a legal subject that it takes on the real characteristics of the units after which its legal form has been shaped.

To say that there exists no world social system is a simplification. Some elements normally associated with social systems are highly developed in the world system, while others are almost entirely lacking. Economic exchange relationships are rather well developed. Certain types of cultural norms are very widespread and standardized in the world. This is true of norms which relate to science and technology, and also to economic transactions to some extent. It might well be argued that the world is in a very rapid process of becoming culturally integrated. As a social organization, however—in terms of membership groups and political leadership—the process is much slower and more uneven, in part characterized by developments which lead away from an integrated world society.

One implication of this differential development of the cultural and the organizational aspects of the world social system is that international conflict resolution will tend to be restricted to methods which rely heavily upon the shared intellectual tools and norms and upon the divided national bases of force and authority. This favors traditional diplomacy, or mediation if third parties are brought into the conflict. It also favors attempts to reach a consensus on important conflict issues between those who participate most actively in a worldwide culture: the natural scientists. The Pugwash movement is a particularly striking example of the latter tendency.

If we turn to the more specific points in our analysis of the operation of national courts as a means to solve conflicts, some further implications may be derived from these aspects of the world as a system. Self-righteousness is a characteristic of individuals in conflict. It is also a characteristic of nations, or of their representatives, when they are in conflict. However objectionable self-righteousness may be in disputes between individuals, it has an important function within a legal system: it furnishes the courts with the cases needed to reassert the authority of law, and to elaborate upon the implications of legal norms. But, while individual self-righteousness leads to the courts, national self-righteousness diminishes the chances that a country will bring the international court, or other court-like proceedings, into operation. To take a case to the national courts is normally perceived as an expression of a "firm attitude," of self-confidence, and of fighting spirit. To accept an international court proceeding or the good offices of intermediaries may also be praised, but for the opposite reasons.

This reversal of the role of the courts on the international level is a consequence of the lack of authority of international bodies. It is also closely related to the fact that those who act on behalf of nations in international disputes have, as their most important reference groups, their compatriots: other politicians, civil servants, journalists, or an electorate. These audiences are apt to perceive a willingness to enter into legal types of conflict resolution as an admission of weakness. Although it might be eminently rational for the nation to admit weakness, it need not be rational to do so for those who make the decisions. There is a lack of synchronization between the needs of the representatives and the needs of the bodies which they represent. We even lack criteria of need-satisfaction for nations.

This phenomenon has another aspect which is more encouraging. An implication of the above considerations is that the representatives of nations may be free from some of the sources of irrationality which becloud the judgment of parties to private litigation. Many individuals can very well sustain their self-respect, even enhance it, when they perceive some flaw in the position taken by the nation they belong to or which they represent. This may increase the likelihood of concessions in the course of negotiations, provided the negotiators believe that these concessions can be camouflaged or justified *vis-à-vis* their national audience. While self-righteousness internationally is unlikely to lead to legal conflict resolution, neither will self-righteousness make it as difficult to negotiate between nations as may be the case between individuals. From both points of view, international court proceedings seem less likely to occur.

It was claimed above that an asymmetry between parties might be conducive to litigation, that is, when one of the parties has a strong interest in predictability per se, more or less irrespective of loss or gain in the trial case. This type of situation may be less common in the relationships between states. States are units of the same order, and it is not easy to point to conflicts where one of the states might be interested in buying predictability at the cost of a loss in an individual case.

The relationship between client and counsel changes character when we move from the traditional situations within national legal systems to international litigation. When legal counsel is a citizen of his client state, he is in a sense the subordinate of his client. This is not unlike the relationship between company lawyers who work in the firm and their client, but it is strikingly different from the situations which, during a long tradition, shaped the legal profession and the role of its members. In many situations where individuals are in conflict, the attorney fulfills a quasi-judicial function by virtue of his independent authority. Although a representative of one party, he is not a dependent or a subordinate of the client. He has strong reasons to guard his independence and protect himself against the suspicion that he is a partisan of certain types of clients and that his services are unavailable to others.

The fact that a lawyer is privately hired and paid to further the interests of his client makes the client prone to listen to his advice. The client may accept an interpretation of legal rules which he would object to if it had been presented to him by someone who was not looking after his interests, or who represented what he perceived as an "enemy." A civil servant representing the state in a tax case would be perceived as an adversary, whereas the client's lawyer would be perceived as an ally, notwithstanding the fact that they might both present the client with the same inescapable demands. The credibility of the private attorney is higher under these circumstances. Thus the legal profession provides for a cushioning between the demands of the state and the private interests of the citizens. It tends to ameliorate conflicts without having recourse to litigation, which merely lurks as a threat in the back of the client's mind.

The private practitioners of the legal profession are not civil servants and do not, at least in their occupational role, share formal political power in nations. But they constitute an essential part of the conflict-solving machinery which is built up around the courts. It is difficult to see how a modern legal system could function without the independent legal profession. And it may well be that the establishment of an independent legal profession with supranational loyalties creates more formidable problems than the creation of an international court system. One impediment to such a development is the extreme parochialism of legal education in the legally developed countries. Law as an academic discipline is national in a sense which would be unthinkable in the natural sciences, and which exceeds the not inconsiderable nationalism of the other social sciences, including history. To be trained in law is not merely to be trained in the mastery of a set of intellectual tools and techniques. It involves also the inculcation of a set of loyalties, rigorously circumscribed by national boundaries. This is, of course, not to deny that lawyers over large parts of the globe may share certain basic academic assumptions and premises, e.g., some of those derived from Roman law.

An interesting aspect of the (very slowly) developing interchange between law and the other social sciences is that it may further an internationalization of the subculture of the legal profession. A decision of the legislator may at any time introduce or eliminate a difference or a similarity between the legal systems of two nations.[2] But no national decision-maker can change the causal and functional regularities which sociologists of law may discover in their respective countries. From this point of view the development of a sociology of law might in the long run exert a balancing effect upon the international legal system, by widening the common ground between experts on law from different nations.

Law and Science

This brings us back to a theme which was broached in the introduction to this paper: the relationship between law and science. Law as well as science aim towards predictability. During the long historical period when national legal systems developed, science was undeveloped by comparison with its present status. Whatever predictability could be achieved in the interaction between citizens of a state was to a high degree based upon man-made laws and upon other types of normative structures regulating social life. No doubt, experience with natural phenomena contributed to predictability in social exchange. Exaggerated claims have probably been made for the thesis that "tradition reigned" in folk or peasant societies. Compared to modern

[2] Cf. the statement by von Kirchmann: "Ein Federstreich des Gesetzgebers, und Bibliotheke werden Makulatur" (1848, p. 19).

social life, however, the thesis points to a highly significant difference. It could be said that man-made laws, and other social norms, represented an attempt to secure some predictability in man's life as a "functional alternative" to the insight into natural laws and social mechanisms which was much less developed than it is today. The use of the term "law" in both contexts is not without significance.

With increased scientific knowledge about the regularities of nature and also of economic and social life, the relative importance of law as a way of achieving predictability has been receding in modern societies. A process of "delegalization" can be observed in many social spheres. Our trust that the doctor will heal us in the case of sickness does presuppose a legal and moral duty on the part of the doctor. More important, however, it presupposes extensive medical knowledge. When we buy an air-ticket from London to New York, we expect to land in New York on time, less because the company has taken on an obligation to do so than because we have confidence in the technical know-how of air transport personnel. To a businessman a program of investment is dependent upon the assumption that agreements will be fulfilled, but increasingly also upon factual predictions of the development of the market in the future, derived from economics as a branch of science.

The present era, in which international law meets its severe tests and takes fumbling steps toward a system which the citizens of the world may trust, is characterized by a much higher development of scientific thinking. Thus, also, modern thinking about world problems has been dominated by scientific disciplines; biology, medicine, botany, economics, demography, strategic studies, etc. The most popular models of the future world are rarely legal utopias; most of them are "systems" derived, with more or less rigor, from more or less tenable empirical premises. It looks as if this international development has bypassed the legal stage in man's attempt to furnish predictability and has plunged right into the stage where predictions, and the flickers of hope and trust, are derived from science. But there is nothing in the development within modern states which suggests that law is superfluous, only that it is increasingly insufficient to furnish on its own the kind of predictability in social life which is needed if conflicts are to be avoided or, if not avoided, solved.

Apart from the basic political and organizational obstacles to the development of a world social system, there may also be some intellectual difficulties involved. Law has in the most developed states lost much of its old appeal to intellectually gifted and enterprising youth. Law as a science is widely distrusted or scorned, sometimes feared, by representatives of other scientific disciplines as some kind of secular priesthood. This is not surprising. Nor is it wholly unjustified. But this attitude to law ought not to be encouraged by the other social sciences. I believe that a considerable amount of modesty is called for on the part of other scientific disciplines if the concern is to develop methods of conflict avoidance and conflict resolution. The cooperation between law and the other social sciences is important in the national social system. But it is probably even more important to the development of the international social system. In this perspective the development of an adequate scientific understanding of law as a structure of action and roles with a specified set of social functions takes on increased practical significance.

REFERENCES

AUBERT, VILHELM. "The Structure of Legal Thinking." In: *Legal Essays. Festskrift til Frede Castberg*. Oslo: Universitetsforlaget, 1963a, pp. 41–63.

———. "Competition and Dissensus: Two Types of Conflict and of Conflict Resolution," *Journal of Conflict Resolution*, 7, 1 (March 1963b), 26–42.

———. *The Hidden Society*. Totowa, N.J.: Bedminster Press, 1965.

VON KIRCHMANN, J. H. *Die Wertlosigkeit der Jurisprudenz als Wissenschaft*. 3rd edn. Berlin, 1848.

Part II
Alternative Dispute Resolution

[4]

University of Florida Law Review

VOLUME XXXVII | WINTER 1985 | NUMBER 1

ALTERNATIVE DISPUTE RESOLUTION SYMPOSIUM

ALTERNATIVE METHODS OF DISPUTE RESOLUTION: AN OVERVIEW

FRANK E.A. SANDER*

I. INTRODUCTION**

Beginning in the late sixties, American society witnessed an extraordinary flowering of interest in alternative forms of dispute settlement. This interest emanated from a wide variety of sources ranging from the Chief Justice of the United States Supreme Court to corporate general counsel, the organized Bar and various lay groups.[1] Following a decade or so of virtually unabashed enthusiasm, serious questions and doubts are now being raised. Additionally, we are slowly accumulating limited data concerning viable models and empirical effects. Hence, this may be an opportune time for evaluating and exploring promising future directions.

Perhaps a good place to begin is with some definitions. What exactly do we mean by "alternative dispute resolution mechanisms" (ADRMs)? Alternative to what? Presumably "alternative" is used as a substitute for the traditional dispute resolution mechanism, the court. Interestingly enough, however, courts do not resolve most disputes. The literature on dispute processing and dispute transformation has delineated ways in which grievances may be turned into ongoing disputes, and the myriad ways in which disputes may be resolved by means other than court adjudication.[2] In fact, disputes that cannot be readily adjusted may be presented initially to a whole host of dispute processors such as arbitrators, mediators, fact-finders or ombudsmen. If the dispute is ultimately filed in court, approximately 90-95 percent of these disputes are settled by negotiation, with little or no court litigation. Hence, the argument for "alternatives" is not based on the need to find a substitute for court adjudiciation.

---

* Bussey Professor, Harvard Law School. B.A., 1949, Harvard; LL.B., 1952, Harvard.

** This paper is a revision of a draft paper prepared for a conference on the lawyer's changing role in dispute settlement, held at Harvard Law School in October 1982. The paper differs somewhat from that delivered at University of Florida College of Law in Fall 1984.

1. J. MARKS, E. JOHNSON, JR. & P. SZANTON, DISPUTE RESOLUTION IN AMERICA: PROCESSES IN EVOLUTION (Nat'l Inst. for Dispute Resolution 1984).

2. Felstiner, Abel & Sarat, *The Emergence & Transformation of Disputes: Naming, Blaming, Claiming*, 15 L. & SOC'Y REV. 631 (1980-81); Galanter, *Justice in Many Rooms*, 19 J. OF LEGAL PLURALISM 1 (1981).

Rather, it is based on the need to gain a better understanding of the functioning of these alternative mechanisms and processes.

Alternatives to courts are not a new phenomenon.[3] Yet, the current resurgence of alternative dispute resolution seems to have a freshness about it. The movement appears to have a much broader theoretical and practical base. It might therefore be useful briefly to speculate on the confluence of events that have led to the current renewal of interest in alternatives.

The sixties were characterized by considerable strife and conflict, emanating in part from the civil rights struggles and the Vietnam War protests. An apparent legacy of those times was a lessened tolerance and a greater tendency to turn grievances into disputes. Also relevant was a significant increase in the statutory creation of new causes of action.

A noteworthy development from these events was that courts found themselves inundated with new filings, triggering cries of alarm from the judicial administration establishment. This judicial congestion led to claims that equal access to justice had been denied.[4] Spurred in part by these conditions, parties attempted to resolve some of these disputes through alternative dispute resolution mechanisms. In the 1964 Civil Rights Act Congress established the Community Relations Service in the United States Department of Justice to aid courts and others in settling intractable racial and community disputes. The Ford Foundation established the National Center for Dispute Settlement and the Institute of Mediation and Conflict Resolution to study dispute settlement mechanisms.[5]

Any attempt to isolate the roots of a complex and ill-understood movement is bound to suffer from oversimplification. One can readily identify a number of other social forces that contributed to the recent flowering of the alternatives movement. One contributor is the waning role of some of society's traditional mediating institutions such as the family, the church, and the wardhealer. A second influence is the discernible recent mood of anti-professionalism.[6] Both these conditions point towards the creation of alternative indigenous mechanisms such as community mediation centers and family dispute settlement tribunals.[7] Of course, need alone does not always lead to constructive solutions. Fortunately, for the alternatives movement, the Law Enforcement Assistance Administration (LEAA) took a firm interest in developing and testing ADRMs, even if the required nexus with the criminal law system at times distorted the proper emphasis.

Certain intellectual developments paralleled these social forces. Over the past 15-20 years some cultural anthropologists have attempted to apply their study of foreign dispute settlement to the local scene.[8] Contemporaneous with that effort has been the work of other legal scholars, most notably the late Lon

3. *See* J. AUERBACH, JUSTICE WITHOUT LAW? RESOLVING DISPUTES WITHOUT LAWYERS (1983).

4. *See* ACCESS TO JUSTICE AND THE WELFARE STATE 147 (M. Cappelletti ed. 1981).

5. Ford Foundation, New Approaches to Conflict Resolution 25 (1978).

6. Compare the return to midwives in medicine. *See* Smith, *A Warmer Way of Disputing: Mediation & Conciliation*, 26 AM. J. OF COMP. L. 205 (Supp. 1978).

7. *See* J. MARKS, E. JOHNSON, JR. & SZANTON, *supra* note 1.

8. *See, e.g.*, Nader, *Disputing Without the Force of Law*, 88 YALE L.J. 998 (1979).

Fuller, who have attempted to analyze characteristics of various dispute processes such as mediation and arbitration. These scholars proposed some useful conclusions about the strengths and limitations of particular processes for particular types of disputes.[9]

From this brief and fragmentary history, four goals of the alternatives movement emerge:

1) to relieve court congestion, as well as undue cost and delay;
2) to enhance community involvement in the dispute resolution process;
3) to facilitate access to justice;
4) to provide more "effective" dispute resolution.[10]

These goals might overlap and conflict. Consider, for example, the problem of "excessive" access. If society is too ready to provide access for all kinds of disputes, this will lengthen the queue and aggravate the congestion problem. Similarly, measures aimed at relieving court congestion would take a very different form from measures designed to enhance community control over dispute settlement. Hence, it is essential to think clearly and precisely about the reasons for pursuing ADRMs.

Considering the complex social conditions that have led to court congestion and concomitant delay,[11] it seems specious to assume an appropriate use of alternatives can significantly affect court case loads. This is not to say that a cautious and informed use of ancillary mechanisms to screen court cases is not worth undertaking. On the contrary, such a program holds considerable promise. But the notion that a pervasive use of arbitration and mediation will solve "the court crisis" seems misguided. The principal promise of alternatives stems from the third and fourth goals set forth above. Our primary efforts should be directed toward these two goals. And since the access goal can only be fulfilled by providing access to an ADRM that is appropriate for the particular dispute, the third and fourth goals in effect coalesce.

II. Current Types of Disputes and Programs

This section presents a brief overview of the rich variety of ADRMs presently in use. Of necessity the picture will be somewhat fragmentary and conclusory.[12]

---

9. *See, e.g.*, Fuller, *The Forms and Limits of Adjudication*, 92 Harv. L. Rev. 353 (1979) [hereinafter cited as Fuller, *Adjudication*]; Fuller, *Mediation, — Its Forms and Functions*, 44 S. Cal. L. Rev. 305 (1971) [hereinafter cited as Fuller, *Mediation*]; Fuller, *Collective Bargaining and the Arbitrator*, 1963 Wis. L. Rev. 1 [hereinafter cited as Fuller, *Collective Bargaining*].

10. Although no definitive work has been done with respect to how to measure "effectiveness," presumably to be taken into account are such factors as cost, speed, satisfaction (to the public and the parties) and compliance. *Cf.* Getman, *Labor Arbitration and Dispute Resolution*, 88 Yale L.J. 916 (1979).

11. *See* J. Lieberman, The Litigious Society (1981); Manning, *Hyperlexis, Our National Disease*, 71 Nw. U.L. Rev. 767 (1977); *see also* Council on the Role of Courts, The Role of Courts in American Society (J. Lieberman ed. 1984) [hereinafter cited as CORC].

12. For further elaboration, see E. Green, S. Goldberg & F. Sander, Dispute Resolution (1985); J. Marks, E. Johnson & P. Szanton, Dispute Resolution in America: Processes in Evolution (1984) (National Institute for Dispute Resolution pamphlet); Singer, *Non-Judicial Dispute Resolution Mechanisms: The Effects on Justice for the Poor*, 1979 Clearinghouse Rev. 569. E. Johnson,

Because many mechanisms involve a blend or sequence of different dispute processes, it might be useful first to provide a brief restatement of the basic processes.

The most common and familiar form of dispute settlement between two parties is bargaining or negotiation. Negotiation offers the great advantage of allowing the parties themselves to control the process and the solution. Sometimes, however, disputants are unable to settle the dispute, and a third party must be engaged. If a third party joins the negotiations, the parties must determine whether he or she has power to impose a solution on the parties, or whether the third party is simply to help the disputants arrive at their own solution. The latter role is commonly referred to as conciliation or mediation. The former might entail some form of adjudication, by a court, an administrative agency, or a private adjudicator, also known as an arbitrator.[13]

A. *Labor Mediation and Arbitration*

The model for many of the current mechanisms is the system developed during World War II for handling grievances arising under collective bargaining agreements. Typically, such agreements provide for a series of steps whereby an employee with a grievance first complains to his foreman. Next a meeting occurs between the Union Committee and the Plant Committee. Finally, if the matter cannot be resolved within the plant by negotiation, the parties select an outside arbitrator, often with the assistance of the American Arbitration Association or the Federal Mediation and Conciliation Service. This procedure is comparatively expeditious and inexpensive, even though recent complaints suggest it is becoming more formal, costly, and time-consuming. In short, it is too much like the court system it was originally designed to circumvent.[14]

This procedure for dealing with disputes arising under collective bargaining agreements should be contrasted with disputes which arise in reaching such agreements. With collective bargaining, negotiation and mediation are the principal dispute settlement tools, because economic terms of employment are rarely externally imposed on the parties. Hence, if an agreement cannot be achieved by these means, the principal economic weapon, the strike, might be deemed necessary. However, in certain public sector industries where strikes cannot be tolerated fire departments, police departments and schools, compulsory arbitration is sometimes utilized.[15]

Troublesome questions have also been raised when employees present claims arising under recent enactments guaranteeing non-discrimination on account of sex, race or age. Such cases have often created bitter contests, with sharply

---

V. Kanter & E. Schwartz, Outside the Courts: A Survey of Diversion Alternatives in Civil Cases (1977).

13. There are of course a host of hybrid processes, such as fact finding, inquiry and final offer selection. E. Green, S. Goldberg & F. Sander, *supra* note 12.

14. *See generally* E. Teple & R. Moberly, Arbitration and Conflict Resolution (1979); Getman, *supra* note 10.

15. Occasionally in these situations final offer arbitration is used. Here the arbitrator can select only one side's or the other's best offer, nothing in between. An obvious effect of this mechanism is to induce more serious bargaining. E. Green, S. Goldberg & F. Sander, *supra* note 13.

differing factual assertions. Therefore, some commentators have suggested that adjudication is unsuitable because of its "win-lose" nature and have argued for resolving some of these cases by a process of mediation.[16]

B. *Commercial Arbitration*

Long before the rise of labor arbitration, commercial contract disputes were submitted to arbitration by a panel of experts in the industry. This mechanism works particularly well in industries where a continuing relationship exists between the parties. Such cases necessitate an expeditious and amicable method by which one or more individuals familiar with the trade practices can resolve the disputes. The American Arbitration Association now handles close to 10,000 of these disputes each year. In addition, an untold number are handled similarly under private industry agreements.

C. *Consumer Disputes*

In a sense, consumer disputes could be subsumed under the category of commercial arbitration. Consumer disputes, however, typically involve smaller claims. Additionally, consumer contract agreements rarely provide for arbitration of disputes.[17]

In recent years several mechanisms have been developed for extra-judicial handling of consumer disputes. Some states have created consumer protection divisions within the attorney general's office, where such claims are sought to be mediated, often by volunteers.[18] Likewise, some industry groups, such as the Better Business Bureaus, have established procedures for arbitrating such claims. Some industries (e.g., automobiles and major appliances) even set up panels providing free arbitration of the consumer's claim.[19] Of course, consumer claims also can be presented in small claims court[20] and, where available, to media action programs such as Call for Action, where the service provided is not really dispute resolution but information and referral. Because of the clout wielded by these latter groups, they sometimes act in effect like mediators or ombudsmen in adjusting consumer grievances. A recent study, however, suggests the effectiveness and accessibility of some of these mechanisms may be suspect.[21]

16. *See, e.g.*, Meacham, *The Use of Mediation to Resolve Employment Discrimination Complaints*, 28 Bost. Bar J. 21 (May-June 1984); A. Westin, Corporate Programs for Handling Employee Discrimination Complaints: An Analysis of Current Mechanisms to Resolve EEO Disputes Through Internal or Voluntary Mechanisms (1983) (unpublished mimeo by the Educational Fund for Individual Rights, Columbia University Law School).

17. One exception is medical care agreements that provide for the handling of malpractice claims by an arbitration tribunal. *See* Henderson, *Contractual Problems in the Enforcement of Agreements to Arbitrate Medical Malpractice*, 58 Va. L. Rev. 947 (1972).

18. E. Johnson, V. Kantor & E. Schwartz, *supra* note 12, at 67.

19. F. Sander, American Bar Association Report on the National Conference on Minor Disputes Resolution, May 1977 (1978). Manufacturers of automobiles and major appliances are among the industries utilizing free arbitration panels. *Id.*

20. *See infra* notes 40-41 and accompanying text.

21. No Access to Law: Alternatives to the American Judicial System (L. Nader ed. 1980).

D. *Interpersonal Disputes*

One of the best examples of the need for new dispute resolution mechanisms can be seen with respect to various types of interpersonal disputes. Here, the tendency of courts to look backwards and produce winners and losers is least responsive to the needs of the parties, who usually are seeking to resolve present controversies and avoid future disputes. Mediation, which helps the parties settle their problems jointly, is far more suited to this task than adjudication.[22]

1. Neighborhood Justice Centers

In the past decade well over two hundred community dispute centers have been created.[23] These are known by various names, ranging from "citizen complaint center" to "neighborhood justice oenter." These centers are either free-standing institutions or are affiliated with the court.[24] Center referrals are received from the court, prosecutor, police or other community agencies; some disputants also come on a walk-in basis. The kinds of cases handled varies widely, from landlord-tenant disputes to domestic and neighbor quarrels.[25]

Although dispute centers vary greatly, two differing prototypes deserve exploration. One, commonly attached to a prosecutor's office, features rapid screening of a large number of cases to determine whether quick settlement might be possible and desirable. These programs involve high-volume processing in very short sessions, which law students often conduct. Whether this process should be viewed as true mediation is open to question.

In contrast to this approach is the more typical mediation, conducted by a professionally trained mediator or by a person drawn from the neighborhood who has received mediation training. Two or three mediators often conduct these mediations, which typically last three to four hours. These meetings allow disputants a full opportunity to present their views, and permit the mediators to meet with each of the disputants separately before attempting to reach agreement.

On the whole, the experience with these projects has been encouraging, although further public education is needed to stimulate greater resort to these unfamiliar institutions. Americans appear too prone to presume that anyone engaged in a dispute should take it to a lawyer or court. Ironically, the individuals who do use the new projects find them helpful and satisfying, and the agreements reached appear to endure.[26] New York recently became the first state to recognize the value of these agencies by providing public funding for them.[27]

---

22. Fuller, *Mediation, supra* note 9.

23. American Bar Association Special Committee on Alternative Dispute Resolution, Dispute Resolution Directory (1983).

24. Recently, a number of church groups have also sponsored such programs. *See, e.g.*, R. Kraybill, Repairing the Breach, Ministering in Community Conflict (1982).

25. *See* Neighborhood Justice: Assessment of an Emerging Idea (R. Tomasic & M. Feeley eds. 1982).

26. R. Cook, J. Roehl & D. Sheppard, Neighborhood Justice Field Test: Final Evaluation Report (1980).

27. *See* 1981 N.Y. Laws, ch. 847.

2. Divorce Mediation

Although some neighborhood justice centers handle divorces, these cases often present more challenging problems of dispute settlement because complex legal and tax issues arise, as well as difficult questions of child custody. In 1981, California became the first state to require mediation to resolve all child custody disputes. In a number of other jurisdictions, mediation services are available in court-connected agencies. The principal development in divorce mediation, however, has occurred outside the courts, as lawyers and mental health professionals perform mediation as a private service. Although public interest in this alternative to the traditional legal process is widespread, the insitution of divorce mediation remains in a state of infancy. Questions yet to be resolved include: Who should be the mediators? What kind of training should they receive? How should their services be compensated? How, if at all, will representative lawyers fit into this process? Should a new form of regulation be developed for this newly emerging profession?[28]

3. Parent/Child Disputes

Another subcategory of cases that might be heard in neighborhood justice centers, but is sometimes handled in separate projects, involves various types of parent/child disputes. A recent study attempted to inventory such projects.[29] One such project is the Children's Hearing Project in Cambridge, Massachusetts, which is patterned on a similar proceeding in Scotland. Both projects utilize citizens from the community to help parents and children settle their disputes.[30]

E. *Intra-institutional Disputes*

Some institutions have recently applied the grievance machinery model of the labor sector to their intra-institutional settings. For example, a California prison established a grievance committee comprising prisoners and supervisory personnel to air prisoner complaints. If the case could not be resolved internally, it would be submitted, at least in an advisory capacity, to an outside arbitrator. This process features intitial consideration by a group with respresentation from both sides, and the possibility of ultimate submission to an outside authority.[31] This process has been replicated in other correctional facilities[32] and other institutional settings, such as schools.[33]

28. *See* ABA, ALTERNATIVE MEANS OF FAMILY DISPUTE RESOLUTION (1982); ABA, DIVORCE MEDIATION: READINGS (1985); J. HAYNES, DIVORCE MEDIATION: A PRACTICAL GUIDE FOR THERAPISTS AND COUNSELORS (1981); Winks, *Divorce Mediation: A Nonadversary Procedure No-Fault Divorce*, 19 J. FAM. L. 615 (1981); J. LEMMON, FAMILY MEDIATION PRACTICE (1985).

29. E. VORENBERG, STATE OF THE ART SURVEY OF DISPUTE RESOLUTION PROGRAMS INVOLVING JUVENILES, (A.B.A. Special Committee 1982).

30. *See, e.g.*, CHILDREN'S HEARINGS (F. Martin & K. Murray eds. 1976).

31. For elaboration of other essential aspects of such a grievance mechanism, see Keating & Kolze, *An Inmate Grievance Mechanism: From Design to Practice*, 39 FED. PROBATION 42 (1975).

32. *See, e.g.*, G. COLE, R. HANSEN & J. SILBERT, ALTERNATIVE DISPUTE RESOLUTION MECHANISMS FOR PRISONER GRIEVANCES (NAT'L INST. CORRECTIONS 1984).

33. *See* RESOLVING CONFLICT IN HIGHER EDUCATION (J. McCarthy ed. 1980).

Despite the analogy to the collective bargaining context, there are obvious differences between labor and prison contexts. In the prison all power is on one side, and that side is often reluctant to surrender any power, even to an outside arbiter's advisory review. Hence, the success of grievance mechanisms in the more complex prison setting has been questioned.[34] Alternative ways of resolving prisoner disputes, which make up a very large proportion of the recent caseload growth in the federal courts, are voluntary mediation of prisoner grievances, and ombudsman mechanisms.[35] The latter method involves a third party of great ability and integrity who is empowered to investigate complaints or grievances. Following completion of the inquiry, the ombudsman makes recommendations to the individual in charge of the institution. Usually an ombudsman has no coercive power, but if he is highly regarded, his judgment is given considerable respect. It would be difficult for the institution's presiding authority wholly to ignore a prestigious ombudsman's report that a meritorious grievance had been unfairly ignored. Therein, of course, lies a principal reason for institutional resistance to this mechanism.

F. *Claims Against the Government*

The ombudsman institution first arose in Scandinavia in response to citizen's complaints against the government. A number of American states and municipalities now have ombudsmen.[36] An analogue of the ombudsman concept has been the development of media action lines such as Call for Action on television.[37]

G. *Public Disputes*

Most of the controversies considered previously involve two disputants, with relatively concrete, defined concerns. In recent years, however, more large-scale disputes have arisen involving a multiplicity of parties and interests. Examples of such disputes are community conflicts over whether a facility should be built in the area, certain racial controversies, major claims to land holdings by native Americans, and environmental disputes.[38] Such cases have proved to be far more intractable, and have often required a combination of litigation and mediation. A number of organizations, most of them privately sponsored, have sought to develop special expertise in the handling of such cases.[39]

H. *Court-Annexed Mechanisms*

Most of the mechanisms discussed thus far are primarily found in the private dispute resolution sector and are not a part of the formal court structure. In an attempt to make courts more responsive to the emerging alternatives movement, ADRMs have been incorporated in one way or another into the court

34. *See* G. COLE, R. HANSEN & J. SILBERT, *supra* note 32.

35. *See id.*

36. *See* W. GELLHORN, WHEN AMERICANS COMPLAIN (1966); Frank, *State Ombudsman Legislation in the United States*, 29 U. MIAMI L. REV. 397 (1975).

37. *See* Palen, *Media Ombudsmen: A Critical View*, 13 L. & SOC'Y REV. 799 (1979).

38. *See* ROUNDTABLE JUSTICE: CASE STUDIES IN CONFLICT RESOLUTION (R. Goldmann ed. 1980).

39. *See, e.g.*, G. BINGHAM, RESOLVING ENVIRONMENTAL DISPUTES: A DECADE OF EXPERIENCE (1985).

system. In that respect, these developments represent a partial foreshadowing of the "multi-door courthouse" notion more fully explored in Section III below.

1. Small Claims Adjudication and Mediation

Over fifty years ago courts were recognized as too elaborate and expensive for simple cases involving only small claims. This led to the creation of small claims court, where litigants themselves, without lawyers, can present their disputes. These actions normally involve claims of not more than $1,000 and result in a type of quick, rough justice. Some scholars have recently raised serious questions about the efficacy of small claims courts.[40] Nevertheless, the institution appears to be an essentially durable one that has carved a place in the catalog of useful dispute settlement mechanisms. An interesting recent variant has been utilization of mediation in small claims court.[41]

2. Compulsory Arbitration

Following a 1950's experiment in Philadelphia a number of jurisdictions have recently passed legislation requiring all monetary claims cases up to a certain limit (generally around $10,000-$15,000) to be initially processed by arbitration. In view of the prevailing right to trial by jury, a right to *de novo* review must then be accorded in the courts. However, such recourse to the courts might be subjected to cost sanctions if the petitioner does not prevail in court. Absent such a sanction, the net result might be to substitute two proceedings for the previous one. A similar program was begun on an experimental basis in three federal district courts.[42] Preliminary data from these experiments are encouraging, and show that even where a sizeable percentage of the cases are appealed to court, very few proceed to trial.[43]

3. Malpractice Screening

Following the malpractice "crisis" in the mid-seventies, a number of states set up special procedures for malpractice actions. Often the parties are initially required to arbitrate their differences. In other jurisdictions, such as Massachusetts, a screening panel is established, consisting of a doctor, lawyer and judge. The panel determines whether a *prima facie* case is established. If not, the plaintiff may proceed only by putting up a bond for the defendant's costs.[44]

---

40. *See, e.g.*, J. RUHNKA & S. WELLER, SMALL CLAIMS COURTS: A NATIONAL EXAMINATION (1978); F. SANDER, *supra* note 19; Yngvesson & Hennessey, *Small Claims, Complex Disputes: A Review of the Small Claims Literature*, 9 L. & SOC'Y REV. 219 (1975).

41. McEwen & Maiman, *Small Claims Mediation in Maine: An Empirical Assessment*, 33 ME. L. REV. 237 (1981).

42. *See* Lind & Shapard, *Evaluation of Court-Annexed Arbitration in Three Federal District Courts*, FED. JUD. CENTER (1981); Levin, *Alternative Dispute Resolution in the Federal Courts*, 37 U. FLA. L. REV. 29 (1985).

43. *See, e.g.*, J. ADLER, D. HENSLER & C. NELSON, SIMPLE JUSTICE: HOW LITIGANTS FARE IN THE PITTSBURGH ARBITRATION PROGRAM (1983) (published by Rand Corp.).

44. *See* Note, *Recent Medical Malpractice Legislation — A First Checkup*, 50 TUL. L. REV. 655 (1976); Comment, *An Analysis of State Legislative Reponses to the Medical Malpractice Crisis*, 1975 DUKE L.J. 1417.

The success of these experiments has varied. In some states, the special procedures have been abandoned or declared unconstitutional. In others, the mechanisms have worked well to screen out spurious claims.

4. Large Litigation

Many of the devices discussed above are applicable only to what has sometimes been referred to as "minor disputes." Some devices have also been developed to deal specifically with large and complex litigation.

a. Rent-a-Judge

Arbitration often employs experienced individuals such as retired judges to arbitrate difficult cases. Such use of arbitration, by consent of the parties, is quite different from that discussed in Section 2 above, where reference to arbitration is compulsory rather than consensual.

A variant of this practice has developed in some jurisdictions, notably California. It calls for parties to select a retired judge to hear the case, much as an arbitrator would. The procedures applied are the same as those that would apply in court, except as otherwise modified by the parties. Most notably, the judge's decision has the same force and effect as a judgment entered by a regular court.

The Rent-a-Judge procedure raises important policy questions. For example, should parties be able to hire the best available judges under circumstances where their decision has the full force of law, just as if the case had been decided in court? How does this practice square with the notion of equal access to the courts regardless of means? What will be the impact of such a practice on the regular judiciary? These questions and others deserve more discussion than they have received thus far.[45]

b. Mini-Trial

Ten years ago some imaginative litigants in the federal district court in California developed an innovative extrajudicial mechanism to aid in the settlement of complex and protracted litigation.[46] The procedure calls for the parties to select an experienced individual to preside at a two-day information exchange. Each party has one day to present its case in any form it desires, including questions for the opposing side. The highest official of each party, assuming a corporate litigant, must attend this hearing. At the end of the proceeding, the two top officials confer, without their lawyers, to evaluate the case. In the seminal case utilizing this innovative procedure, the parties promptly settled.[47] If an agreement is not reached, then the presiding official will give his view

---

45. *See* E. Green, Avoiding the Legal Logjam — Private Justice California Style, 1982 Corporate Dispute Management; Note, *The California Rent-A-Judge Experiment: Constitutional and Policy Considerations of Pay-As-You-Go Courts*, 94 Harv. L. Rev. 1592 (1981).

46. Green, Marks & Olson, *Settling Large Case Litigation: An Alternative Approach*, 11 Loy. L.A.L. Rev. 493 (1978).

47. *Id.*

concerning how the case would be resolved in court. The parties then use this additional information to discuss settlement. If settlement is not achieved, the procedure has no evidentiary effect and the case returns to court. In virtually all cases which have utilized this procedure, however, settlement has been achieved.[48] The procedure has the additional virtue that it can be readily adapted to different situations (e.g., the presider can be dispensed with, more or less time can be allowed for the presentations).

III. Problems and Prospects

As noted earlier, the recent resurgence of the alternatives movement has now passed through several phases. After the initial period of exhuberant expansionism, a more critical and reflective phase has ensued, and a number of difficult and fundamental questions are emerging. The remainder of this paper will attempt to address some of these questions.

A. *Relation of ADRMs to Each Other and to the Court System*

Implicit in the preceding discussion is the notion that dispute resolution mechanisms are dispersed throughout the social fabric. The mechanisms are either public or private, mandatory or optional. Wherever disputes arise among individuals or organizations, a complex network of possible grievance mechanisms appears to be available for the venting of these grievances.[49] The question which naturally arises is what, if any, relationship should exist among the different types of mechanisms. This question assumes importance not only for the disputant who might benefit from some guidance concerning where to take any particular dispute, but also for a society seeking to provide a coherent response to these grievances.

One can envision a system possessing a hierarchy and structure within the formal public dispute resolution system, complemented by a vast and ill-understood network of indigenous dispute mechanisms. In essence, that is our present system. Disputants might first try to utilize the array of informal mechanisms provided in the particular arena where the dispute arises. Then, as a last resort, disputants might take the controversy to the public forum, the court.[50] That is the paradigm but in fact, informal private mechanisms are frequently not available, or if they are, they are not resorted to. The result is often the typically American tendency to take the case immediately to court. The net effect is that

48. E. Green, The C.P.R. Mini-Trial Handbook, 1982 Corporate Dispute Management.

49. *See* Galanter, *supra* note 2.

50. At present, it is almost accidental if community members find their way to an appropriate forum other than the regular courts. Several other modes of dispute resolution already are available in many communities. Still, since they are operated by a hodge-podge of local government agencies, neighborhood organizations, and trade associations, citizens must be very knowledgeable about community resources to locate the right forum for their particular dispute.

Johnson, Toward a Responsive Justice System, State Courts: A Blueprint for the Future 107, 122 (1978) (publication of National Center for State Courts).

many disputes presented to court are not appropriate for court adjudication and could be better handled by some other mechanism.[51]

This situation led me to suggest, in a paper delivered at the Pound Conference in 1976, a more comprehensive and diverse mechanism known as a Dispute Resolution Center.[52] This center would provide a variety of dispute resolution processes, according to the needs of the particular dispute. This concept was later termed "the multi-door courthouse" (MDC).[53]

What would such an institution look like? A provisional first-step type of MDC could consist essentially of a screening and referral clerk who would seek to diagnose incoming cases and refer them to the most suitable ADRMs. Depending on the available mechanisms in the particular community, referrals might be made to mediation, arbitration, court adjudication, fact finding, malpractice screening, media action lines or an ombudsman. Such a model would be subject to all the familiar deficiencies of a referral scheme. For example, slippage often occurs between the act of referral and the receiving agency's actual handling of the case.

A more ideal model would contain all the "doors" under one roof, as part of an integrated dispute resolution center. Such a mansion might feature the following doors:

(1) effective and accessible small claims adjudication;
(2) services for family, landlord/tenant, and other continuing relations cases;
(3) ombudsmen for the processing of disputes between citizens and large bureaucracies;
(4) social service agencies providing mental health counseling and treatment of alcohol and drug related problems;
(5) trial court of general jurisdiction for novel statutory and constitutional claims, as well as major criminal cases; and
(6) compulsory arbitration for small monetary claims.

Additional dispute processing forums might include those mediating or arbitrating juvenile matters and those handling ordinance violations such as bad checks and health code and building code violations.[54]

Recently, under the auspices of the American Bar Association, three cities, Tulsa, Houston and Washington, D.C., have been selected for experimental multi-door courthouse projects. These programs are now in their initial eighteen month pilot phase. At the end of that period mid-course corrections will be made in the structure of the referral scheme to take account of malfunctioning or missing "doors." In a final six month phase, the ABA hopes to draw on the learning of these experiments to develop a nationally replicable model.

An integrated multi-door courthouse would have a number of benefits as well as potential pitfalls. First, such a full-service MDC would provide an efficient way of availing a wide range of dispute processes. It could also serve

51. *See* Sander, *Varieties of Dispute Processing,* 70 F.R.D. 111 (1976).

52. *Id.*

53. *See* E. Green, S. Goldberg & F. Sander, *supra* note 13, at 514.

54. *See* McGillis, *Minor Dispute Processing: A Review of Recent Developments,* in Neighborhood Justice, *supra* note 25, at 60.

as a major source of information and referral, transcending the particular "doors" that are available. Second, bringing such diverse ADRMs under the court umbrella would solve the increasingly difficult question of how to fund alternative mechanisms. Likewise, it would avoid the pro-court adjudication bias inherent in the present system where the state pays the costs of court adjudication but not those of other, often more suitable, mechanisms.

Third, because of the predominant emphasis on courts in our society, most alternatives are seldom used. This caseload drought is ironic in light of the generally high satisfaction rate among those parties using alternative mechanisms.[55] Thus, a major difficulty appears to be popular unfamiliarity with these mechanisms. This requires additional public education, but it also argues for building ARDMs into an expanded court system.[56]

These are some of the substantial benefits that might be derived from such an ADRM experiment. However, major obstacles exist as well. A critical feature would be the initial screening which would require a highly skilled intake worker rather than a bureaucratic court functionary. Accordingly, a crucial question is whether ADRM specialists presently have sufficient knowledge of the particular characteristics of various dispute processes and mechanisms. This knowledge is necessary to confidently refer particular types of cases to one or another mechanism. While this science is at a primitive stage, one could posit a number of plausible criteria for determining the suitability of various dispute mechanisms.[57]

1. Nature of Case

ADRMs should be designed to handle a novel claim challenging the constitutionality of a statute quite differently from a claim applying established principles to a specific set of facts. Only the former merits the unique skills and resources of a court. The latter can be more expeditiously and inexpensively dealt with by arbitration.

2. Relationship of Disputants

Adjudication typically seeks to make a definitive determination with respect to past events, while mediation attempts to restructure the relationship of the disputants.[58] Thus, mediation best resolves cases involving long-term relationships extending into the future. For example, a mediator is more likely to resolve effectively a mid-contract dispute between a landlord and tenant, or even a divorce, than is a judge. Not only will a mediator be better equipped to restructure future relationships, but the open-ended and non-coercive process of mediation is also more likely to teach the parties to recognize and resolve

55. *Cf.* Cook, Roehl & Sheppard, *supra* note 26; Pearson, *How Child Custody Mediation Works in Practice*, 20 JUDGES J. 11 [hereinafter cited as *Child Custody Mediation*]; Pearson, *An Evaluation of Alternatives to Court Adjudication*, 7 JUST. SYS. J. 420 (1982) [hereinafter cited as *An Evaluation of Alternatives*]; McEwen & Maiman, *supra* note 41.

56. Cratsley, *Community Courts: Offering Alternative Dispute Resolution Within the Judicial System*, 3 VT. L. REV. 1 (1978).

57. *See* E. GREEN, S. GOLDBERG, & F. SANDER, *supra* note 12; CORC, *supra* note 11.

58. *See* Fuller, *Mediation*, *supra* note 9.

future controversies. Mediation thus gives maximum durability to the settlement the parties have crafted.

A significant qualification, however, is presented in the case where the two disputants have substantially disparate bargaining power. In such a case, mediation is either pointless, or worse yet, threatens to take undue and unfair advantage of the weaker party. ADRM specialists must learn far more about the optional combination of formal adjudicative and informal mediation processes for this type of case.[59]

3. Size and Complexity of Claim

Society has already taken some account of the size and complexity criterion in establishing, on an optional basis, small claims courts for the processing of minor disputes. Some states have even experimented with the use of different tracks for cases of different complexity.[60] Generally, however, transaction costs in processing disputes have largely been ignored. To be sure, certain cases (e.g., a serious crime or a major constitutional challenge) should not be measured by the amount in controversy. Beyond those cases and others raising similar considerations, however, should not we lawyers be more attuned to the immense public cost every time a lawsuit is processed in court? If a case involves only $1000 and does not raise larger issues of public policy, should society not *require* such a case to be processed in small claims court or its functional equivalent? The counterargument, of course, is that for the low-income consumer a claim of $1000 over his defective refrigerator is as important as a multi-million dollar claim is for General Motors. That argument, however, misses the point. If the larger claim is also a straightforward collection action, it also does not deserve access to the deluxe adjudication model. These factors and others need further exploration. Indeed, one of the potential benefits of such a tentative typology is that it will permit the acquisition of significant additional data to test some of the stated hypotheses.

In addition to the cited general criteria, certain programmatic channels might also be proposed. For example, medical malpractice claims would be directed to the appropriate screening tribunal. Prisoners' claims might be sent to an internal grievance mechanism to be initially processed.[61] And if the jurisdiction had an ombudsman, claims against the government would be directed there.

As appealing and efficient as such a scheme might be, it would undoubtedly have its costs. First, intelligent central referral presumes the intake official is

59. For example in an environmental dispute where the situational power resides predominantly in the polluter, an initial adjudication might be required to more nearly equalize the power relationship and bring the more powerful respondent to the bargaining table.

60. *See* Action Commission to Reduce Court Cost and Delay, Attacking Litigation Cost and Delay 7 (ABA 1984).

61. *Cf.* 42 U.S.C. 1997e (1982), authorizing stay of a federal civil rights action up to 90 days to permit exhaustion of an internal grievance mechanism, provided such remedy has been found to be "plain, speedy, and effective." This statute suggests the desirability of developing procedures for certifying certain ADRMs as meeting minimal requirements of fairness and efficacy — a kind of "Good Dispute Processing Seal of Approval." Such ADRMs might be given priority in funding and referrals. *Id.*

completely aware of all the facts. However, disputants are often notoriously inarticulate in voicing their real grievances. In such a case, the true complaint does not surface until much later in the proceeding. Second, any new institution also runs the risk of sinking to the lowest bureaucratic level, and thereby eliminating the benefits that emanate from decentralized, indigenous dispute resolution. A related bureaucratic nightmare has the MDC simply shunting difficult and undesirable cases to an endless series of "alternatives" from which the disputants emerge dissatisfied and disillusioned.

A final question is whether the referral process should be optional or compulsory. A system of mandatory referral raises different questions of law and policy than would a merely advisory reference. No single uniform answer to this question is required. At the outset, referral should undoubtedly be voluntary, while necessary information is obtained about the workings of the system. But once that level of experience and understanding is attained with respect to a particular class of cases, that particular referral process might become mandatory. For example, sufficient data now exist to warrant the initial compulsory referral of small monetary claims to arbitration.[62] However, ADRM specialists must first learn more about what types of cases are particularly suitable for such treatment, and what types of cases are not.[63]

B. *Data Drought*

Despite all of the recent developments in alternative modes of dispute settlement, relatively little is known about the critical questions of ADRMs.[64] For example, ADRM specialists have essentially no sophisticated data concerning the relative time and cost of alternative dispute settlement mechanisms such as arbitration and mediation. No doubt this problem is due to the difficult questions that would be posed by such an inquiry. What, for example, are the appropriate ingredients of cost? What is the aggregate cost to the system? What is the cost to the parties? And how does one determine the comparative cost of a case in court? Should cost be determined on a marginal or an average basis? What is the appropriate time frame?

Suppose, for example, that a particular court case cost $462, while a mediated solution cost $597. Does this show that mediation is more costly, even if the effect of the mediation were not only to settle the present dispute but to prevent future ones? This question suggests the difficulty of measuring potential benefits to be derived from particular forms of dispute settlement. Perhaps these questions explain why so little sophisticated research has been published.

Nevertheless, reliable data now exist confirming one's intuitive assumption that mediation leads to higher disputant satisfaction — even where no settlement is reached — and concomitantly to greater compliance with the terms of the settlement. Although such results might be suspect in situations where the mediated cases resulted from self-selection, some of the studies involve a process

62. *See* J. Adler, D. Hensler & C. Nelson, *supra* note 43, at 524.
63. *See An Evaluation of Alternatives*, *supra* note 55.
64. *See* E. Green, S. Goldberg & F. Sander, *supra* note 13, at

akin to random assignment.[65] Hence, these results are extremely important and encouraging, particularly in fields like child support enforcement where non-compliance is a significant problem.[66]

C. *Critiques*

In recent years the alternatives movement has been severely attacked from a number of quarters. Perhaps the most pervasive of these has emanated from the political left. The argument suggests that providing ADRMs for the poor and powerless constitutes the establishment's attempt to "cool out" legitimate grievances by negotiating or mediating away poor people's legal rights.[67]

To the extent that this argument rests on implicit premises of distributive justice, it goes well beyond the issues of formal versus informal justice. In fact, little evidence suggests that the courts can, barring very exceptional situations, bring about major redistributions of wealth and power. Indeed, given the existing constraints of restricted access to the courts and the summary treatment accorded many litigants, it is far from clear that disputants fare less well in the informal system.[68] Moreover, the limited empirical evidence supports the conclusion that disputants prefer the informal system.[69] Perhaps, from a radical perspective, this only proves that the courts themselves are an instrument of capitalist domination. However, that argument takes us considerably beyond the issue of formal versus informal justice.

If the focus is narrowed to the actual operation of the informal system, a number of legitimate issues arise. Particularly where alternatives are considered for minor criminal cases, questions arise concerning the availability of various procedural and constitutional protections.[70] Perhaps this question becomes essentially one of fair notice and free choice. If the "defendant" prefers the informal process after having been fully apprised of the protections and consequences in each system, there can be little complaint. This goal, however, might be difficult to achieve in practice. In fact, some programs fail to fully disclose the different procedures and consequences of each system. Occasionally,

---

65. *See Child Custody Mediation, supra* note 55. *See also* W. FELSTINER & L. WILLIAMS, COMMUNITY MEDIATION IN DORCHESTER, MASSACHUSETTS (1979, 1980); Cook, Roehl & Sheppard, *supra* note 26; McEwen & Maiman, *supra* note 41.

66. *See* J. CASSETTY, CHILD SUPPORT AND PUBLIC POLICY: SECURING SUPPORT FROM ABSENT FATHERS (1978); *but cf.* D. CHAMBERS, MAKING FATHERS PAY: THE ENFORCEMENT OF CHILD SUPPORT (1979).

67. *See* THE POLITICS OF INFORMAL JUSTICE (R. Abel ed. 1982); R. HOFRICHTER, *Justice Centers Raise Basic Questions*, in NEIGHBORING JUSTICE, *supra* note 25.

68. *See* Rosenberg, *Civil Justice and Civil Reform*, 15 LAW & SOC. REV. 473 (1980-1981); Johnson, *supra* note 50.

69. *See, e.g.*, R. COOK, J. ROEHL & D. SHEPPARD, *supra* note 26. It is also somewhat puzzling that the communitarians who share many of the goals of the radical critics seek precisely the opposite result (i.e., delegalization and community-controlled dispute settlement). *See* R. SHONHOLTZ, NEIGHBORHOOD JUSTICE SYSTEMS: WORK, STRUCTURE, AND GUIDING PRINCIPLES, 5 MEDIATION Q. 3 (1984).

70. *See* Snyder, *Crime and Community Mediation — The Boston Experience: A Preliminary Report on the Dorchester Urban Court Program*, 1978 WIS. L. REV. 737; Rice, *Mediation and Arbitration as a Civil Alternative to the Criminal Justice System — An Overview and Legal Analysis*, 29 AM. U.L. REV. 17 (1979).

those programs effectively push the complainee into the informal system, for example, by sending him a letter on District Attorney stationery so "suggesting."[71] Where the program is overtly compulsory, in court-annexed arbitration, different types of issues arise, such as whether the legally required right of access to the courts, following exhausion of the alternative mechanism, can be significantly burdened, as by imposing various "costs" on the judicial petitoner.

Other problems stem from inadequate conceptualization of ADRM processes. For example, if a substantial power disparity exists between disputants then mediation will be inappropriate because it threatens to exploit the apparent powerlessness of one disputant.[72] Perhaps here again it is largely a question of full information coupled with free choice.[73] Or, as noted with respect to a comparable situation in an environmental dispute, we need to learn more about the optimal interrelationship between the formal and the informal legal processes. ADRM specialists should strive to combine the court's power-equalizing role with the greater participation, flexibility and range of choices offered by the mediative process.[74]

D. *Role of Lawyers in ADRMs*

What is the proper role of attorneys in alternative dispute resolution mechanisms? First, ADRMs must distinguish between a lawyer's role as a representative of the disputants, and a lawyer's role as a dispute resolver. With respect to the former, much turns on the nature of the proceeding. If, for example, the dispute is a low-key squabble between two neighbors, lawyers might not be needed. However, if the dispute is a complex divorce case involving technical issues in a zero sum context, the argument for legal representation becomes much more compelling. In short, the issue of legal representation in ADRMs is not unlike that in court. The mere fact that the

---

71. *See* F. Sander, *supra* note 19.

72. Consider the power inequity between an overweaning husband, with access to professional resources, and a meek, subservient wife. *See* M. Levine, Power Imbalances in Vermont Law School Dispute Resolution Project, A Study of Barriers to the Use of Alternative Methods of Dispute Resolution 137 (1984).

73. For example, in the marital example in the previous footnote, the wife would first have to receive competent legal advice concerning her "rights" in court. If she then, for her own good reasons, knowingly opts for the informal system that should be no cuase for objection.

74. The individually tailored quality of most mediative solutions, however, might prove to be a disadvantage when dealing with recurring violations. For example, if a vendor has committed various consumer regulation violations, and settlement by mediation is considered for each claim, the underlying issues are never likely to be rectified. What is needed here is some form of "aggregate" remedy, akin to the "pattern and practice" litigation the Massachusetts Attorney General sometimes brings as a result of repeated complaints to the mediation branch of the Consumer Protection Division. See also the operation of the Swedish Consumer Complaint Board described in M. Eisenstein, *The Swedish Public Complaints Board: Its Vital Role in a System of Consumer Protection*, in 2 Access to Justice 491 (Cappelletti & Weisner eds. 19). This is another task that might be better fulfilled in the Multi-Door Courthouse central screening intake. Of course that could not deal with the problem of multi-jurisdictional violations; other techniques would be needed there. *Cf.* T. Ehrlich & J. Frank, Planning for Justice (1977) (published by Aspen Institute).

alternative process is nonadversary does not necessarily indicate that lawyers have no legitimate role.[75]

When the lawyer's role as dispute resolver is considered, the lawyer's claimed expertise must rest on a different footing. Unfortunately, much of a law student's training is in adversary dispute settlement rather than accommodative problem-solving. This situation is rapidly changing, however. Increasingly, legal education encompasses mediation and other ADRM training.[76] Hence, lawyers should be neither specially qualified or disqualified for alternative dispute resolution. Depending on the case in question, lawyers with appropriate training might often possess excellent credentials for alternative dispute resolution.

The new roles outlined above present an exciting challenge to the legal community. If it is to be successfully met, the new system will require

1) the continued support of the legal education community (include the continuing legal education establishment);

2) an open mind on the part of the legal ethics committees who will be asked to sanction the work done by these newly created professionals;

3) some institutional mechanisms capable of providing training and possibly financial support to aid traditional lawyers in making appropriate vocational changes; and

4) possible regulation and certification of the new professionals.

IV. Conclusion

The alternative dispute resolution movement is at a critical turn in the road. Too often in the past, hopes of a coordinated program of experimentation and research have been dashed as the dispute resolution program fell victim to the budgetary ax. The establishment of the National Institute of Dispute Resolution may represent the final opportunity for the sound development of this promising movement.

Successful ADRMs require a broad effort to expand our presently limited understanding of the field. Progress will require continued experimentation and research, as well as further attempts to conceptualize the field. Enhanced public education about the benefits to be derived from alternative modes of dispute settlement will be necessary. Above all, the ADR movement will require the broadened involvement and support not only of the legal and legal education establishments, but also of the political and social orders and the public at large.

75. Consider, for example, the varying possible roles for representative lawyers in divorce mediation. *See* J. Folberg, & A. Taylor, Mediation (1984); Silberman, *Professional Responsibility Problems of Divorce Mediation*, 16 Fam. L.Q. 107 (1982). A lawyer might act simply as adviser to the mediator. *See, e.g.*, O. Coogler, Structured Mediation in Divorce Settlements (1978). Alternatively, each spouse could be urged to consult an attorney after a tentative agreement has been reached, or even at the outset of the entire process. *See* Samuels & Shawn, *The Role of the Lawyer Outside the Mediation Process*, 2 Med. Q. 13 (1983).

76. *See, e.g.*, Riskin, *Mediation and Lawyers*, 43 Ohio L.J. 29 (1982). A 1982 conference for law teachers engaged in or interested in dispute settlement drew well over 100 participants, and questionnaires sent out to all ABA-accredited law schools showed a sizeable proportion having some curricular and/or extra-curricular program in alternative dispute settlement.

[5]

MEDIATION—ITS FORMS AND FUNCTIONS

LON L. FULLER*

It is characteristic of the experienced mediator that he often proceeds most effectively to his goal, especially during the early stages of his efforts, by circumlocution and indirection. Perhaps I may be forgiven, therefore, if my approach to the subject of mediation itself displays something of those qualities. I have, in any event, thought it expedient to preface my analysis by putting mediation in the wider context of some assumptions of methodology that appear to shape our efforts to comprehend social phenomena generally.

I

In every branch of human study that has achieved or aspires to the name of science there seems to repeat itself a fundamental difference in the assumptions men make as to the nature of the thing they are examining. This schism in basic orientations extends over a wide range of subjects. Something of its pervasiveness becomes apparent when we recall the slogan-like terms conventionally employed in describing this opposition of viewpoints: structure *versus* process, substance *versus* procedure, statics *versus* dynamics and—on a more elevated plane—Being and Becoming. As these terms indicate, this recurring difference is not so much thought of as a quarrel about the most profitable posture of the mind as it is about the essential nature of the thing being studied.

There are, of course, thinkers who with some difficulty—and often with some attendant obscurity—attempt to straddle the choice. Certain paradoxes also often emerge when we compare closely related subjects. For example, social anthropology, which has traditionally dealt with the more "static" primitive societies, tends, I believe, to be more "process-oriented" than its sister science of sociology, practitioners of the latter subject being inclined to stick with "social structure" without displaying much curiosity about how it got there.

Legal scholarship has, on the surface at least, been spared the

* Carter Professor of General Jurisprudence, Harvard University.

anguish of choice visited on the practitioners of related disciplines. For one thing, law does not pretend to be a "science" and hence can permit itself a certain obscurity about its basic premises, attributing this condition simply to the nature of its subject. Legal reasoning is, in general, quite happy to proceed eclectically, fitting its methods and starting assumptions to the problem at hand. Then, too, American law teachers may assert that the case method combines in a happy mixture an analysis of both structure and process; it studies not only the established rules, but also, to the frequent discomfort of the beginning student, examines painstakingly and at great length the dialectical processes that bring them into being. Finally, a defense of legal scholarship against the charge of being one-sided can be derived from a glance at the law school catalogue where will be found listed, not only courses in "substantive law," but also courses in "procedure."

With respect to this last point it should be pointed out that law school courses dealing explicitly with procedure are concerned with the highly structured procedure observed in the trial of cases in court. It tells the student, for example, something about the problems of proving a contract in court; it tells him little about the extracurial procedures by which contracts come into being. In the case of the highly formal written contract, this omission may be quite innocent. But what of the contract "implied-in-fact?" Here any attempt to articulate clearly the modes by which contractual obligations arise tacitly out of human interactions would present structure and process in an incomfortably intimate embrace, for in this case the thing that emerges from the process—"the contract"—is, as it were, simply an aspect of the process itself.

As for the case method as practiced in American law schools it can indeed be said of it that it combines in a felicitous mixture a study of both process and structure. The structure of the law of contracts as it goes into Restatements and textbooks is viewed as being in large measure a product of the judicial process. That process is in turn viewed as being shaped by the existing structure of rules and by the tensions that may arise between that structure and the court's conception of the proper disposition of the controversies (often of "novel impression") that are brought before it for decision. Thus, structure and process are viewed as interacting, each serving to shape the other.

The trouble with the case method, for all its explicit and perceptive orientation toward process, is that there is not enough of it in the law school curriculum. It is largely confined in practice to a particular kind of law-making, a species of legal ordering that for historical reasons has come to be known as "the common law," though a more apt designation would have been "adjudicative law." The adjudicative process is, however, only one way of bringing human relations into a workable and productive order. Other processes include statutory enactment, administrative direction, contractual ordering effected by the parties themselves, and the tacit accommodations that ripen into something equivalent to customary law. These various forms of social ordering are interrelated in complex ways; formal adjudication may of course serve as an adjunct to any of them for purposes of interpretation and enforcement.

The standard law school curriculum deals with the *results* of all these forms of social ordering; we do indeed teach students a little bit about customary law and a great deal about statutory law, administrative law and contracts. We do not, however, spend much time exploring the social processes by which these various forms of "law" come into being. Because these processes are neglected we inevitably lack a perspective from which to appraise the relative aptness, for solving a given problem, of the various competing forms of social ordering.

No one has contributed more to a correction of this defect, and to an enlargement of this perspective than the late Henry M. Hart. His mind had a strong bent toward process and procedure. The famous course he created, which is now taught (still from multilithed materials) in some two dozen law schools, was and is called *The Legal Process.* The course consists in a series of diagnostic and prescriptive exercises. Instead of asking, "What is the rule?" or even, "What is the best rule?" it asks, "What is the nature of the basic problem and how shall we choose among the various procedures of social ordering that might be applied to it?"

II

I like to think there is a special appropriateness in dedicating an article on mediation to the memory of Henry Hart. For of mediation one is tempted to say that it is all process and no structure.

Casual treatments of the subject in the literature of sociology tend to assume that the object of mediation is to make the parties aware of the "social norms" applicable to their relationship and to persuade them to accommodate themselves to the "structure" imposed by these norms. From this point of view the difference between a judge and a mediator is simply that the judge orders the parties to conform themselves to the rules, while the mediator persuades them to do so. But mediation is commonly directed, not toward achieving conformity to norms, but toward the creation of the relevant norms themselves. This is true, for example, in the very common case where the mediator assists the parties in working out the terms of a contract defining their rights and duties toward one another. In such a case there is no pre-existing structure that can guide mediation; it is the mediational process that produces the structure.

It may be suggested that mediation is always, in any event, directed toward bringing about a more harmonious relationship between the parties, whether this be achieved through explicit agreement, through a reciprocal acceptance of the "social norms" relevant to their relationship, or simply because the parties have been helped to a new and more perceptive understanding of one another's problems. The fact that in ordinary usage the terms "mediation" and "conciliation" are largely interchangeable tends to reinforce this view of the matter.

But at this point we encounter the inconvenient fact that mediation can be directed, not toward cementing a relationship, but toward terminating it. In a form of mediation that is coming to be called "marriage therapy" mediative efforts between husband and wife may be undertaken by a psychoanalyst, a psychiatrist, a social worker, a marriage counsellor, or even a friendly neighbor. In this situation it will not infrequently turn out that the most effective use of mediation will be in assisting the parties to accept the inevitability of divorce. In a radically different context one of the most dramatically successful uses of mediation I ever witnessed involved a case in which an astute mediator helped the parties rescind a business contract. Two corporations were entrapped by a long-term supply contract that had become burdensome and disadvantageous to both. Cancelling it, however, was a complicated matter, requiring a period of "phasing out" and various financial adjustments back and forth. For some time the parties had been chiefly engaged in reciprocal threats of a law suit. On the advice of an attorney for one of the parties, a mediator (whose previous experience had been almost entirely in the field of labor relations) was brought in. Within no time at all a severance of relations was accomplished and the two firms parted company happily.

Thus we find that mediation may be directed toward, and result in discrepant and even diametrically opposed results. This circumstance argues against our being able to derive any general structure of the mediational process from some identifiable goal shared by all mediational efforts. We may, of course, indulge in observations to the effect that the mere presence of a third person tends to put the parties on their good behavior, that the mediator can direct their verbal exchanges away from recrimination and toward the issues that need to be faced, that by receiving separate and confidential communications from the parties he can gradually bring into the open issues so deep-cutting that the parties themselves had shared a tacit taboo against any discussion of them and that, finally, he can by his management of the interchange demonstrate to the parties that it is possible to discuss divisive issues without either rancor or evasion.

But can we go beyond generalities of this sort? I believe we can, but to accomplish this we shall have to begin by examining in detail the functions mediation can perform in a specific illustrative situation. If this illustrative case is aptly chosen we may then, with appropriate adjustments, extend our conclusions to other situations that vary in specific ways from the model adopted for detailed analysis. The model I propose here is that presented by mediational efforts serving to facilitate the negotiation of a collective bargaining agreement between an employer and a labor union. Aside from the fact that this use of mediation happens to be one in which I have had some personal participation, I believe it to be especially suited to our present purpose because it combines in a single illustrative instance a number of the quite diverse functions a mediator can perform.

I begin, then, by supposing that an employer—say, a corporation engaged in manufacturing—and a labor union representing its production force are about to enter into negotiations concerning the terms of a collective bargaining agreement. I assume that these negotiations will range over a wide variety of issues, either because a collective bargaining agreement is being entered by the parties for the first time, or because an existing agreement has come open for renegotiation and the issues raised by the parties extend over a wide range of subjects, such as rates of pay, seniority provisions, grievance procedures and the timing and length of annual paid vacations.

Now among the characteristics of this relationship that are relevant to our purposes, the *first* lies in the obvious fact that the parties mediated are two in number, they constitute a dyad, not a triad or more numerous group. To be sure, during the mediational effort some differences of opinion within the union and, less commonly, within the company, may come to the surface, but basically the mediator's efforts are directed toward an ordering of the relations between the company and the union and he will generally be at pains to stay out of quarrels arising within either of the participating groups.

The *second* characteristic of concern here lies in the circumstance that normally neither of the parties, the employer or the union, has any real choice but to reach an agreement with the other. The two parties are locked in a relationship that is virtually one of "bilateral monopoly"; each is dependent for its very existence on some collaboration with the other. The employer is not only under economic pressure to reach a contract with the union, but in the United States is normally subject to a legal compulsion "to bargain in good faith" with the elected representative of his employees. The union, on the other hand, being organized for the purpose of collective bargaining, must, if it is to fulfill its reason for being, reach an agreement with the employer.

This "tied-in" relation, it should be noted, extends not only to the union as a collective entity, but in some measure to the individual union member as well. If, dissatisfied with what his union has achieved for him, he considers taking a job with another employer he is likely to be reminded that in his new position he will find himself at the bottom of the seniority ladder and vulnerable to lay-off at the first slackening of production. Furthermore, moving into a new employment may forfeit for him any nontransferable "fringe benefits" his union has obtained for him through collective bargaining, these benefits relating to such things as retirement pay, health benefits, paid vacations proportioned to length of service, and the like. We commonly find, then, between the unionized employer, on the one side, and the labor union and its members, on the other, a relationship that may be called one of heavy interdependence: they simply must find some way of getting along with one another.

The *third* characteristic of the relationship that is relevant here lies in the obvious fact that the negotiation of the collective bargaining agreement has elements of an economic trade. This is plainly true, of course, where rates of pay are being negotiated. But it is also true where "non-monetary" provisions of the contract come under discussion. For example, a manufacturer might be willing to accept a revision of the grievance procedure proposed by the union, in return for some expansion of the clause removing certain management decisions from arbitrational review. The question, "Will this help or hurt *us?*" is one the parties constantly put to themselves as they negotiate the contract—sometimes even when the issue is simply where a comma ought to be inserted. Into every aspect of the negotiations, then, there is likely to enter some calculation of relative "payoff."

The *fourth* characteristic of our illustrative situation stands in some contrast to that just described. The enterprise in which the parties are engaged is not simply one in which each seeks to attain the contractual language that will most favor his immediate interests. The parties are also caught up in the task of drafting a constitution, of putting on paper words by which they can in the future live together successfully. A perception of this aspect of their joint endeavor must temper and often redirect their efforts toward the achievement of their separate goals. A clause with hidden ambiguities that invite endless disputes will carry a heavy price tag for both parties, even though the party securing its adoption may at the time have congratulated himself on having served well his own advantage.

The fact that the actual negotiation of the collective bargaining agreement is conducted, not by principals, but by agents or representatives constitutes a *fifth* characteristic of the situation we are discussing. The employer is an abstract entity called a corporation; those who represent that entity act in a representative capacity and they are by no means commonly the chief executives of the corporation itself. Likewise, of course, the entire membership of the union does not and cannot participate directly in the negotiations; these are commonly conducted on their behalf by an out-of-town expert from the national union headquarters, assisted by a local committee.

The *sixth* and final characteristic of the relationship we are examining lies in the fact that one of the parties, the company, occupies toward the membership of the union a dual role. In the negotiation of the collective bargaining agreement the parties meet each other as equals, with neither having any recognized authority over the other; in the day-to-day management of the plant, however, the company is boss. Its foremen and superintendents, not the labor union, direct the manufacturing process. Indeed, experienced labor leaders exercise a canny reserve about invading this prerogative, for the responsibilities that go with it could be quite inconvenient for them and any sharing of those responsibilities would tend seriously to compromise their role as representatives of the union membership.

These, then, are six characteristics of the collective bargaining situation that have suggested to me it might be useful as a model in analysing the functions of mediation generally. By way of a recapitulation: the parties concerned (1) being two in number, find themselves (2) in a relationship of heavy interdependence exerting a strong pressure to reach an agreement, an agreement that will (3) combine elements of an economic trade with (4) elements of a written charter or constitution for the governance of their future relations; this agreement is (5) negotiated by agents, not principals, and (6) the employer occupies throughout a dual role, being, on the one hand, director of the enterprise and, on the other, a coequal with the union in the negotiation and administration of the collective bargaining agreement.

In what immediately follows I shall attempt an analysis of the ways in which these six characteristics affect the need for, and the functions performed by a mediator. Following that analysis I shall attempt to draw some analogies between the situation I have taken as my illustrative model and the uses of mediation in quite different social contexts. One context I shall discuss is that presented generally by "primitive" societies, where (in various guises) mediative processes play a prominent role in preserving (and sometimes in creating) a functioning social order. (By way of anticipation, I suggest that if the reader will glance through the summary presented in the last paragraph, he will discern that some of the six characteristics I have attributed to the collective bargaining situation bear a striking resemblance to those present in primitive societies; others, to be sure, are less obviously present, if they are at all.)

III

The first question is, then, how the need for a mediator, and the role performed by him, are affected by the fact that the parties whose relations constitute the subject of mediation are two in number. Here Simmel's famous discussion of the dyad and the triad becomes relevant.[1]

Simmel observes that among groups ranked in terms of the number of their members, the group of two, the dyad, is peculiarly handicapped in resolving problems of internal order. Even the triad confronting internal difficulties can be governed openly or tacitly by the majority principle; this is an expedient from which, of course, the dyad is excluded. Then, too, one member of a triad can often undertake to mediate between the other two, having perhaps preserved a posture of detachment precisely in order to assume this role;

1. THE SOCIOLOGY OF GEORG SIMMEL 118-169, (Wolff ed. 1950).

A seeing trouble brewing between *B* and *C* may initially have been inclined to favor *B* but decided to remain neutral in order to qualify for the role of mediator. This is obviously another resource denied to the dyad.

The dyadic relationship is, then, one eminently suited to mediation and often dependent on it as the only measure capable of solving its internal problems. Indeed, one may ask whether mediation in the strict sense is really possible in ordering the internal affairs of any group larger than two. If *A*, *B* and *C* are all at odds with one another, it is extremely difficult for an outsider, say, *X*, to undertake a mediative role without becoming a participant in the internal maneuvers of the quarreling members. If *X* asks *A*'s acquiescence in a proposed solution, *A* may reply that he will give his assent if *X* will undertake to persuade *B* to withdraw a concession *B* made in favor of *C*. *X* may thus end by becoming the manipulated tool of those he sought to guide. In this predicament he may face the alternative of retaining the empty title of mediator or becoming, in effect, a fourth member of the group and a participant in its internal games. If he chooses the latter alternative, his accession to membership may not increase, but rather tend to diminish the chance for achieving a functioning order since it introduces for the first time the possibility of a deadlock of two against two, in other words, it impairs an advantage the triad enjoys over the dyad, the capacity to resolve internal difficulties by something like a majority vote.

There is perhaps one situation in which an outsider may, with skill and good luck, serve usefully as a mediator among three. This would be where three different measures are proposed as the solution for some problem faced by the triad. *A* favors *Solution X*, *B* favors *Solution Y*, while *C* favors *Solution Z*. Here the mediator might discuss with each of the parties the grounds upon which, and the degree of conviction with which, he supports his preference for one solution as against the other two. There are thus opened up, in somewhat embarrassing abundance, six separate entries for the mediator's intervention. Exploring these conscientiously he might discover that *A*'s preference for *X* over *Y* was based on a mistake of fact; with this mistake corrected *A* might then be ready to join with *B* in supporting *Y*. Or, the mediator might discover that *B*'s preference for *Y* over *Z* was very slight and that he was almost indifferent between the two. The mediator might then persuade *B* to join with *C* in supporting *Z*, thus restoring the triad as a functioning entity. These happy outcomes are certainly possible, but it is obvious that the relationships involved are so complex, and the opportunities for misunderstanding so great, that the mediator may find it extremely difficult to maintain the integrity of his role as he makes the rounds among *A*, *B* and *C*. Certainly if the mediational process can be said to have a home ground, it is to be found in the dyad.[2]

In my analysis of the characteristics of the collective bargaining situation I noted that it involved not only a dyad, but a dyad the members of which stood toward one another in a relation of "heavy interdependence." Perhaps this observation served only to emphasize a characteristic that must be present before a resolution of the internal problems of the dyad becomes a matter of sufficient concern to justify mediative efforts. It is fairly obvious that mediation has scarcely any role to play in human relationships fluidly organized on what may be broadly described as the market principle. If *X* finds *A*, *B* and *C* all competing to supply his needs through rival contractual arrangements, he may need the services of an expert adviser, but he will scarcely have occasion to call on those of a mediator. Likewise, in a society where transient and freely terminable sexual alliances took the place of marriage it is hardly likely that there would develop any institutional practice comparable to "marriage therapy." Mediation by its very nature presupposes relationships normally affected by some strong internal pull toward cohesion; this is true whether the mediative efforts in question be directed toward the formation, modification or dissolution of such relationships.

Those whose minds are intent on the "structure of authority," rather than on an analysis of social processes, are apt to ask of the mediator not, "What does he do?" but, "Whence comes his capacity or authority to arrange the affairs of others?" In this mood the inquiry is likely to be whether his power rests on a tacit contract with the affected parties, or derives from some charismatic qualities possessed by the mediator himself, or should be attributed to some role or office assigned to him by tradition or higher authority. Now an inquiry along

2. This does not mean, it should be observed, that a single mediator might not have occasion to cope with internal difficulties arising within a collectivity forming one member of a dyad. For example, in the course of mediating the negotiation of a contract between an employer and a union it might turn out that one of the chief obstacles to agreement lay in a clash between two factions within the union. An experienced (and courageous!) mediator might in some measure mediate the dispute within the union as the first step necessary toward mediating the dispute between the union and the employer. This would involve, however, dealing successively with two dyads and not with any attempt to put in order a three-cornered pattern of opposed interests.

these lines is certainly not meaningless, but taking it too seriously may lead us to ignore the fact that the mediator's "power" may largely derive from the simple fact that he is there and that his help is badly needed. Thomas Schelling has some vivid and perceptive things to say about this aspect of the mediator's job:

> When there is no apparent focal point for agreement . . . [the mediator] can create one by his power to make a dramatic suggestion. The bystander who jumps into an intersection and begins to direct traffic at an impromptu traffic jam is conceded the power to discriminate among cars by being able to offer a sufficient increase in efficiency to benefit even the cars most discriminated against; his directions have only the power of suggestion, but coordination requires the common acceptance of some source of suggestion. Similarly, the participants of a square dance may all be thoroughly dissatisfied with the particular dances being called, but as long as the caller has the microphone, nobody can dance anything else. The white line down the center of the road is a mediator, and very likely it can err substantially toward one side or the other before the disadvantaged side finds advantage in denying its authority.[3]

A serious study of mediation can serve, I suggest, to offset the tendency of modern thought to assume that all social order must be imposed by some kind of "authority." When we perceive how a mediator, claiming no "authority," can help the parties give order and coherence to their relationship, we may in the process come to realize that there are circumstances in which the parties can dispense with this aid, and that social order can often arise directly out of the interactions it seems to govern and direct.

The third characteristic I found present in the collective bargaining situation lies in the fact that in reaching agreement each party is constantly calculating the relative advantage or disadvantage to him of any particular proposal. There is, in other words, a pervasive evaluation of "payoffs"; this evaluation extends even to provisions of the contract that seem unrelated in any direct way to monetary costs. In terms of the mediator's function, this means that the mediator participates in a bargaining situation where each party seeks to get as much for himself as he can at as small a cost as possible, the "cost" involved being, of course, that entailed in some concession to the opposing party.

3. T. Schelling, The Strategy of Conflict 144 (1960).

In approaching this aspect of the situation I should like to begin with a quotation from a great student of the sociology of organization. It should be noted that in this passage the author makes it clear that his chief interest is not in something like a trade of economic goods, but in the calculations of utility that enter into any bargaining situation—sometimes even, as I have suggested, when the issue is where a comma ought to be inserted.

> . . . the rule must be that you give, so far as possible, what is less valuable to you but more valuable to the receiver; and you receive what is more valuable to you and less valuable to the giver. This is common sense, good business sense, good social sense, good technology, and is the enduring basis of amicable and constructive relations of any kind. This does *not* mean that you give as little as you can from the *receiver's* point of view. In terms of money, you give a man dollars for his services which are worth more to you than the dollars. No sane man would admit anything else. If you give services for dollars it must be that the dollars are worth more to you than the services. Unfortunately for simplicity, neither side of the transaction can be confined to or measured completely in dollars, even in commercial enterprises; and in non-commercial enterprises the exchange is extremely intangible.
>
> What conceals this simple fact of experience so often is that subsequent evaluations may change, though this is then beside the point. I may pay a man $10 today with pleasure, and find tomorrow that I need $10 very badly, but cannot use the services I paid for. I am then perhaps disposed to think I made a bad exchange. I read the past into the present. This leads to the false view that what exchanges *should* be is as little as possible of what the *receiver* wants, regardless of its value to me. This philosophy of giving as little as possible and getting as much as possible in the *other man's values* is the root of bad customer relations, bad labor relations, bad credit relations, bad supply relations, bad technology. The possible margins of cooperative success are too limited to survive the destruction of incentives which this philosophy implies.[4]

The closing sentences of the passage just quoted plainly suggest one function the mediator can perform in the collective bargaining situation, that of reminding the parties that their negotiations constitute a cooperative enterprise and that one does not necessarily make a gain for himself simply because he denies to the other fellow something he wants. In conveying this message the mediator only supplies

4. C. BARNARD, THE FUNCTIONS OF THE EXECUTIVE 254-255 (1953).

the insight that the parties ought to have brought to the bargaining table without his aid. He simply makes them see, in Barnard's words, that "the rule must be that you give, so far as possible, what is less valuable to you but more valuable to the receiver; and you receive what is more valuable to you and less valuable to the giver." Plainly it is this divergence between the cost of giving and the gain realized by receiving that makes possible the reciprocal advantages that can result from a properly negotiated exchange.

But if it is relatively easy to see that an apt exchange can yield advantages to both parties, it is much more difficult to discern the actual processes of discussion and negotiation that will maximize these gains of reciprocity. Suppose, for example, that one party reveals, intentionally or inadvertently, that he is desperately eager to secure some particular concession from his opposing number. It happens that granting this concession would visit very little disadvantage on the party from whom it is demanded. Does he at once reveal this fact, or does he hold back his concession as a resource on which to draw when he wants something badly that the other party is reluctant to give? Which course of action will, in fact, serve ultimately to maximize the gains of reciprocity for both parties?[5] In judging this last question it should be recalled that gratuitous concession falling outside the frame of normal bargaining are apt to arouse suspicions as to their motivation and may be interpreted as requiring the benefited party to volunteer some counter-concessions, which may itself be unguided by any accurate understanding of its value to the other party—the "exchange" of Christmas presents is notoriously a poor example of maximizing utilities.

An obvious, but mistaken expedient would be to have both parties at once disclose to each other their internal evaluations of all the items under discussion. But there are many difficulties with this. As Barnard remarks, the values may be extremely intangible; there is no yardstick that can convert them into numbers. Furthermore, the items on a negotiating agenda may be interrelated in various complex ways. For example, suppose that one party, *A*, asks for concessions *X*, *Y*, and *Z*. Now it might be that if *Y* and *Z* were granted, *X* would become wholly

5. I am aware that it is generally accepted in game theory that there is no objective way of defining an optimum settlement between two persons standing in a relationship of bilateral monopoly. Hence, when I speak of "maximizing the gains of reciprocity" I have in mind a settlement that would appeal to a reasonable man, familiar wtih the general posture of the utilities on both sides, as a close approximation to something that could be called an optimum settlement.

unnecessary. On the other hand, if the other party were willing to concede both *X* and *Y* this concession might yield a return much higher than the value of *X* alone, say, roughly its double, although *Y* taken by itself would produce only a small fraction of the value that a grant of *X* by itself would yield, etc., etc.

Where the bargaining process proceeds without the aid of a mediator the usual course pursued by experienced negotiators is something like this: the parties begin by simply talking about the various proposals, explaining in general terms why they want this and why they are opposed to that. During this exploratory or "sounding out" process, which proceeds without any clear-cut offers of settlement, each party conveys—sometimes explicitly, sometimes tacitly, sometimes intentionally, sometimes inadvertently—something about his relative evaluations of the various items under discussion. After these discussions have proceeded for some time, one party is likely to offer a "package deal," proposing in general terms a contract that will settle all the issues under discussion. This offer may be accepted by the other party or he may accept it subject to certain stipulated changes.[6]

Now it is obvious that the process just described can often be greatly facilitated through the services of a skillful mediator. His assistance can speed the negotiations, reduce the likelihood of miscalculation, and generally help the parties to reach a sounder agreement, an adjustment of their divergent valuations that will produce something like an optimum yield of the gains of reciprocity. These things the mediator can accomplish by holding separate confidential meetings with the parties, where each party gives the mediator a relatively full and candid account of the internal posture of his own interests. Armed with this information, but without making a premature disclosure of its details, the mediator can then help to shape the negotiations in such a way that they will proceed most directly to their goal, with a minimum of waste and friction.

The fourth characteristic of the collective bargaining situation to

6. Probably the cautious and indirect approach just described is characteristic of all complex negotiations. This is certainly suggested in Walder's brilliant fictional account of the negotiation of the Peace of St. Germain. The following passage reports advice given to one of the negotiators:

> You must mask your intentions, uncover them only a little at a time, tentatively, to find out where they agree. You must be able, behind your reserve, to change projects, purposes, allow your opinion the necessary fluidity, if there is to be the best possible outcome of our labors! Above all, do not commit yourselves, do not bind yourselves prematurely! Nothing is said, nothing is done until the very last moment.

WALDER, THE NEGOTIATORS 91-92 (Folliot trans. 1959).

be examined here lies in what I have called its "constitution-drafting" aspect. It should be kept in mind that the collective bargaining agreement serves, in effect, as the charter of a miniature government; it assigns functions, establishes procedures for the presentation of claims, and, in its provisions relating to arbitration, institutes what amounts to a private judiciary. Drafting such a document is a demanding exercise, not only in the accurate and unambiguous use of language, but in the apt design of institutional arrangements.

When I first mentioned this aspect of the collective bargaining situation I remarked that it stood in some contrast to that we have just examined at length. When the parties have reached the point where they are ready to express their future relationship in written words, their efforts will generally be directed toward an achievement of shared objectives, rather than toward a workable compromise of divergent aims. However, it is obvious that some elements of trade-off are likely to reappear when the parties undertake to reduce to numbered paragraphs an oral agreement previously reached "in principle."

For one thing, there is often an inescapable compromise between what might be abstractly desirable and what can be clearly defined in words and effectively realized through formally instituted procedures. In exploring the reasons why this should be so, a hypothetical illustration drawn from a quite different field may be useful here. Let us suppose that for a century, two peoples, divergent in language and religion, have been united under one emperor. The empire is being dissolved and the two peoples will henceforth constitute separate nations. Under the empire, *People A* in general inhabited the area to the west of a large winding river, while the area to the east of the river was largely populated by *People B*. This simple line of division was, however, marred by some anomalies; at certain points on the river there were populations, as it were, "on the wrong side." Now plainly there would be long-run advantages if the plainly visible, permanent boundary provided by the river could be established as the line dividing the new nations. On the other hand, the presence of these pockets of people on "the wrong side" of the new boundary might itself become a source of renewed friction and discord. An appraisal of relative advantages and disadvantages might be made differently by the two peoples; a skillful mediator might work out some acceptable compromise, which could, of course, include some relocation of populations.

Now the forms of language, like rivers, have a certain inertia of their own; they cannot always be readily bent to accommodate every nuance of thought and a clause overloaded with qualifications may forfeit its meaning as a clear guidepost for human interaction. In the drafting of any complex agreement there is often an inescapable compromise between what can be simply expressed and what might be abstractly desirable. The mediational process plainly has a place in dealing with such problems.

There is another service that a mediator can render when the parties' efforts toward a formal agreement have reached the drafting stage. The mediator can bring to problems of drafting a third-party perspective; in George Herbert Mead's famous phrase he can serve as "the generalized other." This is important because the generalized other may in fact shortly appear on the scene in the person of Mr. *X*; six months after the contract is signed Mr. *X* may become personnel manager of the company in succession to the man who actually negotiated the contract on behalf of the employer and who was familiar with all the considerations that entered into its phrasing. The negotiators must keep in mind, not only what the words mean to them, but what they may mean to one who was not a participant in their deliberations and tacit adjustments. The mediator can help to supply that perspective.

We reach now the fifth aspect of the collective bargaining situation having some significance for the role of the mediator and the contribution he can make to a successful contract. This aspect lies in the circumstance that the contract is negotiated, not by principals, but by representatives or agents.

My first observation here relates to limitations, real or pretended, on the agent's authority. Let us suppose that the representative of one of the parties opens the first bargaining session by stating that he has been instructed by his principal that he may not, under any circumstances, make certain specified concessions. The excluded concessions will naturally relate to matters that might reasonably be expected to fall within the scope of the negotiations; the agent is hardly likely to warn the opposite party that his principal will sign no contract requiring him to commit a capital offense. In the collective bargaining situation the limitation on the agent's authority might, in the case of the employer, exclude a provision granting any version of the closed shop, or, in the case of the union, anything like a "management prerogative" clause.

Obviously the mediator will usually serve the cause of effective bargaining by freeing the negotiations from shackles imposed before any discussion of issues has begun and in abstraction from what the negotiations may later reveal about the actual posture of the two parties' interests. If the limitations on the agent's authority are feigned, the mediator can more readily and gracefully penetrate the pretense than can the opposing party. If the limitations have in fact been imposed by the principal, the mediator may induce the agent to ask for their removal and assist him in bringing about that result. None of this means, of course, that in the contract finally signed the principal will inevitably concede things he hoped to prevent from becoming subjects of bargaining; it simply means that the issues sought to be excluded will, in fact, enter into the discussions and be considered as possible ingredients in the final settlement, where, if included, they may of course undergo some modification.

The exploitation of feigned incapacities for the purpose of securing a bargaining advantage has been analysed at some length in "game theory."[7] Long before the device was subjected to any such sophisticated treatment it was familiar to lawyers and businessmen as the technique of "the wicked partner." *A* and *B* are discussing the terms of a contract. *B* demands some concession of *A*. *A* replies, "I wish very much I could let you have this. But my partner, who is in Europe and unfortunately cannot be reached, is dead set against it." In analysing the implications of this bargaining stratagem, it is important to realize that it becomes a serious problem only in situations I have described as those of "heavy interdependence," where the needs of the parties and the intertwining of their interests creates a strong pressure toward some sort of accommodation between them. It should also be noted that even in such situations it is a device that may miscarry and disserve the interest of the party who attempted to exploit it. When *A* refuses in advance even to consider making a particular concession he will realize that he might receive something in return for this concession, but he thinks he has grounds for believing that this counterconcession could not possibly compensate him for what he gave to secure it. This judgment may be misinformed for it has been reached before the internal structure of the other party's interests has been exposed through an open-ended exploration of the different ways in which the parties' diverse interests can be fitted together. But even if the party exploiting the wicked-partner technique is correct in his assumption that he will gain by forestalling in advance any granting

7. *See* SCHELLING, *supra* note 3, index entry, "commitment."

of the concession, the bargaining process itself is distorted and it becomes impossible to secure the general and uninhibited exploration of diverse interests essential to a realization of the maximum gains of reciprocity. The scars left by this distortion may affect adversely the future relations between the parties.

All of this means that where the agent pleads in advance a lack of power to grant certain concessions and where the granting of these concessions would normally form an appropriate subject for bargaining between the parties, the mediator, by securing the removal of such restrictions, may make a substantial contribution, not only to the interests of the immediate parties, but to the integrity of the bargaining process considered as an essential in a functioning society.

So much for limitations, real or pretended, on the agent's power. There is a second and quite different implication for the mediator's role deriving from the fact that the parties to the negotiations are represented by agents. This lies in the observation that if there is no mediator the parties' agents may be forced, in effect, to join together in assuming the mediational role.

The negotiation of a collective bargaining agreement is commonly opened by a general session attended by delegations of persons representing both sides. On behalf of the union there may appear an attorney, a field representative from national headquarters and a committee of the local. Management may be represented by an attorney, the personnel manager, the treasurer and perhaps several other officers concerned with labor relations. Plainly this wide and miscellaneous audience constitutes a very poor human milieu in which to conduct the delicate sounding-out procedures by which the two parties' interests are revealed and gradually fitted together into some workable pattern. Spokesmen for both sides may be deterred, for example, from making anything like definite proposals by the fear of audible or visible dissents coming from their associates in the audience. The result is that the general opening session normally serves only a ceremonial and ritualistic purpose.

What is the next step? If a mediator is available, this is not difficult. Each of the two groups will, in turn, meet alternately with the mediator out of the presence of the other. At these repeated meetings each side will make, perhaps with some initial hesitancy but by degrees more openly, a relatively candid disclosure of the posture of its interests and preferences. Any differences within the ranks that may come to the surface during these meetings need not be damaging; on the contrary, some insight into these differences may furnish the mediator useful guidance as he works his way toward an accommodation of the parties' interests that will furnish a workable charter for their future relations.

What happens in the absence of a mediator? As I have previously expressed it, what not uncommonly occurs is that the two opposing agents join to take over the mediational function. This means that they meet together privately, explore possible ways of bringing to some workable accommodation the diverse interests of their principals, interrupt their discussions to secure advice from their colleagues, return to their joint sessions, and finally agree on the outlines of a settlement which they will propose for acceptance by their respective principals.

Obviously this procedure requires a degree of trust and mutual respect between the two negotiating agents. A good agent does not antagonize his opposite number, but is at pains to keep on good terms with him. When a lawyer representing industry has occasion over time to deal repeatedly and in different contexts with the same labor representative, a certain comaraderie will normally and quite usefully develop between them. This intimacy may, however, easily drift into a tacit reciprocity in the granting of favors that may in time become detached from the interests of the particular clients being represented. Thus, if a lawyer representing industry was forced by the intransigence of his client to deal rather harshly with his opposite number in Centerville, the question may arise, should he make up for this when the two representatives next meet in Zenith, where the employer is quite generous toward labor and ready to grant any reasonable concession recommended by his lawyer? I once heard an employer express himself in terms that left no doubt as to how he thought the lawyer would answer that question. He said, "You lawyers that represent industry and the labor people are like professional wrestlers. You travel around together and when you're in one town you agree on who'll take the fall in the next."

This was a harsh judgment, but it points to a real problem, a problem that the services of a mediator may do much to alleviate. The mediator can, by his explicit assumption of the mediational role, help those purporting to act as representatives remain what they offer themselves as being.

It should be noted that the problem here suggested is not a new one; it is by no means a sordid by-product of our complex modern industrial age. It was some one hundred and eighty years ago that Edmund Burke wrote the following lines:

> The world is governed by go-betweens. These go-betweens influence the persons with whom they carry on the intercourse, by stating their own sense to each of them as the sense of the other; and thus they reciprocally master both sides.[8]

Burke's remarks contain important implications for the ethos of the mediator's office as well as for that of the agent; indeed, Burke seems to have in mind primarily the man who openly assumes the role of "go-between." Is it in fact a common practice of mediators, in communicating the positions of the parties back and forth, to state "their own sense to each of them as the sense of the other?" Certainly when he receives from one party a statement of his position, the mediator, before conveying it to the other party, will normally strip it of vituperation and recrimination; his duty is to convey the substance of what was said, not its tone or the facial expression that accompanied it. But it is not always easy to effect this separation, especially since the depth with which a party feels about an issue is something that enters into the valuations that shape the final adjustment of diverse interests. At the same time an agreement obtained through an outright misrepresentation of the parties' own reasons for their proposals will certainly furnish an insecure basis for future relations, if indeed it does not lead to an immediate collapse of the agreement as soon as the false ground on which it was accepted becomes evident.

Like everyone else concerned with the mediational process, the mediator needs to reflect on his proper role and on the sources of his power. Mediators often pride themselves, and receive much newspaper publicity, for solving "tough" cases. But sometimes what makes the cases "tough" lies in the high stakes involved and the strong compulsion both parties are under to reach agreement. When he "solves" such a case, the mediator needs to reflect that his powers may derive as much from the urgency of the situation as from any special gifts of his. He may usefully recall Schelling's amateur who volunteers to call the dances at a square dance; the couples may follow his calls, not because the calls are especially apt, but because if they are not followed the dance cannot go on.

The sixth and final aspect of the collective bargaining situation

8. THE WORKS OF EDMUND BURKE 189-190 (1904). The quotation is from "An Appeal from the New to the Old Whigs," 1791.

requires only brief mention. This aspect lies in the fact that the employer occupies toward the union a dual role, being, on the one hand, director of an economic enterprise employing the union membership and, on the other, confronting the union as a coequal in negotiating and administering the collective bargaining agreement. In the present climate of labor relations in the United States this duality of role cannot be said to present any special problem for the discharge of the mediator's function. A few peripheral issues may arise; an example would be in working out the rules relating to lay-off in the case of reduced operations. The union is likely to seek formalized rules based on seniority, while management may want to retain some discretion in order to preserve a workable balance of specialized skills within the reduced force. The role of the mediator in helping to solve this sort of conflict is not different from that we have already analysed at length with respect to other problems.

There are other contexts, however, in which this duality of role may create serious problems for the mediator. An example would be presented by a conflict between a municipality and some of its employees, as where teachers, firemen or police threaten to go on strike—a strike that may be illegal. In solving such problems successfully the mediator will have to enlarge considerably the range of his concerns and in the process have to content himself with something short of perfection in the achievement of his more familiar objectives. So one may also suppose that in societies organized on a hierarchic principle, where personal status plays an important and diffuse role, the mediational process might have to be diverted to subsidiary issues (such as "saving face") that are only indirectly related to the task of establishing a workable framework for future relations.

IV

Elaborate as the analysis just concluded has been, it has dealt only inferentially and indirectly with what may be said to be the central quality of mediation, namely, its capacity to reorient the parties toward each other, not by imposing rules on them, but by helping them to achieve a new and shared perception of their relationship, a perception that will redirect their attitudes and dispositions toward one another.

This quality of mediation becomes most visible when the proper function of the mediator turns out to be, not that of inducing the parties to accept formal rules for the governance of their future relations, but that of helping them to free themselves from the encumbrance of rules and of accepting, instead, a relationship of mutual respect, trust and understanding that will enable them to meet shared contingencies without the aid of formal prescriptions laid down in advance. Such a mediational effort might well come into play in any of the various forms of mediation between husband and wife associated with "family counseling" and "marriage therapy." In the task of re-establishing the marriage as a going concern the mediator might find it essential to break up formalized conceptions of "duty" and to substitute a more fluid sense of mutual trust and shared responsibility. In effect, instead of working toward achieving a rule-oriented relationship he might devote his efforts, to some degree at least, in exactly the opposite direction.

Because it does not bring this aspect of mediation into relief the illustrative model to which I have just devoted so many pages may seem inaptly chosen. The negotiation of an elaborate written contract, such as that embodied in a collective bargaining agreement between an employer and a labor union, does indeed present a special set of problems for the mediator. But in defense of the choice of this model it may be observed that complexity and formality of the processes involved may enable use to discern distinctive aspects of the mediator's task which, though present in more informal contexts, would there have been blurred and resistant to separate analysis.

Furthermore, it should be remembered that the primary function of the mediator in the collective bargaining situation is not to propose rules to the parties and to secure their acceptance of them, but to induce the mutual trust and understanding that will enable the parties to work out their own rules. The creation of rules is a process that cannot itself be rule-bound; it must be guided by a sense of shared responsibility and a realization that the adversary aspects of the operation are part of a larger collaborative undertaking. The primary task of the arbitrator is to induce this attitude of mind and spirit, though to be sure, he does this primarily by helping the parties to perceive the concrete ways in which this shared attitude can redound to their mutual benefit.

It should also be noted that the benefits of a collective bargaining agreement do not lie simply in the aptness of the numbered paragraphs that appear over the parties' signatures, but derive also from the mutual understanding produced by the process of negotiation itself. I once heard an experienced and perceptive lawyer observe, speaking of complex business agreements, "If you negotiate the contract thoroughly, explore carefully the problems that can arise in the course of its administration, work out the proper language to cover the various contingencies that may develop, you can then put the contract in a drawer and forget it." What he meant was that in the exchange that accompanied the negotiation and drafting of the contract the parties would come to understand each other's problems sufficiently so that when difficulties arose they would, as fair and reasonable men, be able to make the appropriate adjustments without referring to the contract itself.

Certainly this beneficial by-product of carefully conducted negotiations is present in some measure in the case of the collective bargaining agreement. At the same time, it should be noted that the contractual relations between a labor union and an employer are not like a business deal where the relationship is scheduled for liquidation so soon as the reciprocal performances have been rendered. I have suggested that in one aspect the collective bargaining agreement is like a constitution; it must serve as a charter of government, if not for "generations as yet unborn," at least for a period that will in all likelihood extend beyond changes in the personnel administering the agreement. Since those who may have to administer the contract will not have had a chance to participate in the unverbalized understandings and expectations that went into its construction, I suggested that the mediator might usefully bring the perspective of "the generalized other" to the task of drafting the instrument. In this connection it should be observed that it may, paradoxically, sometimes be fortunate if disputes arise promptly under the new contract so that they may be resolved by those who participated in the negotiation of it and shared the perceptions that went into, and at the same time came out of, that process.

V

It is time now to bring mediation into some closer relation with the order-producing and order-restoring processes of society as a whole and in particular with those of state-made law. Some paragraphs back I spoke of the "central quality of mediation, namely, its capacity to reorient the parties toward each other, not by imposing rules on them, but by helping them to achieve a new and shared perception of their relationship, a perception that will redirect their attitudes and dispositions toward one another." This suggests a certain antithesis between mediational processes, on the one hand, and the standard procedures of law, on the other, for surely central to the very notion of law is the concept of *rules*.

Insofar as our concern is with the problem of bringing laws into existence, this "antithesis" presents no difficulty at all. It is a commonplace of democratic government that statutes quite generally express some measure of compromise between opposing points of view. Individual legislators often find themselves, at times with some reluctance, cast in the essential mediative role that will effect this compromise. The crucial problem arises when we ask, not what role mediation should play in creating law, but how far and in what respects should it enter into the administration of laws. A general answer to this question is easy: once a law has been duly enacted its interpretation and enforcement is for the courts; courts have been instituted, not to mediate disputes, but to decide them.

It is not difficult to see why, under a system of state-made law, the standard instrument of dispute settlement should be adjudication and not mediation. If the question is whether *A* drove through a red light, or has paid his grocery bill, or has properly reported his earnings to Internal Revenue, even the most ardent advocate of conciliative procedures would hardly recommend mediation as the standard way of dealing with such problems. A pervasive use of mediation could here obliterate the essential guideposts and boundary markers men need in orienting their actions toward one another and could end by producing a situation in which no one could know precisely where he stood or how he might get where he wanted to be. As between black and white, gray may sometimes seem an acceptable compromise, but there are circumstances in which it is essential to work hard toward keeping things black and white. Maintaining a legal system in functioning order is one of those occasions.

It is, then, not in the making of legal rules, but in their enforcement and administration that a certain incompatibility may be perceived between mediative procedures and "the rule of law." We may express something of the nature of this incompatibility by saying that, whereas mediation is directed toward *persons*, judgments of law are directed toward *acts*; it is acts, not people, that are declared proper or improper under the relevant provisions of law. This distinction is not quite so simple as it seems on the surface, for there are routine occasions within the operations of a legal system when judgment must be passed on persons. This necessity arises, for example, when a court must decide whether a convicted criminal should be admitted to probation or when a judge must determine which of two contesting parents should be given custody of a child. But in its core operations, in deciding, for example, whether a man has committed a crime or broken a contract, the standards of legal judgment are derived from rules defining the consequences of specific acts or failures to act; these rules do not attempt or invite any general appraisal of the qualities or dispositions of the person, exception being made, of course, for cases where the problem of legal accountability is raised, as when the defense if insanity is pleaded.[9]

The distinction just taken has been blurred in modern sociology by the indiscriminate use of the term "social norm." This expression seems to be so used as to embrace indifferently, on the one hand, rules attributing legal or social consequences to overt and specifically defined acts, and, on the other, precepts eliciting dispositions of the person, including a willingness to respond to somewhat shifting and indefinite "role expectations." The word "norm" seems, indeed, to owe its popularity precisely to the circumstance that it lifts from the user the responsibility for making any such distinction. Complex and difficult as taking this distinction may in some contexts become, it is vitally important to keep it in mind in any inquiry directed toward discerning the limits of the effectiveness of "law," or toward defining the proper place and function of the various forms of social ordering, including mediation.

With reference to the uncertainties of our conventional vocabulary, I should also remark that there is a considerable ambiguity in the word "rule" itself. The Golden Rule is a magnificent expression of principle, but the "rule" that one should do unto others as one would be done by could hardly serve as a statutory injunction to be applied by courts. When in the remainder of this essay I speak of rules I shall have in mind rules requiring, prohibiting, or attaching specific consequences to acts. Such rules are characteristic of enacted law; they are even more characteristic of what may be called contractual law, that is, of the legal regulation of the parties' relationship achieved through a contract. Though we do not speak of the "rules" contained in a contract, it is clear that contracts typically prescribe acts or performances, not resolutions of the will or dispositions of the spirit. Both

9. I have attempted some analysis of the person-act distinction in *Two Principles of Human Association*, 11 NOMOS (VOLUNTARY ASSOCIATIONS) 3, 17-19 (1969); and in *Human Interaction and the Law*, 14 AM. J. JURIS. 1, 34-36 (1969).

the laws of the state and the requirements of a contract characteristically represent rules that may be called "act-oriented."

In seeking now to delineate, within the processes of society as a whole, the proper domain of mediation, I suggest that we may usefully apply two tests; the first of these tells us when mediation *should not* be used, the second tells us when it *cannot* be used. The two tests are as follows: *First,* is the underlying relationship such that it is best organized by impersonal act-oriented rules? If so, then mediation will generally be out of place except as it is employed to create or modify rules. *Second,* is the problem presented amenable to solution through mediational processes? Mediation is itself subject to intrinsic limitations; I have discerned two of these: (1) it cannot generally be employed when more than two parties are involved; (2) it presupposes an intermeshing of interests of an intensity sufficient to make the parties willing to collaborate in the mediational effort.

In attempting an appraisal of the role of mediation in the total processes of society the most appropriate starting place is, I believe, offered by the institution of marriage. As I have already suggested, mediation has always played, and seems now to be playing an increasing role in the ironing out of marital difficulties. There is no mystery in this, for by the tests proposed here marital problems qualify on all counts for mediational solution. Marriage is, with us, a dyadic relation—one hesitates to think what it would be like to mediate the tangled affairs of a harem! The deterrents to separation or divorce, with the material and emotional costs either would entail, are generally sufficient to make the parties willing to collaborate in the mediational effort. Finally, the internal affairs of the marriage have generally been thought to be inappropriate material for regulation by a regime of formal act-oriented rules, whether imposed by law or by contract. There are, for example, no laws in the books prescribing which spouse is responsible for helping the children with their school work or allocating between husband and wife the right to invite their respective relatives to make weekend visits. In the few cases that have come to court where the spouses have attempted some contractual apportionment of rights and duties within the marriage relationship the courts have generally refused to lend their powers of enforcement to such agreements.[10]

10. Miller v. Miller, 78 Iowa 177, 42 N.W. 641 (1889); Graham v. Graham, 33 F. Supp. 936, 938 (E. D. Mich., 1940); Foote, Levy & Sander, Cases and Materials on Family Law 297-366 (1966); Note, *Litigation Between Husband and Wife,* 79 Harv. L. Rev. 1650 (1966).

The inappropriateness of formal, act-oriented rules as a means of organizing the internal affairs of a marriage can be rested on two grounds: *first*, that a "legalistic" conception of the relationship would be destructive of the spirit of mutual trust and confidence essential for the success of a marriage; *second*, that the shifting contingencies of married life—illness, pregnancy, loss of a job, the necessity for housing an indigent relative, etc.—would require reading so many tacit exceptions into the rules that they would, in any event, forfeit their efficacy as an organizing principle of the relationship. In refusing to enforce contracts between husband and wife regulating the details of their internal relationship, the courts have understandably had some difficulty in explaining just why such contracts should not be legally enforceable. The best one court could do was to say that "judicial inquiry into matters of that character, between husband and wife, would be fraught with irreparable mischief, and [is] forbidden by sound considerations of public policy."[11]

Recently there seems to have developed among students of marriage a greater inclination to approve an explicitly contractual organization of the relationship.[12] One physician has, indeed, recently proposed a kind of model contract to be entered before the marital vows are taken.[13] It includes a provision for three bank accounts: "a joint checking account for the payment of household bills and expenses, and a savings account for the husband and one for the wife." (One is tempted to ask, if the husband drinks and the wife does not, is a supply of liquor and a cocktail shaker a "household expense?") There are other provisions about the religion in which the children are to be reared, custody of children in the event of separation, etc. The contract makes no explicit provision for mediation except to state that when difficulties develop the parties will seek "counselling." On the other hand, the agreement expressly provides that when "a dispute arises that defies mutual solution, both parties agree to subject it to com-

---

11. Miller v. Miller, 78 Iowa 177, 182, 42 N.W. 641, 642 (1889).

12. McDowell, *Contracts in the Family*, 45 Boston U. L. Rev. 43 (1965).

13. Javert, *Guidelines for a Marriage Contract*, Trial Magazine, Dec.-Jan. 1967-1968, at 46-47. For a more extreme proposal, *see* Schulman, *A Marriage Agreement*, 1 Up From Under 5-8 (1970). The recommended contract contains a detailed apportionment of household duties between husband and wife; the following extract illustrates the general tenor of the document: "8. Cooking: Wife does all dinners except Sunday nights; husband does all weekend breakfasts (including shopping for them and dishes), Sunday dinner, and any other dinners on his nights of responsibility if wife isn't home. Breakfasts are divided week by week. Whoever invites the guests does shopping, cooking, and dishes; if both invite them, split work."

petent arbitration and to abide by the decision of the arbitrators." The references to "arbitrators" in the plural suggests an arbitrational board, truly a formidable (and expensive!) way of bringing the relationship of husband and wife within the Rule of Law. Whether a general adoption of this conception would for the first time elevate the marital relationship to a level worthy of human dignity or would, in the language of the Iowa Supreme Court, "be fraught with irreparable mischief," is something that perhaps only experience can answer.[14]

A recent general reform in the law of divorce deserves brief mention here. It reveals with unusual clarity the tensions that can develop between the act-oriented perspective characteristic of legal processes and the person-orientation implicit in mediation. Though, as we have just observed, the marital relationship itself has generally been regarded as unsuited to regulation by act-oriented rules, the dissolution of marriage by divorce was, until recently, entirely dominated by the conventional legal approach; to secure a divorce the petitioning party had to prove the commission of a "marital offense" by the other spouse. The most obvious of such offenses was, of course, the act of adultery. Then, following an irregular pattern, different jurisdictions gradually began expanding the list of marital offenses in directions that tended to compromise its original act-orientation. The not-easily-defined act of mental cruelty might be added. Again, separation for a specified period of time, say, five years, was in some jurisdictions made of itself, and without regard to fault, a ground for divorce.

It is not necessary to describe here the hypocrisies and abuses that have developed out of this system; even when the only ground for divorce has been the act of adultery, the required act, when both parties wanted a divorce, might be feigned and proved in court by perjured testimony. As a cure for this and numerous other evils, the reform in question has introduced the concept of "a complete and permanent breakdown of the marriage." In some jurisdictions this has been added to the conventional "marital offenses" as a ground for divorce; in others it has been made the sole basis for granting a divorce. This reform does not mean, in theory at least, that the parties can get a divorce simply by mutual consent; even if both declare that they wish a divorce they must convince the court that their marriage has in fact suffered "a complete and permanent breakdown." One asks at once, how does a judge go about deciding a question like

14. Miller v. Miller, 78 Iowa 177, 182, 42 N.W. 641, 642 (1889).

that? What evidentiary proof will suffice to demonstrate that a given marriage has in fact broken down irretrievably?

Fortunately we now have a perceptive sociological study of the actual functioning of the new system as it operates in Poland.[15] It appears that if both parties want a divorce it is extremely difficult for the judge to penetrate behind their own self-serving declarations that their marriage has broken down. It would seem that the most logical way of going about deciding this issue would be to attempt reconciliation; if the parties do not succumb to skillful mediational efforts then it may be accepted that the marriage has indeed broken down. In a machine shop if the question arose whether a particular machine had broken down so completely that it ought to be consigned to the junkyard, one would certainly answer that question by asking a competent mechanic whether he could put it back in running condition; there would indeed be no other way of testing the matter. It appears that under Polish law the test of the breakdown of the marriage is not explicitly made its unamenability to conciliation. In fact, however, the courts commonly make repeated efforts during the divorce proceedings to accomplish a reconciliation, and it seems inevitable that they should take a failure in these efforts as the primary proof of the irremediable character of the "breakdown."

What purports to be a finding of objective fact, that the marriage has broken down beyond repair, involves in fact a judgment of persons. Insofar as inquiry is directed toward finding out whether the two spouses are personally compatible, this is wholly in keeping with the spirit of the new law. But there is a third person involved, the judge himself. Górecki's study found that there was a very considerable difference in mediational skill among the judges of the divorce courts; a "factual" finding that the marriage is beyond repair may in reality reflect incapacities in the judicial mechanic attempting the repairs.

Experience in Poland has demonstrated that the new conception of divorce has by no means abolished the hypocrisies and abuses surrounding the old conception of "the marital offense." It appears that where both spouses want a divorce they may plead and attempt to prove a breakdown of their marriage for a great variety of reasons. In the reported experiences of attorneys their clients "had claimed and obtained divorce in order to get a better flat, to escape the liability for the other spouse's debts, to retain a professional position endangered

15. J. Górecki, Divorce in Poland (1970).

by an offense committed by the other spouse."[16] In one case the parties to a very happy marriage obtained a divorce so that the husband could get a visa to a foreign country where the wife planned later to join him.[17]

What has just been reported in no way represents any attempt to suggest that the reform in question was a mistake, or that the absurdities and abuses of the new system are any worse than those of the old. I have simply tried to suggest that in solving problems in the design of social institutions, as in those of engineering, compromises sometimes have to be made and that every advantage is likely to carry some cost. Unlike engineering, however, legal sociology, with its heavy orientation toward law as a simple exercise of "authority," has devoted little attention to the problems of institutional design or to a comparison of the pros and cons of rival processes of social ordering.

Resuming our more general inquiry into the proper place and function of mediation in the processes of society as a whole I should like to turn now to a subject that may seem remote from any we have so far considered. I refer to the problem of allocating scarce irrigation waters among competing uses.[18]

We are dealing, let us say, with a system of canals supplying perhaps a hundred different farmers with the water essential for growing their crops. The situation is one typical of areas where irrigation is necessary, that is, the available supply of water will fluctuate from year to year and even from week to week. During acute shortages an even distribution of water might result in a total failure of everyone's crop. In such an emergency, and in others less drastic, some decision has to be made as to how a vital resource shall be allocated among competing needs that exceed the available supply. The responsibility for making this allocation is generally placed in the hands of an official known as the watermaster. Can his decisions be brought within "the rule of law?" Is it possible to lay down in advance impersonal, act-prescribing rules that will determine just how much water each farmer shall receive? The answer is plain; no such system is possible.

In discussing the internal ordering of the family I spoke of the "shifting contingencies" of married life as precluding any regime

16. *Id.* at 56.

17. *Id.* at 55.

18. In what follows I am drawing on sources cited in my article, *Irrigation and Tyranny*, 17 STAN. L. REV. 1021 (1965).

wholly founded on fixed rules of duty and entitlement. The unpredictable dislocations to which the management of the household is subject are fully matched or exceeded by those affecting an agricultural system based on irrigation. The ability of the farmer to produce a satisfactory crop is not only dependent on the availability of canal water at the right time and in the right amount, but also on local conditions of rainfall, heat, light, wind and atmospheric humidity, and on the balance of these factors as between night and day. Then there are the possible destructive effects of insect invasions and plant diseases. All of these factors may enter into the watermaster's decision. It would be foolish, for example, to give scarce water to a farmer whose crop will be destroyed by insects that have already begun their invasion; it would be equally foolish to save a crop if the same crop has in nearby areas come on in such abundance that there is no market for it and it lies unharvested in the fields. Typically the consideration of factors like these will be complicated by uncertainties that require a weighing of probabilities. The watermaster may also confront difficult and embarrassing questions of judging the person. One farmer can manage emergencies better than his neighbor; is that a reason for favoring the neighbor because he is handicapped or should his lack of expertise be a ground for denying him water? Again, another farmer notoriously tends to get drunk when a drought threatens his crop; during his conversation with the watermaster he seems already a bit tipsy. Should he be denied water because if he becomes drunk (as it now seems very likely he will) his condition will prevent him from operating effectively the system of ditches that serve to distribute the water over his land?

The problems involved in allocating irrigation waters are, then, not even remotely suited to solution through a regime of impersonal, act-oriented rules. Can these problems be solved by mediation? Plainly not. An irrigation system serving only two farmers would be a thing virtually unheard of ; the number competing for the scarce supply may run into hundreds. Even if we were to assume that the users of the system formed a dyad, any mediational efforts between them would be unassisted by any felt sense of interdependence; far from standing in a relation of bilateral monopoly, they would be caught in a locked-in relationship of diametrically opposed interests. Where there are two farmers and only enough water for one of them, a solution in the mood of "game theory" might suggest itself—let them toss for it to see who gets the water; let the resulting crop be divided between them. Even this sort of solution, which is hardly "mediative" in any usual sense, could scarcely be extended beyond a quite small number.

Despite what has just been said one encounters in the literature references to the use of "mediation" in dealing with problems of irrigation, though generally without any indication of the kind of problems involved or the mode of their solution. Why is it that "mediative" procedures should thus have been associated with problems of irrigation? I think this association becomes understandable when we consider how a conscientious watermaster would view the nature of his responsibilities. The discharge of his duties requires not simply an inspection of the farmer's fields; it requires active consultation with the farmer himself as to his needs, plans and wishes. The watermaster cannot just look at a crop and decide for himself how long it can go without water; the ability to withstand drought depends on the nature of the crop and the peculiarities of its location; these are matters likely to be better known to the farmer than to the watermaster. Furthermore, it may be desirable to give the farmer options and let him choose the one he considers most suited to his situation. The watermaster might ask the farmer, for example, whether he would rather be given today a certain amount of water or wait a week when there is a two-to-one chance he can be alloted twice as much.

In his relations with the persons affected by his decisions the watermaster occupies a role quite different from that, say, of the sanitary inspector, who has rules to enforce and can generally see for himself whether they are being observed. The "mediational" aspect of the watermaster's task lies in the fact that, though he issues administrative orders, those orders are informed and directed by consultation with the man whose interests are at stake. The official whose task it is to divide the waters seeks to accomplish this division, insofar as the relevant limitations permit, in a way that will suit the needs of the individual farmer as those needs are perceived by the farmer himself.

I suggest that in our modern society, where individual interests are becoming every day more interwoven and interdependent, we are witnessing a drastic increase in problems that resemble closely those of administering an irrigation system. Consider, for example, the numerous similarities between that undertaking and the administrative task of dispensing scarce public welfare funds to those most in need of them. Or consider the problem of the crowded public hospital which has to allocate, not utilities, but disutilities, when it has to ask a certain number of its patients, not yet entirely well, but on the mend, to give up their beds and go home to make room for patients more seriously ill. The discharge of responsibilities that cut as deeply into human lives as these certainly needs to be at least "mediative" (that is, as open-mindedly consultative) as those of the man who apportions scarce waters.

The standard American solution for problems of the sort just suggested is to move toward "judicializing" or "legalizing"[19] the administrative tasks they involve.[20] The obvious cost of this expedient is that it reduces inevitably the consultative and mediative elements in the operation. To say that "the law is no respecter of persons" can, not unreasonably, be construed to mean that those exercising powers conferred by law need not bother to consult the preferences of persons and, indeed, that there would be some impropriety in doing so. This construction is likely to be especially appealing to the overburdened bureaucrat, who will find his task easier if he can confute those who press their special needs on him simply by saying, "Sorry, I have to follow the rules."

VI

At an early point in this essay I spoke of the possible implications of the analysis it presents for primitive systems of law. I believe that the three models of mediation offered her—the mediation of a collective bargaining agreement, marriage "therapy," and the consultative aspects of the watermaster's task—all have analogues in societies that would be called "primitive."

Perhaps the aspect of mediation discussed here which seems most remote from early forms of social ordering is that I have described as an adjustment of interests designed to obtain optimum "pay-offs" for the participants. Yet Malinowski discerned in the principle of reciprocity a fundamental aspect of the ordering systems of "savage societies."[21] If he had in mind an explicit trade in which one party withholds his contribution until an opposite number has promised some reciprocal benefit, he would seem to be contradicted by his own report of relationships among the Trobriand Islanders. But we must remember that the silent slowdown is a more ancient phenomenon then the openly declared strike and that tacit contracting and trading

19. "le-gal-ize . . . 2. to interpret or apply in a legalistic spirit (you persist to legalize the gospel—J. W. Fletcher)." WEBSTER'S THIRD NEW INTERNATIONAL DICTIONARY (1966).

20. A perceptive sociological study of the gradual "legalization" of the functions of the California Industrial Accident Commission will be found in P. NONET, ADMINISTRATIVE JUSTICE (1969).

21. B. MALINOWSKI, CRIME AND CUSTOM IN SAVAGE SOCIETY (1926).

were known and practiced centuries before the explicit verbal contract was perceived as an available expedient for arranging human affairs.

If we were to distinguish broadly among the various processes that contribute to social ordering we might discern six: legislation, adjudication, administrative direction, mediation, contractual agreement, and customary "law"—it being recalled of the last of these that it is often the intended product of a relegation of emergent issues to the tacit accommodations foreseen as developing out of future interactions. Even in modern societies these forms are interrelated in various complex ways and at times tend to shade into one another. In primitive society, I would suggest, they appear in still more mixed and muted forms; generally any scruple about blending or mixing them seems to be absent, perhaps because they are simply not perceived as separate processes.

Something of the ambiguity of the social processes by which primitive societies are ordered is suggested in Barton's famous study of the Ifugao *monkalun* or "go-between." Barton refers to the parties who invoke the *monkalun's* office as "litigants"; the services rendered by the *monkalun* himself are described as follows:

> The office of the *monkalun* is the most important one to be found in Ifugao society. The *monkalun* is a whole court, completely equipped, in embryo. He is judge, prosecuting and defending counsel, and the court record. His duty and his interest are for a peaceful settlement . . . To the end of peaceful settlement he exhausts every art of Ifugao diplomacy. He wheedles, coaxes, flatters, threatens, drives, scolds, insinuates . . . The *monkalun* has no authority. All he can do is to act as a peace making go-between. His only power is in his art of persuasion, his tact and his skillful playing on human emotions and motives.[22]

What appear to us as hopelessly confusing ambiguities of role were probably not perceived as such either by the occupant of the role or by those subject to his ministrations. In analysing the social processes of primitive societies this often makes it an exercise in futility, as Gluckman has cogently observed, to try to sort out those processes that deserve to be called "law."[23]

---

22. R. BARTON, IFUGAO LAW 87 (1969). (The first edition of this work was published in 1919.)

23. M. GLUCKMAN, POLITICS, LAW AND RITUAL IN TRIBAL SOCIETY 211-216 (1965). Henderson's study of the history of conciliation in Japanese law is instructive for its

One might have been inclined to assume that as, in the course of history, the various forms of social ordering and dispute-settlement became separated in practice, they would become the subject of an earnest discussion among scholars as to their distinctive functions and their most appropriate applications. Instead of this, however, we find the substitution of one simplifying obfuscation for another. Now the tendency is to convert every form of social ordering into an exercise of the authority of the state, or, among sociologists, into a projection of "norms" by an abstract entity called "society." Legislation, adjudication, and administrative direction, instead of being perceived as distinctive interactional processes, are all seen as unidirectional exercises of state power. Contract is perceived, not as a source of "law" or social ordering in itself, but as something that derives its whole significance from the fact that the courts of the state stand ready to enforce it. Custom is passed over in virtually complete silence by sociologists and is viewed by legal scholars as becoming worthy of attention only when it has been recognized by the courts and thus been converted into "law." Only mediation seems to resist this tendency to subsume every kind of ordering under the rubric of "power" or "authority." Perhaps the attempt made in this essay—tentative and imperfect as it is—to analyse the forms and functions of mediation may help in some small measure to stimulate a more general interest in the analysis and comparison of the competing forms of social ordering.

---

analysis of the way in which roles familiar to us were combined and intermixed in Japan. D. HENDERSON, CONCILIATION AND JAPANESE LAW—TOKUGAWA AND MODERN (no date, *circa* 1966). *See*, especially, Chapter III, *The Tokugawa Concept of Law and the Role of Law in Tokugawa Society*, at 47-62.

[6]

Competition and dissensus: two types of conflict and of conflict resolution

VILHELM AUBERT
University of Oslo and Institute for Social Research, Oslo, Norway

The present paper sets out to develop a simple typology of interpersonal conflicts. The evolving scheme of classification is based upon sources of conflicts as well as upon the modes of their settlement. Some systematic relationships between sources of conflicts and their settlements are suggested. Certain sources of conflict may tend to call forth a certain type of mechanism for conflict resolution, but the form of the conflict may also frequently be determined by the available means of solution.

On the basis of such considerations an attempt will be made to describe the essentials of the legal method in conflict resolution. Law will be described in terms of a specific way of perceiving the participants in a conflict and the relationship between them. At the same time it will be shown how the legal approach to conflict resolution is accompanied by, and springs out of, certain simple numerical arrangements of actors. The basic event from this point of view is the transition from the dyad of the conflicting parties to the triad, where an intermediary who stands outside the original conflict has been added to the dyad. The position of the third person and the choices which are open to him furnish the most fruitful starting point for an analysis of the development of conflict resolution within law.

Conflict

The term *conflict* is ambiguous. It is applied to neural processes, to internal psychic states and to individual choice of action (Murphy, 1947, pp. 296 ff.). The conflicts with which we are concerned are those which may obtain between individuals or groups. Even so the usage of the concept oscillates between various referents. It seems fruitful to distinguish between three concepts basic to an understanding of conflicts. They refer to various stages in the development of conflicts and of their settlement. The starting point must be sought in a state existing between two (or more) individuals characterized by some overt signs of antagonism. The term conflict will here be reserved for this state of tension between two actors irrespective of how it has originated and how it is terminated. A more precise definition of this state of tension is hard to achieve. As a minimum, it must be demanded that at least one of the actors, in words or action, gives expression to a motive to frustrate Alter, or that he actually frustrates him. Thus, a state characterized by Ego's futile attempts to frustrate Alter, may be called a conflict, although Alter may suffer no loss, real or perceived. On the other hand, a state characterized by Ego's unintended actions contrary to Alter's interests, may be termed a conflict although Ego feels no aggression and no wish to harm Alter. The explanation of such types of conflicts may obviously be very different, and the modes of solution appropriate to each one of them may vary. But this seems no valid reason why any one of them should be given precedence in the definition of conflict itself. The definition of conflict should be true to the troubles people actually experience in their relationships, and thus be wide enough to cover the most common empirical cases.

For the present purposes it does not seem germane to attempt a further specification of what types of frustrations and what kinds of hostility may constitute a conflict. What is important is to distinguish between this state of conflict and its basis. By the *basis of conflict* is meant the condition of the system which has led to the overt signs of hostility or to the objectively frustrating deeds or words. Much confusion, e.g., in the discussions of class conflicts, is due to a failure to distinguish between the actual state of hostility and its underlying conditions (Dahrendorf, 1959). Now, a restriction has already been placed upon our concern with the antecedents of conflicts, when we define the basis of conflict as a condition prevailing in the conflict-ridden system itself. Obviously, the search for causes of conflicts may lead to the location of factors in one of the participants long before he became a member of this conflict-system. Or, the causes may be sought in natural conditions of resources completely outside the control of the individuals in conflict, or in the historical processes, etc. Here, however, by the *basis of conflict,* we mean a condition which must be described as a state of the system of interacting individuals. It might also be termed the *conflict potential.*

A state of hostility and/or inflicted frustration between two individuals does not only have antecedents, it also has an aftermath. It is often solved, and at least terminated. It is no simple matter to single out those modes of termination which can be termed settlements or solutions (Coser, 1962). We are not particularly interested in those endings to conflicts which are due to death or the passing of time. As *modes of resolving conflicts* will be considered only those ways of channelizing conflicts which result in reduction of expressed hostility and/or inflicted frustration. It seems necessary to emphasize, however, that the concept of conflict resolution should be kept so wide as to include also settlements which seem unjust, unstable, or in violation of other goals more important than avoidance of the strife in question. It seems that conflicts characteristically develop into certain more or less institutionalized forms, which often, but not necessarily lead to reduction of tension. A classification of these modes of conflict resolution, and their relationship to the bases of conflicts, will be a main concern in the present analysis.

Conflicts of Interest

Two kinds of conflict are readily distinguished in terms of their bases, the conflict of interest and the conflict of values or belief, although the classification of concrete cases as belonging either to the one or to the other, may be different or impossible. A conflict of interest between two actors stems from a situation of scarcity. Both A and E want "the same thing," but there is not enough of it available for each to have what he wants. In this general sense the basis for a conflict is present in all trading transactions. The seller would like to have more money than the buyer is willing to part with, or he would like to withhold a quantity of the produce which the buyer wants to acquire. This conflict potential is eliminated through the operation of the market, usually so smoothly that no overt signs of conflict appear. If a conflict comes into the open, the solution will often be a compromise. Each party concedes to reduce his demands until an agreement is reached, although possibly still believing that he is contributing too much. This agreement is, therefore, not to be interpreted as an ethical commitment to the price as an expression of the just terms of exchange. It is merely to be interpreted as an expression of what A or E, under the given market conditions, find it in their own interests to do.

The opposing interests have been brought together because of a wish to minimize the likelihood of maximal loss on both sides. For the buyer not to buy at all, and for the seller not to sell at all, is often the gravest contingency, at least under modern conditions. Therefore they will be prepared to make considerable compromises, relative to their own real preferences. More important, they will compromise with what they consider to be the just terms of exchange. It is a type of social interaction in which it seems that solutions are reached by discouraging the actors from getting morally involved in a major aspect of the interaction, the condition being that the interests are not diametrically opposed. The gain of one party is not wholly a loss to the other.

The possibilities for avoiding conflicts through this method are sharply reduced when new and destructive incidents occur in the relationship. If the supply of the contribution which one of the parties was to yield disappears after the interaction has begun, but before the exchange is completed, a conflict may arise. Let us say that a car dealer has placed a sold car, locked, at the curb outside the house of the buyer, but that the car has vanished before the buyer comes home. Is he still to pay for the car or not? In such a case, and in the absence of law, one party would have no interest in making any compromises at all. There is no longer anything he can achieve from the other party. His gain would be the other party's loss. Since he cannot get any contribution from Alter in the future, he is unconcerned with trying to motivate his behavior, and is interested solely in terminating the interaction. Were there no law and no force in society, the person who wanted to terminate the interaction would have all the cards in his hand in situations where transactions had gone wrong, and there was no longer a question of sharing goods, but of sharing losses. Society, however, has been unwilling to accept that in the case of mishaps of this kind, the sheer accident of who physically possesses the undestroyed part of the exchange should always determine the solution of the conflict of interest over the sharing of a loss.

The way in which society, through law, solves conflicts of interest is such that the parties will often find it advantageous to go on with a negotiation in a spirit of compromise. The legal solution, in common with the solution which accident, fate, or ill will may give to a transaction, tends to ignore the minimax principle and gives all to one party. But it is typical of many such cases that although one of the parties may stand to gain by rejecting compromise, it is uncertain which party it will be. Therefore the one who wants to be *sure* that he will not lose everything, will also make some compromise in conflicts of this kind where something has gone wrong, thus preventing that *both* sides may change the situation to their advantage. We shall deal later with the problem of why legal solutions have this all-or-none character, and why it is that some people prefer such solutions in spite of the strong reasons for avoiding maximum loss. The first problem is the question of why we have courts, and the second, why anyone should want to make use of them.

Dissensus

Competing or contrasting interest does not in itself imply any disagreement between

Ego and Alter concerning values. It may even be claimed that a conflict of interest presupposes a consensus, at least on the value of the good which is sought after by both parties. Let us assume that the object of the interest conflict is a position of leadership or superior rank within a group. Such a conflict can arise only if the contestants agree that incumbency of the position has value. The case of sexual rivalry may be even more to the point. Often the area of consensus is sharply limited. But its very presence as a condition of any interest conflict is significant, as it does, paradoxically, draw together the conflicting parties. In this sense a conflict of interest is less fundamental than certain conflicts of values, which may amount to mutual denial of membership in the human race. Interest conflicts emphasize the similarity of the contestants, their common needs and aspirations. In this lies, no doubt, one reason why politicians who compete fiercely with each other for office nevertheless often get along very well. It seems as if this particular kind of inverse interplay between interest conflict and value conflict serves as a major brake on the outward and destructive manifestations of both kinds of conflict. For it also works the other way around. A profound conflict of values will tend to keep the antagonists apart. They do not value the same things and tend therefore to encounter each other less frequently than would otherwise have been the case.

A conflict of value is based upon a dissensus concerning the normative status of a social object. In itself there is nothing about a dissensus that should lead individuals to attack each other. Nevertheless there is no doubt that disagreements over values as well as over facts have often contributed to overt and aggressive conflict behavior, most blatantly in religious and ideological wars. Such conflict behavior, however, seems almost always to be accompanied by some conflict of interest which derives from the scarcity of power and authority.

One may raise the question whether conflicts of values can be avoided in the same fashion as interest conflicts, e.g., by compromise and mutual resignation relative to what seems the ideal solution. It is no doubt possible to formulate statements that contain some elements from one system of values or description and some from another. Such compromises are frequently reached in negotiations between organizations who want to substitute cooperation for competition. The terms of exchange are, however, very uncertain in such dealings. A scent of the illicit often pervades such dealings: "one cannot trade in values," "ideas are not for sale," "no bargain with the truth," etc. This illicit nature of compromise on the level of value and of empirical truth makes it hard to discuss matters quite candidly, thereby decreasing the chances of reaching a solution. One reason for this, I suppose, is that on the level of dissensus it is hard to tell what is "give" and what is "take." Is the one who gives in on a point of value or fact making a sacrifice or a gain? This is uncertain, because norms are double-edged, making demands upon the self as well as upon others. Consequently it is difficult to measure compromises of value as exchanges of sacrifices and advantages. Neither are those who negotiate on ideological questions supposed to dispose freely of values. There is no private ownership of values. That would contradict their communal origin. The same is the case with respect to scientific truth.

A type of dissensus which often leads to conflict is the one concerned with the application of values and norms. Political feuds often take this form, whatever their ultimate basis may be. A accuses his opponent E of being responsible for a specific policy which has been in opposition to some important value, say full employment. The feud may then take on a factual character, turning around the question of whether E actually was responsible for the policy, or whether the policy actually led to unemployment. But it may also take on a purer ideological character, E admitting his responsibility for some unemployment, but maintaining that this was a price one had to pay for achieving a value with higher priority, increased efficiency and higher production. It is especially when these questions of factual responsibility, of guilt and merit, become parts of value-conflicts, and they usually do, that a solution through compromise becomes so difficult. Whether, and how they can be solved is, of course, also dependent upon the interrelations between the dissensus and the interests of the parties. For the dissension, which appears to be the immediate basis of hostilities, may in its own turn be derived from, or intermingled with, a conflict of interests.

Some Conflict "Careers" Based Upon Competing Interests

Opposition of interests, derived from a shared desire for scarce goods, may develop into a bargain. In that case there may be no reason to speak about a conflict at all. The conflict is avoided because the strategic plans of the two parties coincide at a point at which both consider the exchange desirable from their own points of view. Normative considerations about the just terms of exchange need not intrude, but norms may have entered into their deliberations, for instance in the form of a reference to the market price or to some precedent set in a previous exchange. The parties agree, most often tacitly, that it is reasonable to stick to the market price and disregard more subtle calculations of who stands to gain and to lose by applying the set price. Thus, a normative consensus may further a bargain, and consequently avoidance of conflict, even in situations where bargaining based upon mutual adjustments of needs and plans is perfectly permissible.

Opposing interests do, however, as mentioned above, frequently lead to conflicts because of certain asymmetries in the strategic positions of the adversaries. They may do so with or without the intervention of dissensus over facts or values. The clash of interests may develop into a pure conflict of interests in the sense that the adversaries simply maintain their interests and their unwillingness to compromise, without seeking any justification in normative principles. Thus, two competing shopkeepers may inflict frustrations upon each other, and yet their cognitions and evaluations may be closely similar on all points, the only difference being that the "I" in their respective calculations refers to two different persons. Liberalistic economic ideologies encourage businessmen to feel no hostility in such situations of competition, and discourage attempts to interpret the conflict as a matter of principle, of guilt and merit.

In real life, conflicts of interest may often take a somewhat different course. The opposing interests call forth dissensus over values or dissensus over facts, or both. During such transformations the question of personal antagonistic interests may be forgotten, or at least omitted from the debate, or the debate links the question of interests to normative structures dealing with distributive justice. In many cases the conflict becomes harder to solve when a strong dissensus has been expressed. As we shall soon see, however, the expression of dissensus may also open up for mechanisms of conflict resolution inapplicable to "pure" conflicts of interests. To put it very simply: As long as a conflict of interest remains relatively pure, it is amenable to solutions through bargaining and compromise, on the condition that there is something to give and something to take on both sides. (This condition need not always be fulfilled, however.) When a clash of interests has become associated with a dissensus, bargaining and compromise may be harder to achieve, while the conflict has, on the other hand, become amenable to a solution through the intervention of law in the broadest sense.

The development of a dissensus in connection with a clash of interests may be described in two ways, depending upon the stage of the conflict at which the dissensus appears. It may appear at an early stage, early in the sense that the dissensus further aggravates hostilities and frustrations between the contestants. Thus, the development of the dissensus cannot be considered as a part of the mechanism for conflict resolution, but this latter is the case when a pure conflict of interest is brought before a court of law. The adversaries will then be forced by the conflict-solving mechanism to formulate their opposing interests as a dissensus, over facts or law or both. Thus, a dissensus may arise out of opposing interests, either as a consequence of the conflict and hostility or as a consequence of the structure of the conflict-solving mechanism. The former is perhaps the most likely alternative.

In the present scheme of stages in a conflict, from opposing interests via hostilities and frustrations to conflict-terminating mechanisms, bargaining has a dual role. The bargaining which goes on in shops every day cannot be very meaningfully termed conflict-solving mechanisms, although an element of opposing interests is always present. The communality of interests does in such cases normally overshadow the area of possible conflict. Bargaining in shops must properly be viewed as an institutionalized way of exchanging values while *avoiding* conflicts. But, it may also sometimes be justified to talk about bargaining as a way of solving conflicts, namely when the method is applied to a situation where hostility has developed, frustrations have been inflicted, and the communality of interests is less apparent than the antagonism. It is, however, not easy to distinguish clearly between these two stages, neither is it very important to do so in abstract terms.

Some Conflict "Careers" Based Upon Dissensus

Let us now consider the possible developments from an initial dissensus, originally unconnected with competing interests. In a certain sense dissensus, as such, is somewhat less germane to the problem of interpersonal and social conflict than is a clash of interests. Clashing interests derive from a common desire for scarce goods, and therefore draw the competitors closer together, making conflicts more imminent and increasing the need for mechanisms of settlement. There is a centripetal force in conflicts of interest. Dissensus may, however, be largely irrelevant to the problem of conflict and conflict resolution, because it is most often a question of disagreements between people who live in their separate worlds and never meet. Their dissensus will not bring them together; on the contrary, it keeps them apart, thus making conflicts less likely and mechanisms of conflict resolution less relevant. However, the dissenting persons or groups may be brought closer to each other through the operation of other factors, e.g., due to a development of nation-wide or even world-wide communications. This has raised the existence of vast cultural dissensions to a significance for world peace which was previously unheard of.

As a pure dissensus we can consider a situation where the adversaries have no other interests to defend than to keep the essentials of their own system of values and cognition intact. If the adversaries don't meet as a consequence of factors irrelevant to their disagreement, this modest interest will not lead them into a conflict. If they are in communication, however, being members of the same community, or meeting for some other reason, dissensus will very easily lead to attack, hostility, and frustration. An agreement to disagree is possible, but represents a marginal case with various approximations. To defend one's own values or beliefs without attacking, or throwing doubt upon those of others with differing views, is well nigh impossible.

Under what conditions a debate between disagreeing partners becomes a conflict is very hard to determine in general terms. For our present purposes it does not seem necessary to make a decision with respect to this problem. What concerns us here is (a) how dissensus may lead to conflicts of interest, and (b) how conflicts arising out of a dissensus may be solved.

When people hold strong convictions, religious, moral, political or even scientific, they often want to convert others into true believers. The reason why they want to do so may often be connected with other kinds of interests. Thus, a dissensus over religion may appear to cause crusades and religious wars, although a closer scrutiny may reveal that this had probably not happened unless there had been some clash of interests underlying the strife. For the moment this kind of relationship between dissensus and interest conflict will be disregarded, as it has been implicitly dealt with above. Another type of relationship between dissensus and interests will concern us here. It seems, namely, that if two adversaries who disagree strongly, each want to propagate their faith, they will have to compete for scarce goods. Potential true believers may be numerous, but are still limited. Adherents won are, at least potentially, won over from the camp of the adversary. Even more important, the contestants will compete for positions of power and authority. Each side will attempt to achieve control of resources which puts them in a more advantageous position for the propagation of their beliefs. These resources are scarce, and the competition for them may be fierce. Disagreements with institutional implications seem, especially, to develop into hostility and conflict when they are combined with competition for power.

Such competition may, of course, be viewed as a phenomenon which aggravates a conflict based upon a dissensus. The addition of opposing interests to the dissensus belongs then to the early stages in the evolution of conflicts, but the transformation of a "pure" dissensus to a conflict based upon a mixture of dissensus and competition, may also be seen as a preliminary to a solution of the conflict. It has already been mentioned that bargaining and compromise in a contest over values and truth may often meet with normative obstacles and psychological impediments. Through a transformation into competition for power the road has been paved for compromise solutions, e.g., through a distribution of power positions among ideological opponents in accordance with a principle of representativity. This may be a much more palatable solution than for everybody to subscribe to a compromise formulation combining fragments from all of the competing ideologies. Another question is whether, or under what conditions, a bargain with respect to distribution of power (an aspect of democracy) paves the way for consensus among representatives on a middle of the road ideology.

The Scheme of Analysis

The scheme of analysis which emerges from the considerations advanced above is rather simple. Sources of conflict are classified in two broad categories, dissensus and competing interests. All conflicts in our sense can be traced back to either one or the other, or both of these conditions. The conditions may be present, however, without leading to a conflict in the sense of expressed hostility or inflicted frustration. The presence of dissensus and/or competing interests is a necessary, but not a sufficient, condition for the emergence of conflict. If conflicts move towards a solution they may do so in one of two major ways, through bargaining and compromise and through law and the application of norms to established facts. In a sense the former conflict-solving mechanism presupposes that the conflict is handled as a conflict of interest, while the latter presupposes that it be handled as a dissensus over facts or norms, although the underlying opposition of interests may be fully recognized. Thus, there is a correspondence between the two sources of conflict and the two mechanisms for solution, but we have no reason to assume that the source of the conflict will fully determine the mechanism of solution. It is an empirical problem to discover what sources of conflict lead, and under what additional conditions, to what kinds of conflict-solving mechanisms. Conflicts may be transformed when they pass from the stage of aggravation to the stage of solution, and this may often be dependent upon the availability and effectiveness of the existing apparatus for conflict resolution. But it may also depend upon other factors. The preceding must not be interpreted to exclude the possibility that conflicts may be terminated without the application of any conscious conflict-solving method. Such cases do not particularly interest us, however. But a variety of conflict-solving mechanisms, intermediary between law and bargaining, are of great interest. A market price may solve conflicts in a way reminiscent of law, as may arbitration, while mediation must be considered a modified type of bargaining.

Law as a Conflict-solving Mechanism

I shall now consider the possible transformation of conflicts which occur, or have already occurred, when they are handed over to the law. At the same time certain possible relationships between the nature of legal conflicts and the numerical aspects of the interaction situation will be suggested.

When a conflict of interests is turned over to the law it must from now on be formulated as a dissensus, a conflict of value or belief. It may be that this transformation has already occurred in the heat of the conflict previous to the intervention of lawyers and courts, thus making it insoluble through compromise. But if the transformation has not already occurred it must be effected before the parties can enter into effective litigation. When a conflict turns into a lawsuit and litigation, something else is also bound to happen: The basic interaction situation changes from a dyad to a triad. Between these two transformations there exists some kind of functional relationship. Let us first see what it implies when a contrast of interests is turned into a dissensus. The clash of interests is from now on formulated as a disagreement concerning either certain facts in the past or concerning what norms apply to the existing state of affairs, or both, in a way which often makes it hard to distinguish clearly between questions of fact and questions of law. The needs of the parties, their wishes for the future, cease to be relevant to the solution. Whether the solution harmonizes two contrasting sets of needs and plans for the future is no longer material. The problem has become objectivized in the sense that a solution can be reached by an outsider who knows the rules of evidence and is able to perform logical manipulations within a normative structure. By comparing the available facts with the norms he can reach a verdict. As long as an interest conflict remains pure, no outsider, no third person can, alone, arrive at any conclusion. A solution means a natural adjustment of needs.

The preceding suggests one superiority of law to the market: it permits others and in advance, abstractly to determine how certain conflicts are to be solved. This is what makes it possible in law to combine the function of creating predictability with the function of solving individual conflicts. Under certain conditions the "free market" also does that, but only when the objects of the interest conflicts are replaceable or standardized. Otherwise, a solution of interest conflicts through the reciprocal adjustment of needs is ill suited to serve the need for predictability. Likewise the adjustment mechanism leaves out of consideration the notion that the solution which the parties reach may affect the rest of society.

From the point of view of the contestants, the transformation from a pure conflict of interests to one of values and belief imposes certain restrictions. They are no longer free to disregard the past, to let "the dead ones bury their dead." Questions of law can only be solved through a settlement of guilt, or whether the factual bases of alleged rights or duties actually exist, whether a contract was actually signed, whether it did say what it is claimed to say, etc. In the mutual adjustment of needs in the market the question of what has been said or done previously can be left unsettled if it suits the parties. In such negotiations, furthermore, the parties can often (but not always) disregard the precedent implications of the settlement. There is no necessary implication that it should be interpreted as an application of generally valid rules, applicable to other, similar cases. This obviously gives an amount of freedom which is absent in the typically legal situation. A bargain struck leaves no mark upon the normative order, it is not a consequence of it, nor does it become a constituent part of it. In this lie both its advantages and its disadvantages.

Society often has a stake in what goes on between two conflicting parties, especially when they have reached a point where only one will stand to gain in the future by a change of the *status quo*. This is usually the case after a loss, whether the loss is due to an accident, to fraud or negligence, to inability or to a crime. A bargain may still be struck, but there is also a danger that aggression will make for new losses, including the possibility of murder in revenge. The history of many primitive societies, and also of some civilized ones, shows that such revenge may exact a heavy toll and become the concern of others than the parties involved. As a matter of fact, methods for handling conflicts have evolved so as to ward off such possible outcomes. They usually consist in the institutionalized intervention of some third party in the dispute. In this lies the embryo of the legal phenomena, and the basic happening is that the dyad has become a triad.

From Dyad to Triad

Hoebel has shown how the third person has been introduced in different forms in a number of primitive tribes (Hoebel, 1954). Where law is least developed, this third party is vaguely defined, has little special authority and can only function when invited by the parties to do so. Among the Eskimo it is frequently only the whole community which functions, rather vaguely, as a mediator or "judge." It used to do so, e.g., when acting as audience to the song- and drum-contests which took place between conflicting parties. In some cases a blood-feud was prevented by society's demand that a relative of the murderer should execute the revenge. His overlap in group membership would serve the same function as the intervention of a third party who enjoyed the confidence of both of the conflicting parties. In summary it must be stated, however, that the triadic situation in cases of conflict was very poorly developed in most Eskimo tribes.

Among the Ifugao of Luzon the intervention of third persons in litigation has become more firmly institutionalized. There is no superior governmental agency with independent resources of power and sanctions. The parties to a conflict are required by the norms of society to utilize a go-between, who is not a civil servant, nor a full time expert, nor a judge. But the go-between is an upper-class person with power who may draw upon the resources of his kinfolk in case of need. Normally conflicts would be settled through the go-between's ability to whittle down the claims on both sides, until a basis for peaceful settlement was attained. The reason why this so often succeeded must in no small part have been due to the fact that if one of the parties rejected the procedural norms or was intransigent, he would face an alliance of his opponent and the go-between and their families. This would usually mean having to fight against an overpoweringly strong enemy, and with no practicable road to victory in the suit. Hoebel's analysis of Ifugao Law offers one of the most clear-cut demonstrations of the functions of the triadic arrangements *as such*, because the third person need not be more powerful or differently qualified from the parties to the conflict.

This is no longer true if we follow him to the Cheyenne, where political authority is institutionalized and invested with its own resources of power and sanctions. It belonged to the office of the chief to settle disputes together with the council of headmen. These offices did not constitute specialized judgeships, but comprised diverse functions. It is, however, very clear that the existence of a definitely legal element in the social structure of the Cheyenne was tied to the existence of third persons who would intervene in conflicts, on their own initiative or after being invited to do so.

What must always happen when a third party intervenes in a conflict between two, is that there arises a possibility of an alliance (Simmel, 1950, pp. 135 ff.). Instead of the stalemate 1 to 1, it can now become 2 to 1. One possibility is, of course, that the two original contestants both become antagonistic towards the third person and decide to agree so as not to let the newcomer influence the settlement. This mechanism, bringing conflict partners together in a common antipathy against outside interference, operates in many situations, but mostly where a developed legal or administrative system already exists (Pitt-Rivers, 1961, pp. 160 ff.). For the original crystallization of legal techniques it must have been a more significant eventuality that the newcomer might join one of the parties, thereby creating a definitive overweight in power, and making it unnecessary to compromise with the one found to be in the wrong.

The possibility of an alliance makes it possible, although not necessary or even likely, that the one side will have to carry the total loss involved in the case, that is, conform completely to the demands of the other party. Such will rarely be the outcome when there are only two parties, unless the power differential between them is very great. Usually it takes the participation of a third person to enforce a dichotomous view on the rights and wrongs of the case. Only when one person can be defined as guilty, liable, or responsible, does the settlement take on a clear normative meaning. It becomes something more than the settlement between E and A; it also becomes a demonstration of the validity of a rule of behavior and a statement on past facts.

With the third person the norm of objectivity has been institutionalized, although it may well remain unrealized. When two partners meet and reach a settlement on their conflicting interests they do not necessarily have to (although they may) agree on either norms or facts, but only on the single point in space and time on which their interests converge. The result is subjective in somewhat the same sense as the "I-Thou" encounter in Martin Buber's writings (Buber, 1956, pp. 43 ff.). With the third person the original relationship will almost necessarily become objectified as an It, subsumable under general norms. One reason why it may have to become objectified in this sense, is the great increase in the difficulty of settling the relationships in a triad simply, and without reliance upon general norms. It may be questioned whether the "I-Thou" method of mutually adjusting opposing interests can be extended beyond the dyad. The introduction of a third person may inevitably imply a change of technique for conflict resolution if settlement is to be reached (Caplow, 1956).

Modes of Cognition in the Triad

In a triad each of the participants can look upon the relationship of the other two as an object, something to be described and classified. It is not directly experienced, and nothing can be done about it without some conceptualization. Since we are for the moment considering the general properties of the triad, irrespective of the qualifications and mode of recruitment of the third person, it may be asked why this conceptualization should tend to be normative and not causal or functional. There is probably nothing inherent in the triad to prevent such a mode of perception of others and of the relationship between the others. The two modes of perception, the normative and the causal (Aubert and Messinger, 1958) share the requirement of a general classification of the relationship and a grasp of certain past facts. If the third person, however, is recruited to the triad with the explicit purpose of effecting a settlement between the two original members, there are good reasons why he would soon abandon a causal-functional approach to their problem. To pursue a causal approach would often mean to attempt a "cure" of the relationship, parallel to the one a doctor tries to effect on his patient by removing the cause of his trouble. Some "causes" of an unresolved conflict of interests are easy to perceive, e.g., that one, or both, of the parties are too greedy, too negligent, too lazy. Already these terms indicate that the "curer" of interpersonal conflicts will find it very hard to pursue a causal line of thinking without committing himself to normative judgments. Whenever he looks for causes of interpersonal conflicts, he is likely to find acts which imply responsibility and lie open to evaluation in normative terms.

We have in the cited paper outlined some of the perceptual implications of taking the criminal law as a starting point when selecting and describing certain people as criminals (Aubert and Messinger, 1958). These perceptual consequences, which give a key to the understanding of the sociological difference between the criminal and the sick, between legal and medical thinking, will not be repeated here. In this context we are concerned with the perceptual implications of the structure of the triad, without assuming that a criminal law, or a legal system in the modern sense, has been established. Even so the causal approach meets with formidable obstacles, which becomes evident when social scientists try to develop cures for interpersonal relations, based upon schemes of thought in the causal-functional tradition.

This is in part a direct consequence of differences in the availability of scientific knowledge on intraorganismic and interpersonal processes respectively. The more we move from the study of human problems as physiological processes within individual organisms to the study of interaction and social systems, the greater the lack of adequate scientific knowledge. But this purely cognitive difference must not be viewed in isolation. It is related to the difference between a situation where it is necessary for the advisor or expert to consider problems of justice, and one where the expert may leave such considerations, if they are relevant at all, to the "client."

Let us assume that the third party attached to the dyad in conflict is able to assess some of the causes of the conflict. It might so happen that the removal of the causes of the conflict would involve a certain balance in the distribution of burdens and sacrifices among the contestants. In that case his "cure" may be accepted by the parties on the basis of a feeling of justice, as they might also have accepted a purely normative plan for getting the conflict out of the world. Suppose, however, that the conflict-solver concludes that an economic feud is caused by the pathological stinginess of one of the parties, in the sense that the conflict would never have arisen unless this factor had been present. Or he concludes that a marriage conflict would never have arisen if it were not for the very pronounced moralism and sense of duty of one of the parties. In such cases the attempt to remove the causes is apt to meet with formidable obstacles.

To cure a person of pathological stinginess will, initially at least, appear to impose a burden upon him and it will appear to be a completely one-sided approach to the conflict, very likely to arouse a feeling of injustice. If the object of the conflict was a small amount of money, it may furthermore be felt that the sanction is out of all proportion to the issue at stake. This feeling may sometimes, perhaps rather routinely, arise also in ordinary medical consultation. Minor ailments may turn out to be caused by habits of living to which the patient feels dedicated. When the doctor has given his diagnosis, he may leave it to the patient to decide which value to give priority, his health or his habitual style of life. This intrapersonal conflict may need expert assistance to become cognitively clarified but once that is done, the individual has mechanisms available for settling the conflict on his own. In intrapersonal conflicts this is not so. The third person is called in precisely because such mechanisms do not work.

Removal of the cause of a conflict may appear to impose undue burdens upon the party exposed to cure but it may also appear irrelevant and unsatisfactory from the point of view of the "blameless" party. If the relationship between the contestants is a short-term one, he is interested in having a value restored to him, which is a different matter from removing the cause of the conflict. What is troubling him is not the unpleasantness of the conflict, but simply that he does not get what he wants and feels entitled to. In more stable relationships this may be different. For this reason they are also somewhat more amenable to the causal approach, as we can see in marriage counseling. Here the conflict in itself may be experienced as the real trouble, and the "blameless" party may want a removal of the causes more than anything else. But the causal approach will also here meet with objections based upon a sense of justice if it directs the cure in only one direction. It may, furthermore, lead to an impasse if otherwise valuable qualities are diagnosed as causes of conflicts. There is no reason to assume a perfect symmetry between cause and guilt, in the sense that conflicts are always caused by negative traits in one or both of the parties.

It is only this assumption of identity of cause and guilt which gives the appearance that interpersonal conflicts can be solved purely on the basis of an analysis of causes and by their consequent removal. Such removal of causes can only be successful when based upon considerations of justice, either in the sense of equitable distribution of the costs of the cure, or in the sense that the cure is directed towards the guilty, that is, the morally deviant party.

Modes of Cognition in the Dyad

Before going further, let us raise the question of the possibility of solving conflicts in the dyad through the application of causal-functional schemes of cognition. In the "I-Thou" encounter, settlements can be effected without the explicit classification or description of the relationship or of the participants. However, there is nothing in the dyad to hinder one of the members from beginning to perceive the other person as an organism moved by needs, purposes, internal states, previous experiences, group memberships. This is supposedly one of the things that happen when one, or both, of the members becomes a "diplomat," weighing words and actions for their probable effects upon the other person. It might as truly be said that he has become a scientist, a psychologist, sociologist, or political scientist, as the case may be. Through the mutual application of such schemes of perception and inference the members of a dyad may come to understand each other's needs, and thereby, how far they can be expected to go in a bargain. It may thus serve to resolve or prevent conflicts. It is not easy empirically to distinguish this process behind a settlement from the spontaneous "I-Thou" process of reciprocal adjustments. Whether the one or the other is likely to prevail, will depend a great deal upon the intimacy and permanency of the relationship and the magnitude of the object of the conflict. In a marriage conflict it is not unlikely that the partners have some perceptions of each other which follow the pattern of causal explanation and prediction. Such relationship will frequently be characterized by normative schemes of interpretation: A shirks his duty, E has a right to expect a certain behavior and sentiment, considering what E has contributed to the relationship, etc. These arguments are essentially based upon comparison processes (Festinger, 1954) and are normative in character. It is an interesting problem whether the normative or the descriptive-causal mode of perceiving the other, is the more conducive to the settlement of interest conflicts, or rather, under what conditions the one or the other is the most functional from this point of view.

Whenever E perceives the conflict in causal terms, this implies a danger that E may perceive himself as the cause. In one very trivial sense this would always be correct. Remove E and that particular interest conflict can no longer continue. If the situation were turned around, E would be viewed as usually having it in his power to remove the difficulty by changing his behavior. In this sense he has means available for causal manipulation which the third person does not command since he is outside the original conflict-system. This brings us to another reason why the outsider has to resort to normative judgments: Only for such judgments can he enlist the support needed to effect any change in the system. His membership alone gives him no status as "cause" of the trouble. He is free from blame, but therefore also without intrinsic ability to manipulate the state of the conflict by his own behavior.

The Role of the Third Person

This feeling of power to change the state of the conflict on the part of E or A often depends upon the view that "it takes two to make a quarrel." One may raise the question as to whether the third person, by virtue of his position, will tend towards the opinion that there must be "some wrong on both sides." He *can* ally himself with one of the parties, and *can* thereby enforce a completely asymmetrical view of the responsibility for the conflict, but there may be reasons intrinsic in the triadic situation as to why he should try to avoid this. If he sides fully with one of the contestants, he has brought his status as an outsider into some jeopardy. He has sacrificed his unique moral standpoint in the little group. Although his interests differ from those of the other two, he has in normative terms become one in a sub-group of two. It seems that in terms of power and authority he will generally stand to gain by assuming a position somewhere between the claims of the two parties, possibly maximizing his own moral superiority the nearer the solution lies towards the golden mean. If he does suggest a middle-of-the-road settlement, he comes out of the conflict as the only one of the three who has taken the normatively correct position. The two others have presented themselves as extremists, exaggerating the importance of this or that point, or having somewhat misrepresented the facts.

Precisely in outcomes of this kind lies one of the attractions of letting oneself be used as a third person, a middleman, a mediator in disputes between others. It affords the chance of enhancing one's prestige, by showing oneself to be a little more right than other people who get themselves involved in conflicts which they cannot settle on their own. This tendency may, of course, often be overridden by other factors, by the actual merits of the case, by the opinion of the rest of society, by bribery or particularistic attachments, but as a force it seems to inhere in the triadic situation when this is built up on the basis of a dyad in a state of conflict. Through this mechanism the triadic situation may come to settle the conflict at very much the same point where the two parties would have converged if they had been able and willing to carry on with their bargaining and adjustment. To the interest of the two in reaching a compromise, is added the interest of the third person in keeping his unique role and avoiding a complete alliance.

In a triad, however, the possibility of such a full normative alliance does exist, and in many cases society's interests seem to demand a full alliance, as between the victim of a crime and the prosecution. We would today say that any inherent tendency in the judicial system towards distributing blame evenly between the criminal and his victim is a perversion of justice. This is not objectivity, although objectivity requires that the factual story as rendered by the victim should be received with as much doubt as that of the defendant. However, the conclusion will usually, although not always, be that all the blame rests with the one side, even if the court does not side wholeheartedly with the claims of the prosecution. That is a different matter.

This view on the relationship between the criminal and the victim does not seem to have been universally dominant. It seems, rather, to be a fairly modern development to look upon the criminal and the victim as belonging to two different and opposing moral spheres of society, the deviants and the law-abiding citizens. The normative asymmetry in the perception of criminals and victims reaches its apex in the notion of the criminal as someone who, without considering his relationship to the victims, can be classified as belonging to a certain type, not only in normative, but also in causal-genetic terms. Criminality should then be amenable to diagnosis without knowledge of any particular conflicts of the kind defined as crime.

Such a conception is strikingly different from the notion of crime as we glimpse it from the Old Norse Sagas. Crimes occurred in Old Norse society in the sense of breach of laws or other people's interests. But it is characteristic that these crimes are described as elements in feuds, as parts of interpersonal conflicts, unintelligible without detailed knowledge of the history of the individuals and their interrelationships. The most heinous crimes took place in the "best society," between equals. Like war, they must be considered as the diplomacy of conflicts "carried on with different means." They were undistinguishable from the feuds out of which they arose. Murder was often settled by the payment of compensation, the fine (wergild) being agreed upon after bargaining between the sibs of the criminal and his victim. Implicit in this procedure, where a third party is vaguely discernible, seems to lie an assumption that there might be some wrong on both sides.

In the intrinsic tendency of the third party to take a middle-of-the-road view, may lie one of the most primitive roots of an hierarchical moral ordering of society. If people in conflict fail to settle their differences and need a third person's intervention, they can hardly fail to bestow upon him a higher status than he had before. He performs a social service by removing stalemates and receives almost automatically a kind of moral "tax" in addition to the actual economic rewards which he has often been given for his performance. Still, this tendency may also introduce a bias, since there is no intrinsic reason why one party to a conflict should not be predominantly right in his claims. Here lies a strong reason why the third person should be made independent both of the need for alliance with one of the parties, and of the opportunity to enhance his own social position by middle-of-the-road-ism. Hence a need for social agencies that are sufficiently strong to handle the two conflicting parties independent of alliances, and whose status is permanently secured in their professional role, independent of the outcome of individual cases.

This is what the genuine courts attempt to establish, through organs which dispose of sufficient resources of power, thus enabling them to solve conflicts without resorting to alliances. The third party is firmly institutionalized, his social status independent of the outcome of any one case. His independence will often be demonstrated through an evening out of decisions in the long run. He may rule in favor of the insurance company in some cases, and find for the insured in some others. He may decide in favor of the wife in some divorce cases, but in favor of the husband in others.

Organizational Triads

In the preceding we have considered triadic relationships of a specific kind. The third person is assumed to have been added to the dyad *because* of the conflict and with the purpose of terminating the strife. It has furthermore been assumed that the third person disposes of no resources in addition to those of the two others, except his possible power to effect a solution to the conflict. There exist, however, eminently practical situations, where two parties may be in conflict, while a third person is in a position to distribute rewards and sanctions between the contestants. Such is the case if we consider the relationship between two applicants for promotion and their superior who makes the choice, or a governmental agency determining which one of several competing firms should be granted a contract or a license.

Eckhoff has pointed out that in administrative triads of this kind, the superior third person may try to maximize goals very different from those implied in the above analysis of the third person in conflict-solution (Eckhoff, 1962). There is this initial difference from the legal model that the administrative executive is not coopted to the system of the two in order to solve a conflict, although it may be recognized in the organizational blueprint that it is one of his tasks to settle disputes between his subordinates or his clients. Furthermore, *he* is in command of the relevant resources, not the competitors. By his decisions he may bestow new rewards upon one of the parties, or both, not merely influencing upon the distribution of a given scarce value.

From the point of view of the "distributor," his subordinates or "clients" may be considered as "resources" to be manipulated, encouraged to choose certain courses of action rather than others, with the purpose of attaining the goal of the organization. He may, at least originally, be primarily interested in efficiency. Whether this implies injustice, unequal distribution of values as between subordinates or competitors, is in itself irrelevant. His scheme of thinking is one in the terms of cause and effect, of ends and efficient means to secure the ends. His policy will often engender conflicts, between himself and his clientele or his subordinates, as well as between the latter. He may avoid the latter types of conflict if he can successfully keep the recipients of his resources from considering themselves as belonging to a common system. Such will often be the case with clients of private professionals, doctors, attorneys, architects. Whatever the professional does to any one of his clients, need not be perceived by the others, or at least not considered a relevant comparison, although it may be so perceived. Conflicts may nevertheless arise, since each client may feel that there is some lack of balance in the relationship between his contribution and that of the professional.

Now, it is typical of bureaucracies that subordinates and clients tend very easily to make comparisons between what they receive and what others receive. Discrepancies will be evaluated in terms of merit. If those who receive more than others are considered to be without any particular merit, which can explain their advantages, conflicts may arise. These conflicts will be of two kinds, conflicts based upon a sense of imbalance between the contributions of distributor and recipient, and conflicts based upon a feeling of distributive injustice between the competitors (Eckhoff, 1962). Actually the latter kind of felt injustice may be the most frequent source of conflict with superiors, since just distribution is one major contribution expected from an executive. Possibly, this is one of the most fundamental asymmetries in the mutual expectations of superiors and subordinates: the subordinates expect just distribution of rewards and sanctions, while distributive justice is often felt as a great nuisance and as an impediment to efficient administration from the point of view of the executive and distributor.

In most organizations a strong force will operate in the direction of adopting to some extent the subordinate point of view. Thus, many bureaucracies may become, at least partially, transformed into machineries for settling disputes between subordinates or clients, while efficiency must recede into the background. I shall not here attempt an analysis of the forces which may bring about this partial transformation, which has been described by Eckhoff and others (Eckhoff and Jacobsen, 1960). The result of such a transformation, however, is of direct concern to us in the analysis of conflict-resolution through the intervention of a third party. For it means that some bureaucratic conflicts may approach the model of private litigation and a court decision. The subordinates or clients consider themselves as having some minimal *right* of access to resources or privileges, and it is considered to be the prime duty of the superior to make decisions, and just decisions, in cases where conflicts arise over the distribution of these scarce values. A system of precedent and quasi-legal thinking may come to permeate what was originally set up as an organization devoted to effective furtherance of specified goals, and with freedom for the executive to choose the means considered most efficient to maximize the goal.

It seems possible, then, that the mere existence of triadic relationships, which will always be a characteristic of large scale organization, tend to foster definitions of conflicts as questions of dissensus, as disagreements over rights and over operative facts. When this happens the executive is in danger of becoming a judge, and he will have strong reasons to accept some of the challenge. For how can a big organization work effectively unless the staff feel that they will be rewarded and sanctioned in accordance with the demands of justice? Justice and quasi-juridical behavior has become an element in an even more comprehensive system of means-end thinking.

REFERENCES

AUBERT, V. and MESSINGER, S. S. "The Criminal and the Sick," *Inquiry*, 1 (1958), 137–60.

BUBER, M. *The Writings of M.B.* Will Herberg (ed.). New York: Meridian Books, 1956.

CAPLOW, T. "A Theory of Coalitions in the Triad," *American Sociological Review*, 21 (1956), 489–93.

COSER, L. "The Termination of Conflict," *The Journal of Conflict Resolution*, 5 (1961), 347–53.

DAHRENDORF, R. *Class and Class Conflict in Industrial Society*. Stanford, Calif.: Stanford University Press, 1959.

ECKHOFF, T. *"Justice."* Unpublished manuscript. Oslo, 1962.

ECKHOFF, T. and JACOBSEN, K. DAHL. *Rationality and Responsibility in Administrative and Judicial Decision-Making*. Copenhagen: Munksgaard, 1960.

FESTINGER, L. "A Theory of Social Comparison Processes," *Human Relations*, 7 (1954), 117–40.

HOEBEL, E. ADAMSON. *The Law of Primitive Man*. Cambridge, Mass.: Harvard University Press, 1954.

MURPHY, G. *Personality*. New York: Harper & Bros., 1947.

PITT-RIVERS, J. *The People of the Sierra*. Chicago: Phoenix Books, The University of Chicago Press, 1961.

SIMMEL, G. *The Sociology of G.S.* Kurt H. Wolff (ed.). Glencoe, Ill.: The Free Press, 1950.

[7]

Disputing Without the Force of Law

Laura Nader†

Americans have no access to law for certain types of problems. Starting with Dean Roscoe Pound, commentators[1] have documented the reasons for lack of access: entry to the legal system demands an amount of time, money, and knowledge that many people do not have;[2] the courts have contrived devices to control their dockets;[3] and certain harms have not been accorded a legal remedy.[4] Proposed reforms to

† Professor of Anthropology, University of California, Berkeley. The author wishes to thank Christopher Shugart for invaluable assistance in the preparation of this article. For a more complete discussion of the subject of this article, see No Access to Law (L. Nader ed. forthcoming); in many respects, law review form is not conducive to the expression and development of ideas by persons trained in other disciplines.

1. *E.g.*, Fox, *Providing Legal Services for the Middle Class in Civil Matters: The Problems, the Duty, and a Solution*, 26 U. PITT. L. REV. 811 (1965); Maguire, *Poverty and Civil Litigation*, 36 HARV. L. REV. 361 (1923); Pound, *The Administration of Justice in the Modern City*, 26 HARV. L. REV. 302 (1913).

2. Pound, *supra* note 1, at 310-11. Commentators have observed that entry into the legal system also demands a willingness to submit to a complex and cumbersome procedure that may fail to address underlying problems and may prevent disputants from acquiring quick response after telling their own stories. *E.g.*, AMERICAN BAR ASSOCIATION, REPORT OF THE NATIONAL CONFERENCE ON MINOR DISPUTES RESOLUTION 2 (1977) (prepared by F. Sander).

3. *See* Friedman, *Legal Rules and the Process of Social Change*, 19 STAN. L. REV. 786, 798-810 (1967) (reviewing jurisdictional and procedural rules developed by legal system to control volume of litigation). *But cf.* Sykes, *Cases, Courts, and Congestion*, in LAW IN CULTURE AND SOCIETY (L. Nader ed. 1969) (judicial autonomy limits judges' desires to develop administrative devices to control dockets).

4. Some consumer complaints concern risks of harm that have not yet occurred but that still cause constant worry. *See* p. 1002 *infra*. In addition, although consumers may be misled by marketing schemes even if they do not complete a transaction, actual economic injury is usually required to sustain a legal cause of action. *See* Rice, *Remedies, Enforcement Procedures and the Duality of Consumer Transactions Problems*, 48 B.U. L. REV. 559, 561 (1968).

Although judicial and legislative inroads have expanded legal protection for consumers during the past two decades, D. RICE, CONSUMER TRANSACTIONS 86-329 (1975), many such reforms have been criticized as inadequate. The Uniform Consumer Sales Practices Act, for example, is designed to provide restitution to consumers harmed by abusive sales practices, but it has been criticized for imposing sanctions only against knowing violations and for failing to create balanced incentives for settlement. Rice, *Uniform Consumer Sales Practices Act—Damage Remedies: The NCCUSL Giveth and Taketh Away*, 67 NW. U.L. REV. 369, 375-82 (1972). Moreover, burdensome time limitations and costs of meeting notice requirements impede class action suits under this and other legislative provisions. *See* McCall, *Due Process and Consumer Protection: Concepts and Realities in Procedure and Substance—Class Action Issues*, 25 HASTINGS L.J. 1351 (1974).

The Truth-in-Lending Act, 15 U.S.C. §§ 1601-1677 (1976), is designed to guard against deceptive credit practices, but critics note the shortcomings resulting from its reliance on disclosure requirements. *E.g.*, Kripke, *Gesture and Reality in Consumer Credit Reform*, 44 N.Y.U. L. REV. 1, 2-9, 51-52 (1969). The increasing stringency of products liability law

address access problems have at times stimulated broad political movements. Thus, the small claims court movement,[5] the regulatory movement,[6] the legal services movement, including federally funded legal assistance and prepaid legal services,[7] and the public-interest movement,[8] have each promised to provide previously unavailable legal help. None of these efforts alone, nor all of them combined, has satisfied the demand for access to legal relief which, by the turn of the century, became acute for a range of problems arising in the everyday lives of individuals.

Scholarly discussions of the problem of access, and reform proposals, have seldom focused on what people actually do when they have complaints but no access to law. Citizen action—and inaction—outside the legal system must be reviewed to determine whether the inaccessibility of legal relief for some problems is a serious deficiency. One particular class of cases commonly falls outside the channels of access to law in this country—complaints about the defects in purchased items and public services that interfere with life as usual and that often go un-

offers little assistance to consumers with problems that are frequent and relatively inexpensive. D. RICE, *supra*, at vii.

The Federal Trade Commission (FTC) regulates deceptive and abusive consumer practices, but the Commission's focus on halting undesired conduct and its own workload and bureaucratic delays limit its ability to provide effective redress for individual consumers. *See, e.g.*, Lurie, *Consumer Complaints: A Proposed Federal Trade Regulation Rule*, 5 J. L. REF. 426 (1972). Thus, even when legal relief may be available for some of the complaints described in this article, the practical barriers to effective redress can effectively interfere with access to law.

5. For a comprehensive discussion of the literature on small claims, see Yngvesson & Hennessey, *Small Claims, Complex Disputes: A Review of the Small Claims Literature*, 9 LAW & SOC'Y REV. 219 (1975). Recent studies criticize the enforcement process used by small claims courts. *See* AMERICAN BAR ASSOCIATION, *supra* note 2, at 309.

6. *See* D. RICE, *supra* note 4, at 6-10; R. WIEBE, THE SEARCH FOR ORDER 164-95 (1967). For discussions of current movements to reform regulatory efforts, see COMMISSION ON LAW AND THE ECONOMY, AMERICAN BAR ASSOCIATION, FEDERAL REGULATION: ROADS TO REFORM (1978) (exposure draft); Bruff, *Presidential Power and Administrative Rulemaking*, 88 YALE L.J. 451, 454-56 (1979).

7. Approximately 320 legal services programs in local communities throughout the country serve 29 million Americans who live at or below the poverty threshold determined by the Office of Management and Budget. Ehrlich, *Giving Low-Income Americans Minimum Access to Legal Services*, 64 A.B.A.J. 696, 696-97 (1978). The Legal Services Corporation was established to ensure that those who are otherwise unable to afford legal assistance have access to it. *Id.*

Group legal services plans seek to provide a range of legal services to middle-income recipients. Like group medical insurance, these plans spread the cost among a large number of people in order to minimize the cost to the individual participant. In August 1976, approximately 125 such plans covered an estimated 1,250,000 members from $12 to $250 per member yearly. Murphy, *The Prepaid Legal Services Picture*, 62 A.B.A.J. 1569, 1570 (1976). For a description of various bar-sponsored prepaid legal service plans, see SPECIAL COMMISSION ON PREPAID LEGAL SERVICES, AMERICAN BAR ASSOCIATION, REVISED HANDBOOK ON PREPAID LEGAL SERVICES (1972).

8. *See* Note, *The New Public Interest Lawyers*, 79 YALE L.J. 1069 (1970).

The Yale Law Journal Vol. 88: 998, 1979

corrected. What do Americans do with such complaints when they perceive that they cannot obtain legal relief?[9]

This article considers the importance of these complaints and examines an array of alternatives to the legal system that has developed to process consumer and citizen grievances. A pervasive pattern of unsatisfied complaints and inadequate relief emerges from research on extrajudicial complaint settings.[10] The article suggests some of the causes and societal consequences of this pattern of failure;[11] it concludes that, at least in this country, ultimate access to the legal system is crucial if extralegal processes are ever to provide effective relief for consumer and citizen complaints.

I. Complaints about "Little Injustices"

A. *Why Care About Complaints?*

One reason for an interest in little injustices is that people care about them; they are a great part of everyday living in a consumption-oriented society. Another reason for an interest in such complaints is that ignoring them encourages criminal behavior: when complaints go unaddressed, producers are in effect stealing small amounts from large numbers of people and escaping sanctions for such behavior. Traditional techniques for dealing with unfair treatment simply are no longer in use. English towns in the Middle Ages could rely heavily on public opinion to deter abuses in the marketplace; dishonest craftsmen and merchants were paraded through the streets and placed in stocks for all to see, and their wares were publicly burned.[12] In a modern, industrialized society dominated by large corporations and sprawling governmental bureaucracies, public opinion and interpersonal ties can no

9. Consumer dissatisfaction is increasing. A survey of consumer attitudes commissioned by the Sentry Insurance Co. in 1976 found that 61% of consumers interviewed thought that the quality of goods and services had worsened in the preceding 10 years, and 78% said that products did not last as long as they did a decade ago. Sentry Insurance Co., Consumerism at the Crossroads 22, 23 (July 1976) (available from Sentry Insurance Co., Stevens Point, Wis.).

10. This article draws on research conducted over the past eight years. *See* p. 1003 *infra.*

11. For one judicial appraisal of causes and consequences, see Johnson v. Avery, 393 U.S. 483, 491 (1969) (Douglas, J., concurring):

> The increasing complexities of our governmental apparatus at both the local and the federal levels have made it difficult for a person to process a claim or even to make a complaint. Social security is a virtual maze; the hierarchy that governs urban housing is often so intricate that it takes an expert to know what agency has jurisdiction over a particular complaint; the office to call or official to see for noise abatement, for a broken sewer line, or a fallen tree is a mystery to many in our metropolitan areas.

12. Hamilton, *The Ancient Maxim Caveat Emptor*, 40 YALE L.J. 1133, 1152 (1931).

Disputing Without Law

longer serve as effective mechanisms of social control. The increasing availability and complexity of goods and services create more occasions for things to go wrong, such as defects in products and delays in the provision of public services.

Lacking other effective methods for solving such problems, a citizen may hope for relief from the legal system. Yet individual complaints about consumer goods and governmental benefits seldom reach courts.[13] Even if there is a plausible legal argument, the money, time, and knowledge necessary to pursue a claim through official legal channels may be beyond the claimant's reach. The consumer suffers from a doubly disadvantaged position: he has to bear the full cost of legal fees, while businesses can deduct litigation costs as a business expense[14] and the public bureaucracy's legal costs are ultimately paid by the consumer.

Speaking more generally, the legal system is seldom responsive in a complex industrial society to issues that affect the quality of everyday life.[15] In fact, the legal system may define a problem as relatively unimportant if the monetary amount in controversy is small, if one of the parties is too poor to wage a legal battle, or if the issue itself simply seems to be trivial.[16] Yet from other perspectives, such problems are important. From the vantage point of a low-income family expecting a baby, the landlord's failure to return a security deposit could impose severe damage to the family's well-being.[17] If the legal system is un-

13. Many complaints seldom reach any third party. *See* Best & Andreasen, *Consumer Response to Unsatisfactory Purchases: A Survey of Perceiving Defects, Voicing Complaints, and Obtaining Redress*, 11 LAW & SOC'Y REV. 701, 713-14 (1977) (only 3.7% voiced complaints studied reached any third party; only 16% of those brought to third parties were brought to lawyer or court).

14. Legal expenses incurred in producing or collecting income and managing income-producing property are deductible under I.R.C. § 212. *See, e.g.*, Commissioner v. Estate of Bartholomew, 4 T.C. 349, *appeal dismissed*, 151 F.2d 534 (9th Cir. 1945).

15. *See* THE DISPUTING PROCESS: LAW IN TEN SOCIETIES 38 (L. Nader & H. Todd eds. 1978); L. Nader & Combs-Schilling, *Restitution in Cross-Cultural Perspective*, in RESTITUTION AND CRIMINAL JUSTICE 27 (J. Hudson & B. Galaway eds. 1977).

16. *See* R. SMITH, JUSTICE AND THE POOR 41 (1924) ("Our legal system has taken too literally the ancient maxim, 'de minimis non curat lex.' ")

17. Chief Justice Burger has observed:

> [W]e do not need to call on psychiatrists or clinical psychologists to tell us that a sense of injustice rankles and festers in the human breast and the dollar value of the conflict is not always the measure of tension and irritation produced. A landlord who delays unduly in repairing a defective radiator or refrigerator can produce unhappy chain reactions on children and adults. A defective roofing or siding job on the home, defective work on the family car sometimes can produce serious consequences comparable to those of a major illness.

Burger, *Our Vicious Legal Spiral*, JUDGES' J., Fall 1977, at 48; *see* SMALL CLAIMS STUDY GROUP, LITTLE INJUSTICES: SMALL CLAIMS COURTS AND THE AMERICAN CONSUMER 5 (1972) (J. Weiss, project director) ("The person of modest income, barred from seeking redress for a real grievance by the cost of legal assistance, may feel a sense of powerlessness just as great as the unattended patient.")

The Yale Law Journal Vol. 88: 998, 1979

responsive to such everyday problems, it becomes irrelevant to its citizens. If the alternatives to legal relief are also ineffective, the inadequacy of law is felt even more profoundly.[18] What may seem to be a minor problem thus can be significant because its resolution—or lack thereof—influences people's attitudes about law and social order.

Further, complaints about little injustices may serve to signal broader problems affecting many people. Even though companies may tend to believe that people use general complaints as a strategy to solve an individual problem, people often complain in order to encourage the company to change its production policy or improve the quality of its product.[19] A company that ignores or misunderstands such complaints may fail to perceive the seriousness of underlying product defects. Such was the case when one woman complained to a company that made diapers that distintegrated in use. She asked that the company do something to guard against the risk that a child might swallow a piece of diaper and choke to death; she received in response a new box of diapers.[20]

An examination of numerous similar individual complaints in the aggregate may expose the extent of a problem and highlight the need for a systemic response. Consumer complaints can alert regulatory agencies to the widespread presence of product defects. For example, problems encountered by women and minorities who attempt to obtain credit can become apparent through examination of the level of individual complaints registered at the FTC.[21] If all individual com-

18. In this sense, judicial and extrajudicial mechanisms can be seen as parts of one interrelated system of social control; together, they define the availability of solutions to people's problems.

19. A review of over 5,000 complaint letters revealed that people of all socioeconomic brackets write such letters and that they are often motivated by a sense of injustice and a desire to improve products, as well as by a desire to have their own loss redressed. *See* L. Nader, Introduction to No Access to Law (L. Nader ed. forthcoming) [hereinafter cited without cross-references as No Access to Law].

20. *Id.* A similarly inadequate response occurred when a complainant convinced the New York Department of Consumer Affairs to respond to a company's fraudulent disc-brake special. The Department simply imposed a $50 fine on the company; it did not put an end to the scheme. *Id.*

21. The FTC, the agency with overall enforcement authority under the Equal Credit Opportunity Act, 15 U.S.C. § 1691c(c) (1976), receives consumer complaints and inquiries regarding the vast majority of the creditors affected by the Act; other complaints are directed to other agencies. Although the FTC does not intervene in individual disputes regarding credit rejections, it responds to consumer inquiries. The agency files all inquiries and complaints under the complainant's name, the name of the creditor, and the statutory provision that governs the problem described in the complaint. Although the FTC does not tabulate complaints, FTC attorneys try to investigate creditors about whom large numbers of complaints accumulate or who appear to be engaged in particularly egregious violations. Telephone Interview with Jean Noonan, attorney, Division of Credit, FTC (Feb. 5, 1979).

Disputing Without Law

plaints to congressional representatives about social security were channeled from case-work staff to legislative action, perhaps the entire benefit system would be streamlined. This aggregate approach to individual complaints is seldom taken, however, partly because politicians benefit personally from the handling of cases individually and because complainants rarely see themselves as members of a class sharing the same problems.

B. *Studying Complaints*

A systematic study of people who voice complaints in extrajudicial settings was launched eight years ago.[22] Locating complainants for study is difficult because they are dispersed and often hidden by virtue of the confidentiality maintained by companies and nonjudicial dispute-settlement mechanisms.[23] After reviewing several hundred letters sent to a national citizen-action organization,[24] the study focused on the complainant's perspective on organizations whose manifest goal is to handle complaints. A team of researchers used participant-observation methods and other data-gathering techniques employed by anthropologists to acquire a panoramic view of the range of mechanisms that has been developed to handle complaints about products and services. In recent years, such programs have sprouted in the form of city consumer departments, consumer fraud divisions of attorneys general offices, private company toll-free hotlines, advertising review boards, professional associations, consumer complaints centers, media action lines, and neighborhood legal services. Some institutions developed by the business community were selected for detailed examination: a branch of the Better Business Bureau (BBB),[25] the consumer-action

22. Following preliminary study, in 1973 a proposal was submitted to the Carnegie Corporation from the Center for the Study of Responsive Law in Washington, D.C., for the establishment of a Consumer Complaint Research Center. The purposes of such a research center were to learn in greater detail about the actual operation of existing grievance mechanisms and to determine American attitudes about these processes. The work was conducted jointly by the Center and the University of California, Berkeley.

23. As testimony to the attempt of companies to keep complaints secret, General Motors displayed avid interest in buying 19 boxes of microfilmed complaint letters originally sent to the Chevrolet customer relations department that accidentally wound up in the hands of two scrap dealers. It would be overgenerous to presume that GM quickly paid $20,000 out of a desire to better understand the nature of customer dissatisfaction. *See* San Francisco Chronicle, Apr. 29, 1971, at 2, col. 1.

24. Freedman, "Dear Mr. Nader": A Study of Consumer Complaint Letters, in No Access to Law. Freedman's study analyzes recurrent patterns in several hundred complaint letters written directly to Ralph Nader, or written to corporations or government agencies with carbon copies sent to Mr. Nader.

25. Eaton, The Better Business Bureau: "The Voice of the People in the Marketplace," in No Access to Law. Beginning in 1971, Eaton analyzed the performance of a BBB branch. Her study substantiates a congressman's findings that documented the tension

panels sponsored by six trade associations,[26] and the complaint-management systems developed by six urban department stores to satisfy steady customers.[27] The open-return policy adopted by some of these stores was also examined.[28] In addition, the research team studied the Public Review Board of the United Auto Workers—another institution managed directly by the organization complained about.[29] Although the union does not deal with either product or service complaints, its board is reputed to be the best developed mechanism for handling worker-

between the BBB's financial dependence on local businesses and its goal of serving consumers. *See* 117 Cong. Rec. 47,781 (1971) [hereinafter cited as Rosenthal Report].

The BBB remains one of the most frequently used complaint-processing mechanisms. A 1974 Roper Report asked consumers where they would turn should they fail to get satisfaction from a seller or manufacturer. Over 50% responded that they would go to the BBB. Conference Board, The Consumer Affairs Department: Organizations and Functions 6 (1973); *see* D. King & K. McEvoy, A National Survey of the Complaint-Handling Procedures Used by Consumers (1976) (Nat'l Technical Information Serv., U.S. Commerce Dep't) (BBB more familiar to consumers than 19 of 21 public and private organizations; only Post Office and Social Security Administration better known).

26. Greenberg & Stanton, Business Groups, Consumer Problems: The Contradiction of Trade Association Complaint Handling, in No Access to Law. The research for this study was conducted from 1974 to 1976.

Consumer action panels aim to decrease overt dissatisfaction at the smallest cost and without alienating the businesses that constitute their memberships. Their purpose is to forestall government regulation through industry self-regulation. *Id.* For another discussion of complaint handling by trade associations, see Jones & Boyer, *Improving the Quality of the Marketplace: The Need for Better Consumer Remedies*, 40 Geo. Wash. L. Rev. 357, 370-72 (1972).

27. Karikas & Rosenwasser, The Department Store: Face-to-Face Complaint Management, in No Access to Law. This study was carried out in 1972. The research is particularly interesting because it deals with complaints directed against the seller. One survey found that 87% of households that complained went to the seller first. *See* D. King & K. McEvoy, *supra* note 25, at 10. Best and Andreasen found that only 3.7% of all complaints were taken to third parties, and noted that "[t]he limited role of third parties suggests that our first priority should be improvement in the way sellers handle complaints." Best & Andreasen, *supra* note 13, at 132.

28. Despite the commonly expressed fear that an open-return policy would produce an avalanche of unsubstantiated complaints that in turn would reduce corporate profits, the study's preliminary review of retailers and manufacturers found numerous businesses that have maintained such a policy and still earned respectable profits. *E.g.*, Telephone Interview with Gordon Serman, former president of Midas Muffler (Apr. 22, 1974); Interview with regional spokesman, Sears Roebuck, Inc. (Oakland, Cal., Oct. 3, 1978). Sears Roebuck has used an open-return policy since the 1890s, and has also instituted a system for identifying and dealing with patterns of complaints. *Id.* Reports on every complaint are sent to the Sears headquarters in Chicago and compiled. Sears then tries to work with manufacturers to improve products that continually fail to satisfy customers. The open-return system gives each store an increased incentive to carry only products that will please. *Id.*

29. *See* Combs-Schilling, Grieving and Feuding: The Organizational Dilemma of a Labor Union, in No Access to Law.

Combs-Schilling studied the UAW's formal mechanisms for handling complaints during two separate periods: in 1973, when the auto industry was in relatively good health, and in 1975, when it was not. In describing the procedures used for processing complaints, she notes that they resemble American legal procedures in their formality and complexity: they include the initiation of charges, the choosing of a trial committee, a trial, and several levels of appeal. Her most important finding is that the system was hardly ever used. *Id.*

Disputing Without Law

union complaints; it was chosen for study with the hope that some of its ideas could be applied to the handling of consumer complaints.

Other complaint-processing devices use an intermediary to act as a clearinghouse, troubleshooter, or watchdog. Two such programs received close consideration: the handling of constituent complaints by the district office of a popular United States congressman,[30] and the Policy Service Bureau (PSB) of the California Department of Insurance.[31] San Francisco Consumer Action, a private voluntary organization created to help citizens with their grievances, was also researched in depth.[32] Another study compared a business organization, a private voluntary organization, and a city government organization as they operate in a Washington, D.C. ghetto.[33] Finally, four media action lines that solicit and pursue complaints were examined.[34]

Each of these techniques is devoted to receiving and responding to an individual's dissatisfaction with a product or service; each is supposed to offer speedy, simple, and inexpensive access to relief. At various times, some of the devices have successfully satisfied individual complainants. Department-store customers—especially those with good credit records—who persist in their complaints by confronting upper-level management can obtain favorable resolution.[35] The congressman's wide network of influential contacts enabled him to process constituent complaints effectively.[36] San Francisco Consumer Action added pro-

30. Karikas, Solving Problems in Philadelphia: An Ethnography of a Congressional District Office, in No Access to Law; *see* W. GELLHORN, WHEN AMERICANS COMPLAIN: GOVERNMENTAL GRIEVANCE PROCEDURES (1966). Congressman William Barrett, who held office from 1945 to 1946 and from 1949 until his death in 1976, operated in the style of the political machine that in the past prevailed in many cohesive ethnic communities in American cities. Machine politics were based on reciprocal favors within the local ward: Barrett's constituents delivered the votes in return for his personal aid. *Id.*

31. *See* Serber, Resolution or Rhetoric: Managing Complaints in the California Department of Insurance, in No Access to Law. Research on the Department was completed during 1971 and 1972. The Insurance Department is the only agency, public or private, in California that takes complaints about insurance; it is authorized to suspend an insurer's state certification upon a finding of unfair practices. Most of the Department's work is conducted by an insurance officer who mediates between the customer and the company. *Id.*

32. *See* Wilson & Brydolf, Grass Roots Solutions: San Francisco Consumer Action, in No Access to Law. A study by Wilson in 1973 was followed up three years later by Brydolf. The organization had undergone significant changes during that time. *Id.*

33. Greenberg, Easy Terms, Hard Times: Complaint Handling in the Ghetto, in No Access to Law (comparing Consumer Development Group and Service Area Committee (SAC), and a department store, all in Washington, D.C.).

34. Mattice, Media in the Middle: A Study of the Mass Media Complaint Managers, in No Access to Law. The media action lines studied included one managed by a newspaper, one associated with a television station, and two associated with radio stations. The research was initiated in 1972. By the early 1970s, over 350 action-line columns appeared in newspapers alone. *Id.*

35. Karikas & Rosenwasser, *supra* note 27.

36. Karikas, *supra* note 30.

grams to its switchboard hotline to promote public education, train consumers to help themselves, and undertake political lobbying demonstrations.[37] Public faith in the organization was always very high; in a survey, eighty-eight percent of complainants polled said that they trusted the organization.[38] Media action lines sometimes have publicized recurrent complaints about business and government, and have stimulated corrective action.[39]

Yet in spite of particular successes of some of these organizations, in general a rather dismal pattern emerges from the study. Instead of providing easy access to swift relief, many of the programs obstruct the complainants' path with complex procedures[40] and repeated delays.[41] Some fail to disclose to the complainant the steps necessary in order to process a grievance;[42] some department stores even hide their customer-service offices from view.[43] Intermediary organizations are often understaffed, underfinanced, and overworked,[44] and the resulting backlogs and inefficiency can discourage consumers from pressing their complaints.[45] There is evidence that some organizations deliberately dissuade individuals from pursuing relief.[46] In sum, complaint-processing methods often make it so difficult for complainants to persist that they are likely to "lump it,"[47] and even likely to avoid raising claims in the future.[48]

37. Wilson & Brydolf, *supra* note 32.

38. *Id.*

39. Mattice, *supra* note 34.

40. *E.g.*, Combs-Schilling, *supra* note 29 (union workers may be discouraged by paperwork involved in trial-type complaint procedures).

41. *E.g.*, Greenberg & Stanton, *supra* note 26 (resolution of complaints by trade association panels takes months, "especially when the panels needlessly send consumers back to dealers or manufacturers").

42. Combs-Schilling, *supra* note 29 (union workers uninformed about available procedures); Greenberg & Stanton, *supra* note 26 (trade association panels do not systematically inform unsatisfied complainants that they can continue to pursue relief).

43. Karikas & Rosenwasser, *supra* note 27 (complaint departments often on top floor of store; customer service sign at one store partially hidden).

44. *E.g.*, Serber, *supra* note 31.

45. *Id.*

46. Greenberg, *supra* note 33 (ghetto store that sells on credit and deals with customer complaints about payment terms uses intimidation as last resort to prevent customer from complaining to third party); *see* Eaton, *supra* note 25; Greenberg & Stanton, *supra* note 26.

47. "Lumping it" refers to the failure of an aggrieved party to press his complaint so that the problem that gave rise to the disagreement is ignored. Felstiner, *Influences of Social Organization on Dispute Processing*, 9 LAW & SOC'Y REV. 63-94 (1974). This behavior is typical of persons who lack access to information or to law, and persons who perceive that the costs of pursuing a complaint are too high or that the potential gains are too low. *See* Galanter, *Why the "Haves" Come Out Ahead: Speculations on the Limits of Legal Change*, 9 LAW & SOC'Y REV. 95, 124-25 (1974).

48. The self-reported success rates of complaint organizations are thus often misleading because of the large number of persons who initially seek assistance and then drop out. In a 1975 report, for example, one trade-association complaint panel claimed that 97% of

Disputing Without Law

A survey of 2,419 respondents in 34 cities was conducted in 1975 in order to discover how consumers respond to unsatisfactory purchases.[49] A remarkable finding was that buyers did not complain at all about 57.7% of their problems that concerned more than only price. In 30.7% of the cases in which buyers perceived problems, the only complaint made was to the seller. In only 1.2% did the buyer take his grievance to a third party. One might think there was no need to resort to third parties because the sellers were so quick to give redress, but the data show otherwise. Only 56.5% of the voiced complaints—disregarding the few that concerned only price—were settled to the satisfaction of the purchaser. This means that many consumers who complained to the seller without success did not contact a third party. One reason for consumer reluctance to complain to third parties is the inprobability of success.

The failure to devise successful processes to receive and respond to complaints is even more severe when measured against the societal benefit that could accrue if complaints were handled satisfactorily. Besides resolving individual grievances quickly and fairly, an ideal complaint-handling system would disclose aggregate patterns of abuse or injustice and would support systemic reform. An ideal system would improve the quality of goods and services by alerting producers about defects and by providing administrative agencies with data to guide and support enforcement. The systems that exist, however, do not prevent or deter abuses. At best, they satisfy isolated individuals[50] and only rarely is systematic reform stimulated.

The remainder of this article examines the results of our study which revealed the inadequacy of complaint processes in nonjudicial settings. It identifies competing constituencies and structural flaws that contribute to the limited responsiveness of complaint-handling systems.

II. Constraints on Third-Party Complaint Handlers

A few years ago I attended a ceremony in San Francisco to celebrate the opening of a complaint-mobile by the city district attorney's office.

its cases were resolved during the first phase of its procedures. Greenberg & Stanton, *supra* note 26. Less than half, however, were actually resolved in a way that the complainants considered satisfactory. *Id.; cf.* R. Darmstadter, All You Ever Want to Know About the Office of Consumer Affairs (unpublished 1973) (on file with *Yale Law Journal*) (White House Consumer Office labeled complaint procedure "success" whenever company responded to inquiry).

49. *See* Best & Andreasen, *supra* note 13.

50. *See, e.g.*, Karikas & Rosenwasser, *supra* note 27 (individual complaints at department stores rarely affect general store policy and rarely reach manufacturers); Karikas, *supra* note 30 (congressman handled cases on isolated basis and did nothing to create lasting changes that would avoid identical future complaints).

On a city street, the public was invited to present their complaints—access was certainly easy. An agitated woman hurried forward and sat down in front of the complaint handler. "I haven't received my social security check for six months," she said. The complaint handler put down her pencil: "I'm sorry, we don't handle social security problems." The woman walked away. There was a problem of misleading advertising; the sign on the truck did read "Complaint-Mobile."

This anecdote is not an isolated example. It summarizes problems inherent in most complaint-handling devices: they are not tailored to the needs of individual users. False expectations are encouraged in the advertising and labeling of complaint mechanisms. Those expectations are disappointed in the actual provision of services. This pattern perhaps should not be surprising. It replicates the problems of consumer goods and services that give rise to complaints. From the automobile industry[51] to public educational systems,[52] technology often is not designed to meet the needs or constraints of the individual user.

The plight of the consumer to some extent was created by the disintegration of a market system of exchanges between parties having equal power and information.[53] Government regulation designed to protect the consumer constitutes one attempt to compensate for market disintegration.[54] Complaint mechanisms, at least overtly, constitute another. The development of these mechanisms suggests that individuals need the additional leverage offered by intermediaries to register their interests and to obtain satisfaction. On closer examination, however, it appears that complaint handlers in fact do not compensate for the inequalities that impair the operation of a market system. Instead, complaint handlers reinforce those inequalities and respond to interests other than those of individual complainants. Seldom funded or created by complainants, complaint mechanisms are able to survive without responding fully or successfully to consumer or citizen grievances. As a result, most extrajudicial settings for resolving consumer and citizen complaints deliberately or unintentionally discourage complainants and diffuse pressures for systemic change.

51. *See* R. NADER, UNSAFE AT ANY SPEED (1965) (describing design deficiencies of Corvair and Mustang automobiles).

52. *See, e.g.*, D. TYAK, THE ONE BEST SYSTEM 39-59 (1974) (historical roots of educational systems designed to promote order and conformity).

53. For general discussions of the rise of giant corporations and the transformation of the traditional market system, see J. GALBRAITH, ECONOMICS AND THE PUBLIC PURPOSE 38-51 (1973); R. HEILBRONER, THE WORDLY PHILOSOPHERS 252-76 (2d ed. 1961); G. LODGE, THE NEW AMERICAN IDEOLOGY 234-64 (1975).

54. *See, e.g.*, Fair Packaging and Labeling Act, 15 U.S.C. §§ 1451-1461 (1976); Truth in Lending Act, *id.* §§ 1601-1677; M. WEIDENBAUM, BUSINESS, GOVERNMENT AND THE PUBLIC 24-59 (1977) (reviewing consumer-product regulation).

Disputing Without Law

A. *Powerful Interests v. Individual Complainants*

Organizations are attentive to the people who provide for their funding and continued survival. When these supporting organizations have interests contrary to those of complainants, the complaint mechanisms will have at best limited effectiveness. Even absent conflicting interests, patrons who do not share the goals of complainants can distract the organization from satisfying complainants. This pattern appears in media action lines, in self-regulation efforts of the business community, and in programs sponsored by governmental agencies.

Media action lines have the capacity to act as intermediaries, to take advantage of informal networks of favors, to create bad publicity, and to translate complaints into calls for general reform.[55] Yet, regardless of the action line's independence from the parent newspaper or broadcaster, it will be constrained by the goals of its media host: pleasing the audience and the advertisers. Although obtaining a solid victory for a consumer can make good news, complaints may be rejected because they are repetitive and no longer engage the audience.[56] Furthermore, the interests of advertisers can ultimately supervene those of both the audience and the consumer. The staff of one television action line was told to discontinue the use of company names because advertisers felt threatened.[57] An auto association in Atlanta reacted to a local television station's proconsumer broadcasts with a one-year advertising boycott.[58] Thus, media action lines may disregard the interests of consumers in order to maintain their primary audience and to avoid antagonizing their benefactors, the business community.

Self-regulation efforts established by the business community in response to consumer complaints are even more directly tied to the

55. Mattice, *supra* note 34. The intermediary role served by action lines resembles a function performed in other legal systems. *See* Barton, *Igugao Law*, 15 U. CAL. PUBLICATIONS IN AM. ARCHAEOLOGY & ETHNOLOGY 1, 57-58 (1919) (all important transactions consummated with aid of intermediary). For example, "Action 4," part of a television news program in New York City, had trouble convincing a department store to settle consumer complaints until reporter Betty Furness discussed the problem on the air. N.Y. Times, Mar. 29, 1976, at 55, col. 1.

56. An advertisement placed in a newspaper by "Action 7" of KGO-TV in San Francisco announced that the station was "looking for unusual problems that can't seem to get resolved in usual ways." San Francisco Chronicle, Aug. 28, 1972, at 11, col. 5.

57. NEWSWEEK, Sept. 15, 1975, at 69-70. In another instance, a local lawyer worried that a newspaper action line was treading too close to the practice of law. He brought the issue to the state bar association; in response, the newspaper adopted the policy of excluding legal items from its action-line column. Bowler, *Action Line Gets Answers*, COLUM. JOURNALISM REV., July/Aug. 1971, at 29, 32. One observer has suggested that to be safe, action lines should avoid giving specific answers to individuals' questions and instead devote themselves to general advice. *See* EDITOR & PUBLISHER, Nov. 15, 1969, at 56.

58. NEWSWEEK, Sept. 15, 1975, at 69-70.

interests of the businesses about which complaints are received.[59] Unless independent nonbusiness members are included in the governing structure of a complaint-processing organization,[60] or unless its work is recorded on an open public record, such an organization has little incentive or power to address complaints by responsibly incorporating the consumer perspective.

Complaint mechanisms established and funded by government avoid the immediate pressure of conflicting interests. Yet, even though funds come from the taxpayer, they are funneled through legislatures in which business lobbies exert persistent influence.[61] Key positions in public agencies are often filled by persons with close ties to the businesses under regulation.[62] An informal channel may exist between jobs in an agency and jobs in the industry under surveillance. Staff loyalties are also colored by past experiences or hopes of future employment.[63] In addition, mechanisms established by government to deal with complaints about government services resemble private industry efforts at self-regulation. Dependent on the government for its continued existence, a public complaint agency has little or no incentive to respond to grievances, and instead may divide the community,

59. Motivated by dwindling consumer confidence and by hopes of forestalling government regulation, business groups created and financed the BBB and trade-association complaint mechanisms. *See* Rosenthal Report, *supra* note 25, at 47,782 (describing origin of BBB); Greenberg & Stanton, *supra* note 26 (describing trade association devices). The personnel of these organizations may be ardent consumer advocates, but their activities will be influenced by the continuing financial support of the businesses they are supposed to monitor. Moreover, the BBB is accorded little power; it forwards consumer complaints to the offending business, but cannot compel settlement. Instead, it relies on the business to resolve complaints voluntarily. Eaton, *supra* note 25.

Similarly, consumer action panels sponsored by trade associations chiefly transmit complaints from the consumer to the company and can only issue nonbinding, advisory opinions. The panels attempt to decrease consumer dissatisfaction without alienating the businesses that constitute their membership. Thus, they exist primarily to serve trade association members, not consumers. Greenberg & Stanton, *supra* note 26.

60. An exceptional trade-association program, the Office of the Impartial Chairman (OIC), was authorized to resolve disputes within the moving industry in New York City through the use of binding arbitration. It helped to prevent complaints by screening the estimates of moving costs submitted by members of the industry. This organization differed in one crucial way from most trade association programs: it was set up jointly by the mover's trade association and a local chapter of the Teamsters Union. Responsive to a different constituency, OIC was given more power and independence than other systems, and was better equipped to respond to consumer interests. Greenberg & Stanton, *supra* note 26.

61. 3 SENATE COMM. ON GOVERNMENT OPERATIONS, 95TH CONG., 1ST SESS., STUDY ON FEDERAL REGULATION 1-22 (Comm. Print. 1977) (describing lobbying expenditures).

62. *See* R. NOLL, REFORMING REGULATION 99-100 (1971); Robinson, *The Federal Communications Commission: An Essay On Regulatory Watchdogs*, 64 VA. L. REV. 169, 185-93 (1978) (even when appointees are not from regulated industry, they seldom represent public interests; even if regulators are not captured by industry, regulation itself often is).

63. Serber, *supra* note 31 (personal and political connections between California's insurance-regulating agency and regulated insurance companies).

Disputing Without Law

lower complainants' expectations, and continue to be perceived as legitimate despite its inadequate resolution of complaints.[64]

B. *Monopoly, Power, and Public Scrutiny*

A complaint mechanism may also be able to insulate itself from complainants by monopolizing complaints.[65] It may be the only organization receiving complaints in a given area or it may be sponsored by the only producer of the goods or services that engender complaints. A store that sells on credit and deals with customer complaints about payment terms has a near-monopoly on easy credit in the community.[66] Thus, despite dissatisfaction, customers will return. The store's purpose is not to resolve complaints but to keep customers and to prevent their going elsewhere to complain. It achieves its purpose because of its market power and its ability either to pacify or to manipulate customers.[67]

A similar phenomenon may explain some conduct of organizations like the PSB.[68] As the only bureau in the state that hears complaints about insurance companies, it has a monopoly on knowledge about such grievances. Perhaps due to its monopoly position, the PSB does not make complaint information public, and it thereby avoids public scrutiny of its conduct.

The UAW's mechanism for processing worker complaints[69] is the

64. This pattern appeared in the conduct of the Service Area Committee (SAC), which is funded by the city government of Washington, D.C. SAC brings together community leaders and city agency personnel to discuss complaints about municipal services. Greenberg, *supra* note 33. Because SAC is dependent on the city for its continued existence and has little influence over resource allocation, it has been a largely inadequate mechanism for resolving complaints. Weekly meetings are congenial gatherings of well-intentioned people, all doing their best to solve problems. The informal atmosphere helps shift the focus from the formal rights of citizens and the duties of government, and lowers the expectations of community members. Community leaders tend to accept the rationalizations given by city officials who, in turn, often place blame on the community. In addition, SAC at times divides the community by causing local leaders to compete for limited resources. *Id.*

65. Problems arise even when there are many available third-party complaint handlers, because consumers cannot always determine which one to consult. Consequently, although diversity theoretically permits better choices, the consumer is unlikely to distinguish the truly helpful intermediaries from the crowd of worthless ones, particularly because complaint handlers sometimes change their names, or cease to exist.

66. *See* Greenberg, *supra* note 33. *See generally* D. CAPLOVITZ, THE POOR PAY MORE 15-30 (1967) (describing practices of retailers in low-income neighborhoods).

67. *See* Greenberg, *supra* note 33.

68. Serber, *supra* note 31. PSB rarely challenges the final arrangement that results from mediation between the complaining customer and an insurance company. PSB seldom requests public hearings, although it is authorized to do so. Furthermore, PSB's bias toward the insurance industry is apparent in its reluctance to launch investigations of large companies. *Id.*

69. *See* Combs-Schilling *supra* note 29.

only forum within the union for the expression of worker grievances about the union; its use is intimately connected to the union's role as exclusive representative of the workers to the management. The mechanism is cumbersome and unresponsive,[70] and workers have disincentives to complain during economic downswings.[71]

A striking contrast is offered by the complaint systems of department stores in one urban area. A study of six systems identified variations in their organization and concluded that persistent customers generally obtain satisfaction even if their complaints seem unreasonable.[72] A major reason for this could be the face-to-face nature of department store complaint encounters. Such encounters may give the complainant an advantage over the individual who complains by mail or telephone. Another reason for success may be that department stores in competitive markets believe the benefits of keeping the steady customer satisfied are worth the costs.

C. *The Organization as Con Artist*[73]

Complaint intermediaries often serve the interests of organizations complained about by resolving only the most blatant cases of unfair treatment and by satisfying only the most persistent complainers. The intermediary diverts all but the real troublemakers and thus diffuses the anger felt by those whose complaints remain unaddressed. Through psychological ploys and functional unresponsiveness these intermediaries serve the interests of organizations stimulating complaints.

Third-party intermediaries, in contrast to in-house complaint departments, are particularly well situated to divert and pacify complainants. Third parties give a gloss of legitimacy to complaint handling; their apparent neutrality suggests an impartiality that puts the

70. *See* note 29 *supra*. From the perspective of the workers, "[t]he more paperwork involved, the less likely the men are to use the procedure." Combs-Schilling, *supra* note 29. There are also pressures from union officials that discourage worker complaints; one official observed that workers who complain are usually those who "kiss ass" with the company and are antiunion. *Id.* But the most entrenched disincentive derives from the union's position as the workers' exclusive bargaining representative. Most of a line-worker's grievances arise against the district committeeman who initially receives the worker's complaints. Because the worker cannot afford to alienate the committeeman, he is often forced to "lump" his grievance. *Id.*

71. Combs-Schilling found that union members used the complaint mechanism less in a period of economic hardship than in a period of relative economic health. *See* note 29 *supra*.

72. Karikas & Rosenwasser, *supra* note 27.

73. This section draws on Goffman, *On Cooling the Mark Out: Some Aspects of Adaptation to Failure*, 15 PSYCH. 451 (1952), which identifies the elements of con artists' techniques and notes their appearance in other social interactions. For a persuasive account of the identical structure of con games and all commercial transactions, see A. LEFF, SWINDLING AND SELLING (1976).

complainant off guard. As a result, the third party can often convince the complainant to drop the complaint or to accept a less than satisfactory resolution.

A kind of symbiosis exists between the organizations that provide goods and services and third-party complaint handlers. The organizations are the sources of problems that the third parties process, and the third parties help the organizations by managing the complaints. Most third parties are probably unaware of this functional fit; nonetheless, unresponsive complaint handling often serves the interests of the organization complained about.

Complaint mechanisms, whether run by third parties or by the offending organizations, can be unresponsive simply by making complaining difficult. Complex and time-consuming procedures[74] that put the burden on the complainant at each successive step[75] are likely to discourage individuals from bringing or pursuing grievances. Such obstacles and failure to monitor compliance in "settled" grievances[76] may be part of a deliberate effort to placate the complainant until the grievance is no longer urgent and the complainant is ready to let it go. In another context, Goffman refers to this strategy as "cooling out."[77] The consumer is initially pacified with a sympathetic response; next, he is met with delay. As his frustrated expectations fade and his anger diminishes, the complainant may voluntarily give up. The strategies are to give the complainant hope in the beginning and then slowly take it away,[78] or to symbolize concern while not accomplishing anything lasting.[79] Other approaches let the complainant vent anger by exploding at the complaint handler, by making routine telephone calls, and by completing routine forms. Even if the problem is not resolved, the complainant feels better because he has done something and has been

74. For example, extensive paperwork is required by the UAW's Public Review Board procedures. *See* Combs-Schilling, *supra* note 29.

75. For example, trade-association consumer action panels transmit a complaint to the offending organization and take no further action until the consumer contacts the intermediary again. Greenberg & Stanton, *supra* note 26.

76. Action lines, for example, rarely check to see if a complainant has been satisfied. *See* N.Y. Times, Mar. 29, 1976, at 31, col. 4.

77. Goffman, *supra* note 73, at 451-52. "Operators" cool out the "mark" or prospective victim of planned exploitation; "[a]n attempt is made to define the situation for the mark in a way that makes it easy for him to accept the inevitable and quietly go home." *Id.* at 452.

78. *See* L. Nader, *The Direction of Law and the Development of Extra-Judicial Processes in Nation State Societies*, in CROSS-EXAMINATIONS: ESSAYS IN MEMORY OF MAX GLUCKMAN 93-94 (P. Gulliver ed. 1978) (illustrating "hot-cold treatment" in linguistic techniques used by telephone supervisor to cool out complainant).

79. The SAC, *see* note 64 *supra*, was able to cool out complainants consistently by implementing "special projects" designed to demonstrate concern. The projects ultimately proved unsuccessful. *See* Greenberg, *supra* note 33.

heard. He may even acquire a desired sense of control by viewing the act of dropping the complaint as his own calculated decision.[80]

The complaint processer may actively work to lower the complainant's expectations or to force him to reevaluate his initial sense of injustice. In some instances, informal meetings communicate a friendly atmosphere and an impression that all that can be done to solve the problem is being done.[81] The intermediary actually may mislead the complainant to believe that all avenues of relief have been exhausted,[82] or that the offending business practices are reasonable. The BBB, for example, may incorrectly tell a consumer that unwritten agreements are not binding and thereby persuade him that he has no basis for complaint.[83] Short of dismissing the grievance altogether, the complaint handler often helps the complainant reformulate the grievance through a process variously called clarification, objectification, or interpretation.[84]

By thus conveying problems "strip[ped] of their hostile emotional content"[85] complaint handlers may cause consumers to reevaluate their initial feelings. In this process, the complaint handler may shift blame to the complainant.[86] Further, the complainant may be blamed simply for complaining; for example, he may be told that he has no cause to complain. He may watch himself give up in the face of delays, and conclude it was petty to demand redress for a minor problem. He may learn to see people who complain as deviants.[87] Indeed, in this culture, people are commonly reluctant to see themselves as complainers.[88] This

80. If the complainant feels powerless in seeking satisfaction, he may rationalize his decision to give up as being at least one act within his own control.

81. Greenberg, *supra* note 33; *see* note 64 *supra* (complainants develop sympathetic attitudes toward those handling complaints in informal meetings).

82. Eaton, *supra* note 25.

83. *Id.* (customer billed for unwanted services was told relief unavailable absent written contract).

84. *See* Steele, *Fraud, Dispute and the Consumer: Responding to Consumer Complaints*, 123 U. Pa. L. Rev. 1107, 1156 (1975) (clarification, objectification); Mattice, *supra* note 34 (interpretative communication).

85. Steele, *supra* note 84, at 1155.

86. Greenberg describes how a sanitation department representative to a community complaint forum blamed the trash in vacant lots on the lack of community participation, when, in reality, the community was unable to discover procedures or times for trash removal. Greenberg, *supra* note 33.

87. Combs-Schilling found that reluctance to complain to the UAW's complaint mechanism was due in part to the negative image union members associated with complaining. Combs-Schilling, *supra* note 29. The peculiarly American value placed on self-reliance, *see* Hsu, *American Core Value and National Character*, in Psychological Anthropology 248 (F. Hsu ed. 1972), may contribute to the sense that complaining is an undesirable sign of weakness.

88. *See* Best & Andreasen, *supra* note 13, at 720-21 (voicing complaint seems generally disfavored; complaining to third parties even more disfavored). One commentator has encouraged people to overcome the negative image of complaining: "Most of all, com-

attitude accompanies what appears to be a pervasive perceptual handicap: the inability to identify individual complaints as part of an aggregate that calls for systemic response.

D. *Failure to See the Forest*

Individuals with complaints tend to think that they are alone, even when numbers of other people have the same problem. Perhaps this sense and the related reluctance to complain stem from a pattern linked with industrialization: the atomizing of the social organization into smaller and smaller consuming units. In addition, the demands of conformity—an equally powerful part of the American ideology—argue against identifying oneself as a troublemaker, even as others swallow the same complaints.[89]

In the context of complaint mechanisms, individuals tend to accede to the suggestion that their complaints are petty and not worth pursuing.[90] Some, willing to see themselves as whistleblowers, may pursue their claims. Yet the prevailing rate of unsatisfactory resolution conveys the message that an individual complaint is generally not worth pressing.[91] Reinforcing a sense of individual powerlessness, this failure rate may contribute to the view that only isolated individuals, as opposed to classes of people, have complaints.

One consequence is that only limited numbers of complaints are voiced, and these complaints do not provide strong pressures for systemic change. Even when large numbers of related complaints are ex-

plainers as individuals should not lose heart. They should learn to suppress that feeling of embarrassment, the worry about what other people will think of them." Baker, *Time Essay: Louder! The Need to Complain More*, TIME, July 3, 1972, at 33.

89. Tocqueville was one of the first to describe American intolerance of deviant behavior. *See* A. DE TOCQUEVILLE, DEMOCRACY IN AMERICA 399-40 (J. Meyer & M. Lerner eds. 1966) (immense power of public opinion in democracy).

90. This article has considered only a few of the possible sources of discouragement. Given a variety of pressures, a potential complainant may often decide to "exit" rather than "voice" his grievance. *See* A. HIRSCHMAN, EXIT, VOICE, AND LOYALTY 105 (1970). Hirschman argues that decisions about whether to voice or to exit are related to perceptions of the probability of influencing a decision, of the calculated advantage of success, and of the availability of alternative products and services. *Id.* at 37-38, 41. The tendency to voice also depends on a population's general readiness to complain and on the availability of mechanisms for communicating complaints cheaply and effectively. *Id.* at 42-43. The exercise of voice for handling everyday complaints can be treated as an index of the degree to which people believe they are powerful, regardless of the actual distribution of power in society. *See* L. Nader, *Powerlessness in Zapotec and United States Societies*, in THE ANTHROPOLOGY OF POWER (R. Fogelson & R. Adams eds. 1977).

91. Best and Andreasen found that when consumers take their problems to third parties, they come away satisfied only one-third of the time. Best & Andreasen, *supra* note 13, at 125; *see* p. 1007 *supra*.

pressed, most complaint handlers are not equipped to perceive or respond to group problems.[92]

Few federal agencies, for example, actually have offices responsible for handling citizen-initiated complaints;[93] few publicize their procedures or tabulate incoming complaints.[94] One researcher noted that "[w]ithout statistical records of the nature, categories, frequencies, distributions, and dispositions of complaints, agencies can hardly be expected to integrate complaint data into their regular operations or sustain standards of meritorious performance in their direct relationship with the public."[95] It is not surprising, then, that federal agency practices are seldom changed in response to complaints.[96]

Other complaint mechanisms fail to respond to problems in the aggregate because they are not empowered to do so or because it is not in their own interest to respond with systemic reforms. Some mechanisms, particularly those created as a form of self-regulation, lack any authority to resolve complaints and simply act as couriers that carry complaints to the proper party.[97] Lacking sufficient ties to the parties they are supposed to scrutinize,[98] these intermediaries do not have the structural capacity to respond to problems on an aggregate level. Some complaint handlers shy away from challenging general practices in order to garner enough power to achieve success in individual cases.[99] Others, fully aware of their limited authority, may even try to separate complainants who initially come to them with shared interests.[100] Such intermediaries hold little authority or power and must depend on unobtrusive, uncontroversial measures. The grant of little authority is often due to the presence of interests more powerful than the consumer or citizen groups supposedly served by complaint programs.[101]

92. *See, e.g.*, Steele, *supra* note 84, at 1180-86 (Illinois Consumer Fraud Bureau primarily solves concrete disputes rather than enforcing antifraud laws systemically).

93. One study found that of 64 agencies responding to a questionnaire, 51 reported having no office specifically responsible for handling citizen-initiated complaints, aside from formal adjudicative procedures. Rosenblum, *Handling Citizen Initiated Complaints: An Introductory Study of Federal Agency Procedures and Practices*, 26 AD. L. REV. 1, 10 (1974).

94. *Id.* at 10-12.

95. *Id.* at 12.

96. *Id.* at 11.

97. For example, the BBB and the complaint panels created by trade associations for the most part simply carry complaints to the offending business. *See* note 59 *supra*.

98. In fact, most trade-association mechanisms represent less than half of their particular industry. As a result, they are hampered from fulfilling even the limited task of conveying complaints to the proper parties. *See* Greenberg & Stanton, *supra* note 26.

99. The Community Development Group, a private service organization in Washington, D.C., relies on the influence it gains through informal contacts with public agency personnel to facilitate certain cases. Therefore it refrains from aggressive challenges to the agencies. *See* Greenberg, *supra* note 33.

100. *See* note 64 *supra*.

101. *See* pp. 1009-11 *supra*.

Disputing Without Law

Some complaint mechanisms do not gather or respond to complaints on an aggregate basis even when they have the power to act systemically. Media action lines are a prime example. Capable of arousing public pressure and generating group consciousness,[102] media organizations are fundamentally limited by dependence on audience interest and advertiser support. These limitations often impede systemic reforms,[103] even though media action lines remain one of the most effective complaint handlers outside of courts.

Another effective complaint handler, a congressman, was free of conflicting interests and depended to a great extent on the satisfaction of complaints for reelection.[104] In a sense, the congressman had a stake in the continuation of his constituent's problems.[105] For his own political survival, it made sense to respond on a case-by-case basis, rather than to push legislative action. Even in relation to problems potentially shared by a class of constituents, such as recipients of social security or veterans benefits, the congressman guaranteed votes by arranging for individualized relief.

Most intermediaries screen complaints in order to select those that should be addressed. Although they are meant to serve as alternatives to law, complaint processors often screen out complaints that do not raise legal claims. Moreover, complaint handlers sometimes screen complaints according to the personal characteristics of the complainant. The PSB, for example, pays more attention to the complainant who is calm, articulate, white, male, and middle-class than to the excited, nonwhite, or female complainant.[106] Intermediaries may try to determine whether the subject of the complaint is "important" or "valid"; they may reject a case that appears complex and costly to process.

This ad hoc approach to complaint handling permits unfair treatment and fails to stimulate extensive reforms. Secrecy, intimidation, and distancing mechanisms all protect self-interested groups. Rather than responding to all complainants, grievance organizations find it less expensive to treat isolated cases and to allow complainants to drop

102. One complainant reported that she persevered in her complaint about a particular brand of stove when she received supportive letters from other purchasers following a newspaper story about her complaint. Citation withheld to protect confidentiality.

103. *See* p. 1009 *supra*.

104. Karikas, *supra* note 30. The need to cultivate votes gave the congressman a direct incentive to aid complainants; the need to develop helpful local contacts to ensure his ability to solve complaints gave him reason to lobby in Washington for the local industries that assisted his constituents. *Id.*

105. *See* W. GELLHORN, *supra* note 30, at 75-76 (congressional representatives respond to constituent complaints to help themselves get reelected).

106. Serber, *supra* note 31 ("deselection" of complaints based on complainants' sex, race, affluence, articulateness, and degree of calm).

their grievances or to avoid voicing them; yet the costs of this approach are real, if sometimes hidden, and they are pervasive.

E. *The Costs of Inadequate Complaint Processing*

The immediate cost of inadequate complaint processing is borne by the consumer. If his complaint remains unsatisfied, he continues to suffer the injustice that stimulated it, as well as cumulative effects of that injustice. Particularly if the complainant is poor, even a small dollar loss can be serious. Individuals of any income level are not immune to larger costs such as those associated with defects in automobiles, mobile homes, or nursing home services.

The psychological strains of living with an unreliable product or service[107] are compounded by the emotional toll of the complaint process itself. Delays and confrontations accompany even responses to complaints that are finally successful; unsuccessful complainants have to deal with increased frustration and humiliation, even when "cooled out" by the intermediary. The consequent sense of powerlessness is a cost to both the individual and society.[108] People who feel powerless tend to become apathetic and uninvolved. This response short-circuits the ideal chain of communication that could alert producers of goods and services to defects and inefficiencies.

As a result, the kind of information loop that could improve products and services does not develop, and instead an inefficient and unsuccessful process of chain referrals is maintained. The cost of dealing with an average product or service failure is often as large or larger than the original purchase price and consumers absorb the greater part of such costs. Effective complaint resolution would cause firms to internalize these costs when they make repairs, replacements, or refunds. Thus they would have a stronger incentive than they do now to improve the quality of products and services. In other words, mass redress of individual consumer complaints could have a powerful effect in improving the quality of American products. Further, institutions for which complaint handling is only a secondary function could then devote more time to the performance of their primary tasks.

107. Even though small amounts of money may be involved, the breakdown of a washing machine can be a real crisis for a family without an automobile. A low-income individual who refuses to pay a bill for a defective item may face the possibility of garnishment of his wages. A delay in repairing a set of false teeth has emotional costs for a patient that exceed the money involved. *See* note 17 *supra*.

108. The Small Claims Study Group concluded that small grievances "are the stuff of everyday life and the outcome of the attempt to redress them has much to do with whether people feel empowered, active agents controlling their own destinies, or exploited, victims of forces beyond their control." SMALL CLAIMS STUDY GROUP, *supra* note 17, at 9.

Disputing Without Law

Some observers have suggested that the cumulative effect of little injustices is endemic lawlessness.[109] Even if complaint mechanisms do not cause disorder and lawlessness, they fail to help remedy the corruption and ineptitude of landlords, loan sharks, health inspectors, public service bureaucrats, and private producers. One obvious reform would be to increase the role of law in addressing the low-profile, petty exploitation suffered by large segments of the population. But that solution, most often associated with the small claims court movement, has also failed to realize stated goals.[110]

III. Complaints and the Law

Several concluding observations result from the studies of alternatives to courts that have been described here. First, the relative power between purchasers and providers is a key variable with respect to the ability of nonjudicial complaint mechanisms to resolve disputes satisfactorily.[111] The fundamental problem that constrains the performance

109. *See, e.g.*, P. Schrag, Counsel for the Deceived (1972). Schrag, a professor at Columbia Law School, described his attempts to deal with everyday problems in New York City. He perceived a breakdown in law evidenced by nonenforcement of consumer-protection legislation.

110. *See* Yngvesson & Hennessey, *supra* note 5, at 268 (small claims courts remain ineffective for poor).

111. The relative bargaining power of the parties can determine the fairness of the terms of the exchange. The law has already recognized the danger of a "contract of adhesion," described as

> a standardized contract proposed entirely by one party to the transaction for the acceptance of the other; such a contract, due to the disparity in bargaining power between the draftsman and the second party, must be accepted or rejected by the second party on a "take it or leave it" basis, without opportunity for bargaining and under such conditions that the "adherer" cannot obtain the desired product or service save by acquiescing in the form agreement.

Steven v. Fidelity & Cas. Co., 58 Cal. 2d 862, 377 P.2d 284, 27 Cal. Rptr. 172 (1962) (citations omitted).

Courts have used the unconscionability clause of U.C.C. § 2-302 to invalidate onerous provisions of such contracts. *See, e.g.*, Williams v. Walker-Thomas Furniture Co., 350 F.2d 445 (D.C. Cir. 1965); Zabriski Chevrolet, Inc. v. Smith, 99 N.J. Super. 441, 240 A.2d 195 (Super. Ct. Law Div. 1968). As one critic noted, however, contract remedies secured through adjudication do not address the "inefficiencies and inequities of exorbitant prices and oppressive clauses" of form contracts. Kornhauser, *Unconscionability in Standard Forms*, 64 Calif. L. Rev. 1151, 1183 (1976). Nor are judicial remedies responsive to those who do not sue because they do not expect relief or to those who decide not to purchase because of unfair contract terms. *Id.* at 1180.

Unequal bargaining power is especially troubling when the seller uses vastly unequal bargaining power to disclaim warranties or limit remedies. *See* Henningsen v. Bloomfield Motors, Inc., 32 N.J. 358, 404, 161 A.2d 69, 95 (1960) ("The lawmakers did not authorize the automobile manufacturer to use its grossly disproportionate bargaining power to . . . impose on the ordinary buyer, who in effect has no real freedom of choice, the grave danger to himself and others that attends the sale of such a dangerous instrumentality as a defectively made automobile.") Legislative efforts to protect consumers against such harm include 15 U.S.C. §§ 2301-2312 (1976), which requires that warranties for con-

of alternative complaint mechanisms today derives from their inability to compensate adequately for the ineffective bargaining position of the individual who confronts large corporations and government bureaucracies. Many complaint handlers reinforce these unequal bargaining positions; others are powerless to reorder them. Disputes between people of unequal power are unlikely to be settled fairly by mediation or arbitration unless the force of law is available as a last resort.[112]

Courts should be available, especially in cases in which the parties have unequal power; parties with relatively equal power are more likely to resolve disputes without the aid of the judiciary. Access to court for parties of unequal power could itself shape opportunities for satisfactory settlement without the exercise of legal authority. Even now, settlements of claims that could have been resolved legally almost universally reflect the level of awards available in small claims court.[113] Expanding judicial relief for minor claims could lead to better nonjudicial solutions.

A second observation is that no matter how alternative complaint mechanisms are strengthened, their case-by-case approach cannot remedy all the harms identified by consumer and citizen complaints. Expanding automatic return policies, simplifying small claims court, and extending consumer arbitration in the shadow of the courtroom door are reforms that would provide some limited relief, but they would not contribute to the identification of widespread problems or to the prevention of future disputes. Only when numerous complaints are viewed together can a pattern emerge—for example, a pattern of automobile-repair fraud. Handling such complaints in the aggregate may lead to effective preventive reforms; it may also be less expensive than a case-by-case approach. Aggregate solutions are available through class-action litigation and regulation,[114] yet business and government, for the most part, do not construct aggregate solutions to classes of complaints and instead persist in approaching each grievance individually.

Ways must be found to compensate for the perceptual handicap that

sumer products be more readily understandable and enforceable by the consumer. This statute ultimately may fail to serve consumer interests because its provisions could encourage sellers to issue oral warranties that are difficult to enforce or to issue limited rather than full warranties. Hymson, *The Magnuson-Moss Warranty-Federal Trade Commission Improvement Act: Should the Consumer Rejoice?* 15 J. FAM. L. 77 (1976).

112. Giving parties access to court ensures that they have an effective technique to resolve their dispute; access may also influence the way in which the same problems are resolved out of court. *See* Lempert, *Mobilizing Private Law: An Introductory Essay*, 11 LAW & SOC'Y REV. 173, 173-74 (1976).

113. L. Nader & Shugart, in No Access to Law (chapter 2, untitled).

114. *But see* note 4 *supra* (noting barriers to class-action litigation and limitations of regulation).

so often restricts problemsolving to this case-by-case approach.[115] One technique would start with the recognition that, as in most cultures, the most powerful tool of law reform is public opinion. The mass nature of this society requires the use of innovative techniques to inform and rally public opinion. Although seldom employed for this purpose, existing communication technologies could be used to publicize the records of varied complaint organizations. Such records could be published; complaints could be metered or banked.[116] Further, if all public and private complaint organizations were required to have open records, strategies for aggregate reform could be formulated more easily.

A third observation is an initial response to the question posed at the beginning of this article: are problems of access to law causing a serious deficiency in our justice system? The answer is yes. Estimates of the economic and psychological costs of unattended complaints can only hint at the loss to society that results when little injustices accumulate without judicial relief. Yet the courts are unable to provide complete justice even to those who enter their doors. A comparison of two trial courts in California between 1890 and 1970 concludes that the function of courts has changed from dispute settlement to routine administration.[117] The institutions that have replaced the courts, some of which have been described here, do not operate very well for the powerless.

Disputing without law is not a very satisfactory experience for most consumers and citizens in this country, yet it is unlikely that the force of law can be marshaled to address "little injustices" unless they are reconceptualized as collective harms. For official action in that direction to have any likelihood of yielding more than symbolic victories, an active and vital grass-roots citizen and consumer movement must be encouraged.

115. *See* pp. 1015-18 *supra.*

116. L. Nader & Singer, *Dispute Resolution . . . Law in the Future: What are the Choices?* 51 CAL. ST. B.J. 281, 314 (1976).

117. Friedman & Percival, *A Tale of Two Courts: Litigation in Alameda and San Benito Counties*, 10 LAW & SOC'Y REV. 267, 302 (1976).

[8]

TOWARD ANOTHER VIEW OF LEGAL NEGOTIATION: THE STRUCTURE OF PROBLEM SOLVING

Carrie Menkel-Meadow*

"To sue is human, to settle divine"
—Sign in U.S. Magistrate's Office

TABLE OF CONTENTS

---

* Acting Professor of Law, University of California, Los Angeles; A.B., Barnard College; J.D., University of Pennsylvania.

So many of my colleagues and friends have read and commented on earlier drafts of this Article that it is difficult to give credit where credit is due. On the other hand, the spirit with which my friends tried to solve the problems I encountered working on this piece amply demonstrates the advantages of the collaborative processes described in the text. I therefore must express my appreciation to those who entered into my problem-solving world and made some contribution to the final product or to my thinking: Richard Abel, Paul Bergman, David Binder, Victoria Bonebakker, Paul Brest, Carole Goldberg-Ambrose, Daniel Lowenstein, William McGovern, Robert Meadow, Patrick Patterson, Gary Schwartz, Murray Schwartz, Mark Spiegel and Stephen Yeazell. In addition, I must give special thanks to my Dean and friend, Susan Westerberg Prager, and to my colleague and husband, Robert Meadow, without whose support I would be solving no problems at all.

And finally, I would like to express my gratitude to my editors Janet Kobrin and Sharon Nolfi. I think I can say that never has a law review editorial process been so pleasurable and supportive as we "negotiated" the words that follow.

INTRODUCTION

When people negotiate they engage in a particular kind of social behavior; they seek to do together what they cannot do alone. Those who negotiate are sometimes principals attempting to solve their own problems, or, more likely in legal negotiation, they are agents acting for clients, within the bounds of the law.

When lawyers[1] write about this frequent social activity they

1. Law professors have written most of the legal literature on negotiation. *See, e.g.*, G. BELLOW & B. MOULTON, THE LAWYERING PROCESS: NEGOTIATION (1981); L. BROWN & E. DAUER, PLANNING BY LAWYERS: MATERIALS ON A NONADVERSARIAL LEGAL PROCESS (1978); H. EDWARDS & J. WHITE, THE LAWYER AS A NEGOTIATOR (1977); H. FREEMAN & H. WEIHOFEN, CLINICAL LAW TRAINING (1972); K.

join commentators from other disciplines[2] in emphasizing an adversarial[3] or zero-sum game[4] approach to negotiation. In their view, what one party gains the other must lose. Resources are

HEGLAND, TRIAL AND PRACTICE SKILLS IN A NUTSHELL (1978); J. KELNER & F. MCGOVERN, SUCCESSFUL LITIGATION TECHNIQUES: STUDENT EDITION (1981); M. MELTSNER & P. SCHRAG, PUBLIC INTEREST ADVOCACY: MATERIALS FOR CLINICAL LEGAL EDUCATION ch. 13, (1974) [hereinafter cited as M. MELTSNER & P. SCHRAG, MATERIALS]; M. MELTSNER & P. SCHRAG, TOWARD SIMULATION IN LEGAL EDUCATION: AN EXPERIMENTAL COURSE IN PRETRIAL LITIGATION (1975) [hereinafter cited as M. MELTSNER & P. SCHRAG, COURSE]; C. PECK, CASES AND MATERIALS ON NEGOTIATION (2d ed. 1980); G. WILLIAMS, EFFECTIVE LEGAL NEGOTIATION (1979); G. WILLIAMS, LEGAL NEGOTIATION AND SETTLEMENT (1983); Lowenthal, *A General Theory of Negotiation Process, Strategy, and Behavior*, 31 U. KAN. L. REV. 69 (1982); Mathews, *Negotiation: A Pedagogical Challenge*, 6 J. LEGAL EDUC. 93 (1953). Some of the lay texts, however, have been written by practicing lawyers. *See, e.g.*, H. COHEN, YOU CAN NEGOTIATE ANYTHING—HOW TO GET WHAT YOU WANT (1980); C. KARRASS, GIVE & TAKE: THE COMPLETE GUIDE TO NEGOTIATING STRATEGIES AND TACTICS (1974) [hereinafter cited as C. KARRASS, GIVE & TAKE]; C. KARRASS, THE NEGOTIATING GAME (1970) [hereinafter cited as C. KARRASS, GAME]; D. LEWIS, POWER NEGOTIATING TACTICS & TECHNIQUES (1981); G. NIERENBERG, FUNDAMENTALS OF NEGOTIATING (1982) [hereinafter cited as G. NIERENBERG, FUNDAMENTALS]; G. NIERENBERG, THE ARE OF NEGOTIATING (1981) [hereinafter cited as G. NIERENBERG, ART.].

2. The authors of the "non-legal" literature on negotiation include social scientists and business people. *See, e.g.*, R. FISHER & W. URY, GETTING TO YES: NEGOTIATING AGREEMENT WITHOUT GIVING IN (1981) (Roger Fisher is a law professor but this work was written for a more general audience.); J. ILICH, THE ART AND SKILL OF SUCCESSFUL NEGOTIATION (1973); J. ILICH & B. JONES, SUCCESSFUL NEGOTIATING SKILLS FOR WOMEN (1981); H. RAIFFA, THE ART AND SCIENCE OF NEGOTIATION (1982); M. SCHATZKI, NEGOTIATION: THE ART OF GETTING WHAT YOU WANT (1981); T. SCHELLING, THE STRATEGY OF CONFLICT (1960); T. WARSCHAW, WINNING BY NEGOTIATION (1980); J. WILT, HANDLING YOUR DISAGREEMENTS: A CHILDREN'S BOOK ABOUT DIFFERENCES OF OPINION (1980) (a charming way to introduce children to some of the concepts discussed herein); I. ZARTMAN, THE 50 PERCENT SOLUTION: HOW TO BARGAIN SUCCESSFULLY WITH HIJACKERS, STRIKERS, BOSSES, OIL MANAGERS, ARABS, RUSSIANS, AND OTHER WORTHY OPPONENTS IN THIS MODERN WORLD (1976); I. ZARTMAN & M. BERMAN, THE PRACTICAL NEGOTIATOR (1982).

3. I have chosen the term "adversarial," to describe the traditional and competitive idea of negotiation that dominates the literature. This model of negotiation could be called "competitive," "zero-sum" and "individualistic." The term "adversarial," however, best captures one of the arguments of this Article: the courtroom litigation model dominates in negotiations, even when parties desire to accomplish things a court could not do. In addition, "adversarial" avoids confusion with the term "competitive" which has come to be associated with negotiation styles or tactics, rather than a total conception of negotiation which this Article addresses.

4. A zero-sum game is, strictly speaking, one where the total winnings for one party minus the total losses for the other party equal zero. Cooter, Marks & Mnookin, *Bargaining in the Shadow of the Law: A Testable Model of Strategic Behavior*, 11 J. LEGAL STUD. 225, 227 (1982). *See also* M. BACHARACH, ECONOMICS AND THE THEORY OF GAMES (1976). The conception of zero-sum games comes from the now classic J. VON NEUMANN & O. MORGENSTERN, THE THEORY OF GAMES AND ECONOMIC BEHAVIOR (1944). See L. THUROW, THE ZERO-SUM SOCIETY (1980) for a discussion of how a such conception affects the way in which we "solve" economic problems.

limited and must be divided. Information about one's real preferences must be jealously guarded. If the negotiation fails, the court will declare one party a winner, awarding money or an injunction. Successful negotiations represent a compromise of each party's position on an ordinal scale of numerical (usually monetary) values. This Article suggests that writers and negotiators who take such an adversarial approach limit themselves unnecessarily because they have not fully examined their assumptions.

Recently, several analysts[5] have suggested that another ap-

---

5. G. BELLOW & B. MOULTON, *supra* note 1, at 146–54; R. FISHER & W. URY, *supra* note 2; H. RAIFFA, *supra* note 2; G. WILLIAMS, LEGAL NEGOTIATION & SETTLEMENT, *supra* note 1; Lowenthal, *supra* note 1, at 72. This literature is vague and imprecise in its definitions of problem solving. Some commentators provide processes or sets of strategies or behaviors; others present a conception which, like the definition offered in this Article, is meant to orient the reader to negotiation or objectives sought by the negotiator. Fisher and Ury and Raiffa make the best efforts at describing problem solving as both a conceptualization of the purpose of negotiation and as a process but there are still areas where the distinctions blur. *See, e.g.*, R. FISHER & W. URY, *supra* note 2, at 101–49.

There have been threads of problem-solving approaches in the legal literature over the years, *see* H. HART & A. SACKS, THE LEGAL PROCESS: BASIC PROBLEMS IN THE MAKING AND APPLICATION OF LAW ch. 2 (tent. ed. 1958), but adversarial notions of negotiation have dominated the teaching of negotiation in law school courses. *See, e.g.*, H. EDWARDS & J. WHITE, TEACHERS MANUAL FOR THE LAWYER AS A NEGOTIATOR (1977); G. WILLIAMS, TEACHERS' MANUAL FOR LEGAL NEGOTIATION AND SETTLEMENT (1983); Ortwein, *Teaching Negotiation: A Valuable Experience*, 31 J. LEGAL EDUC. 108 (1981); White, *The Lawyer As Negotiator: An Adventure in Understanding and Teaching the Art of Negotiation*, 19 J. LEGAL EDUC. 337 (1967). *See also* H. RAIFFA, *supra* note 2, at 25–32. There is a remarkable lack of literature on transactional negotiation, although threads of problem-solving themes run through many discussions of contract law, *see, e.g.*, C. FRIED, CONTRACT AS PROMISE: A THEORY OF CONTRACTUAL OBLIGATION (1981), and the law and economics literature, at least in the sense that efficiency may be produced by such transactions, *see, e.g.*, R. POSNER, ECONOMIC ANALYSIS OF LAW (2d ed. 1977).

The conception of problem-solving negotiation is not new; non-legal literature has long recognized this approach to negotiation. *See, e.g.*, BARGAINING: FORMAL THEORIES OF NEGOTIATION (O. Young ed. 1975) [hereinafter cited as BARGAINING]; O. BARTOS, PROCESS AND OUTCOME OF NEGOTIATIONS (1974); A. CODDINGTON, THEORIES OF THE BARGAINING PROCESS (1968); CONFLICT RESOLUTION: CONTRIBUTIONS OF THE BEHAVIORAL SCIENCES (C. Smith ed. 1971); COOPERATION AND COMPETITION IN MIXED MOTIVE GAMES (L. Wrightsman ed. 1972); J. CROSS, ECONOMICS OF BARGAINING (1968); A. DOUGLAS, INDUSTRIAL PEACEMAKING (1962); R. FISHER, INTERNATIONAL CONFLICT FOR BEGINNERS (1969); G. MAXWELL & D. SCHMIDT, COOPERATION: AN EXPERIMENTAL ANALYSIS (1975); E. MCGINNIES, SOCIAL BEHAVIOR: A FUNCTIONAL ANALYSIS (1970); I. MORLEY & G. STEPHENSON, THE SOCIAL PSYCHOLOGY OF BARGAINING (1977); NEGOTIATIONS: SOCIAL-PSYCHOLOGICAL PERSPECTIVES (D. Druckman ed. 1977) [hereinafter cited as NEGOTIATIONS]; E. PETERS, STRATEGY AND TACTICS IN LABOR NEGOTIATIONS (1966); D. PRUITT, NEGOTIATION BEHAVIOR (1981); J. RUBIN & B. BROWN, THE SOCIAL PSYCHOLOGY OF BARGAINING AND NEGOTIATION (1975); SOCIAL CONFLICT: READINGS IN RULE STRUCTURES AND CONFLICT RELATIONSHIPS (P. Brickman ed. 1974); THE NEGOTIATION PROCESS: THEORIES AND APPLICATIONS (I. Zartman ed. 1975); THE SOCIAL INFLUENCE PROCESS (J. Tedeschi ed. 1972); THE STRUCTURE OF CONFLICT (P. Swingle ed. 1970); R. WALTON & R. MCKERSIE, A BEHAVIORAL THEORY OF LA-

proach to negotiation, an approach I will call problem-solving, might better accomplish the purposes of negotiation. This problem-solving model seeks to demonstrate how negotiators, on behalf of litigators or planners,[6] can more effectively accomplish their goals by focusing on the parties' actual objectives and creatively attempting to satisfy the needs of both parties, rather than by focusing exclusively on the assumed objectives of maximizing individual gain. Unfortunately, some of this new literature tends to confuse collaborative negotiation styles or strategies[7] with what must be antecedent to any negotiation behavior—a conception of negotiation goals.[8] These recent analysts have also failed to fully explore their own assumptions concerning the objectives in nego-

BOR NEGOTIATIONS (1965); Black & Morton, *The Intergroup Dynamics of Win-Lose Conflict and Problem Solving Collaboration in Union-Management Relations*, in INTERGROUP RELATIONS AND LEADERSHIP (M. Sherif ed. 1962); Schlenker & Goldman, *Cooperators and Competitors in Conflict: A Test of the "Triangle Model,"* 22 J. OF CONFLICT RESOLUTION 393 (1978). For an excellent bibliography of the social psychology literature see D. PRUITT, supra, at 237–49 (1981). What is remarkable is the persistence of the adversarial model in legal negotiation literature, given the far richer approach to the process developed in other fields.

6. The discussion of negotiation in this Article focuses primarily on negotiation in the litigation or dispute resolution context, although there is some discussion of transactional negotiations. Transactional, or "rulemaking," negotiations may be sufficiently different from dispute resolution to require a different conceptual framework, *see, e.g.*, Eisenberg, *Private Ordering Through Negotiation: Dispute-Settlement and Rulemaking*, 89 HARV. L. REV. 637 (1976); Paul, *A New Role For Lawyers in Contract Negotiations*, 62 A.B.A. J. 93 (1976). On the other hand, it may be that, to the extent that they are different, transactional negotiation more often employs a problem-solving conceptualization and dispute resolution negotiations may benefit from application of transactional models to settling disputes. While adversarial negotiation may be dysfunctional in litigation negotiations, it is likely to be even more dysfunctional in transactional negotiations, especially where the parties are forming a long term relationship. *See* Eisenberg, *supra*, at 649; *infra* text accompanying notes 32–154. There may, of course, be differences along a continuum of contexts in transactional as well as litigation negotiation. Negotiations for contracts in the entertainment industry, for example, where the resources to be divided may be more limited, are likely to be more "adversarial" than those between commercial buyers and sellers who do business together regularly. *See* Klein, *The Put Up or Shut Up Strategy in Business Negotiation*, 17 U.C.D. L. REV. 341 (1983).

7. Both Lowenthal, *supra* note 1, and G. WILLIAMS, LEGAL NEGOTIATION AND SETTLEMENT, *supra* note 1, focus primarily on the execution of negotiation processes and do not discuss the planning or conceptualization of solutions. Much of this literature takes the solutions or "demands" as given and focuses on the negotiators' interactions. This is important work but it should not exclude focusing on the goals of a particular negotiation.

8. Negotiation goals, in general, encompass that which the client seeks to accomplish. It could mean "maximizing gain" but in many negotiations the client will have particular substantive goals that may not include maximizing individual gain. Thus, the particular goals should be considered before any given set of strategies or behaviors are utilized.

9. R. FISHER & W. URY, *supra* note 2, does an excellent job of presenting the problem-solving arguments in a simple fashion for a wide variety of practitioners of negotiation. This work, which is not meant to be a scholarly treatment of the issues,

tiation.[9] This Article explores those assumptions and elaborates on a framework for problem-solving negotiation that responds to the limitations of the adversarial model.

In order to contrast the adversarial model with the problem-solving model several key concepts must be defined and criteria for evaluation of the models made explicit. The negotiation models described here may seem unduly polarized, yet they represent the polarities of approach exemplified both by the conceptions of negotiation we construct as well as by the strategies and behaviors we choose.[10] The models described here are based on orientations to negotiation, that is, how we approach our purpose in negotiation, rather than on the particular strategies or tactics we choose. It must be noted, however, that the tactics and strategies we choose may well be affected by our conception of negotiation.[11] A

---

however, does not fully explore how the authors' proposals can be adapted to the special characteristics of legal negotiation. It is an important beginning but its simplicity may be deceptive. *See* Washington, Book Review, 48 BROOKLYN L. REV. 647 (1982) (reviewing R. FISHER AND W. URY, GETTING TO YES (1981)). *See also* White, *The Pros and Cons of Getting to Yes*, 34 J. LEGAL ED. 115 (1984). R. FISHER & W. URY, *supra* note 2, presents a number of important issues that could productively be explored by legal scholars.

10. Given the conceptualization in the literature of two essentially polarized orientations to negotiation, *see* R. FISHER & W. URY, *supra* note 2, at 9; G. WILLIAMS, LEGAL NEGOTIATION AND SETTLEMENT, *supra* note 1, at 15-69, it is not surprising that polarized behaviors such as Hard/Soft and Competitive/Cooperative have been documented in the empirical work done on negotiating attorneys. *Id.* On the other hand, behaviors as well as orientations are more likely to be "mixed" or to exist on a continuum. Just as negotiators' behaviors are affected by their conceptions, the researcher's polarized conception may well bias the coding of the behaviors studied. *See* Menkel-Meadow, *Legal Negotiation: A Study of Strategies In Search of A Theory*, 1983 A.B. FOUNDATION RESEARCH J. No. 4 at text accompanying notes 72, 109-10. Anthropologist Gulliver, on the basis of cross-cultural studies of dispute negotiations, has observed that there may be a cycle to negotiation processes in which competitive and cooperative behaviors are alternated as the parties identify their differences and then attempt to find their points of agreement. P.H. GULLIVER, DISPUTES AND NEGOTIATIONS: A CROSS CULTURAL PERSPECTIVE (1979).

11. As the discussion in the text illustrates, the orientation of the negotiator with respect to the purpose of the negotiation can strongly affect the behaviors chosen. *See* Pruitt & Lewis, *The Psychology of Integrative Bargaining*, in NEGOTIATIONS, *supra* note 5, at 161, 169-70. Without presenting my own formal empirical data on the matter, I have observed hundreds of negotiations in clinical courses in which students' behaviors were clearly affected by what they perceived as their purpose. In a sense, negotiation conceptions are like paradigms, *see* T. KUHN, THE STRUCTURE OF SCIENTIFIC REVOLUTIONS (1962), that imprison their creators in a unidimensional view until a different paradigm is presented; then behaviors may be radically altered to fit the new paradigm.

Conceptions and behaviors about negotiation do not always match. *See* H. RAIFFA, *supra* note 2, at 344-55. Therefore it is important, as Professor Raiffa has stated, that there be a "cadre of researchers who will attempt to bridge the chasm between theory and practice." *Id.* at 334. This Article is, in part, such an effort. More, clearly, is needed.

general model demonstrates the relationship of negotiation orientations to negotiation results:

Orientation→ Mind-set→ Behavior→ Results.

The orientation (adversarial or problem solving) leads to a mindset about what can be achieved (maximizing individual gain or solving the parties' problem by satisfying their underlying needs) which in turn affects the behavior chosen (competitive or solution searching) which in turn affects the solutions arrived at (narrow compromises or creative solutions).

The primary, but not exclusive, criterion for evaluation of a negotiation model is the quality of the solution produced.[12] This includes the extent to which the process utilized contributes to or hinders the search for "quality" solutions.

In elaborating on approaches to negotiation I shall consider the following criteria of evaluation:

1. Does the solution reflect the client's total set of "real" needs,[13] goals and objectives, in both the short and the long term?

2. Does the solution reflect the other party's full set of "real" needs, goals and objectives, in both the short and long term?[14]

3. Does the solution promote the relationship the client desires with the other party?

4. Have the parties explored all the possible solutions that might either make each better off or one party better off with no adverse consequences to the other party?[15]

5. Has the solution been achieved at the lowest possible

---

12. This criterion of evaluation is common among game theorists, decision scientists and economists. *See* M. BACHARACH, *supra* note 4; H. RAIFFA, *supra* note 2. It is less familiar to legal clinicians who have focused most of their attention on negotiation processes. *See* G. BELLOW & B. MOULTON, *supra* note 1; M. MELTSNER & P. SCHRAG, PUBLIC INTEREST ADVOCACY, *supra* note 1; G. WILLIAMS, LEGAL NEGOTIATION & SETTLEMENT, *supra* note 1.

13. *See infra* text accompanying notes 155–185 for a discussion of the parties' "real" and total needs in contrast to the wants or desires that are articulated in legal proceedings.

14. From a utilitarian perspective this criterion is important for the acceptability and enforcement of the agreement reached. It may also be utilitarian and satisfy criterion number 1 if one's own client desires the other party to be satisfied because of the relationship goals reflected in criterion number 3. From a humanitarian perspective, the purpose of a negotiation may be conceived as making both parties as happy as possible with the negotiation, including satisfying the other party.

15. This criterion simply asks the parties to look for all Pareto optimal solutions, forcing them to consider solutions that may be less obvious and also may increase the size of whatever pie might eventually have to be divided. Related to this criterion is the evaluation of the solution achieved in comparison to other solutions possible—what the court would do in litigation or what the "common business practice" is in transactional negotiation. A Pareto optimal solution is one in which a party cannot be made better off if doing so harms the other party. *See infra* note 172.

transaction costs relative to the desirability of the result?[16]

6. Is the solution achievable, or has it only raised more problems that need to be solved? Are the parties committed to the solution so it can be enforced without regret?

7. Has the solution been achieved in a manner congruent with the client's desire to participate in and affect the negotiation?[17]

8. Is the solution "fair" or "just"? Have the parties considered the legitimacy of each other's claims and made any adjustments they feel are humanely or morally indicated?[18]

Criteria one through seven are all based on a utilitarian justification of negotiation. By satisfying these criteria, a negotiation may produce results which are more satisfactory to the parties, thus enhancing commitment to and enforcement of the agreement.[19] The final criterion is applicable to those negotiators who wish to consider the effects of their solution on the other party

---

16. Suppose that a negotiator has achieved a $10 settlement with an effort costing $1. With an additional $3 of effort she might increase the settlement to $13 (net gain of $1) but to do so will take another two hours. The cost of settlement could be determined by evaluating the time as well as monetary costs and deciding whether it is worth the additional expenditure. This type of calculation may not be easy when the gain is difficult to translate into quantifiable terms, as, for example, the "gain" in making a child happier with a joint custody award. Such measurements become even more complex when considering the additional costs of making the other party happier. In the above example negotiator A could increase the pie with an additional expenditure of $1 to give the other party an additional $2 without any decrease to his own gain except for the additional transaction cost. Should the effort be made? *See infra* text accompanying notes 236–41.

17. This is a process criterion related to numbers 3 and 6. The client may want to be involved in the negotiation or may have a preference about the manner in which the negotiation is conducted. The client's satisfaction with the process might affect her satisfaction with, and commitment to, the result.

18. Note that these criteria of evaluation consider the effect of the solution on the other party from both the utilitarian and humanitarian perspectives. A satisfactory solution for the other side may be necessary to achieve agreement and to enforce settlement, aside from any considerations of doing good or doing right. Thus, one could evaluate the success of a solution on the basis of its responsiveness to the other party's needs, not necessarily out of genuine altruistic interest in the other party, but because it is an indication that an effective agreement has been reached. *See* Pruitt & Lewis, *supra* note 11, at 175.

In some sense all of the evaluation criteria can be considered subsets of 1 and 2. The relationship, cost, justness, and process of the negotiation are all aspects of the client's needs or goals to be considered in evaluating the solutions. Listing the goals separately, however, forces us to consider whether particular negotiation models are more or less likely to encourage attention to these issues.

This last criterion asks the negotiator to step back from a client-centered stance and consider whether the result achieved is, apart from the client's perspective, a fair one to the other side, or to additional parties who may be affected by the solution. Thus, the evaluation criteria are addressed both to those negotiators who stand inside a negotiation and have to decide what to do and to those who stand outside a negotiation and want to decide whether a good result has been achieved.

19. *See infra* text accompanying notes 166–76.

from a humanitarian or ethical perspective.[20]

This Article will first explore the structure, process and assumptions of traditional adversarial negotiations.[21] Second, it will describe, with examples, the problem-solving model of negotiation.[22] Finally, it will discuss the limits of the problem-solving conception of negotiation.[23]

In writing about legal negotiation it is difficult to separate the descriptive from the prescriptive. Part II is, in many ways, a description not only of the negotiation literature, but of the pedagogy of legal clinicians who teach negotiation. Part III, which presents the model for problem solving, is largely prescriptive for legal clinicians; yet I think it also describes how some lawyers conceive of negotiation at the present time.[24] The impetus for this Article came from many years of watching teachers and students in clinical programs struggle to understand negotiation, primarily through strategic and tactical considerations. What we lack are sufficiently clear overarching theories or frameworks which would enable us to understand better the complexity of legal negotiations.[25] There is a danger of some bias when conclusions about legal negotiation are drawn from the clinical data. This is due to the limited contexts in which clinical teachers and students negotiate—generally in the area of "public interest" or representation of those who otherwise would have no lawyers. The reader is well advised to consider whether it is possible to develop negotiation models with general applicability to a variety of contexts.[26]

---

20. See *infra* text accompanying notes 236–41 for a discussion of what the content of those standards might be. The application of humanitarian, moral or ethical standards to a negotiation result obviously requires a dialogue between client and lawyer. *See* MODEL CODE OF PROFESSIONAL RESPONSIBILITY EC 7-8 (1983); MODEL RULES OF PROFESSIONAL CONDUCT Rule 1.4 (1983); Lehman, *The Pursuit of A Client's Interest*, 77 MICH. L. REV. 1078 (1979); Spiegel, *Lawyering and Client Decisionmaking: Informed Consent and the Legal Profession*, 128 U. PA. L. REV. 41 (1979).

21. *See infra* text accompanying notes 32–154.

22. *See infra* text accompanying notes 249–58.

23. *See infra* text accompanying notes 290–348.

24. *See, e.g.*, R. FISHER & W. URY, *supra* note 2. Empirical data on how lawyers actually negotiate is almost non-existent. *Cf.* G. WILLIAMS, LEGAL NEGOTIATION & SETTLEMENT, *supra* note 1.

25. *See* Menkel-Meadow, *supra* note 10; Weiss-Wik, *Enhancing Negotiators' Successfulness: Self-Help Books and Related Empirical Research*, 27 J. CONFLICT RESOLUTION 706 (1983).

26. *See* Marshall, *Lawyers, Truth and the Zero-Sum Game*, 47 NOTRE DAME LAW. 919 (1972). The writings derived from clinical legal education and public interest advocacy may be particularly adversarial in focus because of the need of the "underdog" to learn how to fight. *See, e.g.*, M. MELTSNER & R. SCHRAG, PUBLIC INTEREST ADVOCACY, *supra* note 1, at 231–40.

Those who have done the most writing on negotiation have been clinicians with litigation backgrounds. There is a dearth of literature on transactional or organiza-

This Article is addressed to readers on two levels. First, individual negotiators may seek prescriptive advice about how to behave in legal negotiations if they choose to adopt a problem-solving conception of negotiation. In this sense the Article provides some suggestions for how to conceive of negotiations differently; it does not, however, provide specific behavioral or strategic suggestions. Second, and on another level, the Article looks at legal negotiations from the perspective of the larger legal system. What, in the aggregate, would our system of dispute resolution and transaction planning look like if problem solving were the more usual model? How would it affect the parties, the legal system and society? It is important when examining the processes engaged in by lawyers that we look at both the micro and macro implications of those processes, though the former is emphasized in this Article.[27]

Thus, the Article is addressed to a number of different readers. For legal clinicians it should broaden the conceptual and behavioral base of our teaching of legal negotiation. For practitioners it should give some guidance on how to rethink goals and behaviors in negotiation. For legal scholars it should raise, if not answer, some basic questions about the structure of the legal system and the role of lawyers' micro level activities in the macro structure.

This effort is motivated by a desire to see the legal system work in a way which promotes and maximizes human interactions that are creative, enfranchising, enriching and empowering, rather than alienating and conflict-provoking.[28] Problem[29] solving offers

---

tional negotiation in the legal context. Thus, in many ways my analysis is similar to that of Professor Simon's in Simon, *Homo Psychologicus: Notes on a New Legal Formalism*, 32 STAN. L. REV. 487 (1980), which I have criticized elsewhere. *See* Menkel-Meadow, *The Legacy of Clinical Education: Theories About Lawyering*, 29 CLEV. ST. L. REV. 555, 565 n.61 (1980). My analysis relies on the published writings of a few who have written on negotiation and may not fairly represent the conceptualization of negotiation as it is taught. Although, in my experience, most clinical teaching of negotiation is based almost exclusively in the litigation context. *See also infra* note 288.

27. *See* Menkel-Meadow, *supra* note 26.

28. In reading an earlier draft of this Article, my late colleague Donald Hagman remarked that the problem-solving conception of negotiation described herein was the product of a feminist conception of dispute resolution and transaction planning. To the extent that some of the elements of problem solving, such as trying to satisfy the needs of all parties and addressing the relational aspects of negotiation, seem to represent women's concerns, this is so. *See* C. GILLIGAN, IN A DIFFERENT VOICE: PSYCHOLOGICAL THEORY AND WOMEN'S DEVELOPMENT 2 (1982) (presenting an argument, supported by data, that girls and women engage in a different mode of moral reasoning when faced with issues of choice and judgment, than do men). Women are more likely to emphasize the relational and interpersonal aspects of moral decision-making, while men are more likely to reason with universal, abstract principles that are hierarchically arranged. Gilligan points out that her observations about gender are empirically based but that elements of both modes may be found in both genders.

an opportunity to produce results that are better for the parties as well as for the legal system.[30] Such results are better in the sense that they more closely meet the parties' needs and are potentially more "just."

Much of what is said here may appear commonsensical, but it is actually counterintuitive, countercultural, and contrary to the assumptions and myths currently infusing legal negotiations. The pressures to "win" are far greater than we think[31] and the rewards for solving problems are few and far more subtle.

I. Assumptions of the Traditional Model: Adversarial Negotiation

Much of the legal negotiation literature emphasizes an adversarial model,[32] implying an orientation or approach that focuses on "maximizing victory."[33] This approach is based on the as-

---

Id. On the other hand, many scholars presently studying negotiation and offering problem-solving-like insights, such as Fisher and Ury, do not seem to have conceived of or observed negotiation processes with a feminist consciousness. Furthermore, data on gender differences in negotiation motivation and behavior are as yet inconclusive. *See infra* note 111; H. Raiffa, *supra* note 2, at 122-26; J. Rubin & B. Brown, *supra* note 5, at 169-74. *See also* E. Maccoby & C. Jacklin, The Psychology of Sex Differences (1974).

29. I have used "problem" throughout this Article to connote the legal event, transaction, relationship or occurrence about which parties conduct negotiations. I use this term advisedly as in earlier research I discovered that legal clients do not like to describe themselves as people with "problems." C. Menkel-Meadow, The 59th Street Legal Clinic: Evaluation of the Experiment 40 (1979). In addition, in any "problem" involving more than one party there will be different perceptions of what the "problem" is.

30. The text focuses on how conceptions of negotiation affect the parties. An analysis of these conceptions raises a number of significant questions about our legal system: Does it promote a particular orientation of negotiation? Why does adversarial negotiation seem to dominate our system of dispute resolution? Can questions about the most effective negotiation model be separated from questions about the relative power of the parties, both in the legal system and in the larger society? How do aggregations of individual negotiations affect the character of the larger system? How do the characteristics of the larger system affect individual lawyer choices in negotiation? Answers to these questions await further study.

31. *See* Rosenberg, *Alternatives to Litigation: Long Term Solutions or Short-Term Fads?*, UCLA Mgmt. Fall 1983, at 7-8.

32. *See supra* notes 1 and 2. Not all of the existing literature has this emphasis, however. More recent works on negotiation, both legal and general, have begun to explore other negotiation processes. *See, e.g.*, R. Fisher & W. Ury, *supra* note 2; G. Williams, Legal Negotiation and Settlement, *supra* note 1.

33. "Maximizing victory" involves two separate goals; one is to "maximize the likelihood the client will prevail," Schwartz, *The Professionalism and Accountability of Lawyers*, 66 Calif. L. Rev. 669, 675-77 (1978) [hereinafter cited as *Accountability*], and the other is to maximize the amount the client receives upon prevailing.

In game theoretic terms, one can maximize gain in several different ways. For example, in some zero-sum games both sides may gain something but each incremental gain is zero-sum. As in a sporting match, only one player can win each point and the game in toto, but both parties win points along the way. In other zero-sum games,

sumption that the parties desire the same goals, items, or values. It is assumed that the parties must be in conflict and since they are presumed to be bargaining for the same "scarce" items, negotiators assume that any solution is predicated upon division of the goods. In the language of game theorists, economists, and psychologists, such negotiations become "zero-sum" or "constant-sum" games[34] and the bargaining engaged in is "distributive" bargaining.[35] Simply put, in the pure adversarial case, each party wants as much as he can get of the thing bargained for, and the more one party receives, the less the other party receives.[36] There is a "winner" in the negotiation, determined by which party got more.[37]

Legal negotiations, at least in dispute resolution cases, are marked by another adversarial assumption. Because litigation ne-

---

see M. DEUTSCH, THE RESOLUTION OF CONFLICT (1973), victory is measured by the relative gain over the other party. Thus, there is "individualistic" gain in which one party simply wins and doesn't care by how much and "competitive" gain in which one party not only wins, but hopes to prevent the other party from as much gain as possible. In some legal disputes the resources available may not be scarce, but, to the extent they are limited, one party may hope to win as much as possible and prevent the other party from gaining as much as possible. In other disputes a simple "majority" win may be all the parties desire.

34. For a definition of zero-sum games, see *supra* note 4. Constant-sum games, like the zero-sum game, are those in which the players' pay-offs total some constant number. In another formulation, the players, upon losing or winning, will have to pay out or receive certain fixed amounts. The strategies or conceptions of constant-sum games are essentially the same as those of zero-sum games. A total sum of money or other items possessed by both parties is constant and the sole purpose of the game is to redistribute this amount among the players, where the players' utility functions are linear in these values. Game theory also recognizes the court model of negotiation, *see infra* text accompanying notes 129–130, as a zero-sum game because there are only two possible and mutually exclusive outcomes for each party—victory or defeat. In this situation, no assumptions of linear utility to the parties are required. Where there is a third possibility, such as a "draw," the game is not zero-sum unless there are special assumptions about how the parties would differentially value the "draw" outcome. J. HARSANYI, RATIONAL BEHAVIOR AND BARGAINING EQUILIBRIUM IN GAMES AND SOCIAL SITUATIONS 98–99 (1977); R. LUCE & H. RAIFFA, GAMES AND DECISIONS: INTRODUCTION AND CRITICAL SURVEY 158–59 (1957); M. SHUBIK, GAMES FOR SOCIETY, BUSINESS AND WAR: TOWARDS A THEORY OF GAMING 64–65 (1975).

35. As the definitions above make clear, a distributive bargaining strategy is one in which the parties negotiate in order to distribute among themselves the constant sum of what is available. Distributive bargaining strategies have also been identified more generally in the literature as those in which the aim of the bargainer is to elicit concessions from the other bargainer in order to obtain a larger portion of the goods to be divided. Pruitt & Lewis, *supra* note 11. Distributive bargaining is distinguished from integrative bargaining in that the latter seeks new solutions which may not require division of a limited amount of materiel. *Id.*

36. *See supra* note 34; H. RAIFFA, *supra* note 2, at 33.

37. *See supra* note 33.

gotiations are conducted in the "shadow of the law,"[38] that is, in the shadow of the courts, the negotiators assume that what is bargained for are the identical, but limited, items a court would award in deciding the case. Typically, it is assumed that all that is bargained for is who will get the most money and who can be compelled to do or not to do something. Indeed, it may be because litigation negotiations are so often conducted in the shadow of the court that they are assumed to be zero-sum games.

In transactional negotiation, the "common business practice" or "form provision" may serve the same limiting function. If the parties cannot resolve a particular point but still prefer to consummate the transaction, they may permit a form provision or common business practice to decide the issue. This may be true even where an unusual provision would more closely meet the parties' needs. Clauses which assign or allocate risks routinely to one side of a transaction are one example.[39] Although transactional negotiations differ from dispute negotiations because in the former no court can force a solution, the two types of negotiation may be analogous where the shadow of the court or the "shadow of the form contract" encourage a habit of mind in the negotiators to rely on common solutions, rather than to pursue solutions which may be more tailored to the parties' particular needs.

These basic adversarial assumptions affect not only the conceptions of negotiations that their proponents assert, but the behaviors that are recommended for successful negotiation.[40] Indeed, a good portion of the negotiation literature[41] focuses principally on behavioral admonitions, but never examines with any sophistication the sources or assumptions of such tactical injunctions and what their limitations might be.

The next section describes these admonitions and the process they produce so that their underlying assumptions may be examined in the succeeding sections. The basis of the description is the negotiation literature; there is at the present time little empirical data on how lawyers actually behave,[42] though the existing

38. This phrase is borrowed from Mnookin & Kornhauser, *Bargaining in the Shadow of the Law: The Case of Divorce*, 88 YALE L.J. 950, 950 (1979).

39. For example, insurance clauses frequently allocate the risk to one class of parties such as owners or landlords, when in particular cases lessees or others might either be better able to bear the risk or at least pay for insuring against it.

40. *See supra* text accompanying notes 10–11.

41. *See, e.g.*, G. BELLOW & B. MOULTON, *supra* note 1; H. EDWARDS & J. WHITE, *supra* note 1; C. KARRASS, GIVE & TAKE; *supra* note 1; C. KARRASS, GAME, *supra* note 1; M. MELTSNER & P. SCHRAG, MATERIALS, *supra* note 1; M. MELTSNER & P. SCHRAG, COURSE, *supra* note 1; G. NIERENBERG, FUNDAMENTALS, *supra* note 1; G. NIERENGERG, ART, *supra* note 1.

42. *See supra* note 26. Video tape and other training materials prepared to demonstrate how lawyers negotiate also emphasize adversarial processes. *See, e.g.*,

literature seems to assume that most lawyers either already do or need to behave in adversarial ways to accomplish their goals. The purpose in beginning with these behavioral admonitions is not to focus on negotiation strategies but to illustrate how the literature implicitly, if not explicitly, assumes a unidimensional conception of negotiation goals.

A. *The Structure and Process of Adversarial Negotiation*

The literature of negotiation presents a stylized linear ritual of struggle—planned concessions after high first offers, leading to a compromise point along a linear field of pre-established 'commitment and resistance' points.[43] In such legal negotiations the compromise settlement point is legitimized by comparing it to the polarized demands of plaintiff and defendant and the relatively improved "joint gain" of the compromise point in comparison to the "winner take all" result achieved in court.[44] In the most reductionist form of this adversarial model, analysts predict that the final outcome of any distributive bargaining problem will be at the "focal point" midway between the first offers of each party.[45]

This section reviews the descriptions and prescriptions of adversarial negotiation found in the literature in order to demonstrate their weaknesses and limitations in achieving the types of solutions which might better meet the evaluation criteria suggested above.[46] Several preliminary caveats are in order. First, much of this literature confuses the descriptive and prescriptive

JACKER, EFFECTIVE NEGOTIATION TECHNIQUES FOR LAWYERS (1983) (available from National Institute for Trial Advocacy). *Cf.* ABA Lawyering Skills Program, Instructor's Manual (1982). The training materials used by such programs as NITA may not reflect actual lawyer practice any more than the literature. Yet the fact that the simulations created specifically to teach lawyers replicate adversarial assumptions and approaches indicates what many lawyers think they should strive for. These teaching materials may, in fact, be as similar to actual negotiation as Perry Mason is to real trial practice.

43. G. BELLOW & B. MOULTON, *supra* note 1, at 27-63; H. RAIFFA, *supra* note 2, at 33-77. This analysis of the adversarial negotiation process can be considered in the structuralist mode. This Article, in essence, conducts a decomposition of the negotiation process both as described in the literature and as manifested in its familiar practice forms. Thus, the revealed structures, offer-rejection and concession along a linear field of compromise, expose the underlying assumptions of the negotiation process when conducted this way.

44. This makes evaluation of a negotiation result easy. With only a 50/50 chance of achieving either of the bipolar results, the compromise point achieves a result without the transaction costs of trial. Thus, in a sense the settlement avoids the potential "minus-sum" game of one party winning all but both parties paying substantial court and attorneys fees. *See* R. Fisher, *What About Negotiation as a Specialty?*, 69 A.B.A. J. 1221, 1221-24 (1983).

45. H. RAIFFA, *supra* note 2, ch. 3; T. SCHELLING, *supra* note 2, at 57.

46. *See supra* text accompanying notes 13-18.

aspects of negotiation. It is unclear, for example, whether the negotiator should make a high first offer because that is what is commonly done and therefore expected,[47] or because a high first offer assures a "focal point" or "compromise" closer to the negotiator's beginning point.[48] Second, descriptions of the structure of negotiation[49] with its "bargaining range"[50] and offer and counteroffer "concession patterns"[51] should be distinguished from the rather specific tactical exhortations commonly found in the literature. While the former may serve an explanatory purpose, such as describing what zero-sum negotiations look like, the tactical literature has limitations even within its own assumptions. This is explored more fully below.[52]

1. The Structure of Adversarial Negotiation: Linear Concessions on the Road to Compromise

Most disputes are settled out of court.[53] Describing how this majority of cases is settled, writers depict a remarkably uniform negotiation model.[54] Because the parties fear the cost, the length of time to judicial resolution, and the winner-take-all quality of the judicial result, most cases are settled somewhere mid-range between each party's initial demand.[55] Thus, the structure of adversarial negotiation consists of: 1) the setting of "target points"[56] or

47. *Id.*; H. EDWARDS & J. WHITE, *supra* note 1, at 115–17; H. MELTSNER & P. SCHRAG, MATERIALS, *supra* note 1; M. MELTSNER & P. SCHRAG, COURSE, *supra* note 1.

48. *See* H. COHEN, *supra* note 1.

49. *See infra* text accompanying notes 53–129.

50. G. BELLOW & B. MOULTON, *supra* note 1, at 58-63; H. RAIFFA, *supra* note 2, at 45–50.

51. G. BELLOW & B. MOULTON, *supra* note 1, at 108–19; H. RAIFFA, *supra* note 2, at 44–65.

52. *See infra* text accompanying notes 106–15.

53. It is estimated that as many as 91% of civil cases are settled out of court and 85% of criminal cases are resolved without trial. *See* Rubin, *A Causerie on Lawyers' Ethics in Negotiation*, 35 LA. L. REV. 577 (1975). *See also* L. ROSS, SETTLED OUT OF COURT: THE SOCIAL PROCESS OF INSURANCE CLAIMS ADJUSTMENT (2d ed. 1980); D. ROSENTHAL, LAWYERS AND CLIENT: WHO'S IN CHARGE? (1974). *See also* Galanter, *Reading the Landscape of Disputes: What We Know and Don't Know (And Think We Know) About Our Allegedly Contentious and Litigious Society*, 31 UCLA L. REV. 4 (1983). Statistics also indicate that approximately 90% of divorces are settled without court trials. Mnookin & Kornhauser, *supra* note 38, at 951 n.3.

54. "The simplest characterization of the bargaining process is a sequence of offers and counteroffers for dividing the stakes," Cooter, Marks & Mnookin, *supra* note 4, is an example of a typical definition of the negotiation process. Another is "a process through which two teams try to resolve their differences and arrive at an agreement. Typically, the differences are resolved when each side makes some concessions, so that the agreement lies somewhere between the original positions of the two teams." O. BARTOS, *supra* note 5, at 3–4.

55. H. RAIFFA, *supra* note 2, at 66–77; L. ROSS, *supra* note 53.

56. G. BELLOW & B. MOULTON, *supra* note 1, at 58–63.

"aspiration levels"[57]—what the parties would like to achieve (target points may be set at the initial demand in the complaint or reduced slightly by a more realistic appraisal of what is possible); 2) the setting of "resistance points"[58] or "reservation points,"[59] the points below which the party seeks not to go (preferring to risk the possibility of winning the polarized game in court); and 3) the ritual of offer and demand with patterns of "reciprocal concessions."[60] The process results in 4) a compromise solution at some point along the scale where target or resistance points overlap for the two parties. This structure, mapped below, as developed in Bellow & Moulton's *Lawyering Process* text,[61] expresses graphically the assumption that negotiations are linear win/lose games where X's gain is Y's loss:

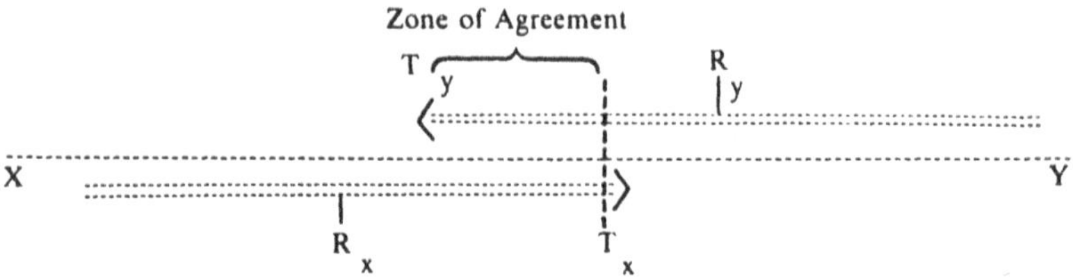

T= Target point (or aspiration point)
R= Resistance point (or reservation level)

FIGURE 1

In this negotiation game, X and Y attempt to assess each other's "target points" and "resistance points"[62] in order to determine whether there is a "bargaining range."[63] The resemblance of

---

57. H. Raiffa, *supra* note 2, at 41.

58. G. Bellow & B. Moulton, *supra* note 1, at 58-63; H. Edwards & J. White, *supra* note 1, at 186.

59. H. Raiffa, *supra* note 2, at 37.

60. G. Bellow & B. Moulton, *supra* note 1, at 108-19; H. Raiffa, *supra* note 2, at 47-65.

61. G. Bellow & B. Moulton, *supra* note 1, at 58-63. The graphic representation of the negotiation structure in the text is found in one form or another in most of the negotiation literature. H. Raiffa, *supra* note 2, at 46, 48, 57-59; L. Ross, *supra* note 53. The source of this representation is the Walton & McKersie book on labor negotiation. *See* R. Walton & R. McKersie, *supra* note 5. It is questionable whether this representation is particularly accurate for multi-issue labor negotiations, but it is interesting to note how quickly one model of negotiation in one particular context has become the model for analyzing all negotiations. Raiffa's explanation of this model more accurately describes how it applies to cases where there are two parties and only one issue. H. Raiffa, *supra* note 2, at 44-65.

As a matter of intellectual history it would be interesting to trace the original sources of the clinical literature's statements about the lawyering processes, including but not limited to negotiation.

62. Otherwise known as "bottom lines" or "minimum dispositions." H. Raiffa, *supra* note 2, at 44-65.

63. *Id.*

adversarial negotiations to a football field and goals is hardly coincidental. The first issue in the negotiation process is likely to be on whose side of this linear field the negotiation game will be played and who will ultimately "win" or be paid. This issue is covered in the largely contradictory "first offer" literature.[64] Following "resolution" of the first offer controversy, the parties proceed in a pattern of offer-counteroffer[65] or demand-response[66] resulting in "reciprocal concessions"[67] which can be analyzed to give each party information about the other's target and resistance points. The process continues until a compromise solution is reached somewhere within the bargaining range.[68]

Given this linear conception of the structure of negotiation it is easy to see why results are perceived as compromises along this linear scale and why "split the difference" solutions are so common in conventional negotiations.[69] In order to avoid the costs

64. *See, e.g.*, P. Hermann, Better Settlements Through Leverage (1965); D. Lewis, *supra* note 1, at 203; C. Peck, *supra* note 1, at 254–55; C. Stevens, Strategy and Collective Bargaining Negotiation 32–35 (1963); Chertkoff & Conley, *Opening Offer and Frequency of Concession as Bargaining Strategies*, 1 J. of Personality & Soc. Psychology 181 (1967); Hinton, Hammer & Pohlen, *The Influence Of Reward Magnitude, Opening Bid And Concession Rate On Profit Earned In A Managerial Negotiation Game*, 19 Behav. Sci. 197 (1974); Liebert, Smith, Hill & Keiffer, *The Effects of Information and Magnitude of Initial Offer on Interpersonal Negotiation*, 1 Experimental Soc. Psychology 431 (1968).

65. G. Bellow & B. Moulton, *supra* note 1, at 100–08.

66. Although on one level the use of different vocabularies for the same thing (offer-counteroffer and demand-response) connotes a very similar conception of negotiation there may be some difference in the negotiation dynamics between an "offer" and a "demand" depending on the specific language used in making offers.

67. *See supra* note 60.

68. This model has been applied to both civil and criminal cases:

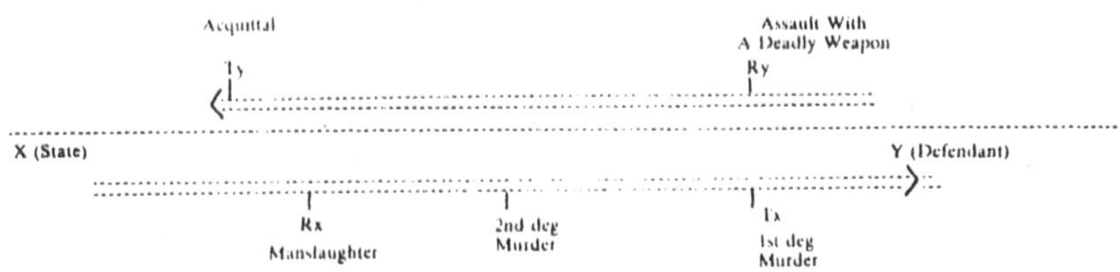

FIGURE 2

G. Bellow & B. Moulton, *supra* note 1, at 59.

69. "Splitting the difference" as a negotiation strategy is a much discussed, H. Edwards & J. White, *supra* note 1, at 121; C. Karrass, Give & Take, *supra* note 1; C. Karrass, Game, *supra* note 1; G. Nierenberg, Fundamentals, *supra* note 1; G. Nierenberg, Art, *supra* note 1, and much criticized, *see* R. Fisher & W. Ury, *supra* note 2, approach in which the parties agree overtly to compromise on a point halfway between their demands. Criticisms, like Fisher & Ury's, are based on the fact that this position cannot be principled or justified in any way that is related to the merits of the dispute, either legally or by the parties' underlying objectives. Although I generally agree with the criticism of this technique, "splitting the difference" may be

and risk of polarized results in court the parties choose compromise, after a culturally appropriate time of debate and concessions.

Although such a model encourages compromise at some midway point, it frequently fails to provide a satisfactory solution for the parties. Consider the example of two children arguing over a piece of chocolate cake. The parental compromise solution, cutting the piece in half, will not be satisfactory to either child if one prefers the cake and the other the icing.[70] Compromises may be highly dysfunctional in cases where one needs a pair, rather than a single shoe[71] to do the necessary walking.

A linear negotiation structure might work in those few cases where there is really only one issue,[72] but it is clearly insufficient when the issues in a negotiation are many and varied.[73] For instance, in negotiating a personal injury case one party may seek

---

a useful technique at the conclusion of a negotiation when the parties have completed their "principled negotiation" and still remain somewhat apart. In problem solving, "the difference" may be "split" over a number of different issues, i.e. more in the nature of a trade-off.

70. The literature abounds with examples of parties arguing about something without exploring their complementary interests. Thus, arguments about dividing an object fail to take account of different desires: for potato and skin, orange and peel, and open and closed windows. *See* R. Fisher & W. Ury, *supra* note 2, at 41; H. Raiffa, *supra* note 2, at 102.

71. Silver, *The Imminent Failure of Legal Services for the Poor: Why and How to Limit Caseload*, 46 J. Urb. Law 217, 222 (1969). I do not mean to suggest that all compromise is bad. Compromise may be necessary as a convention for resolving disputes when it is not possible to do anything else. Our political system and the legal system of which it is a part are based on the necessity and "morality" of compromise. *See* Coons, *Compromise as Precise Justice* in Nomos XII, Compromise in Ethics, Law, and Politics 190 (1979); Coons, *Approaches to Court Imposed Compromise—The Uses of Doubt and Reason*, 58 Nw. U.L. Rev. 750 (1964).

72. It is argued in the text that we must look behind the money demanded in a case to see what the real needs of the parties are. Others have argued, however, that it is money's function as a proxy for other things that might be indivisible that permits the legal system to function:

> The common law consistently converts indivisible disputes, that is, disputes over injury to person and property and disputes over the fulfillment or nonfulfillment of obligations into disputes over sums of money. Mediate solutions are always possible in disputes about money. Even a judge who must declare that one party is legally right and the other legally wrong need not resort to winner-take-all solutions. Typically he will award money damages that amount to more than the loser wants to pay but less than the winner claims he deserves.

M. Shapiro, Courts: A Comparative And Political Analysis 10 (1981). I have no argument with the fact that money as proxy permits us to resolve many disputes in common currency that might otherwise go unresolved. Historically, the development of money has greatly increased our ability to resolve conflicting claims. On the other hand, we may have gone too far, so that by looking at the "easy" way to measure what we value, we almost never look behind the currency to see what it might buy. Notice how Shapiro's formulation—"more than the loser and less than the winner"—contemplates a linear compromise.

73. *See infra* text accompanying notes 126–27.

an apology, as well as lost earnings, rehabilitation costs, and pain and suffering damages. The "concession" of an apology from the other side may or may not reduce the amount of money to be negotiated as compensation for the other things. Similarly, in the formation of a partnership a "concession" on one issue of control does not necessarily move the "result" away from or toward one of the parties, especially if unaccompanied by an equivalent "trade" of contribution. Indeed, it may be impossible to represent graphically the negotiation of a complex, multi-issue transaction as a two dimensional structure, without imagining a many-planed axis with hundreds of potential coordinates.[74]

Perhaps an example, familiar to most teaching clinicians,[75] will illustrate this point. Ms. Brown buys a car from Mr. Snead, a

74. Game theorists have come closest to mapping a legal negotiation with multiple solutions by using a two dimensional axis with coordinates representing pairs of potential outcomes. These maps demonstrate that there are many possible points of solutions along the efficiency frontier:

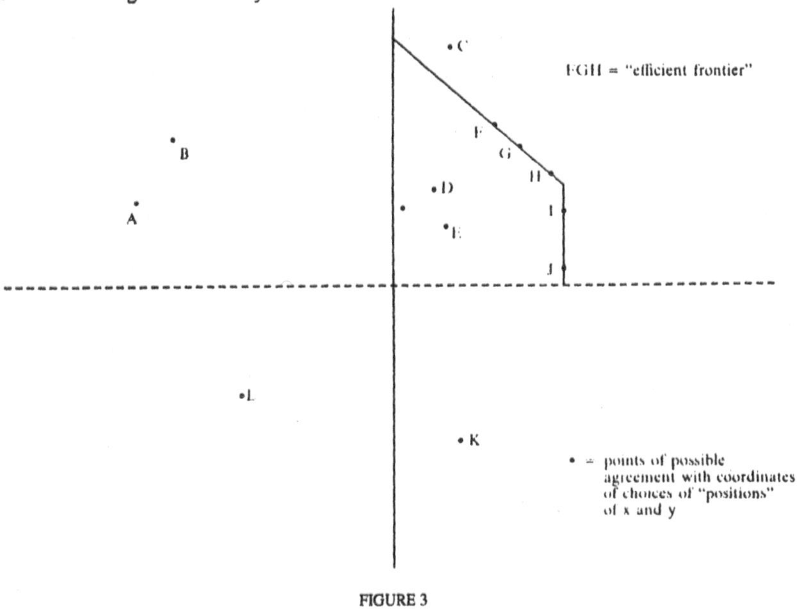

FIGURE 3

See M. BACHARACH, *supra* note 4, at 85, 90; H. RAIFFA, *supra* note 2, at 100, 138. This map still reduces all possible outcomes to single pairs of coordinates, assuming that for all the factors that determine a particular outcome point there is an equivalent quantitative measure of each outcome in relation to other outcomes. In legal negotiations where there may not be such clear utility measures even this model may be somewhat inaccurate in depicting the reality.

75. This example is based on the hypothetical case of Valley Marine Bank v. Terry James developed by the Legal Services Corporation, Office of Program Support (1975), for training legal services attorneys and currently used as a teaching problem in many law school clinical programs.

used car salesman. After a short period of time the car ceases to function, despite repeated attempts by Ms. Brown to have the car repaired. Ms. Brown, therefore, sues Mr. Snead for rescission of the sales contract, claiming misrepresentation in the sale of the car or, in the alternative, breach of warranty, with consequential damages including lost income from the loss of a job due to repeated latenesses and absences as a result of the malfunctioning car. Mr. Snead counterclaims for the balance due on the car, claiming that the warranty period has ended and the dealership was given insufficient time in which to cure any possible defects. Suppose the car was purchased for a total of $2500, Ms. Brown received $500 as a trade-in allowance, and she has made one monthly payment of $50. Her lost income from losing time at work, and ultimately her job, is approximately $2000, and she has spent approximately $400 in her attempts to repair the car. By the terms of the sales contract, Mr. Snead is entitled not only to the unpaid balance on the car but to attorneys fees for any collection action required to recover the unpaid balance.[76]

Following the filing of the lawsuits described above, the parties, if engaged in conventional adversarial negotiation, would structure their negotiations around the value of their respective monetary claims.[77] Ms. Brown's attorney would evaluate the

---

76. Attorneys fees provisions in such contracts are common, though attacks have been made on them as "unconscionable" under U.C.C. § 2-302 in form or adhesion contracts where the percentage fee does not accurately reflect the legal collection work actually performed. In the Brown-Snead case this claim might be raised as one of the legal issues about which the parties would negotiate.

77. Such bargaining could be represented on the same bargaining grid discussed above, *see supra* text accompanying notes 61–68, as follows:

$ 2,950 +	0	$2,600
Brown's Claims		Snead's Claims

Brown's Claims		Snead's Claims	
$2,000	lost income	$2,500	contract price
500	trade-in value returned	-500	trade-in
400	repairs	- 50	monthly payment
50	monthly payment		
+	punitives (fraudulent misrepresentation)	1950	
		+ 650	(1/3 attys fee)
2,950 +		2,600	

FIGURE 4

There is a total dollar value of $5,550 + at stake. The parties would first negotiate about who would pay whom and then concede increments of dollar values based either on the validity of the legal claims ("principled negotiations"), or in simple compromise, or some combination of both.

When negotiated by law students the most common result in this case is the simple "wash-out"—settlement by dropping all claims, with no payments by either party—which does not meet either of the parties' needs as fully as other possible solutions might.

amount her client had spent on the car, how much she has lost in income and repairs, and the cost of the lawsuit itself. Mr. Snead's attorney would compute the balance due on the car, subtract payments made, and add the fees to recover the balance due. Both parties might then discount their target and resistance points by an estimate of how likely it is that they would prevail in court, subject to a further discount of the cost of achieving that result through adjudication.[78] The attorneys would then engage in a bargaining process of reciprocal concessions based on their assessments of the values and probabilities of recovery on each of the claims, until they reached some dollar amount on which they might agree.[79] Such a settlement would be a compromise with respect to the "scarce" resource in this case–money.[80] In addition to the money, the parties might also negotiate to return their relationship to the *status quo ante*. The difficulty with this solution is that the real goals or objectives sought by the parties might not be accomplished at all. Ms. Brown wants a reliable car to take her to work and Mr. Snead a profitable sale and a satisfied customer who will make recommendations to her friends.

If, however, the parties considered what they had initially desired from this transaction, they might arrive at other solutions. Alternatives could be found that would more completely and efficiently satisfy their needs, solutions not necessarily arising from compromise. If, for example, Ms. Brown's problem is transportation to work, Snead might repair her present car or substitute another car at little or low cost to a dealer who has large inventory. At the same time, Snead could continue to hold Ms. Brown to her contract, or a new contract could be negotiated.[81] With this solution, both parties meet their objectives—a car for Ms. Brown and

78. Litigation negotiation literature is replete with models and checklists for economic and non-economic case evaluation. *See, e.g.*, G. Bellow & B. Moulton, *supra* note 1, at 50–79; Personal Injury Valuation Handbooks (updated); G. Williams, Legal Negotiation & Settlement, *supra* note 1, at 110–35; Werchick, *Settling the Case-Plaintiff*, 4 Am. Jurisprudence Trials 289, 319–22 (1966); Note, *An Analysis of Settlement*, 22 Stan. L. Rev. 67 (1969). Such case evaluation is essential for informed predictions of what the court will do and may be especially important for providing accurate information to the client in a counseling situation, D. Binder & S. Price, Legal Interviewing and Counseling 143–47 (1977). But, to the extent that evaluation models based on legal merits form the basis for settlement proposals, they may reinforce the polarized model with limited results of court adjudication. The parties will negotiate by arguing over whose evaluation is more accurate.

79. *See, e.g.*, Legal Services Corp. Training Tapes, Edited Negotiation, VMB v. James (1977).

80. *See supra* note 77.

81. Snead will be able to resell Brown's first car if he supplies her with a new one. The cost to Snead might be somewhat greater if Snead has to repair the original car before resale to someone else.

a continued profit for Mr. Snead[82]—at considerably less legal expense, lower transaction cost in the negotiation, and avoidance of litigation.[83] Note how in the compromise solution above, Ms. Brown could receive a settlement dollar amount that would be insufficient to permit her to buy a new car and Mr. Snead would receive less than an adequate profit, either by having to pay Ms. Brown or by receiving less than the contract price as his settlement. Note also that most courts would not be authorized to order the non-compromise arrangement, although particular judges or settlement officers in some courts might encourage the parties to "work out" such a settlement in private where the court does not have the authority to order such relief.[84]

2. The Process of Adversarial Negotiation: Unproductive Competition

Adversarial assumptions affect not only the quality of solutions to negotiated problems but also the process by which these solutions are reached. This is especially important because the type and quality of solutions may depend a great deal on the process used.[85] The adversarial conception of negotiation produces a

82. The new solution reflects both clients' underlying needs, in the long run and in the short run, and results in the best possible arrangement for each party without hurting the other. The solution appears to be easily implemented and enforceable as long as the parties assume the same trust of performance that was in effect at the beginning of the first contract. It is possible, of course, that the parties would prefer not to deal with each other at all, and thus would not wish to enter into another contract.

83. There may, of course, be additional transaction costs in some situations, making the new solution undesirable and returning the negotiators to the more traditional model. Clients might be unwilling to pay the additional fees that "problem solving" would cost if it appeared to take more time than traditional negotiations. *See* Spiegel, *supra* note 20, at 110–12. Ultimately, the client's preferences and concerns for the cost and manner of achieving the solution, and its "fairness," would have to be compared to how the client would judge a more "adversarial" result.

84. In some sense courts are engaged in problem solving when they require or encourage settlement conferences and when judges, magistrates or other settlement officers suggest or "encourage" arrangements which might be beyond the court's official power but which courts are pleased to approve informally. *Cf.* Resnick, *Managerial Judges*, 96 HARV. L. REV. 374 (1982) (reporting on the role of judges and masters in managing cases by assuming long term responsibilities for solving and monitoring institutional problems in major litigation); Walker & Thibaut, *An Experimental Examination of Pre-Trial Conference Techniques*, 55 MINN. L. REV. 1113 (1971) (an empirical study of what judges and magistrates do to encourage pre-trial settlement). A good example of these informal arrangements is provided by the many quota or goal settlements in employment discrimination cases decided before the power of courts to require them in certain circumstances was made clear in United Steelworkers of Am. v. Weber, 443 U.S. 193 (1979) (holding that affirmative action goals were appropriate when voluntarily set by employers).

85. The effect of the process on the solutions may be so important that it can explain why most of the writing on negotiation focuses on negotiation processes rather than evaluation of solutions or results. Even R. FISHER & W. URY, *supra* note

particular mind-set concerning possible solutions which then tend to produce a competitive process. This, in turn, may cause the parties to miss opportunities for expanding the range of solutions.[86] Thus, by encouraging competitive strategies important information may not be communicated and the parties may arrive at unsatisfactory and inefficient solutions. This section briefly explores the processes of adversarial negotiation, both in terms of their most common stages and phases and in terms of tactics and strategies,[87] in order to examine the limiting effects of these processes on the outcomes.

What is astounding about the conventional literature on tactics and strategies[88] is the assumption of universal applicability. Strategic exhortations are offered without reference to how negotiations might vary in different contexts or under different circumstances, such as under the influence of various clients' desires.[89] Negotiators are admonished to never make the first offer[90] and to always draft the final agreement[91] as if there were a few simple rules negotiators should obey in order always to maximize individual gain.

Commentators on the adversarial negotiation process have described a remarkable uniformity of stages and phases of negotiation that all appear to be derived from the linear negotiation

---

2, which discusses criteria for evaluating solutions, *id.* at 4, is primarily concerned with techniques or strategies for a different negotiation process.

86. *See supra* text accompanying notes 11–18.

87. Indeed, the very words "tactics" and "strategies" derive from purely militaristic uses for winning battles. *See* X OXFORD ENGLISH DICTIONARY 1087 (1933) (strategies); XII OXFORD ENGLISH DICTIONARY 22 (1933) (tactics).

For an effort to devise an analytic framework for choosing among different strategies in legal negotiation, see Lowenthal, *supra* note 1. Unfortunately, this piece too is focused primarily on "cooperative" vs. "competitive" strategies without linking the strategies to particular negotiation goals. There is some effort, however, to analyze the choice of strategies within the context of different case types—a significant effort, and one which should be pursued.

88. *See, e.g.*, H. COHEN, *supra* note 1; H. EDWARDS & J. WHITE, *supra* note 1, at 112–41; M. MELTSNER & P. SCHRAG, PUBLIC INTEREST ADVOCACY, *supra* note 1; H. RAIFFA, *supra* note 2, at 119–30.

89. Most of these works are devoid of any analysis of how particular contexts might affect negotiation strategies. *But see* G. WILLIAMS, LEGAL NEGOTIATION AND SETTLEMENT, *supra* note 1, at 66–67. Social scientists studying negotiation have been much more systematic about considering under what circumstances particular negotiation strategies, tactics, or objectives may differ. *See, e.g.*, A. STRAUSS, NEGOTIATIONS, VARIETIES, CONTEXTS, PROCESSES AND SOCIAL ORDER (1978). For an analysis of how different contexts may affect negotiation goals and strategies, see *infra* note 288.

90. *See supra* note 47. Note how often such rules are framed with unqualified "always" or "never" formulations. *See, e.g.*, H. COHEN, *supra* note 1.

91. M. MELTSNER & P. SCHRAG, PUBLIC INTEREST ADVOCACY, *supra* note 1, at 238.

structure described above.[92] Thus, for Raiffa[93], Williams[94], Meltsner & Schrag,[95] and Gulliver[96] the phases of an adversarial negotiation will generally proceed along these lines: 1) prenegotiation strategizing or planning to determine target and resistance points, location, and timing of negotiation (Gulliver's "arena,"[97] Raiffa's "logistics"[98] and Williams' "orientation");[99] 2) offers and responses (expression of differences and issue definitions); 3) information exchange (positions, arguments and objectives "presented"); 4) bargaining (Raiffa's negotiation dance),[100] where concessions are made and analyzed; 5) closure or agreement, where agreements are made and parties allocate final responsibilities for negotiated relations. These stages and phases of negotiation are intended to lead negotiators of divergent and polarized objectives through the process of argument and concession, to the point of compromise and agreement.

The difficulty with such a description of the stages and phases of negotiation is not one of accuracy.[101] The problem is that the stylized ritual of offer/response, counteroffer/counterresponse and concessions may not be of assistance when the issues are multi-dimensional and the parties seek to discuss a variety of solutions at the same time.[102] Furthermore, these descriptions of negotiations emphasize an argumentative, debate form of discussion

---

92. *See supra* text accompanying notes 53–129.

93. H. Raiffa, *supra* note 2, at 126–30. Raiffa's stages are: Preparation, Opening Gambits, The Negotiation Dance, and End Play.

94. G. Williams, Legal Negotiation and Settlement, *supra* note 1, at 70–90. Williams' stages are Orientation and Positioning, Argumentation, Emergence and Crisis, and Agreement or Final Breakdown.

95. M. Meltsner & P. Schrag, Public Interest Advocacy, *supra* note 1, at 232–39. Meltsner & Schrag's stages are Preparatory, Initial Tactics, General Tactics and Post-Negotiation Tactics.

96. P. Gulliver, *supra* note 10, at 122. Gulliver's stages are search for arena, agenda definition, exploring the field (emphasis on differences), narrowing differences, preliminaries to final bargaining, final bargaining, ritualization of outcome, and execution of outcome.

97. "Arena," as Gulliver defines it, is both the place in which the negotiation will take place and the social, legal and cultural rules which the parties agree will govern their negotiations. *Id.* at 122–26. The negotiation about the size and shape of the negotiation table at the Viet Nam peace talks is an example of the search for arena. This involved the very significant decision about who would be a party to the negotiation. Similar issues are currently being negotiated with respect to the role of the Palestine Liberation Organization in Mid-East peace talks.

98. H. Raiffa, *supra* note 2, at 126.

99. G. Williams, Legal Negotiation and Settlement, *supra* note 1, at 70.

100. H. Raiffa, *supra* note 2, at 128–29.

101. I base my own teaching on such models of stages and phases of negotiation, *see* D. Binder & C. Menkel-Meadow, American Bar Association Lawyering Skills Program § 12, at 2–3 (1982).

102. How problem-solving processes may differ from adversarial processes is discussed *infra* text accompanying notes 249–289.

that may force the parties into attack and defensive postures which then may inhibit creativity in finding solutions.[103] In short, this form of negotiation debate may lead to competitive reactive dynamics rather than to creative proactive dynamics. For example, commitment to a particular offer may keep the adversarial negotiator from seeing variations of that offer that might be more advantageous for the parties. By arguing for a particular proposal the adversarial negotiator may lock himself into a "mind-set" about why that offer must be accepted. Adversarial negotiation processes are frequently characterized by arguments and statements rather than questions and searches for new information.[104]

The recommended strategies may not work even on their own terms. Many commentators have offered a number of competitive strategies designed to force the other side to capitulate.[105] The difficulty with all of these strategic exhortations is the assumption that the other side can be bullied, manipulated or deceived. It is true, for example, that some will wilt under pressure, but others are likely to respond in kind. Moreover, even those who wilt at the negotiation table may be resentful later and exercise their power either by failing to follow through on the agreement or by seeking revenge the next time the parties meet.

Many of these strategic exhortations may work against the negotiator, even in an adversarial negotiation. For example, if as Meltsner & Schrag suggest,[106] the negotiator chooses his own office for greater comfort in negotiating, the other side may be less comfortable and less amenable to open discussions. In addition, choosing one's own office for comfort minimizes the chances of learning about the other party by not negotiating on their "turf" or by keeping the other party from its sources of information, such as office files. On a more mundane level, the choice of one's own office for comfort may actually increase discomfort by encouraging interruptions from co-workers and telephone calls. Thus,

103. *See* Walcott, Hopmann & King, *The Role of Debate in Negotiations* in NEGOTIATIONS, *supra* note 5. The sample transcript which Fisher & Ury present to demonstrate how principled negotiations work, R. FISHER & W. URY, *supra* note 2, at 96-98, demonstrates how good arguments or principles help to "win"—for example, a higher payment from the insurance adjustor—rather than restructure transactions or solve problems. As another solution to the problem, the insurance adjustor might find a satisfactory car for the claimant, rather than argue about the money.

104. *See* LEGAL SERVICES CORPORATION TRAINING TAPES, EDITED NEGOTIATION, VMB v. JAMES (1977); ABA CONSORTIUM FOR PROFESSIONAL EDUCATION, LAWYERING SKILLS, MODEL NEGOTIATION 1, BRIGHT v. GOLD (1979).

105. H. COHEN, *supra* note 1; M. MELTSNER & P. SCHRAG, PUBLIC INTEREST ADVOCACY, *supra* note 1, at 231; H. RAIFFA, *supra* note 2, ch. 9.

106. M. MELTSNER & P. SCHRAG, PUBLIC INTEREST ADVOCACY, *supra* note 1, at 232.

these strategic exhortations, designed to put the other party at a disadvantage, may not even be effective on their own terms.

The literature is replete with advice to overpower and take advantage of the other side.[107] But as one of the popular guides to negotiation has so wisely stated, "a tactic perceived is no tactic."[108] If two competitive negotiators read the same literature it is

107. *See supra* note 105. The Meltsner and Schrag negotiation tactics piece is a good example of this literature. *See id.* at 231-39. It was originally written as a guide for public interest litigators who negotiated with parties presumed to be adversarial and more powerful, such as government entities and large corporations. The authors intended to teach novice negotiators how to fight fire with fire. The Meltsner and Schrag "rules" are still interesting to study as an example of unstated assumptions about the uniformity of negotiations and their presumed, necessarily adversarial character. The "rules" assume, of course, that the other side is not privy to the same tactical guide.

In addition to the example cited in the text, Meltsner and Schrag advise negotiators to "outnumber the other side" on the assumption that there is power in numbers and never any confusion over bargaining authority. Negotiators are urged to bargain when the other side is pressed for time, to make "prenegotiation demands," and to "lock themselves in" to positions, all of which assume that taking a rigid early position will be advantageous and will not cause the other party to call off negotiations or use similar tactics. *Id.* at 231.

Meltsner and Schrag also suggest that the other side be encouraged to make the first offer and that first offers, when made, be high. *See supra* note 64 and accompanying text. Similarly, concessions should be extracted from the other side because first concessions encourage others. In addition, tactics such as "be irrational," "be tough," "invoke law or justice," M. MELTSNER & P. SCHRAG, PUBLIC INTEREST ADVOCACY, *supra* note 1, at 233, are suggested on the theory that harsh, competitive and aggressive tactics will produce an advantage in negotiation. Several of these suggestions, such as "raising demands during the negotiations" and "claiming no authority to compromise," *id.* at 234, may raise questions of ethics or at least observance of negotiation cultural norms, but all are advised on the assumption that such "power tactics" will intimidate the other side into agreement. Little attention is paid to the risk of stalemate or termination of negotiation if these tactics prove offensive to the other side.

In the end the negotiator is urged to make the adversary feel good about the result achieved, *id.* at 234, so that enforcement of the agreement can proceed smoothly, although it is difficult to imagine how this can be accomplished after using the tactics described above. The negotiator is urged to draft the agreement so that ambiguities can be resolved to the drafter's advantage. *Id.* at 235. This is, of course, contrary to the rules of construction if the agreement is subsequently litigated. *See* Havighurst, *Principles of Construction and the Parole Evidence Rule as Applied to Releases*, 60 NW. U.L. REV. 599 (1965); Havighurst, *Problems Concerning Settlement Agreements*, 53 NW. U.L. REV. 283 (1958).

These exhortations, although expressly written for a limited audience, are still typical of much of the negotiation literature. *See* H. COHEN, *supra* note 1, and sources cited *supra* note 2. The rules are based on assumptions that the other party can be overpowered into submission, that the other party is not using similar tactics (one wonders how many lawyers would fill each negotiating room if every lawyer obeyed the injunction to "outnumber the other side") and that such "always" and "never" rules are equally applicable in all negotiation contexts. Thus, even assuming a zero-sum adversarial negotiation, these tactics are not likely to be successful on their own terms and if the objective of the negotiation is other than to "maximize victory," these tactics are likely to be counterproductive.

108. H. COHEN, *supra* note 1, at 138.

difficult to see how these strategies will be employed to maximize individual gain. Who will win when both sides know all the same tricks?

The one strategic exhortation that seems to dominate most descriptions of adversarial negotiation is the admonition that the negotiator should never reveal what is really desired. Thus, the process of exaggerated offers is designed to cloak real preferences so that one negotiator cannot obtain unfair advantage over another by knowing what the other really wants.

> In any negotiation, and particularly in lawsuit settlement negotiation, the opposing negotiators may have widely different views of the same case. . . . The logical corollary to the foregoing principle is that one should not reveal his own settling point. . . . Presumably in the optimal negotiation, one will determine his opponent's settling point without revealing his own.[109]

The assumption here, of course, is that in every negotiation each side will attempt to thwart what the other really wants, and therefore the negotiator does well to refuse the adversary such leverage.

The principle that one should hide information about one's real preferences is based on unexplored assumptions of human behavior[110] that negotiators are manipulative, competitive and adversarial.[111] The danger of acting on such assumptions is that

109. H. EDWARDS & J. WHITE, *supra* note 1, at 112-13.

110. These assumptions have been least explored in the legal literature, which has focused primarily on litigation negotiation, *see supra* note 1, and has assumed an adversarial or hostile negotiating environment. This might be accurate if lawyers negotiating in litigation conceived of themselves as trial lawyers. Whatever the limitations of these assumptions for litigation negotiations, they may be totally inappropriate for transactional negotiations. The social psychological literature, on the other hand, has at least attempted to test such behavioral assumptions. *See infra* note 111.

111. Social psychologists, particularly those engaged in game theory experimentation, have tested these assumptions of human behavior by alternating behaviors, such as cooperative and competitive, in simulated games like Prisoner's Dilemma in order to test the interactive aspects of personality and behavior in bargaining situations. *See, e.g.*, J. RUBIN & B. BROWN, *supra* note 5; BARGAINING, *supra* note 5. The findings, while inconclusive and somewhat contradictory, have indicated that:

1) bargaining behavior, while dependent on some individual personal factors, K. LEWIN, PRINCIPLES OF TOPOLOGICAL PSYCHOLOGY (1936), is an interactive process, Deutsch, *The Effect of Motivational Orientation Upon Trust and Suspicion*, 13 HUM. REL. 123 (1960). *See generally* M. DEUTSCH, *supra* note 33;

2) there are many complex relationships between "interpersonal orientations" and "motivational orientations" along competitive and cooperative scales. J. RUBIN & B. BROWN, *supra* note 5, at 158-258;

3) age is related to bargaining competency in that children are less likely to have interpersonal competency, Fry, *A Developmental Examination of Performance in a Tacit Coordination Game Situation*, 5 J. PERSONALITY & SOC. PSYCHOLOGY 277, 280-81 (1967);

4) negotiators are more likely to behave cooperatively with an opponent of the same race, *see* Baxter, *The Effects of Information About Other Player and Race of*

opportunities for better solutions may be lost (remember the choc-

Other Player Upon Cooperation in a Two-Person Game, 30 DISSERTATION ABSTRACTS INT'L 4544-A (1970), with blacks being slightly more likely to bargain cooperatively. Berger & Tedeschi, *Aggressive Behavior of Delinquent, Dependent, and "Normal" White and Black Boys in Social Conflicts*, 5 J. EXPERIMENTAL SOC. PSYCHOLOGY 352, 358, 362 (1969); Sampson & Kardush, *Age, Sex, Class, and Race Differences in Response to a Two-Person Non-Zero-Sum Game*, 9 J. CONFLICT RESOLUTION 212, 219 (1965);

5) while the studies are legion and findings plentiful and contradictory, in general, gender is not systematically correlated with bargaining behavior, *see* J. RUBIN & B. BROWN, *supra* note 5, at 169-74 (collecting the findings of over 100 studies). Some of the contradictory findings, however, are interesting. Some studies suggest that males are more cooperative than females, and others that females are more cooperative than males, *id.* at 170-71. Rubin and Brown have attempted to reconcile this contradiction by arguing, based on hundreds of Prisoner's Dilemma game studies, that women are more sensitive and reactive to the interpersonal aspect of their relationship to the other bargainer. Men, on the other hand, orient themselves not to the other negotiator but "to the impersonal task of maximizing their own earnings. When earnings can best be maximized through the use of a competitive strategy, males tend to compete, on the other hand, when a cooperative strategy seems most likely to maximize own earnings, males cooperate.". *Id.* at 173;

6) personality factors such as tolerance of ambiguity, self-concept, cognitive complexity and risk-taking propensity are all associated with tendencies to competitive or cooperative orientations. *Id.* at 174-94;

7) competitors tend to behave competitively, regardless of the other's behavior, while those who are cooperative tend to react and to behave cooperatively with other cooperators and competitively with competitors. *Id.* at 185; Kelley & Stahelski, *Social Interaction Basis of Cooperators' and Competitors' Beliefs About Others*, 16 J. PERSONALITY & SOC. PSYCHOLOGY 66, 69 (1970).

The Prisoner's Dilemma game, *see* A. RAPOPORT & A. CHAMMAH, PRISONER'S DILEMMA (1965), has been used to test theories of human motivation with both real bargainers and simulated or pre-programmed bargainers. In the game, two people accused of a crime are faced with the dilemma of confessing. If neither confesses there will be insufficient evidence to convict. If one confesses and the other does not, one will get an especially high sentence. If both confess they will get medium sentences. Since they are separated and cannot communicate they are faced with a strategic dilemma of what to do, based on assumptions about what the other will do. Whatever the choice, the "solution" is produced by their "joint" activity. Researchers can vary the play by "programming" the players to engage in particular choices. The larger significance of these studies has been, first of all, that the bargaining process is so clearly interactive that generalizations about particular personality types may have low explanatory purchase, particularly when the combinations of factors are mixed, matrix-like, in the course of any negotiating dyad. Secondly, bargainers seem to respond to the process itself and change their behaviors. For example, experimental subjects have been perceived to change behavior, simply out of boredom in a simulation exercise, or out of hostility to a non-human bargainer, Enzle, Hansen & Lowe, *Humanizing the Mixed Motive Paradigm: Methodological Innovations from Attribution Theory*, 6 SIMULATION & GAMES 151, 163-64 (1975).

What, then, can be concluded from this complex series of findings? It is tempting to take the view that since the factors are so many and so varied it is impossible to develop a coherent approach to human bargaining behavior. When the pieces missing in the game-theory simulations are added, notably variable subject matters, verbal communication between the parties, and complex social environments that exist in legal negotiations, the difficulties seem insurmountable. Yet it seems to me that given the consistency of some of the findings in game research (see #7 above) legal negotiators must attempt to develop a more sophisticated analysis of the variability of negoti-

olate cake!) and that when one party behaves in this way, the other side may be more likely to reciprocate with competitive and manipulative conduct of its own.[112] Like many of the other assumptions of the adversarial model, the notion that one should hide information is based on a conception of the court outcome. Trial lawyers may fear releasing information in pre-trial negotiations because of the presumed loss of advantage at trial. In this era of discovery, however, this fear may be misplaced.[113] Although thoughtless revelation of "all the facts" may not lead to satisfactory solutions either,[114] failure to disclose real preferences has been shown to foreclose some of the most efficient and mutually satisfactory solutions.[115] Moreover, revealing preferences or needs is not the same thing as revealing "evidence."

Competitive descriptions of negotiations foster a perception of the negotiator as the principal actor in legal negotiations. Be-

---

ating behavior. At the very least, legal negotiators cannot assume similar motives of behavior on the part of all negotiators as a way of simplifying the principles, tactics, or strategies to be used. Because the game theory findings are restricted to bargaining tactics and strategies, especially where the parties are not engaged in verbal communication, they may be of limited value in assessing models of negotiation described here.

Williams has at least attempted to examine legal negotiators' bargaining orientations empirically. *See* G. WILLIAMS, LEGAL NEGOTIATION AND SETTLEMENT, *supra* note 1. He has identified six types of negotiators: effective cooperators, effective competitors, ineffective cooperators, ineffective competitors, average cooperators and average competitors. *Id.* at 18–40. Unfortunately, the data are based not on observations, but on interview and survey data, with the exception of seven videotaped simulations. *Id.* at 15–18.

112. Many of the Prisoner Dilemma studies have demonstrated that once competitive, distrustful behavior is initiated it will beget more competition. J. RUBIN & B. BROWN, *supra* note 5, at 173; Braver & Barnett, *Perception of Opponent's Motives and Cooperation in a Mixed-Motive Game*, 18 J. CONFLICT RESOLUTION 686, 697–99 (1974); Pruitt & Lewis, *supra* note 35, at 170. *See* R. FISHER & W. URY, *supra* note 2, at 101–49 for practical suggestions to reverse this behavior.

113. Beyond the requirements of formal discovery, it may be bad lawyering not to reveal and seek information long before trial begins. As Binder and Bergman point out, evidence sought by one side in order to prevail will depend greatly on what theories and particular evidence the other side intends to pursue. D. BINDER & P. BERGMAN, FACT INVESTIGATION: FROM HYPOTHESIS TO PROOF (1984). To use Wigmore's original categories, J. WIGMORE, THE SCIENCE OF JUDICIAL PROOF (1937), without sharing some information, the litigator will not know whether to prepare for an explanation, denial, or rebuttal unless some information is shared prior to the trial. Thus, medieval notions of trial by surprise make little sense in the context of a fully adversarial trial and still less sense in the context of the pre-trial negotiation process.

It might be argued, however, that revealing particular pieces of evidence or facts is different from revealing the parties' ultimate preferences or desires. Again, the assumption is that if each party knows what the other really wants, it will be withheld. Whether or not it is wise to act on such motivations, it surely has little to do with the ultimate trial result if the parties know each other's underlying objectives. If the case is litigated it will be decided on the legal merits, not on the parties' needs or objectives.

114. *See infra* text accompanying notes 268–269.

115. H. RAIFFA, *supra* note 2, at 300–03, 307, 309.

cause legal negotiations are so stylized and are based on understanding of a special culture, the lawyer becomes the provider of what the court would order if the case went to trial, or what the law allows in transaction planning. The client, intimidated by these adversarial and specialized proceedings, depends on the lawyer to structure solutions that are "legal" rather than what the client might desire if the client had free rein to determine objectives.[116] The client may also assume that the lawyer knows the only "right" way to accomplish the result and may therefore be hesitant to suggest other alternatives. Although clients generally engage lawyers to do what they cannot do themselves, they do not necessarily wish to relinquish all control over either the desired outcomes or the process by which they are achieved.[117] This is especially true where the negotiation involves parties who will have to continue a relationship with one another, such as partnership or post-dissolution custody relationships. The client may also have an interest in how the negotiation is pursued because, if competitive processes are used, the client may have trouble enforcing the agreement or in continuing a relationship with the other party.

B. *The Underlying Assumptions of the Adversarial Model*

1. The Zero-Sum Game: Assumptions of Win/Lose with Equally Valued Limited Resources

Certain beliefs about human and legal behavior underlie ad-

116. *See* D. ROSENTHAL, *supra* note 53; Spiegel, *supra* note 20, at 79. There are, of course, clients who will go too far in their participation or negotiation demands. In such cases the lawyer may have to intervene to exercise her professional judgment about what is appropriate. This is a difficult issue and one which is beyond the scope of this Article. Indeed, although some skeptics think the difficulty with the problem-solving model is how the other lawyer will respond, my own view is that in many cases it is the client who will want to engage in adversarial negotiation. There is a real chicken and egg problem in attempting to discover whether it is adversarial clients who have forced lawyers to create an adversarial model of negotiation or lawyers who have built adversarial expectations for their clients. *But see infra* text accompanying notes 229–41.

117. *See* D. ROSENTHAL, *supra* note 53; Bellow, *Turning Solutions Into Problems: The Legal Aid Experience*, 34 NLADA BRIEFCASE 106 (1977); Lehman, *supra* note 20; Spiegel, *supra* note 20, at 77–81. Much of the literature decrying the professional dominance of lawyers comes out of representation models of individuals, especially those who are indigent or otherwise powerless, like personal injury claimants. There may be other problems in entity representation or when the client is particularly strong or has the power over the attorney. The client may seek a hired gun who will do everything the client wishes. In such circumstances there may be problems of client dominance in the negotiation and the decision making dynamics may be quite different but equally problematic. *See* G. WILLIAMS, *supra* note 1, at 59–69. Thus, it may be that such issues require a more sophisticated social structural analysis of lawyer-client relations before we can formulate accurate generalizations. *See* Heinz & Laumann, *The Legal Profession: Client Interests, Professional Roles, and Social Hierarchies*, 76 MICH. L. REV. 1111 (1978).

vice about appropriate and effective negotiation behavior. This section uncovers the assumptions behind the adversarial model.

The difficulty with the literature described above is that it is based on *one* conception of negotiation goals—maximizing individual gain of a particular kind. What the parties want and how they can best achieve it, however, may vary greatly depending on the subject matter of the dispute, the past relationship of the parties, the costs of "maximizing gain," and a number of other factors.[118]

The adversarial paradigm is based almost exclusively on the simple negotiation over what appears to be one issue, such as price in a buy-sell transaction, or money damages in a personal injury or breach of contract lawsuit. The common assumption in these cases is that the buyer wants the lowest price, the seller the highest; the plaintiff wants the money demanded in the complaint and the defendant wants to resist paying as much as possible. Each dollar to the plaintiff is a commensurate loss to the defendant; the same is true with the buyer and seller. Given this description of the paradigmatic negotiation, the negotiator's goal is simply to maximize gain by winning as much of the materiel of the negotiation as possible. Underlying this general assumption are really two assumptions: first, that there is only one issue, price; and second, that both parties desire equally and exclusively the thing by which that issue is measured, in most cases, money.

The difficulty with this zero-sum approach to negotiation is not that it is necessarily wrong in all cases, but that it has become the tail that wags the dog. First, true zero-sum games are empirically quite rare. Even in game theory

> the interests of the two players have to be precisely opposed for a game to be "zero-sum." There must be no possible outcome which both would prefer, however slightly, to some other possible outcome. In other words, for every pair of outcomes if one player prefers the first the other must prefer the second. . . . Even in a game whose outcome is a division of a fixed sum of money between two players, the two players' interests are not generally opposed in this diametric way if there are chance elements in the game and if the players have 'risk aversion'.[119]

Strictly speaking, a zero-sum game loses its zero-sum qualities and its assumptions when more than one issue is negotiated because trade-offs between issues are possible. In the paradigmatic pricing problem, if one party cares slightly more about

118. *See* Lowenthal, *supra* note 1; *infra* note 288. Some commentators have developed a typology of negotiation dependent on the voluntariness of the negotiation. M. SCHWARTZ, LAWYERS AND THE LEGAL PROFESSION 196–209 (1979 & Supp. 1982) [hereinafter cited as LAWYERS]; *Accountability*, *supra* note 33; Eisenberg, *supra* note 6.

119. M. BACHARACH, *supra* note 4, at 7–8, 41.

when the payment is made (a form of risk aversion) the timing issue will have discount values that render the game less zero-sum. If a dollar is worth more to me today I will take fewer dollars to settle today than next week. This is not necessarily a loss to me and a gain to you since you may or may not have the same preferences as to the timing of payment.

While there may be some paradigmatic zero-sum games in legal negotiations,[120] most are not zero-sum. For example, in a random search of 240 cases taken from 15 federal and state reporters[121] most cases, in terms presented to the court, were not zero-sum disputes. Those that could be characterized as zero-sum were those which required a definitive ruling–evidentiary rulings in

120. These would include, for example, strict pricing problems, or a situation requiring a definite and authoritative ruling. Analysts of legal negotiation processes, myself included, have been grappling with a typology of cases that would lend itself to zero-sum-non-zero-sum analysis. *See, e.g.*, Lowenthal, *supra* note 1, at 95–96. In Raiffa's more general formulation, negotiations must be considered zero-sum when there are two parties and one single issue, such as price. H. RAIFFA, *supra* note 2, at 33–35. Legal negotiations encompass cases where the materiel of the negotiation is actually finite—children in child custody, assets available for division in marital dissolution or bankruptcy. In addition, there are many situations in which the parties require a third party definitive ruling. This occurs in constitutional cases, environmental cases, some personal injury cases, and criminal cases. There is yet another category of cases in which the parties may seek vindication from or retribution against the other party, and reaching "efficient" results may be irrelevant to such nonprofit maximizers.

My earlier efforts to develop such a typology of cases, however, has led me to conclude that although some case types may seem to be more determinately zero-sum, there are within each case type many individual cases that may be subject to non-zero sum resolutions. These would include joint child custody cases, reorganization, and receivership. I prefer, at the present time, to avoid the stigmatizing effect of labeling certain case types as uniformly zero-sum. The stereotyping of cases may limit solutions in the very cases we hope to solve more creatively.

Finally, even in the "simple" pricing situation there are likely to be a number of issues which, although not as important as price, may modify the zero-sum nature of such negotiations. *See, e.g.*, H. RAIFFA, *supra* note 2, at 35–43 (issues such as timing, conditions, etc. may alter the negotiation environment).

121. These cases are derived from class exercises in which students in a negotiation course select 5 cases at random from a court reporter, state or federal, and analyze the zero-sum or non-zero-sum aspects of the cases. As an exercise in building problem-solving creativity, the students are asked to go further and craft solutions to the cases that the court did not or could not use.

Examples of the case-types so categorized are as follows, as taken from the original random sample of 240 cases:

Zero Sum	*Non-zero-sum*
Evidentiary rulings in criminal cases	Joint or shared child custody
Sentencing—whether to imprison	Sentencing—alternative service, probation
Constitutional issues (definitive ruling required)	Alimony/child support (alternative methods of computation, *see e.g. Sullivan v. Sullivan*)
Duty of Liability-Insurer	Zoning, variance, fines for alternative uses
Contract Interpretation (seeking definitive ruling)	Attorneys' fees
Libel/Slander (seeking vindication)	Extent of Liability
Some environmental disputes (prohibited uses, fines)	Taxation
Procedural rulings (requiring definitive ruling - does not confront underlying subject matter of dispute)	Name Change*
	Tortious Interference with Business
	Some environmental disputes (cost-benefit analyses)
	Allocation of Fishing Rights**
	Contract Disputes

* The name change case presents an interesting example of how a seemingly zero-sum dispute can easily be transformed to a non-zero-sum issue. In a particular case, a mother sought to change her illegitimate daughter's last name from that of the putative father's, which was on the birth certificate, to her own. She did not want her daughter subjected to questions about the difference between her last name and her mother's. The court refused to grant the request because of a state policy against illegitimacy, as evidenced, apparently, by the use of the father's name on the certificate—a zero-sum, polarized, and limited remedies approach to the problem. On the other hand, the court would have entertained a motion to change the mother's name to the daughter's, or putative father's, name. This might not be exactly what the mother wanted, i.e. loss of her own identity, but it does solve the problem of different names. Fortunately, many states now permit parents in such circumstances to select any name. *See, e.g.*, 28 PA. HEALTH & SAFETY CODE § 1.6 (1976).

** In one case, a dispute between sport and commercial fishermen over allocations of fishing rights was initially viewed as zero-sum, with the limited resource being the fish in the sea. By dividing or classifying the fish into categories or species which met the different needs of commercial and sport fishermen, some aspects of the dispute were eliminated. This is not a compromise solution limiting the specific numbers of fish which could be caught by each group. The solution permits the effort and "sport" of fishing to be retained.

Note that many of these cases have already been transformed to zero-sum by presentation to a trial court. A sample based on reported cases from the appellate courts is already over-representative of cases which may have been positive sum games but which have been converted into zero-sum games by the decision of the trial court. To obtain a fair sample of dispute cases we would, at the very least, have to look at cases before decision, perhaps at time of filing, and ideally find disputes before they even are transformed into lawsuits. *See* Felstiner, Abel & Sarat, *The Emergence and Transformation of Disputes: Naming, Blaming, Claiming . . .*, 15 LAW & SOC'Y REV. 631 (1980-1981); Miller & Sarat, *Grievances, Claims & Disputes: Assessing the Adversary Culture*, 15 LAW & SOC'Y REV. 525 (1980-1981).

criminal cases,[122] determinations that constitutional rights were infringed, or findings that contracts were applicable in particular situations. Most, however, presented multi-issue situations. Child custody can become joint custody, zoning cases permit variances, and bankruptcy can become financial reorganization. Not every legal dispute or transaction can be transformed into a non-zero sum or cooperative[123] game, but zero-sum games in legal negotiations may be more the exception than the rule. Our conceptualization of the negotiation process ought not to be based on the exceptions. Since zero-sum games are, in some sense, the hardest to resolve and perhaps the least fair,[124] these rare cases should not control those which permit more flexible resolutions. As it is, the court may have to resolve the dispute in a win/lose zero-sum fashion if the negotiations fail. Thus negotiators could better use the negotiation process to explore the possibility of solutions which may be different and perhaps more advantageous to the parties than those the court has to choose.

Second, at the core of the zero-sum conception is an assumption that parties value the fixed resource equally. The negotiator may assume, for example, that all parties value money equally, rather than finding out how parties value what that money can buy. This may unduly limit the solutions to negotiated problems both in terms of the numbers of possible solutions and the quality of those solutions. If, in a personal injury case, the plaintiff wants money to buy a new car, the defendant might be able to provide

---

122. Even evidentiary rulings may not be zero-sum when evidence is admitted for some purposes, but not for others.

123. In game theory a non-zero-sum game is not necessarily the same as a cooperative game. A non-zero-sum game is one in which the parties do not have strictly competing utilities or values for particular outcome choices. In cooperative games the parties can effect their strategies by communicating and sharing preferences or choices with each other. Thus, the zero-sum nature of the game depends on the desired or possible outcomes. The cooperativeness of the game has to do with the parties' communication (or use of means) with each other. In the classic cooperative game, Battle of the Sexes, a husband desires to go to a prize fight and a wife to the ballet. Both prefer to go together than do either activity alone. The parties will improve their outcomes if they openly share preferences and choices. H. RAIFFA, *supra* note 2, at 88-90; M. BACHARACH, *supra* note 4, at 84.

Of course, even if there are many issues they could all be zero-sum issues and the nature of the game would still be zero-sum. On the other hand, the likelihood that the parties have absolutely competitive preferences on all the issues so that trade-offs will not be possible is extremely unlikely. *See* H. RAIFFA, *supra* note 2, at 148-65; Pruitt & Lewis, *supra* note 11, at 174-77.

124. Coons, *supra* note 71, suggests that where facts are truly indeterminate or when there are two equally compelling rules of law an award of winner-take-all is totally unjust in 50% of the cases. We can decrease this unfairness by reducing the zero-sum aspects of distribution. For Coons, even a 50-50 compromise in the context of a court decision would be "fairer" than awarding the whole item—in his case a cow or a watch—to one party.

such a car directly to the plaintiff at a lower cost than the market price of a new car which defendant would have to pay in settlement.[125]

Third, by assuming that there is only one issue, such as price, other issues or concerns of the parties may be masked and remain unresolved. In a simple "pricing" problem such as Bedding and Swealy in the Edwards & White Teacher's Manual for Negotiation,[126] many teachers and students of negotiation see the price of mattresses to be sold as the only issue. More astute negotiators will recognize that in addition to price there are issues relating to quantity (with the potential for large quantity discount on price), delivery, timing, and manner of payment. There is also the potential of creating a longer term business relationship. Thus, single issue, zero-sum negotiations are quite rare because even simple, single issue situations may contain other issues or needs of the parties which may destroy the strictly zero-sum nature of the dispute.[127]

Finally, by assuming that the materiel of the negotiation is fixed or limited in some way, the parties may lose opportunities to expand the materiel before some division is necessary. For example, by assuming that there is a zero-sum dispute about the parties' assets to be divided in a dissolution proceeding, the parties may miss an opportunity to hold a major asset, such as the couple's residence, until such time as the market price rises. While division may be necessary at some point, both parties may increase their eventual share by deferring division and treating timing as another issue in their negotiation.

To the extent that our negotiation models assume limited or fixed resources, valued equally by all parties to a negotiation, we miss opportunities to find solutions that ultimately might be more

---

125. The example is not as unrealistic as it seems. Many insurance company defendants may retain an inventory of cars from prior claims or through subsidiary businesses such as car rentals, etc. Notice that in this example the cost of settlement is reduced with the same net gain to plaintiff at a lower cost to the defendant. The defendant may, therefore, be more likely to settle.

126. H. EDWARDS & J. WHITE, *supra* note 1, at 11-15. Legal clinicians are well advised to craft carefully the instructions to students in negotiation simulations in order to avoid prematurely or inaccurately "characterizing" a problem or the relationship of the parties in ways which limit the real world complexity of the problem or unconsciously type the case and narrow the range of solutions.

127. Although this is not an example from litigation, all cases involving the payment of money will have a number of dimensions and potential for conversion to non-zero-sum games, if only on the questions of payment. There will be issues of timing of payment, the payor (who), and cash or cash substitutes. Thus, in some personal injury cases a structured settlement with payouts over time converts an otherwise zero-sum into a non-zero-sum situation, particularly where the plaintiff may neither want nor know how to manage a large lump sum.

satisfactory to the parties.[128] Assumptions of total competition of interests and zero-sum outcomes foreclose exploiting the potential for creative solutions inherent in situations where parties attribute differing values to the issues.[129]

2. Negotiating in the Shadow of the Court: Assumptions of Polarized Results and Limited Solutions

The assumption that only limited items are available in dispute resolution occurs because negotiation takes place in the shadow of the courts. Negotiators too often conclude that they are limited to what would be available if the court entered a judgment. To the extent that court resolution of problems results in awards of money damages and injunctions, negotiators are likely to limit their crafting of solutions to those remedies.[130] To the extent that a court would not allow a particular remedy such as barter, exchange, apology, or retributory action, negotiators may reject or not even conceive of these solutions.

Similarly, because courts often declare one party a winner and the other a loser,[131] negotiators often conceive of themselves

128. In the Pareto optimal sense one party can be made better off without worsening the condition of the other party. Thus, one party could choose to expand the pie, *see infra* text accompanying notes 209–241, for the sole purpose of increasing his own share of the total profits. It should be clear that if the pie is increased in size, the pieces are usually, though not always, likely to be bigger for both parties, even if one party gets more pieces.

129. *See infra* text accompanying notes 226–228 for ways of exploiting value differences as a source of potential solutions. In addition to different values attributed to items involved in a negotiation, the parties may have different costs associated with obtaining the same item. They thus have different utilities for similar outcomes which can be exploited to find more or different solutions. *See* H. RAIFFA, *supra* note 2, at 148–65.

130. *See* Eisenberg, *supra* note 6, at 658. In legal negotiations the parties must always consider what the court will do if they do not reach an agreement. Too often what the court would do determines the agenda for the negotiation. The court result might better be used in one of the senses of Fisher & Ury's BATNA (Best Alternative to a Negotiated Agreement), R. FISHER & W. URY, *supra* note 2, at 104–11. Is what the court would do better than what we can accomplish in negotiation? If it is we may choose to go to court; but we need not be confined in the negotiation to what the court might order if we conclude we can do better in a negotiation than in court.

131. Judicial declaration of a winner and a loser may be characterized as "binary results." Eisenberg, *supra* note 6, at 654. As P.H. Gulliver has commented in his discussion of the role of norms in negotiation where the rule of law is heavily emphasized:

> Related to the matter of norms is the contention that "all or nothing is a characteristic feature of the ordinary judicial method. An action is proven and sustained or not proven and dismissed . . . ." Similarly, the "verdict of the court has an either/or character; the decision is based upon a single, definite conception of what has actually taken place and upon a single interpretation of the legal norms . . . ." This implies that adjudication operates largely in terms of black and white: This is the rule, that is not; this rule is superior to or more compelling

as winners and losers, and in court games, the result is usually "winner take all." Although some have argued that courts do or should compromise,[132] the more common structure of court resolution of disputes, such as "plaintiff wins $25,000" or "defendant acquitted," tends to narrow the conceptions of negotiation solutions since all solutions are judged against what the court is likely to do. Negotiations, therefore, proceed as an earlier version of court resolution, without the judge.

A clear example of how this court model affects negotiation can be found in the literature which suggests that negotiators set "goals, minimum/maximum dispositions, target points, reservation points and aspiration levels"[133] at levels which are based on assessments of what the court might do if the case goes to trial. This is especially true in the personal injury literature which suggests numerical formulas for setting goals at such values as "three times the specials" or "midway between the maximum recovery potential and minimum recovery expectation."[134] Thus, even though the eventual solution may be one of compromise within the bargaining range, this settlement is based on the presumed limits set by the court. To the extent that courts do "compromise" through doctrines such as comparative negligence, even parties' "split the difference" solutions may be based, at least in part, on what the court would do.[135]

One of the strengths of the legal system—definitive, precedential rulings to promote clarity, certainty, and order—may actually be dysfunctional for the creation of innovative and

---

> than that one and therefore the latter is overridden; these facts are more probably correct, those are less probably, and therefore the latter are rejected; this disputant is in the right, the other is in the wrong. Conversely, it is implied, negotiators are able to, indeed almost must, take less of an either-or stance. They can compromise and take account of a spectrum of shades between extremes.

P.H. GULLIVER, *supra* note 10, at 13 (quoting O. Schmidt and V. Aubert).

Gulliver goes on to point out that there are some adjudicators who compromise by "taking account of the degrees of culpability, factual correctness, and applicability of norms." *Id.*

132. Coons, *supra* note 71. *See also* Farago, *Intractable Cases: The Role of Uncertainty in the Concept of Law*, 55 N.Y.U. L. REV. 195 (1980). Others have argued that courts do order detailed and complex rulings to fit the requirements of the parties, if only in special kinds of litigation. Eisenberg & Yeazell, *The Ordinary and the Extraordinary in Institutional Litigation*, 93 HARV. L. REV. 465 (1980).

133. G. BELLOW & B. MOULTON, *supra* note 1, at 55-66; H. EDWARDS & J. WHITE, *supra* note 1, at 123-26; H. RAIFFA, *supra* note 2, at 35-43.

134. *See* G. BELLOW & B. MOULTON, *supra* note 1, at 63-66.

135. *Id.* at 55-66. There are, of course, differences in what the court will do depending on whether the court is the judge or a jury. Juries may be more likely to compromise, either by splitting the difference or on some other basis. However, juries are still limited in their solutions by the law or by the parameters set by the court, and still must declare one party a "winner" and the other a "loser."

idiosyncratic solutions to problems that may never reach judicial resolution. To the extent that negotiations in the shadow of the court are limited by conceptions of what the court would do, negotiation may present no real, substantive alternative to trial. Lawyers may prefer this limited conception because it makes evaluation of possible outcomes clearer and easier, especially when discussing alternatives with clients. If this is so, then the large number of settlements[136] can only be explained by the lower cost and relative speed of completion, rather than the superior substantive justice that is done.[137] The limited remedial imagination of courts, when extended to negotiation, narrows not only what items might be distributed but also how those items might be apportioned.

The process described above is strongly influenced by a court conception of dispute resolution.[138] Although there is no third party adjudicator present in most negotiations, the negotiators will frequently adopt adversarial postures, engaging in debate with the hope that they will persuade the other party that it will lose in court, and thus should concede now, without further ado or expense. While debate and some exaggeration may be tolerable in a trial with a third party to "mediate" the truth, such forms may be dysfunctional for achieving the best results in a situation where two parties negotiate voluntarily, without a third party to evaluate their relative claims.[139] If adversarial processes limit one's ability

136. *See supra* note 53.

137. *See* R. Fisher & W. Ury, *supra* note 2. Negotiation of disputes offers the possibility of more and different types of results precisely because, unlike adjudication, the arguments as well as the solutions need not be *binary*, but can be *graduated* and *accommodative*. No one party need be declared the victor and remedies may be individualized in a manner which fits the dispute and disputants. In addition, because there is no need for a third-party adjudicator to reach a final decision, the facts on which solutions may be based can be more accurately and flexibly "found." Eisenberg, *supra* note 6, at 657–58. There is an interesting empirical question underlying this point. Why do parties prefer negotiation to adjudication? The standard argument is the cost and speed of resolution in negotiation versus that of adjudication. Others have suggested that parties prefer negotiation because they know their cases better than the judges will, so they effectuate "better" settlements with their own expertise. C. Rosenberg, *The Culture of Settlement*, (talk delivered to UCLA Faculty Colloquium, March, 1983) (on file at UCLA Law Review). Martin Shapiro has argued persuasively that those things which we presume to be unique to courts—an independent judge, pre-existing legal norms, adversary proceedings and a dichotomous decision—are, in many cases, no longer true, if they ever were, so that courts offer very little to litigants that is different from negotiation. M. Shapiro, *supra* note 72. It would be interesting, as an empirical matter, to investigate whether parties still view courts as providing aspects of dispute resolution that are different from negotiation, besides the cost and timing. In other words, if the costs and timing of litigation and negotiation were equal, which would parties prefer and why?

138. See *infra* Section C for a fuller discussion. *See also* Eisenberg, *supra* note 6, at 665.

139. *See* M. Schwartz, Lawyers, *supra* note 118, at 3-45. See also H. Raiffa, *supra* note 2, and M. Bacharach, *supra* note 4, for discussions of how "dishonest"

to conceive of creative solutions[140] then it may be unwise to have trial lawyers conduct pretrial negotiations.[141] In effect, the ten percent of cases which are tried control the types of solutions which are achieved in the other ninety percent of cases.[142]

Transactional negotiations may be similarly limited in the types of solutions considered plausible due to previous litigation about particular clauses, or because of "industry practices" or form provisions which are common in usage and seldom questioned by successive negotiators.[143] Thus, although the use of form terms can be likened to precedent in the guidance and efficiency it offers the parties, it can also produce a limiting or "channeling" effect.[144] The parties to a commercial lease, for example, may adopt the convention of a percentage of gross sales for rent, though they might both be better off with a more secure and stable fixed rent. Although, as Eisenberg suggests, these form terms are most likely to be used in the subsidiary terms[145] which are not crucial to the transaction, their use even in this capacity may limit the possible trade-offs of more creative solutions between and among subsidiary terms and "deal points." Thus, in the commercial lease example above, a subsidiary term allocating property maintenance costs could have some bearing on the possible rent terms. Finally, as the theme of this Article should make clear, differing needs or values of the parties may make one party's subsidiary term another party's crucial term. Thus, the choice of use of common terms may itself become an important aspect of the negotiation, requiring less limited conceptions of what might be

---

representations and positions produce inefficient results in two-party negotiation. See also Davis, *The Courtroom Mystique and Legal Education*, 23 ARIZ. L. REV. 661 (1981) for a discussion of how trial norms and values may have come to dominate legal education and the consciousness of lawyers.

140. *See* Pruitt & Lewis, *supra* note 11, at 181; Aubert, *Competition and Dissensus: Two Types of Conflict and of Conflict Resolution*, 7 J. CONFLICT RESOLUTION 26 (1963) (noting the reciprocal relationship between objectives and mechanisms). Social psychologists using Prisoner's Dilemma simulations have found that competitive, adversarial players have the greatest difficulty coordinating choice behavior and reaching outcomes. *See* studies collected in J. RUBIN & B. BROWN, *supra* note 5, at 201–06.

141. If trial orientations and skills are sufficiently different from negotiation skills it might be wise to separate those functions. Others have suggested that functional differences in the type of lawyering work done should result in different rules of conduct, such as for the lawyer as adversary and the lawyer as advisor. *See Accountability*, *supra* note 33. *See also* ABA Model Rules of Professional Conduct (Final Draft, 1983).

142. *See supra* note 53.

143. Eisenberg, *supra* note 6, at 671 n.101. *See also* H. HART & A. SACKS, *supra* note 5, ch. 2.

144. P.H. GULLIVER, SOCIAL CONTROL IN AN AFRICAN SOCIETY 235 (1963).

145. Eisenberg, *supra* note 6, at 671.

possible.[146]

C. *Consequences of the Adversarial Assumptions: The Limits of Linearity*

When negotiators adopt zero-sum conceptions of the problems or transactions they seek to resolve or plan, they unnecessarily limit themselves in a number of ways. First, by assuming single-issue negotiations in which parties value the single item equivalently, they may fail to consider whether the parties have other needs or issues that consequently may go unresolved. Second, by focusing on maximizing immediate, individual gain, negotiators may fail to appreciate the long-term consequences of a particular solution. For example, in the Bedding/Swealy problem[147] the seller may "win" by gaining a high price for the mattresses, but this may discourage the purchaser from engaging in business in the future with the "victorious" seller. Third, zero-sum, single-issue conceptions of negotiation problems often fail to consider transaction costs, both in terms of process costs to the client in the use of an adversarial approach[148] and the costs of a less than optimal solution. The adversarial negotiation conception narrowly limits potential solutions by encouraging negotiators to develop mind-sets about possible solutions which include only court solutions or commonly used solutions that may not meet the parties' needs.[149]

The adversarial model can lead to stalemate or no agreement by failing to exploit differences in values that could broaden the range of possible solutions[150] or even increase the gain to one party without decreasing the gain to another.[151] By focusing too exclusively on how only one side can gain, the parties may miss

146. Form provisions are undoubtedly used because it is cheaper not to renegotiate every term and because common practice has demonstrated the viability of particular terms. In some cases, however, focusing on the cheaper process of using form terms may prevent the more expensive but desired tailoring of terms to meet particular or idiosyncratic needs.

147. *See supra* text accompanying notes 126-127.

148. For a vivid example of the process costs in having lawyers with strong adversarial conceptions negotiate see Legal Services Corporation Training Program Video Tape-Negotiation-VMB v. James (1977). These training tapes use "real" lawyers to negotiate a simulated problem. In the tapes, lawyers' egos and desires to "win" come to dominate any client interest in settling the case.

149. Note how these consequences fail when measured against the evaluative criteria described above, *see supra* text accompanying notes 13-18.

150. For example, by bargaining very hard over the amount of money to be paid as a wage in labor negotiations the parties may reach a stalemate and strike without exploring the trade-off of fringe benefits for increments of wages.

151. It may be possible to "sweeten" a settlement and make it more acceptable to one party by offering something which comes at no cost to the other party.

opportunities to expand what they must divide or to trade off unequally valued items.

Seeing negotiation as an arena with only one victor may result in withdrawal, submission, dependence, and, ultimately, resentment on the part of the party which perceives itself as the weaker. Enforcement of agreements made under such circumstances may be impaired by failure to comply, causing forced compliance costs or new negotiations about compliance.

Adversarial orientations lead to competitive strategies, and thus may produce inefficiencies by taking more time and costing more money.[152] Escalation in negotiation strategies may not only intensify the conflicts in the situation by increasing rigidity of positions, but also may prevent the creation and realization of solutions which more closely meet the needs of the client.[153]

The adversarial structure encourages compromise in its conventional sense; that is, both parties must give something up in order to reach agreement. In contrast, the problem-solving model substitutes a negotiation structure that does not require unnecessary compromise[154] but permits the parties to come to agreement without having to give up their preferences.

II. TOWARD A MODEL OF PROBLEM SOLVING NEGOTIATION: A THEORY OF NEEDS

Problem solving is an orientation to negotiation which focuses on finding solutions to the parties' sets of underlying needs and objectives.[155] The problem-solving conception subordinates strategies and tactics to the process of identifying possible solutions and therefore allows a broader range of outcomes to negotiation problems.

This section provides a framework for understanding problem-solving negotiation by discussing 1) the principles which underlie this alternative model; 2) the structure of problem solving, including how the parties' full sets of underlying needs and objectives are identified and how solutions may be conceived to meet

152. Pruitt & Lewis, *supra* note 11.

153. R. FISHER & W. URY, *supra* note 2, at 29; H. COHEN, *supra* note 1; Pruitt & Lewis, *supra* note 11, at 181; *supra* note 85.

154. *See supra* note 71.

155. By "real" problem or objective I mean that which the client wants to accomplish, not how those needs are translated into legal remedies. In disputes it is often useful to look not only at what the dispute is about, but what brought the parties into a relationship in the first place. Thus, in the Brown and Snead example above, *see supra* text accompanying notes 75–84, the dispute concerns a defective car and the failure to make payments on a contract, but the case focuses on the purchase of a car for the mutual gain of both parties. For a discussion of how lawyers frequently fail to ascertain or act on client's real needs see Lehman, *supra* note 20.

these underlying needs and 3) what negotiation processes may facilitate the creation of solutions that meet the criteria outlined at the beginning of this Article.[156]

A. *The Underlying Principles of Problem Solving: Meeting Varied and Complementary Needs*

Parties to a negotiation typically have underlying needs or objectives–what they hope to achieve, accomplish, and/or be compensated for as a result of the dispute or transaction. Although litigants typically ask for relief in the form of damages, this relief is actually a proxy for more basic needs or objectives. By attempting to uncover those underlying needs, the problem-solving model presents opportunities for discovering greater numbers of and better quality solutions. It offers the possibility of meeting a greater variety of needs both directly and by trading off different needs, rather than forcing a zero-sum battle over a single item.

The principle underlying such an approach is that unearthing a greater number of the actual needs of the parties will create more possible solutions because not all needs will be mutually exclusive. As a corollary, because not all individuals value the same things in the same way, the exploitation of differential or complementary needs will produce a wider variety of solutions which more closely meet the parties' needs.[157]

A few examples may illustrate these points. In personal injury actions courts usually award monetary damages. Plaintiffs, however, commonly want this money for specific purposes. For instance, an individual who has been injured in a car accident may desire compensation for any or all of the following items: past and future medical expenses, rehabilitation and compensation for the cost of rehabilitation, replacement of damaged property such as a car and the costs of such replacement, lost income, compensation for lost time, pain and suffering, the loss of companionship with one's family, friends and fellow employees and employer, lost opportunities to engage in activities which may no longer be possible, such as backpacking or playing basketball with one's children, vindication or acknowledgment of fault by the responsible party, and retribution or punishment of the person who was at fault.[158] In short, the injured person seeks to be returned to the same physical, psychological, social and economic state she

156. *See supra* text accompanying notes 11–20.

157. This is known in psychology as the Homans Principle. *See* I. ZARTMAN & M. BERMAN, *supra* note 2, at 13–14, 66, 175–76.

158. M. FRANKLIN, INJURIES AND REMEDIES: TORT LAW AND ALTERNATIVES (2d ed. 1979); Abel, *A Socialist Approach to Risk*, 41 MD. L. REV. 695 (1982); Abel, *A Critique of American Tort Law*, 8 BRIT. J. OF L. AND SOC'Y 199 (1981).

was in before the accident occurred. Because this may be impossible, the plaintiff needs money in order to buy back as many of these things as possible.

In the commercial context, a breach of contract for failure to supply goods might involve compensation for the following: the cost of obtaining substitute goods, psychological damage resulting from loss of a steady source of supply, lost sales, loss of goodwill, any disruption in business which may have occurred, having to lay off employees as a result of decreased business, restoration of good business relationships, and retribution or punishment of the defaulting party. In the Brown and Snead case described above,[159] the litigation model structured the parties' goals in terms of the payment of money, when in fact one party sought to purchase and own a reliable form of transportation and the other sought a profit. It may be more useful in any contract case to think of the parties' needs in terms of what originally brought them together—the purpose of their relationship. Can the parties still realize their original goals? Charles Fried describes the classic function of contracts as attempts by the parties to mutually meet each other's needs:

> You want to accomplish purpose A and I want to accomplish purpose B. Neither of us can succeed without the cooperation of the other. Thus, I want to be able to commit myself to help you achieve A so that you will commit yourself to help me achieve B.[160]

Some of the parties' needs may not be compensable, directly or indirectly. For example, some injuries may be impossible to fully rehabilitate. A physical disability, a scar, or damage to a personal or business reputation may never be fully eradicated. Thus, the underlying needs produced by these injuries may not be susceptible to full and/or monetary satisfaction. The need to be regarded as totally normal or completely honorable can probably never be met, but the party in a negotiation will be motivated by the desire to satisfy as fully as possible these underlying human needs. Some parties may have a need to get "as much X as possible," such as in demands for money for pain and suffering. This demand simply may represent the best proxy available for satisfying the unsatisfiable desire to be made truly whole-that is to be put back in the position of no accident at all. It also may represent a desire to save for a rainy day or to maximize power, fame or love.[161]

---

159. *See supra* text accompanying notes 75-84.

160. C. Fried, *supra* note 5, at 13.

161. Although legal negotiations tend to bring us into contact with those who seek to maximize money, there are others who seek to maximize other human goals—fame, love, power, security, maybe even altruism. These are still needs, and although

It is also important to recognize that *both* parties have such needs. For example, in the personal injury case above, the defendant may have the same need for vindication or retribution if he believes he was not responsible for the accident. In addition, the defendant may need to be compensated for his damaged car and injured body. He will also have needs with respect to how much, when and how he may be able to pay the monetary damages because of other uses for the money. A contract breaching defendant may have specific financial needs such as payroll, advertising, purchases of supplies, etc.; defendants are not always simply trying to avoid paying a certain sum of money to plaintiffs. In the commercial case, the defendant may have needs similar to those of the plaintiff: lost income due to the plaintiff's failure to pay on the contract, and, to the extent the plaintiff may seek to terminate the relationship with the defendant, a steady source of future business.

As Carol Gilligan noted in her study of gender differences in moral reasoning, there may be more solutions when one takes account of both parties' needs than when one tries to evaluate the moral hierarchy of whose needs are more deserving.[162] When asked, as part of a larger study on rights and responsibilities, whether a man should steal a drug to save his wife's life when a pharmacist demands a price the man cannot afford, a boy sees the problem as one of property versus life and argues that the drug should be stolen. A girl, in seeking to meet the needs of the man, his wife, and the pharmacist, tries to find other solutions such as borrowing money (either from the pharmacist or a third party) or trying to persuade the druggist to give the man the drug because he comes to see the importance of the woman's life. Amy, the girl in the study, is confident that " if Heinz (the man) and the druggist had talked it out long enough, they could reach something besides stealing."[163]

---

they will be hard to "meet" when the other side also seems to have the same insatiable demand, it is important to understand them at their most basic level. If a demand for money is really masking a strong need for security, there may still be other ways to meet the security need. The board game *Careers* (copyright Milton Bradley) captures wonderfully these basic human desires, permitting each player to identify for herself which of these things she will attempt to maximize in the game.

162. In her discussion of how a boy and girl attempt to decide what is morally correct in Heinz's dilemma (a moral problem developed by Kohlberg to establish the stages of moral development) the boy reasons hierarchically and must come up with "a" solution. The girl attempts to figure out if there are other possibilities that would permit the man to obtain the drug and would also provide payment for the pharmacist. C. GILLIGAN, *supra* note 28, at 24–32.

163. *Id.* at 29. In Gilligan's study girls and women saw such problems as relational and situational; they tried to meet the needs of *all* of the people involved. Boys and men, on the other hand, needed to resolve the dilemmas with *an* answer produced by logic or mathematical niceties—there must be a "right" way to solve the

Whether a focus on the needs of both parties is a particularly female mode of problem solving is still unknown. To the extent that it focuses on a broader way to solve problems it obviously should be of use to all legal negotiators–male or female.

To the extent that negotiators focus exclusively on "winning" the greatest amount of money, they focus on only one form of need. The only flexibility in tailoring an agreement may lie in the choice of ways to structure monetary solutions, including one shot payments, installments, and structured settlements. By looking, however, at what the parties desire money for, there may be a variety of solutions that will satisfy the parties more fully and directly. For example, when an injured plaintiff needs physical rehabilitation, if the defendant can provide the plaintiff directly with rehabilitation services, the defendant may save money and the plaintiff may gain the needed rehabilitation at lower cost. In addition, if the defendant can provide the plaintiff with a job that provides physical rehabilitation, the plaintiff may not only receive income which could be used to purchase more rehabilitation, but be further rehabilitated in the form of the psychological self-worth which accompanies such employment.[164] Admittedly, none of these solutions may fully satisfy the injured plaintiff, but some or all may be equally beneficial to the plaintiff, and the latter two may be preferable to the defendant because they are less costly.

Understanding that the other party's needs are not necessarily as assumed may present an opportunity for arriving at creative solutions. Traditionally, lawyers approaching negotiations from the adversarial model view the other side as an enemy to be defeated.[165] By examining the underlying needs of the other side, the lawyer may instead see opportunities for solutions that would not have existed before based upon the recognition of different, but not conflicting, preferences.[166]

---

problem. Gilligan has observed empirically these different modes of moral reasoning as gender linked without commenting on the origin of these differences. She points out that these modes may simply be two different ways of making choices so that we need not see them as exclusively male or female modes of problem-solving. *Id.* at 2. The "male mode" bears a striking resemblance to the court model of binary solutions and adversarial negotiations.

164. This solution is not as far fetched as it seems. It is taken from an actual negotiation and is a relatively common solution in some types of cases. For example, both employer and employee have an interest in finding another job for a worker's compensation claimant who would like to return to work but can no longer do the original job. See Keppel, *Goods, Not Cash, Settle Loss Claims*, L.A. Times, Feb. 19, 1983, at 1, col. 1 for other examples of non-cash settlements of "real" objectives.

165. *See supra* Section II.

166. See D. Binder & C. Menkel-Meadow, *supra* note 101, for a fuller discussion of how this material can be used to structure and plan problem-solving negotiation.

The implication of this for clinical teachers of negotiation is that parties' needs

An example from the psychological literature[167] illustrates this point. Suppose that a husband and wife have two weeks in which to take their vacation. The husband prefers the mountains and the wife prefers the seaside. If vacation time is limited and thus a scarce resource, the couple may engage in adversarial negotiation about where they should go. The simple compromise situation, if they engage in distributive bargaining, would be to split the two weeks of vacation time spending one week in the mountains and one week at the ocean. This solution is not likely to be satisfying, however, because of the lost time and money in moving from place to place and in getting used to a new hotel room and locale. In addition to being happy only half of the time, each party to the negotiation has incurred transaction costs associated with this solution. Other "compromise" solutions might include alternating preferences on a year to year basis, taking separate vacations, or taking a longer vacation at a loss of pay. Assuming that husband and wife want to vacation together, all of these solutions may leave something to be desired by at least one of the parties.[168]

By examining their underlying preferences, however, the parties might find additional solutions that could make both happy at less cost. Perhaps the husband prefers the mountains because he likes to hike and engage in stream fishing. Perhaps the wife enjoys swimming, sunbathing and seafood. By exploring these underlying preferences the couple might find vacation spots that permit all of these activities: a mountain resort on a large lake, or a seaside resort at the foot of mountains.[169] By examining their underlying needs the parties can see solutions that satisfy many more of their preferences, and the "sum of the utilities"[170] to the

must not be rigidly stated on printed instructions before negotiation simulations. If law students are to develop an understanding of the "real" needs of clients they must have an opportunity to interview "real" clients whose needs are dynamic and may be altered by the information given to them by their lawyers. For the last two years I have used volunteers, other students, real clients, and myself as the "client" in negotiation simulations rather than distributing rigid negotiation instructions which do not permit the students to learn why a client may desire particular things. *See generally* M. MELTSNER & P. SCHRAG, COURSE, *supra* note 1, at 59-123.

167. This example was suggested by Pruitt & Lewis, *supra* note 11.

168. Many couples today might prefer separate vacations. This example would then be limited to those who value the taking of joint vacations or who value the preservation of the relationship over their preferences for particular activities. It may be of limited utility in litigation contexts where the parties do not have long-term relationships to preserve, though it still illustrates how differing interests can be dealt with without compromising.

169. Constructing this example while writing in Southern California it is very easy to find a mutually satisfactory solution: Santa Barbara.

170. The "sum of utilities" here refers to the measure of the acceptability of each notice. In a "joint gain" situation such as the one described in the text the utilities, or

couple as a whole is greater than what they would have achieved by compromising.

In addition, by exploring whether they attach different values to their preferences they may be able to arrive at other solutions by trading items.[171] The wife in our example might be willing to give up ocean fresh seafood if she can have fresh stream or lake trout, and so, with very little cost to her, the couple can choose another waterspot where the hikes might be better for the husband. By examining the weight or value given to certain preferences the parties may realize that some desires are easily attainable because they are not of equal importance to the other side. Thus, one party can increase its utilities without reducing the other's.[172] This differs from a zero-sum conception of negotiation because of the recognition that preferences may be totally different and are, therefore, neither scarce nor in competition with each other. In addition, if a preference is not used to "force" a concession from the other party (which as the example shows is not necessary), there are none of the forced reciprocal concessions of adversarial negotiation.

The exploitation of complementary interests occurs frequently in the legal context. For example, in a child custody case the lawyers may learn that both parties desire to have the children some of the time and neither of the parties wishes to have the children all of the time. It will be easy, therefore, to arrange for a joint custody agreement that satisfies the needs of both parties.[173]

---

sum of the wins and losses, are additive rather than zero- or constant-sum. *See* Pruitt & Lewis, *supra* note 11, at 161–62.

This type of joint gain solution may more likely be achieved in long term relationships. Note that here the parties would like to vacation together, just as the husband and wife in the Battle of the Sexes game want to attend the same event. In situations where the parties do not have such a commitment to the relationship or transaction itself, it may be less easy to arrive at these solutions.

171. Trading is a common problem-solving device. Known also in game theory and politics as "logrolling," the parties simply trade items which are of different value. Each bargainer gets something he values highly because it is not valued as highly by the other side, and gives in trade another item valued highly by the other side. Pruitt & Lewis, *supra* note 11, at 164. This type of negotiation behavior is possible because of the Homans Principle, G. HOMANS, SOCIAL BEHAVIOR: ITS ELEMENTARY FORMS (1961), which says that because people have different preferences or values it is possible to increase the number of outcomes in situations where several differentially valued items are at stake. I. ZARTMAN & M. BERMAN, *supra* note 2, at 13–14. Unlike strict compromises these trades do not necessarily result in equivalent win-loss functions for both parties. By effectuating such trades with differentially valued items, there is a net gain for both parties.

172. This is known as a Pareto optimal result. *See* M. BACHARACH, *supra* note 4; R. LUCE & H. RAIFFA, *supra* note 34, at 193; H. RAIFFA, *supra* note 2, at 138–39.

173. Joint custody may present its own problems. In one sense it can be seen as a "compromise" or avoidance of making a decision, and the allocation of time, unlike responsibility, may have elements of a zero-sum game. There has been criticism recently that joint custody may represent an abdication of judicial responsibility in

Similarly, in a commercial matter, the defendant may want to make payment over time and the plaintiff, for tax purposes or to increase interest income, may desire deferred income.[174]

B. *The Structure of Problem Solving*

1. Identifying the Parties' Underlying Needs and Objectives

Unlike the adversarial model which makes assumptions about the parties' desires to maximize individual gain, problem solving begins by attempting to determine the actual needs of particular clients. The problem-solving model seeks to avoid a lawyer who acts for a hypothetical, rather than a real, client by creating a "standardized person to whom he attributes standardized ends."[175]

Ascertaining the client's needs will, of course, begin with the initial interview. This is not the place to review the extensive interview literature,[176] but in thinking ahead to the negotiation which might occur, a lawyer might begin by asking the client such general questions as "how would you like to see this all turn out?" or "what would you like to accomplish here?" before channelling the client's objectives in directions the lawyer knows are legally possible. The client may be the best source of ideas that go beyond what the court or the legal system might commonly permit. Once the client's ideas are brought to the surface, the lawyer can explore the needs they are meant to satisfy, and the legal and nonlegal consequences of these and other solutions.

Since so many legal problems are reduced to monetary solutions, consideration of the economic needs and objectives of the client faced with a dispute or transaction is a good place to begin. What are the monetary requirements now—compensation, return on investment, liquidity for payment? What might be the future monetary needs? What is the money needed for? Are any cheaper means available? Are there cash substitutes that are available and acceptable? What are the tax consequences of pay-

making important custody decisions. Steinman, *Joint Custody: What We Know, What We Have Yet to Learn, and the Judicial and Legislative Implications*, 16 U.C.D. L. Rev. 739 (1983).

174. Tax consequences are among the reasons structured settlements have become such popular problem-solving devices. Plaintiffs may not be able to pay taxes on or manage a large lump sum. By fixing liability discounted for present value, the insurance company is permitted its deduction in the present and the plaintiff can take his income over time, both for tax purposes and for ease of management.

175. Lehman, *supra* note 20, at 1087 (paraphrasing Simon, *The Ideology of Advocacy: Procedural Justice and Professional Ethics*, 1978 Wis. L. Rev. 29).

176. *See, e.g.*, D. Binder & S. Price, Legal Interviewing and Counseling (1977); T. Schaffer, Legal Interviewing and Counseling in a Nutshell (1976); Schoenfield & Schoenfield, *Interviewing and Counseling Clients in a Legal Setting*, 11 Akron L. Rev. 313 (1977).

ment/receipt now? Later? What payment structure is desirable—lump sum, installments? Why? What are the transaction costs or solution costs of negotiation as opposed to litigation?

Next the lawyer might consider that with which she is most familiar—the legal issues. What legal regulations govern the parties' situaton? Must there be an admission of liability? Is a legal judgment necessary? Why? Is a formal document evidencing agreement desirable or required? What are the likely future legal consequences of actions taken? What are the parties likely to do if one of them breaches an agreement? What assets will be available in the future for legal action, if necessary?

The negotiator might consider how any solution affects the client's relationship to others. What are the social needs of the parties? How do others feel about this dispute or transaction? Will family members,[177] friends, business associates, employers, employees be affected by actions taken by the parties? If not affected now, how will any of these people feel if things change in the future?

The negotiator might also ask the client to consider the personal feelings generated by the dispute or transaction. What are the psychological needs of the parties? Does one desire vindication, retribution, power? Why? What will be the long-term psychological consequences of satisfying or not satisfying these needs? How risk averse are the parties? What are their motivations for pursuing their aims in the negotiation? How might some of these feelings change if they forego litigation now or if they insist on obtaining some advantage?[178]

Finally, the negotiator might also consider the ethical concerns of the parties. How fair do they desire to be with each other? What are the consequences of acting altruistically or dishonestly now? In the future? Will there be feelings of guilt later for "taking advantage" or the other side?

For each of these basic categories of needs[179] the negotiator should also consider how the needs may change over the long run. There may be additional needs which the client has not articulated and which have as yet unrealized consequences. Frequently,

177. For example, consider the importance of taking account of the needs of the children in determining the needs of the parents in negotiating custody matters. J. GOLDSTEIN, A. FREUD, & A. SOLNIT, BEYOND THE BEST INTERESTS OF THE CHILD (1979).

178. For a guide to determining clients' needs and objectives in interviewing and counseling sessions, see D. BINDER & S. PRICE, *supra* note 176, and D. BINDER & C. MENKEL-MEADOW, *supra* note 101.

179. There may be other categories of needs to pursue, *see* MASLOW, THE FARTHER REACHES OF HUMAN NATURE (1972); T. SCHAFFER, *supra* note 176, at 3-5 ("feelings are facts").

some of the latent needs or concerns can be ascertained by simply following up a client's statement of need with an inquiry as to why that item or thing is desired.[180] For each stated need, the lawyer should engage in a systematic inquiry into long and short run consequences and the latent concerns behind those which are manifest.

Ideally, this framework for determining the parties' needs must be considered from both parties' perspectives.[181] At the very least, it should encourage lawyers and clients to consider whether all the potential needs presented by a negotiation have been canvassed.[182] The following chart summarizes this identification or inventory of needs:

	Now (Short Run)	Later (Long Run)	Manifest (Articulated)	Latent (Unstated)
Economic (Including Transaction Costs)				
Legal				
Social (Relationships)				
Psychological (Feelings) (Risk Aversion)				
Ethical/Moral (Fairness)				

As important as ascertaining the parties' needs is the consideration given to the weight or value of client's needs and preferences. Professor Lehman illustrates the sad consequences of lawyers' assumptions that legal or economic needs are always preeminent in importance to clients. In one case he tells us of a couple whose desire to make a gift was thwarted. Listening to their lawyer's advice about deferring the gift for tax reasons, they decided not to make the gift and died before the tax year was over.[183] In another case, a grieving widow headed toward alcoholism in her marital home, refused to consult a lawyer about selling the house. She feared the lawyer would urge her to stay until she reached age 55, an additional year, in order to avoid capital

180. The role the lawyer plays in counseling the client about negotiations is extremely important, although a full exploration of this subject is beyond the scope of this Article. See *infra* notes 233–41 and accompanying text. For other conceptions of the lawyer's role in counseling or representing clients see *Accountability*, *supra* note 33; Fried, *The Lawyer as Friend: The Moral Foundations of the Lawyer-Client Relation*, 85 YALE L.J. 1060 (1976); Simon, *The Ideology of Advocacy*, 1978 WIS. L. REV. 29; Wasserstrom, *Lawyers as Professionals: Some Moral Issues*, 5 HUMAN RIGHTS 1 (1975).

181. *See supra* text accompanying notes 164–66.

182. *See infra* text accompanying notes 188–209.

183. Lehman, *supra* note 20, at 1088.

gains taxation.[184] The lesson of such unfortunate tales is that, as Lehman tells us: "the lawyer needs to be careful to discover what it is the client is really about, to give [the] fullest possible opportunity for her interests to be explored, and to avoid the over-bearing assertion of simple money saving."[185]

In negotiation, as in counseling, the lawyer should be certain that she acts with full knowledge of the client's desires. Within the suggested framework, the lawyer ranks the client's preferences in terms of what is important to the client rather than what the lawyer assumes about the "typical" client.

In order to engage in problem-solving negotiation the lawyer must first ascertain her clients' underlying needs or objectives. In addition, the lawyer may want to explore whether there are unstated objectives, pursue those which she thinks appropriate to the situation, or probe the legitimacy and propriety of particular goals. It should be noted, however, that the lawyer's role in exploring latent concerns or discussing the propriety of objectives can come dangerously close to the role of the lawyer in the adversarial model who imposes his own values or makes assumptions about what the client wants to accomplish.[186] Finally, in order to pursue solutions that will be advantageous for both parties, the lawyer must ascertain the likely underlying needs and objectives of the other party. The client is a primary source for this information, but the lawyer should pursue other sources throughout the negotiation process.[187]

2. Creating solutions

a. Meeting the Parties' Needs Having identified the parties' needs one can begin the search for solutions with those that are suggested by the parties or that otherwise directly meet the parties' needs.

For example, in a personal injury case the injured plaintiff may have economic needs for compensation and rehabilitation costs that extend into the future. In such cases, structured settlements, paid over time, and according to a variety of formulas,[188] may more closely meet the needs of the parties than a single lump sum payment. Conversely, given the difficulty of enforcement of spousal support[189] the parties to a dissolution might prefer a single

184. *Id.* at 1089.

185. *Id.* at 1089-90.

186. *See infra* notes 229-48 and accompanying text.

187. *See infra* notes 249-89 and accompanying text.

188. *See supra* note 174.

189. Blank & Rone, *Enforcement of Interspousal Support Obligations: A Proposal*, WOMEN'S RTS. L. REP., June 1975, at 13; *See* Mnookin & Kornhauser, *supra* note 38.

payment, if it can be afforded, in order to avoid the transaction costs of enforcement proceedings. The failure of conventional court solutions to return the parties to the *status quo ante* demonstrates how negotiated solutions may meet other needs of the parties. In some recent products liability cases, for example, plaintiffs who could not be fully returned to their previously uninjured selves have requested that the defendants rewrite their warnings in order, at least, to prevent similar injuries to others. These plaintiffs have altruistic objectives in addition to their needs to be compensated, which likely would be unattended to in a court-decided solution.

In the transactional context, consider an example of a negotiation of a standard commercial real estate lease in which the lessor demands the usual five percent of gross revenue for rent.[190] Suppose the prospective tenant is opening a new fast-food restaurant in a shopping center and would prefer to keep the rent low in the early months when profit will be low and start-up costs may be high. A conventional, adversarial lawyer for the tenant might simply attempt to negotiate a lower percentage rent or perhaps a low fixed monthly rent. By asking the client to identify his needs, the lawyer might discover that this particular client would prefer a lower-than-standard percentage at the beginning of the rental period but would be willing to pay a higher-than-standard percentage at a later time, perhaps after a certain profit figure is reached. A sliding percentage rent may be quite acceptable to the lessor, depending on his particular financial needs.[191] In short, by engaging in a conventional adversarial negotiation, attempting to reduce the standard rent provision, the lawyer might have missed an opportunity to arrive at another solution which more effectively meets the parties' needs. This is particularly important in cases such as the one in the example where the parties are likely to have a long-term relationship.

The power of parties' underlying interests in suggesting solutions is vividly demonstrated in international relations negotiation. The proposals for treatment of the Sinai peninsula during the Mid-East negotiations provide an excellent demonstration of

190. This example is derived from a problem, Berger/Jones, written by the author and David Binder for the ABA Lawyering Skills Institute, D. BINDER & C. MENKEL-MEADOW, *supra* note 101. Note that the now standard percentage of gross provision was regarded as a creative solution to commercial leases in 1958. *See* H. HART & A. SACKS, *supra* note 5, at 212-32.

191. For example, if the fast food restaurant is going to attract a great deal of business to the shopping center the landlord might be willing to accept this arrangement because he anticipates increased income from the percentage of gross arrangements he has with his other tenants. Note that if this is so, the solution is also a resource-expanding solution. *See infra* text accompanying notes 210-28.

the importance of ascertaining a client's needs.[192] A compromise "split-the-territory" approach was considered undesirable by both parties because of the geographic integrity of the land and the different values the parties associated with it. As the negotiations progressed,[193] it became clear that while Israel's primary concern was security, for Egypt the issue was territorial sovereignty. Rather than compromise by splitting the difference, the parties crafted an alternative solution, based upon information gained through the negotiations. The resulting formula of neutralization returned the land to Egypt, meeting the sovereignty need, but also prohibited armaments and provided for a UN or other neutral security force, thereby meeting Israel's need for security.[194]

Such solutions may have their analogues in legal disputes where the materiel of the negotiation cannot easily be severed or divided and the parties have different but not mutually exclusive needs for the materiel. Joint custody of a child is a variant of this solution; at least one jurisdiction has ordered divorcing spouses to alternate living in the marital residence so that the children could remain at home while the parents shared custody.[195] These solutions, derived from the parties' respective needs, can be called non-possessory or sharing solutions. They are particularly useful in cases where the parties' needs coalesce around the same desired and potentially unique item.[196] In these situations, compromises or splits need be used only as a last, rather than as a first resort. In Zartman's[197] and Raiffa's[198] terms these types of solutions are possible when parties choose not to argue about the different values but to exploit the differences in order to arrive at solutions.[199]

The following illustrates a more common legal problem that can be solved by looking directly at the parties' underlying needs. Suppose two neighbors are engaged in a simple neighborhood dispute about noise. Mr. Tony Smith, a 23 year old auto mechanic, works long hours and lives in an apartment. Dr. Margaret Meade,

---

192. I. Zartman & M. Berman, *supra* note 2, at 91–96; R. Fisher & W. Ury, *supra* note 2, at 42–43; H. Raiffa, *supra* note 2, at 205–17.

193. J. Carter, Keeping Faith: Memoirs of a President (1982); *see supra* note 192.

194. I. Zartman & M. Berman, *supra* note 2, at 96. In Zartman and Berman's terms this was the creation of a "neutralization formula."

195. Church v. Church, 8 Fam. L. Rep. 2252 (Mich. Cir. Ct. 1981).

196. These solutions might be particularly useful in property disputes about "unique" realty or personal property.

197. I. Zartman & M. Berman, *supra* note 2, at 12–13.

198. H. Raiffa, *supra* note 2, at 148–65.

199. There is an interesting irony here in that different goals and values actually facilitate solutions, rather than thwart them. Contrast this with the assumption of the adversarial model that the parties value equally the same item, usually money, thus forcing competition for one solution. *See supra* text accompanying notes 32–42.

a middle-aged woman in her third year of a medical residency program, lives next door. When the young man comes home from his hard day of physical labor he unwinds by playing loud rock music on his new and very expensive stereo. When Dr. Meade comes home from her noisy and tension-filled days at the hospital, she prefers quiet reading and early bedtime as her relaxation. Dr. Meade has asked Mr. Smith many times to turn down his stereo, to no avail, and the two have been engaged for many weeks in loud arguments which are upsetting the entire neighborhood. One evening, in desperation, Dr. Meade calls the police to complain about the noise. The police arrive and threaten to arrest Mr. Smith for disturbing the peace. The next night Mr. Smith again plays his loud music; an altercation develops with Dr. Meade. In her frustration and anger, Dr. Meade throws a flower pot at Mr. Smith. It misses him, but breaks his window. Mr. Smith files a criminal assault charge and a civil small claims action against Dr. Meade.[200]

The dispute has now found its way into two courts—one civil and the other criminal. Note that regardless of the outcome in either court, the underlying problem will not be resolved.[201] Neither the criminal court nor the civil has the authority to establish rules about quiet hours in the neighborhood.[202] Any last, particular incident may be dealt with, but except for its precedential value in the event of future violent altercations there is nothing in either court's decision that will improve life for Mr. Smith or Dr. Meade. Even an injunction ordering the parties to cease and desist from disturbing each other is unlikely to resolve the problem because it is likely to be worded in a general and negative fashion[203] and to entail complex enforcement problems.[204] The solutions more likely to resolve the problem and meet the parties' needs can be achieved only by negotiation or, perhaps, by third party mediation.[205]

---

200. This example was suggested by a real case fictionalized for film purposes, *see* PEACEWORK (motion picture written, directed and produced by Enos, Laruccia, & Lincoln 1979) and further elaborated upon by this author.

201. In the criminal action Dr. Meade will either be found guilty and serve a jail sentence, pay a small fine, or be placed on probation. If she is found innocent Mr. Smith will get nothing. In the civil action Dr. Meade will either be ordered to pay the costs of damaging the window and perhaps some damages for the assault or she will have to do nothing.

202. Rules of the house may be specified in the lease or normative expectations of quiet in the neighborhood. But these rules regarding right to quiet are not self-enforcing and even if brought to a court in a justiciable fashion, the court would not have authority to set particular quiet hours for the parties.

203. Imagine the enforceability of an injunction which says "Do not disturb each other," rather than specifying particular hours of quiet or permissible activities.

204. Enforcement might require multiple "contempt" hearings.

205. Indeed, the case on which this example is based was submitted to mediation.

Mr. Smith and Dr. Meade could view this problem as an adversarial, zero-sum dispute, dividing up the scarce resource–time–with one half time allocated for quiet and one half for music. If the parties were aware of each other's underlying needs, however, they might create solutions that would permit Mr. Smith to have more than half music time and Dr. Meade more than half quiet time. Mr. Smith might be willing to give up some nights of music knowing that Dr. Meade needs quiet on the nights she is home because she is frequently in the hospital overnight and gets no sleep at all.[206] Conversely, if Dr. Meade learns that Mr. Smith uses loud music to unwind from his day she might be more tolerant of his needs. She might also be able to think of other solutions, such as buying him headphones.

Focusing on the actual, rather than assumed, needs of the parties leads to solutions other than those which courts would order or which would result from compromising in adversarial negotiation. With the above set of facts the problem has easy solutions; change a few facts and the problem can become more difficult. Suppose that an examination of the parties' goals, needs or preferences reveals a value conflict. Mr. Smith insists upon raucous music without headphones so he can dance and move freely about his apartment. By rejecting the headphone solution, Mr. Smith has revealed a preference that may actually compete with Dr. Meade's needs. The value dissensus forces a consideration of other solutions. One or both parties could move, but that wouldn't prevent similar problems from occurring with new neighbors. Attempts to argue or persuade each other to change values[207] are unlikely to work in this case because both parties have real and persuasive reasons for their preferences.

The parties could try other solutions that would not force them to give up their preferences. They could change work schedules to minimize contact hours at home. Dr. Meade could use earplugs several nights a week and Mr. Smith could use headphones on the others. They could allow a third party to mediate noise levels or evenings on which music could be played. In other words, they could search for alternative solutions that keep stated value preferences constant, but attempt to take account of both

Much of what is said here about problem-solving negotiation is equally applicable to mediation. *See* H. RAIFFA, *supra* note 2, at 218-34; Riskin, *Mediation and Lawyers*, 43 OHIO ST. L.J. 29 (1982).

206. For example, he might forego music on the nights when she is home because on the other nights he can be assured of playing his music without her complaining. Of course, there is always the problem that other neighbors will complain and the problem will repeat itself.

207. Indeed, this is what occurs in most conventional negotiations. Walcott, Hopmann & King, *supra* note 103.

parties' needs. Regardless of how limited the possible solutions may appear to be, they are, in this context, far more likely to satisfy the parties and effectuate a more permanent agreement than would most results achieved in court or in adversarial negotiations.

The needs of the parties, therefore, may serve as a springboard for potential solutions to the problem. By focusing on economic needs the parties may discover ways to cut costs,[208] dovetail short- and long-term interests, or minimize tax consequences. By discovering that they have different values about social needs, for example, time spent with children, they may be able to agree to child custody arrangements. By determining that a client's need to give a gift is more important than the economic consequences something may be given without demanding a trade. And, by ascertaining that the parties value some items differentially, it may be possible to trade or "logroll" one item for another.[209]

b. Expanding the Resources Available Of course, the parties' needs will not be sufficiently complementary in all cases to permit direct solutions. Needs may conflict or there may be conflict over the materiel required to satisfy the needs. In addition to focusing on the parties' needs as a source of solutions, negotiators can attempt to expand the resources that the parties may eventually have to divide.[210] In essence, this aspect of problem-solving negotiation seeks wherever possible to convert zero-sum games into non-zero-sum or positive-sum games.[211] By expanding resources or the materiel available for division, more of the parties' total set of needs may be satisfied. Indeed, as the literature on legal transactions and the economic efficiency of such transactions makes clear,[212] the parties come together to transact business precisely because their joint action is likely to increase the wealth available

208. D. Pruitt, *supra* note 5, at 142.

209. *Id.* at 153–54.

210. This effort at expanding resources before dividing should be attempted in all negotiations, including those thought to be simple and paradigmatic zero-sum situations. Even if needs cannot be met directly, an attempt to expand resources may satisfy more of the parties' needs.

211. M. Bacharach, *supra* note 4, at 58-156; H. Raiffa, *supra* note 2, at 131-47; I. Zartman & M. Berman, *supra* note 2, at 12. The typology of games by game theorists begins with two person zero-sum games and proceeds through two person non-zero-sum non-cooperative games (non-competitive in utilities but no coordination of choice), two person cooperative games, n-person games with transferable utility, and n-person games without transferable utility. M. Bacharach, *supra* note 4, at 58-156. The utility of game theory in helping to develop typologies of negotiation is not as great as it would appear given the interactive, interdependent and uncertain characteristics of legal negotiations.

212. The literature focuses primarily on contracts, *see* R. Posner, *supra* note 5, at 65-100.

to both. To the extent that principles of wealth creation and resource expansion from transactional negotiation can be assimilated to dispute negotiation,[213] the parties to a negotiation have the opportunity to help each other by looking for ways to expand what is available to them.

Various substantive strategies may increase the materiel available for distribution. Resources can be expanded by exploring *what* could be distributed, *when* it could be distributed, *by whom* it would be distributed, *how* it could be distributed and *how much* of it could be distributed. The following examples are illustrative. In the personal injury example above[214] resources can be expanded by providing the plaintiff with a job, rather than money (*what*), and money payments over time which would result in tax savings for both parties (*when*). In exploring the *what* for distribution it is often useful to determine whether the defendant can satisfy the plaintiff's needs more directly and at less expense than with a money payment which the plaintiff must use to purchase an item on the open market. As in the above example, it may be less costly for the defendant to provide the plaintiff with a job, and thus earnings, to satisfy rehabilitation needs than if the defendant simply pays the plaintiff to purchase these items. Also, in exploring the *what* of distribution the parties should examine whether there are substitute goods or other forms of exchange that could be used to expand what is available for division.[215]

By whom and *when* solutions can be illustrated by the following solution drawn from an actual legal negotiation.[216] In the settlement of a large anti-trust case against drug manufacturers an original settlement figure of $100 million was considered inadequate when a group of drug wholesalers and retailers requested more than the $3 million originally allocated to them. A change in the distribution of the settlement fund would have been a time consuming and costly process given the nature of the classes of litigants. The settlement terms required that no one receive payment until the time for appeal had run. A solution was devised whereby the defendant drug companies placed a large portion of the total settlement in a bank account in trust for the plaintiffs.

213. The extent to which notions of wealth creation through contracts and transactions, *see, e.g.*, C. FRIED, *supra* note 5, can be applied to dispute resolution is an important question to be explored further. It is the thesis of this Article that dispute resolution offers the parties many of the same opportunities to enhance each other's position and to create rather than destroy surplus.

214. *See supra* text accompanying notes 158-60.

215. *See supra* note 164. Such settlements are becoming increasingly common as "structured settlements" in personal injury litigation. G. WILLIAMS, LEGAL NEGOTIATION AND SETTLEMENT, *supra* note 1, at 131-32 and sources cited therein.

216. *See* G. BELLOW & B. MOULTON, *supra* note 1, at 149; G. NIERENBERG, FUNDAMENTALS OF NEGOTIATION, *supra* note 1.

Thus, the defendants were able to take a corporate tax deduction in one year and by accruing interest the plaintiffs received an augmented settlement award one year later. In this solution, the bank, as a third party, increased the resources by paying interest to the plaintiff.[217] The use of third parties to expand resources available to the negotiating parties is a common device for solving problems. In real estate transactions, for example, a buyer and seller can expand the materiel of their negotiation by persuading the broker to take a reduced commission.[218]

Variations on the *how* and *how much* of distribution are illustrated by the types of creative sharing arrangements discussed above, such as joint custody, shared ownership, and preservation of items with geographic or other integrity.[219]

In addition to these devices the growing negotiation literature is replete with other suggestions for expanding resources or exploiting trade-offs between the parties so that more solutions will be available on the "efficient frontier."[220] For example, in a one item pricing problem, the parties can both be made better off by aggregating items. In one of the classic negotiatiation problems in the literature a tourist enters a grocery store with the intention of

---

217. Note that the bank gains as well by being able to use the money in making loans during the appeal period.

218. In this case the third party gets less by taking a reduced fee, but it expands the bargaining range available to the two principals.

219. *See supra* text accompanying notes 192-95. The Law of the Sea treaty is another example of a creative sharing arrangement. In the proposed solution for deep sea mining, nations are to choose sites which they will share with an international mining entity. Thus, parallel mining permits multiple parties to benefit from a limited resource. R. FISHER & W. URY, *supra* note 2, at 87-88; H. RAIFFA, *supra* note 2, at 275-87. As of this writing the United States has refused to participate in the Law of the Sea treaty.

Another example of using the *how* and *how much* to craft solutions can be found in the novel and film of J. CAIN, *The Postman Always Rings Twice* (1934) at 117-31. There, three insurance companies recognized their potential liability if the death of one character was considered murder, thus enabling another character to collect on an intentional misconduct guest liability provision for injuries suffered during commission of the murder. The insurance companies each contributed amounts less than their total liability to settle a third company's claim. In return, the murder is recharacterized as an accident, permitting the character to be released from jail and the insurance companies from further liability. Once again, there is greater benefit to one party at a lower cost to the other, in this case produced by third party payments and, just incidentally, by obstruction of justice through inability to prosecute without the insurance company's testimony.

220. H. RAIFFA, *supra* note 2, at 139. The "efficient frontier" or Pareto Optimal Frontier is the locus of achievable joint evaluations from which no further joint gains are possible and is represented by an arc on a two-axis coordinate. *Id. See also* M. BACHARACH, *supra* note 4, at 88-90; *supra* note 74. Note that there are many points along the efficient frontier. That is, in most two party non-zero-sum games with cooperation, that is, coordination of choice, there exists a variety of equally efficient solutions, a phenomenon known as indeterminacy, *see* M. BACHARACH, *supra* note 4, at 89.

buying a single can of beans. By focusing on the low price the tourist wants to pay for one can and the seemingly high price the grocer wishes to charge, the parties discern no range of agreement. But by buying more than one can of beans, the tourist is able to get a lower unit price and the grocer a reasonable profit. This is a simple case of producing a better or more economically efficient result by searching for ways to increase each party's gain without hurting the other side.[221] Aggregating units may also be seen as taking advantage of a long-term conception of needs. While at the moment the tourist is concerned with buying only one can and the seller with the short-term profit, the parties can meet their long-term needs by buying a larger quantity of food for the future and taking a long- rather than short-term profit. As a corollary, in some cases where the parties are focused on larger units in the negotiation, disaggregation may also lead to a greater number of items or solutions.

As another device for broadening the conception of a problem and expanding resources, Fisher and Ury have recently suggested that negotiators examine how problems would be solved by those with expertise in another field.[222] For example, hotly contested public interest litigation against public agencies such as departments of welfare, prisons, and schools focuses not only on liability but also on the availability of funds to accomplish institutional changes.[223] One of the major issues in such cases is to look at the problems from the perspective of financiers or legislators who must find a source of funds to pay for a particular project.

This device can be used productively by examining the checklist of needs and seeing how fundraisers, tax lawyers, and economists might solve the economic problems, psychologists the psychological problems, and so on. The approach requires law-

221. A tourist enters a grocery store desiring to purchase some beans. There are five dusty cans of beans. The tourist would buy all five, but would settle for one. He would like to pay 8 cents (the home price) but would pay as much as 22 cents if necessary. The shopkeeper won't sell at less than cost (10 cents) and is confident that all could be sold eventually for prices between 10 and 25 cents. A sale at any price between 10 cents and 22 cents would be more satisfactory to both parties than no sale. C. KARRASS, THE NEGOTIATING GAME, *supra* note 1, at 140–45. However, only by focusing on arranging a sale of more than one can the parties increase their satisfaction without hurting each other. Thus, a better deal is struck if the tourist buys five cans for 63 cents. (The buyer pays 21.6 cents per can and the grocer earns 13 cents). In a negotiation where the parties may not know each other's preferences and costs it might be more difficult to arrive at efficient solutions. *See* G. BELLOW & B. MOULTON, *supra* note 1, at 16–35. Note also that in this type of negotiation problem the parties maximize their chances for an efficient solution if they honestly share information about their preferences and costs. *See* H. RAIFFA, *supra* note 2, at 303–07.

222. R. FISHER & W. URY, *supra* note 2, at 71; H. RAIFFA, *supra* note 2, at 352.

223. *See* Frug, *The Judicial Power of the Purse*, 126 U. PA. L. REV. 715 (1978); Eisenberg & Yeazell, *supra* note 132.

yers to step out of their own worlds of expertise and control and may lead to additional expense. Although learning to break through the paradigms of professional training and ways of looking at the world may be difficult, there is a rapidly growing literature on increasing creativity by exploring new or different paradigms.[224]

The key to finding solutions that are not simply compromises of the original demand is to develop ways of expanding the resources available before division, if division is indeed necessary. The linear conception of negotiation does not serve well in this endeavor. The dilemma of non-zero-sum games is that there is no single, totally optimal solution, although game theorists and economists have tried to locate them in theory and in simulation.[225] In summary, by using substantive strategies such as exploring shared interests,[226] by exploiting value differences in needs,[227] by looking to third parties, by sharing, by aggregating or disaggregating, by neutralizing, by seeking substitute goods, by exploring long- and short-term values, and by using other specific devices[228] a greater number of solutions may be found. In addition, the particular solutions may be better, and the parties may be more likely to have all or a greater number of their total needs satisfied.

c. Just or Fair Solutions For those who seek the most effective or efficient solutions from a utilitarian perspective, it is enough to settle at a point where no party can gain without hurting the other party. This is the best solution that can be reached when all preferences and needs are taken into account. But legal negotiations leave us with two special non-Pareto optimal[229] problems. First, should the zealous advocate pursue a gain for his client that would cause a loss to the other side? Second, when might the negotiator choose to pursue less gain for his client or actually cause his client to suffer some loss so as to benefit or not

224. C. GILLIGAN, *supra* note 28; R. OLSON, THE ART OF CREATIVE THINKING (1978); M. GARDNER, AHA! GOTCHA: THE ART OF BREAKTHROUGH THINKING (1983).

225. See M. BACHARACH, *supra* note 4, at 89–91 and H. RAIFFA, *supra* note 2, at 133-204 for an excellent explication and application of game theory concepts to real world negotiation problems.

226. For example, time deferrals for mutual tax benefit.

227. Such differences can either be linked or traded, or themselves lead to a solution, such as in the husband-wife vacation example. There is a variety of dimensions on which value differences can be exploited for an increased number of solutions. Raiffa suggests there may be differences with respect to perceptions of risk, probabilistic projections, beliefs, utilities, and items valued, all of which can lead to increasing numbers of solutions by varying terms to comport with differences, rather than trying to achieve agreement on values. H. RAIFFA, *supra* note 2, at 156.

228. H. RAIFFA, *supra* note 2, at 133–65. Pruitt & Lewis, *supra* note 11, at 163.

229. *See supra* notes 14, 172 and accompanying text.

hurt the other side? In some sense these questions are on opposite sides of the same coin. Without solving either definitively,[230] the problem-solving model of negotiation may provide some avenues of inquiry.

In the first case the lawyer and client together can consider whether the pursuit of an additional gain at an equivalent or higher cost to the other side is likely to effect the result in an adverse way. The second party may be so hurt, angry or defeated that the solution will be difficult or more expensive to implement. Having answered the utilitarian question, the legal negotiator must then take into account the rules of her profession. If she abides by the rules which require her to be a zealous advocate[231] for her client, she may pursue the "harsh" result. As Bellow, Moulton & Kettleson have noted,[232] there appears to be nothing in the Code of Professional Responsibility which prohibits a lawyer from achieving a result which even she may regard as unfair.[233] Murray Schwartz has suggested that, at least in non-litigation matters, a slightly different standard of conduct ought to be applied; that the lawyer not necessarily extract that last gain if to do so would be unconscionable as measured by the law in other areas.[234] Still, as a matter of current rules a tough negotiator could (indeed some would say she must) pursue with impunity that additional gain unless, of course, her client instructs otherwise.[235]

Regarding the second case, and as part of the first, the following formulation is offered to those who wish to take the evaluation

230. While there is no definitive solution to this problem; a growing body of literature attempts to deal with the question of what is fair or just in legal negotiation. *See, e.g.*, G. BELLOW & B. MOULTON, *supra* note 1, at 258–73; G. HAZARD, ETHICS IN THE PRACTICE OF LAW (1978); WILLIAMS, LEGAL NEGOTIATION AND SETTLEMENT, *supra* note 1, at 62–64; Rubin, *A Causerie On Lawyers' Ethics in Negotiation*, 35 LA. L. REV. 577 (1975); White, *Machiavelli and the Bar: Ethical Limitation on Lying in Negotiation*, 1980 A.B. FOUNDATION RESEARCH J. 921. *See also* S. BOK, LYING (1978). The discussion in the text is only a beginning; this is an important topic which requires further treatment.

231. MODEL CODE OF PROFESSIONAL RESPONSIBILITY Canon 7 (1980).

232. G. BELLOW & B. MOULTON, *supra* note 1, at 263–73.

233. There is, however, a body of law which prescribes when settlements may be set aside under fraud doctrines. *See* G. WILLIAMS, LEGAL NEGOTIATION AND SETTLEMENT, *supra* note 1, at 90–109. RESTATEMENT (SECOND) OF CONTRACTS § 205 (1979). The proposed Model Rules of Professional Conduct included a requirement that lawyers in negotiations engage in "fair dealing" and truth telling. PROPOSED RULES OF PROFESSIONAL CONDUCT Rules 4.1, 4.2, 4.3. These requirements have been dropped from the latest draft, which was adopted by the ABA in August of 1983. *See* MODEL RULES OF PROFESSIONAL CONDUCT (1983).

234. Schwartz, *Accountability*, *supra* note 33, at 678–90.

235. *Id.* MODEL CODE OF PROFESSIONAL RESPONSIBILITY EC 7-7 (1980); MODEL RULES OF PROFESSIONAL CONDUCT Rules 1.2, 1.4 (1983).

of a problem-solving solution beyond a utilitarian analysis.[236] In considering the acceptability of a particular solution, both lawyer and client might engage in a dialogue about the fairness or justness of their proposals. Putting aside for the moment philosophical debates about the appropriate measures of justness or fairness,[237] lawyer and client might simply ask each other what, if any, detrimental effect their solution has on themselves, the other party, third parties, or the larger society. No current rule requires[238] the lawyer or her client to act on such a dialogue. However, in considering whether the negotiation problem has been solved in a way which meets the underlying objectives of the parties, asking such questions might prevent clients and lawyers from seeking objectives that they ought not or do not want.[239] Under the present Code, the withdrawal rules[240] will govern those lawyers and clients who may have a differing sense of justice or fair-

236. *See supra* text accompanying note 18.

237. The negotiation literature contains some very good discussions of the relationship between justice or fairness and negotiation. *See* D. PRUITT, *supra* note 5, at 61–66; G. WILLIAMS, LEGAL NEGOTIATION AND SETTLEMENT, *supra* note 1, at 62–66; I. ZARTMAN & M. BERMAN, *supra* note 2, at 102–09. These discussions focus on the various forms justice can take—procedural, equitable, equal, compensatory, distributive and allocative. For the philosophical foundations of such discussions, see, e.g., B. ACKERMAN, SOCIAL JUSTICE IN THE LIBERAL STATE (1982); R. DWORKIN, TAKING RIGHTS SERIOUSLY (1977); J.S. MILL, UTILITARIANISM (G. Sher ed. 1979); J. RAWLS, A THEORY OF JUSTICE (1971). *See also* R. FISHER & W. URY, *supra* note 2, at 84–98 for a more pragmatic and less philosophical view of how negotiation results can be measured for fairness.

238. This is not, strictly speaking, true. The lawyer cannot assist the client in achieving illegal objectives. MODEL CODE OF PROFESSIONAL RESPONSIBILITY DR 7-102 (1980). The lawyer is also prohibited from certain specific conduct such as using perjured testimony, making false statements of law or fact, and creating evidence known to be false. *Id.*

239. I do not supply any answers here for what the lawyer and client ought not do. In my view the lawyer and client should hold each other in some kind of moral check or accountability. Achieving the client's objectives, both in its adversarial and problem-solving formulations, ought not, in my judgment, permit the lawyer to do everything the client seeks to do. See Postema, *Moral Responsibility in Professional Ethics*, 55 N.Y.U. L. REV. 63 (1980), for one view of how the lawyer can monitor the "hired gun" model. *See also* Lehman, *supra* note 20. *See also* E. DVORKIN, J. HIMMELSTEIN & H. LESNICK, BECOMING A LAWYER: A HUMANISTIC PERSPECTIVE ON LEGAL EDUCATION AND PROFESSIONALISM 200–02 (1981). John Stuart Mill may be instructive in applying a moral standard, even within the context of a utilitarian code:

> The great majority of good actions are intended not for the benefit of the world, but for that of individuals, of which the good of the world is made up; and the thoughts of the most virtuous man need not on these occasions travel beyond the particular persons concerned, except so far as is necessary to assure himself that in benefiting them he is not violating the rights, that is the *legitimate* and authorized expectations, of anyone else. The multiplication of happiness is, according to utilitarian ethics, the object of virtue . . . . (emphasis supplied)

J.S. MILL, *supra* note 237, at 18–19.

240. MODEL CODE OF PROFESSIONAL RESPONSIBILITY DR 2-110, EC 7-9; MODEL RULES OF PROFESSIONAL CONDUCT Rule 1.16 (1983).

ness and who choose to part company over their differences.[241]

In one sense this moral dialogue[242] is simply part of ascertaining the client's needs and thus falls squarely within the problem-solving model. By not discussing these issues with her client, the lawyer may be assuming the standardized, self-interested profit maximizer that dominates the adversarial model. Thus, to the extent that the client does have a need to act fairly, morally, or justly, the lawyer must determine such needs as carefully as she determines how much money the client needs.

Consideration of the justness or fairness of a solution, however, may go beyond a simple needs analysis of the problem. Or, as Fisher & Ury suggest, meeting needs may be secondary to achieving just and objective results. To the extent that the Fisher & Ury model of "principled negotiation" depends on reaching a fair agreement measured by objective standards as a way of avoiding the costs of positional negotiation, it places a greater emphasis on an "objective" agreement than on meeting the parties' needs.[243]

In a sense, consideration of the justness of the solution may be a "need" of the lawyer who seeks to participate in a process that accomplishes just results, or at least is conducted in a manner which gives full expression to the autonomy and dignity of the participants. Some commentators would go further and suggest that consideration of the justness or fairness of a solution is not a need, but an obligation derived either from the special duties and obligations of our profession, or from the ordinary duties and ob-

241. This may, of course, lead to the "last lawyer in town" problem discussed in *Accountability*, *supra* note 33, and Schwartz, *The Zeal of the Civil Advocate*, in THE GOOD LAWYER (D. Luban ed. 1983).

242. Lehman, *supra* note 20, at 1097.

243. In their chapter on "Insist on Objective Criteria" Fisher and Ury emphasize the use of objective criteria as a way of deciding issues involving conflict so that a fair solution can be reached. R. FISHER & W. URY, *supra* note 2, at 84-98. This notion is premised on the fact that a fair solution is better than none at all and that an objective measure may help the parties arrive at a solution without the cost of positional argumentation. To the extent that parties use objective criteria, while not meeting their needs they may nonetheless arrive at compromise-like solutions. Thus, a fair solution may be different from and in some cases give the parties less than what they could get by trying to meet needs. Fisher and Ury could be read to apply a sequential approach to negotiation. First, parties attempt to meet needs. If they can't meet needs, or the needs are truly in conflict, then parties might resort to objective criteria to achieve a fair solution without resorting to litigation or positional bargaining.

Separating out these alternatives suggests four different approaches to negotiation: 1) conventional adversarial; 2) problem solving (meeting needs); 3) fair or objective negotiation (solutions mediated by outside standards where needs are not the only criteria); and 4) conventional cooperative (compromise). More work needs to be done to determine whether these categories are empirically or theoretically distinct. See *infra* note 250 for other division of negotiation models.

ligations of our humanity.[244]

For the lawyer who engages in problem-solving negotiation, assessment of the fairness of the solution may be made easier by all that has gone before. Professor Gilligan points out that moral judgments may be more deeply embedded in the contexts and relationships of the moral dilemmas[245] than in any abstract principles. To the extent that this is true, the problem-solving negotiator who has canvassed a richer set of needs will know more about the context and relationships affected by the problem than the negotiator who simply tries to maximize financial gain.

Negotiations result in agreements which affect the lives of the parties. Parties and their lawyers must finally decide what they want to do. They may consider the rightness of what they do or they may avoid such issues. There is nothing in the problem-solving model which necessarily compels parties to consider the justice of their solutions, unless that is a need, expressed or unstated, of one of the parties. But, if the purpose of the problem-solving model is to accomplish a result which most satisfies the parties, there is no reason why satisfaction shouldn't include knowing that one has done right.[246]

The justness or rightness of a negotiation can be considered not only from the ends produced, but also from the process–the acts of which it consists. This aspect of negotiation is beginning to be explored with some seriousness.[247] Aside from whether one is justified in lying or in overstating preferences in negotiation, the question of how one feels about the process used to accomplish negotiated solutions is not unrelated to the justness of the solution. A problem-solving orientation toward negotiation may lead not only to better solutions, but to a process which could be more creative and enjoyable than destructive and antagonistic.[248]

C. *The Process of Problem-Solving Negotiation*

The process of problem-solving negotiation is likely to be very different from the linear, reciprocal concession patterns leading to compromise in adversarial negotiation. This section reviews how problem-solving negotiation processes are likely to differ from adversarial negotiation.[249]

244. *See* Lehman, *supra* note 20; Wasserstrom, *supra* note 180; Postema, *supra* note 239; Wolf, *Legal Ethics and the Ethics of Law*, in THE GOOD LAWYER, *supra* note 241.

245. C. GILLIGAN, *supra* note 28, at 24–63.

246. J.S. MILL, *supra* note 237.

247. *See supra* note 230.

248. Fox, *Goodby to Game Playing*, JURIS DR., Jan. 1978, at 37–42; Rosenberg, *The Lawyer As Hired Gun*, L.A. LAW., July-Aug. 1979 at 10.

249. This is a brief overview of ways in which the problem-solving process is

1. Planning

As the discussion thus far should indicate, the crux of the problem-solving approach is the conceptualization and planning which precede any execution of the negotiation. A problem-solving conception of negotiation should be distinguished from cooperative or collaborative negotiation. The latter refers to particular behaviors engaged in during the negotiation, such as "being flexible, disclosing information and establishing good relationships with the other negotiator."[250] These behaviors may be useful in problem-solving negotiations, but they can also be used as tactics in adversarial negotiations where their purpose is to achieve greater individual gain. The conceptualization used in planning problem-solving negotiation is useful in all negotiation, regardless of the particular behaviors chosen in the executory stages. Planning may indicate that needs are truly incompatible and call for the use of adversarial strategies to maximize individual gain, or that resort to adjudication is necessary.[251]

Although economic evaluation of the case[252] and some prediction of how a court would rule in a dispute resolution will still be appropriate,[253] potential solutions need not be limited to some

likely to differ significantly from adversarial processes. Because this Article is concerned primarily with orientations to negotiation, a more detailed description of problem-solving processes and strategies awaits further elaboration. *See* R. FISHER & W. URY, *supra* note 2.

250. G. WILLIAMS, LEGAL NEGOTIATION AND SETTLEMENT, *supra* note 1, at 18–23; Lowenthal, *supra* note 1, at 74. Lowenthal and Williams talk about the goals or objectives of cooperative negotiators but they do so in the context of talking about cooperative strategies. Too many commentators conflate the ends and means of negotiation. Negotiators may have a problem-solving conception of negotiation and still not engage in cooperative means or behavior. The classic four-fold table illustrates:

		ENDS	
		ADVERSARIAL	PROBLEM-SOLVING
MEANS	Competitive	Rigidity (Potential Stalemate)	Closed or Limited Problem Solving
	Cooperative	Compromise	Open Problem Solving

FIGURE 6

See Pruitt & Lewis, *supra* note 11, at 183 for a slightly different formulation.

251. This occurs, for example, when the parties seek diametrically opposed interpretations of a rule of law or when the client's ultimate aim is to maximize financial gain.

252. *See supra* note 78.

253. Such analyses are required for two purposes in problem-solving negotiations. First, the likely court results must be compared with any possible negotiated solution

prediction of the mid-point compromise between estimated first offers. Instead, the planning stages of a problem-solving negotiation resemble the brainstorming process decribed by Fisher & Ury in *Getting To Yes*. The process emphasizes exploring and considering both parties' underlying needs and objectives and the devices suggested earlier in this Article for expanding resources. The problem solver who has engaged in a brainstorming planning session is likely to approach a negotiation with a number of possible proposals[254] which can be offered for two-sided brainstorming with the other party.[255] While the planning stages of an adversarial negotiation may narrow and make the offers more precise,[256] the problem solving planning stages are more likely to result in a broadening of solutions. As Fisher & Ury point out, the key to creative problem solving is to separate the creative stages of planning from the necessarily more rigid judgment stages.[257] The more potential solutions a negotiator is able to bring to the bargaining table, the more probable it is that agreement will be reached; stalemate and rejection are less likely to occur. In the legal context these brainstorming sessions should include the client, as she may have some solutions of her own, as well as important insights into what the other party desires.[258]

The planning discussed above is primarily substantive planning focused on potential solutions rather than strategic planning focused on what positions to take in the negotiation.[259] Strategic planning may depend on how willing the other party is to depart

---

to determine whether negotiation or trial will best meet the party's needs. Second, an analysis of how the court is likely to resolve the issues should provide the negotiator with some of the principles for explaining and justifying particular proposals. *See infra* text accompanying notes 272–83.

254. The use of particular terminology is significant. The "offer and response" language connotes binary acceptance or rejection reactions. "Proposals" on the other hand are intended to connote suggestions which may be modified as well as accepted or rejected.

255. R. FISHER & W. URY, *supra* note 2, at 62–72. By conceiving of the negotiation process as a brainstorming session, the negotiators hope to discover solutions in addition to those they have planned for. Thus, the adage "two heads are better than one" captures the sense of synergy accompanying a negotiation session which is more problem-solving than adversarial.

256. The adversarial literature suggests planning for a negotiation by mapping out offers and concessions in advance so that concessions can be made asymptotically to confuse the other party. *See* H. COHEN, *supra* note 1; Craver, Basics of Effective Legal Negotiating (CEB Course Materials 1982); Ury, Negotiator's Checklist (Harvard Negotiation Project).

257. R. FISHER & W. URY, *supra* note 2, at 62–66.

258. For those teaching negotiation this means that negotiations should ideally be preceded by client counseling sessions in which clients discuss negotiation goals and strategies with their lawyers. *See supra* note 166; D. BINDER & C. MENKEL-MEADOW, *supra* note 101.

259. Although I have discussed some strategic aspects of negotiation, this Article is addressed primarily to substantive planning and conceptualization of negotiation.

from the more familiar adversarial negotiation process.[260] At the intersection of substantive and strategic planning are considerations of what information about the other party's needs is necessary to plan for solutions acceptable to the other party. An example best illustrates this point.

Suppose that in a lawsuit based on concealment of a leaky roof in the sale of a residence, the plaintiff has sued for $10,000, the cost of repairing the roof. However, a more extensive portion of the roof was repaired than that which seemed necessary to prevent leaks. The plaintiff has been forced to take out a bank loan in order to repair the roof. This is a further encumbrance on the property, and the plaintiff is having a great deal of difficulty making all of the payments on the house. In addition, the plaintiff is concerned that her parents will learn she bought the house without following their advice to have an inspection made. The defendant seller of the house needs to make payments on her own house and is worried about the possibility of rescission. A bona fide dispute about the facts is whether the defendant mispresented the facts, and if so, whether he did so negligently or intentionally. The seller holds a second mortgage on the house and the plaintiff now threatens to withold payment. The plaintiff has taken the deposition of the defendant's former housekeeper who does remember a leaky roof when the defendant was in possession.[261]

Assuming that we represent the plaintiff in this case, there are a number of needs that can be identified. Economically, the plaintiff would like to recover the cost of the roof repair, probably with a minimum of transaction costs. Depending on her dealings and relationship with the defendant, the plaintiff might wish to have the defendant's actions declared legally fraudulent. Recall, however, that in this example the defendant holds a second mortgage on the house so that the plaintiff and the defendant will have a continuing relationship if the plaintiff remains in the house. The plaintiff's social needs may include preventing her parents from discovering that she bought the house without an inspection. Psychologically, it is possible that the plaintiff feels both foolish for not discovering the leak and angry because it was hidden. Furthermore, the plaintiff may feel that the defendant's deception was morally wrong and she may want an apology, payment as punishment, and/or an assurance that this is the only undisclosed defect.

At this point all we know of the defendant's needs may be what we learned from our client, the plaintiff. We know, for example, that the defendant needs the money from the second mortgage to pay the mortgage on her own new home. We may know

260. *See infra* text accompanying notes 262-71.

261. Evans v. Bollinger from D. BINDER & C. MENKEL-MEADOW, *supra* note 101.

that the defendant would prefer not to have a legal judgment of fraud entered against her because it will damage her credit rating. Similarly, the defendant may not want a lawsuit for fraud to become public because it could damage her relationship with business associates or her reputation in the community. Finally, it is possible that because the housekeeper has already given testimony against her, the defendant fears losing a lawsuit and may feel regretful or guilty about what she has done. Note that many of the assumptions or speculations about the defendant's needs have to be more fully discovered, either in pretrial discovery or in informal investigation, or tested in the negotiation.

Having identified the parties' needs, we can now begin to consider a number of general solutions. These may include such things as settling the case privately because both parties fear publicity, an apology and new promise that nothing else is defective, and perhaps a delayed or installment payment from defendant to plaintiff, or a reduction on the plaintiff's obligation on the second mortgage. The one remaining issue which is likely to result in conflicting views, the amount of the settlement, can be made less difficult either by having an independent determination of the proper amount to repair the original damage or by expanding the resources through time payments and tax structures that may permit the plaintiff to realize more dollars than the defendant actually pays out.

The structure of this example may not work in all cases, but it illustrates how the analysis of both parties' needs may lead to a number of possible solutions.

2. Execution

To the extent that both parties engage in a problem-solving negotiation structure, the negotiation is likely to resemble a fluid brainstorming session. Even if only one party has engaged in a problem-solving planning process, the negotiation need not be reduced to an adversarial exercise.[262] First, the parties may begin with a greater number of possible solutions simply because two heads are better than one. In addition, as empirical research has demonstrated, when both parties approach negotiation with the objective of working collaboratively, more of the information re-

262. *See infra* text accompanying notes 321–48. Those with a problem-solving orientation may still try to solve problems with those who have adversarial conceptions or employ competitive means. Learning the other party's needs may be more difficult if the negotiation is undertaken without coordination ("information sharing" in game theory terminology) so that problem-solving may be "closed"—that is, undertaken in the absence of complete or optimal information. It is still possible, however, to strive for solutions which meet the parties' needs, even if they are only perceived or incomplete needs.

flecting the parties' needs may be revealed, facilitating the search for solutions.[263] Thus, in the case of the leaky roof, the amount of damages might be easier to determine if both parties approached the problem by looking for ways to reach agreement than if one approached the problem as simply maximizing or minimizing payment, using litigation as a threat. On the other hand, even a single problem solver can propose alternative ways of measuring liability that may eventually be successful, if she has accurately determined the other party's needs.

When the problem solver is able to present a number of different solutions which potentially satisfy at least some of the other party's needs, it is more likely that the adversarial concession and argumentation pattern can be avoided than if she presents a single demand. The parties can consider variations of each of the proposals using the techniques of game theorists who simply alter the coordinates slightly at each play to see if a more efficient solution can be achieved. Thus, the negotiation game may be played on a multi-dimensional field rather than on one that is linear, or two dimensional.[264] In the leaky roof case one party may suggest a number of different methods of payment, such as reduction of the second mortgage, lump-sum, or installment payments at different discount factors, rather than simply demanding $10,000.

In addition to the different offer structure, problem-solving negotiations are likely to have different information sharing processes. As discussed above, many conventional works on negotiation urge the negotiator not to reveal information.[265] The problem solver recognizes that he is more likely to develop solutions which meet the parties' needs by revealing his own needs or objectives, while at the same time trying to learn about the other party's. In short, there is no incentive to dissemble.[266] When this is the goal, the process consists of asking questions in search of clarification and information, rather than making statements or arguments designed to persuade the other party to accept one's own world view.[267]

On the other hand, totally uninhibited information sharing may be as dysfunctional as withholding information. In experi-

263. *See* R. FISHER & W. URY, *supra* note 2, at 84–98.

264. *See supra* text accompanying note 74.

265. *See supra* text accompanying notes 109–11.

266. *See* H. RAIFFA, *supra* note 2, at 143.

267. *See supra* note 103. At least one commentator has suggested that lawyers may have particular difficulty behaving in such a searching or "additive" mode. Lawyers, he argues, are trained to respond to statements, proposals, or positions with argumentation and persuasion, rather than listening or making requests for clarification. Condlin, *Socrates' New Clothes: Substituting Persuasion for Learning in Clinical Practice Instruction*, 40 MD. L. REV. 223 (1981).

mental simulations Pruitt & Lewis found that there was not necessarily a correlation between free information exchange and joint profit.[268] Instead, joint profit was associated with information processing—that is, the ability to listen to, receive, and understand the information and how it related concretely to the problem. Furthermore, information sharing in a thoughtless and unrestricted fashion may lead to the sharpening of conflict as value differences are revealed in competing goals and needs.[269] In problem-solving negotiation it is crucial to understand the usefulness and function of particular pieces of information—such as exploring how strongly one party desires something—because each piece is related to possible solutions. Problem solvers must determine what information is needed and why, and must be able to absorb information from the other side to test assumptions about needs, goals or objectives.

An example taken from my negotiation course can illustrate. In negotiating a partnership agreement, students are given information about each of the prospective partners. One partner has an immediate need for a relatively high salary because he must provide for a disabled child. The other partner would also like a high salary, but is more concerned about creating the partnership because he is excited about entering a new business. Students, who in my experience are more likely to be adversarial negotiators,[270] have tended to approach the salary negotiation as a conventional zero-sum negotiation. When, as happens occasionally, one side reveals why the salary is needed, a greater variety of solutions seem to come unlocked, such as sliding scales, deferred versus immediate compensation, special provisions for the child, and salary trade-offs for other items. In this situation the party who learns of the disabled child either may be moved by sympathy or by the more instrumental realization that if this is of concern to his future partner it should be dealt with now so it is not a future drain on the partnership. Whatever the motivation, the new information can serve as a source of new solutions ending an otherwise stalemated salary negotiation. Obviously, not all negotiation problems will contain such useful information, but the problem solver is willing to share information about needs that may facilitate such solutions. Thus, problem solving produces a more sophisticated calculus concerning what information should be revealed.[271]

268. Pruitt & Lewis, *supra* note 11, at 170–72.

269. *See* Brehmer & Hammond, *Cognitive Factors in Interpersonal Conflict*, in NEGOTIATIONS, *supra* note 5, at 79.

270. Condlin, *supra* note 267.

271. For example, problem solving may reveal needs that must be met for there to be any agreement, or needs that may be better met by disclosure during negotiation

Related to the information flow is the process by which the proposals are evaluated during the negotiation. Fisher & Ury describe this process in a problem-solving environment as principled movements[272] which are reasoned, justified statements about why a particular proposal is important. Fisher & Ury distinguish such movements from the arguments over position which occur in conventional adversarial negotiation. In conventional negotiation, each party takes a position such as the first offer or target position,[273] argues for it, and then makes unprincipled concessions to reach a compromise.[274]

Even conventional adversarial negotiation, however, may be justified by principled movements. One of the most valuable contributions of the growing clinical literature on legal negotiation has been the analysis of using reasons for concessions.[275] Thus, in order to avoid the pitfalls of totally unjustified concessions, negotiators are told that "it is important that the pattern and content of . . . justifications [for concessions] be well thought out in advance" as "the justification offered for a particular concession invariably will be assessed by one's opponent . . . ."[276] These suggestions about principled movement in the adversarial context, however, have been used largely to justify movements up and down the limited linear plane. Thus, although useful even in adversarial negotiation, principled movements are of a different sort and used for different purposes in a problem-solving negotiation.

According to Fisher & Ury, in the problem-solving context the negotiator will use principled movements to justify proposals and suggestions in terms of their relationship to the parties' underlying interests or objectives.[277] Reconciling interests will be more effective than arguing over positions, they say, because "for every interest there usually exist several possible positions that could satisfy it. . . . Reconciling interests rather than compromising between positions also works because behind opposed positions lie

than at trial, where they may be beyond what a court could consider. For teaching purposes I have developed a series of hypotheticals that are designed to test whether revealing information is harmful or helpful to the case. Students are asked to consider whether any rules can be derived from the examples. In general, students recognize that some facts will necessarily have to be revealed if they are needs which must be met or which the court couldn't consider. In other cases, revelation of a fact in negotiation must be compared to the effect revelation would have at trial, for example, evidentiary facts or cost facts, now or later. This is clearly an area in which much more work needs to be done.

272. R. FISHER & W. URY, *supra* note 2, at 3–14, 41–57.

273. *See supra* text accompanying notes 53–68.

274. R. FISHER & W. URY, *supra* note 2, at 1.

275. G. BELLOW & B. MOULTON, *supra* note 1.

276. *Id.* at 119.

277. R. FISHER & W. URY, *supra* note 2, at 11, 41–57.

many more shared interests than conflicting ones."[278]

In the process of considering possibilities, the problem solver articulates reasons why a particular solution is acceptable or unacceptable, rather than simply rejecting an offer or making a concession. Articulating reasons during the negotiation facilitates agreement in a number of ways. First, it establishes standards for judging whether a particular solution is sensible and should be accepted. If the reason is focused on the parties' underlying needs, the negotiator can consider whether the proposal is satisfactory to the parties. She need not be concerned with such conventional evaluation as "Is this the most I can get?" or its counterpart, "Is this the least I can get away with?" Second, principled proposals focus attention on solving the problem by meeting the parties' needs, rather than winning an argument. Furthermore, continuously focusing justification on the parties' needs may cause negotiators to see still other solutions, rather than simply to respond with arguments about particular offers. The use of principled proposals can decrease the likelihood that unjustified and unnecessary concessions will be made simply to move toward agreement. Finally, the use of principled proposals causes the parties to share information about their preferences that they might otherwise be reluctant to reveal.

Principled negotiations in the legal context may be more complex, however. In addition to proposals based on the parties' underlying needs, negotiators can focus on the legal merits as a justification for a particular proposal. Indeed, negotiators are told to use "the law" or "the facts" to make arguments or justify positions in analyzing how concessions can be justified in adversarial negotiations.[279] For example, in deciding whether to accept a particular settlement offer a negotiator might say: "We might not agree on the percentage of responsibility, but in this jurisdiction there is comparative negligence so it is unlikely that our contributory negligence will bar recovery. My client is entitled to something." In some sense, all legal negotiations are measured against the legal merits because, in deciding whether to accept a particular proposal, the negotiator must also decide whether the negotiated agreement is better than the one which would be achieved at trial or in a form contract.[280] In Fisher & Ury's parlance this is termed one of the BATNAs (Best Alternative to a Negotiated Agreement.[281] All proposals in litigation negotiations will be measured

---

278. *Id.* at 43.

279. M. Meltsner & P. Schrag, Public Interest Advocacy, *supra* note 1, at 236.

280. *See supra* text accompanying notes 12-18.

281. R. Fisher & W. Ury, *supra* note 2, at 104.

against predictions about what the court might order.

Proposals justified by the legal merits can be problematic. Given a dispute where the parties have widely divergent views of the merits and how they will be determined by a factfinder, negotiators may find themselves involved in precisely the sort of unproductive argumentation inherent in adversarial negotiation. Indeed, as some have argued, one of the primary advantages of negotiation over adjudication is that no judgment need be made about whose argument is right or wrong. Parties can agree to settle on principles such as community norms or values that are broader than those the court can consider.[282] On the other hand, focusing on the merits as a justification still may be more productive than adhering to arbitrary positions simply out of competitive stubbornness.

Ideally, of course, proposals should be justifiable on a basis which integrates the parties' needs and the legal merits. Returning to the leaky roof example, consider how a demand by the plaintiff for $10,000 "because your client defrauded mine" contrasts with the following proposal to the defendant:

"One solution here might be for your client to pay my client $7,000 by reducing the monthly payment on the second mortgage over the term of the five year mortgage. It seems to me that this is fair because if we go to trial I think the court will find the defendant liable for at least $7,000 of the damages to the roof. The housekeeper's testimony will make it clear the defendant knew of the leak and the court will believe the housekeeper because she has no reason to lie. A payment of $7,000 is fair because it cost $3,000 to repair the roof, $3,000 to replaster the room and $1,000 to replace the ruined rugs. The proposal seems fair because it fits the needs of both of the parties. My client needs a reduction in her total monthly payments to meet all of her obligations, including the second mortgage payment to your client, and your client won't be out of any immediate cash to settle this case. If you prefer some other method of payment or other formulation, I'd be happy to discuss it with you."

The defendant's lawyer is now able to respond to the assessment of the legal merits and his client's needs and may modify this proposal, perhaps by offering a small cash payment with less of a reduction on the second mortgage to insure some future income. In addition, by presenting proposals with such justifications, each party reveals its assumptions about the other party's needs and legal positions, and can be corrected where wrong. When proposals are not justified in this way, the problem-solving

282. Eisenberg, *supra* note 6, at 638, 649.

negotiator should ask on what basis the proposal is made to be sure the principles are articulated and not assumed. Notice that the proposal is sufficiently flexible and indeterminate in terms of how the $7,000 second mortgage reduction will be structured. Both parties, therefore, can modify the proposal and contribute to the final solution without having to accept or reject the general principle of the solution.

Thus, although the relationship of the legal merits to the parties' underlying needs may be more problematic and complex than a simpler justification on the basis of the parties' underlying interests,[283] these articulated rationales for negotiation proposals may be more likely to produce acceptable solutions.

Finally, a word should be said about the process of problem-solving negotiation from the perspective of the behavior of the parties. Problem-solving conceptions of negotiation do not necessarily result in weak or conciliatory strategies or tactics. As Fisher & Ury have stated, "being nice"[284] is not the answer to unproductive adversarial negotiations. Negotiating styles and behaviors are the means or procedures by which negotiation results and solutions are achieved, but they are not synonymous concepts. An overly cooperative negotiator may be just as likely to produce an ineffective compromise by giving in without basis as would a competitive negotiator who stubbornly holds to an unreasonable position. Some game theory suggests that cooperative strategies positively affect joint outcomes.[285] Empirical studies of the effectiveness of cooperative versus competitive behaviors, however, are more complex and as yet inconclusive, both in legal negotiation[286] and in more general negotiations studied by social psychologists.[287] It is beyond the scope of this Article to discuss particular behaviors, other than in the context of negotiation structure. Furthermore, the state of negotiation art and science is not sufficiently advanced to permit accurate generalizations about specific behav-

283. Extrapolating Fisher and Ury's principled arguments to the legal environment might call for arguments based primarily on the parties' underlying interests, rather than the legal merits. Such principled arguments are not likely to work in legal disputes where the principle itself is the party's underlying interest—i.e. being vindicated, or having a constitutional principle interpreted as being applicable to a particular situation. Thus, some attention will have to be paid to the legal merits in principled negotiations as well as to the underlying interests.

284. R. Fisher & W. Ury, *supra* note 2, at 8.

285. *See supra* note 111. Hofstadter, *Metamagical Themas: Computer Tournaments of the Prisoner's Dilemma Suggest How Cooperation Evolves*, Sci. Am., May 1, 1983, at 16; R. Axelrod, The Evolution of Cooperation (1984).

286. *See* G. Williams, Legal Negotiation and Settlement, *supra* note 2, at 15–58.

287. *See supra* note 111.

ioral choices.[288]

---

288. This is the single biggest dilemma addressed in the negotiation literature. Negotiation analysts seek theories of behavior that are sufficiently general to be applicable in all negotiations. As soon as such rules are drafted, however, they must be qualified or modified to take into account different circumstances, situations, or contexts in which negotiations take place. *See* G. WILLIAMS, LEGAL NEGOTIATION AND SETTLEMENT, *supra* note 1, at 66–69. To those who characterize negotiations as consisting of two styles or strategies—cooperative or competitive—the significant question is when each of these strategies should be used. Is it possible to construct a typology of case types or circumstances in which one uses cooperative strategies versus competitive strategies? *See* Lowenthal, *supra* note 1, at 92–112.

I began my own taxonomy of case types or circumstances under which problem solving was most likely to be possible and concluded that even within case types, individual cases were still always capable of being analyzed as having the potential for resource expansion or party needs satisfaction. *See supra* note 120 and accompanying text.

On the other hand, it seems useful in considering whether resources can be expanded or the parties' needs satisfied, to examine certain circumstances, contexts, or factors influencing the negotiation that may affect choices. Thus, I suggest that the following factors in the negotiation context should be considered in assessing ways of solving the parties' problems. The list is both suggestive and tentative. We need much more sophisticated analyses of negotiation contexts based on empirical evidence than is currently available.

1. *Subject Matter of the Dispute*. Is the negotiation about dispute resolution or about transaction planning? Is a definitive court ruling or precedent necessary? What materiel is at stake in the negotiation?

2. *Content of the Issues Involved*. What are the real issues to be negotiated? How many issues are there? Are there any which may be important but are latent and not yet defined? Are there short-term and long-term issues? Do these differ from each other? Do the parties see the same issues?

3. *Voluntariness*. Do the parties have a choice about negotiating or is negotiation compelled, either formally or informally, such as in plea bargaining?

4. *Relationship*. What are the relationships of the parties to each other? Is the relationship long-term, such as in partnerships or personal relationships, or one-shot, as in car accidents? What is the relationship of the lawyers to each other?

5. *Visibility*. Will the negotiation be conducted in a private or public arena? Note the potential for rigid adversarial negotiations when the parties bargain in public—e.g., the air traffic controller strike, the NFL strike, and some sports contracts (such as Fernando Valenzuela's). *See* L.A. Times, Feb. 26, 1982, § III, col. 1, ed. 1; L.A. Times, Feb. 27, 1982, § III, at 1, col. 1; L.A. Times, Feb. 28, 1982, § III, at 1, col. 1.

6. *Accountability*. To whom is the negotiator accountable? When a lawyer acts for a client the lawyer is always responsible to the client. Are there other, more complex constituencies—labor union memberships, family members, or others who may be affected by negotiation results? Who is responsible for assessing proposals and potential strategies?

7. *Stake*. Does one party have a greater stake in the negotiation—e.g. wanting to preserve the relationship or wanting a definitive ruling?

8. *Routineness of the Transaction*. Is the type of problem to be solved settled routinely in a certain way (e.g. plea bargaining, reasonable business practice) so that efforts to depart from the routine will be difficult?

9. *Power*. How do the parties assess their relative power in the negotiation on a number of dimensions—law, facts, financial resources, moral rightness? How do the parties' perceptions of each other's power affect the potential solutions?

10. *Personal Characteristics of Negotiator*. What is the experience level of each negotiator? What are the social structural factors that affect the negotiator—size of

Because problem-solving negotiations are likely to result in a greater number of potential solutions not contemplated in advance, the client in such negotiations is more likely to become involved in evaluating proposals. This will be particularly true where a client's objectives or needs may change over time, or need to be reevaluated as new proposals are forthcoming. Thus, the increased fluidity and emphasis on the parties' underlying interests may result in greater client involvement in the legal negotiation process.[289] One of the key differences between the conventional adversarial model and the problem-solving model is the extent to which the parties and their lawyers engage in a continually interactive negotiation process, using the opportunity to seek new solutions rather than simply moving along a predetermined linear scale of compromise.

III. Limits of a Problem-Solving Model of Negotiation: Negotiating in a Competitive World

Several difficulties may confront the skeptical problem solver. First, there is the problem of perceiving resources as finite. In some legal disputes, for example, a case involving a simple transfer of limited dollars or other valued items from one side to the other, it may appear impossible to expand what is available to both parties.[290] A second barrier may be the perceived inequality of power between the negotiating parties. If one side has power in the legal, economic or psychological sense during the negotiation,

law firm, type of practice, method of payment (retainer, contingency fee, salary)? *See infra* text accompanying notes 321–28.

11. *Medium or Arena of Negotiation*. Are there to be several face to face or "side by side," R. Fisher & W. Ury, *supra* note 2, at 39, encounters, or will the negotiations take place without interpersonal interaction, for example, by telephone. What are the cultural differences that are likely to affect the negotiation? Will clients or principals be present?

12. *Alternatives or Options to Negotiation*. What can the parties do if they don't negotiate—court ordered solution, developing business deal with someone else, no settlement?

This list is not exhaustive. Williams, for example, considers the parties' motivations an important factor in considering behavioral choices. G. Williams, Legal Negotiation and Settlement, *supra* note 1, at 67. The list is meant to suggest some of the factors which require study and attention in analysis of the dynamics of particular negotiation strategies and behaviors, as distinguished from the negotiation orientations described in the text. *See also* Weiss-Wik, *supra* note 25.

289. Because clients must be consulted about all settlement offers, Model Code of Professional Responsibility EC 7-7, there is a greater likelihood that problem-solving negotiation, if it results in a greater number of potential solutions, will increase the number of lawyer-client contacts concerning settlement. There is thus some danger that costs of problem-solving negotiation would thereby be increased.

290. The personal injury case is considered by some to be a paradigmatic zero-sum game of negotiation over dollars. *But see supra* text accompanying notes 158–64, 215.

the weaker party may have insufficient leverage[291] to use problem-solving techniques where the stronger party knows it can gain a great deal by exercising power in a conventional negotiation. Third, an attempt to satisfy needs may itself thwart the problem-solving approach in a situation where, for example, one of the parties has a need for revenge or punishment. Fourth, there may be limited psychological resources. Where one of the parties is used to a competitive style of negotiation, the execution of a problem-solving method may be viewed as impossible unless the other party becomes a problem solver. Finally, a problem-solving model based on a theory of needs has its own limitations. It will not solve all negotiation dilemmas, but it still offers a potentially more systematic and effective way of thinking about negotiation.

A. *Limits of Inequality*

Because problem solving is so often erroneously confused with cooperative processes, skeptics raise questions about its usefulness when the parties are unequal. Inequalities can exist in a number of ways, which are discussed below, but at the outset it is important to consider the effects of these inequalities in adversarial negotiations as well.

1. Wealth

Where the case appears to be one involving the simple transfer of money, such as in a personal injury action[292] or the limited economic allocations that must be made between industrial polluters and the neighboring public,[293] it may seem impossible to solve the problem with anything other than an all-out win for one party or at best a compromise.

The problem-solving conception of negotiations may, however, change our perception of even these difficult situations. For example, the personal injury case has become a zero-sum negotiation over money because of the way our legal system and the substantive law have defined the problem. It is impossible, our court

291. Until this point I have purposefully avoided the term "leverage." In the traditional adversarial literature, *see, e.g.*, G. BELLOW & B. MOULTON, *supra* note 1, at 67–79, leverage is defined as the "power or influence" that one can exercise over the opponent, *id.* The notion of leverage is clearly an adversarial one. The negotiator who has it, uses it, usually to obtain concessions from the other party. The use of leverage as a threat is unlikely to foster an atmosphere conducive to joint problem solving.

292. *But see supra* text accompanying notes 158–64.

293. But see H. RAIFFA, *supra* note 2, at 310–17 for use of problem-solving approaches to resolving environmental conflict. *See also* A. TALBOT, SETTLING THINGS: SIX CASE STUDIES IN ENVIRONMENTAL MEDIATION (1983); Cooter, *Law and the Imperialism of Economics: An Introduction to the Economic Analysis of Law and A Review of the Major Books*, 29 UCLA L. REV. 1260, 1263–64 (1982).

system tells us, to administer a court of apology in which the party at fault demonstrates its contrition and thereby satisfies some of the needs of the injured, beyond the recompense of the pain and suffering.[294] If the negotiation were conducted outside of the legal process, other items might be bargained for[295] and the problem could be converted into more than a zero-sum game with more than a limited dollar agenda.

Furthermore, to the extent that the legal system is not meeting the real needs of the parties in the limited remedies it provides, the increased use of negotiation may tell us something about how problems may be solved outside of the system. Indeed, as commentators Coons[296] and Eisenberg & Yeazell[297] have argued, the courts are already providing more sophisticated and less polarized remedies, at least in part because of the pressure to more effectively meet the parties' needs or solve legally indeterminate or socially difficult problems. Several examples of this phenomenon include joint custody,[298] which began as an out-of-court problem-solving alternative to the zero-sum nature of custody disputes, and recent proposals for changes in the zero-sum awards of tort claims.[299] There are also the neighborhood court and mediation movements[300] which seek to remove many local disputes from the

294. Indeed, some have argued that the multipliers by which pain and suffering are measured are based on compensation for items, such as apologies, which the official legal arena cannot provide. Abel, *A Critique of American Tort Law*, 8 BRIT. J. OF L. & SOC'Y 199 (1981). In other cultures apologies may serve to directly meet the need of one party to know the other party is sincerely sorry. This apparently is what some victims of legal malpractice desire as well.

295. *See supra* text accompanying notes 158-64, 215.

296. Coons, *supra* note 71.

297. Eisenberg & Yeazell, *supra* note 132.

298. The now common court order of joint custody originally began as a party-initiated effort at problem solving. In California, for example, joint custody began as a voluntary remedy agreed to by the parties in their own dissolution agreements. The merits of this solution have been considered so beneficial to the parties and children involved that the California legislature has now mandated joint custody as the preferred judicial order in custody matters. CAL. CIV. CODE §§ 4600(b)(1), 4600.5 (West 1983). Obviously, legislatures have been able to draft, and courts to enforce, other types of problem-solving solutions. Doctrinal changes, such as the move from contributory negligence to comparative negligence, are also efforts at minimizing the harsh effects of polarized results. Too often, however, these efforts may simply legitimate the compromises that the parties reach by splitting the difference. Joint custody may differ from these developments because it truly solves the problem by giving the child two parents, not by compromising. On the other hand, recent criticism of joint custody asserts that it is being granted too automatically, in cases where it is not appropriate, and represents some judicial abdication of decisionmaking in this difficult area. *See Divorce American-Style*, NEWSWEEK, Jan. 10, 1983, at 42-48.

299. *See supra* note 294.

300. Abel, *Conservative Conflict and the Reproduction of Capitalism: The Role of Informal Justice*, 9 INT'L J. SOC. LAW 245 (1981); Hofrichter, *Neighborhood Justice and the Social Control Problems of American Capitalism: A Perspective*, in 1 THE POLITICS OF INFORMAL JUSTICE (R. Abel ed. 1982); Riskin, *supra* note 205.

zero-sum rule of traditional courts. This movement away from traditional court resolution of zero-sum disputes demonstrates some unwillingness on the part of the legal culture to have its disputes resolved in this manner. It also suggests pressure toward changes in the substantive law to make accommodations for non-zero-sum solutions, both as substantive remedies and as procedural devices.

Even the archetypal zero-sum or limited resource cases may not be as limited as is commonly believed. The mechanism for reorganizations under the Bankruptcy Act,[301] for example, demonstrates the need to consider ways of preserving the bankrupt entity's operation so that the pie can be increased for the benefit of the creditors, debtors, and third parties. Thus, what may appear to be a limited pie requiring competitive negotiation on division can yield to creative problem solving in cases where deferral of division or some other problem-solving device benefits all the parties at a later date.[302]

In short, we cannot really know whether a particular dispute or transaction is a limited resource problem until we have tried a more searching and creative analysis of the problem from the perspective of the parties' real needs and opportunities for enhancing the resources available. Although it seems realistic to assume that the needs are the payment of money, the money available may be increased in a number of ways,[303] or it may really be a proxy for something else. This kind of problem-solving orientation to negotiations is seen in a variety of other areas such as labor negotiations,[304] which make use of shared lay-offs and flextime as work-sharing devices,[305] and deferred compensation and other forms of fringe benefits as nontaxable or delayed taxable income incre-

301. Even a bankrupt's assets available for division may be expanded when the creditors are willing to temporarily subordinate their claims and allow the business to continue, perhaps under receivership. This is the principle underlying corporate reorganization, 11 U.S.C. § 1325(a) (Supp. V 1982).

302. An example of this can be seen in present depressed real estate markets, such as Southern California's. Given the high cost of interest, the single most important term, price, has been modified by creative financing arrangements. Typically, the owner finances some portion of the purchase price at a lower interest rate. Thus, the terms of creative financing can become as significant as price in negotiation.

At the time of this writing, such solutions seem to be running into their own problems, as the worsening economy and the failure of interest rates to drop substantially are resulting in defaults on creatively financed sales.

303. *See supra* text accompanying notes 210-28.

304. Examples of this include the creative arrangements, sometimes called "givebacks," employed by the United Auto Workers in their negotiations with Chrysler during threatened bankruptcy. For example, the UAW suggested a consumer rebate program to increase sales with a delayed wage increase in order to increase profits.

305. Summers & Love, *Work Sharing As An Alternative to Layoffs By Seniority: Title VII Remedies in Recession*, 124 U. PA. L. REV. 893 (1976).

ments. If all negotiations are viewed initially as presenting these possibilities, it is difficult to establish that any single classification of dispute or transaction can never be transformed into a problem-solving negotiation, though some individual cases surely cannot.[306]

2. Power

Regardless of the susceptibility of particular case types to problem-solving negotiation, some will argue that the larger context of the case will make problem solving difficult or impossible in that solving the problem by mutual gain is not the desired end. These arguments are based on conclusions about the distribution and legitimacy of power within our legal system.[307] Critics would argue that problem solving cannot work where one party is so powerful that it will not accede to demands or requests to bargain for joint or mutual gain. The government, large corporations, and powerful or wealthy individuals all represent "haves" in the legal system who may have no incentive to bargain with a less powerful adversary to accomplish mutual gain. For example, government agencies sometimes refuse to negotiate at all, either because of the low incremental cost of negotiation where all attorneys are on salary, or because the government seeks a precedential ruling to clarify rules and avoid litigation costs elsewhere.[308]

However, I cannot agree with the assumption that it is necessarily ineffective to at least attempt problem-solving negotiation. This is so particularly where the cost of not making the attempt is either to break off relationships altogether or to resort to the litigation model where all of the characteristics that make one party more powerful will certainly continue to operate. Indeed, as Galanter has argued, the powerful will repeatedly do well in the for-

306. *See supra* note 120. One of the potential difficulties here, however, is that needs or objectives may be manufactured to produce a problem-solving agenda. To the extent that such needs are "created," the problem-solving model can be used as just another device to manipulate for competitive gain. The key to satisfactory problem solving is to focus on real, not manufactured, needs.

307. *See, e.g.*, Bellow, *Turning Solutions Into Problems: The Legal Aid Experience*, 34 NLADA BRIEFCASE 106 (1977); Galanter, *Why the "Haves" Come Out Ahead: Speculations on the Limits of Legal Change*, 9 LAW & SOC'Y REV. 95 (1974).

308. Negotiations with such entities may require an entirely different negotiation model—bureaucratic negotiation—which has some elements of adversarial negotiations (limited resources) but for different reasons (limited authority for bureaucrats to "solve" their own problems, another form of the accountability problem, *see supra* note 288). Bureaucratic or administrative negotiation may require a different model because the negotiators are multiple (an agency with a constituency) and the interests or needs may be more difficult to ascertain (the "public" interest, what policies are appropriate, etc.).

mal court structure.[309] Does the addition of a judge or the formal rules of court adequately diminish the advantage of the powerful or equalize the parties before problem resolution?[310] Where the parties are so truly unequal that one party can avoid, manipulate, or refuse a problem-solving approach, any advantage may make itself felt in court as well.[311] In the case of non-litigation transactions, the fear that the powerful will take advantage of the less powerful is no different because there is even less chance that a court can equalize the parties.

Fisher & Ury have suggested that when one party is more powerful than the other, principled negotiations[312] can at least be attempted as long as the less powerful party has calculated its Best Alternative to a Negotiated Agreement (BATNA).[313] This enables the less powerful negotiator to set limits and understandings of when it is likely to be taken advantage of. When this bottom line is reached the party can realistically appraise the costs and benefits of terminating negotiations and subjecting the problem to a non-negotiated resolution. In those cases where power is equalized by third party adjudication, or a definitive ruling is sought, the better alternative for problem resolution is to refuse negotiation and proceed to adjudication. Fisher & Ury argue that the clearer, more specific, and creative the BATNA, the stronger one can become in the negotiation by creating an environment and attempting to have the other side see the advantages to problem-solving negotiation. In addition, to the extent that a negotiator can apply objective criteria in evaluating solutions,[314] some of the inequality may be minimized or subject to the control of an outside evaluation. This could, of course, compromise the parties' needs, but might still be preferable to no agreement.

B. *Limits of Ideology and Personality*

Some of the potential difficulties with problem solving inhere in the context of particular problems. Parties or their lawyers may seek particular political aims that go beyond the facts of the case or the relationship of the parties. Or, the parties involved may

309. Galanter, *supra* note 307.

310. *See* Abel, *supra* note 300; Galanter, *supra* note 307.

311. This is evident in the "paper wars" of large scale litigation.

312. Such arrangements are Fisher and Ury's equivalent of problem-solving negotiation.

313. R. FISHER & W. URY, *supra* note 2, at 101-11. The BATNA is intended to be a *single* real alternative. Too often negotiators consider all of the potential alternatives and aggregate these as the one alternative to be compared to the negotiation proposal. Fisher and Ury argue that this aggregation is unrealistic as the negotiator will likely have to choose among the alternatives if the negotiation fails. *Id.* at 105.

314. R. FISHER & W. URY, *supra* note 2, at 84-98.

present barriers to problem solving that also go beyond the particular problem at issue by virtue of their own personal characteristics.

1. Definitive Rulings and Punishment

In some negotiations mutual benefit is not perceived as desirable, either by the parties themselves, or on the basis of some larger social, political or moral assessment of right in the particular case. In short, when one side is perceived as wrong or bad, the results should be dichotomous or zero-sum. The bad side should lose, be punished,[315] or be forced to give something to the other side. Maximizing joint gain is sometimes inappropriate. Legal services class actions against governmental bodies, environmental cases, and intentional infliction of serious bodily injury are examples of such cases. In some instances the parties' needs and objectives will be simply revenge, vindication, victory, or even total annihilation of the other party. Divorce, neighborhood disputes, and some employer-employee suits fall into this category.

The argument that not all situations or cases ought to be solved may be a persuasive one in some instances. In identifying those cases, one should consider whether the conflict or antagonism produced by achieving the zero-sum, polarized victory is outweighed by the righteousness of the result or victory. If the parties must deal with each other again, as in ongoing relations between divorced parents, victory or vindication may be Pyrrhic. In antitrust actions, for example, victory which results in inefficient market and company divisions may have an overall negative impact on the industry and consumers.[316] In a sense, this too is an application of the needs theory; forcing the parties to carefully canvas the long-term effects of their preferred solutions requires them to consider their needs. It is also an application of the Fisher and Ury BATNA concept,[317] as long as the parties consider fully all of the implications, including long-term and perhaps latent consequences of the desired BATNA.

Nonetheless, some disputes will be appropriately settled by total victory—one-shot cases or cases where the law must be clear, as in abortion, school busing, etc. There is no simple answer here; one is simply thrown back on moral or political philosophies of

315. Criminal cases are paradigmatic. But even in criminal cases, if the parties could fashion more creative solutions within the limits defined by our judicial system, creative solutions such as restitution and alternative service would be possible. Plea bargaining is an example, though admittedly a special case, of creative solutions in the criminal system. *See Special Issue on Plea Bargaining*, 13 LAW & SOC'Y REV. 189-687 (1979).

316. R. POSNER, *supra* note 5, at 195-237.

317. *See supra* note 313.

justice to determine when problem solving ought not be pursued in the interest of accomplishing a morally just, dichotomous win.

On the other hand, some disputes which require the polarized results of a court order may still benefit from a problem-solving conception both before and after the decree. In institutional litigation, for example,[318] efforts such as voluntary desegregation plans which seek to avoid litigation can be attempted before resort to the judicial process. Pre-litigation experiments or trials of solutions may be particularly important in cases where parties or other experts believe they know the field better than the judges.[319] An order that institutional practices must change, following litigation, frequently requires the parties to negotiate the changes or, at the very least, to find a way to finance the court-ordered changes. It may be important to assign blame and responsibility in an authoritative manner so as to insure compliance and the continuity of the social order. Many of the details of the ruling, however, will still be negotiated social change, such as in the school desegregation and prison conditions lawsuits requiring years of compliance and masters' hearings.[320]

2. Negotiator Personality

Problem solving may appear difficult when it is viewed as a process only, rather than as a conception or paradigm. Suppose the other negotiator won't play this new game. The popular texts offer many strategies for personality transformation: persuasion that this is the best way to accomplish results; negotiation jujitsu or aikido[321] where one simply listens to the other side and credits its demands as possible solutions, rather than as competitive demands; flexibility or passive resistance so that the other side sees that one is not going to participate in the escalation of the conflict.[322] Fisher & Ury suggest that adversarial negotiators can most effectively be tamed by making the negotiation tactics explicit and calling attention to what is making the negotiation competitive and ineffective; under some circumstances one will need to walk away.[323]

318. In cases concerning such problems as prison conditions, school desegregation, welfare reform, and housing discrimination, negotiation may be necessary over the long run to effectuate the parties' objectives. Seldom will a single court order be sufficient to terminate the problem.

319. The growth of corporate "mini-trials" is one example. Koenig, *More Firms Turn to Private Courts to Avoid Expensive Legal Fights*, Wall St. J., Jan. 4, 1984, at 25 col. 4.

320. *See* A. STRAUSS, *supra* note 89; Resnick, *supra* note 84.

321. R. FISHER & W. URY, *supra* note 2, at 112-18.

322. *Id.* at 114-18, 145.

323. *Id.* at 134-49.

The key to the psychological or interpersonal problem is not to hope for the transformation of competitive personalities, but to focus on the problem.[324] If the problem solver tries too earnestly to wrest a concession from the other party concerning the process itself, there is a danger that the concession will be interpreted in conventional adversarial ways and traded off against particular proposals or solutions. The personality of the other party or other negotiator itself may become a problem to be solved.

The problem-solving model can be applied here. Why is the negotiator or other party behaving this way? What are his needs or objectives within the negotiation context? How can those needs be satisfied here? Why are they important? The behaviors or motivations can be examined in the assessment of psychological needs within the needs framework. If the other lawyer as negotiator must demonstrate that he won something to justify his fee, how can we demonstrate victory or solution of the problem to his principal? It may be necessary to undertake an analysis of the needs or objectives of the negotiator, as well as of the principal party. By dealing with these elements of the problem of the parties or their negotiating agents in the same manner as the underlying substantive problem is dealt with, the party problem is solved just as the legal problem is—directly—by looking for solutions to that problem.[325]

The problem solver might be able to persuade an adversarial negotiator that it really is in his best interest to explore both parties' actual needs,[326] if for no other reason than by doing so he will accomplish a solution that will be satisfactory to his client. Note that whether or not the other party plays the game, the problem solver can consider solutions that may rank higher on our list of

324. In their chapter entitled "Separate the People From the Problem," *id.* at 17–40, Fisher and Ury discuss techniques for crediting the other person's personality needs and dealing with them as part of the problem. However, in their concluding chapters, *id.* at 101–49, they tend to speak of separating the people from the problem by ignoring them or forcing them to focus exclusively on the substance of the problem. Although this inconsistency could be explained by noting that the concluding chapters deal with difficult negotiators, I think some of the techniques suggested therein could lead to escalation. It is my view that, even in very difficult negotiations, the negotiators must be regarded as part of the problem to be solved. In some situations culture, personality, or both make this very difficult and require great analytic ability and sensitivity. *See* Lowenthal, *supra* note 1, at 109–12.

325. Some conflict may be important for resolution and legitimacy of the resolution of the problem, Druckman, Rozelle & Zechmeister, *Conflict of Interest and Value Dissensus: Two Perspectives*, in NEGOTIATIONS, *supra* note 5, at 105–31, or for political reasons, *see* Abel, *The Contradictions of Informal Justice*, in 1 THE POLITICS OF INFORMAL JUSTICE, *supra* note 300.

326. *See* H. RAIFFA, *supra* note 2, at 143, 300–06. In many cases the most efficient result for either party can be achieved only by honestly revealing actual preferences and avoiding strategic misrepresentations that may distort the solution. *Id.* at 142–47.

criteria than those which would be produced by two parties playing a conventional adversarial game. The achievement of better solutions may be enhanced if both parties are problem solvers,[327] but a problem-solving conception need not be abandoned simply because both parties don't use the same negotiation behaviors.[328]

C. *The Limits of a Needs Analysis*

A focus on an analysis of the parties' needs and an attempt to meet those needs has its own limitations. To the extent that the problem-solving model is based on utilitarian philosophical or economic justifications, the most powerful and trenchant criticisms can be found in the literature which criticizes utilitarian justifications for human endeavor. In a sense there are two criticisms. The first, an economic claim, states that there is yet no proof that maximizing joint gain is more efficient either for the parties or for the larger sphere in which transactions occur.[329] This may be true, but we also can't say that adversarial negotiations have been either more efficient or more wealth-creating.

The second, a moral claim, is that trying to satisfy the parties' needs, like maximizing happiness or pleasure,[330] is not a morally correct measure of our actions.[331] The legal analog of this critique would be that meeting parties' needs is not much different from the hired gun conception of the adversarial model; lawyers are merely conduits of their clients' needs. The only differences between problem solvers and adversarial negotiators are that problem solvers attempt to meet two sets of needs, and that problem solvers act on stated, rather than "presumed" needs. As discussed more fully above, my response to these objections, like John Stuart Mill's, is that notions of morality, justness, and rightness are part of the pleasure or happiness we seek and should be part of

327. Cooperative games in game theory, those where coordination and joint choices are possible, require cooperative behavior and coordination to produce the best results. M. Bacharach, *supra* note 4, at 81-117; H. Raiffa, *supra* note 2, at 142-47, 300-06.

328. In my view, unlike others', it doesn't "take two to tango." A problem solver can seek to expand resources and attempt to meet the parties' underlying needs even if the other party won't play. In some cases the better solution offered by the problem-solver will be its own reward. It may be helpful to keep in mind a pedagogical concept which informs my teaching—delayed learning. If the problem-solver sees the purpose of a negotiation as convincing the other party to play his game, he has fallen into an adversarial trap. If problem-solving does produce better results the negotiator who won't play may realize its strength long after the negotiation is over. This is much like students who understand the value of what they have been taught only when they have to use what they have learned. For those seeking immediate gratification through proselytizing, neither problem-solving nor teaching is the answer.

329. *See* R. Posner, *supra* note 5.

330. J.S. Mill, *supra* note 237.

331. *See* R. Dworkin, *supra* note 237, at vii-xv.

any utilitarian calculus of need.[332]

On the other side of the hired gun debate is the criticism that client satisfaction is an insufficient measure of negotiated outcomes. Gary Bellow has argued that some clients set their need or satisfaction levels too low[333] and that some lawyers fail to consider whether more or better solutions are possible. This is a real problem, but one which may be addressed by a dialogue engaged in by both client and lawyer about needs, if they both seriously and fully canvas those needs. The lawyer and client moral dialogue may also address some of these problems.[334]

Finally, as discussed above, in some cases focusing on needs may present more problems than it solves. The client who says he needs as much money as possible to be compensated for his pain and suffering or security needs, or the business negotiator who simply wants to make as much money as possible, may articulate needs that look no different than adversarial negotiation demands. I have discussed some ways in which a problem-solving negotiation conception can attempt to deal with this,[335] but I am reluctant to claim too much. When faced with these situations, there are other ways of resolving the disputes—the use of some convention or custom, if all else fails, or, as Fisher & Ury suggest, the use of some objective criteria[336] to mediate the parties' needs.[337] At worst, it is possible to return to adversarial dispute resolution. It may be appropriate in some limited cases, but at least it should come after other possibilities have been explored.[338]

Attempting to satisfy needs does not guarantee foolproof solutions. Many of the creative solutions suggested above may create new problems of their own. Solutions must always be analyzed in terms of how they will work in individual cases and in both the short and long run.[339] There clearly are occasions in le-

332. *See supra* text accompanying notes 230–41.

333. G. Bellow & B. Moulton, *supra* note 1, at 60.

334. As a clinician I cannot resist the opportunity to point out that lawyers will get better at this with more instruction and attention paid to such matters, both in law school and in continuing education programs. *See also* H. Raiffa, *supra* note 2, at 344–55.

335. *See supra* text accompanying notes 160–74.

336. R. Fisher & W. Ury, *supra* note 2, at 84–98.

337. "The Law," by the way, may be one source of objective criteria.

338. It may be far easier to escalate a negotiation into an adversarial process than to de-escalate from an adversarial approach to a problem-solving one.

339. Some solutions such as joint custody, *see supra* note 298, and structured settlements may present their own problems. Parents may use joint custody as a split-the-difference solution, or use it for their own advantage rather than for the children, *see* Mnookin & Kornhauser, *supra* note 38. The recipient of a structured settlement may suddenly need a large amount to compensate for some non-recurring treatment. The key to problem solving, as indicated in the text, is not to mechanically focus on a solution, but to be sure any particular solution is appropriate in a particular case.

gal negotiation when problem solving will not solve all problems. More work on these issues is needed,[340] but problem solving at least presents us with some hope of systematically exploring what we are trying to accomplish in negotiation.

Conclusion

This Article has outlined a systematic approach to legal negotiation premised on the notion that agreements will be more effective when the parties conceive of their purposes as solving the problem or planning the transaction, rather than winning or gaining unilateral advantage. The creative problem-solving approach outlined here depends on two structural components: (1) identifying the parties' underlying needs and objectives, and (2) crafting solutions, first by attempting to meet those needs directly, and second, by attempting to meet more of those needs through expanding the resources available. By utilizing such a framework for negotiations, the parties should recognize the synergistic advantage of such an approach over the adversarial and manipulative strategies of zero-sum negotiations. Parties should be able to achieve solutions to disputes that would not have been possible in court-ordered resolutions.

The argument for problem-solving negotiation depends on two major propositions. The first is that in a court system which is authorized primarily to award only polarized decisions and limited remedies, the parties will be able to better craft solutions outside of the official legal arena where greater variability can be achieved. Second, by seeking to expand resources before dividing them, the parties may accomplish better results for themselves individually and increase the joint gain to both.

This Article has explored some of the major difficulties presented by such a constructive model of negotiation. For example, in planning for solutions, knowledge of one's own needs and those of the other party raises important and complex issues of disclosure and of the function of information in the negotiation process. Revelation may, for example, lead to disagreement about values or conflict[341] which can defeat the entire process. Motivating others to participate in such a new paradigm of negotiation may be difficult. Integrating the problem-solving approach with particular behavioral and strategic negotiation processes also may be difficult, or at best causally unclear. Knowing when one has a true zero-sum problem of scarce resources may be difficult.

340. As a social scientist I cannot resist closing this Article with a plea for more empirical research.

341. *See supra* note 325.

The argument presented here does not claim that these difficulties can be entirely overcome, either in the abstract or in the practice of negotiation. Instead, it offers some criteria for analyzing whether particular negotiated solutions are all that they could be in terms of client satisfaction, efficiency, and fairness. The alternative model for negotiation offered here suggests that a focus on party needs will increase party satisfaction over solutions commonly achieved by the more conventional approach to negotiation, and will more often than not be realizable.

The argument explores two of the major issues raised by legal negotiations—the problem of unequal power and the personalities of the negotiators—by suggesting that these are part of the problem to be solved. Unlike Fisher & Ury,[342] I suggest that the people cannot be separated from the problem because as long as negotiators are people, they will be part of the problem to be solved. Similarly, unequal power is not uniquely problematic to negotiations.[343] While there is some fear that negotiated settlements will diffuse important political conflicts,[344] negotiations will continue to be used in a system with a marketplace of legal services and access to official arenas, both public and private. Strategies for solving problems in an unequal negotiation environment are as important, if not more so, than looking to litigation to solve all important legal and political disputes.[345]

The attraction of the problem-solving approach to negotiations is that it returns the solution of the problem to the client and forces the lawyer to perform her essential role in the legal system—that of solving problems. By using her professional expertise to canvas possible solutions to the problems and by constantly referring back to the client's real needs and objectives, the lawyer can make the negotiation process more responsive, while at the same time reducing the client's desire for potentially destructive unilateral victory. By utilizing a problem-solving approach the lawyer may be able to avoid the analog of iatrogenic illness, refusing to make worse or increase the costs of the legal problem by her intervention. The client will not, then, experience his dispute or transaction as getting worse simply because of his entrance into

342. R. FISHER & W. URY, *supra* note 2, at 17–40.

343. Galanter, *supra* note 307.

344. *See generally* Abel, *supra* note 325; Bellow, *supra* note 307.

345. *See generally* J. LIEBERMAN, THE LITIGIOUS SOCIETY (1981) (discussing the disadvantages of relying on litigation to solve difficult social problems). On the other hand, some argue that too much negotiation will remove important cases from the system, thus distorting the cases available for adjudicatory rulemaking. *See* O. Fiss, "Dispute Resolution and Relation to Legal Theory," talk presented to AALS Workshop on Alternative Dispute Resolution (Cambridge, Mass., 1982), and "Some Doubts About Alternative Dispute Resolution," talk presented to AALS Section on Civil Procedure and Alternative Dispute Resolution (San Francisco, Cal., Jan. 1984).

the legal system.[346]

In focusing on problem solving for mutual gain, the lawyer will execute one of her obligations to the society that charters her profession. By decreasing the pressure on the official dispute resolution machinery in situations where mandatory, authoritative, and dichotomous results are not required, the lawyer increases the efficiency of the total dispute resolution system.[347] And, perhaps by helping the parties articulate their real needs and objectives, legal negotiators will increase participation in the decision-making process with less destructive conflict between all those involved than currently exists within our assumptions of adversarial bargaining. By viewing legal negotiation as an opportunity to solve both the individual needs and problems of their clients, and the broader social needs and problems of the legal system, negotiators have an opportunity to transform an intimidating, mystifying process into one which will better serve the needs of those who require it. Whether or not this will work, we don't yet know. But what can we lose by trying?[348]

346. Menkel-Meadow, The Transformation of Disputes By Lawyers: What the Dispute Paradigm Does and Does Not Tell Us (paper presented to 1983 Law and Society Association meeting) (on file at *UCLA Law Review*).

347. One problem, not related to efficiency, however, may be that with a greater number of settlements there will be fewer or unrepresentative cases left in the system from which courts must "make" the law, or that only a certain class of cases will remain to receive whatever justice the legal system dispenses, *see* Abel, *supra* note 325. It may be that we have already reached this point, *see supra* note 153.

348. In future work I hope to examine the particular behavioral choices—the means or processes by which this conceptual model can be implemented—and to assess the empirical successes or failures of these choices. In addition, I hope to examine how transactional negotiation orientations may differ from litigation negotiations.

Part III
The Critics

[9]

Comment

Against Settlement

Owen M. Fiss†

In a recent report to the Harvard Overseers, Derek Bok called for a new direction in legal education.[1] He decried "the familiar tilt in the law curriculum toward preparing students for legal combat," and asked instead that law schools train their students "for the gentler arts of reconciliation and accommodation."[2] He sought to turn our attention from the courts to "new voluntary mechanisms"[3] for resolving disputes. In doing so, Bok echoed themes that have long been associated with the Chief Justice,[4] and that have become a rallying point for the organized bar and the source of a new movement in the law. This movement is the subject of a new professional journal,[5] a newly formed section of the American Association of Law Schools, and several well-funded institutes. It has even received its own acronym—ADR (Alternative Dispute Resolution).

The movement promises to reduce the amount of litigation initiated, and accordingly the bulk of its proposals are devoted to negotiation and mediation prior to suit. But the interest in the so-called "gentler arts" has not been so confined. It extends to ongoing litigation as well, and the advocates of ADR have sought new ways to facilitate and perhaps even pressure parties into settling pending cases. Just last year, Rule 16 of the Federal Rules of Civil Procedure was amended to strengthen the hand of the trial judge in brokering settlements: The "facilitation of settlement"

---

† Alexander M. Bickel Professor of Public Law, Yale University. This essay is based on a speech I gave in San Francisco on January 6, 1984, at a joint session of the Civil Procedure and Alternative Dispute Resolution Sections of the American Association of Law Schools.

1. Bok, *A Flawed System*, HARV. MAG., May-June 1983, at 38, *reprinted in* N.Y. ST. B.J., Oct. 1983, at 8, N.Y. ST. B.J., Nov. 1983, at 31; *excerpted in* 33 J. LEGAL EDUC. 570 (1983).
2. Bok, *supra* note 1, at 45.
3. *Id.*
4. *See, e.g.*, Burger, *Isn't There a Better Way?*, 68 A.B.A. J. 274 (1982); Burger, *Agenda for 2000 A.D.—A Need for Systematic Anticipation*, 70 F.R.D. 83, 93-96 (1976).
5. The *Journal of Dispute Resolution*, published by the University of Missouri-Columbia School of Law, is scheduled to begin publication in June, 1984.

became an explicit purpose of pre-trial conferences, and participants were officially invited, if that is the proper word, to consider "the possibility of settlement or the use of extrajudicial procedures to resolve the dispute."[6] Now the Advisory Committee on Civil Rules is proposing to amend Rule 68 to sharpen the incentives for settlement: Under this amendment, a party who rejects a settlement offer and then receives a judgment less favorable than that offer must pay the attorney's fees of the other party.[7] This amendment would effect a major change in the traditional American rule, under which each party pays his or her own attorney's fees.[8] It would also be at odds with a number of statutes that seek to facilitate certain types of civil litigation by providing attorney's fees to plaintiffs if they win, without imposing liability for the attorney's fees of their adversaries if they lose.[9]

---

6. FED. R. CIV. P. 16. In a similar spirit, the Second Circuit has instituted a Civil Appeals Management Plan (CAMP), which empowers a court officer to direct the parties to a civil appeal to appear at a pre-argument conference "to consider the possibility of settlement," before their case is scheduled for argument. CAMP ¶¶ 4-5, *reprinted in* 2D CIR. R. 54. Conferences are held in approximately 90% of the cases assigned to CAMP; staff counsel grant requests by the parties not to hold pre-argument conferences because of "unsettleable issues" in fewer than one in ten cases. Letter from Vincent Flanigan, Management Analyst, Second Circuit Judicial Conference, to Owen M. Fiss (Apr. 12, 1984). For a review of the debate over CAMP's success, see Hoffman, *The Bureaucratic Spectre: Newest Challenge to the Courts*, 66 JUDICATURE 60, 70 & nn.42-44 (1982). For a discussion of the problems which arise when judges become deeply involved in pre-trial attempts to facilitate settlement, see Resnik, *Managerial Judges*, 96 HARV. L. REV. 374 (1982).

7. In pertinent part, Rule 68 currently provides:

> At any time more than 10 days before the trial begins, a party defending a claim may serve upon the adverse party an offer to allow judgment to be taken against him for the money or property or to the effect specified in his offer, with costs then accrued . . . . If [the offer is rejected and] the judgment finally obtained by the offeree is not more favorable than the offer, the offeree must pay the costs incurred after the making of the offer.

FED. R. CIV. P. 68. The term "costs" has been interpreted not to include attorneys' fees. Roadway Express v. Piper, 447 U.S. 752, 759-63 (1980); Chesny v. Marek, 720 F.2d 474, 480 (7th Cir. 1983), *cert. granted*, 52 U.S.L.W. 3770 (U.S. Apr. 23, 1984) (No. 83-1437).

The proposed amended rule would provide, in pertinent part:

> At any time more than 30 days before the trial begins, any party may serve upon an adverse party an offer, denominated as an offer under this rule, to settle a claim for the money or property or to the effect specified in his offer and to enter into a stipulation dismissing the claim or to allow judgment to be entered accordingly . . . .
>
> If the judgment finally entered is not more favorable to the offeree than an unaccepted offer . . . , the offeree must pay the costs and expenses, including reasonable attorneys' fees, incurred by the offeror after the making of the offer . . . . The amount of the expenses and interest may be reduced to the extent expressly found by the court, with a statement of reasons, to be excessive or unjustified under all of the circumstances. In determining whether a final judgment is more or less favorable to the offeree than the offer, the costs and expenses of the parties shall be excluded from consideration. Costs, expenses, and interest shall not be awarded to an offeror found by the court to have made an offer in bad faith.
>
> . . . . This rule shall not apply to class or derivative actions under Rules 23, 23.1, and 23.2.

Committee on Rules of Prac. & Proc. of the Judicial Conference of the United States, *Preliminary Draft of Proposed Amendments to the Federal Rules of Civil Procedure*, 98 F.R.D. 339, 361-63 (1983).

8. *See* Alyeska Pipeline Serv. Co. v. Wilderness Soc'y, 421 U.S. 240, 247 (1975).

9. The Civil Rights Attorney's Fees Awards Act of 1976 provides that, in a variety of civil rights

Against Settlement

The advocates of ADR are led to support such measures and to exalt the idea of settlement more generally because they view adjudication as a process to resolve disputes. They act as though courts arose to resolve quarrels between neighbors who had reached an impasse and turned to a stranger for help.[10] Courts are seen as an institutionalization of the stranger and adjudication is viewed as the process by which the stranger exercises power. The very fact that the neighbors have turned to someone else to resolve their dispute signifies a breakdown in their social relations; the advocates of ADR acknowledge this, but nonetheless hope that the neighbors will be able to reach agreement before the stranger renders judgment. Settlement is that agreement. It is a truce more than a true reconciliation, but it seems preferable to judgment because it rests on the consent of both parties and avoids the cost of a lengthy trial.

In my view, however, this account of adjudication and the case for settlement rest on questionable premises. I do not believe that settlement as a generic practice is preferable to judgment or should be institutionalized on a wholesale and indiscriminate basis. It should be treated instead as a highly problematic technique for streamlining dockets. Settlement is for me the civil analogue of plea bargaining: Consent is often coerced; the bargain may be struck by someone without authority; the absence of a trial and judgment renders subsequent judicial involvement troublesome; and although dockets are trimmed, justice may not be done. Like plea bargaining, settlement is a capitulation to the conditions of mass society and should be neither encouraged nor praised.

---

actions, a "court, in its discretion, may allow the prevailing party . . . a reasonable attorney's fee as part of the costs." 42 U.S.C. § 1988 (1976 & Supp. V 1981). The Supreme Court has read the Act to mean that prevailing plaintiffs should normally recover their attorneys' fees, while prevailing defendants are not normally entitled to such awards. *See* Christiansburg Garment Co. v. EEOC, 434 U.S. 412, 416-18 (1978).

In Delta Air Lines v. August, 450 U.S. 346 (1981), the Court held that Rule 68 does not allow a prevailing defendant to recover any costs (including attorney's fees) from a Title VII plaintiff even though the defendant had proposed a settlement prior to trial. The Court found that such an application of Rule 68 would be contrary to the concept of the private attorney general underlying Title VII. *Id.* at 360 n.27. Given the Court's insistence in *Alyeska Pipeline* that any expansion of the concept of the private attorney general would require specific statutory authorization, 421 U.S. at 263-64, and given Congress' response—the 1976 Act—it would be ironic for the Supreme Court to use its rulemaking power to constrict the use of private attorneys general by amending Rule 68. In Chesny v. Marek, 720 F.2d 474, 479 (7th Cir. 1983), *cert. granted*, 52 U.S.L.W. 3770 (U.S. Apr. 23, 1984) (No. 83-1437), Judge Posner interpreted the "costs" provision of current Rule 68 to exclude attorney's fees. He found that including them would deter private attorneys general, would thus involve "substantive" not "procedural" effects, and would therefore exceed the bounds of the Rules Enabling Act, 28 U.S.C. § 2072 (1976). Judge Posner also noted that by the mid-1970's, Congress had enacted between 75 and 90 separate fee-shifting statutes. *Id.* at 477.

For statutes in other fields of law that award attorney's fees to prevailing plaintiffs but not to prevailing defendants, see, e.g., 5 U.S.C. § 552a(g)(B) (1982) (Privacy Act); 15 U.S.C. § 15 (1982) (antitrust).

10. Martin Shapiro provides one formulation of the dispute-resolution story. *See* M. SHAPIRO, COURTS: A COMPARATIVE AND POLITICAL ANALYSIS 1-2 (1981).

THE IMBALANCE OF POWER

By viewing the lawsuit as a quarrel between two neighbors, the dispute-resolution story that underlies ADR implicitly asks us to assume a rough equality between the contending parties. It treats settlement as the anticipation of the outcome of trial and assumes that the terms of settlement are simply a product of the parties' predictions of that outcome.[11] In truth, however, settlement is also a function of the resources available to each party to finance the litigation, and those resources are frequently distributed unequally. Many lawsuits do not involve a property dispute between two neighbors, or between AT&T and the government (to update the story), but rather concern a struggle between a member of a racial minority and a municipal police department over alleged brutality, or a claim by a worker against a large corporation over work-related injuries. In these cases, the distribution of financial resources, or the ability of one party to pass along its costs, will invariably infect the bargaining process, and the settlement will be at odds with a conception of justice that seeks to make the wealth of the parties irrelevant.

The disparities in resources between the parties can influence the settlement in three ways. First, the poorer party may be less able to amass and analyze the information needed to predict the outcome of the litigation, and thus be disadvantaged in the bargaining process. Second, he may need the damages he seeks immediately and thus be induced to settle as a way of accelerating payment, even though he realizes he would get less now than he might if he awaited judgment. All plaintiffs want their damages immediately, but an indigent plaintiff may be exploited by a rich defendant because his need is so great that the defendant can force him to accept a sum that is less than the ordinary present value of the judgment. Third, the poorer party might be forced to settle because he does not have the resources to finance the litigation, to cover either his own projected expenses, such as his lawyer's time, or the expenses his opponent can impose through the manipulation of procedural mechanisms such as discovery. It might seem that settlement benefits the plaintiff by allowing him to avoid the costs of litigation, but this is not so. The defendant can anticipate the plaintiff's costs if the case were to be tried fully and decrease his offer by that amount. The indigent plaintiff is a victim of the costs of litigation even if he settles.[12]

11. *See* Posner, *An Economic Approach to Legal Procedure and Judicial Administration*, 2 J. LEGAL STUD. 399 (1973); Priest, *Regulating the Content and Volume of Litigation: An Economic Analysis*, 1 SUP. CT. ECON. REV. 163 (1982); Shavell, *Suit, Settlement, and Trial: A Theoretical Analysis Under Alternative Methods for the Allocation of Legal Costs*, 11 J. LEGAL STUD. 55 (1982).

12. The offer-of-settlement rule of the proposed Rule 68 would only aggravate the influence of distributional inequalities. It would make the poorer party liable for the attorney's fees of his adver-

Against Settlement

There are exceptions. Seemingly rich defendants may sometimes be subject to financial pressures that make them as anxious to settle as indigent plaintiffs. But I doubt that these circumstances occur with any great frequency. I also doubt that institutional arrangements such as contingent fees or the provision of legal services to the poor will in fact equalize resources between contending parties: The contingent fee does not equalize resources; it only makes an indigent plaintiff vulnerable to the willingness of the private bar to invest in his case. In effect, the ability to exploit the plaintiff's lack of resources has been transferred from rich defendants to lawyers who insist upon a hefty slice of the plaintiff's recovery as their fee. These lawyers, moreover, will only work for contingent fees in certain kinds of cases, such as personal-injury suits. And the contingent fee is of no avail when the defendant is the disadvantaged party. Governmental subsidies for legal services have a broader potential, but in the civil domain the battle for these subsidies was hard-fought, and they are in fact extremely limited, especially when it comes to cases that seek systemic reform of government practices.[13]

Of course, imbalances of power can distort judgment as well: Resources influence the quality of presentation, which in turn has an important bearing on who wins and the terms of victory. We count, however, on the guiding presence of the judge, who can employ a number of measures to lessen the impact of distributional inequalities. He can, for example, supplement the parties' presentations by asking questions, calling his own witnesses, and inviting other persons and institutions to participate as amici.[14] These measures are likely to make only a small contribution to-

sary, which are likely to be greater than the plaintiff's own legal fees when the defendant retains higher-priced counsel. Thus, fee shifting presents a greater risk to plaintiffs than to defendants. In cases where the prevailing plaintiff is entitled to attorney's fees pursuant to a specific statute, the defendant already has an incentive to settle, namely, to avoid becoming responsible for the plaintiff's legal expenses at trial. (He would still be liable for the plaintiff's pre-trial expenses if the court found that the settlement was sufficiently favorable to make the plaintiff a prevailing party, *see* Maher v. Gagne, 448 U.S. 122, 129-30 (1980), but these expenses are presumably significantly lower than the expenses of actually completing pre-trial preparation and proceeding to trial.) Rule 68 thus does not make the defendant more amenable to settlement. It does, however, place additional burdens on plaintiffs, because under Rule 68 they would risk incurring the attorney's fees of the defendant. *See* Bitsouni v. Sheraton Hartford Corp., 33 Fair Empl. Prac. Cas. (BNA) 898, 901-02 (D. Conn. 1983).

13. *See* 42 U.S.C. § 2996f(b)(3), (6), (8), (9) (Supp. V 1981) (restricting use of Legal Services Corporation funds for, *inter alia*, political, abortion-rights, and desegregation litigation).

14. In a case challenging conditions in Texas' state prison system, for example, Judge Justice ordered the United States to appear as an amicus curiae "[i]n order to investigate the facts alleged in the prisoners' complaints, to participate in such civil action with the full rights of a party thereto, and to advise this Court at all stages of the proceedings as to any action deemed appropriate by it." *In re* Estelle, 516 F.2d 480, 482 (5th Cir. 1975) (quoting unpublished district court order), *cert. denied*, 426 U.S. 925 (1976). The decree which was eventually entered found systemic constitutional violations and ordered sweeping changes in the state's prisons. *See* Ruiz v. Estelle, 503 F. Supp. 1265 (S.D. Tex. 1980), *motion to stay order granted in part and denied in part*, 650 F.2d 555 (5th Cir. 1981), *add'l motion to stay order granted in part and denied in part*, 666 F.2d 854 (5th Cir. 1982).

ward moderating the influence of distributional inequalities, but should not be ignored for that reason. Not even these small steps are possible with settlement. There is, moreover, a critical difference between a process like settlement, which is based on bargaining and accepts inequalities of wealth as an integral and legitimate component of the process, and a process like judgment, which knowingly struggles against those inequalities. Judgment aspires to an autonomy from distributional inequalities, and it gathers much of its appeal from this aspiration.

The Absence of Authoritative Consent

The argument for settlement presupposes that the contestants are individuals. These individuals speak for themselves and should be bound by the rules they generate. In many situations, however, individuals are ensnared in contractual relationships that impair their autonomy: Lawyers or insurance companies might, for example, agree to settlements that are in their interests but are not in the best interests of their clients, and to which their clients would not agree if the choice were still theirs.[15] But a deeper and more intractable problem arises from the fact that many parties are not individuals but rather organizations or groups. We do not know who is entitled to speak for these entities and to give the consent upon which so much of the appeal of settlement depends.

Some organizations, such as corporations or unions, have formal procedures for identifying the persons who are authorized to speak for them. But these procedures are imperfect: They are designed to facilitate transactions between the organization and outsiders, rather than to insure that the members of the organization in fact agree with a particular decision. Nor do they eliminate conflicts of interests. The chief executive officer of a corporation may settle a suit to prevent embarassing disclosures about his managerial policies, but such disclosures might well be in the interest of the shareholders.[16] The president of a union may agree to a settlement as a way of preserving his power within the organization; for that very reason, he may not risk the dangers entailed in consulting the rank and file or in subjecting the settlement to ratification by the membership.[17] More-

15. In Glazer v. J.C. Bradford & Co., 616 F.2d 167 (5th Cir. 1980), for example, the court held that the plaintiff was bound by his attorney's offer of settlement simply because he had earlier instructed his attorney to investigate the possibility of settling the case.

16. In Wolf v. Barkes, 348 F.2d 994 (2d Cir. 1965), *cert. denied*, 382 U.S. 941 (1966), Curtis Publishing Company, one of whose stockholders had brought a derivative suit against several corporate officers alleging mismanagement and waste, settled privately with those officers. This settlement effectively eliminated the stockholders' ability to get an accounting of managerial behavior.

17. For a general discussion of how unions often bind their members to collective bargaining agreements without allowing members any role in the negotiating process or any right to ratify the contract eventually agreed to, see Hyde, *Democracy in Collective Bargaining*, 93 YALE L.J. 793 (1984).

Against Settlement

over, the representational procedures found in corporations, unions, or other private formal organizations are not universal. Much contemporary litigation, especially in the federal courts, involves governmental agencies,[18] and the procedures in those organizations for generating authoritative consent are far cruder than those in the corporate context. We are left to wonder, for example, whether the attorney general should be able to bind all state officials, some of whom are elected and thus have an independent mandate from the people, or even whether the incumbent attorney general should be able to bind his successors.[19]

These problems become even more pronounced when we turn from organizations and consider the fact that much contemporary litigation involves even more nebulous social entities, namely, groups. Some of these groups, such as ethnic or racial minorities, inmates of prisons, or residents of institutions for mentally retarded people, may have an identity or existence that transcends the lawsuit, but they do not have any formal organizational structure and therefore lack any procedures for generating authoritative consent. The absence of such a procedure is even more pronounced in cases involving a group, such as the purchasers of Cuisinarts between 1972 and 1982, which is constructed solely in order to create funds large enough to make it financially attractive for lawyers to handle the case.[20]

The Federal Rules of Civil Procedure require that groups have a "representative";[21] this representative purports to speak on behalf of the group, but he receives his power by the most questionable of all elective procedures—self-appointment or, if we are dealing with a defendant class,

18. According to Judge Gilbert Merritt, almost half of the cases in the Sixth Circuit involve suits against government agencies or officials. Merritt, *Owen Fiss in* Paradise Lost: *The Judicial Bureaucracy in the Administrative State*, 92 YALE L.J. (1983) (forthcoming).

19. In March of this year, the Civil Rights Division announced its intention to support the position of white municipal employees in Birmingham, Alabama, who are attacking the city's affirmative action policy, even though that policy was initiated under a consent decree that the Division had previously negotiated and obtained in a suit to eliminate discrimination against blacks, United States v. Jefferson County, Civ. Act. No. 75-P-0666-S (N.D. Ala. Aug. 21, 1981) (approving consent decree). *See U.S. to Support Whites in Suits On Bias Decree*, N.Y. Times, Mar. 5, 1984, at A1, col. 2.

In the fall of 1982, the Reagan Administration announced that it would not defend the Internal Revenue Service's policy of withholding tax-exempt status from private educational institutions that discriminated on the basis of race. The IRS had initiated the policy after a three-judge district court had issued an injunction prohibiting the IRS from exempting such schools. Green v. Kennedy, 309 F. Supp. 1127 (D.D.C.), *appeal dismissed sub nom.* Cannon v. Green, 398 U.S. 956 (1970). The Supreme Court appointed a private attorney, William Coleman, essentially to defend the decree when the Reagan Administration announced its position. *See* Bob Jones Univ. v. United States, 102 S. Ct. 1965 (1982) ("invit[ing]" Coleman to brief and argue case "in support of the judgments below"), 103 S. Ct. 2017 (1983) (affirming IRS' policy); N.Y. Times, Apr. 20, 1982, at A1, col. 5; *id.* at D21, col. 1 (describing government's actions and Coleman's appointment).

20. *See In re* Cuisinart Food Processor Antitrust Litig., [1982-83 Transfer Binder] TRADE REG. REP. (CCH) ¶ 65,680 (D. Conn. Oct. 24, 1983).

21. FED. R. CIV. P. 23(a).

appointment by an adversary. The rules contemplate notice to the members of the group about the pendency of the action and the claims of the representative, but it is difficult to believe that notice could reach all members of the group, or that it could cure the defects in the procedures by which the representative gets his power. The forces that discourage most members of the group from stepping forward to initiate suits will also discourage them from responding to whatever notice may reach them. The sponsors of the amendment to Rule 68 recognize the nature of class actions and exempt them from its special procedures.[22] But this exemption does little more than create an incentive for casting all civil litigation as class actions, with their attendant procedural complexities, and leaves the problem of generating authoritative consent for organizational parties unsolved. The new Rule 16 does not even recognize the problem.

Going to judgment does not altogether eliminate the risk of unauthorized action, any more than it eliminates the distortions arising from disparities in resources. The case presented by the representative of a group or an organization admittedly will influence the outcome of the suit, and that outcome will bind those who might also be bound by a settlement. On the other hand, judgment does not ask as much from the so-called representatives. There is a conceptual and normative distance between what the representatives do and say and what the court eventually decides, because the judge tests those statements and actions against independent procedural and substantive standards. The authority of judgment arises from the law, not from the statements or actions of the putative representatives, and

22. 98 F.R.D. at 363; *see supra* note 7. The Advisory Committee Note explains that Rule 23 class actions are exempted from new Rule 68's scope because "the offeree's rejection [of an offer] would burden a named representative-offeree with the risk of exposure to heavy liability for costs and expenses that could not be recouped from unnamed class members. The latter prospect, moreover, could lead to a conflict of interest between the named representative and other members of the class." 98 F.R.D. at 367. The danger the Committee points to, however, is not confined to class actions, but would exist whenever an individual plaintiff represents a group, for example, as a private attorney general.

The failure of the Committee to comprehend fully the concept of the private attorney general is further revealed by its insistence that the result at trial be "more favorable *to the offeree* than an unaccepted offer . . . ." 98 F.R.D. at 362 (emphasis added). Private attorneys general vindicate important societal interests as well as their own private concerns, *see, e.g.*, Fortner Enters. v. United States Steel Corp., 394 U.S. 495, 502 (1969); Newman v. Piggie Park Enters., 390 U.S. 400, 401-02 (1968) (per curiam), and yet, any benefits of an individual plaintiff's suit that redound to the public at large rather than to the named plaintiff may not be weighed in the Rule 68 determination. For example, in an employment discrimination case, an individual plaintiff might seek $25,000 in damages for past harm and an injunction against the continuation of discriminatory practices. He may reject the defendant's offer to settle for $5000, go to trial, and receive an injunction and $1000. Under Title VII, he would be able to recover attorney's fees as a prevailing party. *Cf.* McCann v. Coughlin, 698 F.2d 112, 128-29 (2d Cir. 1983) (nominal damages of $1 sufficient to justify attorney's fees). By contrast, under the proposed Rule 68, he stands in danger of incurring liability for his opponent's attorney's fees on the theory that the injunction he obtained is of less value *to him* than the defendant's offer of settlement.

Against Settlement

thus we allow judgment to bind persons not directly involved in the litigation even when we are reluctant to have settlement do so.

The procedures that have been devised for policing the settlement process when groups or organizations are involved have not eliminated the difficulties of generating authoritative consent. Some of these procedures provide a substantive standard for the approval of the settlement and do not even consider the issue of consent. A case in point is the Tunney Act. The Act establishes procedures for giving outsiders notice of a proposed settlement in a government antitrust suit and requires the judge to decide whether a settlement proposed by the Department of Justice is in "the public interest."[23] This statute implicitly acknowledges the difficulty of determining who is entitled to speak for the United States in some authoritative fashion and yet provides the judge with virtually no guidance in making this determination or in deciding whether to approve the settlement. The public-interest standard in fact seems to invite the consideration of such nonjudicial factors as popular sentiment and the efficient allocation of prosecutorial resources.[24]

Other policing mechanisms, such as Rule 23, which governs class actions, make no effort to articulate a substantive standard for approving

---

23. Antitrust Penalties & Procedures Act of 1974, Pub. L. No. 93-528, § 2, 88 Stat. 1706, 1707 (codified at 15 U.S.C. § 16(e) (1982)). In pertinent part, the Act provides:

> Before entering any consent judgment proposed by the United States under this section, the court shall determine that the entry of such judgment is in the public interest. For the purpose of such determination, the court may consider—
>
> (1) the competitive impact of such judgment, including termination of alleged violations, provisions for enforcement and modification, duration or relief sought, anticipated effects of alternative remedies actually considered, and any other considerations bearing upon the adequacy of such judgment;
>
> (2) the impact of entry of such judgment upon the public generally and individuals alleging specific injury from the violations set forth in the complaint including consideration of the public benefit, if any, to be derived from a determination of the issues at trial.

24. In Maryland v. United States, 103 S. Ct. 1240 (1983), the Supreme Court summarily affirmed the district court's approval of a consent decree proposed by the government in the AT&T antitrust case. In dissent, Justice Rehnquist, joined by the Chief Justice and Justice White, questioned the constitutionality of § 16(e). The District Court had interpreted § 16(e) to mean that the proposed consent decree should be accepted "if it effectively opens the relevant markets to competition and prevents the recurrence of anticompetitive activity, all without imposing undue and unnecessary burdens upon other aspects of the public interest . . . ." United States v. American Tel. & Tel. Co., 552 F. Supp. 131, 153 (D.D.C. 1982), *aff'd sub nom.* Maryland v. United States, 103 S. Ct. 1240 (1983) (per curiam). Justice Rehnquist, however, said: "It is not clear to me that this standard, or any other standard the District Court could have devised, admits of resolution by a court exercising the judicial power established by Article III of the Constitution." 103 S. Ct. at 1242. He continued:

> The question whether to prosecute a lawsuit is a question of the execution of the laws, which is committed to the executive by Article II. There is no standard by which the benefits to the public from a "better" settlement of a lawsuit than the Justice Department has negotiated can be balanced against the risk of an adverse decision, the need for a speedy resolution of the case, the benefits obtained in the settlement, and the availability of the Department's resources for other cases.

Id. at 1243.

settlements, but instead entrust the whole matter to the judge.[25] In such cases, the judge's approval theoretically should turn on whether the group consents, but determining whether such consent exists is often impossible, since true consent consists of nothing less than the expressed unanimity of all the members of a group, which might number in the hundreds of thousands and be scattered across the United States. The judge's approval instead turns on how close or far the proposed settlement is from what he imagines would be the judgment obtained after suit. The basis for approving a settlement, contrary to what the dispute-resolution story suggests, is therefore not consent but rather the settlement's approximation to judgment. This might appear to remove my objection to settlement, except that the judgment being used as a measure of the settlement is very odd indeed: It has never in fact been entered, but only imagined. It has been constructed without benefit of a full trial, and at a time when the judge can no longer count on the thorough presentation promised by the adversary system. The contending parties have struck a bargain, and have every interest in defending the settlement and in convincing the judge that it is in accord with the law.

THE LACK OF A FOUNDATION FOR CONTINUING JUDICIAL INVOLVEMENT

The dispute-resolution story trivializes the remedial dimensions of lawsuits and mistakenly assumes judgment to be the end of the process. It supposes that the judge's duty is to declare which neighbor is right and which wrong, and that this declaration will end the judge's involvement (save in that most exceptional situation where it is also necessary for him to issue a writ directing the sheriff to execute the declaration). Under these assumptions, settlement appears as an almost perfect substitute for judgment, for it too can declare the parties' rights. Often, however, judgment is not the end of a lawsuit but only the beginning. The involvement of the court may continue almost indefinitely. In these cases, settlement cannot provide an adequate basis for that necessary continuing involvement, and thus is no substitute for judgment.

The parties may sometimes be locked in combat with one another and view the lawsuit as only one phase in a long continuing struggle. The entry of judgment will then not end the struggle, but rather change its terms and the balance of power. One of the parties will invariably return to the court and again ask for its assistance, not so much because condi-

25. "A class action shall not be dismissed or compromised without the approval of the court, and notice of the proposed dismissal or compromise shall be given to all members of the class in such manner as the court directs." FED. R. CIV. P. 23(e).

tions have changed, but because the conditions that preceded the lawsuit have unfortunately not changed. This often occurs in domestic-relations cases, where the divorce decree represents only the opening salvo in an endless series of skirmishes over custody and support.[26]

The structural reform cases that play such a prominent role on the federal docket provide another occasion for continuing judicial involvement. In these cases, courts seek to safeguard public values by restructuring large-scale bureaucratic organizations.[27] The task is enormous, and our knowledge of how to restructure on-going bureaucratic organizations is limited. As a consequence, courts must oversee and manage the remedial process for a long time—maybe forever. This, I fear, is true of most school desegregation cases, some of which have been pending for twenty or thirty years.[28] It is also true of antitrust cases that seek divestiture or reorganization of an industry.[29]

The drive for settlement knows no bounds and can result in a consent decree even in the kinds of cases I have just mentioned, that is, even when a court finds itself embroiled in a continuing struggle between the parties or must reform a bureaucratic organization. The parties may be ignorant of the difficulties ahead or optimistic about the future, or they may simply believe that they can get more favorable terms through a bargained-for agreement. Soon, however, the inevitable happens: One party returns to court and asks the judge to modify the decree, either to make it more effective or less stringent. But the judge is at a loss: He has no basis for assessing the request. He cannot, to use Cardozo's somewhat melodramatic formula, easily decide whether the "dangers, once substantial, have become attenuated to a shadow,"[30] because, by definition, he never knew the dangers.

The allure of settlement in large part derives from the fact that it avoids the need for a trial. Settlement must thus occur before the trial is complete and the judge has entered findings of fact and conclusions of law. As a

26. Domestic relations cases form the largest subject-matter category of cases on state court dockets. *See* NAT'L CENTER FOR STATE COURTS, STATE COURT CASELOAD STATISTICS: THE STATE OF THE ART 53 (1978). Much of this litigation occurs after the entry of initial decrees. *See* Oldham, Book Review, 54 U. COLO. L. REV. 469, 478-80 (1983) (reviewing L. WEITZMAN, THE MARRIAGE CONTRACT (1981)).

27. I define the relationship between structural reform and the dispute-resolution story more fully elsewhere. *See* Fiss, *The Social and Political Foundations of Adjudication*, 6 L. & HUM. BEHAV. 121 (1982).

28. *See, e.g.*, Clark v. Board of Educ., 705 F.2d 265 (8th Cir. 1983) (continuation of Little Rock desegregation case); Brown v. Board of Educ., 84 F.R.D. 383 (D. Kan. 1979) (seeking intervention in original Topeka desegregation case on behalf of class represented by Linda Brown's daughter).

29. In United States v. United Shoe Mach. Corp., 391 U.S. 244 (1968), for example, the government successfully reopened a decade-old decree because competition in the shoe machinery market had not yet been attained.

30. United States v. Swift & Co., 286 U.S. 106, 119 (1932).

consequence, the judge confronted with a request for modification of a consent decree must retrospectively reconstruct the situation as it existed at the time the decree was entered, and decide whether conditions today have sufficiently changed to warrant a modification in that decree. In the Meat Packers litigation, for example, where a consent decree governed the industry for almost half a century, the judge confronted with a request for modification in 1960 had to reconstruct the "danger" that had existed at the time of the entry of the decree in 1920 in order to determine whether the danger had in fact become a "shadow."[31] Such an inquiry borders on the absurd, and is likely to dissipate whatever savings in judicial resources the initial settlement may have produced.

Settlement also impedes vigorous enforcement, which sometimes requires use of the contempt power. As a formal matter, contempt is available to punish violations of a consent decree.[32] But courts hesitate to use that power to enforce decrees that rest solely on consent, especially when enforcement is aimed at high public officials, as became evident in the Willowbrook deinstitutionalization case[33] and the recent Chicago desegregation case.[34] Courts do not see a mere bargain between the parties as a sufficient foundation for the exercise of their coercive powers.

Sometimes the agreement between the parties extends beyond the terms of the decree and includes stipulated "findings of fact" and "conclusions of law," but even then an adequate foundation for a strong use of the judicial power is lacking. Given the underlying purpose of settlement—to avoid trial—the so-called "findings" and "conclusions" are necessarily the products of a bargain between the parties rather than of a trial and an independent judicial judgment. Of course, a plaintiff is free to drop a lawsuit altogether (provided that the interests of certain other persons are not compromised), and a defendant can offer something in return, but that bargained-for arrangement more closely resembles a contract than an injunction. It raises a question which has already been answered whenever

31. *See* United States v. Swift & Co., 189 F. Supp. 885, 904, 910-12 (N.D. Ill. 1960), *aff'd* 367 U.S. 909 (1961). For a history of the Meat Packers' consent decree over a fifty-year period, see O. Fiss, Injunctions 325-99 (1972).

32. *See* D. Dobbs, Handbook on the Law of Remedies § 2.9, at 93-94, 99 n.25 (1973).

33. New York State Ass'n for Retarded Children v. Carey, 631 F.2d 162, 163-64 (2d Cir. 1980) (court unwilling to hold governor in contempt of consent decree when legislature refused to provide funding for committee established by court to oversee implementation of decree). The First Circuit explicitly acknowledged limitations on the power of courts to enforce consent decrees in Brewster v. Dukakis, 687 F.2d 495, 501 (1st Cir. 1982), and Massachusetts Ass'n for Retarded Citizens v. King, 668 F.2d 602, 610 (1st Cir. 1981).

34. In United States v. Board of Educ., 717 F.2d 378, 384-85 (7th Cir. 1983), the Court of Appeals found that the district court had acted too hastily in ordering the United States to provide additional financial support for Chicago's voluntary desegregation program pursuant to the consent decree which the federal government and the school board had entered into with the plaintiffs. The Seventh Circuit instead instructed the district court to give the federal government time to comply voluntarily with its obligations.

Against Settlement

an injunction is issued, namely, whether the judicial power should be used to enforce it. Even assuming that the consent is freely given and authoritative, the bargain is at best contractual and does not contain the kind of enforcement commitment already embodied in a decree that is the product of a trial and the judgment of a court.

Justice Rather Than Peace

The dispute-resolution story makes settlement appear as a perfect substitute for judgment, as we just saw, by trivializing the remedial dimensions of a lawsuit, and also by reducing the social function of the lawsuit to one of resolving private disputes: In that story, settlement appears to achieve exactly the same purpose as judgment—peace between the parties—but at considerably less expense to society. The two quarreling neighbors turn to a court in order to resolve their dispute, and society makes courts available because it wants to aid in the achievement of their private ends or to secure the peace.

In my view, however, the purpose of adjudication should be understood in broader terms. Adjudication uses public resources, and employs not strangers chosen by the parties but public officials chosen by a process in which the public participates. These officials, like members of the legislative and executive branches, possess a power that has been defined and conferred by public law, not by private agreement. Their job is not to maximize the ends of private parties, nor simply to secure the peace, but to explicate and give force to the values embodied in authoritative texts such as the Constitution and statutes: to interpret those values and to bring reality into accord with them. This duty is not discharged when the parties settle.

In our political system, courts are reactive institutions. They do not search out interpretive occasions, but instead wait for others to bring matters to their attention. They also rely for the most part on others to investigate and present the law and facts. A settlement will thereby deprive a court of the occasion, and perhaps even the ability, to render an interpretation. A court cannot proceed (or not proceed very far) in the face of a settlement. To be against settlement is not to urge that parties be "forced" to litigate, since that would interfere with their autonomy and distort the adjudicative process; the parties will be inclined to make the court believe that their bargain is justice. To be against settlement is only to suggest that when the parties settle, society gets less than what appears, and for a price it does not know it is paying. Parties might settle while leaving justice undone. The settlement of a school suit might secure the peace, but not racial equality. Although the parties are prepared to live under the terms they bargained for, and although such peaceful coexistence may be a necessary precondition of justice,[35] and itself a state of affairs to be valued, it is not justice itself. To settle for something means to accept less than some ideal.

I recognize that judges often announce settlements not with a sense of frustration or disappointment, as my account of adjudication might suggest, but with a sigh of relief. But this sigh should be seen for precisely what it is: It is not a recognition that a job is done, nor an acknowledgment that a job need not be done because justice has been secured. It is instead based on another sentiment altogether, namely, that another case has been "moved along," which is true whether or not justice has been done or even needs to be done. Or the sigh might be based on the fact that the agony of judgment has been avoided.

There is, of course, sometimes a value to avoidance, not just to the judge, who is thereby relieved of the need to make or enforce a hard decision, but also to society, which sometimes thrives by masking its basic contradictions. But will settlement result in avoidance when it is most appropriate? Other familiar avoidance devices, such as certiorari,[36] at least promise a devotion to public ends, but settlement is controlled by the litigants, and is subject to their private motivations and all the vagaries of the bargaining process. There are also dangers to avoidance, and these may well outweigh any imagined benefits. Partisans of ADR—Chief Justice Burger, or even President Bok—may begin with a certain satisfaction with the status quo. But when one sees injustices that cry out for correction—as Congress did when it endorsed the concept of the private attorney general[37] and as the Court of another era did when it sought to enhance access to the courts[38]—the value of avoidance diminishes and the agony of judgment becomes a necessity. Someone has to confront the betrayal of our

35. Some observers have argued that compliance is more likely to result from a consent decree than from an adjudicated decree. *See* O. FISS & D. RENDLEMAN, INJUNCTIONS 1004 (2d ed. 1984). But increased compliance may well be due to the fact that a consent decree asks less of the defendant, rather than from its creating a more amicable relationship between the parties. *See* McEwen & Maiman, *Mediation in Small Claims Court: Achieving Compliance Through Consent*, 18 LAW & SOC'Y REV. 11 (1984).

36. *See generally* A. BICKEL, THE LEAST DANGEROUS BRANCH 111-99 (1962) (discussing "the passive virtues"). For an analysis of the doctrines of vagueness and overbreadth as techniques for avoidance, see Note, *The Void-for-Vagueness Doctrine in the Supreme Court*, 109 U. PA. L. REV. 67 (1960).

37. For a discussion of the role of the private attorney general, see *supra* notes 9 & 22. The Federal Question Jurisdictional Amendments Act of 1980, Pub. L. No. 96-486, 94 Stat. 2369 (codified at 28 U.S.C. § 1331 (Supp. V 1981)), which eliminated the jurisdictional amount in federal question cases, reflects a similar sentiment: A claim's significance cannot be measured simply by the amount of money involved. *See* H.R. REP. NO. 1461, 94th Cong., 2d Sess. 2, *reprinted in* 1980 U.S. CONG. CODE & AD. NEWS 5063, 5063-64.

38. For a discussion of the Supreme Court's decisions during the 1960's and early 1970's suggesting that access to the courts and the opportunity to litigate are essential due process rights, see Michelman, *The Supreme Court and Litigation Access Fees* (pts. 1 & 2), 1973 DUKE L.J. 1153, 1974 DUKE L.J. 527.

Against Settlement

deepest ideals and be prepared to turn the world upside down to bring those ideals to fruition.

THE REAL DIVIDE

To all this, one can readily imagine a simple response by way of confession and avoidance: We are not talking about *those* lawsuits. Advocates of ADR might insist that my account of adjudication, in contrast to the one implied by the dispute-resolution story, focuses on a rather narrow category of lawsuits. They could argue that while settlement may have only the most limited appeal with respect to those cases, I have not spoken to the "typical" case. My response is twofold.

First, even as a purely quantitative matter, I doubt that the number of cases I am referring to is trivial. My universe includes those cases in which there are significant distributional inequalities; those in which it is difficult to generate authoritative consent because organizations or social groups are parties or because the power to settle is vested in autonomous agents; those in which the court must continue to supervise the parties after judgment; and those in which justice needs to be done, or to put it more modestly, where there is a genuine social need for an authoritative interpretation of law. I imagine that the number of cases that satisfy one of these four criteria is considerable; in contrast to the kind of case portrayed in the dispute-resolution story, they probably dominate the docket of a modern court system.

Second, it demands a certain kind of myopia to be concerned only with the number of cases, as though all cases are equal simply because the clerk of the court assigns each a single docket number. All cases are not equal. The Los Angeles desegregation case,[39] to take one example, is not equal to the allegedly more typical suit involving a property dispute or an automobile accident. The desegregation suit consumes more resources, affects more people, and provokes far greater challenges to the judicial power. The settlement movement must introduce a qualitative perspective; it must speak to these more "significant" cases, and demonstrate the propriety of settling them. Otherwise it will soon be seen as an irrelevance, dealing with trivia rather than responding to the very conditions that give the movement its greatest sway and saliency.

Nor would sorting cases into "two tracks," one for settlement, and another for judgment, avoid my objections. Settling automobile cases and leaving discrimination or antitrust cases for judgment might remove a

39. *See* Crawford v. Board of Educ., 46 Cal. App. 3d 872, 120 Cal. Rptr. 334 (Ct. App. 1975), *aff'd*, 17 Cal. 3d, 551 P.2d 28, 130 Cal. Rptr. 724 (1976). For a recent recounting of the history of the 20 years of litigation, see Crawford v. Board of Educ., 103 S. Ct. 3211, 3214-15 (1982).

large number of cases from the dockets, but the dockets will nevertheless remain burdened with the cases that consume the most judicial resources and represent the most controversial exercises of the judicial power. A "two track" strategy would drain the argument for settlement of much of its appeal. I also doubt whether the "two track" strategy can be sensibly implemented. It is impossible to formulate adequate criteria for prospectively sorting cases. The problems of settlement are not tied to the subject matter of the suit, but instead stem from factors that are harder to identify, such as the wealth of the parties, the likely post-judgment history of the suit, or the need for an authoritative interpretation of law. The authors of the amendment to Rule 68 make a gesture toward a "two track" strategy by exempting class actions and shareholder derivative suits, and by allowing the judge to refrain from awarding attorney's fees when it is "unjustified under all of the circumstances."[40] But these gestures are cramped and ill-conceived, and are likely to increase the workload of the courts by giving rise to yet another set of issues to litigate.[41] It is, moreover, hard to see how these problems can be avoided. Many of the factors that lead a society to bring social relationships that otherwise seem wholly private (e.g., marriage) within the jurisdiction of a court, such as imbalances of power or the interests of third parties, are also likely to make

---

40. 98 F.R.D. at 362.

41. It is far from clear that either the current offer-of-judgment rule or the proposed amendments are likely to reduce the overall volume of litigation. Although such a rule increases the potential costs a plaintiff faces should he lose, and thus means a plaintiff will be willing to settle for a smaller amount than he would demand if there were no potential liability for the defendant's expenses, it also increases the potential benefits a defendant will receive should his offer exceed the amount the plaintiff recovers at trial (since the defendant will both retain the difference between the offer and the amount actually recovered and will recover his expenses), and thus means a defendant will offer less in a settlement. There is no reason to assume that the gap between the plaintiff's demand and the defendant's offer will be relatively smaller because of the offer-of-judgment rule. *See* Priest, *supra* note 11, at 171.

Moreover, Rule 68 makes no exception for cases seeking non-monetary relief, such as injunctions. It thus requires the court to decide whether the injunction actually obtained was in fact "better" or "more favorable" than the decree the defendant was willing to enter prior to trial.

The "reasonability" language of the proposed rule, *supra* note 7, creates potential attorney-client conflicts that may also spark litigation. By implication, a court which grants an offeror all of his expenses has decided that the offeree was unreasonable in his refusal. If the offeree based that refusal on the advice of counsel, then that advice was unreasonable, and a malpractice suit can be expected to recover fees assessed against the client in the original case.

The proposed rule's exclusion of costs and attorney's fees from the assessment of whether an offer is more or less favorable than an eventual judgment, 98 F.R.D. at 362, may cause additional conflicts between plaintiffs and their attorneys. Suppose that a defendant offers a plaintiff $100,000 as full relief including attorney's fees and costs. If the plaintiff accepts this offer, then his attorney forfeits the right to attorney's fees under a statutory fee-shifting scheme. If, however, the plaintiff refuses the offer, then the plaintiff may be liable to the defendant for the defendant's attorney's fees and costs, even though the plaintiff's total "recovery" at trial—for example, $80,000 on the merits and $30,000 in attorneys' fees—exceeds the defendant's offer because the plaintiff recovered less on the merits. In these circumstances, the lawyer may press his client to litigate because this will assure the lawyer his fee, even though the client will thereby be exposed to possible liability for the defendant's costs and expenses.

settlement problematic. Settlement is a poor substitute for judgement; it is an even poorer substitute for the withdrawal of jurisdiction.

For these reasons, I remain highly skeptical of a "two track" strategy, and would resist it. But the more important point to note is that the draftsmen of Rule 68 are the exception. There is no hint of a "two track" strategy in Rule 16. In fact, most ADR advocates make no effort to distinguish between different types of cases or to suggest that "the gentler arts of reconciliation and accommodation" might be particularly appropriate for one type of case but not for another. They lump all cases together. This suggests that what divides me from the partisans of ADR is not that we are concerned with different universes of cases, that Derek Bok, for example, focuses on boundary quarrels while I see only desegregation suits. I suspect instead that what divides us is much deeper and stems from our understanding of the purpose of the civil law suit and its place in society. It is a difference in outlook.

Someone like Bok sees adjudication in essentially private terms: The purpose of lawsuits and the civil courts is to resolve disputes, and the amount of litigation we encounter is evidence of the needlessly combative and quarrelsome character of Americans. Or as Bok put it, using a more diplomatic idiom: "At bottom, ours is a society built on individualism, competition, and success."[42] I, on the other hand, see adjudication in more public terms: Civil litigation is an institutional arrangement for using state power to bring a recalcitrant reality closer to our chosen ideals. We turn to the courts because we need to, not because of some quirk in our personalities. We train our students in the tougher arts so that they may help secure all that the law promises, not because we want them to become gladiators or because we take a special pleasure in combat.

To conceive of the civil lawsuit in public terms as America does might be unique. I am willing to assume that no other country—including Japan, Bok's new paragon[43]—has a case like *Brown v. Board of Education*[44] in which the judicial power is used to eradicate the caste structure. I am willing to assume that no other country conceives of law and uses law in quite the way we do. But this should be a source of pride rather than shame. What is unique is not the problem, that we live short of our

42. Bok, *supra* note 1, at 42.

43. *Id.* at 41. As to the validity of the comparisons and a more subtle explanation of the determinants of litigiousness, see Haley, *The Myth of the Reluctant Litigant*, 4 J. JAPANESE STUD. 359, 389 (1978) ("Few misconceptions about Japan have been more widespread or as pernicious as the myth of the special reluctance of the Japanese to litigate."); *see also* Galanter, *Reading the Landscape of Disputes: What We Know and Don't Know (And Think We Know) About Our Allegedly Contentious and Litigious Society*, 31 UCLA L. REV. 4, 57–59 (1983) (paucity of lawyers in Japan due to restrictions on number of attorneys admitted to practice rather than to non-litigousness).

44. 347 U.S. 483 (1954); 349 U.S. 294 (1955).

ideals, but that we alone among the nations of the world seem willing to do something about it. Adjudication American-style is not a reflection of our combativeness but rather a tribute to our inventiveness and perhaps even more to our commitment.

[10]

Articles

The Mediation Alternative: Process Dangers for Women

Trina Grillo†

CONTENTS

---

† Assistant Professor of Law, University of San Francisco. J.D., University of Minnesota, 1974; A.B., University of California-Berkeley, 1969.

I have received incalculable help from others. I thank Harlon Dalton, Richard Delgado, John Denvir, Dolores Donovan, Jay Folberg, Alan Freeman, Gary Friedman, Evelio M. Grillo, Michele Hermann, Marilyn L. Ray, Antoinette Sedilla-Lopez, Jean Stefancic, and Catharine Wells for their generous and thoughtful readings and suggestions. Thanks also to Eric Landis-Brenman, Phyllis Rosen, Sandra Schutz, and University of San Francisco Librarians Lee Ryan and Marian Shostrom for research assistance. I owe much gratitude to Catherine Grillo, my mother, who supported me with advice, concern, and childcare throughout the time I was writing this Article. Finally, I thank Paul Baum and Stephanie Wildman for their friendship, careful criticism, and constant encouragement.

INTRODUCTION: THE PROMISE OF MEDIATION

The western concept of law is based on a patriarchal paradigm[1] characterized by hierarchy, linear reasoning, the resolution of disputes through the application of abstract principles, and the ideal of the reasonable person.[2] Its fundamental aspiration is objectivity, and to that end it separates public from private, form from substance, and process from policy.[3] This objectivist paradigm is problematic in many circumstances, but never more so than in connection with a marital dissolution in which the custody of children is at issue, where the essential question for the court is what is to happen next in the family. The family court system, aspiring to the ideal of objectivity and operating as an adversary system, can be relied on neither to produce just results nor to treat those subject to it respectfully and humanely.

There is little doubt that divorce procedure needs to be reformed, but reformed how? Presumably, any alternative should be at least as just, and at least as humane, as the current system, particularly for those who are least powerful in society. Mediation has been put forward, with much fanfare, as such an alternative. The impetus of the mediation movement has been so strong that in some states couples disputing custody are required by statute or local rule to undergo a mandatory mediation process if they are unable to reach an agreement on their own.[4] Mediation has been embraced for a number of

1. *See* Menkel-Meadow, *Portia in a Different Voice: Speculations on a Woman's Lawyering Process*, 1 BERKELEY WOMEN'S L.J. 39, 50 (1985) ("[T]here is a tendency for the male-dominated or male-created forms and values to control [our present legal structures] . . . ."); Polan, *Toward a Theory of Law and Patriarchy*, in THE POLITICS OF LAW 294, 296 (D. Kairys ed. 1982) (discussing relationship of legal system to patriarchy); Rifkin, *Mediation from a Feminist Perspective: Promises and Problems*, 2 LAW & INEQUALITY 21, 22 (1984) (describing "the patriarchal paradigm of law as hierarchy, combat, and adversarialness") [hereinafter Rifkin, *Mediation*]; Rifkin, *Toward a Theory of Law and Patriarchy*, 3 HARV. WOMEN'S L.J. 83, 87 (1980) (patriarchy will not be eliminated unless male paradigm of law is transformed) [hereinafter Rifkin, *Toward a Theory*].

2. *See, e.g.*, Bender, *A Lawyer's Primer on Feminist Theory and Tort*, 38 J. LEGAL EDUC. 3, 5-8 (1988); Donovan & Wildman, *Is the Reasonable Man Obsolete? A Critical Perspective on Self-Defense and Provocation*, 14 LOY. L.A.L. REV. 435 (1981). These articles suggest that, despite the change in terminology from "reasonable man" to "reasonable person," the standard was never intended to include women or members of minority groups, whether male or female. As Bender has said: "Our legal system . . . resolves problems through male inquiries formulated from distanced, abstract, and acontextual vantage points." Bender, *supra*, at 10-11; *see also* G. CALABRESI, IDEALS, BELIEFS, ATTITUDES, AND THE LAW: PRIVATE LAW PERSPECTIVES ON A PUBLIC LAW PROBLEM 26-28 (1985) (discussing race and gender implications of "reasonable person").

3. *See* C. MACKINNON, TOWARD A FEMINIST THEORY OF THE STATE 62-63 (1989) [hereinafter C. MACKINNON, TOWARD A FEMINIST THEORY]; MacKinnon, *Feminism, Marxism, Method, and the State: Toward Feminist Jurisprudence*, 8 SIGNS 635, 655-56 (1983) [hereinafter MacKinnon, *Feminism, Marxism*].

4. In some states mediation is a prerequisite to a judicial hearing. *See* CAL. CIV. CODE § 4607 (West 1983 & Supp. 1990); DEL. FAM. CT. C.R. (16)(a)(1); ME. REV. STAT. ANN. tit. 19, § 752 (West 1981 & Supp. 1990); N.C. GEN. STAT. § 50-13.1 (1989) (mediation required if custody or visitation issue involved); OR. REV. STAT. ANN. §§ 107.755-.795 (Butterworths 1990). Other states permit the court to order mediation. *See* ALASKA STAT. § 25.24.060 (Michie 1983); FLA. STAT. ANN. § 44.101 (Harrison Supp. 1989); ILL. REV. STAT. ch. 40, ¶ 607.1(c)(4) (Smith-Hurd 1980 & Supp. 1990); IOWA CODE ANN. §§ 598.41, 679.1-.14 (West 1987 & Supp. 1990); KAN. STAT. ANN. §§ 23-601 to -607 (1989); LA. REV. STAT. ANN. §§ 9:351-:356 (West Supp. 1990); MICH. COMP. LAWS § 552.505 (West 1988 & Supp. 1990); MINN. STAT. ANN. § 518.619 (West 1990); N.H. REV. STAT. ANN. § 328-C (Butterworths Supp. 1989); N.M. STAT. ANN. § 40-

reasons. First, it rejects an objectivist approach to conflict resolution, and promises to consider disputes in terms of relationships and responsibility. Second, the mediation process is, at least in theory, cooperative and voluntary, not coercive. The mediator does not make a decision; rather, each party speaks for himself.[5] Together they reach an agreement that meets the parties' mutual needs. In this manner, the process is said to enable the parties to exercise self-determination and eliminate the hierarchy of dominance that characterizes the judge/litigant and lawyer/client relationships. Third, since in mediation there are no rules of evidence or legalistic notions of relevancy, decisions supposedly may be informed by context rather than by abstract principle. Finally, in theory at least, emotions are recognized and incorporated into the mediation process. This conception of mediation has led some commentators to characterize it as a feminist alternative to the patriarchally inspired adversary system.[6]

Whether mandatory mediation, required as part of court proceedings, fulfills these aspirations, or instead substitutes another objectivist, patriarchal, and even more damaging form of conflict resolution for its adversarial counterpart, is the subject of this Article. Many divorcing couples seem pleased with their mediation experiences.[7] Indeed, studies have shown that mediation clients are more

---

12-5 (1988); R.I. GEN. LAWS § 15-5-29 (1988); TEX. CIV. PRAC. & REM. CODE ANN. §§ 152.001-.004 (Vernon 1985); WASH. REV. CODE ANN. § 26.09.015 (West Supp. 1990); WIS. STAT. § 767.11(3) (West Supp. 1990).

5. I have made an effort in this Article to maintain gender neutrality in my use of pronouns. As the Article makes apparent, however, the sexes are not always affected the same way by certain flaws in mediation or adjudication. Where a party of one gender appears particularly likely to play a certain role, I have cast my description of that role in that gender. This Article is about how women are endangered by the mediation process. I should emphasize, however, that the flaws of mediation I discuss ultimately work to the detriment of *both* sexes. For, if either party is disadvantaged or silenced in the mediation process, the other party loses some of the most significant of mediation's potential benefits; he is deprived of the opportunity to gain an understanding of the other party, to learn to communicate honestly with her, and to work together to construct an agreement that creatively and precisely attends to their shared concerns.

6. *See, e.g.*, Rifkin, *Mediation*, *supra* note 1, at 23. See also Menkel-Meadow, *supra* note 1, at 53, where she states that "an ethic of care and a heightened sense of empathy in women suggests that women lawyers may be particularly interested in mediation as an alternative to litigation as a method of resolving disputes." Menkel-Meadow, however, adds that "mediation as a process is not necessarily good or bad for women's interests; it depends on who the mediator is and what model of mediation is being used." *Id.* at 53 n.78. In any event, given its potentially profound implications for women's lives, the study of mediation introduces, and even requires, a feminist pedagogy—one that is fundamentally different from traditional legal pedagogy. *See* Rifkin, *Mediation*, *supra* note 1, at 24. *But see* Fineman, *Dominant Discourse, Professional Language, and Legal Change in Child Custody Decisionmaking*, 101 HARV. L. REV. 727, 760-68 (1988) (arguing that "legal model" in custody cases is preferable to one in which "professional helpers" such as mediators influence decisions related to divorce).

7. For example, Jessica Pearson and Nancy Thoennes found that more than three-quarters of the mediation clients in their studies expressed satisfaction with the process and would recommend it to others. Pearson & Thoennes, *Divorce Mediation: Reflections on a Decade of Research*, in MEDIATION RESEARCH 9, 19 (1989); *see also* J. PEARSON & N. THOENNES, FINAL REPORT OF THE DIVORCE MEDIATION PROJECT 1 (1984) [report as whole hereinafter J. PEARSON & N. THOENNES, FINAL REPORT] (submitted to the Children's Bureau, Administration for Children, Youth and Families, U.S. Dept. of Health and Human Services) (citing studies showing higher levels of participant satisfaction in divorce mediation than in conventional legal proceedings); Pearson & Thoennes, *Mediating and Litigating Custody Disputes: A Longitudinal Evaluation*, 17 FAM. L.Q. 497 (1984) (although many refuse to mediate disputes, those who do mediate tend to be extremely pleased with results) [hereinafter Pearson & Thoennes, *Mediating and Litigating*].

satisfied with their divorce outcomes than persons using the adversary system.[8] Although there are significant methodological problems with each of these studies,[9] the existence of substantial client satisfaction with some models of mediation cannot be completely discounted.

Nonetheless, I conclude that mandatory mediation provides neither a more just nor a more humane alternative to the adversarial system of adjudication of custody, and, therefore, does not fulfill its promises. In particular, quite apart from whether an acceptable result is reached, mandatory mediation can be destructive to many women and some men[10] because it requires them to speak

---

8. Joan Kelly found that mediation clients were, on the whole, more satisfied with their divorce outcomes than persons using the adversary system, although her study was limited to persons voluntarily using a private mediation service to mediate integrated agreements not restricted to child custody. *See* Kelly, *Mediated and Adversarial Divorce: Respondents' Perceptions of Their Processes and Outcomes*, MEDIATION Q., Summer 1989, at 71, 77-87; *see also* Bautz, *Divorce Mediation: For Better or For Worse*, MEDIATION Q., Winter 1988, at 51, 56-59 (couples who used divorce mediation more satisfied with settlement than couples who contested their divorce; only 12 mediated cases were in the sample, however, and only 2 cases were referred by court); Irving & Benjamin, *A Study of Conciliation Counselling in the Family Court of Toronto: Implications for Socio-Legal Practice*, in THE RESOLUTION OF FAMILY CONFLICT 268 (1984) (discussing need for and appropriateness of conciliation counseling); Waldron, Roth, Fair, Mann & McDermott, *A Therapeutic Mediation Model for Child Custody Dispute Resolution*, MEDIATION Q., March 1984, at 5, 11-19 (child custody mediation by child therapists can enhance parents' ability to coparent and improve the mental health of their children). Some commentators have noted, however, that men were more satisfied with the mediation process than women. *See* Emery & Jackson, *The Charlottesville Mediation Project: Mediated and Litigated Child Custody Disputes*, MEDIATION Q., Summer 1989, at 3, 10-17 (couples more satisfied with mediation than litigation, but men show greater satisfaction with mediation, and mothers more likely to feel they fared better in litigation); Emery & Wyer, *Child Custody Mediation and Litigation: An Experimental Evaluation of the Experience of Parents*, 55 J. CONSULTING & CLINICAL PSYCHOLOGY 179, 183 (1987) (most of gains in satisfaction from mediation accrued to men).

Use of the mediation process does not necessarily improve communication between the parties. According to Kenneth Kressel, a large proportion of persons who have undergone mediation said that it had no effect on their ability to cooperate or communicate with the other parent, and a sizable minority (10%) said that it made things worse. Kressel, *Research on Divorce Mediation: A Summary and Critique of the Literature*, in THE ROLE OF MEDIATION IN DIVORCE PROCEEDINGS: A COMPARATIVE PERSPECTIVE 219, 220 (Vermont Law School Dispute Resolution Project ed. 1987) [article hereinafter Kressel, *Research*; volume as whole hereinafter THE ROLE OF MEDIATION] (discussing United States, Canada, and Great Britain); *see also* K. KRESSEL, THE PROCESS OF DIVORCE: HOW PROFESSIONALS AND COUPLES NEGOTIATE SETTLEMENTS 226 (1985) (positive impact of mediation upon respondents dubious six months after mediation); *cf.* Pearson & Thoennes, *Mediation Versus the Courts in Child Custody Cases*, 1985 NEGOTIATION J. 235, 241 (1985) (only 30% of couples who reached agreement in mediation and 7% of those who did not credited process with improving relationship with spouse, while close to 15% of couples in mediation indicated that it hurt relationship; in general, however, respondents viewed mediation as less damaging than going to court).

9. In each of the studies, either the mediation involved was voluntary, or the sample of clients was small. The simple design used in these studies typically compares a mediation group with an adversary group, making it difficult to assess any placebo effects caused by the enthusiasm with which mediation is administered. *See, e.g.*, Bautz, *supra* note 8, at 54-55. Moreover, preexisting differences between the mediating and adversarial couples are not addressed. Finally, neither "mediation" nor "the adversarial system" is a monolith; thus, neither group of clients is receiving homogeneous and absolutely distinct treatment. *See* Kressel, *Research*, supra note 8, at 219.

10. Although mandatory mediation harms some men in the same ways that it harms significant numbers of women, many more women than men share the emotional orientation, worldview, and economic circumstances I describe. In addition, women are often expected to act in a particular way because they are women. *See* Williams, *Deconstructing Gender*, 87 MICH. L. REV. 797, 813 n.61 (1989).

Carol Gilligan, in her pathbreaking work, *In A Different Voice*, has described two different, gendered modes of thought, a "male" mode and a "female" mode. She has observed that even though she is not

in a setting they have not chosen and often imposes a rigid orthodoxy as to how they should speak, make decisions, and be. This orthodoxy is imposed through subtle and not-so-subtle messages about appropriate conduct and about what may be said in mediation. It is an orthodoxy that often excludes the possibility of the parties' speaking with their authentic voices.

Moreover, people vary greatly in the extent to which their sense of self is "relational"—that is, defined in terms of connection to others. If two parties are forced to engage with one another, and one has a more relational sense of self than the other, that party may feel compelled to maintain her connection with the other, even to her own detriment. For this reason, the party with the more relational sense of self will be at a disadvantage in a mediated negotiation. Several prominent researchers have suggested that, as a general rule, women have a more relational sense of self than do men, although there is little agreement on what the origin of this difference might be.[11] Thus, rather than being a feminist alternative to the adversary system, mediation has the potential actively to harm women.

Some of the dangers of mandatory mediation apply to voluntary mediation as well. Voluntary mediation should not be abandoned, but should be recognized as a powerful process which should be used carefully and thoughtfully. Entering into such a process with one who has known you intimately and who now seems to threaten your whole life and being has great creative, but also enormous destructive, power. Nonetheless, it should be recognized that when two people themselves decide to mediate and then physically appear at the mediation sessions, that decision and their continued presence serve as a rough indication that it is not too painful or too dangerous for one or both of them to go on.[12]

Although this Article cautions against mediation's dangers, I should emphasize at this juncture that mediation is the work I most like to do. Few professional experiences can compare to the moment when the world of possibilities seems to expand for a couple, and hope and optimism coexist, at least tempo-

---

ascribing the male mode exclusively to men and the female mode exclusively to women, most women do appear to operate in the female mode. C. GILLIGAN, IN A DIFFERENT VOICE: PSYCHOLOGICAL THEORY AND WOMEN'S DEVELOPMENT 24-63 (1982). *See also infra* notes 259-61 and accompanying text (discussion of male and female modes of thought).

Another essay could no doubt describe how mediation hurts particular groups of men: that is not my task. For a discussion of the claim that nonformal mechanisms, including mediation, injure the poor and disempowered generally, see Delgado, Dunn, Brown, Lee, & Hubbert, *Fairness and Formality: Minimizing the Risk of Prejudice in Alternative Dispute Resolution*, 1985 WIS. L. REV. 1359, 1360-61, 1375-91 [hereinafter Delgado, *Fairness and Formality*].

11. *See, e.g.*, N. CHODOROW, THE REPRODUCTION OF MOTHERING: PSYCHOANALYSIS AND THE SOCIOLOGY OF GENDER 176-80, 200 (1978); D. DINNERSTEIN, THE MERMAID AND THE MINOTAUR 156 (1976); C. GILLIGAN, *supra* note 10, at 64-105; J. MILLER, TOWARD A NEW PSYCHOLOGY OF WOMEN 83-89 (1976); A. SCHAEF, WOMEN'S REALITY: AN EMERGING FEMALE SYSTEM IN WHITE MALE SOCIETY 28-33 (1981).

12. The decision to enter mediation, however, may not be truly voluntary if dictated by an unequal power balance in the relationship as it existed prior to the mediation. Thus even voluntary mediation can be coercive.

rarily, with pain and anger. It is from my experiences mediating and listening to the stories of those who have been participants in the mediation process, and out of concern for the integrity of that process, that this Article has been written.[13]

Part I of this Article describes the rise of child custody mediation, focusing on the version currently required by California law. California has led the country in both the substance and procedure of divorce reform, beginning with no-fault divorce, continuing with the statutory embrace of joint custody, and, most recently, in legislating the use of divorce mediation.[14] Part II describes the promises of mediation: reliance on context rather than exclusively on abstract rules; the inclusion of emotions along with rational self-interest; and the introduction of self-determination in the place of an outside decisionmaker. Part III discusses the particular dangers to women of mandatory mediation's requirement of direct engagement with their adversary. Part IV suggests alternatives to a system of mandatory mediation. While the focus of my discussion is mandatory mediation, many of the observations in the Article also have implications for voluntary mediation, which in many cases also fails to fulfill its promise to be a gentler alternative to the adversarial system.

I. The Rise of Mandatory Custody Mediation in California

The movement for voluntary mediation of divorce disputes began several decades ago as lawyers and therapists offered to help their clients settle their cases in a nonadversarial manner.[15] Some clients reported that, by meeting together with a third party to help facilitate their communication, they were able

13. At various points in this Article there are descriptions of mediation sessions, and of the perspectives of mediators and parties in court-ordered mediations, which are denoted by blocked italic text. Because the mediation process and settlements that flow from it are not public, there are no transcripts and only limited records of settlements available. The descriptions of mediation sessions are therefore based on actual cases which have been related to me by the participants themselves, though the names and identifying details have been changed. The descriptions of participants' perspectives on mediation are composites, drawn from my observation of many mediation sessions. One of the descriptions of a mediation session (that of Joe and Elaine, see *infra* text accompanying note 194) is also a composite, combining the details of two cases.

14. *See* Deis, *California's Answer: Mandatory Mediation of Child Custody and Visitation Disputes*, 1 Ohio St. J. Dispute Resolution 149, 152 (1985) (understanding and analysis of California's mandatory mediation statutes important because many states expected to follow California's lead in this area, just as they did in area of no-fault divorce); Fineman, *supra* note 6, at 741 n. 59 ("California was a pioneer in no-fault legislation."); Folberg & Milne, *The Theory and Practice of Divorce Mediation: An Overview*, in Divorce Mediation, Theory and Practice 3, 5 (1988) (court personnel providing conciliation services in California probably first to offer mediation services).

Deis comments that "approximately eighteen states are using mediation to resolve these [child custody and visitation] disputes." Deis, *supra*, at 171 (citing Jenkins, *Divorce California Style*, 9 Student L. 30 (1981)). She continues: "It is difficult to estimate how many other states allow mediation of child custody and visitation disputes because this has been accomplished in some states through a general provision giving judges the power to provide counseling or alternate means of decision making for the parties." *Id.*

15. Conversation with Gary Friedman, Center for the Development of Mediation in Law, Mill Valley, California (Dec. 14, 1988); *see also* O. Coogler, Structured Mediation in Divorce Settlements at xv (1978) (structured mediation process developed in mid-1970's); Folberg & Milne, *supra* note 14, at 5 (handful of attorneys began offering nonadversarial legal services in early 1970's).

to reach agreements that met everyone's needs and leave their marriages without the acrimony and fear they had anticipated from the adversarial divorce process.

As mediation caught on, it began to be heralded as the cure for the various ills of adversary divorce. It was touted as a process in which the parties would voluntarily cooperate to find the best manner of continuing to parent their children. Consumers, however, were not embracing the mediation cure. Whether because of lack of familiarity with the process, the hostility of the organized bar, or some more considered reluctance, few divorcing couples chose to enter mediation.[16] In order to bypass this consumer resistance, some state legislatures established court-annexed mediation programs, requiring that couples disputing custody mediate prior to going to court.[17]

As noted earlier, California law is the focus of this Article because California has been the trendsetter in both substantive and procedural divorce reform.[18] California was the first state to enact a statute that required mediation of child custody and visitation disputes.[19] California's mandatory mediation law, which first became effective in 1981, requires that all custody and visitation disputes be mediated prior to being considered by the county Superior Court.[20] The mediation is intended to "reduce acrimony" between the parties and lead to an agreement that assures the children "close and continuing contact with both parents."[21] The court is required to appoint a mediator, who may be a member of the professional staff of a family conciliation court, probation department, or mental health services agency, or some other person or agency

---

16. *See* Pearson, *An Evaluation of Alternatives to Court Adjudication*, 7 JUST. SYS. J. 420, 427 (1982). Pearson indicates that participation in mediation varies with program coercion. *Id.* at 428-29.

17. *Id* at 428-29; *see also* Deis, *supra* note 14, at 151 n.21 (citing California and Delaware statutes requiring mediation for divorce disputes).

California's family mediation model was adopted in 1980, quite early in the trend toward mediation in court-annexed programs. When I describe mediation procedures, I will rely on the California model. For a review of other states' models, see ABA STANDING COMMITTEE ON DISPUTE RESOLUTION, LEGISLATION ON DISPUTE RESOLUTION 7-71 (1988).

18. *See supra* note 14 and accompanying text.

19. *See* Deis, *supra* note 14, at 149. Deis describes mediation as "flawed" but as more advantageous than the adversary system, and says that mediation fosters "privacy and self-determination." *Id.* at 151. For a discussion of how mediation, by suppressing the expression of anger, does not foster self-determination see *infra* section II.C.

20. The California statute provides:

> In any proceeding where there is at issue the custody of or visitation with a minor child, and where it appears on the face of the petition or other application for an order or modification of an order for the custody or visitation of a child or children that either or both such issues are contested . . . the matter shall be set for mediation of the contested issues prior to or concurrent with the setting of the matter for hearing. . . . The purpose of the mediation proceeding shall be to reduce acrimony which may exist between the parties and to develop an agreement assuring the child or children's close and continuing contact with both parents. The mediator shall use his or her best efforts to effect a settlement of the custody or visitation dispute that is in the best interests of the child or children . . . .

CAL. CIV. CODE § 4607(a) (West Supp. 1990) (emphasis omitted). For a listing of other similar state laws, see *supra* note 4.

21. CAL. CIV. CODE § 4607(a) (West Supp. 1990).

the court decides is appropriate.[22] Mediators must have a master's degree in psychology, social work, or another behavioral science; experience in counseling or psychotherapy; knowledge of the California court system and family law procedure; and knowledge of adult and child psychology, including the effects of divorce on children.[23]

In practice, the qualifications of mediators provided by the California courts vary widely.[24] In some urban counties, there are large professional staffs of mediators, all of whom are experienced mental health professionals; in other counties, there may be only one mediator with little professional training.[25] Similarly, some counties have extensive office facilities in which to house their mediation program and provide the opportunity to have several meetings with the mediators; in others, mediation takes place in the twenty minutes before court in a hallway.[26] The California Judicial Council has prepared standards of practice for mediators which should increase uniformity among the counties.[27] Nonetheless, nine years after the introduction of mandatory mediation in California, the services offered are frequently inadequate at best, even from the perspective of proponents of mandatory mediation.[28]

---

22. CAL. CIV. CODE § 4607(b) (West Supp. 1990).

23. CAL. CIV. CODE § 4607(b) (West Supp. 1990) provides that mediators must meet the requirements of CAL. CIV. PROC. CODE § 1745 (West Supp. 1990), which sets forth these requirements. State statutes that have similar requirements include: KAN. STAT. ANN. § 23-602 (1988); LA. REV. STAT. ANN. § 9:356(A) (West Supp. 1990) (additional requirements, including bar membership); MINN. STAT. ANN. § 518.619(4) (West Supp. 1990). State statutes with lesser or agency-created requirements include: MICH. COMP. LAWS § 552.513 (1988); W. VA. CODE § 48A-2-2 (Supp. 1990); WIS. STAT. § 767.11 (Supp. 1990). State statutes that empower the courts to set standards include: ALASKA STAT. § 25.24.060(b) (1983); CONN. GEN. STAT. § 46-53a (Supp. 1990); FLA. STAT. ANN. § 44.302(3) (West Supp. 1989); N.H. REV. STAT. ANN. § 328-C (Supp. 1989); N.M. STAT. ANN. § 40-12-5 (1989); N.C. GEN. STAT. § 7A-494(a) (1989); OKLA. STAT. tit. 42, § 109H (1989); OR. REV. STAT. § 107.755 (1989); WASH. REV. CODE ANN. § 26.09.015 (Supp. 1990). States whose statutes are silent on the requirements include Illinois, Iowa, Montana, Rhode Island, and South Dakota.

24. *See* Folberg & Milne, *supra* note 14, at 21; Bruch, *And How Are the Children? The Effects of Ideology and Mediation on Child Custody Law and Children's Well-Being in the United States*, 2 INT'L J.L. & FAM. 106, 118 (1988); Milne, *Divorce Mediation: The State of the Art*, MEDIATION Q., Sept. 1983, at 15, 21; D. Saposnek, Remarks at the Meeting of the Northern California Council for Mediation, San Francisco, California (Oct. 28, 1989). Donald Saposnek is one of several consultants hired by the California Family Court Services/Administrative Office of the Courts to study the mandatory mediation systems of the various counties and develop a mediation training manual for use throughout California. In his talk, attended by the author, Saposnek described findings from his survey of how mediation operates in California.

25. D. Saposnek, *supra* note 24.

26. *Id.* Saposnek stated that although some counties had well-run programs, others were providing very poor service. For example, in one county a single mediator typically handled 10 mediations in a morning. This is certainly not enough time for anything resembling the joint problem-solving that mediation advertises itself to be. In other counties, mediations were held in places where there was no privacy. Saposnek also stated that some mediators had little concern for confidentiality and/or an incomplete understanding of the statutory scheme for confidentiality. For the statutory language on confidentiality, see *infra* note 29 and accompanying text.

27. The California Civil Code required the Judicial Council to adopt standards and offer training on them by January 1, 1991. *See* CAL. CIV. CODE § 4607.1 (West Supp. 1990).

28. In arguing for mandatory mediation, proponents often assume the mediation services that are being provided resemble those of the larger counties, such as San Francisco, Santa Clara, Los Angeles, and Alameda, where mediators are for the most part well-trained and highly qualified. As this Article points out, however, there are serious problems with the mandatory system even in such counties. What is more,

In California, mediations are held in private and communications to the mediator from the parties are deemed "official information" protected from disclosure by the Evidence Code.[29] The mediator has discretion to exclude counsel from the mediation,[30] whether or not the parties wish to have them present.

Local courts have the option of requiring mediators to make a recommendation to the court regarding custody or visitation.[31] If the parties do not reach

---

in many areas of the state, mediation services are poor by any standard. It is callous to expect parties to participate in these services in the hope that at some future date mediators will be properly trained.

29. CAL. CIV. CODE § 4607(c) (West 1983) provides: "Mediation proceedings shall be held in private and shall be confidential, and all communications, verbal or written, from the parties to the mediator made in a proceeding pursuant to this section shall be deemed to be official information within the meaning of Section 1040 of the Evidence Code."

CAL. EVID. CODE § 1040(b) (West Supp. 1990) provides:

> A public entity has a privilege to refuse to disclose official information, and to prevent another from disclosing official information, if the privilege is claimed by a person authorized by the public entity to do so . . . .
>
> (2) Disclosure of the information is against the public interest because there is a necessity for preserving the confidentiality of the information that outweighs the necessity for disclosure in the interest of justice . . . .

At least seven states other than California have enacted legislation specifically providing that mediation proceedings shall be confidential. *See* COLO. REV. STAT. ANN. § 13-22-307 (1986); CONN. GEN. STAT. ANN. § 46b-53 (West 1985); IOWA CODE ANN. § 679.12 (West 1987); MASS. GEN. LAWS ANN. ch. 233, § 23C (West 1986); N.Y. JUD. LAW § 849-b (Consol. 1983); OKLA. STAT. ANN. tit. 12, § 1805 (West 1991); TEX. CIV. PRAC. & REM. CODE ANN. § 154.073 (Vernon Supp. 1991). Because these statutory approaches to confidentiality vary so greatly, however, there exists much uncertainty as to how they can best be applied. Other states rely on the limited privilege given to offers to compromise. For an illustration of this privilege, see FED. R. EVID. 408. A discussion of the limitations of the privilege is contained in DONOVAN LEISURE NEWTON & IRVINE ADR PRACTICE BOOK 127-32 (J. Wilkinson ed. 1989); *see also* L. FREEDMAN, C. HAILE & H. BOOKSTAFF, CONFIDENTIALITY IN MEDIATION: A PRACTITIONER'S GUIDE 87-90 (1985) (discussing the ethical and legal duties that may compel a mediator to disclose confidential information); Folberg, *Confidentiality and Privilege in Divorce Mediation*, in DIVORCE MEDIATION, THEORY AND PRACTICE, *supra* note 14, at 319 (survey of statutory and common law regulations relating to confidentiality and privileged communications).

30. Under California law, the mediator can exclude counsel from mediation proceedings if the mediator deems this to be appropriate or necessary. CAL. CIV. CODE § 4607(d) (West Supp. 1990); *see also infra* note 246 (quoting statute). Different states, however, vary considerably in their rules as to whether attorneys may attend mediation sessions. There are states such as Kansas, which permit only the parties to attend mediation sessions. KAN. STAT. ANN. § 23-603(a)(6) (1988). Connecticut also prohibits attorneys from attending mediation over custody and visitation issues as a matter of court policy. *See* McCrory, *Legal and Practical Issues in Divorce Mediation: An American Perspective*, in THE ROLE OF MEDIATION, *supra* note 8, at 144, 152. Other states, such as Maine, actively encourage attorneys to attend the mediation sessions. Orbeton, *Domestic Relations Mediation in Maine*, in THE ROLE OF MEDIATION, *supra* note 8, at 52. In Florida some courts order attorneys to attend their clients' mediations. Talcott, *Court-Ordered Mediation in Florida*, MEDIATION Q., Spring 1989, at 77, 80. Some states leave it up to the discretion or policy of the mediation services provider as to who should attend. *See, e.g.*, WIS. STAT. ANN. § 767.11(10)(a) (West Supp. 1990).

31. CAL. CIV. CODE § 4607(e) (West Supp. 1990) provides in pertinent part: "The mediator may, consistent with local court rules, render a recommendation to the court as to the custody or visitation of the child or children . . . ." Only Minnesota has a similar provision. MINN. STAT. § 518.619(1) (1990). For discussions of the impact of having the mediator make recommendations, see McIsaac, *Confidentiality: An Exploration of the Issues*, 23 CONCILIATION CTS. REV. 63 (1985); M. Duryee, Open Mediation: A Systemic View *passim* (Dec. 3, 1987) (paper presented at winter meeting of Association of Family and Conciliation Courts, Las Vegas, Nevada, on file with author); E. Kodituwakku, Outcome Satisfaction in Mediation of Child Custody and Time Sharing as a Function of Confidentiality, Personality, and Family Dysfunction 40-45 (1989) (unpublished dissertation abstract, University of New Mexico, on file with author).

an agreement, the mediator may also make a recommendation that an investigation be conducted or mutual restraining orders be issued.[32] More than half of California counties have opted to require mediators to make such recommendations.[33] In these counties, a mediator meets with the parties and, having assured them of confidentiality, attempts to help them reach an agreement. Should they not reach an agreement, however, the mediator uses what happened in the mediation session to make a recommendation to the court. In some counties, I have observed that the recommendations of mediators are almost always accepted by the judge; indeed, some mediators disclose this fact in an effort to pressure the parties into reaching an agreement.

II. The Betrayal of Mediation's Promises

A. *The Informal Law of Mediation*

> *The good woman: She comes into mediation ready to be cooperative. She does not deny her feelings, but does not shift them onto her children. She realizes her problems are her problems, that she should not use the children as a way of solving them, and that it is critically important that her husband stay involved in the lives of the children. She does not play victim, but realizes what she is entitled to and insists on it calmly. She is rational, not bitter or vengeful, and certainly not interested in hurting her husband. She understands that she played a role in whatever harms he inflicted on her, since in a family no one person is ever at fault.*
>
> *The bad woman: She is bitter and wants revenge for things that have happened to her in the past. She fights over the most trivial, petty things. She is greedy and ready to sacrifice her children as a tool against her husband. She is irrational and unwilling to compromise. When a specific, focused response is called for, she responds by bringing up a completely unrelated matter. It is hard to keep her on track. She keeps venting her anger instead of negotiating constructively.*[34]

In even the most mundane settings there develops a type of informal law, shared expectations that there is a right way of acting, that departures from this way are wrong, and that an offender should be sanctioned.[35] The "law" that develops in these "microsocial" settings[36] is often both complex and necessary

32. Cal. Civ. Code § 4607(e) (West Supp. 1990).

33. D. Saposnek, *supra* note 24.

34. For the origin of these descriptions, see *supra* note 13.

35. *See* Reisman, *Looking, Staring and Glaring: Microlegal Systems and Public Order*, 12 Den. J. Int. L. & Pol'y 165, 172 (1983); *cf.* Wildman, *Integration in the 1980's: The Dream of Diversity and the Cycle of Exclusion*, 64 Tul. L. Rev. 1625, 1669-70 (all institutions operate through informal and formal rules, which become incorporated into a group dymanic).

36. Microsocial settings are settings in which a small group of people, as a result of their physical or social proximity, have the opportunity to interact. *See* Reisman, *supra* note 35, at 172.

for human interaction to proceed. Where norms appropriate for a situation are not prescribed or made clear, interaction is impeded and perceived as awkward. The normative components of microsocial settings may be thought of as microlegal systems.[37]

The norms that govern microlegal systems are unwritten and often not consciously perceived, but they are always present. Violation of these norms may produce strong reactions. What makes such norms distinguishable from the mere "shoulds" of daily conversation is the presence of sanctions: additional communications which accompany the "shoulds" and which punish the deviant or reward the conformist. Many of these sanctions might appear trivial at first glance—for example, laughing at or dismissing someone—but they are powerful nonetheless. According to Michael Reisman, an actor enforcing norms within a micro-legal system is often both unaware of the nature of the system and oblivious to his own functional role in it. It is not the actor's motive or self-awareness that renders his reaction a sanction, but the effect of the reaction on those sanctioned.[38]

Persons in the midst of a divorce often experience what seems to them a threat to their very survival. Their self-concepts, financial well-being, moral values, confidence in their parenting abilities, and feelings of being worthy of love are all at risk. They are profoundly concerned about whether they are meeting their obligations and continuing to be seen as virtuous persons and respectable members of society. They are especially vulnerable to the responses they receive from any professional with whom they must deal. Against this backdrop, mediation must be seen as a relatively high-risk process. To begin with, for most people it is a new setting. Its norms are generally not understood by the parties in advance, with the result that the parties are extremely sensitive to cues as to how they are supposed to act; they will look to the mediator to provide these cues. Mediators are often quite willing to give such cues, to establish the normative components of the mediation, and to sanction departures from the unwritten rules. The informal sanctions applied by a mediator can be especially powerful, quite apart from whatever actual authority he might have.[39] These sanctions might be as simple as criticizing the client for not putting the children's needs first, or instructing her not to talk about a particular issue.[40] That these informal sanctions might appear trivial does not mean they will not be as influential in changing behavior as sanctions that might on their face appear more severe; "the microsanctions of microlegal systems to which we are actually susceptible may be much more significant determinants of our

37. *See id.*

38. *See id.* at 174-75.

39. *See infra* notes 215-25 and accompanying text.

40. For an extensive description of the ways in which mediators control the mediation process and the substantive issues that are discussed, see Merry & Silbey, *Mediator Settlement Strategies*, 8 L. & POL'Y 7 (1986).

behavior than conventional macrosanctions which loom portentously, but in all likelihood will never be applied to us."[41]

In the following Section, I discuss the mediation process as a microlegal setting characterized by certain normative components. I examine the "law" of that setting with respect to the parties' relationship and emotions, and the informal sanctions that may be applied by the mediator for departures from the approved way of handling these issues.

B. *The Promise to Contextualize Decisionmaking*

1. *Principles Versus Context as the Basis for Decisionmaking*

Traditional western adjudication is often criticized for its reliance on abstract principles and rules rather than on subjective, contextualized experience.[42] It "aspires to science: to the immanent generalization subsuming the emergent particularity, to prediction and control of social regularities and regulations."[43] It relies on rights, and adopts an abstract hierarchy of rules regulating the interaction of individuals.[44] This objectivist paradigm of law focuses on a specific moment in time—when a lawsuit was filed or when an act was done or injury incurred—and applies supposedly objective principles and rules to that moment to determine who was at fault: that is, who must pay and to whom payment is due.

Of course, under the common law some context, in the form of the facts of an individual case, is also to be considered. The concern for the particular facts of a dispute has been characterized as a feminine search for context, while the pursuit of applicable legal principles has been viewed as a masculine search for certainty and abstract rules.[45] To the extent that its issues are framed merely as questions of law, simply involving precedents and rights, the result in a case may be insensitive to the particular facts of the dispute. The invocation of stare decisis to establish the broad rules of a decision also serves to minimize the importance of the factual context to the resolution of a particular case. Finally, a primary focus on questions of law masks many underlying social and political questions.[46]

Where child custody is being determined, a system that ostensibly brings context—*this* mother, *this* father, *these* children—into the process of dispute resolution, and renders a decision based on the lives of those actually involved in the dispute rather than on the basis of a general rule, has much to offer.

41. Reisman, *supra* note 35, at 177.
42. *See* Rifkin, *Toward a Theory*, *supra* note 1, at 87.
43. MacKinnon, *Feminism, Marxism*, supra note 3, at 655-56.
44. *See* Karst, *Woman's Constitution*, 1984 DUKE L.J. 447, 462.
45. *See, e.g.*, Menkel-Meadow, *supra* note 1, at 49.
46. Rifkin, *Toward a Theory*, *supra* note 1, at 87.

There is, however, a cost to this change in emphasis; for although the language of legal rights may divert public consciousness away from the real roots of anger, the assertion of rights may also clarify and elucidate those roots. The process of claiming rights, by itself, can be empowering for people who have not shared societal power.[47] Thus the risk of mediation is that if principles are abandoned, and context is not effectively introduced, we end up with the worst of both worlds.

a. *Principles and Fault in the Adversary System*

A series of attempts has been made to make the court system more responsive to the actual situation of persons undergoing a divorce and to their children by deemphasizing claims of right and principle. The first of these attempts consisted of reduced reliance on the notion of fault.[48] Before this change, the principles shaping the legal process of divorce were not difficult to discern. In the absence of flagrant misconduct on the part of the spouse, one was to stay in one's marriage. One was not to engage in adultery. A man was to support his wife and children. A mother was to be the primary caretaker of her children.[49]

Bright-line legal rules were based on these principles. At the time of divorce, a determination was made as to who was at fault, and this person could expect legal consequences to arise from his transgression. The injuries and indignities a party might have endured were recognized. In fact, a person who was not at fault could often halt the divorce.[50] A mother ordinarily received custody unless she was shown to be unfit. A man would be ordered to support his ex-wife indefinitely, assuming that the marriage had been of a reasonable duration.[51]

With the advent of "no-fault" divorce, these rules changed, signaling an as yet undefined departure from the principles upon which they had been based. It is now typical for states to allow divorce on grounds that do not require fault by either spouse.[52] For the most part, one spouse need only show that the marital relationship is irreparable. These changes have increased the individual autonomy of married persons and given husbands and wives freedom to extri-

---

47. *See infra* note 90 and accompanying text. *See generally* the minority critiques of Critical Legal Studies compiled in 22 HARV. C.R.-C.L. L. REV. (1987). In particular, see Matsuda, *Looking to the Bottom: Critical Legal Studies & Reparations*, 22 HARV. C.R.-C.L. L. REV. 323, 340-41 (1987) (trust in Constitution has sustained Japanese-Americans in their struggle to transform society), and Williams, *Alchemical Notes: Reconstructing Ideals from Deconstructed Rights*, 22 HARV. C.R.-C.L. L. REV. 401, 404-05 (1987) (criticizing Critical Legal Studies for ignoring the degree to which rights-assertion has benefitted Blacks).

48. *See* L. WEITZMAN, THE DIVORCE REVOLUTION 15-31 (1985).

49. *See id*; *see also* Teitlebaum & DuPaix, *Alternative Dispute Resolution and Divorce: Natural Experimentation in Family Law*, 40 RUTGERS L. REV. 1093, 1096 (1988) (noting that until the early 1970's, child custody disputes were subject to presumption that mother should receive custody).

50. *See* L. WEITZMAN, *supra* note 48, at 10.

51. *See id.* at 11.

52. *See* Freed & Walker, *Family Law in the Fifty States: An Overview*, 20 FAM. L.Q. 439, 460 (1987).

cate themselves from unhappy relationships. They have reduced the oppressiveness of principles which, although written into the law, did not fit the manner in which many persons choose to lead their lives.

But there have been other consequences of these changes. For example, results were once much more predictable than they are now, both in terms of the availability of support and the likelihood of the father's being able to obtain custody of the children.[53] This lack of predictability generally harms the party who has the lesser amount of power in the relationship, or who is most risk averse.[54] Moreover, to a certain extent community values have been eliminated from the process by which the state recognizes marriage and its end. While the principles that formerly controlled the process were outmoded and sexist and resulted in much unnecessary pain for persons whose marriages were ending, they were not replaced by different principles based on different values. Quite suddenly it became close to irrelevant whether one member of the couple had deceived, sexually or financially abused, or otherwise oppressed, the other.[55] As a result of these changes, it became much more difficult for persons to know whether they had complied with their societal responsibilities and to have their efforts to do so recognized.

Still, when people enter the adversary process they generally believe that they are entering an arena in which principles *are* at stake, and in which what transpires is at least partially a matter of right and justice.[56] In addition, the adversarial process itself aspires to a rule of law as its governing principle, a worthy aspiration for any decisionmaking process.[57]

b. *Principles and Fault in Mediation*

The introduction of mediation into family court processes was another part of the effort to make the adversary system fit the realities of divorce more closely. Mediators stepped into the increasingly uncertain legal world of dissolution with a new process which minimized the role of principles and fault. Mediation appeared to provide the opportunity to bring the lessons of context and subjective experience to dissolution proceedings. In mediation, the parties'

---

53. *See* Teitlebaum & DuPaix, *supra* note 49, at 1098.

54. *See* Mnookin & Kornhauser, *Bargaining in the Shadow of the Law: The Case of Divorce*, 88 YALE L.J. 950, 978-80 (1979); Neely, *The Primary Caretaker Parent Rule: Child Custody and the Dynamics of Greed*, 3 YALE L. & POL'Y REV. 168, 177-79 (1984); Teitlebaum & DuPaix, *supra* note 49, at 1099-1100.

55. *See* L. WEITZMAN, *supra* note 48, at 24. In Weitzman's study, most respondents expressed discomfort with the norm, prevalent in the no-fault divorce context, that no consequences whatsoever—including financial sanctions or even courtroom embarrassment—are to be imposed on an adulterous spouse. *Id.*

56. *See* Merry & Silbey, *What Do Plaintiffs Want? Reexamining the Concept of Dispute*, 9 JUST. SYS. J. 151, 153 (1984); Teitlebaum & DuPaix, *supra* note 49, at 1126-27; *see also* S. MERRY, GETTING JUSTICE AND GETTING EVEN 37 (1990) (people who bring disputes to the courts usually do so with some sense of entitlement).

57. For some interesting recent reflections on the rule of law, see Radin, *Reconsidering the Rule of Law*, 69 B.U.L. REV. 781 (1989); Massey, *The Rule of Law and the Age of Aquarius* (Book Review), 41 HAST. L.J. 757 (1990).

legal rights would not be central. Instead of relying solely on abstract principles and rules, parties and mediators could attend to the reality of complex relationships. Precedent, legal rules and a legalized formulation of the facts might be seen as irrelevant to the mediation process and an unnecessary constraint on the mediator.[58] Individuals could be seen in relation to one another, and morality treated as "a question of responsibilities to particular people in particular contexts."[59]

The informal law of the mediation setting requires that discussion of principles, blame, and rights, as these terms are used in the adversarial context, be deemphasized or avoided. Mediators use informal sanctions to encourage the parties to replace the rhetoric of fault, principles, and values with the rhetoric of compromise and relationship.[60] For example, mediators typically suggest that the parties "eschew[] the language of individual rights in favor of the language of interdependent relationships."[61] They orient the parties toward reasonableness and compromise, rather than moral vindication. The conflict may be styled as a personal quarrel, in which there is no right and wrong, but simply two different, and equally true or untrue, views of the world.

(1) *Are All Agreements Equal?*

The reason for the lack of focus on values and principles in many models of mediation is, in part, simply practical. If the essence of mediation entails trading off interests and compromising, each person's interests are important, but which person violated societal values and why he did so, is not. To the extent that principles and faultfinding based on those principles enter into the discussion, reaching an agreement might be delayed or disrupted. Deemphasizing principles also might appear to be the sensible approach in a society that is increasingly pluralistic in terms of cultures, religions, and varieties of family structures.[62] Where there are conflicting moral codes, as there often are when couples divorce, making the only standard for agreement be that it is accepted by both parties means that it will not be necessary for a third party to decide which moral code is superior.[63]

---

58. *See* Rifkin, *Mediation*, *supra* note 1, at 27.

59. Karst, *supra* note 44, at 462.

60. *See* Fineman, *supra* note 6, at 731-34; Merry & Silbey, *supra* note 40, at 29.

61. Merry & Silbey, *supra* note 40, at 29.

62. Traditional nuclear families, that is, families with both a male and female parent who are married to each other and live with their children all under one roof, constitute less than half of U.S. households. As of 1988, U.S. Census Bureau statistics showed that 42.2% of households consisted of married couples with their own children under the age of 18 (the traditional nuclear family); 27.8% of households were married couples without their children under 18; 11.6% of households were headed by women with no spouse present; 3.3% were headed by men with no spouse present; and 13.1% were defined as "non-family." U.S. BUREAU OF THE CENSUS, STATISTICAL ABSTRACT OF THE UNITED STATES: 1990, at 48 (110th ed.).

63. *See* Merry, *Anthropology and the Study of Alternative Dispute Resolution*, 34 J. LEGAL EDUC. 277, 282 (1984).

Sometimes, however, all agreements are not equal. It may be important, from both a societal and an individual standpoint, to have an agreement that reflects cultural notions of justice and not merely one to which there has been mutual assent.[64] Many see the courts as a place where they can obtain vindication and a ruling by a higher authority.[65] It is also important in some situations for society to send a clear message as to how children are to be treated, what the obligations of ex-spouses are to each other and to their children, and what sort of behavior will not be tolerated. Because the mediation movement tends to regard negotiated settlements as morally superior to adjudication, these functions of adjudication may easily be overlooked.[66]

(2) *Conceptual Underpinnings: Family Systems and Circular Causality*

On a more theoretical level, the reluctance to discuss principles is based on the view, held by most mediators, that the family is a self-contained system. Under this view, all parts of the family are equally implicated in whatever happens within it. Each part of this system is simultaneously a cause for, and an effect of, all the other parts. Relationship problems represent "a mutually regulated dance between oppressor and oppressed."[67] Causality is circular; that is, "[n]o specific situation or person is considered the antecedent, cause, or effect of [the] problem."[68] Under this approach, "the mediator can view the interactional system between the husband and wife in such a way that each spouse's behavior appears perfectly complementary to that of the other spouse and the concepts of reasonable and unreasonable no longer apply."[69]

Although this systems approach can be a useful one in understanding how families and other social organizations work, it has some serious shortcomings. Most critically, it obscures issues of unequal social power and sex role socialization. Structures within the nuclear family are viewed in isolation from outside social attitudes and forces. Thus, a person who has been a victim of violence can be seen as deserving her fate because of her self-defeating patterns

64. *See* J. AUERBACH, JUSTICE WITHOUT LAW? 136, 144-46 (1983); Abel, *The Contradiction of Informal Justice*, in THE POLITICS OF INFORMAL JUSTICE 267, 290-93 (R. Abel ed. 1982). Law also plays an important ideological role in our society, encompassing our aspiration to justice.

65. *See* Merry & Silbey, *supra* note 56, at 153.

66. *See* Walker, *Family Conciliation in Great Britain: From Research to Practice to Research*, MEDIATION Q., Summer 1989, at 29, 46-51; *see also* Crouch, *Divorce Mediation and Legal Ethics*, 16 FAM. L.Q. 219, 243 (1982):

> As it is taught today, mediation theory is characterized by the underlying assumption that all issues can and must be compromised. However, there can be cases imagined wherein this is simply irrational. It could be that the compromiser role requires that one make peace with oppression, suffer fools gladly, redefine black as white, and meet utter nonsense halfway.

67. Libow, Raskin & Caust, *Feminist and Family Systems Therapy: Are They Irreconcilable?*, 10 AM. J. FAM. THERAPY 3, 8 (1982).

68. Enns, *Dilemmas of Power and Equality in Marital and Family Counseling: Proposals for a Feminist Perspective*, 67 J. COUNSELING & DEV. 242, 243 (1988).

69. D. SAPOSNEK, MEDIATING CHILD CUSTODY DISPUTES 180 (1983).

of behavior and participation in cyclical negative interactions with her spouse.[70] In this manner, the family systems approach imposes a value-free universe. It does not leave room for the situation in which one parent is complying with the legitimate expectations of society and the other is not.[71] Yet the family systems approach would suggest that both parents, as well as the children, are all somehow responsible for a family's ills.

In sum, the notion that people are jointly responsible for their interactions is only partly true. Moreover, an unrefined family systems perspective can deprive a divorcing spouse of the opportunity to appear virtuous in society's eyes and her own. No matter how much she struggles, her good works are for naught so long as she is connected to someone who is acting irresponsibly.[72] To the extent mediation incorporates such a family systems perspective, the spouse who is doing "good work" must bear the burden of the other spouse's noncompliance.

2. *The Destroyers of Context: Prospectivity and Formal Equality*

a. *Prospectivity*

> *Kenny had spent ten days with his father Jerry and was scheduled to return to his mother on a flight arriving on Thanksgiving afternoon. That morning, Jerry called Linda and told her that flying was expensive, and that he was returning to his ex-wife's area at Christmas anyway. He said he intended to keep Kenny with him until then; Kenny's stepmother would care for Kenny at their home. Linda, her Thanksgiving dinner in the oven and relatives scheduled to arrive, thought of going*

---

70. *See* Enns, *supra* note 68, at 243; *see also* Rice, *Mediation and Arbitration as a Civil Alternative to the Criminal Justice System—An Overview and Legal Analysis*, 29 AM. U.L. REV. 17, 22-23 (1979) ("[B]oth parties may be culpable when an entire dispute or relationship is considered .... Mediation/arbitration programs ... emphasize the personal responsibility of each party rather than the narrow assessment of legal fault.").

71. *See* Kressel, Butler-DeFreitas, Forlenza & Wilcox, *Research in Contested Custody Mediations: An Illustration of the Case Study Method*, MEDIATION Q., Summer 1989, at 55 [hereinafter Kressel, *Custody Mediations*]. These authors measured parents for characteristics of a profile they labeled an "Interpersonally Dysfunctional Parent" (IDP). *Id.* at 59. Measures in this profile included narcissistic preoccupation, dismissiveness toward the other parent—particularly with respect to childcare arrangements—and general irresponsibility. *Id.* They found that often only one parent in a relationship fit the profile, and that in 8 of the 12 cases they studied, one parent (the father in all but one case) was therefore primarily responsible for the problems in the coparenting relationship. *Id.*

72. In the discussion of their findings, Kressel and his coauthors state that

> [a]lthough one can find occasional reference to the fact that some divorce conflicts are rooted in one spouse's highly disturbed behavior, it is far more typical for the causes of destructive divorce to be described as mutual to both husband and wife. The "equal blame" perspective is encouraged by family systems theory (in which divorce mediation has significant roots) ....

Id. at 65. Although the authors expected to find support for the equal blame theory, they found the opposite. The use of equal blame theory in mediation causes the nondysfunctional partner (usually the mother) to share the responsibility for the dysfunctional partner's behavior in a way that adversely affects the mediation outcome for the nondysfunctional partner.

herself to pick up Kenny or going to court, but decided that the worst thing for Kenny would be a custody battle.

When Kenny returned at Christmas, his behavior was odd; for the first time in his life he was violent and aggressive toward other children. Upon questioning Kenny, Linda discovered that he had not been cared for by his stepmother during the day as promised, but had instead been sent to unlicensed daycare where the teacher had regularly used corporal punishment, to which Linda was passionately opposed and to which Kenny had never before been subjected.

In mediation, Linda asks that she be given primary custody of Kenny. She says that Jerry has been untruthful, unreliable, and has risked Kenny's emotional and physical well-being. She tries to argue that such a young child needs one home base, and that should be her home since she was effectively his sole parent for most of his first three years of life. The mediator does not allow her to make these points. Instead, she says that the past is not to be discussed; rather, they must plan together about the future. She says that whether Jerry participated in Kenny's life for his early years is irrelevant; he is here now. The Thanksgiving situation is past history, and she is sure that they both have complaints about the past. Blaming one another is counterproductive. The mediator tells Linda that she must recognize that the parent who has the child is responsible for choosing daycare. Linda must learn to give up control.[73]

The chief means by which mediators eliminate the discussion of principles and fault is by making certain types of discussion "off-limits" in the mediation. Mediation experts Jay Folberg and Alison Taylor propose the following as one of the "shared propositions" upon which nearly all mediators agree:

> *Proposition 5.* In mediation the past history of the participants is only important in relation to the present or as a basis for predicting future needs, intentions, abilities, and reactions to decisions.[74]

It is typical for mediators to insist that parties waste no time complaining about past conduct of their spouse, eschew blaming each other, and focus only on the future. For example, one of the two essential ground rules mediator Donald Saposnek suggests a mediator give to the parties is the following:

> There is little value in talking about the past, since it only leads to fighting and arguing, as I'm sure you both know . . . . Our focus will be on your children's needs for the future and on how you two can

73. For the origin of this mediation story, see *supra* note 13. After a year spent in a custody arrangement under which Kenny lived alternate months with Linda and with Jerry, and following a second mediation, Linda gave up physical custody of Kenny to Jerry. She believed that the schedule was traumatic to Kenny, and felt that the mediator would recommend in Jerry's favor in a custody battle anyway based on the friendly parent principle.

74. J. FOLBERG & A. TAYLOR, MEDIATION 14 (1984).

> satisfy those needs. . . . [U]nless I specifically request it, we will talk about plans for the future.[75]

Thus, while one of the principal justifications for introducing mediation into the divorce process is that context will be substituted for abstract principles, in fact, by eliminating discussion of the past, context—in the sense of the relationship's history—is removed. The result is that we are left with neither principles nor context as a basis for decisionmaking.

In Linda's case, the questions of whether Jerry had been remiss in not returning Kenny or in secretly placing Kenny in an inadequate childcare situation were ruled irrelevant by the mediator. The mediator did not permit discussion of these issues because reaching an agreement was paramount, and because, under family systems theory as interpreted by the mediator, Jerry could not be at fault—Linda and Jerry were equally responsible for everything. That Jerry had virtually disappeared, leaving Linda to struggle to raise her son alone, and that Jerry had not kept his word about returning Kenny after his visit were simply not proper subjects of discussion. There was nothing Linda could say to introduce these concerns into the dialogue. Further, she could not refer to the past to demonstrate she was a responsible and loving parent. Her attempts to protect her son were labelled as controlling.

b. *Prospectivity and the Assertion of Rights*

> *A woman I knew only vaguely from my daughter's school called me, her voice shaking, and asked me if I could mediate her case. I said that I could not, but would be glad to talk to her and refer her to other mediators. She told me that her husband had told her two days previously that he was leaving her and intended to marry someone else. He told her he wanted to have the divorce mediated and wanted joint custody of the children. He told her she would have to start looking for a job right away. He also told his wife that it would hurt the children if he and she were angry at each other, and that he wanted to retain a friendly, cordial relationship and have a rational, peaceful divorce. She cried into the phone that she felt terrible that she was unable to be rational, and that although she was trying hard to be mature, she still had these angry feelings. She still wanted to blame him, although she realized, she said, that nothing is ever black and white, and no one is at fault when a marriage breaks up.*[76]

Felstiner, Abel and Sarat note that some people are apparently able to tolerate substantial amounts of distress and injustice.[77] This "tolerance," they

75. D. SAPOSNEK, *supra* note 69, at 70.

76. For the origin of this story, see *supra* note 13.

77. *See* Felstiner, Abel & Sarat, *The Emergence and Transformation of Disputes: Naming, Blaming, Claiming* . . ., 15 L. & SOC'Y REV. 631, 633 (1980-81).

posit, comes from a failure to perceive that they have been injured. They describe a three-step process by which (1) injurious experiences are perceived (naming), (2) are transformed into grievances (blaming), and, (3) ultimately, become disputes (claiming).[78] "Naming" involves saying to oneself that a particular experience has been injurious.[79] The acquaintance who called me could barely go this far. "Blaming" occurs when a person attributes fault to another (rather than to an impersonal force, such as luck or the weather). One cannot arrive at "claiming," that is, the assertion of rights, without passing through "blaming."[80] By making blaming off-limits, the process by which a dispute is fully developed—and rights are asserted—cannot be completed. Short-circuiting the blaming process may fall most heavily on those who are already at a disadvantage in society. Whether people "perceive an experience as an injury, blame someone else, claim redress, or get their claims accepted . . . [is a function of] their *social position* as well as their individual characteristics."[81]

The cultural commitment to access to justice[82] has focused on the last stage of disputing—claiming. The more critical place at which inequality is manifested, however, is before experiences are transformed into disputes,[83] that is, at the naming and blaming stages. One adverse consequence of de-emphasizing discussion of principle and fault is that some persons may be discouraged from asserting their rights when they have been injured. Even more troubling, some persons may cease to perceive injuries when they have been injured, or will perceive injuries but those injuries will remain inarticulable, because the language to name them will not be easily available. My acquaintance whose husband had an affair and left her did not trust her sense that she had been injured, treated in a way that human beings ought not to deal with each other. She did not have the support of a clear set of legal principles to help her define her injury; rather, she had been exposed to a discourse in which faultfinding was impermissible, so that she ended up unable to hold her husband responsible for his actions, and instead felt compelled to share his fault. To the extent that there is something to be gained by the assertion of rights, especially for women and minorities,[84] this is unacceptable.

---

78. *Id.*

79. *Id.* at 635-36.

80. *Id*; *cf.* Littleton, *Women's Experience and the Problem of Transition: Perspectives on Male Battering of Women*, 1989 U. CHI. L.F. 23, 38 (focusing on woman's psychological reaction to battering rather than on batterer's behavior makes it difficult for legal system to stop violence).

81. Felstiner, Abel & Sarat, *supra* note 77, at 636.

82. Some might dispute whether our society has a real commitment to access to justice. Nonetheless, from Gideon v. Wainwright, 372 U.S. 335 (1963), *see generally* A. LEWIS, GIDEON'S TRUMPET (1964), to the creation of the Legal Services Corporation, *see* Washington Post, Oct. 23, 1977, at C1, col. 3, at least lip service has been paid to the notion that the disadvantaged deserve legal representation.

83. Felstiner, Abel & Sarat, *supra* note 77, at 637.

84. *See* Williams, *supra* note 47, at 427-33.

Many writers have debated recently whether legal rights have some intrinsic value, especially in the context of rights that define the boundaries of state power.[85] Some Critical Legal Studies theorists have suggested that rights claims perpetuate dichotomies such as individual and community, self and other, and family and market, and thus do not promote social reconstruction.[86] They also criticize the "reification" of rights—that is, the conceptualizing of rights as real, or thing-like, resulting in the acceptance of the existing social order as an inevitable fact of life.[87] Feminist critiques of rights have been based on the characterization of rights claims as formal and hierarchical and, therefore, patriarchal.[88] Both critiques emphasize the ways in which discussion of rights can lead to increased alienation and passivity.

In recent years, a number of women and minority scholars have challenged these critiques of rights, suggesting that rights claims may in fact help enhance and develop individual and political growth.[89] Although the debate usually focuses on "rights" in a very different sense from those at stake when, for example, a mother wants sole rather than joint custody, the debate is useful in considering what the consequences might be of making discussion of principles and fault off-limits in the context of custody. In particular, the literature suggesting that the assertion of rights may have a transformative function applies in this context.[90]

For example, Elizabeth Schneider has demonstrated that assertion of rights can aid in the development of individual and group consciousness among women.[91] She notes that Carol Gilligan describes the developmental challenges

85. *See, e.g.*, Gabel, *The Phenomenology of Rights-Consciousness and the Pact of the Withdrawn Selves*, 62 TEX. L. REV. 1563 (1984); Gabel & Harris, *Building Power and Breaking Images: Critical Legal Theory and the Practice of Law*, 11 N.Y.U. REV. L. & SOC. CHANGE 369 (1982-83); Olsen, *The Family and the Market: A Study of Ideology and Legal Reform*, 96 HARV. L. REV. 1497 (1983); Tushnet, *An Essay on Rights*, 62 TEX. L. REV. 1363 (1984).

86. *See, e.g.*, Brest, *The Fundamental Rights Controversy: The Essential Contradictions of Normative Constitutional Scholarship*, 90 YALE L.J. 1063, 1108 (1981); Kennedy, *The Structure of Blackstone's Commentaries*, 28 BUFFALO L. REV. 209, 212-13 (1979); Sparer, *Fundamental Human Rights, Legal Entitlements and the Social Struggle: A Friendly Critique of the Critical Legal Studies Movement*, 36 STAN. L. REV. 509, 516 (1984).

87. *See, e.g.*, Gabel, *supra* note 85, at 1581; Gabel & Harris, *supra* note 85, at 373 n.10; Gabel & Kennedy, *Roll Over Beethoven*, 36 STAN. L. REV. 1, 3-6 (1984).

88. *See, e.g.*, C. MACKINNON, TOWARD A FEMINIST THEORY, *supra* note 3, at 46-47; MacKinnon, *Feminism, Marxism*, supra note 3, at 644-45; Polan, *supra* note 1, at 300; Rifkin, *Toward a Theory*, *supra* note 1, at 86. These writers are critical of rights, but do not suggest that rights claims be given up completely.

89. *See, e.g.*, Dalton, *The Clouded Prism*, 22 HARV. C.R.-C.L. L. REV. 435, 441-47 (1987); Delgado, *The Ethereal Scholar: Does Critical Legal Studies Have What Minorities Want?*, 22 HARV. C.R.-C.L. L. REV. 301, 314-22 (1987); Matsuda, *supra* note 47, at 363-99; Schneider, *The Dialectic of Rights and Politics: Perspectives from The Women's Movement*, 61 N.Y.U. L. REV. 589, 648-52 (1986); Williams, *supra* note 47, at 427-33.

90. Pat Williams has argued that the Critical Legal Studies movement has ignored the degree to which rights-assertion and the benefits of rights have helped Blacks, other minorities, and the poor. As Williams has put it: "[I]t is very hard to watch the idealistic or symbolic importance of rights being diminished with reference to the disenfranchised, who experience and express their disempowerment as nothing more or less than the denial of rights." Williams, *supra* note 47, at 405.

91. *See* Schneider, *supra* note 89, 623-48.

of maturity as very different for men and for women. Men must learn connection and care for others; women must learn to care for themselves. The assertion of rights can aid women in this development, as "[t]he essential notion of rights [is] that the interests of the self can be considered legitimate."[92] Thus, assertion of rights can help women distinguish self from other, and ultimately give them a sense of collective identity.[93]

My acquaintance whose husband abandoned her was unable to view either her needs or her feelings as legitimate; as far as she was concerned, the important players in her own personal drama were her husband and children, but not herself. Both the current state of divorce law and the reigning model of mediation were operating to keep her in a position in which she tried not to blame others and, in the process, lost herself. Whatever the other limitations of Gilligan's work,[94] her suggestion that assertion of rights can be transformative for many women merits careful attention. To the extent that the mediation process makes it difficult to assert rights, the positive implications of rights-assertion for women, the poor, and minorities of either sex will be lost.

Rights assertion cannot take place in a context in which discussion of fault and the past are not permitted, for recognition and assertion of rights are ordinarily based on some perceived past grievance, as well as on some notion of right and wrong. From the point of view of the courts, minimizing conflict is always a good thing: less litigation means less expenditure of court time and resources. From the point of view of the individual, however, conflict sometimes must occur. Conflict may mean that the individual has realized he has been injured, and that he is appropriately resisting the continuation of that injury. The perception of injury arises from a sense of entitlement, which in turn is "a function of the prevailing ideology, of which law is simply a component."[95] If mediation creates a sense of disentitlement, it will interfere with the perception and redress of injuries in cases where they have in fact occurred.

c. *Formal Equality*

Context is also destroyed by a commitment to formal equality, that is, to the notion that members of mediating couples are, to the extent possible, to be treated exactly alike, without regard for general social patterns and with limited

92. *Id.* at 615 (quoting C. GILLIGAN, *supra* note 10, at 149).

93. Schneider suggests that rights can be "an essential way of understanding and experiencing self-in-other, a foundation for selfhood, and can be critical to the growth and development of any movement." Schneider, *supra* note 89, at 617 (footnote omitted). She argues that the assertion of rights in this manner links the individual to a broader social group, helping to transcend the dichotomy of individual and community. *Id.* at 617-18.

94. *See infra* notes 263-68 and accompanying text.

95. Felstiner, Abel & Sarat, *supra* note 77, at 643.

attention to even the history of the particular couples.[96] Thus, it becomes close to irrelevant in determining custody that the mother may have been home doing virtually all the caretaking of the children for years; she is to move into the labor market as quickly as possible.[97] It is assumed that the father is equally competent to care for the children. In fact, it frequently is said that one cannot assume that a father will not be as competent a caretaker as the mother just because he has not shown any interest previously:

> Many women have told me, "He never did anything with the children. If he is given even part-time responsibility for them, he'll ignore them, he won't know what to do."
>
> Research has shown, however, that little correlation exists between men's involvement with the children before and after divorce. . . . When they gain independent responsibility for the children, many men who were relatively uninvolved during the marriage become loving and responsive parents after divorce.[98]

In mediation, insistence on this sort of formal equality results in a dismissal of the legitimate concerns of the parent who is, or considers herself to be, the more responsible parent. Such concerns are often minimized by characterizing them as evidence of some pathology on the part of the parent holding them.[99] The insistence of a mother that a young child not be permitted to stay overnight with an alcoholic father who smokes in bed might be characterized as the mother needing to stay in control.[100] Or the mediator might suggest that it is not legitimate for one party to assume that the other party will renege on her

96. The formal equality to which this discussion refers exists only between the two parties to a particular mediation. Some might argue that mediation lacks a commitment to formal equality, since abstract rights are not incorporated into mediation and people engaged in different mediation processes in similar positions might end up with different outcomes. Yet, mediation does evince a commitment to formal equality as between the participants, treating them as coequals regardless of their history.

This formal equality problem surfaces in the no-fault divorce arena as well, particularly with respect to alimony awards. As Weitzman explains:

> No fault attempts to treat men and women equally—or *as if they were equal*—at the point of divorce. However, it ignores the structural inequality between men and women in the larger society. Divorced women and divorced men do not have the same opportunities: the women are more likely to face job and salary discrimination and more likely to be restricted by custodial responsibilities.

L. WEITZMAN, *supra* note 48, at 35. Weitzman notes that divorced women and their children experience a 73% decline in their standard of living while divorced men experience a 42% rise in their standard of living in the first year after divorce. *Id.* at xii.

97. *See id.* at 33. Although this represents a new expectation for middle- and upper-class women, working-class women, who comprise the majority of the divorcing population, ordinarily did not receive alimony even prior to the changes in the divorce laws. *Id.*

98. R. ADLER, SHARING THE CHILDREN 33 (1988).

99. *See* Fineman, *supra* note 6, at 766 (finding unsettling extent to which allegations of abusive or neglectful behavior by husbands toward their wives or children is trivialized by rhetoric that reduces to pathology mother's desire for custody or control of child); *see also* Lerman, *Mediation of Wife Abuse Cases: The Adverse Impact of Informal Dispute Resolution on Women*, 7 HARV. WOMEN'S L.J. 57, 71-100 (1984) (discussing problems with mediation in context of cases involving wife abuse).

100. Bruch, *supra* note 24, at 119.

obligations, simply because she has done so in the past. In the example above,[101] once Linda was in mediation, she was treated exactly equally with Jerry even though their past parental performance had been dramatically different. The point is not that mothers never inappropriately desire to stay in control, or that people who have not fulfilled their obligations once will continue to fail to do so, but rather that by defining the process as one in which both parties are situated equally, deep, heartfelt, and often accurate concerns either are not permitted to be expressed or are discounted.

Equating fairness in mediation with formal equality results in, at most, a crabbed and distorted fairness on a microlevel; it considers only the mediation context itself. There is no room in such an approach for a discussion of the fairness of institutionalized societal inequality. For example, women do not have the earning power that men have, and therefore are not in an economically equal position in the world. All too often mediators stress the need for women to become economically independent without taking into account the very real dollar differences between the male and female experience in the labor market.[102] While gaining independence might appear to be desirable, most jobs available for women, especially those who have been out of the labor market, are low paying, repetitious, and demeaning.[103] Studies show that women in such dead-end jobs do not experience the glories of independence, but rather show increased depression.[104]

d. *Equal Control, Unequal Responsibility*

> *Linda had taken a low-paying job in a childcare center so that Kenny could be with her while she worked. Jerry continued to work the chaotic schedule required by the railroad. After determining that Linda and Jerry would share custody of Kenny, the mediator asked Jerry what schedule would work for him. Jerry said that he could not be tied down to a particular schedule because his job on the railroad required him to be available at short notice and out of town for long periods of time. When Linda protested that both she and Kenny needed a predictable schedule, and that she had spent her entire married life at the mercy*

101. *See supra* text accompanying note 73.

102. *See, e.g.*, Haynes, *Divorce Mediator: A New Role*, 23 SOC. WORK 5, 8 (1978). This is not to say that all men and all women have equivalent experiences. For example, the comparative positioning of Black women versus Black men in the labor market is very different from that of white women versus white men. *See* U.S. BUREAU OF THE CENSUS, *supra* note 62, at 454 (mean incomes in 1987 were: Black males, $14,391; Black females, $9,919; white males, $23,643; white females, $11,621); *cf.* E. SPELMAN, INESSENTIAL WOMAN 115-32 (1988) (Black men do not have authority over Black women that white men do over white women).

103. Enns, *supra* note 68, at 243.

104. *See* Belle, *Inequality and Mental Health: Low Income and Minority Women*, in WOMEN AND MENTAL HEALTH POLICY 135, 146 (L. Walker ed. 1984); Carmen, Russo & Miller, *Inequality and Mental Health: An Overview*, in THE GENDER GAP IN PSYCHOTHERAPY 17, 23-24 (1984).

of the whims of his employer, the mediator smiled sympathetically and said, "I guess you didn't get to divorce the railroad after all."[105]

The notion of equality, used so effectively to remove control of children from women by treating men as equally entitled to custody regardless of their prior childcare responsibilities, is not nearly so effective when it comes to requiring men to assume responsibility for their children should they choose not to. One rarely hears of joint custody's being used to mandate that a father participate in the raising of his child although many women might desire that help.[106] But fathers who wish to participate even marginally in childrearing are given full rights, and even special privileges to enable them to do so.[107] These privileges are paid for by the mother in terms of inconvenience and instability in her own life. Fathers who do not want to be concerned with raising their children need only pay support, and many do not even do that.[108] Despite the presumption in favor of joint custody, it is assumed, by and large, that the mother will be available to care physically and emotionally for the children for as much or as little time as she is granted.[109]

Western wage labor is based on the availability of an "ideal" worker with no childcare responsibilities.[110] Joan Williams has written that in this system men are raised to believe they have the right and responsibility to perform as ideal workers. Women are raised to believe that they should be able to spend some time with their small children and, upon return to outside employment, must shape their work around the reality that they have continuing childcare responsibilities.[111]

The laws governing custody are now, in theory, gender neutral.[112] Mediators, however, are as likely as others in society to assume that women's work commitments are secondary to those of men, and to give more credence to the work obligations and ambitions of fathers. Women may be encouraged in

---

105. For the origin of this mediation story, see *supra* note 13.

106. *See* L. WEITZMAN, *supra* note 48, at 370. Weitzman points out that there is no legal cause of action to compel fathers to see their children: "The implicit message is that joint parenting—and even parenting itself—is an 'optional' responsibility for fathers." *Id.*

107. *See id.* at 233 (though numbers of fathers requesting custody is small, nearly two-thirds of those who request it are awarded it).

108. *See id.* at 353-54 (data indicate that 25% of fathers make only some of payments required by child support orders, while nearly 30% do not comply at all.).

109. There are, however, occasional situations in which joint custody is settled upon because neither parent wants full custody of the children. *See, e.g.*, J. HAYNES & G. HAYNES, MEDIATING DIVORCE 228-71 (1989).

110. *See* Frug, *Securing Job Equality for Women: Labor Market Hostility to Working Mothers*, 59 B.U.L. REV. 55, 56 (1979); Williams, *supra* note 10, at 822.

111. *See* Williams, *supra* note 10, at 823; *see also Business Forum: Women in the Work Force: The Mommy Track vs. the Fast Track*, N.Y. Times, May 21, 1989, § 3, at 2, col. 3 (discussing need for businesses to accommodate unique needs of female employees who wish to raise families).

112. This was not always the case. Courts in earlier years used the "tender years" doctrine to presume that children younger than seven should be placed with their mothers. *See* J. AREEN, FAMILY LAW 425-33 (1985); *see also* Fineman, *supra* note 6, at 738 (discussing successful challenges to tender years doctrine).

mediation not to think of themselves as ideal workers so that they will be able to take on primary responsibility for the children.[113]

The result of assuming that one parent will make herself available in this way is that disproportionately more attention is paid to ensuring the access of the parent without physical custody (usually the father) to his children than to meeting the needs of the parent who, in all likelihood, will bear the primary responsibility for these children.

Custody decrees frequently specify joint legal or physical custody,[114] or both, when in fact the children are with one parent—generally the mother—as much or more than children who are living under a sole custody arrangement.[115] The result of such a discrepancy under a joint custody arrangement is that the caretaking parent may be subject to the control of the noncaretaking parent without being relieved of any sizeable amount of day-to-day responsibility for the children.

In Linda's case, her having taken a low-paying job to enable her to care for her son while Jerry had a job which took him away from his son was not considered pertinent in determining who would have physical custody of Kenny (although it might have been had Linda been the one who had taken the railroad job). In determining how the joint physical custody would work, however, the mediator expected Linda to be flexible and work around Jerry's schedule, even though the same flexibility was not required of Jerry. Thus, the

---

113. In a similar vein, studies of psychotherapists and counselors have shown that more female than male subjects are expected to compromise career ambitions, as well as make other concessions, to achieve satisfactory relationships. *See* Bowman, *An Analog Study With Beginning Therapists Suggesting Bias Against "Activity" in Women*, 19 PSYCHOTHERAPY: THEORY, RES. & PRAC. 318, 323 (1982); Enns, *supra* note 68, at 244-47. Moreover, studies have shown that men and women who deviate from traditional roles are seen by mental health professionals as suffering from mental illness. Goleman, *Stereotypes of the Sexes Persisting in Therapy*, N.Y. Times, Apr. 10, 1990, at C1, col. 1.

Deference to fathers may not be confined to the area of employment. Emery and Wyer, in noting that most of the increased satisfaction created by mediation was experienced by men, posited that "[b]ecause children are a continuing tie between divorced parents, perhaps the fathers' increased satisfaction will, over time, lead to increased satisfaction for the mothers as well." Emery & Wyer, *supra* note 8, at 185. In other words, it is evidently thought permissible for the mother, the children's primary caretaker, to obtain her satisfaction secondhand.

114. A parent who has physical custody of a child tends to make day-to-day decisions, such as what to feed the child. A parent who has legal custody has decisionmaking power over larger issues in the child's life, such as those involving education or religious upbringing.

115. *See* Emery & Wyer, *supra* note 8, at 185 (although more joint custody settlements were negotiated in mediation, joint legal custody agreements spelled out childcare arrangements resembling those found in traditional sole custody awards); *see also* L. WEITZMAN, *supra* note 48, at 361 ("Although joint custody laws hold the promise of men assuming equal responsibility for post divorce parenting, in practice these laws have given men equal authority, but not equal responsibility."); Koopman, Hunt & Stafford, *Child-Related Agreements in Mediated and Non-Mediated Divorce Settlements: A Preliminary Examination and Discussion of Implications*, 22 CONCILIATION CTS. REV. 19, 23-24 (1984) (maternal custody arrangements due primarily to societal traditions, not attorney influence); Pearson & Thoennes, *Mediating and Litigating*, *supra* note 7, at 504, 507 (1984) (many joint custody arrangements are more conventional than label implies; only 27% of agreements reviewed called for regular alternation of child between parents, while remainder typically delegated day-to-day care to mother); Schulman, *Who's Looking After the Children?*, 5 FAM. ADVOC., Fall 1982, at 31, 36 ("Despite the perception that joint custody equalizes the responsibility of child raising between parents, women are still the primary caretakers of children, even after divorce.").

"equality" that prevailed to give Jerry equal control did not require equal responsibility of him.

C. *The Promise to Include Emotion and the Suppression of Anger*

Another criticism of the traditional adversary method of dispute resolution is that it does not provide a role for emotion. Decisions by adversarial parties are posited as rational, devoid of emotion, self-interested, and instrumental (result-oriented). Some proponents of mediation and other methods of alternative dispute resolution believe these characteristics should be retained in mediation to the extent they permit parties to serve their self-interests efficiently.[116] Others have argued that mediation and other forms of alternative dispute resolution provide an opportunity to bring intuition and emotion into the legal process.[117] This latter group of proponents points out that family conflicts in particular often involve a combination of emotional and legal complaints, so that the "real" issues are often obscured in the adversarial setting. Thus, "there may be a great need for an open-ended, unstructured process that permits the disputants to air their true sentiments."[118]

Although mediation is claimed to be a setting in which feelings can be expressed, certain sentiments are often simply not welcome. In particular, expressions of anger are frequently overtly discouraged. This discouragement of anger sends a message that anger is unacceptable, terrifying and dangerous. For a person who has only recently found her anger, this can be a perilous message indeed. This suppression of anger poses a stark contrast to the image of mediation as a process which allows participants to express their emotions.

Women undergoing a divorce, especially ones from nondominant cultural groups, are particularly likely to be harmed by having their anger actively discouraged during the dissolution process. Women have been socialized not to express anger, and have often had their anger labelled "bad."[119] A woman in the throes of divorce may for the first time in her life have found a voice for her anger. As her early, undifferentiated, and sometimes inchoate expressions of anger emerge, the anger may seem as overwhelming to her as to persons outside of it.[120] And yet this anger may turn out to be the source of her energy, strength, and growth in the months and years ahead. An injunction

116. *See, e.g.*, Merry, *Disputing Without Culture* (Book Review), 100 HARV. L. REV. 2057, 2062 (1987).

117. *See, e.g.*, S. GOLDBERG, E. GREEN & F. SANDER, DISPUTE RESOLUTION 313 (1985) ("Family disputes are also well suited to alternative forums because the conflicts often involve a complex interplay of emotional and legal complaints.").

118. *Id.*

119. *See generally* H. LERNER, THE DANCE OF ANGER 1 (1985) (women have been discouraged from expressing their anger); A. LORDE, *The Uses of Anger: Women Responding to Racism*, in SISTER OUTSIDER 124 (1984) (suggesting that women need to use anger to fight racism and sexism).

120. *See* H. LERNER, *supra* note 119, at 3, 95.

from a person in power to suppress that anger because it is not sufficiently modulated may amount to nothing less that an act of violence.

1. *Anger in Adversary Adjudication*

People are necessarily angry at divorce, in two senses. First of all, anger is inevitable in ending a marriage; almost everyone who obtains a divorce becomes angry sooner or later.[121] This anger may have many different causes: it may be a result of anticipated losses, wrongful treatment, or the myriad compromises of self that may have been made along the way to the marriage's end. Second, some anger is necessary for the disengagement which is essential to the completion of the divorce.[122] It is thus critical that any system of marital dissolution take anger into consideration and establish a means by which it is permitted to enter into the divorce process.

Despite the rational pursuit of self-interest that underlies the adversary system in theory, in practice there is much room for the expression of anger in the adversarial context. Indeed, anger may be the raw material for the adversary fight, with the entire courtroom battle constituting an exercise in controlled anger. The parties' anger is expressed in a formal, contained way through the ritualized behavior of the lawyers. In *Richmond Newspapers, Inc. v. Virginia*,[123] the Supreme Court, in holding that criminal trials must be open to the public even when the prosecutor and defense wish otherwise, explained that "the open processes of justice serve an important prophylactic purpose, providing an outlet for community concern, hostility and emotion."[124] Barbara Babcock describes a primary function of criminal trials as community catharsis.[125] In the case of civil trials, and in particular in family law cases, the catharsis is individual, but it is catharsis nonetheless. Thus, in the adversary system, although the parties' anger is expressed through surrogates, it is neither delegitimated nor denied expression.

The manner in which anger is expressed in the adversary system is not, however, without its imperfections. Frequently it is not the party's actual anger that is being expressed, but rather the anger the party is expected to have. Lawyers handling dissolutions under the adversary system may exacerbate or even create conflicts, and fan the flames of anger—real or manufactured—that arise from them. Mediation has been put forth as an alternative forum in which parties can express their sentiments directly and ensure that only *their* sentiments are expressed.[126]

---

121. *See* J. WALLERSTEIN & S. BLAKESLEE, SECOND CHANCES 6 (1989).
122. *See* Barsky, *Strategies and Techniques of Divorce Mediation*, 65 SOC. CASEWORK 102, 106 (1984).
123. 448 U.S. 555 (1980).
124. *Id.* at 571 (Burger, C.J., plurality opinion).
125. *See* Babcock, *Fair Play*, 34 STAN. L. REV. 1133, 1139-40 (1982).
126. *See, e.g.*, Folberg & Milne, *supra* note 14, at 9.

2. *Anger in Mediation*

> *At a recent meeting of a mediation group, a nationally known mediator was a moderator at a round table discussion. In the course of the discussion, a participant stated that she thought one of the problems that divorcing couples had was that they had never learned to fight with each other in a productive way. Several of those present, including the moderator, objected to the word "fight." The speaker tried to make her point more palatable by substituting the words "handle conflict." But this modification was not enough. There was general agreement that we should talk instead about "problem-solving."*[127]

Some mediation literature suggests that mediators should proceed by discouraging the expression of anger.[128] This literature evinces a profound lack of respect for the anger that divorcing spouses feel. For example, Donald Saposnek suggests that "[i]n many ways, the mediator must act as a parent figure to the parents, since their struggles are often not unlike those of siblings squabbling over joint possessions."[129] Saposnek's depiction of divorcing parents suggests that their struggles are devoid of content. He characterizes their anger and conflict as "squabbling" rather than as arising from substantively important conflicts or as a necessary and important step in the divorce process.

Saposnek suggests that the mediator ask questions of the parties that will imply to them that elaboration of their feelings during conflicts with each other is "irrelevant and counterproductive" and that the mediator is "interested in . . . ideas for solutions to these problems."[130] Saposnek thus views the expression of feelings as antithetical to problem-solving; a mediator must choose one or the other.[131]

In a similar vein, an article by Susan Rogers and Claire Francy concerning the role of communication in mediation concludes that the amount of verbal communication between the parties during a mediation has little impact on the outcome of the mediation.[132] In discussing their findings, they argue that communication in mediation should be circumscribed: "A complainant who dwells

---

127. Meeting of Northern California Council for Mediation, at Golden Gate University School of Law, San Francisco, California (Oct. 29, 1989).

128. *See, e.g.*, Brown, *Divorce Mediation in a Mental Health Setting*, in DIVORCE MEDIATION, THEORY AND PRACTICE, *supra* note 14, at 127, 131-32; D. SAPOSNEK, *supra* note 69, at 176; Mumma, *Mediating Disputes*, 42 PUB. WELFARE 22, 26 (1984); *see also* Merry & Silbey, *supra* note 40, at 8 (two predominant styles adopted by mediators are bargaining, which discourages exploration of feelings, and therapeutic, which encourages exploration of feelings).

129. D. SAPOSNEK, *supra* note 69, at 176.

130. *Id.* at 177.

131. Saposnek's view of the parties' anger reveals his belief that his clients are not his equals but rather his subordinates, like infants.

132. *See* Rogers & Francy, *Communication in Mediation: Is More Necessarily Better?*, MEDIATION Q., Winter 1988, at 39, 47. The study involved mediation in a large, court-affiliated, community dispute resolution center. *Id.* at 41.

on negative feelings caused by past events may find it hard to look toward a constructive relationship with the respondent in the future."[133]

Even when mediation literature does approve of bringing anger into the process, it often recommends doing so in a way that subtly undercuts the legitimacy of the anger. Mediators are encouraged, where necessary, to permit parties to "vent" their anger, after which the parties can move on to discuss settlement.[134] This view does not take anger seriously enough. Because it treats expressed anger as having no long-range impact on the party who is exposed to it, it is not necessarily seen as objectionable to require one party to be present and endure the other party's "venting"—even where the party enduring the venting has been the subject of abuse in the marriage.[135] The effects of exposure to anger in such a case can be devastating.[136] If the privilege of expressing anger has not been distributed equally in the relationship prior to mediation, then the mediator should not grant that privilege equally during the mediation.

Second, and equally critically, the view of anger as something to be "vented" does not take anger seriously as a path to clarity and strength. Anger that is merely vented has lost its potential to teach, heal, and energize; it is ineffective anger, anger that "maintains rather than challenges" the status quo.[137]

Not all writers suggest that anger be suppressed or vented in the service of eventual suppression.[138] Some mediators, however, especially those in mandatory settings,[139] do advocate that parties suppress their anger. The mediator's personal antagonism toward anger and conflict may lead her to urge clients to keep their angry feelings to themselves.

At the same time, there are other forces which may intensify this dynamic of suppression. Mediators working under time pressures recognize that it takes time to express anger, and its full expression might, indeed, jeopardize a quick settlement.[140] More significantly, there are substantial societal taboos against

---

133. *Id.* at 48.

134. *See, e.g.*, C. MOORE, THE MEDIATION PROCESS 129-31 (1986); Barsky, *supra* note 122, at 106.

135. For a discussion of subjecting abused spouses to mediation, see *infra* text accompanying notes 184-89.

136. The expressions of anger might be taken by the abused spouse to be further threats, and thus might frighten her and make her reluctant to express her views.

137. *See* H. LERNER, *supra* note 119, at 10.

138. Two commentators have stated that "anger in our society is hard to acknowledge and even harder to show in socially acceptable ways. Often the participants in mediation deemphasize their anger by calling it frustration." *See* J. FOLBERG & A. TAYLOR, *supra* note 74, at 89. The authors go on to suggest that the mediator describe the party's feelings precisely, "perhaps even setting the stage by normalizing the feelings." *Id.*

139. I was a trainer for a community mediation program in Oakland, California. Among the persons attending the training were two family court mediators from a local court. These mediators were aghast that we brought the expression of feelings into the structure of the process: they stated that they never let any hostile feelings be expressed because the parties would blow up and the chance for an agreement would be lost.

140. The success of a mediation program is often measured by the percentage of cases settled. *See* Bruch, *supra* note 24, at 119.

the expression of anger by women, taboos which have particular force when the disputant is a woman of color.[141] For a woman who has just found her anger, anger which has enabled her to free herself from an oppressive relationship and involve herself and her family in a divorce proceeding, the suppression of the very force that has driven her forward is a devastating message.[142]

3. *Societal Prohibitions Against Female Anger*

It is considered unfeminine to be angry, even angry with good reason: "From birth, the parent's awareness of the child's sex . . . organizes and directs that parent's response to the child's expression of anger, rebelliousness and protest. Despite changes brought about by the recent feminist movement, expressions of anger and aggression are still considered 'masculine' in men, and 'unfeminine' in women."[143]

Women are not immune from the pervasive fear of female anger which is part of Western culture.[144] Thus, from the external, societal prohibition on our anger arises an even stronger set of internal prohibitions. These prohibitions make it difficult for women to be directly, clearly, self-assertively angry. We carry with us two powerful images of female ways of dealing with aggression. The first image is of the "nice lady" or peacemaker: a woman who, "[i]n situations that might realistically evoke anger or protest . . . stay[s] silent—or become[s] tearful, self-critical or 'hurt.'"[145] Women serving this image are vulnerable to victimization and "share deep unconscious anxieties about 'fighting' which interfere not only with their ability to express anger, but with their capacity to be adaptively self-assertive and competitive as well."[146] But under the "nice woman" exterior is much unconscious rage, which, because direct experience of it is forbidden to women, may be experienced as depression, hurt or guilt. "The amount of creative, intellectual and sexual energy that

141. *See generally* A. LORDE, *supra* note 119.

142. While individual men might also experience the suppression of their anger as devastating, the effect on men of the mediator's message is in general likely to be less for two reasons. First, because of cultural support for men's expression of anger, men ordinarily are far less susceptible than women to suggestions that their anger be suppressed. Harriet Lerner points out that, while there are many English terms for women who are angry at men—shrews, man-haters, castrators—there is not a single unflattering term for men who are angry at women. H. LERNER, *supra* note 119, at 2. Second, the mediator herself, as a product of this culture, may notice men's anger less and tolerate it more than women's.

There is one possible advantage to the suppression of anger in mediation: a woman who has been the victim of her husband's anger may be protected from that anger, however briefly, during the mediation session. On further inspection, however, this advantage is illusory; a mediation model that recognizes the usefulness and power of anger may help her both to express her own anger and protect herself from her husband's anger, during the session and long after it has ended.

143. *See* Lerner, *Internal Prohibitions Against Female Anger*, 40 AM. J. PSYCHOANALYSIS 137, 138 (1980). While Lerner discusses men as a homogeneous group, the societal reaction to the expression of anger or aggression in white males is very different from the reaction to the expression of anger or aggression in Black males, at least outside of the arena of sports. *See infra* notes 160-66 and accompanying text.

144. Indeed, I think we are especially sensitive to it.

145. H. LERNER, *supra* note 119, at 5.

146. Lerner, *supra* note 143, at 139.

is trapped by this need to repress anger and remain unaware of its sources is simply incalculable."[147]

The second image imposed on women is that of the "bitch." Bitchiness, descriptive of women who express anger with ease, is characterized by "ineffective fighting, complaining, and blaming that leads to no constructive resolution."[148] This image is forced on women "when intra-psychic and cultural pressures combine to inhibit the direct and appropriate expression of legitimate anger and protest."[149] The alternative presented is not to express anger at all. The "bitch" is willing to experience her anger and communicate it in some sense, but may "get stuck in a pattern of ineffective fighting, complaining and blaming that only preserves the status quo"; she may "unwittingly protect others" at her own expense.[150]

Neither of the alternatives traditionally available to women allows a woman to use her anger to clarify and strengthen herself and her relationships. Rather, both alternatives force her to deny, displace, internalize, or fear it.[151]

4. *Anger and Separateness*

In addition to society's prohibitions on female anger, many women have an additional reason to be threatened by their own anger: they find it difficult to see themselves as independent. Many women view themselves fundamentally in terms of their connections to other people; they long for such relationships and are fearful of being separate. The experience of anger is one that by its

147. H. LERNER, *supra* note 119, at 8.

148. *Id.* at 5, 7-10.

149. Lerner, *supra* note 143, at 138.

150. H. LERNER, *supra* note 119, at 9; *see also* Austin, *Sapphire Bound!*, 1989 WIS. L. REV. 539, 539-40 (describing effective style of being Black "bitch").

151. Women are often correctly perceived as victims. Yet fear of female anger, on the part of both women and men, seems more intense than the fear of patriarchal anger. Some psychologists have located the origins of this fear in most infants' experiences of being raised by their mothers:

> [T]he infant's and child's world is a matriarchal one in which power and authority are predominantly, if not exclusively, in the hands of women. It is mother who not only gratifies the child's impulses, but is also the first to forbid their expression . . . . Most important, it is mother who is the primary object of the child's dependency. It is with this woman that the child must move from the experience of a fused, undifferentiated symbiosis, in the direction of increasing individuation, separateness, and autonomy. The strength of this struggle with mother—i.e., the struggle between regressive dependent wishes and more autonomous strivings toward separation and autonomy—inevitably generates aggression and rage at the object of one's dependency. Because of the child's heavy reliance on primitive projection, one aspect of the early maternal imago which persists in the unconscious of even the most 'rational' adults is that of a vengeful, angry, possessive, all-powerful 'bad mother' who restricts her child's autonomy, freedom, and growth.

Lerner, *supra* note 143, at 139. We need not rely on the work of western psychologists alone to observe this fear of the omnipotently destructive woman: pictures of statuary from India portray the mother eating the head of her child. In mediation, women who are angry, or even those who define themselves clearly, may trigger this fear in the mediator, in their husbands, and even in themselves. They may be seen as "diminishing men [and] hurting children." Lerner, *Female Dependency in Context: Some Theoretical and Technical Considerations*, 53 AM. J. ORTHOPSYCHIATRY 697, 700 (1983), rather than as legitimately protecting their own interests and the interests of their children.

nature includes feelings of being separate and alone. According to psychologist Teresa Bernardez-Bonesatti, women may be afraid of temporary separateness from the object of their anger because of their fear of loss of connection.[152] While not all women experience this fear,[153] it is enough for my present purposes to note that (1) the experience of anger is one of separateness, and (2) viewing oneself as separate and alone is difficult for many women.

Many women are thus afraid of their own anger, either because of a societal proscription on female anger or because it makes them feel cut off from others. Before their divorces, they may only rarely have experienced their anger directly, experiencing it instead as hurt or depression. To feel their anger directly now may be terrifying, and they may be afraid of the consequences of that anger. In addition, at the time of divorce, all women must cope to some degree with being alone, physically, economically, and for all to see, sometimes for the first time in their lives. They must deal with a painful and permanent loss of connection when, for some, the experience of connection has been the hallmark of their lives. At this vulnerable moment, they may be told in a child custody mediation that their anger is not legitimate. This is a message that their worst fears are true: "You are, indeed," they are told, "threatening your own children by expressing your anger."

The literature on mediation does not directly address the question of whether the delegitimation of anger harms women. A study by Robert Emery and Melissa Wyer, however, has shown that women who have participated in mediation are much more likely to be depressed than women who have used the adversary process.[154] In a later article, Emery and Jeanne Jackson explained this result as due to a temporary sense of vindication felt by women after winning in court.[155] They describe anger in the context of divorce as a temporary means of coping with sadness, and they hypothesize that the difference in rates of depression will not be found at longitudinal followup.[156]

Emery and Jackson's conclusion is troublesome in two respects. First, even *temporary* depression of the magnitude noted at this critical time in a woman's life might be dangerously disabling, and should not be dismissed lightly. Second, the authors conflate depression with sadness. Clinical depression, the

---

152. Bernardez-Bonesatti, *Women and Anger: Conflicts With Aggression in Contemporary Women*, 33 J. AM. MED. WOMEN'S A. 215, 216 (1978). Harriet Lerner describes this as symptomatic of the girl's special difficulty of separating from her mother, and of a fear that the girl's separation would leave the mother "emptied out and depleted." Lerner, *supra* note 143, at 141; *see also* N. CHODOROW, *supra* note 11, at 109-10, 168-69 (describing tendency in women toward boundary confusion and lack of sense of separateness); D. DINNERSTEIN, *supra* note 11, at 48-53, 107-08, 111-12, 192-95 (separating oneself from sense of continuity with mother is problem for every child, but is ordinarily much harder for daughter than son).

153. *See* E. SPELMAN, *supra* note 102, at 62-66.

154. Emery & Wyer, *supra* note 8, at 184. This study found that mothers in mediation had a mean score of 11.37, with a standard deviation of 2.57, on the Beck depression inventory. Mothers in litigation showed much less depression, with a mean score of 5.32 and a standard deviation of 1.24. *Id.*

155. *See* Emery & Jackson, *supra* note 8, at 3, 16.

156. *Id.*

condition measured by the instrument they used, is not "sadness," but, rather, a whole complex of symptoms including poor appetite, loss of energy, sleep disturbance, and a loss of pleasure or interest in usual activities.[157] Moreover, many psychologists believe that suppressed anger *is* related to depression.[158] The classical psychoanalytical literature has conceptualized depression as anger turned against the self. More recently, feminist psychologists have viewed depression as a psychological consequence of internal and cultural prohibitions against female anger.[159] Emery and Jackson's explanation for the results is apparently that all women are "sad" at divorce, but that the adversary experience permits some women to use anger to replace temporarily or avoid that sadness. A more accurate analysis may be that all women are angry at divorce, but that the mediation process may require that anger to be suppressed (or at least not to be attended to) or to be directed at themselves, resulting in increased evidence of clinical depression.

5. *Effect on Black Women of Prohibitions Against Anger*

Compounding the fear of feminine anger is the societal fear of anger on the part of racial minorities, especially Blacks.[160] This fear is endemic, shared by sympathetic whites as well as unsympathetic whites, and often by Blacks ourselves. Free-floating hostility toward persons of color[161] may be one form in which this fear manifests itself, as may dehumanizing characterizations of Blacks as animals,[162] or overreactions to aggression by Blacks.[163] In its equally frequent, but arguably more dangerous, manifestation, this fear takes the form of delegitimating anger expressed by Blacks.

Examples of this delegitimation are numerous. In a class in constitutional law, the weariness, discomfort, and scorn is evident in some of the white students' eyes and voices every time a Black student argues for affirmative

157. *See* A. BECK, DEPRESSION 189 (1967); D. PAPALOS & J. PAPALOS, OVERCOMING DEPRESSION 6-7 (1987).

158. *See* H. LERNER, WOMEN IN THERAPY 220 (1988); Freud, *Mourning and Melancholia*, in 4 COLLECTED PAPERS 152, 158, 162-63 (E. Jones ed. 1953).

159. *See* H. LERNER, *supra* note 158, at 221; Bernardez-Bonesatti, *supra* note 152, at 215.

160. The special problems confronted by those who are multiply burdened may be viewed in terms of an "intersectional" experience, which is greater than the sum of racism and sexism. The intersectional experience cannot be understood as the combination of claims arising from discrete sources of discrimination. For three analyses of this insight, see Austin, *supra* note 150, at 554-74; Crenshaw, *Demarginalizing the Intersection of Race and Sex: A Black Feminist Critique of Antidiscrimination Doctrine, Feminist Theory and Antiracist Politics*, 1989 U. CHI. LEGAL F. 139, 152-57; Harris, *Race and Essentialism in Feminist Legal Theory*, 42 STAN. L. REV. 581, 585 (1990).

161. *See* Williams, *Spirit Murdering the Messenger: The Discourse of Fingerpointing as Law's Response to Racism*, 42 U. MIAMI L. REV. 127, 150-55 (1987); *see also* B. HOOKS, AIN'T I A WOMAN 65-72 (1981) (describing complex system of negative myths and stereotypes which socialize white men to regard Black women as unsuitable marriage partners).

162. *See* Decter, *Looting and Liberal Racism*, COMMENTARY, Sept. 1977, at 48, 49.

163. *See* Lawrence, *Dream: On Discovering the Significance of Fear*, 10 NOVA L.J. 627, 632 (1986); Williams, *supra* note 161, at 130-32. Of course, these acts of racism do not arise merely from fear of Black anger; such fear is only one piece of the racism puzzle, albeit a significant piece.

action based on historical oppression: "Do we have to talk about that again? That's history, why are Blacks still carrying on and asking for special recognition?"[164] Publicly, the recent opinions of the United States Supreme Court seem to be proceeding as if racial discrimination were just a distant memory.[165] Blacks who dare to mention societal discrimination, express their anger, and expect some form of redress, are implicitly characterized as ungrateful and greedy. As Justice Blackmun commented recently in his dissent in *Wards Cove Packing Co. v. Atonio*: "One wonders whether the majority still believes that race discrimination—or, more accurately, race discrimination against nonwhites—is a problem in our society, or even remembers that it ever was."[166] The combination of the cultural edicts that it is unfeminine to be angry and that the anger of Blacks is both dangerous and illegitimate leaves Black women in an impossible position. That part of a Black woman's anger that is directed at racism is delegitimated, feared, and used by white men and women as an excuse for locating the "race problem" outside themselves. Audre Lorde tells of "a white academic welcom[ing] the appearance of a collection by nonBlack women of color. 'It allows me to deal with racism without dealing with the harshness of Black women,'" the academic explained.[167] On the other hand, that part of a Black woman's anger that is directed at men may be considered illegitimate by Black men. They may criticize and dismiss her, or, worse, abandon her, for expressing that anger.

Anger as a woman, or as a particular woman in a particular struggle at a particular time, and anger as a person marginalized because of race or color, may be impossible to separate. While the experiences may be indivisible, however, they are often described separately. As a result, the specific and particular concerns of Black women may be left out of many analyses:

> Black women are sometimes excluded from feminist theory and antiracist policy discourse because both are predicated on a discrete set of experiences that often does not accurately reflect the intersection of race and gender . . . . Because the intersectional experience is greater than the sum of racism and sexism, any analysis that does not take intersectionality into account cannot sufficiently address the particular manner in which Black women are subordinated.[168]

---

164. In seven years of teaching constitutional law, I have observed this reaction many times.

165. *See, e.g.*, Patterson v. McLean Credit Union, 491 U.S. 164 (1989) (limiting scope of 42 U.S.C. § 1981 to making and enforcing of contracts); Wards Cove Packing Co. v. Atonio, 490 U.S. 642 (1989) (reformulating order of proof and weight of parties' burdens in disparate impact cases); City of Richmond v. J.A. Croson Co., 488 U.S. 469 (1989) (city minority set-aside programs must demonstrate compelling public interest based on prior discrimination by city and must be narrowly tailored to remedy effects of prior discrimination).

166. 490 U.S. at 662 (Blackmun, J., dissenting).

167. A. LORDE, *supra* note 119, at 126 (citation omitted). The collection referred to is THIS BRIDGE CALLED MY BACK: WRITINGS BY RADICAL WOMEN OF COLOR (1984). Most, but not all, of the writings in the collection are by non-Black women of color.

168. Crenshaw, *supra* note 160, at 140.

Ultimately, when placed in a position in which they must identify with Black men or white women, Black women have chosen Black men;[169] indeed, exposure of conflicts within the community has been regarded by Black people as a sign of disloyalty.[170] In sum, for Black women, the experience of having anger at their mate delegitimated is beset with complications, all of which can lead to paralysis, self-hatred, and a sense of being split off from themselves.[171] To the extent that the mediation process delivers a message that anger is not legitimate, it is thus especially damaging to Black women. Because such a message carries echoes of other cultural messages, from other times and other places,[172] it can be particularly disempowering and disabling.

D. *Mandatory Mediation and the Promise of Self-Determination*

Mediation permits persons to speak for themselves and make their own decisions. This self-determination can be empowering. Patterns of domination characteristic of adversary adjudication are challenged in two ways: no outside decisionmaker is present, and the client need not be the passive recipient of a lawyer's advice and decisionmaking. Instead, he can explore alternatives, create options, and make decisions. In private, voluntary mediation, I have found that many say that they have chosen mediation so that they, and not a lawyer, will be in charge of their own destinies. In this very immediate way, mediation can challenge the hierarchical, professionalized way that family law is usually practiced.[173]

This dynamic is fundamentally altered when mediation is imposed rather than sought or offered. When mandatory mediation is part of the court system, the notion that parties are actually making their own decisions is purely illusory. First, the parties have not chosen or timed the process according to their ability to handle it. Second, they are not allowed to decide themselves how much their lawyers should participate, but instead are deprived of whatever protection their lawyers have to offer. Finally, they are not permitted to choose the mediator,

---

169. *See* Gillespie, *My Gloves Are Off, Sisters: Power, Racism, and that "Domination Thing,"* Ms., Apr. 1987, 19, 19-20 (discussing author's frustration with white women's movement). In response to the dilemma of women of color, Kim Crenshaw has commented: "If any real efforts are to be made to free Black people of the constraints and conditions that characterize racial subordination, then theories and strategies purporting to reflect the Black community's needs must include an analysis of sexism and patriarchy." Crenshaw, *supra* note 160, at 166.

170. The controversy over the movie *The Color Purple* (Warner Bros. 1985) demonstrates this problem. There was much sentiment that by depicting domestic abuse in a Black family, the movie confirmed negative stereotypes of Black men. Thus, the issue of sexism in the Black community was obscured by the debate over whether such an image should be presented on the screen. *See* Crenshaw, *supra* note 160, at 163.

171. This discussion assumes that the couple consists of a Black man and a Black woman; if the man were white, an entirely different, but equally complex, dynamic would be created.

172. Charles Lawrence has described this phenomenon as a cultural chorus: a message that might to an outsider seem easy to dismiss or ignore can become a source of much pain to the recipient if it takes on the resonances of other similar, and perhaps more overtly violent, messages. Lawrence, *If He Hollers Let Him Go: Regulating Racist Speech*, 1990 DUKE L.J. 431, 452-76.

173. *See* Menkel-Meadow, *supra* note 1, at 56; Rifkin, *Mediation*, *supra* note 1, at 30.

and they often cannot leave without endangering their legal position even if they believe the mediator is biased against them.[174]

1. *Choice of Process*

Several writers have noted that most clients do not understand what mediation is and, therefore, absent coercion, are reluctant to enter into it.[175] For example, mediation is almost never represented in the popular culture, whereas television shows which represent the court system are numerous.[176] It has been argued that because of the general ignorance that surrounds mediation, it makes sense to require people to try mediation before their case is heard by the court, so that they can see whether it works for them: "No law is mandating an agreement, but it is requiring a process, however extensive or minimal it may turn out to be in a particular instance."[177] Proponents of this view seldom recognize that, even though an agreement might not be required, a person might agree to something because of the pressures of the situation; or that, even if no agreement is reached, the process itself might be traumatic.[178]

It is presumptuous to assume that the state has a better idea than the parties themselves about whether mediation will work in their particular case. A party may know something the mediator does not: that her spouse is a pathological, but convincing, liar; that years of living with a man have resulted in a pattern in which the woman consistently accommodates him, even when she does not want to; that the woman will lose sight of her own needs in the attempt to appear a cooperative female; or that the woman will sacrifice many of her interests in order to end what may be a psychologically painful process. In sum, there may be an internal wisdom, one that needs to be honored, that mediation is inappropriate in a particular situation.[179] It is true that mandatory mediation

174. In more than half of the California counties, a person who leaves mediation assumes the risk that the mediator will make a recommendation to the court that goes against that person's interests. In some counties, such recommendations are routinely followed by the judge. D. Saposnek, *supra* note 24.

175. *See* Pearson, *supra* note 16, at 428; *see also* Pearson, Thoennes & Vanderkooi, *The Decision to Mediate: Profiles of Individuals Who Accept and Reject the Opportunity to Mediate Contested Child Custody and Visitation Issues*, J. DIVORCE, Fall/Winter 1982, at 17, 20-21, 32 (noting "curious lack of spontaneous demand for mediation services from the general public"); *Warring Couples Shun Divorce Mediation and Opt to Battle It Out in Court Instead*, Wall St. J., Mar. 27, 1990, at B11, col. 3 (quoting family court director in Connecticut as saying, "Basically, you've got to be shoved into it."); S. GOLDBERG, E. GREEN & F. SANDER, *supra* note 117, at 504 (most Americans ultimately turn to courts).

176. From *Perry Mason* and *The Defenders* in the 1960's to *L.A. Law* and *The People's Court* today, the adversary process has captured the public imagination.

177. Ferrick, *Three Crucial Questions*, MEDIATION Q., Fall 1986, at 61, 65; *see also* S. GOLDBERG, E. GREEN & F. SANDER, *supra* note 117, at 504 ("[C]oercion *into* mediation does not seem objectionable, as long as there is no coercion *in* mediation to accept a particular outcome, and as long as unsuccessful mediation does not serve as a barrier to adjudication.").

178. *See infra* notes 276-85 and accompanying text.

179. States vary in the extent to which parties are permitted to withdraw from the mediation proceedings. In Alaska and Wisconsin, either party may withdraw after the first session. ALASKA STAT. § 25.24.060(d) (1983); WIS. STAT. ANN. § 767-11(8) (West Supp. 1990). In Kansas, a party is permitted to terminate after the second session, and the mediator is required to terminate after the second session under

may serve the interests of women who do not wish to enter the adversary process; if opting out of mediation is permitted, some women (as well as some men) will be forced to litigate when their preference would have been to mediate. There is no way around this unfortunate situation. Either some women will be forced to litigate against their will, or some women will be forced to mediate against their will. Mediation poses such substantial dangers, and provides so few benefits to unwilling female participants, however, that to my mind it is indefensible to require mediation, notwithstanding that such a requirement would help women who do want to mediate. In addition, the woman who participates in the mediation process with a reluctant spouse may have gained little.

Often, the time allotted to a mandatory mediation is short.[180] Frequently, an entire mediation is expected to take place in an hour or less. Some take place in the hallways of the courthouse.[181] Given these conditions, it is impossible for the state to ensure that an adequate process is being offered even in cases in which people have chosen it. Where the process is inadequate, its imposition is even more troubling.

Moreover, a person married to a liar or con artist knows that that person is often more persuasive than someone telling the truth. In a relationship in which the wife has been abused, for example, the abuser will often appear dominant, charming, agreeable, and socially facile in comparison to his less assertive wife.[182] In studying the court mediation process in California, Donald Saposnek found pathological liars who fooled everybody into believing that

---

certain circumstances. KAN. STAT. ANN. § 23-604 (1988). In Maine, the court may waive the mediation requirement if extraordinary cause is shown; in all other cases, if the parties do not reach an agreement on an issue, the court is required to determine that they made a good faith effort to do so prior to proceeding with a hearing. Sanctions can be imposed for failing to mediate in good faith. ME. REV. STAT. ANN. tit. 19, § 752(4) (Supp. 1990). In Oregon and North Carolina, the parties may petition the court to waive the requirement of mediation. In North Carolina, the court must hold a hearing and determine if there is good cause for the waiver. N.C. GEN. STAT. § 50-13.1(c) (Supp. 1990). In Oregon, the waiver must be based on a finding that severe emotional distress would result from the mediation. OR. REV. STAT. § 107.179(3) (1989). In Minnesota, mediation is mandatory unless the court determines that a child or one of the spouses has been a victim of physical or sexual abuse. MINN. STAT. ANN. § 518.619(2) (West Supp. 1991). The remainder of the states with mediation statutes are silent on this issue. *See supra* note 4 for a list of these states and their statutory provisions.

180. A study of the Connecticut, Los Angeles, and Minneapolis court-related custody mediation systems showed that cases averaged 1.5 sessions and 2.3 hours in Connecticut, 1.7 and 3.0 hours in Los Angeles, and 3.3 sessions and 4.3 hours in Minneapolis. Many respondents reported attending only one session. Cauble, Thoennes, Pearson & Appleford, *A Case Study: Custody Resolution Counseling in Hennepin County, Minnesota*, in J. PEARSON & N. THOENNES, FINAL REPORT, *supra* note 7, at 12; Pearson, Thoennes & Hodges, *The Effect of Divorce Mediation and Adjudication Procedures on Children*, in J. PEARSON & N. THOENNES, FINAL REPORT, *supra* note 7, at 24-25. In Maine, mediations usually are held in a single session. *See* Orbeton, *supra* note 30, at 51, 53. In Florida, the mediator usually has 2-4 hours in which to help the parties resolve their dispute. Talcott, *supra* note 30, at 82. Donald Saposnek has also acknowledged the brevity of mandatory mediation sessions in California. D. Saposnek, *supra* note 24. In contrast to court-ordered mediations, voluntary integrated mediations (mediations involving all aspects of the dispute, not just the child custody issue) studied by Joan Kelly averaged ten sessions. Kelly, *supra* note 8, at 74.

181. *See supra* note 26 and accompanying text.

182. *See* Germane, Johnson & Lemon, *Mandatory Custody Mediation and Joint Custody Orders in California: The Danger for Victims of Domestic Violence*, 1 BERKELEY WOMEN'S L.J. 175, 188 (1985).

they were reasonable people and wonderful parents.[183] When such a person is believed, the person disagreeing with him may look hysterical, irrational, or silly. Of course, liars show up in court, too; but in an informal process where nothing they say can be disproved, they are in a much stronger position. In sum, a person might decide against mediation because she knows the spouse is not capable of working honestly and productively within the process. Forcing mediation can produce a situation in which the parent with the fewest scruples wins.

A substantial proportion of women who file for divorce state that they do so, at least in part, because they have been the victims of domestic violence.[184] Many mediators agree that mediation is not appropriate in such cases. Others, however, disagree. Some writers suggest that a mediator can discover that abuse has occurred and modify the mediation process accordingly: "The mediator, by carefully directing the process, will make the mediation room a safe place and provide the abused party with a nonthreatening context in which to consider alternatives and come to a personal decision."[185]

Mediation where abuse has occurred is troubling even when mediation is voluntary.[186] Mandatory mediation programs, however, do not always permit abused parties to opt out.[187] Moreover, even where such an exception to the mediation requirement exists, the abused spouse might have trouble showing she is entitled to it; to be relieved from participating in mediation in some

183. D. Saposnek, *supra* note 24.

184. *See* Littleton, *supra* note 80, at 27-28 (while exact figures are difficult to obtain, 50% figure is one many experts subscribe to); Shattuck, *Mandatory Mediation*, in DIVORCE MEDIATION, THEORY AND PRACTICE, *supra* note 14, at 191, 206 (domestic violence had occurred in 32% of families in court mediation sample); *cf.* J. WALLERSTEIN & S. BLAKESLEE, *supra* note 121, at 8 (over half of all children of marriages which end in divorce witness violence between the natural parents); Girdner, *Custody Mediation in the United States: Empowerment or Social Control?*, 3 CANADIAN J. WOMEN & L. 134, 138 n.19 (1989) (Canadian study shows physical violence given as reason for marital separation by 50-75% of women).

185. Ferrick, *supra* note 177, at 66; *see also* Marthaler, *Successful Mediation with Abusive Couples*, MEDIATION Q., Spring 1989, at 53, 65 (special procedures can address concerns of those who claim mediation is inappropriate for couples with history of abuse).

186. *See* Lerman, *supra* note 99, at 73-76; *see also* National Center on Women and Family Law, *Women, Mediation and Family Law*, 18 CLEARINGHOUSE REV. 266, 269 (1984) (mediation unfair because of unequal financial and social power of men and women); Woods, *Mediation: A Backlash to Women's Progress on Family Law Issues*, 19 CLEARINGHOUSE REV. 431, 435 (1985) (protection of one's physical safety too important to entrust to anything other than legal system).

187. Some states do permit a party to opt out, but only under limited circumstances. CAL. CIV. CODE § 4607.2 (West Supp. 1990) requires that where there is a history of domestic violence and a court order is in effect protecting one of the parties, the mediator must meet with the parties separately at the request of the party protected by the order. In Maine, the court may waive mediation for extraordinary cause. ME. REV. STAT. ANN. tit. 19, § 752 (Supp. 1989). The Florida statute provides an exception for "cases where there is any history of domestic violence." FLA. STAT. ANN. § 44.302(c) (West Supp. 1989). In Minnesota, the statute requires that the court "shall not require" mediation where it determines that there is probable cause that one of the parties, or a child of a party, has been physically or sexually abused. MINN. STAT. ANN. § 518.619(2) (West 1990 & Supp. 1991). This provision, however, was interpreted in at least one county to permit the court to *order* the couple into mediation so long as they were permitted later to discontinue the mediation. Despite the clear language of the statute, the abused party was not permitted to forgo mediation altogether. *See* Marthaler, *supra* note 185, at 53-54.

jurisdictions, a woman must come forward with more than her word.[188] In some jurisdictions, then, a woman who has been subject to abuse may finally attempt to take a stand against it, have her word doubted, and then be required to meet face to face with the abuser to decide child custody.[189]

Finally, a person might not want to participate in mediation because the timing is wrong. She might be willing to mediate in the future, but might feel for the present too vulnerable, angry, hurt or fragile to use anything but a formal process with built-in distancing mechanisms. Mandatory mediation takes this crucial decision out of her hands.

2. *Choice of Mediator: Partiality and Unacknowledged Perspective*

Typically in mandatory mediation, the participants cannot choose their mediator or, at best, have a very limited choice of mediators.[190] Some agencies have policies which make it difficult to change mediators when one or both of the parties are dissatisfied with the mediator's handling of the case.[191] Mediators, however, exert a great deal of power. When two people are in conflict, having a third, purportedly neutral person take the viewpoint of one or the other results in a palpable shift of power to the party with whom the mediator agrees. The mediator also can set the rules regarding who talks, when they may speak, and what may be said.[192] The power of the mediator is not always openly acknowledged but is hidden beneath protestations that the process belongs to the parties. This can make the parties feel less, not more,

188. In California some counties routinely hold separate mediation sessions whenever either party has alleged domestic violence. Others require a restraining order against the alleged abuser to have been issued before separate mediation sessions will be held. Telephone interviews with Emily Hancock, Mediator, Alameda County (Jan. 9, 1991); B.J. Herran, Mediator, San Francisco County (Jan. 10, 1991); Dellah Moreno, Mediator, Santa Clara County (Jan. 10, 1991); and David Bradford, Mediator, Los Angeles County (Jan. 10, 1991); *see also* Mahoney, *Legal Images of Battered Women: Redefining the Issue of Separation* 90 MICH. L. REV. (forthcoming Oct. 1991). Mahoney demonstrates that it is difficult for women to self-identify—let alone identify themselves to others—as "battered," even when that is the case, because of their correct perception of themselves as strong.

On a related note, see Littleton, *supra* note 80, at 38-42, who discusses battering from the perspective of the women involved. Littleton demonstrates that if battered women are taken at their word, as they should be, they do not always have the option of leaving their husbands: some women can continue to love the persons who batter them, and hope that their partners will change.

189. *See* Germane, Johnson & Lemon, *supra* note 182, at 188-89. I would be hesitant to say that battered women should never be permitted to mediate, but they certainly should never be penalized for refusing to do so.

190. In California, the court appoints a mediator. *See supra* note 22 and accompanying text. In Alaska, each party has one peremptory challenge of a court-appointed mediator. ALASKA STAT. § 25.24.060 (1983). In Ramsey County, Minnesota, the parties may have the mediator (who is assigned from a court-maintained panel) removed. McCrory, *supra* note 30, at 149.

191. In one California county, the party is required to discuss her dissatisfaction with the mediator, who then may approve or disapprove a change. If the mediator thinks a change is not necessary, the party is required to discuss her objections with the mediator's supervisor. If the problem is still not resolved, the party may approach the Director of Family Court Services and, ultimately, a judge. Interview with Emily Hancock, Mediator, Alameda County (June 9, 1991). For a discussion of mediation practice in various California counties, see Deis, *supra* note 14, at 157-16.

192. *See* Merry & Silbey, *supra* note 40, at 14-18.

in control of the process and its consequences for their lives. There is much room for, but little acknowledgment of, the possibility of the mediator's exhibiting partiality or imposing a hidden agenda on the parties.[193]

a. *The Problem of Prejudice*

George, a Black man, is in the process of divorcing Michelle, a white woman. During the course of the mediation, the mediator asks a number of times whether there is a history of domestic violence. She seems not to believe George or his wife when each insists that although Michelle occasionally has attacked George, he has never fought back.

Elaine is a Black woman, who has worked herself up in the ranks of the local telephone company from an entry level position to her new job, in which she supervises a number of employees. She handles herself with calm and poise, but also a certain coolness. Joe, her husband, who is also Black, is a friendly, gregarious man who has not been reliable in meeting his support obligations or in taking regular responsibility for their two sons. In mediation, Elaine immediately senses that the mediator favors her husband and does not like her. This intuition is confirmed when the mediator permits her husband to interrupt her constantly, but quickly stops her with a sharp lecture when she tries to interrupt him. At one point, the mediator turns to her and says, "I was a single parent too, and I did not have the luxury of an ex-husband who was willing to help me with the children." Five minutes later, the mediator repeats the same statement. When Elaine mentions her debilitating health problems, the mediator laughs and says, "You don't have to act sick to get what you want."[194]

George and Elaine are encountering extreme examples of what is, to some degree, a troublesome aspect of any mediation: the process introduces a third party who is held out to be, but is not, impartial. George's mediator is racially prejudiced; she has some preconceived ideas, sturdy enough to withstand mutual denials, about the likelihood that a Black husband has battered a white wife. Elaine's mediator is clearly partial to Elaine's husband. Whether this partiality is based on racial prejudice, Elaine will never know.[195] Elaine's mediator has also projected[196] some of her own conflicts onto Elaine. Because the mediator feels that her own situation as a single parent was so difficult, it is hard for her to empathize with a woman who has a seemingly lighter burden, but who is still not appreciative.

---

193. *See* D. SAPOSNEK, *supra* note 69, at 26-27.

194. For the origin of this mediation story, see *supra* note 13.

195. Although Elaine's husband is also Black, it is frequently the case that prejudice takes on a particular sharpness with respect to one sex.

196. Projection is "[t]he process whereby an unconscious quality or characteristic of one's own is perceived or reacted to in an outer object or person." S. PERERA, THE SCAPEGOAT COMPLEX: TOWARD A MYTHOLOGY OF SHADOW AND GUILT 118 (1986).

Partiality comes in many forms. In its most virulent form it results from prejudice in favor of or against a person because of his race, gender, sexual orientation, disability, religion, or class. It may also arise, however, from a personal disposition to favor certain outcomes or even from a positive or negative reaction to a particular personality. It is no surprise that mediators are not completely impartial, for, in a very fundamental way, impartiality is a myth. It cannot exist in anything approaching a pure form, although we would like it to, and often we pretend that it does.[197] The concept of impartiality is based on the notion of an observer without a perspective. But any observer inevitably sees from a particular perspective, whether that perspective is acknowledged or not.[198] Mediators, like all other human beings, have biases, values, and points of view. They have all had experiences in their lives that influence how they react to others, independent of anything the others might do. The proper role of these attitudes in mediation is and should be a subject of debate: should a mediator try to keep her own attitudes out of the mediation entirely, or should those attitudes be disclosed? When does disclosure become intrusive; that is, when is it something done to protect the mediator rather than to benefit the parties?

A mediator's attempt to remain neutral is to some extent always doomed to failure, but it is an important effort nonetheless.[199] Neutrality in some form (although not the dispassionate, bloodless neutrality that can give that word a bad name) can remain an aspiration, even if it is one that may never be reached.[200] But aspirations aside, allowances must be made for the inevitable

197. *See* Delgado, *Fairness and Formality*, *supra* note 10, at 1387-91 (discussing how mediation may allow expression of racial and ethnic prejudice); Delgado, *ADR and the Dispossessed: Recent Books About the Deformalization Movement*, 13 L. & SOC. INQUIRY 145, 151-54 (1988) (alternative dispute resolution may expose disputants to higher risk of prejudice) [hereinafter Delgado, *ADR and The Dispossessed*]; Lawrence, *The Id, the Ego, and Equal Protection: Reckoning with Unconscious Racism*, 39 STAN. L. REV. 317, 329 (1987) (law refuses to recognize existence of unconscious racism); Resnik, *On the Bias: Feminist Reconsiderations of the Aspirations for Our Judges*, 61 S. CAL. L. REV. 1877, 1903-05 (1988) (widespread institutional discrimination has been documented but judges continue to speak as if aspirations of impartiality are being met).

198. *See* Minow, *Foreword: Justice Engendered*, 101 HARV. L. REV. 10, 45-50 (1987); Wells, *Situated Decisionmaking*, 63 S. CAL. L. REV. 1728, 1743-44 (1990).

199. *Cf.* Cain, *Good and Bad Bias: A Comment on Feminist Theory and Judging*, 61 S. CAL. L. REV. 1945, 1946 (1988) (discussing need to separate "good" from "bad" bias); Resnik, *supra* note 197, at 1943-44 (feminist perspectives can provide values for role of judging).

200. The shape that neutrality might take is discussed, in the context of judging, in Cain, *supra* note 199, and Resnik, *supra* note 197. Judith Resnik quotes from Learned Hand:

> You must have impartiality. What do I mean by impartiality? I mean you mustn't introduce yourself, your own preconceived notions about what is right. You must try, as far as you can, it is impossible for human beings to do so absolutely, but just so far as you can, not to interject your own personal interests, even your own preconceived assumptions and beliefs.

Resnik, *supra* note 197, at 1943-44 (quoting L. HAND, THE SPIRIT OF LIBERTY, 309-10 (I. Dillard ed. 1958)). Resnik explains that, to Hand, there were two possibilities: "to cease to be in order to hear another's claims, or to be, and then to be impermissibly interested." *Id.* at 1944. She then suggests a third possibility, in which a judge can have an interest—without being corrupted by self-interest—so that "the ordinariness of much that is judging need not be obscured in an effort to privilege the impersonal." *Id.* Pat Cain further suggests that the Hand quote should be interpreted to mean that a judge should transcend his sense of self to listen, and then decide "as a new self . . . for having experienced the story of the other." Cain, *supra*

failures of neutrality. While none of us is neutral, we differ in the degree to which we recognize and are willing to take account of this fact. The most salient feature of a good mediation process is that the failures of neutrality are not denied, but are recognized and addressed.

Various forms have arisen in the adversarial adjudicatory system to take into account, to some extent, the predictable failures of neutrality.[201] Because mediation does not have these forms, its failures must be addressed in a different way. Although there may be many ways in which to do so, giving the parties the choice of whether or not to mediate, and with whom, is surely an indispensable beginning.

b. *Mediators and Judges: The Importance of Form*

Mediators are not supposed to be judges, at least in states that do not permit them to make recommendations to the court.[202] It is assumed, however, that mediators as well as judges can and should be impartial. In the context of judging, Judith Resnik has shown how impartiality among judges is an aspiration, not a reality.[203] Rather, a demonstrable "picture of partiality, of prejudgment, of judges ready to translate racial and sexist views into law" emerges.[204] Even among well-intentioned judges who try to be impartial, the twin

note 199, at 1955.

Kenneth Kressel, Frances Butler-DeFreitas, Samuel Forlenza, and Cynthia Wilcox have suggested that the traditional definitions of mediator impartiality need to be reconsidered: they advocate a "robust" mediator style in which, although the parties are treated evenhandedly, the mediator can have a point of view and will not attempt to be a "passive good Samaritan." Kressel, *Custody Mediations*, *supra* note 71, at 67.

201. *See infra* note 205 and accompanying text.

202. The difference between mediators and judges in their effective, as opposed to formal, decisionmaking power is sometimes remarkably little. Where mediators are permitted to make a recommendation to the court, and that recommendation is routinely followed, it is difficult to differentiate the mediator's authority from the judge's. *See In re* Matthews, 101 Cal. App. 3d 811, 817, 161 Cal. Rptr. 879, 882 (1980) (reversing order of family court judge giving Conciliation Department family counselors "authority of the court" to modify or amend visitation schedule). Martha Fineman has demonstrated how, in many states, mediators and other helping professionals have appropriated decisionmaking in child custody matters from the legal system. *See* Fineman, *supra* note 6, at 740-41 (as custody decisionmaking has become more complex, social workers have replaced judges as "final arbiters of child custody"). Simon Roberts has pointed out that "[m]eanings are . . . going to get muddled in the mind of disputants if processes over which they supposedly retain control are conflated with those which are essentially about externally imposed decision. The beauty of adjudication, if you can call it that, is that we know unambiguously what we are experiencing." Roberts, *The Location and Occasion of Mediation*, in THE ROLE OF MEDIATION, *supra* note 8, at 131, 131-32.

203. Resnik, *supra* note 197.

204. *Id.* at 1904. Several states have considered the issue of sex discrimination in the courts. Most recently, the California Judicial Council's Advisory Committee on Gender Bias in the Courts found widespread and pervasive gender bias at all levels of the California Court system. *See* JUDICIAL COUNCIL ADVISORY COMM. ON GENDER BIAS IN THE COURTS, ACHIEVING EQUAL JUSTICE FOR WOMEN AND MEN IN THE COURTS § 2, at 1-9 (Draft Report 1990); *see also* THE FIRST YEAR REPORT OF THE NEW JERSEY SUPREME COURT TASK FORCE ON WOMEN IN THE COURTS (1984) (investigating gender bias in the New Jersey judicial system); THE SECOND REPORT OF THE NEW JERSEY SUPREME COURT TASK FORCE ON WOMEN IN THE COURTS (1986) (same); *Report of the New York Task Force on Women in the Courts*, 15 FORDHAM URB. L.J. 11, 15 (1986-87) ("[G]ender bias against women litigants, attorneys, and court employees is a pervasive problem with grave consequences.").

dangers of unacknowledged perspective and unrecognized partiality are always present.

These dangers, serious enough in the context of judging, are exacerbated in mediation. There are numerous restrictions on the way the decisionmaker ordinarily relates to parties in the adversarial setting that simply do not apply to mediation. For example, judges (and most other decisionmakers required to be neutral) generally keep both a physical and a psychological distance from the parties, a distance designed to preserve both actual impartiality and the appearance of impartiality. Many formalities of the judicial process serve to maintain this distance. At the most mundane level, judges sit apart from the parties.[205] Ordinarily, they speak to the parties' attorneys rather than directly to the parties. When they do address the parties directly, it is often in a formal manner, and on the record. Judges also do not ordinarily communicate with one side separately, and if there is such communication, they are obligated to notify the opposing party of its substance. Finally, judges can consider only certain sorts of evidence.

By contrast, because the mediator views her role as one of understanding and helping the parties rather than judging them, judicial forms of distancing are dispensed with. Mediators sit close to the parties and speak directly to them. They frequently meet with the parties separately, often without subsequently telling the opposing party what transpired.[206] The session with the mediator is rarely entered on the record or even informally recorded.[207] Finally, no attempt is made to limit the sort of material that may be considered in the session on grounds of privilege or relevancy; something may be considered relevant for the purposes of mediation because it is emotionally—even though not logically—connected to the proceedings. In sum, a mediator establishes what may be a risky relationship of informality and apparent intimacy with the parties.[208]

The informal nature of the mediation setting may make it an environment in which prejudices can flourish. Richard Delgado and his coauthors have shown that people who hold prejudicial attitudes are most prone to act on those

205. *See* Delgado, *Fairness and Formality*, *supra* note 10, at 1387-88. Simple lack of physical distance can have a large effect on the interaction. For example, investigators in Germany found that where youthful offenders sat at the same table as the judge, they were much more likely to confess than when the judge was elevated and at some distance (as told to Professor Alan Freeman by Heino Kolbe, German lawyer-mediator who has studied extensively the impact of theatrical positioning and location on law).

206. Some states, however, do not permit family court mediators to meet separately with the parties except under unusual circumstances. *See, e.g.*, CAL. CIV. CODE § 4607(c) (West 1983 & Supp. 1990).

207. Confidentiality is emphasized in the Model Standards of Practice for Family and Divorce Mediation by the Association of Family and Conciliation Courts: "A mediator shall foster the confidentiality of the process." Bishop, *Standards of Practice for Divorce Mediators*, in DIVORCE MEDIATION, THEORY AND PRACTICE, *supra* note 14, at 403, 422. "The mediator shall maintain confidentiality in the storage and disposal of records." *Id.* at 423.

208. This purported intimacy is necessarily limited by the goal of the mediator to achieve a result.

attitudes in an intimate setting.[209] These authors assert that where prejudicial attitudes conflict with a humane creed, many resolve this conflict by resorting to "situational specificity," that is, by changing their expressed beliefs depending on the circumstances.[210] For example, the average white American exhibits increased prejudice in intimate, as opposed to formal or public settings.[211] The consequence of this tendency is that prejudicial behavior will be discouraged in settings in which institutional expectations and rules of procedure check overt signs of prejudice.[212] In sum, the forms that are required of judges provide some modest, albeit inadequate,[213] protection against bias. Because these forms are not available in mediation, the potential that bias will influence the outcome is increased.

c. *Forms of Partiality*

Most of Richard Delgado and his coauthors' discussion addresses racial and ethnic prejudice, which might be expected to arise as frequently in mediation as in other forms of dispute resolution: that is, frequently indeed.[214] Their basic assertion, however, also applies to other sorts of prejudices, such as those based on gender, social class, and even desired outcome. The very intimacy that renders mediation such a potentially constructive process may facilitate the mediator's projection[215] of her own conflicts onto the parties, and the possibilities and dangers of transference and countertransference.[216]

In psychotherapy, a patient brings with him a view from his past which he then superimposes on the therapist. This superimposed view, referred to as transference,[217] sheds light on the patient's own view of the world in addition to his view of himself.[218] It was Freud who suggested that the patient's picture of the analyst allows great insight into the patient's own personality structure.[219] Freudian psychoanalysis, then, consists largely of studying, and eventually resolving, such transference. For example, a patient might expect to be criticized for even small mistakes, or to be ignored or scorned. On the other hand, he may idealize the therapist or believe he is in love with her. According to Freud, the patient's problems inevitably manifest themselves in the therapeu-

209. *See* Delgado, *Fairness and Formality*, *supra* note 10, at 1386; Delgado, *ADR and the Dispossessed*, *supra* note 197, at 152-54.

210. *See* Delgado, *Fairness and Formality*, *supra* note 10, at 1386.

211. *Id.* at 1386.

212. *Id.* at 1388.

213. *See* Resnik, *supra* note 197, at 1904-05.

214. *See* Delgado, *Fairness and Formality*, *supra* note 10, at 1375.

215. For a definition of projection, see *supra* note 196.

216. It is through projection that transference and countertransference take place. *See* S. PERERA, *supra* note 196, at 41-42.

217. *See* G. WEINBERG, THE HEART OF PSYCHOTHERAPY 134-36 (1984).

218. *See id.* at 134-50.

219. S. FREUD, A GENERAL INTRODUCTION TO PSYCHOANALYSIS 374, 384-86 (1935).

tic relationship;[220] the relationship is a microcosm of the way in which the patient situates himself in the world. A distrustful transference will prepare a person "for a world of thieves but not for love."[221] An extremely trustful transference will make it hard to recognize people who are in reality selfish or cruel.[222]

In a complementary manner, a therapist's response to a patient always, to some degree, arises out of the therapist's own past experiences. That part of the reaction that comes out of the therapist's experience is referred to as countertransference.[223] For instance, a therapist might feel rivalrous with or jealous of the patient, or might be able to see the patient only as a helpless victim. It is considered essential in therapy that the therapist identify and observe her own countertransference and attempt to overcome it.[224]

Countertransference and transference also occur in mediation.[225] When transference occurs in mediation, however, there may not be the time, the commitment, or the expertise to study it and help the client learn what it reveals about her personality structure or orientation to the world. For this reason, a client in mediation might be far more influenced by what the mediator says than would be expected under the circumstances. It is not an answer to the problem of coercion in mediation, then, to say that the party does not have to agree with what the mediator says; she might not agree but go along with it anyway for reasons that are situated in her past and are quite beyond either her or the mediator's understanding. Such a dynamic is particularly troubling when the mediator makes statements that the client believes undercut her competence as a parent or as a human being. In another context, the client might be able to brush such statements off; because of the operation of transference, the particular setting, and what is at stake, however, the potency of the statements is likely to be increased many times.

Similarly, the countertransference that arises in mediation may cause the mediator to react negatively (or positively) to a client for reasons wholly apart from anything that actually happens in the session. Again, the mediator may have neither the time nor the inclination to examine his reaction. The client will have no idea what he has done to elicit the mediator's response, and will be powerless to change it since it arises out of the mediator's past rather than the present interaction. Without the ability to select a mediator or obtain a new one

220. *Id.*

221. G. WEINBERG, *supra* note 217, at 142.

222. *Id.* at 141.

223. *Id.* at 163.

224. *See id.* at 163-69.

225. While transference and countertransference can occur in a number of professional relationships—doctor-patient, lawyer-client, teacher-student—because mediation resembles the therapeutic setting in a number of ways, the likelihood of transference and countertransference reactions is greater. For example, both mediation and therapy are settings in which problems of one's personal life are to be solved through talking. In each process intense emotions are evoked, and the mediator or therapist provides professional listening, sympathy, and guidance.

if he is dissatisfied with the one he has, a client may be unable to avoid biased treatment.

Mediation literature has addressed the problem of unequal bargaining power between the parties by suggesting that the mediator use a variety of techniques to "balance the power."[226] These techniques entail empowering or supporting the less powerful party or disempowering the more powerful party. For example, a mediator might provoke a conflict, forbid the discussion of certain issues, or advise a party who seems to be at an economic disadvantage to see a financial counselor. These suggestions share the premise that the mediator can recognize power disparities when they occur and intervene to lessen their impact. But, as I have attempted to show, benign intervention may not always be possible. When a mediator analyzes and attempts to correct a power imbalance, she can no longer claim to be simply a facilitator of the couple's process; rather, she is taking an active role in affecting the outcome of that process. But the mediator, due to her own internal processes, may not in fact have a sufficiently clear vision of the interaction between the divorcing spouses to make a considered decision about if and how the power needs to be balanced. The existence of partiality, countertransference, and projection on the part of mediators explains why mediators' attempts to redress imbalances cannot necessarily be relied upon to meet the problem of unequal bargaining power.[227]

d. *Implicit Agendas and Defining Fairness*

Apart from the particular dynamic that exists between a mediator and the parties in a given case, a mediator will always be influenced in her mediations by her own values. These values may be personal, or they may be derived from the mediator's professional training or the community in which she lives.[228] The mediator may not disclose, or perhaps even recognize, her reliance on such

226. *See* J. HAYNES, DIVORCE MEDIATION: A PRACTICAL GUIDE FOR THERAPISTS AND COUNSELORS 49-53 (1981); J. HAYNES & G. HAYNES, *supra* note 109, at 17; Bernard, Folger, Weingarten & Zumeta, *The Neutral Mediator: Value Dilemmas in Divorce Mediation*, MEDIATION Q., June 1984, at 61, 65; Haynes, *Power Balancing*, in DIVORCE MEDIATION, THEORY AND PRACTICE, *supra* note 14, at 277 (1988); *see also* Forester & Stitzel, Beyond Neutrality: The Possibilities of Activist Mediation in Public Sector Conflicts, NEGOTIATION J., July 1989, at 251, 256 (activist mediators must dispense with neutrality in order to balance information and participation); Laue & McCormick, *The Ethics of Intervention in Community Disputes*, in THE ETHICS OF SOCIAL INTERVENTION 205, 220 (1978) (intervenor in community dispute should not remain neutral and should help weaker parties to implement their power).

227. Mediators are also likely to share societal assumptions about what roles men and women will play in mediation. *See, e.g.*, Ricci, *Mediator's Notebook: Reflections on Promoting Equal Empowerment and Entitlements for Women*, J. DIVORCE, Spring/Summer 1985, at 49, 52-55, 59.

228. *See* M. Ray, Women and Children After Divorce: Comparing Outcomes from Three Processes for Resolving Disputes 31 (unpublished manuscript on file with author) (expectations of mediators influence custody arrangements).

values.[229] It may appear to the mediator, as to any of us, that her perception of the world is objectively true.

When a mediator imposes an agenda, it is probably because it seems fair to her to do so. In introducing the parties to mediation, mediators frequently emphasize that the goal is a "fair" agreement.[230] Thus, mediators often replace the struggle over legal rights with a struggle over what is "fair."[231] There are some mediators who define a fair agreement as one that closely resembles what the court would have ordered had the case gone to trial. This conception of fairness appears to have the virtue of clarity and permits parties to assert rights within the context of the mediation. But styling what a court would do as the "fair" result limits the room for a party to view the law itself as "unfair."[232] In such a case, it can no longer be said that that party is in control of the normative issues at stake in the mediation. Moreover, if this legalistic conception of fairness is accepted, the only reason to prefer mediation to the adversary system is because it might be less expensive. After all, the "fairest" agreement of all could be reached by going to court and having active settlement judges deal with lawyers, or, arguably, by feeding data about the family into a computer. If this is all mediation is about, then there is little justification for subjecting people to what may be a traumatic process in which their hopes, aspirations, and pain necessarily must enter. Nor is there much reason to tout the process as one of "healing," one in which there is "[c]aring, sharing, mental health, and concern for future functioning."[233]

On the other hand, some mediators regard law as irrelevant to fairness. Rather, they look for an intuitive conception of fairness shared by the parties and, at least to a limited extent, by the mediator. This assumes, of course, that the parties and mediator are able to share a vision of what is fair, and that they can, with the help of the mediator, apply it. Many mediators have had the experience of parties asking them, "Tell me, is this fair? I want to be fair." At such a juncture, the parties themselves are ready to either fall back on the law's definition of fairness, or defer to what the mediator believes to be fair; they are not actively considering their own values.

Finally, some mediators have a more complex view of the role of law in mediation: "[T]he mediator can help the parties consider law not primarily as a set of necessary applied rules, but as providing a relevant reference point, both in terms of a practical alternative and as an expression of societal norms and, perhaps, some underlying principles."[234]

---

229. *See* Teitelbaum & DuPaix, *supra* note 49, at 1125.

230. *See id.* at 1123-25; Center for Development of Mediation in Law, Explanation of Mediation Process 1-3, 6, 8 (Aug. 1983) (training materials).

231. Teitlebaum & Dupaix, *supra* note 49, at 1123-25.

232. *See* Abel, *supra* note 64, at 267-310.

233. Fineman, *supra* note 6, at 757.

234. Center for Development of Mediation in Law, The Place of Law in Mediation 1 (Aug. 1983) (training materials).

The danger inherent in each of these approaches is that, because no community-wide view of fairness exists, the parties may be left with the desire to think of themselves as fair, but have no guiding precepts other than those that may be provided by the mediator to tell them they are behaving justly. Mediators are often far too willing to provide those very "principles."

3. *Joint Custody*

> *Linda and Jerry had been married for five years when Kenny was born. They separated when he was fourteen months old. Even before the separation, Linda had had almost complete responsibility for Kenny since Jerry's job with the railroad took him out of town at least three nights per week on a schedule that was constantly changing. When Jerry was in town, he tended to spend time with his friends rather than with Linda and Kenny. After the separation, Jerry saw Kenny in a sporadic fashion until, when Kenny was two, Jerry moved 1000 miles away to another state. Jerry then kept in only infrequent contact with Kenny and paid little support for him until Jerry moved in with his girlfriend, whom he married when Kenny was three and one-half. Once Jerry remarried, he was anxious to have Kenny with him, and Linda began to send Kenny to Jerry for short visits.*
>
> *Linda was willing for Jerry to have frequent contact with Kenny. She did not feel, however, that it would be good for Kenny to live in two different homes, 1000 miles apart. The mediator told Linda that the most important thing for Kenny's future development was to have frequent and continuing contact with both parents. She said Jerry was entitled to have his son half the time; the only question was which half. Although the mediator recognized the difficulty of arranging for frequent long-distance travel for Kenny, she nonetheless recommended that Kenny spend alternate months with each parent. When Linda protested that, because of Jerry's work schedule, Kenny would have frequent and continuing contact with neither parent when he was staying with Jerry, the mediator made it clear that if Linda did not agree to sharing custody on the terms she suggested, she would recommend to the court that Jerry get sole custody.*[235]

Many mediators state unabashedly that they attempt to steer their clients toward joint custody, regardless of what the clients want.[236] Some go so far

235. For the origin of this mediation story, see *supra* note 13.

236. Donald Saposnek suggests that, in general, "coparenting to the maximal degree possible is the goal towards which the mediator should strive." D. SAPOSNEK, *supra* note 69, at 81. He advises that parents be instructed on the benefits of coparenting, and on the dangers to children of failing to coparent. *Id.* at 69-70. Saposnek further states, however, that should joint custody not be feasible in a certain instance, the mediator should "not even mention it." *Id.* at 78. When the mediator favors coparenting, he may "preempt" a party's position to the contrary. Saposnek, *Aikido: A Systems Model for Maneuvering in Mediation*, MEDIATION Q., Winter 1987/Spring 1988, at 119, 128-29. For example, faced with a woman who wants sole custody, Saposnek suggests that the mediator advise his clients as follows:

> You both need to know that all our research and clinical experience to date lead us to conclude that children of divorce do best when they have regular contact with both parents and that even

as to tell a parent that her refusal to request joint custody may result in an award of custody to the other spouse as the "friendlier" parent.[237] This position is justified on the ground that the mediator should be an advocate for the children. Mediators who take this view do so despite the lack of convincing evidence that joint custody is in fact better for children than sole custody.[238] This position also ignores the disturbing reality that a father may request joint custody to obtain financial concessions from his wife in exchange for permitting her to have sole custody; in fact, some lawyers routinely recommend this tactic.[239]

An influential article by Judith Wallerstein and Joan Kelly[240] helped to shape the views on joint custody held by many mediators. A remarkable leap was made, however, from the results of Wallerstein and Kelly's research to the determination that joint custody is the best of possible custody arrangements. Wallerstein and Kelly did not even study joint custody families; joint custody was barely discussed when they began their research in 1971. Their study simply found that children whose mothers had sole custody did better after divorce when the children had frequent and continuing contact with their fathers.[241] While Kelly has used this early study to endorse a presumption

---

> a parent who was not very involved with the child during the marriage often becomes involved with the child after the divorce in an important and meaningful way.

Id. at 129. Saposnek explains his advice as follows: "Preempting . . . leaves the parent off balance and vulnerable to accepting the mediator's direction . . . ." *Id.*

Robert Emery and Joanne Jackson state that "unlike many mediators, we do not advocate for joint physical custody. . . . Our mediated agreements resulted in more joint *legal* custody awards, but the number of days children were to spend with each parent did not differ for the mediation and litigation families." Emery & Jackson, *supra* note 8, at 8 (emphasis added). These researchers explicitly recognize that their bias against shared physical custody did affect the outcome of agreements. *Id.* In coming out in favor of joint legal custody, however, they do not address the problem of the noncustodial parent's exercising a veto power over the parent who is actually caring for the child or children. *See supra* notes 105-15 and accompanying text. *But see* J. GOLDSTEIN, A. FREUD & A. SOLNIT, BEYOND THE BEST INTERESTS OF THE CHILD 37-39, 48-49 (1973) (custody should be granted to "psychological parent" and custodial parent should have complete decisionmaking power in relation to child).

237. Many court mediators routinely recommend that the parent who does not oppose joint custody be given sole custody where the parties cannot agree on joint custody. *See, e.g.*, Mumma, *supra* note 128, at 30 ("[W]e may recommend custody be given to the parent who is most likely to allow the most frequent or flexible contact with the other parent . . . ."); *see also* Fineman, *supra* note 6, at 751-52 (when choosing between parents, helping professionals prefer parent who most freely allows child access to other parent). Thus, the parent seeking sole custody, usually the mother, risks losing custody entirely if she does not "agree" to joint custody. Mediators who take this position sometimes rely on a "friendly parent" provision in state child custody law. For example, CAL. CIV. CODE § 4600 (West Supp. 1990) provides that in awarding custody, the court should "consider, among other factors, which parent is more likely to allow the child or children frequent and continuing contact with the noncustodial parent." Alaska and Iowa are the two other states which have provisions similar to California's. *See* ALASKA STAT. § 25.20.090(E) (1983); IOWA CODE ANN. § 598.41(1) (West Supp. 1990).

238. *See infra* notes 241-45 and accompanying text.

239. *See* Bruch, *Parenting at and After Divorce: A Search for New Models* (Book Review), 79 MICH. L. REV. 708, 723 n.15 (1981).

240. Wallerstein & Kelly, *Children and Divorce: A Review*, 24 SOC. WORK 468 (1979).

241. Wallerstein and Kelly's research began in 1971. Follow-up research was performed at 18-month and 5-year intervals. *Id.* at 470. The study found that good father-child relationships were pivotal to the psychological well-being of children of divorce. *Id.* at 471. It also found, however, that the mother's emotional well-being was the single best indicator of the children's eventual psychological health. *Id.* at

of joint custody,[242] Wallerstein has cautioned that not enough is known about the effects of shared custody on children to treat it as a presumptively better arrangement.[243]

When Wallerstein some years later actually studied joint custody, she discovered that it does not minimize the negative impact of divorce on children, at least not during the early post-divorce years.[244] Moreover, early studies of joint custody were based only on voluntary joint custody arrangements. When joint custody not based on voluntary agreements was studied, the results were unsettling. Children raised under joint custody arrangements resulting from court orders in cases where there had been significant conflict fared worse than children raised in comparable sole-custody homes.[245] The hope of courts and mediators that joint custody would "force" parents to cooperate has not come to pass.

In the story above, Linda agreed to joint custody to avoid losing her child entirely; for all practical purposes, joint custody was imposed on her. This happened because the mediator was partial to a particular outcome. But even mediators who are careful not to steer their clients toward or away from a particular outcome almost surely have visions of how families are to be structured. Notably, in my reading of the mediation literature I have not come across any substantial discussion of variations in family structure in the United States.

The existence of different values and perspectives makes it dangerous to deprive the parties of the opportunity to choose whether or not to engage in mediation and with whom. Because there are so few formal protections for the clients in mediation, and because the relationship between the mediator and the clients may carry with it the risks that come with intimacy and implicit value-laden agendas, it is essential that the parties retain the right to choose not to participate.

---

470. Even to the extent that this research was relevant to joint custody, the demographics of the study should have given pause. The participants were almost entirely middle-class residents of a wealthy California county, comprising 60 families with 131 children. *Id.* at 470. Eighty-eight percent of the participants were white, 3% were Black, and 9% were interracial. J. WALLERSTEIN & S. BLAKESLEE, *supra* note 121, at 310. It cannot be assumed that the family structures that worked optimally for this group would also be optimal for others with different financial restrictions, values, and cultural backgrounds.

242. *See* Kelly, *Further Observations on Joint Custody*, 16 DAVIS L. REV. 762, 764-65 (1983).

243. *See* J. WALLERSTEIN & S. BLAKESLEE, *supra* note 121, at 258; *see also* Bruch, *supra* note 24, at 109 (noting that while Kelly has endorsed presumption of joint custody, Wallerstein has cautioned against applying research regarding benefits of frequent and continuing contact to arguments supporting joint control).

244. *See* J. WALLERSTEIN & S. BLAKESLEE, *supra* note 121, at 256-73; Kline, Tschann, Johnston & Wallerstein, *Children's Adjustment in Joint and Sole Custody Families*, 25 DEVELOPMENTAL PSYCHOLOGY 430, 437 (1989); *see also* Steinmann, Zemmelman & Knoblauch, *A Study of Parents Who Sought Joint Custody Following Divorce: Who Reaches Agreement and Sustains Joint Custody and Who Returns to Court*, 24 J. AM. ACAD. CHILD PSYCHIATRY 554, 561 (1985) (study of joint-custody families showed wide spectrum of outcomes: for some families joint custody was beneficial option, while for others it was stressful).

245. *See* Johnston, Kline & Tschann, *Ongoing Post-Divorce Conflict: Effects on Children of Joint Custody and Frequent Access*, 59 J. AM. ORTHOPSYCHIATRY 576, 588, 590; *cf.* Bruch, *supra* note 239, at 723 (couples who agree on joint custody as compromise rather than as expression of shared conviction are greatly overrepresented in later custody litigation).

4. *Exclusion of Lawyers*

In California, lawyers typically are excluded from mediation sessions, and the parties are required to speak for themselves, whether or not they wish to do so.[246] Some argue that exclusion of lawyers contributes to client empowerment.[247] In evaluating whether their exclusion actually furthers client empowerment, it is useful to consider the reasons why a person engaged in a divorce might want the services of a lawyer. First, and most obviously, lawyers are hired for their expertise, particularly their expertise in protecting their clients' rights. Of equal importance, however, is the fact that lawyers are hired to provide a buffer, a layer of insulation, between the client and her spouse. Neither of these rationales for the presence of an attorney disappears in the context of mediation.

a. *Lawyers as Protectors of Rights*

A lawyer who is excluded from the mediation sessions may be hampered in protecting her client's rights, particularly if custody is ultimately to be litigated in court. For example, privileged or irrelevant material, which the lawyer does not believe should be disclosed, may mistakenly be revealed in mediation. Once such privileged information is disclosed, it is often impossible to keep it out of a later court proceeding.

In states with an evidentiary privilege protecting mediation,[248] a party would not be able to use in court any documents obtained in mediation. In

---

246. CAL. CIV. CODE § 4607(d) (West 1983) provides in relevant part: "The mediator shall have the authority to exclude counsel from participation in the mediation proceedings where, in the discretion of the mediator, exclusion of counsel is deemed by the mediator to be appropriate or necessary." *Cf.* McCrory, *supra* note 30, at 150-51 (whether lawyers may participate in mediation varies from state to state and in some states is determined by scope of issues being mediated). Attorneys are normally excluded from mediation sessions in California. It is not until an agreement is reached by the parties that counsel become involved: "Any agreement reached by the parties as a result of mediation shall be reported to counsel for the parties by the mediator on the day set for mediation or as soon thereafter as practical, but prior to its being reported to the court . . . ." CAL. CIV. CODE § 4807(e) (West Supp. 1990). For a discussion of other states' approaches to the inclusion of lawyers at mediation sessions, see *supra* note 30.

247. *See* S. GOLDERG, E. GREEN & F. SANDER, *supra* note 117, at 338 (if lawyers are kept out, parties can communicate directly and work out problems themselves); Jaffe, *Divorce Mediation: The Next Decade* in THE ROLE OF MEDIATION, *supra* note 8, at 284, 285 (participants in conference on mediation agreed that lawyers should not take part in mediation sessions). *But see* C. MOORE, *supra* note 134, at 108 (encouraging parties to mediation to consult with lawyer); Folberg, *Divorce Mediation—A Workable Alternative*, in ALTERNATIVE MEANS OF FAMILY DISPUTE RESOLUTION 11, 35-39 (1982) (refuting suggestion that attorneys are ill-equipped to serve as divorce mediators).

248. California is one state with such a privilege. *See supra* note 29 and accompanying text. In California, "official information" cannot be disclosed if an authorized official refuses disclosure pursuant to section 1040(b) of the California Evidence Code. *See supra* note 29. In *In re* Marriage of Rosson, 178 Cal. App. 3d 1094, 1098, 224 Cal. Rptr. 250, 253 (1986), the Court of Appeal held that the official information privilege belongs to the court rather than the parties, and that, by the adoption of local rules permitting a mediator to make a recommendation to the court as to custody or visitation, the court may waive the privilege. Such local rules are specifically authorized by section 4607(e) of the California Civil Code. *See supra* note 31.

many instances, however, he could obtain the documents in some other manner, once he knows of their existence. Moreover, even if the information is not introduced formally, it may nonetheless subtly influence the proceedings at a later date.

Nor does a provision for consulting with attorneys before an agreement is reached, or for stopping the mediation to allow consultation with an attorney, ensure that a client will be adequately protected. Apart from the possibility of harmful disclosure of information, a party may agree to something because he is nervous, intimidated, exhausted, or frightened. Even if the agreement is not final until it has been presented to the attorneys, it will be difficult for a disempowered party to disavow an agreement already tentatively reached. Moreover, the attorneys themselves may be reluctant to be perceived as sabotaging an agreement.

In jurisdictions in which mediators are permitted to make recommendations to the court, the problem of protecting disempowered parties is even more acute. Under California Civil Code section 4607(e), if no agreement is reached in mediation, a mediator "may, consistent with local court rules, render a recommendation to the court" based on information acquired during the mediation.[249] Where such a recommendation is lawful, it may well seem a futile gesture to fail to "agree" to a proposal that the mediator favors or to disavow the agreement before it is approved by the court—especially in a jurisdiction where mediators' recommendations are almost always accepted. This is what happened to Linda in the example above, when the mediator told Linda that if she did not "agree" to the mediator's joint custody terms, the mediator would recommend to the court that Jerry be awarded sole custody.

Even where the judge will evaluate the mediator's recommendation more cautiously, there may be evidentiary problems that make a challenge to the mediator's opinion difficult to mount. In *McLaughlin v. Superior Court*,[250] the California Court of Appeal held that parties must be granted the right to cross-examine a mediator regarding his recommendation. Upon cross-examination, however, some mediators may refuse to disclose the reasons for the recommendation, relying on the "official information" privilege set forth in the

249. More than half of California counties permit such recommendations to be made. *See supra* note 33 and accompanying text.

250. 140 Cal. App. 3d 473, 482-83, 189 Cal. Rptr. 479, 486 (1983). In *McLaughlin*, prior to mediation, counsel for the father had moved, in effect, for a "protective order" which would prohibit the mediator from making a recommendation to the court unless his client were guaranteed the right to cross-examine the mediator. The lower court had denied the motion on the ground that granting the order would violate the local court's policy that mediators not state the basis for their recommendations. *Id.* at 477, 189 Cal. Rptr. at 482. The Court of Appeal upheld the local court policy, reasoning that it was consistent with CAL. CIV. CODE § 4607(c) (West Supp. 1990), which states that mediation proceedings "shall be confidential." *Id.* at 482-83, 189 Cal. Rptr. at 486. But the Court of Appeal went on to hold that the parties must nonetheless be guaranteed the right to cross-examine the mediator in order for the court to receive a recommendation on contested issues, unless they have waived that right. *Id.* at 484, 189 Cal. Rptr. at 487; *cf.* Ohmer v. Superior Court, 148 Cal. App. 3d 661, 668, 196 Cal. Rptr. 224, 228 (1983) (parties found to have waived right to cross-examine court-appointed custody investigator).

Evidence Code.[251] *McLaughlin* did not address the question of whether a mediator can rightfully claim this privilege or refuse to answer specific questions about his recommendation.[252] There is no answer to this dilemma that adequately protects the parties: if the mediator is required to testify fully, the mediation is confidential only in the narrowest sense of that word, and the parties' need for full access to their attorneys *during* the mediation process is apparent. But if the mediator is permitted to limit his testimony, then the parties are deprived of their cross-examination rights just as effectively as if the mediator had never taken the stand.

b. *Lawyers as Providers of Insulation*

Lawyers serve another function in the divorce process, that of insulating the parties from the hand-to-hand combat and self-help that the rule of law is intended to avoid. The presence of a lawyer means that a party does not have to face his adversary directly if he does not wish to do so. Mediation is often put forward as a method of empowering the parties to a dispute, but the words "Don't call me, call my lawyer" are sometimes the most empowering words imaginable. Mandatory mediation, even absent the pressure to reach an agreement that exists when a recommendation to the court can be made, prevents lawyers from performing this protective function.

The usual view is that mediation is at its best where the parties have a close relationship, and one that is likely to continue in some form. The danger of being deprived of the insulation provided by a lawyer is at its greatest, however, under those precise circumstances. At the time of divorce, the hiring of an attorney can be the first step to disengagement, to seeing oneself as separate from one's spouse;[253] the attorney can keep the party from experiencing directly the hostility, pain, or fear of the other party. An attorney may provide a further type of insulation as well. In mediation it is easy for a woman to feel she is being characterized as greedy, selfish, controlling, or unfeminine.[254] Even if the mediator does not mean to do so, many women may be ready to hear those words, or worse, may be using them internally. An attorney can carry the banner for the proposition that there is nothing wrong with the client's wanting what she wants, and that she is entitled, at a minimum, to survive.[255]

It is interesting to contemplate why a mandatory system of mediation should encourage the exclusion of lawyers. Perhaps some believe that lawyers cannot

251. *McLaughlin*, 140 Cal. App. 3d 473, 480, 189 Cal. Rptr. 479, 485. For the relevant text of this provision of the California Evidence Code, see *supra* note 29.

252. *See* Note, *Mandatory Custody Mediation*, 26 SANTA CLARA L. REV. 745, 755 (1986).

253. For a discussion of women's difficulties in asserting a separate self at the time of divorce, see *infra* note 274 and accompanying text.

254. *See infra* notes 272-75 and accompanying text.

255. *Cf.* Swift, *Becoming a Plaintiff*, 4 BERKELEY WOMEN'S L.J. 245 (1989-90) (plaintiff's self-confidence crucial to pursuing and winning litigation).

be relied on to be cooperative and will disrupt the mediation process.[256] In any event, the exclusion of lawyers renders the parties more vulnerable to the exercise of authority—often veiled authority—by the mediator.

III. Mandatory Mediation and the Dangers of Forced Engagement

Emma has been in a marriage which in its early years seemed to be a good one for both Emma and her husband. She has been the primary caretaker of the children, and she is very committed to them. She has lived much of her life through her husband and her children, and has not worked outside her home. Increasingly, however, she has begun to feel that she and her husband have grown apart, and that he does not see her as a person but rather as a repository of various roles. After much agony, she has decided to end her marriage. Her departure from the marriage is a first step toward seeing her life as having separate dimensions from her husband's and children's, but her right to individuation does not seem clear to her; in fact, there are many times when it seems selfish and wrong. It is hard for her even to find the language to describe what is propelling her to turn her life, and her children's lives, upside down, but propelled she is. The marital separation was an early step toward defining her own physical and psychological boundaries. She now finds herself, however, feeling guilty, frightened, and unsure of how she will survive in the world alone.

Joan has been in a marriage in which she has been physically abused for ten years. She and her husband David have two children, whom David has never abused. She is afraid, however, that if she leaves David, he will begin to abuse the children whenever he is caring for them. Joan has been afraid to leave her marriage because David has threatened to harm her if she does so. When she separated briefly from him previously, he followed her and continually harassed her. Each time David beats Joan he shows great remorse afterwards and promises never to do it again. He is a man of considerable charm, and she has often believed him on these occasions. Nonetheless, Joan has finally decided to leave her husband. She is worried about what will happen, economically and physically, to her children and herself.[257]

It might be that mediation would help Emma's family disengage and discover new ways of relating to one another. Mediation could be useful, even transformative, during the divorce process. Significant possibilities of damage

---

256. Martha Fineman describes the image of the legal system held by persons in the helping professions as "adversarial, combative, and productive of divisions, misunderstandings, and hostility." Fineman, *supra* note 6, at 754. She states that those who view mediation as ideal "accuse lawyers and the adversary system of increasing trauma, escalating conflict, obstructing communication, failing to perceive the need for negotiation and counseling, and generally interfering with the development of a process that could help the parties." *Id.* at 754-55 (footnotes omitted); *see, e.g.*, Haynes, *supra* note 102, at 5. Donald Saposnek suggests that clients be requested not to talk to their attorneys about custody or visitation issues during the mediation process. D. SAPOSNEK, *supra* note 69, at 61.

257. For the origin of these stories, see *supra* note 13.

to Emma also exist, however. For example, she might find herself traumatized by a forced engagement with her husband.[258] Or, in the intimate mediation setting, she might find it difficult to withstand criticism of how she is conducting herself in life or in the mediation.

For Joan, the direct confrontation with her husband, with the safety of her children and herself at stake, would surely be psychologically traumatizing and might also put her in physical danger. Because of these possibilities, the chance—even the substantial one—of a beneficial result cannot justify the sort of intrusion by the state that occurs when mediation is mandatory.

While some of mandatory mediation's dangers affect men and women equally, others fall disproportionately on women. A study that compared people who chose to mediate with those who rejected the opportunity found that 44% of the reasons given by women who rejected mediation services offered to them centered around their mistrust of, fear of, or desire to avoid their ex-spouse. In contrast, those men who rejected mediation appeared to do so because they were skeptical of the mediation process or convinced they could win in court. Thus, the requirement of mandatory mediation that the parties meet personally with one another, usually without a lawyer present, presents troubling issues for women. Feminist analyses, looked at alone and together, clarify why this is so.

A. *The Ethic of Care in Mediation*

As discussed earlier, several feminist scholars have suggested that women have a more "relational" sense of self than do men. The most influential of these researchers, Carol Gilligan, describes two different, gendered modes of thought.[259] The female mode is characterized by an "ethic of care" which emphasizes nurturance, connection with others, and contextual thinking. The male mode is characterized by an "ethic of justice" which emphasizes individualism, the use of rules to resolve moral dilemmas, and equality.[260] Under Gilligan's view, the male mode leads one to strive for individualism and autonomy, while the female mode leads one to strive for connection with and

---

258. *See* Pearson, Thoennes & Vanderkooi, *supra* note 175, at 23.

259. Gilligan's work was a response to theories of developmental psychology that defined normal development for both sexes based on tests and observations performed on boys and men. Gilligan conducted interviews by presenting male *and* female subjects with a moral dilemma; she then compared the responses of women and girls to those of men and boys. *See* C. GILLIGAN, *supra* note 10, at 2-3. More recently, Gilligan has completed a five-year study of students at a private school for girls. C. GILLIGAN, N. LYONS & T. HANMER, MAKING CONNECTIONS: THE RELATIONAL WORLDS OF ADOLESCENT GIRLS AT EMMA WILLARD SCHOOL (1990). In that study she found that many girls around the age of 11 are "resisters" who are outspoken and believe in their own integrity; by age 15 or 16, however, they "go underground" and learn to doubt what they had known. *Id.* at 11-15.

260. *See* C. GILLIGAN, *supra* note 10, at 62-63; Dubois, Duchamp, Gilligan, MacKinnon & Menkel-Meadow, *Feminist Discourse, Moral Values, and the Law—A Conversation*, 34 BUFFALO L. REV. 11, 47 (1985) [hereinafter Dubois, *A Conversation*].

caring for others.[261] Some writers, seeing a positive virtue in the ethic of care, have applied Gilligan's work to the legal system.[262] But her work has been criticized by others for its methodology,[263] its conflation of biological sex with gender,[264] and its failure to include race and class differences in its analysis.[265] (Indeed, it is not likely that the male/female differences Gilligan notes are consistent across racial and class lines.[266]) The "ethic of care" has also been viewed as the manifestation of a system of gender domination.[267] Nevertheless, it is clear that those who operate in a "female mode"—whether biologi-

---

261. Gilligan has noted that she is not ascribing the male mode to men and the female mode to women, but rather pointing out a distinction between two modes of thought. *See* Dubois, *A Conversation*, *supra* note 260, at 47. At times, however, she does seem to equate the male mode with men and boys and the female mode with women and girls. *See* C. GILLIGAN, *supra* note 10, *passim*. For the purposes of this Article, it makes little difference whether the distinction made is between males and females or "male" and "female" modes available to either sex, because the female mode is disproportionately used by women. *See id.* at 2.

262. *See, e.g.*, Areen, *A Need for Caring* (Book Review), 86 MICH. L. REV. 1067, 1073 (1988); Finley, *Transcending Equality Theory: A Way Out of the Maternity and the Workplace Debate*, 86 COLUM. L. REV. 1118, 1148 n.135 (1986); Karst, *supra* note 44, at 461-63; Kornhauser, *The Rhetoric of the Anti-Progressive Income Tax Movement: A Typical Male Reaction*, 86 MICH. L. REV. 465, 507 (1987); Menkel-Meadow, *supra* note 1, at 44; Rifkin, *Mediation*, *supra* note 1, at 24-25; Scales, *The Emergence of Feminist Jurisprudence: An Essay*, 95 YALE L.J. 1373, 1380 (1986); Schneider, *supra* note 89, at 597 n.39; Spiegelman, *Court-Ordered Hiring Quotas after* Stotts: *A Narrative on the Role of the Moralities of the Web and the Ladder in Employment Discrimination Doctrine*, 20 HARV. C.R.-C.L. L. REV. 339, 342-44 (1985).

263. *See, e.g.*, Kerber, Greeno, Maccoby, Luria, Stack & Gilligan, *On* In a Different Voice: *An Interdisciplinary Forum*, 11 SIGNS 304, 316 (1986) [hereinafter Kerber, *On* In a Different Voice].

264. *See, e.g.*, Williams, *supra* note 10, at 800-01.

265. *See, e.g.*, Auerbach, Blum, Smith & Williams, *Commentary on Gilligan's* In a Different Voice, 11 FEMINIST STUD. 149, 156-159 (1985); Broughton, *Women's Rationality And Men's Virtues: A Critique of Gender Dualism in Gilligan's Theory of Moral Development*, 50 SOC. RES. 597, 634 (1983).

266. *See* Williams, *supra* note 10, at 844.

267. The notion of the "different voice" can be seen as a means of romanticizing and exalting the consequences of oppression. *See* Hantzis, *Is Gender Justice A Completed Agenda?* (Book Review), 100 HARV. L. REV. 690, 698-71 (1987). Catharine MacKinnon describes the "different voice" as the "voice of the victim speaking without consciousness." Women may claim their identity in relationships because that is what they have been valued for, and because they have not been allowed to have a social identity on their own terms. *See* Dubois, *A Conversation*, *supra* note 260, at 27. In this exchange between Gilligan and MacKinnon, Gilligan indicated that she wished to assimilate the voice of Amy, her typical female, into the mainstream of society. MacKinnon, on the other hand, stated that her goal was to permit Amy to develop a new voice that "would articulate that [which] she cannot now, because [a male] foot is on her throat." *Id.* at 74-75. *See also* C. MACKINNON, *supra* note 3, at 51-52.

In a similar vein, Joan Williams has suggested that the "different voice" is a metaphor based on sex stereotypes, not a description of actual people. Williams, *supra* note 10, at 802-803. Williams identifies the ethic of care as composed of two elements, a critique of absolutes and a critique of possessive individualism. *Id.* at 799-800. She argues that the critique of absolutes did not come from women but was developed primarily by men such as Nietzsche, Heidegger, Wittgenstein, and the American pragmatists. *Id.* at 806.

The critique of possessive individualism, on the other hand, is tied in not only with women, but with the experience of exclusion: "Marginalized groups necessarily have maintained a more critical perspective on possessive individualism . . . than did white males who had most to gain by taking the culture's dominant ideology seriously." *Id.* at 844. Williams views the ethic of care as simply another expression of the gender system that requires women's social existence to be defined in terms of their husbands' need to eliminate their childcare responsibilities in order to function as ideal workers. *Id.* at 839.

cally male or female[268]—will respond more "selflessly" to the demands of mediation.

Whether the ethic of care is to be enshrined as a positive virtue, or criticized as a characteristic not belonging to all women and contributing to their oppression, one truth emerges: many women see themselves, and judge their own worth, primarily in terms of relationships.[269] This perspective on themselves has consequences for how they function in mediation.

Carrie Menkel-Meadow has suggested that the ethic of care can and should be brought into the practice of law—that the world of lawyering would look very different from the perspective of that ethic.[270] Some commentators have identified mediation as a way to incorporate the ethic of care into the legal system and thereby modify the harshness of the adversary process.[271] And, indeed, at first glance, mediation in the context of divorce might be seen as a way of bringing the woman-identified values of intimacy, nurturance, and care into a legal system that is concerned with the most fundamental aspects of women's and men's lives.

If mediation does not successfully introduce an ethic of care, however, but instead merely sells itself on that promise while delivering something coercive in its place, the consequences will be disastrous for a woman who embraces a relational sense of self. If she is easily persuaded to be cooperative, but her partner is not, she can only lose. If it is indeed her disposition to be caring and focused on relationships, and she has been rewarded for that focus and characterized as "unfeminine" when she departs from it, the language of relationship, caring, and cooperation will be appealing to her and make her vulnerable.[272]

---

268. A man who has adopted the female mode, or even part of it, will also be disadvantaged in mandatory mediation and, in light of his potential vulnerablitity, should not be required to participate in a forced engagement with his spouse. When a man who ordinarily operates in the female mode departs from it, however, he is not likely to be explicitly or implicitly criticized for not meeting the expectations associated with his gender identity, as a woman might be. *See* Littleton, *supra* note 80, at 47. Of course, to the extent he is not meeting societal expectations of males, he would be subject to criticism for that.

A particularly unfortunate aspect of this female mode/male mode paradigm is that men or women who depart from the traditional mode for their sex are "denied the dignity of being 'real' men or 'real' women." Williams, *supra* note 10, at 813 n.61.

269. The titles of a number of popular psychology books reflect this fact. *See* R. NORWOOD, WOMEN WHO LOVE TOO MUCH (1985); P. RUSSIANOFF, WHY DO I THINK I'M NOTHING WITHOUT A MAN? (1981); S. FRIEDMAN, MEN ARE JUST DESSERTS (1983). It is hard to contemplate a bestseller entitled *Why Do I Think I'm Nothing Without A Woman?*, although surely there are men who harbor that feeling.

270. *See generally* Menkel-Meadow, *supra* note 1; Menkel-Meadow, *Toward Another View of Legal Negotiation: The Structure of Problem Solving*, 31 UCLA L. REV. 754 (1984).

271. *See* Menkel-Meadow, *supra* note 1, at 49. Menkel-Meadow recognizes, however, that whether mediation is beneficial for women depends on who the mediator is and the model of mediation being employed. *Id.* at 53 n.78. She also notes that some disputes need authoritative rulings to prevent the abuse of power disparities and to provide precedents. *Id.*

272. In a presentation at the Joint Meeting of the Property and the Women in Legal Education Sections of the American Association of Law Schools, San Francisco, California (Jan. 4, 1990), Carol Rose used examples from game theory to demonstrate that, in a negotiation in which cooperation benefits both parties, a person "with a taste for cooperation" will end up less well off relative to a person not disposed to cooperate. To demonstrate her point, Professor Rose relied on a version of the game theory hypothetical "The Tragedy of the Commons." In this hypothetical, there is common grazing land. If both parties

Moreover, the intimation that she is not being cooperative and caring or that she is thinking of herself instead of thinking selflessly of the children can shatter her self-esteem and make her lose faith in herself. In short, in mediation, such a woman may be encouraged to repeat exactly those behaviors that have proven hazardous to her in the past.[273]

In the story above, Emma is asked to undergo a forced engagement with the very person from whom she is trying to differentiate herself at a difficult stage in her life. She may find it impossible to think of herself as a separate entity during mediation, while her husband may easily be able to act on behalf of his separate self. "When a separate self must be asserted, women have trouble asserting it. Women's separation from the other in adult life, and the tension between that separation and our fundamental state of connection, is felt most acutely when a woman must make choices, and when she must speak the truth."[274]

Emma will be asked to talk about her needs and feelings, and respond to her husband's needs and feelings. Although in the past her valuing relationships above all else may have worked to the detriment of her separate self, Emma will now be urged to work on the future relationship between herself and her ex-husband. Above all, she will be asked to put the well-being of the children before her own, as if she and her children's well-being were entirely separate.[275] Her problem in addressing her future alone, however, may be that she reflexively puts her children before herself, even when she truly needs to take care of herself in order to take care of her children. For Emma, mediation may play on what are already her vulnerable spots, and put her at a disadvantage. She may begin to think of herself as unfeminine, or simply bad, if she puts her own needs forward. Emma may feel the need to couch every proposal she makes in terms of the needs of her children. In sum, if she articulates her needs accurately, she may end up feeling guilty, selfish, confused, and embarrassed; if she does not, she will be moving backwards to the unbounded self that is at the source of her difficulties.

---

overgraze the land, both will lose because the land will be depleted; if neither party overgrazes the land, both will be better off. If one party does not overgraze the land, however, and the other does, the latter will be much better off than the party who refrains from overgrazing. A person with a taste for cooperation, according to Professor Rose, might well agree to more restrictions on her grazing rights than will her neighbor because it will take less to convince her to cooperate. Although in so agreeing she will still be better off than if both parties overgrazed the land, she will be worse off in comparison with her less-cooperative neighbor. Thus, in such a negotiation, the gains from cooperation have not been distributed evenly; the cooperator will not end up as well situated as the person who was reluctant to cooperate. In her presentation, Professor Rose indicated that a taste for cooperation might be more characteristic of women than of men, but that whether or not that is true, there is still a cultural expectation that women will be more cooperative. This presumption influences how people behave toward a woman regardless of her individual stance.

273. In a similar vein, Harriet Lerner has remarked that often therapists encourage women clients to be assertive and self-directed *except with the therapists*, to whom they are supposed to defer. H. LERNER, *supra* note 158, at 135-36.

274. West, *Jurisprudence and Gender*, 55 U. CHI. L. REV. 1, 55 (1988).

275. *See* D. SAPOSNEK, *supra* note 69, at 63.

For Joan, the prescription of mediation might be disastrous. She has always been susceptible to her husband's charm, and has believed him when he has said that he would stop abusing her. She has also always been afraid of him. She is likely, in mediation, to be susceptible and afraid once again. She may continue to care for her husband, and to think that she was responsible for his behavior toward her. Joan, and not her husband, will be susceptible to any pressure to compromise, and to compromise in her situation might be very dangerous for both her and her children.

B. *Sexual Domination and Judicial Violence*

Women who have been through mandatory mediation often describe it as an experience of sexual domination, comparing mandatory mediation to rape.[276] Catharine MacKinnon's work provides a basis for explaining why, for some women, this characterization is appropriate. MacKinnon has analyzed gender as a system of power relations, evidenced primarily with respect to the control of women's sexuality.[277] While MacKinnon recognizes the sense in which women are fundamentally connected to others, she does not celebrate it.[278] Rather, she sees the potential for connection as invasive and intrusive. It is precisely the potential for physical connection that permits invasion into the integrity of women's bodies. It is precisely the potential for emotional connection that permits intrusion into the integrity of women's lives.

Men do not experience this same fear of sexual domination, according to MacKinnon; they do not live in constant fear of having the very integrity of their lives intruded upon.[279] Men may not comprehend their role in this system of sexual domination any more than women may be able to articulate the source of their feeling of disempowerment. Yet both of these dynamics are at work in the mediation setting. It may seem a large leap, from acts of physical violence and invasion to the apparently simple requirement that a woman sit in a room with her spouse working toward the resolution of an issue of mutual

276. I have been struck, in the course of conversations with women who have undergone the mandatory mediation process, by how often these women have said, "I felt as if I were raped." (I am aware that many women experience the adversary process similarly.)

277. *See generally* C. MACKINNON, TOWARD A FEMINIST THEORY, *supra* note 3; C. MACKINNON, FEMINISM UNMODIFIED (1987); MacKinnon, *Feminism, Marxism*, *supra* note 3.

278. *See* C. MACKINNON, *Difference and Dominance*, in FEMINISM UNMODIFIED, *supra* note 277, at 32, 39 ("Women value care because men have valued us according to the care we give them, and we could probably use some. Women think in relational terms because our existence is defined in relation to men.").

279. Because the existential and subjective experience of the world differs for men and women, it is sometimes difficult to explain, in legal language, the basis for attention to areas of law that are of particular interest to women such as rape, sexual harassment, and reproductive freedom. For example, rape might be characterized and treated as any other crime of violence if the underlying sexual domination of women by men is not taken into account. Once institutionalized sexual domination is seen as something the law should address, however, rape becomes a very particular harm unlike any other, a combination of violence *and* sexual domination. *See* C. MACKINNON, *Sex and Violence: A Perspective*, in FEMINISM UNMODIFIED, *supra* note 277, at 85, 86-87. For a discussion of the parallel problem in the realm of reproductive freedom, see West, *supra* note 274, at 69.

concern. But that which may be at stake in a court-ordered custody mediation—access to one's children—may be the main reason one has for living, as well as all one's hope for the future. And because mandatory mediation is a *forced* engagement, ordinarily without attorneys or even friends or supporters present, it may amount to a form of "psychic breaking and entering"[280] or, put another way, psychic rape.

There is always the potential for violence in the legal system: "A judge articulates her understanding of a text, and as a result, somebody loses his freedom, his property, his children, even his life . . . . When interpreters have finished their work, they frequently leave behind victims whose lives have been torn apart by these organized, social practices of violence."[281]

The reality of this background of judicial violence cannot be discounted when measuring the potential trauma of the mandatory mediation setting. Although the mediation system is purportedly designed in part to help participants *avoid* contact with the violence that must come from judicial decisions, in significant ways the violence of the contact is more direct. Since the parties are obliged to speak for themselves in a setting to which the culture has not introduced them and in which the rules are not clear (and in fact vary from mediator to mediator[282]), the potential violence of the legal result, combined with the invasiveness of the setting, may indeed end up feeling to the unwilling participant very much like a kind of rape. Moreover, in judging, it is understood that the critical view of the quarrel is that of the judge, the professional third party. Mediation is described as a form of intervention that reflects the *disputants'* view of the quarrel. But having the mediation take place on court premises with a mediator who might or might not inject her prejudices into the process may make it unlikely that the disputants' view will control. Thus, a further sense of violation may arise from having another person's view of the dispute characterized and treated as one's own.[283]

That many reportedly find mediation helpful does not mean everyone does.[284] Consensual sex may take place in a certain setting in one instance but that does not make all sex in that setting consensual; sometimes it is rape. And sometimes it may only seem to be consensual because forced sex is considered par for the course—that is, it is all we know or can imagine.[285]

When I have suggested to mediators that even being forced to sit across the table and negotiate, unassisted, with a spouse might be traumatic, their reaction

280. Singer, Astrachan, Gould & Klein, *Boundary Management in Psychological Work with Groups*, in EXPLORING INDIVIDUAL AND ORGANIZATIONAL BOUNDARIES: A TAVISTOCK OPEN SYSTEMS APPROACH 21, 32 (D. Singer ed. 1979).

281. Cover, *Violence and the Word*, 95 YALE L.J. 1601, 1601 (1986).

282. *Cf. supra* text accompanying notes 24-28 (qualifications of mediators vary widely).

283. *See* David, *The Halls of Justice and Justice in the Halls*, in DIVORCE MEDIATION AND THE LEGAL PROCESS 95, 101 (1988).

284. With at least some models of mediation, participant satisfaction has been high. *See supra* notes 7-8 and accompanying text.

285. MacKinnon, *Feminism, Marxism*, supra note 3, at 648-52.

has been almost uniformly dismissive. Some mediators have denied that this could possibly be the case. Even mediators who acknowledge the possibility of trauma have said, in effect, "So what?" A few hours of discomfort seems not so much to ask in return for a system that, to their mind, serves the courts and the children much better than the alternative. But a few hours of discomfort may not be all that is at stake; the trauma inflicted upon a vulnerable party during mediation can be as great as that which occurs in other psychologically violent confrontations. As such, it should not be minimized. People frequently take months or years to recover from physical or mental abuse, rape, and other traumatic events.[286] Given the psychological vulnerability of people at the time of a divorce,[287] it is likely that some people may be similarly debilitated by a mandatory mediation process.

Moreover, because the mandatory mediation system is more problematic for women than for men,[288] forcing unwilling women to take part in a process which involves much personal exposure sends a powerful social message: it is permissible to discount the real experience of women in the service of someone else's idea of what will be good for them, good for their children, or good for the system.

IV. Alternatives to Mandatory Mediation

It has been said that "[d]isputes are cultural events, evolving within a framework of rules about what is worth fighting for, what is the normal or moral way to fight, what kinds of wrongs warrant action, and what kinds of remedies are acceptable."[289] The process by which a society resolves conflict is closely related to its social structure. Implicit in this choice is a message about what is respectable to do or want or say, what the obligations are of being a member of the society or of a particular group within it, and what it takes to be thought of as a good person leading a virtuous life. In the adversary system, it is acceptable to want to win. It is not only acceptable, but expected, that one will rely on a lawyer and advocate for oneself without looking out for the adversary. The judge, a third party obligated to be neutral and bound by certain formalities, bears the ultimate responsibility for deciding the outcome. To the extent that women are more likely than men to believe in communication as a mode of conflict resolution and to appreciate the importance of an adversary's interests, this system does not always suit their needs.[290]

---

286. *See* S. Estrich, Real Rape 1-3 (1987); Littleton, *supra* note 80, at 28-29.

287. *See* J. Wallerstein & S. Blakeslee, *supra* note 121, at xi-xii; Shattuck, *Mandatory Mediation*, in Divorce Mediation, Theory and Practice, *supra* note 14, at 191, 206 (in sample of mandatory mediation clients in San Francisco, 29% of parents showed marked evidence of serious psychopathology, such as poor reality contact, paranoid ideation, severe depression, and ego decompensation).

288. *See supra* notes 272-73 and accompanying text.

289. Merry & Silbey, *supra* note 56, at 157.

290. *See* Menkel-Meadow, *supra* note 1, at 53-55.

On the other hand, under a scheme of mediation, the standards of acceptable behavior and desires change fundamentally. Parties are to meet with each other, generally without their lawyers. They are encouraged to look at each other's needs and to reach a cooperative resolution based on compromise. Although there are few restrictions on her role in the process, the mediator bears no ultimate, formal responsibility for the outcome of the mediation. In sum, when mediation is the prototype for dispute resolution, the societal message is that a good person—a person following the rules—cooperates, communicates, and compromises.

The glories of cooperation, however, are easily exaggerated.[291] If one party appreciates cooperation more than the other, the parties might compromise unequally. Moreover, the self-disclosure that cooperation requires, when imposed and not sought by the parties, may feel and be invasive. Thus, rather than representing a change in the system to accommodate the "feminine voice," in actuality, mandatory mediation overrides real women's voices saying that cooperation might, at least for the time being, be detrimental to their lives and the lives of their children. Under a system of forced mediation, women are made to feel selfish for wanting to assert their own interests based on their need to survive.

There are, then, many good reasons why a party might choose not to mediate. While some argue that mediation should be required because potential participants lack the information about the process which would convince them to engage in it voluntarily, this is not a sufficient justification for requiring mediation. If the state were committed only to making sure that disputants become familiar with mediation, something less than mandatory mediation—such as viewing a videotaped mediation or attending an orientation program—could be required, and mediators would certainly not be permitted to make recommendations to the court.[292] That more than the simple receipt of information is required under a statutory mediation scheme demonstrates a profound disrespect for the parties' ability to determine the course of their own lives. Perhaps intrusion on the parties' lives might be justified if, in fact, children were demonstrably better off as a result of the process. There is no

---

291. *See supra* note 272.

292. Molly Knowles, Director of the Family Referral Conciliation Service in Kingston, Ontario, Canada, has suggested that the legal system should never play an initiating role in the process of mediation. Rather, mediation services should be available to all divorcing couples at the beginning of the separation process before they go to court. She further argues that the clients alone should decide which issues should be addressed by mediation. Knowles, *Court Annexed Mediation Programs in Canada: Whose Interests Do They Serve?*, in THE ROLE OF MEDIATION, *supra* note 8, at 56, 58-60.

credible evidence, however, that this is so.[293] The legislative choice to make mediation mandatory has been a mistake.

The choice presented today in California and in some other states is between an adversary process with totally powerful legal actors, in which clients never speak for themselves (and often do not know what is going on), and a mediation process in which they are entirely on their own and unprotected. The adversary system admittedly works poorly for child custody cases in many respects. There are, however, some ways to avoid damaging custody battles under an adversary system, such as enacting presumptions that make outcomes reasonably clear in advance,[294] court-sponsored lectures on settlement,[295] and joint negotiation sessions with lawyers and clients present. When in court, lawyers could be held to higher standards with respect to communicating with their clients, and judges could refrain from speaking to lawyers when their clients are not present. (It is difficult to imagine how a client can know whether to trust his lawyer when significant parts of the proceedings take place out of earshot).

The only reason to prefer mediation to other, more obvious alternatives is that the parties may, through the mediation process, ultimately benefit themselves and their children by learning how to communicate and work together. Whether this will happen in the context of a particular mediation is something only the parties can judge.[296]

Any reform proposals, of the adversarial system or of a mediation alternative, should be rejected if they result in further disempowerment of the disempowered. Reform must operate on two simultaneous levels: first, by changing the institutions and rules that govern custody mediation, and second,

---

293. While mediation does seem to serve the courts, there is no evidence that it serves children. Research shows that children whose parents reach a settlement in mediation are no better adjusted following the divorce than children whose parents did not use mediation. *See* J. Pearson, N. Thoennes & W. Hodges, The Effect of Divorce Mediation and Adjudication on Children 27 (1984) (unpublished manuscript on file with author); Kressel, *supra* note 8, at 220.

294. The primary caretaker presumption would in most circumstances result in custody to the parent who has performed the day-to-day care of the child. This rule would maintain the child's bond to the parent more directly involved in her care and make it evident that parenting during marriage, by either parent, is to be valued and rewarded. *See* L. WEITZMAN, *supra* note 48, at 240-45 (presumption decreases ambiguity and emphasizes caretaking ability); Chambers, *Rethinking the Substantive Rules for Custody Disputes in Divorce*, 83 MICH. L. REV. 477, 478-79, 537-38, 569 (1984) (presumption should be limited to preschool children); Fineman, *supra* note 6, at 771-72 (presumption should apply to all contested custody cases); Neely, *supra* note 54, at 180-86 (presumption should apply until child is old enough to decide for himself); Polikoff, *Why Mothers Are Losing: A Brief Analysis of Criteria Used in Child Custody Determinations*, 7 WOMEN'S RTS. L. REP. 235, 241-43 (1982) (presumption desirable and more appropriate than maternal preference). *But see* Schepard, *Taking Children Seriously: Promoting Cooperative Custody After Divorce*, 64 TEX. L. REV. 687 (1985). In this last article, the author argues that post-divorce living arrangements should not reflect an intact family situation: one parent may have acted as the primary caretaker under the "marriage partnership," but that partnership is now dissolved. *Id.* at 724-26, 770-80. Demonstrating an astonishing lack of appreciation for what is involved in raising a child, Schepard goes on to say that "[i]n an increasing number of families, both parents work, and the child's primary caretaker may be a daycare center." *Id.* at 733.

295. *See* Kressel, *Comments*, in THE ROLE OF MEDIATION, *supra* note 8, at 80, 81.

296. *See supra* text accompanying note 179.

by encouraging the respect of each mediator for the struggles and lives of the individuals involved in mediation. Any reforms should evince a concern for the personhood of the mediation clients, a concern that is lacking under current mediation practices.

With respect to institutional changes, an adequate mediation scheme should not only be voluntary rather than mandatory, but should also allow people's emotions to be part of the process, allow their values and principles to matter in the discussion, allow parties' attorneys to participate if requested by the parties, allow parties to choose a mediator and the location for the mediation, allow parties to choose the issues to mediate, and require that divorcing couples be educated about the availability and logistics of mediation so as to enable them to make an intelligent choice as to whether to engage in it.[297]

The second aspect of reform represents more of a personal dynamic, one which is harder to institutionalize or to regulate. But the mediator must learn to respect each client's struggles, including her timing, anger, and resistance to having certain issues mediated, and also must learn to refrain, to the extent he is capable, from imposing his own substantive agenda on the mediation.

CONCLUSION

Although mediation can be useful and empowering, it presents some serious process dangers that need to be addressed, rather than ignored. When mediation is imposed rather than voluntarily engaged in, its virtues are lost. More than lost: mediation becomes a wolf in sheep's clothing. It relies on force and disregards the context of the dispute, while masquerading as a gentler, more empowering alternative to adversarial litigation. Sadly, when mediation is mandatory it becomes like the patriarchal paradigm of law it is supposed to supplant. Seen in this light, mandatory mediation is especially harmful: its messages disproportionately affect those who are already subordinated in our society, those to whom society has already given the message, in far too many ways, that they are not leading proper lives.

Of course, subordinated people can go to court and lose; in fact, they usually do. But if mediation is to be introduced into the court system, it should provide a better alternative. It is not enough to say that the adversary system is so flawed that even a misguided, intrusive, and disempowering system of mediation should be embraced. If mediation as currently instituted constitutes a fundamentally flawed process in the way I have described, it is more, not less, disempowering than the adversary system—for it is then a process in which people are told they are being empowered, but in fact are being forced to acquiesce in their own oppression.

297. For a discussion of institutional concerns in a Canadian context, *see* Knowles, supra note 292, at 56.

[11]

Chapter One

Questioning the Delegalization Movement in Family Law: Do We Really Want a Family Court?

Michael D.A. Freeman

University College,
London, England

Open almost any family law treatise, any report on an issue of family policy, and you will find that it contains at some point a plan for the family court ideal. I too have frequently stressed the need for the establishment of a family court. Indeed, I was a member of the Justice Committee on Parental Rights and Duties and Custody Suits[1] which recommended that a family court be set up in England. As to the structure of the court we were content to adopt the Finer Report's recommendations[2] as our own. That report had noted that submissions to it in favour of the family court ideal offered "more by way of enthusiasm than elucidation,"[3] but that is hardly surprising.

Critics of the existing system seem to agree on what is wrong. Inglis put it well when he said in a public lecture, which was subsequently published,

> Matrimonial litigation is simply one phase in a relationship which must continue in a variety of aspects once the litigation is over. Few matrimonial disputes ever completely end the parties' relationship. It is simply redefined for the future.[4]

We are all, I think, agreed that the adversary system has very severe limitations in the area of family law. Manchester will have spoken for many when he wrote,

> Yet surely we are now agreed upon the basic premise of the family court system . . . a "caring court" with social and welfare services integrated within it as part of a total team operation.[5]

Words constantly repeated are "civilized" and "humane." Very few have cautioned against the family court. The English law lord and former chairman of the English Law Commission, Lord Scarman,[6] is one to have done so. Rereading his address to the Institute of Judicial Administration in Birmingham, nine years after it was given I am struck by the complacency of its tone and the thinness of its argument. I would not expect Lord Scarman to agree with the thesis that I am about to present. We are, however, agreed that the family court concept contains its own dangers. It is easy to be swept along on a tide of euphoria. It is rather more difficult to stand back and take a cool look at what has happened to the family in the twentieth century and to place moves towards the family court ideal within these welfare-oriented policies. This is what, in part, I attempt to do.

I am not concerned with describing in detail or analysing any particular family court or any posited ideal. Proposals are legion and there are in existence in different parts of the world a number of family courts. In my own country, the United Kingdom, proposals for a family court (but not the same one) have come from Royal Commissions,[7] from the Law Society,[8] from the Justices' Clerks' Society[9] and from the Conservative Party.[10] One of the fullest discussions of the concept emanates from Judge Jean Graham Hall.[11] One of the most articulate and sensitive, from Mervyn Murch,[12] a social administration lecturer. But it is accepted in England that we will not get a family court in the foreseeable future. As much divides current proposals and models as unites them. What does, however, unite all critics of the existing system is a desire to render the legal order more "efficient" and more responsive to the perceived needs of the family. These critics, though ideologically poles apart, share with radical critics of the legal order generally a concern over the impersonality, insensitivity and remoteness of law, not to say its excessive rigidity and formality.

This brings me to the second of my themes. Debates about the appropriateness of adversary justice, about the value of integrating adjudicative and welfare roles in the family court, are discourses about the form of law. These are debates with a long heritage and distinguished pedigree: the classical source is, of course, the sociology of Max Weber.[13] There are pervasive delegalization trends in contemporary advanced capitalist societies.[14] It was Weber who first noted that movements towards greater informalism contained the seeds of their own self-contradiction and were ultimately doomed. If this is right, what effect will the move to the family court have? The annals of legal history are strewn with examples of institutions and practices which have had unintended consequences.[15] Programmes which seem to weaken hierarchies of power may actually establish new channels through which they can be expressed or even strengthened. These new programmes may be rendered necessary by, or be more responsive to, technological or economic change. They may be by-products of new patterns of social administration. Observe the way the decline in the criminal sanction[16] has been matched by the growth of the regulatory sanction[17] spawned by the "new property"[18] state; note the way that the therapeutic state has medicalized deviance.[19] The effect is, what Cohen has called, a "dispersal of social control."[20] State involvement may be less, but intervention is more pervasive. We may be moving away from the era of total institutions only to find ourselves enmeshed in total societies.

This is, I think, a likely scenario for the family court. Few of the family court advocates see it this way and many would not find the consequences I describe distasteful. To some, what I am saying will appear far-fetched. But this is where part one of my thesis reemerges. The twentieth century has witnesses, what Philip Rieff has called, the "triumph of the therapeutic."[21] The emphasis on the family has resulted in its greater surveillance and more intensive supervision. The rhetoric is about family autonomy;[22] the reality is of a more pervasive control than existed one hundred years ago. The two parts of my thesis thus converge.

THE FAMILY AND THE STATE

The family has not always been as it is now.[23] The current ideal, which attained its fullest flowering in late Victorian times and now seems to be slowly decaying, rests on the companionate marriage, in which the union is one of two individuals rather than two lineages; on the child-centred household; on the quasi emancipation of women; and on the structural isolation of the nuclear family from the kinship system and the community.

In precapitalist societies and in the early stages of capitalism, work and family life overlapped. The household was the basic unit of production: the home was a place of work. There was no clear distinction between the role of worker and of family member. With industrialization and capitalist production the nature of work and family life changed radically. Productive work now took place in the factory. It became increasingly routinized. The factory system at first used women and children but increasing industrialization brought unemployment and women were driven into dependence upon men. Work done in the home was increasingly restricted to looking after husband-workers and producing children. Eli Zaretsky[24] has described how at the same time the family became idealized, as did the familial role of women. The home became a refuge from the demands of capitalist society. In Lasch's graphic phrase the family became a "haven in a heartless world."

> The family found ideological support and justification in the conception of domestic life as an emotional refuge in a cold and competitive society.[25]

The family became a private place to which people, but especially men, could withdraw.

The family was thus exalted. A "cult of domesticity"[26] was engendered, according to Carl N. Degler,[27] by women themselves. It confined women to the home but at the same time it made them the moral arbiters of the family and of whatever else touched its interests. He argues[28] that demands for the recognition of married women's property rights, for divorce laws favourable to women, for sexual self-control on the part of men, for acknowledgment of women's greater stake in regulating pregnancy, as well as for reforms in the larger social sphere, particularly in relation to "social purity" all arose out of the logic of domesticity itself.

The connection between the "cult of domesticity" and the emancipation of women has also been observed by Jacques Donzelot in his *La Police des Familles*. He sees that:

> Birth control and the "liberation" of women rested on women's old social vocation, and on their function as ambassadresses of culture.[29]

Donzelot also sees what Degler does not, *viz.*: that women's roles as cultural missionaries was to some extent the deliberate creation of doctors seeking to make wives and mothers agents of medical influence. Ideas were spread by "promotional goading and attendant blaming of families who, through their resistance, were ruining the members' chances."[30]

The emotional intensification of family life had, as one of its inevitable consequences, conflict. This, the nascent psychological sciences sought to explain and, of course, to prevent and solve. But, as Lasch has argued:

> To enlightened members of the professional classes — and this includes most feminists — knowledge of this kind, promised a preventive science of sexual and social control, which could be used among other things to civilise the poor, to subject them to new controls sincerely disguised as benevolence, and thus to integrate them more fully into the emerging industrial order.[31]

Women saw the advantage of professional intervention in family life. It undercut patriarchal authority. However, it also eroded the traditional prerogatives of women. Thus, as Ehrenreich and English[32] have also demonstrated, women welcomed the substitution of doctors for midwives in childbirth. The overall result was that professionals continually expanded their jurisdiction over family life. Patriarchal authority may have suffered but so did the authority formerly exercised by women themselves. Lasch makes the point that

> in allying themselves with the helping professions, women improved their position in the family only to fall into a new kind of dependence, the dependence of the

> consumer on the market and on the providers of expert services, not only for the satisfaction of her needs but for the very definition of her needs.[33]

It is easy to see how society came to be governed by doctors, social workers, psychiatrists, juvenile court judges, criminologists, etc., in short, by the modern apparatus of resocialization. The "helping professions" during the first third of this century came to see themselves as doctors to a sick society. This is graphically portrayed in fictional form in D.M. Thomas's *The White Hotel*.[34] Many have written of the growth of the "therapeutic state."[35] Its influence, its impact on the family has been profound. What the cathedral was to medieval times and the legislative chamber was to the nineteenth century, the hospital, the clinic is to our day.[36]

It is all too common to read of the family losing its functions,[37] as if these had formerly been unproblematic and static. In reality what these commentators have observed is the takeover of society playing the nurturing mother of certain roles played by the family, nuclear and extended, at earlier times in history. I think Lasch has grasped this better than anybody. To socialization of production, he believes, we should add "socialisation of reproduction."[38] This, he claims, "proletarianised parenthood, by making people unable to provide for their own needs without the supervision of trained experts." Early proponents of children's rights typify this approach.[39] Contemporary advocates of rights for children, Holt[40] or Farson[41] for example, would not see the child-saving movement as bedfellow to theirs at all. It stressed protecting children while they emphasize the importance of protecting children's rights. The divergence between the two comes out distinctly if we examine the early philosophy in practice.[42] The development of a system of compulsory education fits the turn-of-the-century ethos very well.

> If the state is to have good citizens . . . we must begin to teach the children in our schools, and begin at once, that which we see they are no longer learning in the home,

wrote Ellen Richards[43] in 1910 in a book intriguingly entitled *Euthenics: The Science of Controllable Environment*. Children were to achieve independence from parental control but they fell increasingly, instead, under the control of the state. In Donzelot's words, "family patriarchalism was destroyed at the cost of a patriarchy of the state."[44]

A second example, which is particularly well-documented, though not beyond controversy, is the development of a system of juvenile justice. The juvenile court substituted prevention for punishment, and close surveillance for judgment. It treated the child's or adolescent's crimes as symptoms of an unhealthy, unhygienic home environment, thus justifying enquiries into the morality of his family and his removal from home if this was deemed necessary. Donzelot describes how parents who called in the police or social workers in the hope that outside intervention would strengthen their authority over a wayward child found instead that their authority was tranferred to an outside professional authority.

> Instead of the desired admonition, however, the juvenile judge, after reviewing the results of the social inquiry, decides in favour of an educative assistance that has another purpose altogether, since it brings the adolescent into the sphere of the tutelary complex, leading to his detachment from family authority and transferral to a social authority . . . all in order to prevent him from contaminating his brothers and sisters and to enable his parents to devote themselves to the younger children.[45]

Architects of juvenile justice justified their creation on humanitarian grounds. They may have intended to be humanitarian. They saw themselves as replacing the undoubted barbarities of the criminal law with something better. They argued that the juvenile court was to be a friend of the juvenile offender as well as a confederate of his family. Donzelot describes this reasoning as "pious representations . . . of reasons that are much less 'democratic'."[46] Rothman admits that conscience may have played its part but so, he insists, did "convenience."[47] Donzelot is not the first to have questioned the motives of the reformers. Platt,[48] Fox,[49] Ryerson,[50] and Schlossman[51] have all rejected the orthodox interpretation of the development of the juvenile court. Like Platt, Donzelot sees intervention in the family as a "depoliticising strategy." It was inspired by a fear of class conflict: it belonged to a general attempt to control the poor. It was the liberal state's answer to socialist propaganda. It aimed to convert political debates into administrative procedures. The language used may have been that of hygiene and health, but political considerations were never far below the surface. The parallels between the rhetoric about the juvenile court at the turn of the century and the family court in the last decade are so striking that it is surprising that the implications for the family court ideal have not been drawn, but I would suggest that they are there for all to see.

I have given examples from two areas. Others could be cited. I resist that temptation in order to return to the general issue. Liberals tried to steer a course between what they saw as the Scylla of conservative paternalism, which upheld the family as the foundation of the social order, so that every change was seen as a threat to social integrity, and the Charybdis of socialism, which wanted to replace parenthood with the state. But, "in the end," to quote Lasch once again, "they outflanked their adversaries by creating a therapeutic state which left the family more or less intact yet subjected to non-stop supervision."[52] The liberal state as a result has a system of indirect controls which preserves the appearance, even some of the reality, of private initiative within an overarching structure of professional supervision. The therapeutic state leaves the family "'always' 'justified' in theory and always suspect in practice."[53]

PROFESSIONAL EXPERTISE

The victory of the medical model has meant the elevation of the expert. The effects of this can be seen starkly in the juvenile court. Even where a child has committed a criminal offence, there is reason to believe, and any examination of social enquiry reports reinforces this belief, that in the minds of decision makers the seriousness of his behaviour, what he has *done*, takes a back seat behind an interpretation of what he, and his family, *is*.[54] Individualized justice, the goal of welfare-oriented processes, has been said to result "in a frame of relevance so large, so all inclusive, that any relation between the criteria of judgment and the disposition remains obscure."[55] The social enquiry report is the linchpin of the juvenile court process. Anderson describes it as "the product of an application of social work ideology to the court context."[56] Social enquiry reports are apt to contain value judgments, to make unsubstantiated assertions and often to be based on assumptions which are not supported by the evidence.[57] Writers of the reports, who know no more about the causes of misbehaviour than the rest of us, tend to assemble information which reinforces stereotypes of "causes of trouble" such as broken homes, working mothers, etc., and often to put it into language loosely drawn from psychoanalytic theory.[58] Concepts such as personality disorder, psychopath, impaired bonding, dependency needs are pervasive. The use of theory is random and eclectic.

It is easy to criticize the welfare professionals, social workers, psychologists, child psychiatrists, to attribute this to bad practice. But the problem is deeper than this. As Andrew Sutton has argued, in a recent outstanding article,[59] there has been an unjustified professionalization of issues that are "in fact beyond the present reach of expert understanding."[60] He is not alone in questioning the expertise used by welfare professionals. It would take me too far away from the subject of this paper to give further details of this. Suffice it to say that Sutton, Morgan[61] and others[62] provide considerable evidence of the inadequacy of the knowledge base upon which assessment and treatment of children, the writing of social enquiry reports and similar tasks proceed. There has been, Sutton concludes, an "unjustified reliance on premature professionalism."[63] In Britain the most detailed investigations into social work practice have followed the deaths (or serious injuries) of children at the hands of parents or other caretakers. A common theme running through all the reports[64] of such enquiries is found in the assertion that the system of child care has failed: there has been a lack or ineffectiveness of communication and liaison between welfare professionals, and between them and the police and medical profession. None of these enquiries appears to have grasped the fundamental nettle, the problematic nature of professional expertise.[65] Such is the power of professional mystique.

I have not seen a single proposal for a family court which comes to terms with these issues at all. Take the fullest discussion of the family court in Britain. This is to be found in the Finer report on one-parent families, published in 1974.[66] Though disdainful of American family courts which, it says, are "committed to a social work philosophy which regards family breakdown as a phenomenon to be dealt with primarily by diagnosis and treatment" and which are as much a "therapeutic agency as a judicial institution,"[67] it advocates the use of court social workers. The welfare part of the court would be expected to "demonstrate a commensurate degree of professional integrity and expertise,"[68] commensurate that is with the integrity and formal expertise of the court. But we are talking of different types of expertise: lawyers have formal expertise; social workers aspire to expertise based on empirical knowledge. If Sutton, Morgan and the others are right, the operative words are "aspire to," for it is doubtful whether the knowledge base has as yet been obtained. The Finer report envisages court welfare services providing "assistance for people with marital problems."[69] If by assistance is meant conciliation,[70] so as to civilize the consequences of breakdown, then it is difficult to quarrel with the proposal. The report does not expand on the work tasks it expects welfare services to undertake. It does not, for example, see social workers taking part in the "family court conference," the convening of which it recommends where a maintenance or administrative order has been in operation for two years and the marriage still legally subsists.[71] It does not see social workers as decision makers but rather as handmaidens.[72] They will make social and welfare enquiries and the reports. But the line between informed (or not so informed) opinions and recommendations is a thin one and the experience of juvenile courts, and indeed adult criminal courts which commission reports on defendants, is that they expect, get, and act on recommendations of social workers and probation officers.[73] Indeed, similar evidence is available in the case of courts dealing with family matters where refusals to follow social workers' recommendations are rare and where the courts feel themselves obligated to articulate their reasons for so doing.[74]

DELEGALIZATION

Moves away from adversary justice and towards a family court are in effect moves towards the delegalization of family dispute settlement. Delegalization can take place on a number of levels and can be motivated or inspired by different goals. The simplification of divorce processes with the introduction in England in 1973[75] of the "special procedure" effected a limited measure of delegalization. It was a response to research which had shown that judicial hearings in divorce were perfunctory.[76] It was motivated also by a desire to rechannel money spent by the state through legal aid subsidizing divorce into other areas of unmet legal need.[77] Much discussion of delegalization[78] is in the context of wresting law away from remote authorities and allowing the masses to participate in the processes of justice. Obviously, movements towards deformalization (as indeed towards formalization) take on different meanings depending on cultural, political and historical contexts. Contemporary moves away from formality in the West may well reflect, in part, the decline in the market system and the growth of monopoly capitalism. A consequence of the decline of the market has been the rise of state redistribution as a dominant mechanism for allocation (including the growth of the so-called "new property").[79] The rise of monopoly capitalism has meant that the law does not have to be used to promote the ideal of a self-regulating market.

The temptation to approach formalism and informalism as if the effects of each were opposite to the other must be resisted. Weber saw this. He wrote:

> The position of all "democratic" currents, in the sense of currents that would minimize "authority", is necessarily ambiguous. "Equality before the law" and the demand for legal guarantees against arbitrariness demand a formal and rational "objectivity" of administration, as opposed to the personally free discretion flowing from the "grace" of the old patrimonial domination. If, however, an "ethos" — not to speak of instincts — takes hold of the masses on some individual question, it postulates *substantive* justice oriented toward some concrete instance and person; and such an "ethos" will unavoidably collide with the formalism and the rule-bound and cool "matter-of-factness" of bureaucratic administration. For this reason, the ethos must emotionally reject what reason demands. The propertyless masses especially are not served by a "formal equality before the law" and a "calculable" adjudication and administration, as demanded by "bourgeois" interests. Naturally in their eyes justice and administration should serve to compensate for their economic and social life-opportunities in the face of the propertied classes. Justice and administration can fulfil this function only if they assume an informal character to a far-reaching extent. It must be informal because it is substantively "ethical" ("Kadi-justice"). Every sort of "popular justice" — which usually does not ask for reasons and norms — as well as every sort of intensive influence on the administration of so-called public opinion, crosses the rational course of justice and administration just as strongly, and under certain conditions far more so, as the "star chamber" proceedings of an "absolute" ruler has been able to do.[80]

What Weber is saying is important. To the extent that law is set up to protect the weak, it must be formalistic and impersonal and confined by rules. Yet when it is invoked especially to achieve social justice, to protect the weak against the powerful, it is typically an expression of informal "substantive justice."[81] But this can be very easily subverted by the powerful to their advantage. Both law as form and law as substance may be equated with social justice but neither is able to deliver what it promises.[82]

This should alert us to the danger of falling into the trap of thinking that having created a particular structure, it will operate as we expect it to do. Both movements toward formalism and informalism contain within themselves the capacity to turn into something very different from what they appear. Weber depicted the rise of Western capitalism as a movement towards the dominance of formal rationality over substantive rationality.[83] This destroys popular justice. Instead we get bureaucratic centralization and protest against rational legal authority is seen as "irrational." This is why Weber can conclude that any trend toward greater informalism is doomed. "It is by no means certain," he wrote, "that those classes which are negatively privileged today, especially the working class, may safely expect from an informal administration of justice those results which are claimed for it by the ideology of the jurists."[84]

Further insight into what Duncan Kennedy has called[85] a "regime of rules" may be sought in the contemporary Marxist historian, E.P. Thompson. He is writing of eighteenth century England but some of the comments in his coda are of general application.

> . . . People are not as stupid as some structuralist philosophers suppose them to be. They will not be mystified by the first man who puts on a wig. It is inherent in the especial character of law, as a body of rules and procedures, that it shall apply logical criteria with reference to standards of universality and equity. It is true that certain categories of person may be excluded from this logic . . . and that the poor may often be excluded, through penury, from the law's costly procedures. . . . But if too much of this is true, then the consequences are plainly counterproductive. Most men have a strong sense of justice, at least with regard to their own interests. . . . The essential precondition for the effectiveness of law, in its function as ideology is that it shall display an independence from gross manipulation and shall seem to be just. It cannot seem to be so without upholding its own logic and criteria of equity; indeed, on occasion by actually *being* just . . .[86]

This is an important qualification to what Weber argued and it comes from an unexpected source. By stressing the equivocal character of formal law, Thompson is able to argue for the preservation of the "forms and rhetoric of law . . . which may, on occasion, inhibit power and afford some protection to the powerless."[87] His is a plea not to throw out the "baby" with the "bathwater" and it is one we should heed. We must not let our concern about the rigidity, remoteness, insensitivity of traditional legal mechanisms turn us away from the unqualified good in the rule of law. We may find adversary processes inappropriate, even dehumanizing or alienating. Yet the formalism and rule of law which accompanies them provide a measure of protection to the powerless. In our context they are not, as in Thompson's or Weber's arguments, the working classes, but rather women, and especially, children. The rule of law also inhibits power, not least of welfare professionals. Our experience with the juvenile court provides abundant evidence of what is lost when informal procedures and treatment institutions replace traditional court structures and processes.[88] In the United States, realization of this led to the reintroduction of certain rights for juveniles,[89] in effect a partial relegalization of the juvenile court. But at about the same time in Britain, the decriminalization of "children in trouble" was reaching its high-water mark with the *Social Work (Scotland) Act* of 1968[90] and the English *Children and Young Persons Act* of 1969.[91] The British legislature, it seems, had not noticed *Re Gault*.[92] Are those who hanker for a family court similarly blinkered? The hyperbolical language which greets the family court ideal today is so very reminiscent of descriptions of the juvenile court half a century ago.[93]

Too much must not be read into this analogy with moves to the juvenile court earlier this century. To do so would be to divorce the movements from their historical contexts. The juvenile court emerged during the heyday of classical capitalism. The relationship between capitalism and formalism has been so thoroughly analysed[94] that it need not be elaborated upon further here. Capitalism needed certainty, calculability, stability, and formalism promoted this. In this sense the juvenile court was something of an anomaly, perhaps explained by excepting policies concerned with wayward youth from state initiatives generally.[95] But the economic organization of society has changed in the course of the twentieth century. A postindustrial society, a "third wave"[96] has different needs and expectations. To what extent these have been shaped by legal institutions and ideas and themselves influence legal developments are questions which have exercised the minds of a number of contemporary thinkers.[97] Classical capitalism stressed the division between public and private law and, though many jurists resisted the dualism,[98] the pervasive influence, some would say mystification, of the distinction remains deeply embedded in much liberal legal thinking even today. The separation is not easy to defend today and it is in fact widely under attack.[99] Once again legal rights of the individual are becoming dependent on status.[100] There are any number of manifestations of this trend: the rise in administrative law,[101] "the death of contract"[102] and the "therapeutic state"[103] are some of them. The historical setting for the family court is thus one in which status and hence particularistic relationships have reemerged. It is also one in which the patterns of decision making have shifted. Where once they were determined by reciprocal obligations or the wisdom of the market,[104] now they are centralized. There has been a shift, as Kamenka and Tay put it,[105] from *Gesellschaft* law[106] to bureaucratic administrative regulation. They see

> the contemporary crisis of law and legal ideology . . . [as] a crisis of *Gesellschaft* law, a crisis in its capacity to deal with what are seen as the urgent problems of our time and, consequently in its claim to legitimacy.[107]

Whatever the reason and however one characterizes it, there has been an injection of substantive rationality into the formalized law of advanced capitalist societies. The attenuation of the market has necessitated reliance on other extraeconomic mechanisms to extract and redistribute surplus value. It has led to the rise of state redistribution. The "law" thus plays an affirmative role. Under classical capitalist conditions the law played almost a negative part. It promoted the ideal of a self-regulating market and it afforded a measure of protection to the weaker party. The rule of law has often been said to be a precondition of capitalist competition. With the growth of monopoly capitalism the protection offered by the law becomes a barrier in the way of the expansion of economic power. As capitalism becomes less of a market system the structure and content of law, its institutions and practices, undergo a profound change. For example, general rules give way to vague standards.[108] If we examine what is going on in advanced capitalist societies we can understand why formalism has declined. But this does not mean that we can hope to realize the goals (justice, equality, autonomy or whatever) in whose name formalism was attacked. Formalism has declined but not because of intellectual onslaughts upon it. Can delegalization succeed?

There are many delegalization projects of which those concerned with family dispute settlement make up only a small number. There are initiatives to involve the community in policing[109] and to introduce or strengthen the role of lay personnel in the administration of the lower, usually criminal, courts.[110] All these movements share in common a desire to promote the autonomy and self-sufficiency of local social units, whether these be communities, neighbourhoods[111] or, in our case, families, at the expense of the impersonal, bureaucraticized professional power centres. But the dispersal of control into local and traditional structures is perfectly consistent with the support, indeed the expansion of forms of social control which emanate from these power centres. Prison reform is an apt illustration of the process. The increased involvement of medicine and psychiatry in prisons has meant that

> No longer must such institutions be justified purely in terms of vengeance and punishment but as agencies of positive change the prison becomes a "correctional" institution . . . The scientists and the technicians are beginning to win out, not because of some inherent superiority in their paradigm of crime, but by showing that they have the power to be more effective custodians.[112]

The days of prisons as "human warehouses"[113] may be numbered, for,

> In the very near future, a computer technology will make possible alternatives to imprisonment. The development of systems for telemetering information from censors implanted in or on the body will soon make possible the observation and control of human behaviour without actual physical contact. Through such telemetric devices it will be possible to maintain 24-hour-a-day surveillance over the

subject and to intervene electronically or physically to influence and control selected behaviour. It will thus be possible to exercise control over human behaviour and from a distance without physical contact.[114]

Looked at superficially such changes (it is better not to call them "reforms") might appear to weaken hierarchies of power. In reality what they do is to make control more intrusive, more pervasive and more effective. The river may have burst its banks and the water may now flow in new channels. The water now comes at us from a number of directions and its total force may well be stronger than was the original river. The accepted view has been that control, certainly control within capitalism, required formality and impersonality, bureaucraticization and centralism. But today's advanced capitalism is compatible with decentralized social control. Penal developments draw attention to this in striking fashion but what they tell us can be generalized.

Even where the impetus for reform comes from below, from grass-roots sentiment, as to a large extent it does with moves to delegalize family dispute settlement, there is considerable likelihood that developments will be co-opted by the powerful, so that "bad" form takes over "good" substance. Adorno's remarks seem most pertinent.

Whatever raises from within itself a claim to being autonomous, critical and antithetical — while at the same time never being able to assert this claim with total legitimacy — must necessarily come to naught; this is particularly true when its impulses are integrated into something heteronomous to them, which has been worked out previously from above — that is to say, when it is granted a space in which to draw breath immediately by that power against which it rebels.[115]

Is the result, as Cohen suggests, a "dispersal of social control"? Is the effect, as he argues it is,

to increase rather than decrease the *amount* of intervention . . . and, probably, to increase rather than decrease the total *number* who get into the system in the first place[?][116]

He is writing of the criminal justice system but the parallels are too close to ignore. We can appreciate the proximity of the two when we return to and examine twentieth century policies towards the family.

We find rampant interventionism, a system of indirect controls and pervasive reliance on professional expertise. We find, in other words, policies which the family court legitimates. I believe, and I think my belief is shared, that the family has suffered from these policies. I believe that the family, particularly its weaker members, will suffer further from delegalization. And yet, if my thesis is correct, the move to a deformalized dispute settlement system in family matters has an air almost of inevitability about it. My article is written in the hope of opening our eyes to what we have been doing to the family and what the thrust of contemporary developments will do to the family in the future. Too much has been taken for granted that should be openly debated. Too much that is problematic has been glossed over. I hope my article raises the questions, even if it does not provide the answers.

NOTES

1. London: Justice, 1975, paras. 85 *et seq.*

2. Report of Committee on *One-Parent Families,* Cmnd. 5,629, 1974, London: H.M.S.O., part 4, sections 13 and 14.

3. *Idem*, para. 4.280.

4. "The Family, the Law and the Courts," 47 *Australian Law Journal* 647, 652 (1973).

5. "Reform and The Family Court," 125 *New Law Journal* 984 (1975).

6. In *The Domestic and Matrimonial Jurisdiction of Magistrates' Courts and County Courts,* Institute of Judicial Administration, University of Birmingham, 1973, 56-64, reported in *The Times,* 16 April 1973. See also Sir Leslie Scarman, *Family Law and Family Reform,* University of Bristol, 1966.

7. Finer, *op. cit.*, note 2, and Houghton, Report of Departmental Committee on the *Adoption of Children,* Cmnd. 5,107, 1972, London: H.M.S.O., paras. 276-279.

8. *A Better Way Out,* London: Law Society, 1979, parts III and VIII.

9. *The Case for a Local Family Court — Reform of the Family Jurisdiction of Magistrates,* 1978.

10. *The Case for Family Courts,* London: Conservative Political Centre, 1978.

11. *Proposal for a Family Court,* London: National Council for the Unmarried Mother and Her Child, 1973.

12. *Justice and Welfare in Divorce,* London: Sweet and Maxwell, 1980. I discuss this in "Towards a More Humane System of Divorce," 145 *Justice of the Peace* 1973 (1981).

13. See *Economy and Society* (eds. Guenther Roth and Claus Wittich) Berkeley: University of California Press, 1968, vol. II, pp. 641-900.

14. As to some of these are Richard L. Abel, *The Politics of Informal Justice,* 2 vols., New York: Academic Press, 1982. These volumes were not available in Britain when I wrote this article. Having now seen them, I realize how much my article would have profited from a study of them.

15. *Cf.* R. Merton (ed.), *Unanticipated Consequences of Social Action: Variations on a Sociological Theme,* New York: Academic Press, 1981.

16. See M. Spector, "Beyond Crime: Seven Methods to Control Troublesome Rascals" in (ed.) H. Laurence Ross, *Law and Deviance,* Beverly Hills: Sage, 1981, 127.

17. See Robert Kagan, *Regulatory Justice,* New York: Russell Sage Foundation, 1978.

18. See C. Reich, "The New Property," 73 *Yale L.J.* 733 (1964); M.A. Glendon, *The New Family and the New Property,* Toronto: Butterworths, 1981.

19. See N. Kittrie, *The Right to be Different: Deviance and Enforced Therapy,* Baltimore: Johns Hopkins U.P., 1971; P. Conrad and J. Schneider, *Deviance and Medicalization: From Badness to Sickness,* St. Louis: Mosby, 1980.

20. "The Punitive City: Notes on the Dispersal of Social Control," *Contemporary Crises* vol. 3, 339 (1979).

21. *The Triumph of The Therapeutic: Uses of Faith After Freud*, Harmondsworth: Penguin, 1966.

22. As in J. Goldstein et al., *Beyond The Best Interests of The Child*, New York: Free Press, 1973.

23. See L. Stone, *The Family, Sex and Marriage in England 1500–1800*, London: Weidenfeld and Nicolson, 1977 and E. Shorter, *The Making of the Modern Family*, London: Collins, 1976.

24. *Capitalism, the Family and Personal Life*, London: Pluto Press, 1976. See also A. Foreman, *Femininity As Alienation*, London: Pluto Press, 1977.

25. *Haven in a Heartless World*, New York: Basic Books, 1977, 6.

26. The term is Aileen S. Kraditor's. See *Up from the Pedestal: Selected Writings in the History of American Feminism*, Chicago: Quadrangle Books, 1968.

27. *At Odds: Women and the Family in America from the Revolution to the Present*, New York: Oxford U.P., 1980.

28. Following Nancy Cott, *The Bonds of Womanhood*, New Haven, Yale U.P., 1977 and Aileen Kraditor, *The Ideas of the Women's Suffrage Movement, 1890–1920*, New York: Columbia University Press, 1965.

29. Translated as *The Policing of Families*, New York: Pantheon Books, 1979, 221.

30. *Idem*. See the interesting critique by M. Barrett and M. McIntosh *The Anti-social Family*, London: Verso, 1982, 95 *et seq*.

31. "Life in the Therapeutic State," *The New York Review of Books*, vol. XXVII, no. 16 (12 June 1980) 24 and 27.

32. *For Her Own Good: 150 Years of the Experts' Advice to Women*, Garden City, New York: Anchor Press Doubleday, 1978.

33. *Op. cit.*, note 31, 27.

34. London: Gollancz, 1981.

35. See particularly N. Kittrie, *The Right To Be Different: Deviance and Enforced Therapy*, Baltimore: Johns Hopkins U.P., 1971.

36. *Cf.* P. Rieff, *Freud: The Mind of a Moralist*, London: Gollancz, 1960, 390.

37. See R. Fletcher, *The Family and Marriage in Britain*, Harmondsworth: Penguin, 1973 ch. 5. See also M. Nissel, "The Family and the Welfare State," *New Society*, vol. 53, no. 925 (7 August 1980), 259.

38. *Op. cit.*, note 25, 19.

39. See, e.g., Charlotte Perkins Gilman, *The Home: Its Work and Influence*, New York: McClure, Phillips, 1903, and Jenkin Lloyd Jones, quoted by Christopher Lasch in *Haven in a Heartless World*, *op. cit.*, note 25, p. 16.

40. *Escape From Childhood*, Harmondsworth: Penguin, 1975.

41. *Birthrights*, New York: Macmillan, 1974.

42. For the distinction, see C. Rogers and L. Wrightsman, "Attitudes toward Children's Rights: Nurturance or Self-Determination," *Journal of Social Issues*, vol. 34(2), 1978, 59. See also M. Wald, "Children's Rights: A Framework For Analysis," *University of California Davis L.R.*, vol. 12, 255, (1979) and M.D.A. Freeman, "The Rights of Children in the International Year of the Child," *Current Legal Problems*, vol. 33, 1980, 1; and *The Rights and Wrongs of Children*, London: Frances Pinter, 1983, ch. 2

43. Boston: Whitcomb and Barrows, 1910, 74.

44. *Op. cit.*, note 29, 219.

45. *Idem*, 158.

46. *Idem,* 100.

47. *Conscience and Convenience,* Boston: Little, Brown and Company, 1980.

48. *The Child Savers,* Chicago: University of Chicago Press, 1969 (a second edition was published in 1977).

49. "Philosophy and the Principle of Punishment in the Juvenile Court," 8 *Family Law Quarterly* 373 (1974).

50. *The Best-Laid Plans: America's Juvenile Court Experiment,* New York: Hill and Wang, 1978.

51. *Love and the American Delinquent: Theory and Practice of "Progressive" Juvenile Justice 1825–1920,* Chicago: University of Chicago Press, 1977.

52. *Op. cit.,* note 31, 30.

53. *Idem.*

54. See J. Lofland, *Deviance and Identity,* Englewood Cliffs: Prentice Hall, 1969, 150. See also E. Schur, *Labeling Deviant Behaviour,* New York: Harper and Row, 1971.

55. *Per* D. Matza, *Delinquency and Drift,* New York: Wiley, 1964, 115.

56. R. Anderson, *Representation in the Juvenile Courts,* London: Routledge and Kegan Paul, 1978, 25.

57. See L. Taylor et al., *In Whose Best Interests?* London: Cobden Trust/Mind, 1980; A. Morris et al., *Justice For Children,* London: Macmillan, 1980.

58. It is significant that little serious or sustained attention has been given by professionals to J. Goldstein et al.'s *Beyond the Best Interests of the Child,* revised edition, New York: Free Press, 1980 (first published in 1973), particularly to its idea of the "least detrimental alternative," despite the fact that the book is explicitly psychoanalytical in orientation.

59. "Science in Court" in (ed.) M. King, *Childhood, Welfare and Justice,* London: Batsford, 1981, 45–104.

60. *Idem,* 48.

61. Patricia Morgan, *Child Care: Sense and Fable,* London: Temple Smith, 1975 and *Delinquent Fantasies,* London: Temple Smith, 1978.

62. For example, G. Pearson, *The Deviant Imagination,* London: Macmillan, 1975.

63. *Op. cit.,* note 59, 95.

64. The most famous is the Department of Health and Social Security report into the Maria Colwell case (the Field-Fisher report) published by H.M.S.O., London, 1974. There have been some twenty other reports of enquiries. Eighteen reports are looked at in a new DHSS document, *Child Abuse – A Study of Inquiry Reports 1973–1981,* London: H.M.S.O., 1982. There is a fuller list in D.A. Jones, *Understanding Child Abuse,* Sevenoaks: Hodder and Stoughton, 1982, 290–92.

65. A rather similar point is made by J. Howells, *Remember Maria,* London: Butterworths, 1974.

66. *Op. cit.,* note 2.

67. *Idem,* para. 4.281.

68. *Idem,* para. 4.325.

69. *Idem,* para. 4.328.

70. There is a good description of the Bristol service, the most fully developed in England, in Lisa Parkinson, "Bristol Courts Family Conciliation Service," 12 *Family Law* 13–16 (1982).

71. See, *op. cit.,* note 2, para. 4.390.

72. I use this sexist expression deliberately since I believe it is within the spirit of the report. Also, I am not aware of a neutral term.

73. See J. Thorpe, *Social Enquiry Reports*, London: H.M.S.O., 1979.

74. See generally 9 *Family Law* 50 (1979), particularly the case of *Re C* (1973) discussed therein. See also *R v. R* (1978) 8 *Family Law* 169 and *J v. J* (1979) 9 *Family Law* 91.

75. Extended to all undefended cases in 1977. See Matrimonial Causes Rules, r. 33(3), 48. See S.M. Cretney, *Principles of Family Law*, London: Sweet and Maxwell, 1979, 159-63.

76. E. Elston et al., "Judicial Hearings of Undefended Divorce Petitions," 38 *M.L.R.* 609 (1975).

77. See M.D.A. Freeman, "Divorce Without Legal Aid," 6 *Family Law* 255 (1976).

78. For example, R.L. Abel, "Delegalization: A Critical Review of Its Ideology, Manifestations and Social Consequences," in E. Blankenburg et al. (eds.), *Alternative Rechtsformen und Alternativen Rechtssoziologie und Rechtstheorie*, Opladen: Westdeutscher Verlag, 27-47 (Jahrbuch fur Rechtssoziologie and Rechtstheorie Band 6). See also now, *op. cit.*, note 14, particularly vol. 1, chs. 7 and 10.

79. *Op. cit.*, note 18.

80. *From Max Weber: Essays in Sociology*, edited and translated by H. H. Gerth and C. Wright Mills. Copyright 1946 by Oxford University Press, Inc., renewed 1973 by Hans H. Gerth. Reprinted by permission of the publisher.

81. *Cf.* M. Horkheimer, *Eclipse of Reason*, New York: Seabury, 1974, 6.

82. See M. Galanter, "Legality and Its Discontents" in (ed.) E. Blankenburg et al., *op. cit.*, note 78, 11, and R. Abel, "Conservative, Conflict and Informal Justice," *Int. J. of Sociology of Law*, vol. 9, 245 (1981).

83. That is why "England" was such a problem for him. See A. Hunt, *The Sociological Movement In Law*, London: Macmillan, 1978, 122-28 for a discussion of this.

84. *Economy and Society*, (eds.) Guenther Roth and Claus Wittich, Berkeley: University of California Press, 1968, vol. II, 893.

85. "Form and Substance In Private Law," [1976] 89 *Harvard Law Review*, 1,685-1,778.

86. *Whigs and Hunters*, London: Allen Lane, 1975, 262-63.

87. *Idem*, 266.

88. See M.D.A. Freeman, "The Rights of Children Who Do 'Wrong'," (1981) 21 *British Journal of Criminology*, 210-29; A. Morris et al., *Justice for Children*, London: Macmillan, 1980.

89. See generally W. Vaughan Stapleton and Lee H. Teitelbaum, *In Defense of Youth*, New York: Russell Sage Foundation, 1972.

90. See P. Brown and T. Bloomfield (eds.), *Legality and Community*, Aberdeen: Aberdeen People's Press, 1979 and A. Morris and M. McIsaac, *Juvenile Justice*, London: Heinemann, 1978.

91. Never fully implemented. The current trend is increasingly punitive though a veneer of welfarism remains. The *Criminal Justice Act 1982* reverses some of the trends embodied in the 1969 legislation.

92. 387 U.S.1. (1967). See also *Breed v. Jones* 421 U.S. 519 (1975) and *cf. McKeiver v. Pennsylvania* 403 U.S. 538 (1971).

93. Juvenile courts were once hailed as the best plan "for the conservation of human life and happiness ever conceived by civilised man" *per* C.W. Hoffman, "Organisation of Family Courts, with Special References to the Juvenile Courts," in J. Addams (ed.), *The Child, the Clinic and the Court*, New York: New Republic, 1927.

94. Notably by M.J. Horwitz, *The Transformation of American Law 1780-1860*,

Cambridge: Harvard U.P., 1977. See also D. Kennedy, "Legal Formality," 2 *Journal of Legal Studies* 351–98 (1973) and R.M. Unger, *Law in Modern Society*, New York: Free Press, 1976, 203 *et seq.*

95. Those who propagated the juvenile court may have been moved by other considerations. See Anthony Platt's analysis in *op. cit.*, note 48.

96. Alvin Toffler's phrase (see *The Third Wave*, London: Collins, 1980). In using his expression, I am falling in with his description of a trend, not adopting his agenda, about which I make no comment.

97. See D. Sugarman, "Theory and Practice in Law and History" in (ed.) B. Fryer et al., *Law, State and Society*, London: Croom Helm, 1981, 70.

98. For example, Hans Kelsen, Léon Duguit and Yevgeny Pashukanis.

99. See R.M. Unger, *Law in Modern Society*, New York: Free Press, 1976; Karl Klare, "Law-Making as Praxis," 40 *Telos* 123–35 (1979).

100. Thus reversing the trend from status to contract depicted by Sir Henry Maine in *Ancient Law*. It hardly needs emphasizing that today's "status" is very different from the feudalistic motion in Maine's historical analysis. See, further, A. Fraser, "The Legal Theory We Need Now," *Socialist Review*, no. 40–41, 147–87 (1978).

101. See the two very different treatments of P. Nonet, *Administrative Justice: Advocacy and Change in a Government Agency*, New York: Russell Sage Foundation, 1969 and L. Scarman, *English Law — The New Dimension*, London: Stevens, 1974.

102. See G. Gilmore, *The Death of Contract*, Columbus: Ohio State University Press, 1974.

103. See N. Kittrie, *op. cit.*, note 19.

104. *Cf.* K. Polanyi, *The Great Transformation*, Boston: Beacon Press, 1944, ch. 4.

105. "Beyond the French Revolution: Communist Socialism and the Rule of Law" 21 *University of Toronto L.J.* 109–40 (1971).

106. There had previously been a move from *Gemeinschaft* law. The terms, of course, derive from Ferdinand Tönnies (see translation as *Community and Association*): similar ideas are found in the writing of Karl Renner.

107. "Beyond Bourgeois Individualism: the Contemporary Crisis in Law and Legal Ideology" in (eds.) E. Kamenka and R.S. Neale, *Feudalism, Capitalism and Beyond*, London: Edward Arnold, 1975, 140. *Cf.* D. Neiken, "Is there a Crisis in Law and Legal Ideology?" 9 *J. Law and Soc.* 177 (1982).

108. See R.M. Unger, *op. cit.*, note 94, 216 and F. Neumann, *The Democratic and Authoritarian State*, New York: Macmillan, 1957. Unger refers also to German writing by Friedrich Dessauer, Justus Hedemann and Rudolf Echterholter (see 292–93).

109. See, for example, J. Alderson, *Policing Freedom*, London: Macdonald and Evans, 1979 or "The Case For Community Policing" in (eds.) D. Cowell, T. Jones and J. Young, *Policing the Riots*, London: Junction Books, 1982, ch. 8, *cf.* C. Moore and J. Brown, *Community Versus Crime*, London: Bedford Square Press, 1981.

110. See Z. Bankowski and G. Mungham, "Laypeople and Lawpeople and the Administration of the Lower Courts," *Int. J. of Sociology of Law*, vol. 9, 85–100 (1981).

111. See, for example, D. McGillis and J. Mullen, *Neighbourhood Justice Centers: An Analysis of Potential Models*: Washington D.C.: Govt. Printing Office, 1977; Frank Sander, *Report on the National Conference on Minor Dispute Resolution*, Chicago: American Bar Association, 1977 (also his "Varieties of Dispute Processing," 70 F.R.D. 79 (1976)); L. Nader, *No Access to Law: Alternatives to the American Judicial System*, New York: Academic Press, 1980. See also Benson Royal Commission on Legal Services, London: H.M.S.O. 1979, Cmnd. 7,648, ch. 43. On the concept of "neighbourhood" see

R. Danzig, "Toward the Creation of a Complementary Decentralised System of Justice," 26 *Stanford L.R.* 1 (1973).

112. *Per* Stanley Cohen, "Human Warehouses: The Future of Our Prisons?", *New Society*, vol. 30, no. 632 (14 November 1974), 407 at 410.

113. Stanley Cohen's expression. See "Human Warehouses: The Future of Our Prisons?", *New Society*, vol. 30, no. 632 (14 November 1974), 407.

114. *Per* Barton L. Ingraham and Gerald W. Smith, "The Use of Electronics in the Observation and Control of Human Behaviour, and Its Possible Use in Rehabilitation and Parole," *Issues in Criminology* 35-53 (Fall Issue, 1972).

115. "Culture and Administration," 37 *Telos* 93, 101-102 (1978).

116. *Op. cit.*, note 20, at 347. See also Stanley Cohen, "Prisons and the Future of Control Systems: From Concentration to Dispersal," in (eds.) M. Fitzgerald, P. Halmos, J. Muncie and D. Zeldin, *Welfare in Action*, London: R.K.P., 1977, 217-28.

Part IV
Legal Scholarship and Alternative Dispute Resolution

[12]

Alternative to What? Theories of Litigation, Procedure and Dispute Settlement in Anglo-American Jurisprudence: Some Neglected Classics

*William Twining**

Concern with different institutions and methods of dispute settlement has a long history. But the rapid growth in lawyers' interest in 'alternative dispute resolution' (ADR) is widely perceived to have gathered momentum in the late 1960s in the United States.[1] In the past twenty years there has indeed been a remarkable growth in the 'ADR industry,' exemplified by the development of organisations, courses within law schools, continuing legal education and an extensive literature. The main stimuli appear to have been largely pragmatic and political rather than theoretical or 'scientific.' Three particular concerns seem to have predominated: a feeling on the part of the American legal establishment that the court system was becoming intolerably overloaded by an increased volume of civil claims and criminal prosecutions; a felt need, on the part of professionals and others, for specialised private fora to serve particular interests (eg commercial arbitration); and a view that over and above the concomitant increase in congestion, delay and expense, the system was incapable in more fundamental ways of living up to the ideals of 'access to justice' for all.

When a 'movement' relating to law develops in the United States, one outcome is almost invariably a massive, confusing and largely unsystematic body of literature of variable quality.[2] The ADR movement is no exception. In so far as any general patterns can be discussed from the American ADR literature, perhaps three main strands can be differentiated: first, a body of writing that is concerned with institutional design, in which the central questions relate to the appropriateness of different methods of dispute resolution to various types of 'dispute.' The pioneering work of Lon Fuller in the latter phases of his career is a prominent example.[3] Second, there has been a series of essentially political debates about the desirability and necessity of encouraging and developing ADR on a large scale. The diagnosis, prescriptions and the motives of the enthusiasts were challenged by sceptics of varying political persuasions: for example, radical critics such as Jerold Auerbach and Richard Abel, while doubting that 'justice' was routinely achieved in litigation, argued that the alternatives prescribed by advocates of ADR were no more likely to enhance either access to or delivery of justice in practice and that the net effect of the movement

---

*Faculty of Laws, University College London.
This paper was presented to an Anglo-Soviet Colloquium in Moscow in June 1990 and is published here without revision or adaptation. Some of the ideas are developed at greater length in W. Twining, *Rethinking Evidence* (Oxford: Blackwell, 1990) (hereafter RE), esp chs 3, 5 and 11.

1 eg S. Goldberg, E. Green and F. Sander (eds), *Dispute Resolution* (Boston: Little Brown, 1985) ch 1. Discussions of ADR in the common law world have hitherto tended to be overshadowed by the American debates.
2 cf the American Realist and Law and Literature 'Movements.'
3 L.L. Fuller, 'Mediation — Its Forms and Functions' (1971) 44 S California L Rev 305; 'The Forms and Limits of Adjudication' (1979) 92 Harv L Rev 353.

would be to discourage the disadvantaged from trying to assert their legal rights.[4] From a rather different perspective, Owen Fiss argued forcefully 'against settlement' not only on the grounds that negotiation and mediation tend to favour the powerful, but also because the development of alternatives would undermine the creative role of the courts in developing public policy and inventing new solutions — an optimistic (and perhaps prototypically American) conception of the political role and importance of courts.[5]

A third strand of literature is specifically educational.[6] While some of the most prominent educational works deal with broad issues of institutional design and its political implications, the main thrust is to prepare lawyers for participation in these alternative modes by developing 'skills' in respect of such matters as counselling, interviewing, negotiation, mediation and non-curial advocacy.

The vast bulk of these three bodies of literature is atheoretical. By and large it represents a series of pragmatic and *ad hoc* reactions to some specific perceived problems in the American legal system at a particular period in history. There are two main exceptions to this broad generalisation: first, quite extensive reference is made to the specialised and generally excellent literature of legal anthropology exemplified by such writers as Malinowski, Llewellyn and Hoebel, Gluckman, Gulliver and Nader.[7] Second, a substantial body of detailed empirical research has been done on criminal process, civil litigation and some alternative processes.[8] Most of this research has been informed by contemporary social science methodology and fits within the kind of theoretical framework that is associated with 'the process school' in American jurisprudence — that is to say, a perspective that views litigation and other legal processes as a largely linear and discrete series of decisions and events involving a variety of participants, arenas, procedures, discourses and outcomes.[9]

This characterisation of a vast and complex body of American literature is, of course, a great simplification.[10] However, in so far as it is broadly correct it suggests that this heritage has two characteristics that need to be borne in mind by outsiders. First, it focuses on concerns, institutions and phenomena that are specifically American, despite the de-parochialising influence of anthropology. Second, it is largely divorced from what is widely perceived to be 'mainstream' Anglo-American jurisprudence as exemplified, on the one hand, by English positivists in the tradition of Bentham, Austin, Hart and Raz, and by their, largely American, critics such as Rawls and Dworkin. The two main exceptions to this are, perhaps, Lon Fuller and Karl Llewellyn. However, there is, or at least there is generally thought to be, a disjuncture between these two jurists' 'sociological' writings about

4 R. Abel, *The Politics of Informal Justice* (New York: Academic Press, 1982); J. Auerbach, *Justice Without Law?* (New York: Oxford UP, 1983).

5 Extracts from these debates are collected in L.L. Riskin and J.E. Westbrook, *Dispute Resolution and Lawyers* (St Paul, Minn: West, 1987) ch 1; and Goldberg, Green and Sander, *op cit* pp 485–503.

6 eg *op cit* n 5; and N. Gold, K. Mackie and W. Twining (eds), *Learning Lawyers' Skills* (London: Butterworths, 1989).

7 A useful survey of the literature is F. Snyder, 'Anthropology, Dispute Processes and Law: A Critical Introduction' (1981) 8 *Brit J Law & Society* 141. See also S. Roberts, *Order and Dispute* (Harmondsworth: Penguin, 1979).

8 eg the work of Felstiner, Galanter, Miller and Sarat, and the Wisconsin Dispute Processing Program (1979–).

9 See below, n 37.

10 The ADR movement has been treated here as a largely American phenomenon. The ideas generated have been picked up and developed in common law countries, especially the United Kingdom, Australia and Canada. Of course, most of what is now subsumed under ADR antedates the ADR movement.

dispute settlement and their most memorable contributions to mainstream Jurisprudence. Only a tenuous connection is perceived between Fuller's writings on mediation and adjudication and his attacks on positivism; similarly, Llewellyn's reputation as the spokesman and interpreter of Legal Realism, the architect of the Uniform Commercial Code and the author of *The Common Law Tradition* is generally treated as separate from *The Cheyenne Way* and his 'law jobs theory.' I have argued elsewhere that Llewellyn's thought has a greater unity than this interpretation suggests. The same could probably be said of Fuller.

In so far as there is a perceived disjuncture between the literature on ADR and mainstream Anglo-American jurisprudence, this is puzzling because one of the most persistent concerns of our legal theorists has been about the nature of adjudication. Twentieth-century Anglo-American jurisprudence has been extraordinarily court-centred, with many of the main debates focusing on the role of judges and reasoning about questions of law in hard cases.[11] If *alternative* dispute resolution is mainly concerned with alternatives to civil adjudication, it seems strange that mainstream theories of adjudication do not feature prominently in discussions of ADR.

Two related factors may help to explain this disjuncture, at least in part. First, Anglo-American legal scholarship and legal education have tended to focus on analysis, exposition and argumentation about legal doctrine. In respect of this, the most visible and interesting issues tend to surface in atypical arenas, notably appellate courts. This sometimes obscures the obvious point that in only a tiny percentage of litigated cases is an adjudicative decision required; only a small percentage of adjudicative decisions involves disputed questions of law rather than of fact or disposition; and the percentage of cases that are appealed is strikingly small. The vast majority of civil cases is settled or abandoned before trial; and an even greater percentage of criminal cases involves a guilty plea which precludes an adjudicative decision on either the facts or the law.[12] Accordingly, in so far as a great deal of Anglo-American jurisprudence focuses on the roles and reasonings of appellate judges on questions of law, and treats such judges as the centre-point not only of litigation, but of law in general, it treats statistically insignificant and atypical decisions as central. The phrase 'alternative dispute resolution' is revealing. The word 'alternative' implies exceptional or secondary or even deviant in contrast with something that is normal or standard or ordinary. But alternative to what? To litigation? Hardly — for some of the standard alternatives such as negotiation, compromise and mediation regularly feature as phases *within* litigation. To adjudication? If so, it is not just our theorists who are obsessed with the atypical; rather, court-centred thinking and discourse are deeply ingrained in our legal culture.

For closely related reasons, those enclaves of legal theory which have focused more directly on non-curial legal activities and phenomena — sociology of law, legal anthropology and its precursor historical jurisprudence — have generally been marginalised in our legal culture. Thus, the main parts of our theoretical heritage that are seen as relevant to dispute settlement are largely outside the mainstream of jurisprudence. However, there are some exceptions and in this paper I shall draw attention to some works that help to bridge the gap between marginalised sociological theory and orthodox legal scholarship.

11 The most prominent contemporary example is Ronald Dworkin and his critics.
12 Some statistics on settlement out of court, guilty pleas and appeals in England and Wales are usefully collected in Michael Zander, *Cases and Materials on the English Legal System* (London: Weidenfeld & Nicolson, 5th ed, 1988).

Bentham's Theory of Judicial Organisation and Adjective Law

Jeremy Bentham (1748–1832) is, of course, England's most famous jurist. More written about than read, the general outlines of his thought are well known: a particular version of utilitarianism that is the foundation and driving force of all his thought; his 'theory of fictions' which contains both his general epistemology and his main methods of analysis; his account 'of laws in general' which provides the framework for his jurisprudence; his grand design for a 'pannomion', a complete body of codified law, including a Constitutional Code, a Penal Code and a Civil Code; his theory of punishment and rewards, and so on. Less well known, but among the most extensive of his writings, are his theories of procedure and evidence (adjective law) and of judicial organisation, which deal with what he saw as a crucial part of his grand design, the *implementation* of the whole system of laws founded on utility.[13]

Despite its extent, this aspect of Bentham's work can be summarised quite succinctly. The object of adjudication is the implementation and application of positive law made by the legislator to promote utility. The direct end of adjective laws is rectitude of decision, that is, the correct application of substantive law to true facts. The collateral or subordinate end is avoidance of vexation, expense and delay. Conflicts between the direct and the subordinate ends are to be determined on the basis of utility. The system of procedure best calculated to further these ends is 'the Natural System' as contrasted with the 'Technical System.' The former is characterised by an almost complete absence of artificial (ie man-made) and technical devices, including formal binding rules of evidence and procedure. Rectitude of decision is to be secured by making provision for the forthcomingness of witnesses and the completeness and accuracy of testimony, backed by sanctions; by placing responsibility for each decision on the shoulders of a single judge who is adequately remunerated; the main securities against misdecision are simplicity and, above all, publicity. Questions of fact and the weighing of evidence should be governed by ordinary principles of common sense reasoning. The legislator should provide guidance to judges in the form of 'instructions' addressed to the understanding rather than by general binding rules addressed to the will.[14] The court system should be organised to provide cheap, simple, accessible, local, public justice.[15]

13 For details see W. Twining, *Theories of Evidence: Bentham and Wigmore* (London: Weidenfeld & Nicolson, 1985) ch 2.

14 See generally *Theories of Evidence*, cited in n 13. There is currently a debate among Bentham scholars as to whether Bentham thought that the judge should also treat all substantive law (including the codes) as being subject to the overriding principle of utility in the particular circumstances of each case — in short, whether Bentham had a direct or act-utilitarian theory of adjudication. The main proponent of this view is Gerald Postema, *Bentham and the Common Law Tradition* (Oxford: Oxford UP, 1986); three different interpretations have been advanced by J. Dinwiddy (Review of Postema) (1989) 1 *Utilitas* 283; P. Kelly (Review of *id*) (1989) *History of Political Thought* 366; and W. Twining, 'Reading Bentham' (1989) LXXV *Proc Brit Academy* 97, at n 31.

15 Bentham's list of the evils of procedure as he perceived them to be, in the England of his day, is interesting in this context:

In the penal branch,

1. Impunity of delinquents.
2. Undue punishments, *viz* punishment of non-delinquents, or punishment of delinquents otherwise than due.

In the non-penal branch,

3. Frustration of well-grounded claims.
4. Allowance of ill-grounded claims.

A great deal of Bentham's energy was directed to attacking the complexities and expense of procedure and the confusing technical rules of evidence, which were, he believed, sustained mainly by the sinister interests of lawyers and of judges (who also depended for their income on fees). In the two centuries since he wrote, almost all changes in procedure, evidence and judicial organisation have represented moves in the general direction that Bentham advocated, without going as far as he proposed and in a piecemeal and slow manner that he would have deplored. Similarly, the underlying basic assumptions about what is involved in rational adjudication and in proving facts have been almost universally adopted by specialist writers on the law of evidence. This is in spite of the fact that many of them have defended some of the technical rules that he attacked and even though this ideal type of 'The Rationalist Tradition of Evidence Scholarship' sits less comfortably with adversarial than with inquisitorial modes of procedure.[16] Bentham favoured a system of procedure that cut across the standard distinctions between 'inquisitorial' and 'adversarial' systems: many of his ideas fit the former model better (eg active questioning by the judge), but he also favoured confrontation of parties and witnesses face-to-face in oral proceedings and considered that cross-examination was the redeeming feature of the English tradition.[17]

One reason for Bentham's continuing significance is that he tended to take clear, unequivocal, often extreme positions on fundamental issues. His models of rational adjudication and of the Natural System of Procedure provide useful and rich 'ideal types' for contrasting 'alternative' methods of dispute resolution to adjudication. His attitude to compromise and conciliation are especially suggestive in this context. He studied the Danish Courts of Reconciliation and similar experiments in France, and viewed them with some ambivalence. He recognised some value in the conciliative function, especially in cases in which each side complained of a series of supposed wrongs.[18] But this was rigidly limited by the importance he attached to full implementation of substantive laws, deemed to be consistent with utility. He assumed that reconciliation is best achieved by adjudication in conformity to law: 'The increased facility of extinguishing ill-will, *and at the same time rendering complete justice*, is among the advantages possessed by the natural system of procedure in comparison to the system of technical procedure.'[19]

Bentham considered that the use of the pardon in criminal cases was only justified in exceptional circumstances and it is almost certain that he would have opposed institutionalised plea-bargaining. He was even more uncompromising about compromise. In *Scotch Reform* he wrote: 'Another mode of termination is by what is called *compromise*: which, being interpreted, is *denial of justice*.'[20] This follows from the high value he placed on implementation of law and vindication of rights (expletive justice — ie justice under the law). Compromise, even in situations of equality of bargaining power when parties freely consent, involves the sacrifice of rights and hence a cost, which is only ever justified as the lesser of two evils. He

5. Expense.
6. Vexation.
7. Delay.
8. Precipitation.
9. Complication. (ii *Works* 19, Bowring edition).

16 *Theories of Evidence* ch 2; RE ch 3.
17 *id.*
18 For details see *Theories of Evidence* 94–95, 213, ns 40 and 41.
19 J. Bentham, *Principles of Judicial Procedure*, ii *Works* 47 (Bowring edition) (Italics added).
20 *Scotch Reform* (v *Works* 35).

anticipated modern commentators in doubting whether bargaining is ever really equal or consent truly free. On this interpretation, it seems likely that Bentham would have looked with deep suspicion on modern efforts to promote mediation, negotiation or arbitration (especially in private), and other alternatives to the kind of open, cheap, simple, speedy implementation of the law that would be achieved in his ideal court system.

Some of Bentham's concerns have resurfaced in modern debates, typically divorced from the comprehensive framework of his grand design. For example, Lon Fuller in developing his famous distinction between 'monocentric' and 'polycentric' tasks and arguing that courts should, as far as possible, not take on the latter, assumed a similar conception of courts to Bentham.[21] He saw them as institutions with specific characteristics only suited to applying and implementing law in respect of 'monocentric' tasks. Some critics have challenged this 'traditionalist' view, arguing that courts are much more flexible institutions that have a crucial role to play in adapting laws and politics to changing conditions and in creative problem-solving generally. It is partly because of this 'adaptationist' view of the role of courts that Owen Fiss has argued forcefully 'against settlement,' taking almost as strong a position as Bentham on the basis of a view of the role of courts that Bentham categorically rejected.[22]

Bentham's picture of the Natural System of procedure and his recommendations for access to justice may seem to be simplistic, Utopian and unworkable to some modern eyes; but they contain the clearest and most coherent example of a design theory that vests responsibility for implementation of law and vindication of rights almost exclusively in state courts, and his reasons for this need to be taken seriously in considering alternatives.

Llewellyn's Law-Jobs Theory and Some Successors

Karl Llewellyn's 'law-jobs' theory is rather better known than Bentham's writings on adjective law, but like the latter it represents a relatively neglected part of his thought.[23] It is relevant in the present context because it places dispute prevention and dispute settlement at the centre of a general sociological theory of law-government. The outline of the theory can be summarised as follows[24]: All of us are members of groups, such as a family, a club, a teenage gang, a school or commercial organisation, a trade union, a political party, a nation state, the world community. In order to survive and to achieve its aims, in so far as it has aims, *any* human group has to meet certain needs or ensure that certain jobs are done. The first, perhaps the most important, of these jobs is to channel behaviour and expectations of members of the group in order to avoid conflicts or disputes within it. Second, when disputes arise, they have to be resolved or, at least, be kept at a tolerably low level, or else the group will disintegrate or its objectives will be frustrated or impaired. Third, as the circumstances of the group change, so the behaviour and expectations of members of the group have to be adjusted to such

21 Fuller (1979) *op cit*, cf Goldberg, Green and Sander, *op cit* ch 2.
22 O. Fiss, 'Against Settlement' (1984) 93 Yale LJ 1073. The most important modern defence of compromise is by Stuart Hampshire, *Innocence and Experience* (London: Allen Lane, 1989).
23 See especially K. Llewellyn, 'The Normative, the Legal and the Law-Jobs' (1940) 49 Yale LJ 1355.
24 This formulation is adapted from W. Twining and D. Miers, *How to Things With Rules* (London: Weidenfeld & Nicolson, 3rd ed, 1991) pp 159–160.

changes in order to avoid conflicts and disappointments. Fourth, decision-making in the group needs to be regulated both in respect of who has power and authority to participate in decisions and in respect of the procedures by which decisions are arrived at. This allocation of authority and power is typically the primary function of a 'constitution' of, for example, a club or a nation state. Fifth, in any group, but especially in complex groups, techniques, practices, skills and devices need to be developed for satisfactorily meeting the first four needs. Channelling behaviour, settling disputes, making smooth adjustments to change and providing for acceptable ways of reaching decisions can often be difficult tasks, involving high levels of skill or quite refined or sophisticated devices and institutions.

This last category, which Llewellyn called the 'Job of Juristic Method,' focuses attention on institutional design (eg constitution-making), specific inventions and devices (eg the letter of credit, the trust, mini-trials), individual skills (eg in negotiation, advocacy, fact-management) and more general craft traditions. In bare outline this looks like a fairly orthodox functionalist sociological theory, which provides a convenient characterisation of the main tasks of law, but can hardly be claimed as particularly original except perhaps in repect of the focus on juristic method or legal technology. Moreover, it has been suggested, this is an example of 'extreme functionalism' and hence is vulnerable to standard criticisms of old-fashioned functionalism of the kind associated with Talcott Parsons and Robert Merton.[25]

This is not the place to consider such criticisms in detail. I believe that the theory can be interpreted in a way which exonerates it from the most damaging criticisms and that aspects of it are suggestive and have been fruitfully developed by Llewellyn and others. Here, however, I wish to advance some reasons why this provides a particularly helpful perspective from which to consider dispute settlement.

First, the theory boldly claims to apply to all human groups, from a two-person unit (such as a motor-racing team or a one-parent family) to the world community. It includes submarines, prisons, clubs, tribes, villages and multinational corporations, and regional groupings as well as nation states. Controversy has surrounded how useful it is to treat all human groups as comparables,[26] but in so far as one can ask certain standard questions about how disputes are avoided and handled in any group its claim to comprehensiveness is particularly significant. For example, it helps to free legal theory from focusing exclusively on the nation state and it thus provides a starting point for theories of legal pluralism and 'non-state law.'[27] Second, the theory provides one escape route from obsessive concern with the definition of law. For Llewellyn, 'the institution of law-government' was the main, but not the only, institution specialised to performing the law-jobs in those groups we choose to call 'societies'; conversely, the law-jobs are the main, but not the only, functions of that institution. In specific contexts for particular purposes, it may be useful to distinguish between the 'legal' and 'non-legal,' but these are merely secondary issues of taxonomy. From this perspective it matters little whether, for example, the Kpelle moot, a university disciplinary committee, an Ifugao 'go-between,' a marriage guidance bureau, or a 'rent-a-judge trial' are labelled as 'legal' or not — they are all institutionalised dispute-processing mechanisms that can be compared and

25 A. Hunt, *The Sociological Movement in Law* (London: Macmillan, 1978) ch 3. For a balanced discussion of functionalism in the sociology of law, see R. Cotterrell, *The Sociology of Law: An Introduction* (London: Butterworths, 2nd ed, 1992) ch 3.

26 eg Cotterrell, *op cit* pp 80–83; J. Frank, *Courts on Trial* (New York: Atheneum, 1963) p 77.

27 J. Starr and J. Collier (eds), *History and Power in the Study of Law* (Ithaca: Cornell UP, 1989); Twining (1989) *op cit* n 14, at pp 129–133.

contrasted within a single framework. Third, Llewellyn claimed that all of the law-jobs are essential to group survival and successful achievement of collective goals.[28] But any particular task can be done by a variety of means, singly or in combination. Dispute prevention in most societies, for example, is served by a complex mixture of formal and informal norms, education, rewards and incentives, hedges, barbed wire, physical force and other means of social control. Similarly, in any group, one should expect dispute settlement to be achieved by a variety of means. In a famous passage, Llewellyn summed up the basic insight, which he credited to Max Weber:

> The jobs to be done are jobs to be done: modern complexity of institution serves merely to highlight processes which require to be gone through, in some fashion, in any group. *The jobs, therefore, get themselves done after some fashion* always — or the group simply is no more. Hence if the officially announced imperatives fail to put themselves over, one must look elsewhere for the doing of the jobs . . . Hence to see a Legal regulation which is not working is promptly to face a problem of further inquiry: What *is* working and how?[29]

Finally, as this passage suggests, the law-jobs theory is a contextual theory which requires that any particular institution, device, 'case' or other phenomenon should be viewed in the context of a larger whole. Any decision or event in a process such as litigation should be viewed in the context of the process as a whole. Thinking in terms of total pictures and total processes was part of the basic methodology of Llewellyn's 'realism'. This leads naturally to one of the basic insights and truisms of modern dispute settlement theory: that in any given society only a tiny proportion of all disputes are likely ever to reach those institutions we choose to call 'courts' or even those processes which might be included within the sphere of 'litigation.' A natural starting point for the consideration of any particular dispute settlement method or institution is a realistic demographic total picture of all disputes in the society or group in question and how they are presently being resolved.

The 'law-jobs theory' was developed in a number of directions by Llewellyn and others but, in my view, it has by no means fulfilled its potential. Apart from its direct influence on legal anthropology, four particular developments are of particular interest in the present context.

Law-Crafts and Legal Skills

Llewellyn in his later years elaborated a general theory of the crafts of law, which had both sociological and educational dimensions. It has been particularly influential in respect of the modern emphasis on direct teaching of legal skills (such as negotiation, interviewing, counselling and advocacy) based on systematic job analysis and skills analysis of lawyers' operations and the role of law-trained people in a given society.[32]

---

28 This claim can be interpreted as a useful tautology, if the concept of 'group' is defined in terms of co-ordination and absence of conflict; W. Twining, *Karl Llewellyn and the Realist Movement* (London: Weidenfeld & Nicolson, 1973), at pp 180–182.

29 Llewellyn (1940) *op cit* at pp 1381–1382 (Llewellyn's italics).

30 Twining, 'Talk about Realism' (1985) 60 NYU L Rev 329, at pp 375–380.

31 eg W. Felstiner, R. Abel and A. Sarat, 'The Emergence and Transformation of Disputes: Naming, Blaming and Claiming' (1980–81) 15 Law & Society Rev 631.

32 See *Karl Llewellyn and the Realist Movement*, pp 353–356, 505–512. See especially I. Rutter, 'A Jurisprudence of Lawyers' Operations' (1961) 13 *J Legal Education* 301; Mackie, Gold and Twining, *op cit* n 6.

The Parental Model of Law-Government

Llewellyn also developed a typology of dispute settlement (parental, adversary, inquisitorial), initially in connection with the Pueblo Indians of New Mexico and subsequently in planning a project on Soviet law that was never executed.[33] The idea of 'the parental' was later used by Professor Harold Berman in his writings on Soviet law[34] and may indirectly have influenced Mirjan Damaska's analysis of comparative procedure, which more directly links different ideological structures to systems of legal procedure (see below).[35]

Arbitration

Llewellyn's wife, Soia Mentschikoff, used the law-jobs theory (including the 'parental' concept) in her work on commercial arbitration, including the ambitious Chicago Arbitration Project that was never fully completed.[36]

Theories of Litigation

Llewellyn was also directly and indirectly influential on subsequent theorising about litigation. Perhaps the most sophisticated example of work in this tradition is by John Griffiths, who has developed a total process model that takes account of modern developments in the sociology and anthropology of law.[37] His concern was to construct a general sociological theory of litigation, external to any particular legal system, for the purpose of conducting 'scientific' empirical research, specifically into divorce proceedings and administrative appeals in Holland.

Griffiths usefully draws together some of the main lessons to be gleaned from the sociological and anthropological literature. For example, that concepts such as 'dispute' and 'case' are problematic; that it is a common fallacy to assume that social processes are typically unilinear; that terms like 'dispute settlement' and 'dispute resolution' give a false impression of finality, whereas a particular agreement or decision may be just one phase in a longer process, or feud or story or series of stories: and that 'ADR' is often part of rather than an alternative to litigation. This is just one example of the sociological literature providing salutary reminders of complexities, which are sometimes forgotten in the optimistic discourse of a new movement.

A Comparative Theory of Procedure: Mirjan Damaska

Bentham's theory of adjective law and rational adjudication was an integral part of a prescriptive design theory. It belongs to censorial rather than expository jurisprudence. Llewellyn and the other writers mentioned in the preceding section largely adopt perspectives drawn from social anthropology and sociology. My next

33 *ibid* pp 363–365, 475–476.
34 eg H. Berman, *Justice in the USSR* (Cambridge, Mass: Harvard UP, 2nd ed, 1963), esp at pp 421–423.
35 M. Damaska, 'Evidentiary Barriers to Conviction and Two Models of Criminal Procedure' (1973) 121 U Pa L Rev 506; *The Faces of Justice and State Authority* (New Haven: Yale UP, 1986).
36 S. Mentschikoff, 'Commercial Arbitration' (1961) 61 Columbia L Rev 846.
37 J. Griffiths, 'The General Theory of Litigation — A First Step' (1983) 5 *Zeitschrift für Rechtssoziologie*, Heft 2, 145, discussed in detail in RE ch 11.

example also involves Weberian 'ideal types,' used as tools of analysis and explanation in the comparative study of legal procedure. Mirjan Damaska's important *The Faces of Justice and State Authority*, published in 1986, adopts the perspective and style of a comparative lawyer, but it has potential significance for many specialists whose concerns are more parochial. The author is exceptionally qualified to undertake the task, for he writes with authority and firsthand knowledge of the administration of justice in socialist, civilian and common law systems. A Yugoslav by birth, education and training, Professor Damaska taught and practised law in his own country before moving to the United States in the early 1970s. He is able to draw on literature in several European languages and from several disciplines. Students of Evidence and Criminal Procedure, and many others, will be familiar with Damaska's outstanding article on 'Evidentiary Barriers to Conviction,' published in 1973. The present work is more ambitious and more abstract. It is an attempt to construct a systematic theoretical framework for the study and comparison of 'legal process' in modern Western legal systems.[38]

Throughout, Damaska adopts the standpoint of the *civis peregrinus*, an outside observer who is relatively detached from particular internal debates and disagreements. One of his concerns is to expose some common errors and pitfalls in the discourse of comparative procedure: for example, the conflation of functions of state with structures of government; simple determinist attempts to correlate socio-economic organisation with procedural forms; the equation of Anglo-American procedure with the notion of adversarial 'contest' and civilian procedure with 'inquisitorial' proceedings, when most actual procedural systems are hybrids embodying mixtures of 'inquest' and 'contest' that need to be carefully differentiated; the related error of treating 'contest' and 'inquest' as different means to shared ends, rather than as representing procedural structures which are mainly designed to serve different ends.

Damaska's method is to set up 'ideal types' which are sufficiently precise and detached from historical contingencies to serve as general tools of analysis. The focus is on the design of procedural systems and institutions, their structures, functions and architecture. The treatment is fairly abstract; even the extensive illustrative material is treated at a fairly high level of generality. Damaska sets up three sets of polar models or 'ideal types' relating to systems of government, structures of authority and systems of legal procedure respectively. His three sets of distinctions can be briefly restated as follows[39]: *Systems of Government* can be characterised by the extent to which they approximate to or diverge from pure versions of '*the managerial state*,' in which the role of government is to manage all important aspects of social life, and '*the reactive state*,' in which the role of government is limited 'to provide a framework for social interaction.'[40] This corresponds with familiar distinctions between 'interventionist' and '*laissez-faire*' ideologies of government. Most modern Western societies have hybrid systems of government (and mixed economies) which lie somewhere between the two extremes. Even the United States departs in important respects from the 'ideal type' of the *reactive state*; whereas the United Kingdom, despite recent incursions on the welfare state, is in important respects somewhat closer to the managerial model.

Structures of State Authority can similarly be characterised in terms of a distinction

38 Damaska (1986), *op cit* p 2. Damaska focuses almost entirely on 'Western' systems, but deals with some aspects of the situation in the Soviet Union and the Chinese People's Republic prior to 1985.
39 This summary is adapted from RE, at pp 180–182.
40 Damaska (1986), *op cit* p 71.

between *hierarchical* and *co-ordinate* authority. A reasonably clear example of the former is a bureaucratic state apparatus run by *professionals*, who are in a *hierarchical* relationship to each other, and who purportedly make most important decisions according to *precisely defined standards*. Co-ordinate authority is characterised by extensive *lay* (non-specialist) *participation*, *single levels* of 'horizontal' authority and resort to *undifferentiated community standards* rather than formal rules. Again, most actual systems of authority are hybrids. However, there are clear examples in particular spheres: for example, the English jury closely fits the co-ordinate model in that it is composed of ordinary citizens, its findings are only exceptionally subject to review or appeal ('the sovereignty of the jury') and its decisions, within its allotted sphere, are governed by 'common sense.' Significantly, juries do not, indeed cannot, give reasons for their decisions. This contrasts significantly with the lower judiciary in countries like Italy and France, where the personnel are trained officials, whose decisions even on questions of fact have to be reasoned and are subject to regular review by and appeal to higher authority.

The third distinction, between 'inquisitorial' and 'adversarial' *systems of procedure*, is also commonplace. But Damaska departs from common usage, which tends to be both ambiguous and vague, by distinguishing these categories in terms of purposes rather than treating them as different means to shared ends.[41] The purpose of an 'inquest' is implementation of state policy in order to solve a problem; the purpose of a 'contest' is the legitimated resolution of a single dispute between identifiable parties. It is a truism of procedural scholarship that it is misleading to equate Anglo-American procedure with 'adversary' proceedings or systems influenced by Roman Law with 'inquisitorial' proceedings. English Criminal Procedure, for example, viewed as a total process, can be interpreted mainly in terms of the model of 'inquest' with a few 'adversarial' glosses, especially at the stage of a contested trial — an event which occurs in only a small minority of cases. Damaska goes further than this: he argues that it would be surprising to find any modern state which had only one kind of procedural arrangement and, indeed, that examples of particular institutional arrangements which fit the 'ideal types' exactly are quite exceptional.[42] Most procedural arrangements, let alone most 'systems' of arrangements, are hybrids. Nevertheless, these concepts, if used precisely, have considerable explanatory power.

These distinctions are, of course, potentially controversial; there is also scope for differences in interpreting and applying them to particular examples. That serves to underline the point that it is not possible to give an ideologically neutral account of a legal system. However, Damaska's central thesis may be less controversial. He argues that these different ideal types can combine in practice in a variety of ways: some combinations one would expect to be more 'comfortable,' while others would almost inevitably give rise to serious tensions. For example, the managerial state, hierarchical authority and inquest fit together quite naturally; conversely, there is likely to be regular tension between adversary proceedings and hierarchical authority. However, and this is the central point, there are many more workable combinations of relatively pure types than one might expect; many particular arrangements, as well as whole systems, represent mixes or compromises. For example, there is no necessary incompatibility between 'inquisitorial' procedure and a largely reactive state, on the one hand, or a largely co-ordinate system of authority on the other.[43] Many English tribunals are concerned with implementa-

41 *id* pp 3–6, 10–12; cf 69.
42 *id* pp 224–225.
43 *id* p 69.

tion of law relating to such matters as welfare, tax and immigration: cases typically come before them when a decision is challenged. There is in a sense a 'dispute' and hearings have some 'adversarial' characteristics. We live in a world of hybrids.

Damaska's book has been aptly described as 'a political analysis of Procedural Law.'[44] It brings to the fore questions about the relationship between procedural arrangements and political structures and goals. Damaska deals only incidentally with non-curial proceedings, but his sensitive analysis of the complexities of the relationships between types of political organisation and legal procedures has important implications for broader issues of dispute settlement.[45]

The Faces of Justice and State Authority is undoubtedly the most significant recent contribution in the English language to the comparative study of legal procedure. It contains a number of controversial theses and interpretations which are likely to be debated for many years. Its immediate relevance is that it provides a useful bridge between the specialised and localised Anglo-American literature on dispute settlement and the comparative study of common law, civilian and socialist legal systems; it also provides a broad framework within which to discuss particular institutional arrangements in different political systems. Although Damaska rightly points to the variety of feasible institutional arrangements, he emphasises that the archetypal pattern for the pursuit of the goal of conflict resolution is a system of co-ordinate authority in a reactive state. In this view, alternative dispute resolution institutions will tend to fit uneasily within a managerial regime with a hierarchical structure of state authority.

Conclusion

From this highly selective survey of the stock of Anglo-American theorising that bears on dispute settlement, one might extract the following general obvious and not-so-obvious propositions:

(a) Concepts such as 'alternative,' 'dispute,' 'resolution,' 'case' and even 'adjudication' are problematic and need to be used with caution in particular contexts.
(b) In common law countries not only is a tiny proportion of all disputes litigated, but also only a very small percentage of litigated cases is 'resolved' by adjudicative decisions (on questions of fact or law).
(c) In so far as ADR is concerned with designing institutionalised alternatives to litigation or adjudication in order to reduce vexation, expense and delay, it should not be taken for granted that the benefits of such institutions will necessarily outweigh the costs.
(d) Most systems of legal procedure are hybrids in which a great variety of institutions and procedural forms can be accommodated more or less 'comfortably,' because the relationship between systems of government, systems of state authority and procedural systems is more complex than might be supposed. The same probably applies to institutions of dispute resolution.
(e) A total process perspective underlines the value of looking at particular

44 A. Stein, 'A Political Analysis of Procedural Law' (review of Damaska) (1988) 51 MLR 159.
45 See especially Damaska, *op cit* at pp 78–79.
46 A more comprehensive survey would include, *inter alia*, writings on procedural justice, economic analysis of law, the sociology of the legal profession and recent discussions of the reform of judicial administration and civil procedure.

decisions and events in the context of those that precede and succeed them in time. So-called 'resolutions,' 'settlements' or 'terminations' are frequently not the end of the story of a particular dispute or case, especially in a situation of continuing relationships.

(f) The great bulk of the English language literature on dispute resolution has been stimulated by specifically American concerns and perceived problems. The literature of social anthropology provides some powerful warnings about the complexity of social processes and their relationships to specific cultural and historical contexts.

[13]

DISPUTE PROCESSING IN LAW AND LEGAL SCHOLARSHIP: FROM INSTITUTIONAL CRITIQUE TO THE RECONSTRUCTION OF THE JURIDICAL SUBJECT*

SUSAN SILBEY** AND AUSTIN SARAT***

TABLE OF CONTENTS

I. INTRODUCTION

Though talk about disputing has, for a long time, been common in labor and international relations, as well as on baseball fields and playgrounds, it is only recently that such talk has begun to occupy an important place in law. Arguments in legal scholarship and scholarship about law,[1] as well as struggles over law reform, have increasingly occurred on a terrain marked by language of disputing, dispute processing, and dispute resolution. These arguments and struggles divide legal scholars and practitioners and raise questions about the nature and function of

* The authors wish to acknowledge the helpful comments of Mary Joe Frug, Joel Handler, Christine Harrington, Craig McEwen, Sally Merry, Martha Minow, Elizabeth Spellman, Deborah Stone, and David Trubek. An earlier version of this paper was prepared for the Workshop on Identifying and Measuring Quality in Dispute Resolution Processes and Outcomes which was hosted by the Institute of Legal Studies at the University of Wisconsin School of Law, July 13-14, 1987.

** Professor of Sociology, Wellesley College

*** William Nelson Cromwell Professor of Jurisprudence and Political Science, Amherst College

1. Abel, *Law Books and Books About Law*, 26 STAN. L. REV. 175 (1973). Some have talked about reformulating many important legals concepts and problems using that language. *See* Trubek, *The Construction and Deconstruction of a Disputes-Focused Approach: An Afterword*, 15 LAW & SOC'Y REV. 727 (1980-81). Others resist the incursions of such discourse into the domain of law. *See* Fiss, *Against Settlement*, 93 YALE L.J. 1073 (1984).

courts, the relation of legal scholarship to broader intellectual and political movements, and the status of individual rights and entitlements.

The debate about dispute processing within law entails a competition of ideas about the role of lawyers and a competition of interests within the market for legal services. Some welcome the turn to disputing and dispute processing as a relatively straightforward extension of traditional professional concerns with judicial procedure.[2] They seek to extend the reach of the legal field to encompass new forms of dispute processing and to build alliances with dispute processing professionals.[3] Others believe that thinking about law in terms of disputing and dispute processing threatens basic commitments and values of lawyers and the legal system.[4]

The debate about dispute processing also entails a struggle over appropriate ways to study law. For some researchers, the effort to describe legal practice as a particular form of dispute processing furthers the social scientific ambition to observe and report on social action free of cultural and professional biases. They hope to develop neutral concepts and units of analysis, such as the dispute, to facilitate comparative analysis of the widest range of social behaviors and institutions, including the law, without reproducing the assumptions of those institutions. For these scholars, the turn to dispute processing promotes thus legitimates the role of social scientists in legal scholarship.[5] For others, however, it challenges the singular importance of the legal system in the social order, and threatens the special authority of the legal profession to both study and minister to the law.

This paper describes and assesses struggles over disputing and dispute processing within the legal field. We see the clash between traditional legal authorities and proponents of new forms of dispute processing as a struggle over the definition of the space of law in society.[6] We believe that this contest both transforms the law and reaffirms its importance in social life. As judges and mediators compete within a market for dispute resolution services, the law is challenged and redefined. As Dezalay puts it,

2. *See* Rifkind, *Are We Asking Too Much of Our Courts?* 70 F.R.D. 96 (1976); Sander, *Varieties of Dispute Processing*, 70 F.R.D. 111 (1976).

3. *See* Bordieu, *The Force of Law: Toward A Sociology of the Judicial Field*, 38 HASTINGS L.J. 805 (1987). The term legal field is derived from what Bordieu calls the "juridical field." In his work a field is an area of structured, socially defined activity or practice, especially professional activity. "If one wanted to understand the 'field' metaphorically, its analogue would be a magnet: like a magnet, a social field exerts a force upon all those who come within its range. But those who experience these 'pulls' are generally not aware of their source." Bordieu's conception of the juridical field invites examination of internal conflicts and politics in the legal profession which, in his view, exert a pervasive influence on every aspect of law. Such conflicts are associated with hierarchies of power and prestige within and attached to legal work and legal institutions. Professionals within the legal field are constantly engaged in a struggle with others outside the field to sustain their conception of law's appropriate internal organization and relation to the social whole.

4. *See* Fiss, *supra* note 1.

5. Bok, *A Flawed System*, HARV. MAG. 38 (1983).

6. T. Dunim, The Fear of Law (1989) (to be published in volume 10 of *Studies in Law, Politics and Society*).

> The ceaseless struggle and opposition between these two concepts of justice [adjudication and mediation] must not however conceal their complementarity; it is a division of labor which allows simultaneously for the autonomy of law, its transcendence within time and social space and its permanent updating in accordance with social transformations. Both of these modes of justice, no matter how antagonistic they appear, represent essential components of the belief in law, and from there of the very survival of a field of professional practices.[7]

Like Dezalay, we see dispute processing as an addition to, rather than a displacement of, the legal field. The discourses of dispute processing frame a more layered and complex set of legal practices.

Yet the complementarity of dispute processing within the legal field cannot mask what Dezalay describes as a competition between an array of "goodfellows" who insist upon "a natural pre-existing need for community justice," who seek expanded but less expensive state control of socially troubled persons, and those who want to annex to legal practice and the service of capital techniques previously considered the exclusive prerogative of social welfare practitioners.[8] The dispute processes and programs advocated by this array of reformers, he claims, is a "rationalized, formalized, codified practice set entirely within the scope—albeit in a subordinate place—of the professionalization projects of the legal field."[9]

Dezalay suggests that the struggle over disputing and dispute processing within the field of law is carried out at the level of institutions and turns on the question of who will control them.[10] For Dezalay, the major question is whose idea of "justice" will organize the practices of dispute resolution within courts and in non-judicial institutions. Moreover, in his view, conflict within the legal field over issues of disputing and dispute processing involves ". . . a fundamental opposition between theorists, devoted to pure doctrinal construction, and practitioners, limited to applying law to particular disputes . . . ."[11] That conflict is characterized by the separateness of legal practice and academic law.

We disagree with Dezalay's understanding of the politics of disputing and dispute processing in three ways. First, contestation has not been limited to the question of who will control institutions and develop institutional practices. It has, in addition, been carried out in struggles over the best ways to *study* and *describe* legal institutions and in efforts to define appropriate relations of persons and legal institutions. Analysis of the politics of disputing and dispute processing must be carried out at both of these levels. Second, contestation has not produced a neat divi-

7. Y. Dezalay, Negotiated Justice as Renegotiation of the Division of Tasks Within the Legal Field (June, 1987) (presented to Conference on Dispute Resolution Research in Europe).

8. *Id.* at 7.

9. *Id.* at 24.

10. *Id.*

11. Y. Dezalay, The Forum Should Fit the Fuss . . .: The Economics of Negotiated Justice 4 (December, 1987) (unpublished manuscript presented to the Amherst Seminar).

sion between legal practitioners and theoreticians. On each level of political combat, the interests of scholars and practitioners in a variety of professions have found common ground. Third, by examining several levels of conflict within the legal field and by asking how the interests of practitioners and scholars are simultaneously at issue in debates about disputing and dispute processing, we can see how arguments about institutional practices depend upon, and arise from, the organization of disciplinary activity with the field of academic legal studies. The struggle within the field of institutional practice is enabled by the outcome of a particular struggle among legal scholars. Finally, we argue that competition within the legal field over the place and organization of dispute processing enables and promotes struggle over the meaning of the juridical subject.

In Part II, we describe the politics of dispute processing at the level of legal institutions. We argue that the contemporary alternative dispute resolution ("ADR") movement is held together by a critique of courts and by a concern for judicial competence and capacity. In addition, we suggest that the ADR movement involves an effort to recast the market for dispute resolution services by different interests attempting to advance their own professional projects. Part III describes conflicts within the legal academy precipitated by the growth of the modern social scientific study of law. It is, in our view, the partial success of that movement within academic legal study that fuels the institutional struggle. Thus, attention must be given to the involvement of social scientists in developing the concept of dispute as an alternative way of thinking about law. In Part IV, we suggest that struggles over the organization of legal institutions and struggles among academics to legitimate the scientific study of law are reflected in debates about the nature of the juridical subject. Those debates are then located in the contemporary critique of rights. Locating those debates in the critique of rights, we suggest that the apparent success of ADR reinforces the social power of law by adding to its repertoire of socially efficacious discursive practices. New vocabularies of control and dependency which, at first, appear to be at odds with rights talk play a parallel social role.

II. The Institutional Domain: ADR and The Critique of Courts

Dezalay is surely right to suggest that the ADR movement simultaneously transforms and reaffirms institutional life within the legal field and to direct attention to challenges ADR poses to the activities and organization of judicial institutions.[12] ADR is part of a continuing contest over the dominance of courts in the apparatus of state law. It arises from and requires an argument about the capacity of courts to advance different political and professional projects.

The contemporary ADR movement parallels in important ways sim-

12. Y. Dezalay, *supra* note 7.

ilar disturbances and struggles within law at the turn of the century.[13] In the earlier period, disillusionment with the courts led to the creation of specialized tribunals offering informal procedures for dealing with minor monetary or domestic relations disputes. These tribunals were, however, established within unified court systems and increased the organizational complexity of courts rather than establishing an effective alternative.[14] Although these new courts were responsive to the emerging human sciences, legal professionals retained control, and, as a result, transformations of institutional practice reaffirmed the place of law in society.

The expanded, greatly centralized court system, which grew as a result of the early twentieth century reform movement, itself eventually became an object of criticism for failing to provide responsive and flexible justice. By the 1970s, critics were again advocating systemic alterations, decentralization of the unified courts, and greater "responsiveness to environmental" and community demands.[15] As in the earlier period, reformers also recommended channeling minor disputes into alternatives which would provide participatory and individualized justice.

Contemporary reform efforts have, however, been more than organizational, and have been given a special boost by the "discovery" of, and responses to, a "litigation explosion."[16] Critics of litigiousness claim that reliance upon legal authority is excessive. The responsiveness of courts to demands for redress encourages, in the critics' view, ever more extensive demands and expectations of total justice.[17] Although a "litigation explosion" could be anticipated in a society willing to entrust important decisions to reasoned public argument, critics assert that "the principal thrust of the movement toward a fiduciary social order is the creation of affirmative duties couched in the terminology of ill-defined and often undefined standards."[18] As a result, we create the need for even more litigation, and according to former Chief Justice Warren Burger, "we may well be on our way to a society overrun by hordes of lawyers, hungry as locusts, and brigades of judges in numbers never before contemplated."[19] A former deputy attorney general of the United States complains that "the legal process, because of its unbridled growth, has become a cancer which threatens the vitality of our forms of capitalism and democracy."[20] We suffer, in a word, from hyperlexis, too much law.

13. C. Harrington, Shadow Justice: The Ideology and Institutionalization of Alternatives to Court (1985); Harrington, *Delegalization Reform Movements: A Historical Analysis*, in 1 The Politics of Informal Justice 35 (1982).

14. Harrington, *supra* note 13, at 58.

15. Hays, *Contemporary Trends in Court Unification*, in Managing the State Courts 130 (1977).

16. Galanter, *Reading the Landscape of Disputes*, 31 UCLA L. Rev. 4 (1983).

17. L. Friedman, Total Justice (1985).

18. J. Lieberman, The Litigious Society 29 (1981).

19. *Those #*X!!!! Lawyers*, Time 56 (April 10, 1987).

20. Silberman, *Will Lawyering Strangle Democratic Capitalism?*, 15 Reg. 10 (1978).

While some have advocated abandonment of the judicial form,[21] most contemporary criticisms of litigation and adjudication, like earlier ones, combine claims of shared allegiance to principles of legitimacy for example, equality, justice, liberty, with the search for new and improved procedures. Now, as earlier in the twentieth century, reformers have promised to extend the realm of self-government and "real" community.[22]

The success of the reform movement in creating alternatives to adjudication has depended, in large measure, upon the availability of non-judicial models of decision making and dispute resolution which also seem to serve goals of equality, justice, and autonomy. Thus, anthropologists provided examples of successful non-adjudicatory dispute processing from African tribes, the Zapotec indians of Mexico, Scandinavian fisherman, and some Bavarian villages, each of which offers, proponents say, ways of resolving disputes without the imposition of authority or force characteristic of formal adjudicatory processes. Closer to home, historians described American communities—in Dedham, Massachusetts, Oneida, Chinatown—and business associations in which peace, harmony, and mediation have seemed preferable to conflict, victory, and litigation.

Those latter examples have been particularly notable because they suggest that American history is more than the story of "the glorious triumph of law over inferior forms of communitarian extra-legal tyranny."[23] It appears that American allegiance to the rule of law has been accompanied by "a recurrent dialectic, between legality and its alternatives"[24] which results in repeated efforts to create dispute processing mechanisms outside the courts.[25] These mechanisms are supposed to

21. The turn away from formal legal procedure has also been justified by claims that the extension of legal rights failed to provide substantive justice.

> The principal objection to legal formalism advanced at both points in time is that substantive justice ideals invoked on behalf of *legality* in a liberal democracy (equality, justice, and liberty) come into conflict with *legalization* (the extension of procedure rules governing the processing of disputes). Such a view opposes the extension of legal rights on the ground that formal rationality, the necessary basis of legal legitimacy, fails to provide substantive justice. Consequently, the reform movement favors delegalization . . . . [The] advocates of delegalization justify their proposals as reconciling, harmonizing, and balancing formal and social justice.

Harrington, *supra* note 13, at 36.

22. Santos, *Law and Community: The Changing Nature of State Power in Late Capitalism*, in 1 THE POLITICS OF INFORMAL JUSTICE 249, 265 (1982).

23. J. AUERBACH, JUSTICE WITHOUT LAW? RESOLVING DISPUTES WITHOUT LAWYERS 14 (1983).

24. *Id.*

25. If historical examples of alternatives to law, or justice without procedural formality, encouraged contemporary reformers, some have urged caution to those who would use the historical record to reconstruct—or to transplant—what may be American but are nonetheless culturally alien social arrangements. Auerbach writes:

> The . . . indwelling sense of common purpose that turned communities away from litigation to alternatives like mediation and arbitration is likely to fascinate but ultimately distress modern Americans. It is not easy to empathize with our communitarian forebears. They were too involved in each others lives to satisfy our craving for privacy and solitude. They were mutually supportive, but also intrusive and suspicious; they were cooperative, but also coercive. The strength of a

replace the formality of the court with the informality of the neighborhood, principles of law with general considerations of morality and shared responsibility, win or lose outcomes with compromises, and the coercion and authority of the state with social pressures of the group or community.

In addition to examples of community moots, the contemporary ADR movement also draws upon models of non-judicial decision making within labor relations, especially highly developed and sophisticated techniques of mediation and arbitration. As Getman notes, labor arbitration has been "frequently pointed to as the paradigm of private justice,"[26] offering final, guiding, predictable, efficient, neutral, fair dispute resolution. Because labor arbitration is believed to successfully achieve these values, commentators often conclude "that it offer[ed] a technique for dispute resolution that [could] be routinely applied, with only minor adjustments, in other situations."[27] As a consequence, there has been little reticence about transferring this procedure from its historical and organizational context—collective bargaining between labor and management—to other settings. "Speeches by AAA [American Arbitration Association] officials and AAA pamphlets aggressively sell the process as having something to offer in a variety of circumstances."[28] Arbitration has, as a result, been advocated as a means of dispute resolution for consumer disputes,[29] family disputes,[30] medical malpractice,[31] prisoner grievances,[32] shareholder conflicts in close corporations,[33] community

> unified community, after all, implies the ability to compel adherence to its norms, at the expense of contrary individual preferences. The choice of a non-legal alternative to adjudication never was a decision to replace power with love, or coercion with cajoling. It was the application of power to serve the common interest at the expense of competing individual claims. It was, therefore, the exercise of the power of the community on its own behalf. This was possible because the meaning of justice was clear to its members . . . . Precisely that clarity rendered courts and lawyers not only superfluous but even subversive. Only when there is a congruence between individuals and their community, with shared commitment to common values, is there a possibility for justice without law.

Id. at 15. *See also* Merry, *The Social Organization of Mediation in Nonindustrial Societies: Implications for Informal Community Justice in America*, in 2 THE POLITICS OF INFORMAL JUSTICE (1982).

Despite such cautions, the contemporary ADR movement draws upon examples of both contemporary and historical communities of common value to support the institutionalization of local, community-based informal justice outside, or more accurately, beside, the law. Despite radically different historical and social contexts, some promoters of informal dispute resolution attempt to turn the tide against modernization and formal rationality and to return control of disruptive, injurious, or offensive behaviors and transactions to communities where they could be managed through mediation, compromise and restriction enforced by social sanctions and disputants' desire to settle. *See* Danzig, *Toward the Creation of a Complementary, Decentralized System of Criminal Justice*, 26 STAN. L. REV. 1 (1973).

26. Getman, *Labor Arbitration and Dispute Resolution*, 88 YALE L.J. 916 (1979).

27. *Id.* at 917.

28. *Id. See also* Coulson, *Annual Report: Responding to a Changing World*, 1 AM. ARB. A. NEWS & VIEWS 3-6 (1975).

29. Comment, *Non-Traditional Remedies for the Resolution of Consumer Disputes*, 49 TEMP. L.Q. 385 (1976).

30. Coulson, *Family Arbitration: An Exercise in Sensitivity*, 3 FAM. L.Q. 22 (1969).

31. Nocas, *Arbitration of Medical Malpractice Claims*, 13 FORUM 254 (1977).

32. Goldfarb & Singer, *Redressing Prisoner's Grievances*, 39 GEO. WASH. L. REV. 175 (1970).

or citizen disputes,[34] government contract disputes,[35] and employment disputes in higher education.[36] In all these situations, the labor experience is used to support proposals for alternatives to adjudication.[37]

Finally, in its critique of adjudication, the contemporary ADR movement drew upon and incorporated Freudian/psychoanalytic critiques of rationalism which have achieved a nearly taken-for-granted status in popular and intellectual discourses.[38] At the most obvious level, the psychoanalytic challenge to rationalism derived from its claims to unmask and explore the irrational foundations of human behavior. Beyond this, Freudian perspectives promoted interpretive and imaginative forms of understanding, rather than objective and positivistic marshalling of material evidence associated with science and with law. Integral to both the new subject of study—the irrational aspects of human behavior—and the new emphasis on interpretation and imagination, was a particular process of communication. Although the forms and techniques of therapy were advanced as both a scientific and a professional activity, its widespread acceptance was founded in shared values associated with personal revelation, personality growth, and development.[39] Moreover, such values energized the so-called helping professions and supplied them an outlook and a world view with which to take on, and combat, the allegedly alienating ideologies of legal practitioners.[40]

Armed with the techniques of psychotherapy and labor mediation and with associated ideologies of empowerment and self-knowledge,

33. Leffler, *Dispute Settlement Within Close Corporations*, 31 ARB. J. 254 (1976).

34. Note, *Arbitration of Attorney Fee Disputes*, 5 UCLA-ALASKA L. REV. 309 (1976).

35. Hardy & Cargill, *Resolving Federal Contract Disputes*, 34 FED. B. J. 1 (1975).

36. Finkin, *The Arbitration of Faculty Status Disputes in Higher Education*, 30 SW. L.J. 389 (1976).

37. One prominent labor specialist claims that advocates of alternatives to law who draw upon labor practices and arbitration underestimate the importance of context. *See* Getman, *supra* note 26. Reformers assume that the experience of labor arbitration is universally successful, that its success is attributable to speed and informality, and that it is extractable from the ongoing relationships and organization of collective bargaining.

Moreover, Getman argues that advocates of labor-like alternatives to law are mistaken in their assumption that arbitration is somehow fundamentally different from adjudication or administrative decision making, and he urges caution because "much of the writing describing and evaluating [labor arbitration] has come from practitioners whose professional egos are intertwined with the success of the process." *Id.* at 948. There is a marked tendency by professional associations and practitioners to downplay the critical and to accentuate the importance of the professionalized technique. Getman suggested, very early, a need to attend to the powerful array of interests promoting this "new" reform.

38. P. REIFF, TRIUMPH OF THE THERAPEUTIC (1966).

39. At a more abstract and yet critical level the valorization of intersubjective communication and exchange, which is at the heart of the psychoanalytic model, has been given a political boost by the work of Jurgen Habermas, and others in the Frankfurt School, who have been actively seeking both philosophical and political responses to the apparent dilemmas and injustices—crises—within liberalism and modernity. *See* J. HABERMAS, LEGITIMATION CRISIS (1973); J. HABERMAS, TOWARD A RATIONAL SOCIETY (1970). *See also* R. GEUSS, THE IDEAL OF CRITICAL THEORY (1981). Although the communicative theories of Habermas are themselves challenges to the Freudian paradigm, they nonetheless validate increased attention to the processes of interpersonal, as well as organizational, communication which are central to the ADR movement.

40. *See* Fineman, *Dominant Discourse, Professional Language and Legal Change in Child Custody Decisionmaking*, 101 HARV. L. REV. 727 (1988).

promoters of ADR have abundant resources upon which to draw in mounting their criticisms of courts and adjudication. Indeed, the history of the ADR movement can be told as a story of a series of entrepreneurs, what Howard Becker has called moral entrepreneurs, "whose initiative and enterprise overcame public apathy and indifference and culminated in the passage of federal legislation,"[41] state legislation, and the appropriation of millions of private foundation dollars for the establishment of ADR programs.[42] Here, ADR proponents have combined demands for substantive justice with technocratic concerns for efficiency, adaptability, and cost effectiveness. Indeed, efficiency and substantive justice claims often seem inseparable in this field. Thus, the ADR movement found a variety of models and antecedents to draw upon, and it developed a range of voices promoting dispute resolution as a way to limit, transform or avoid courts and adjudication.

The Teams and the Players

We can identify three major groups each of which has been, during the last decade, actively struggling to establish non-judicial means of dispute resolution. While we recognize that the supporting arguments of each group are not mutually exclusive, they suggest important differences of emphasis within a broad framework of agreement. Professional and institutional support for ADR comes from all positions along the political spectrum; it has produced, nonetheless, a recognizable, if not fully coherent, political movement. The struggle over the place of judicial institutions, and law itself, in the provision of dispute resolution services has enlisted proponents from inside and outside the legal field and legal scholars as well as practitioners.

41. H. BECKER, THE OUTSIDERS: STUDIES IN THE SOCIOLOGY OF DEVIANCE 135 (1963).

42. Moral entrepreneurs work to remedy evils which disturb them. They identify a general cause or harm which threatens all and propose specific remedies to alleviate the social problem thus named. Gusfield writes that reform crusades frequently reveal "the approach of a dominant class toward those less favorably situated in the economic social structure." Gusfield, *Social Structure and Moral Reform: A Study of the Women's Christian Temperance Union*, 61 AM. J. SOC. 223 (1955).

> Moral crusaders typically want to help those beneath them to achieve a better status. That those beneath them do not always like the means proposed for their salvation is another matter. But this fact—that moral crusades are typically dominated by those in the upper levels of the social structure—means that they add to the power they derive from the legitimacy of their moral position, the power they derive from their superior position in society.

H. BECKER, *supra* note 41, at 149.

The obvious consequence of a successful crusade is the creation of new rules and procedures, and with the establishment of organizations of "rule enforcers" or service providers, the crusade—in the case of dispute, the idea—becomes institutionalized. "What started out as a drive to convince the world of the moral necessity of a new rule finally becomes an organization devoted to the enforcement of the rule." *Id.* at 155. While much of the continuing support for the ADR movement has come from those who want to provide expanded dispute resolution services to persons unable to secure access to legal justice, it is important to note that the movement is not solely devoted to providing services to the less powerful and subordinate classes. Merry, *Disputing Without Culture* (Book Review), 100 HARV. L. REV. 2057 (1987).

The Establishment Bar and Legal Elites

We begin with the establishment bar and legal elites who have promoted ADR as a way of dealing with the contemporary crisis of the courts. Theirs is not a critique of the essence or ideals of adjudication; instead, they seek to save adjudication by limiting it, to preserve the space of law by not overtaxing its institutional capacity.[43] Elite lawyers want to conserve judicial resources for the resolution of business and commercial disputes and are willing to see other matters removed from courts if not from the legal field itself. This precipitates conflict with lawyers whose share of legal business would be radically diminished by limitations on adjudication and is reflected in the opposition to ADR by groups like the American Trial Lawyers Association.

Yet the elite bar interest in ADR is not simply a practitioner interest. Scholars and theoreticians have taken up the cause. Foremost among academic proponents is Frank Sander. His work has played a critical role in promoting the study of dispute processing in law schools and in mobilizing the legal establishment's support for ADR. His *Varieties of Dispute Processing*[44] helped set the agenda for efforts both inside and outside the law school. In that article, Sander promoted the dispute processing perspective as a way of thinking about judicial administration and legal procedure. He argued that procedure might be improved if scholars treated adjudication as one of many ways of resolving society's disputes. In his view, legal thought was cabined, and the legal profession was threatened, by an unrealistic view of the limits of adjudication. As a result, lawyers were unable to understand why courts were increasingly swamped with litigation and how to "reserve the courts for those activities for which they are best suited."[45] This concern, as much as any other, animated Sander's early efforts and led to the creation of the American Bar Association's Committee on Minor Dispute Resolution.

For the establishment bar, judicial inefficiency endangers judicial and legal legitimacy by preventing courts from responding appropriately and quickly to important matters. In addition, the inability of legal forums to respond to the accumulated grievances of any or all social groups is perceived to be a source of serious latent instability and a general breakdown in law and order.[46] As Representative Kastenmeier, chairman of the House Judicial Subcommittee on Courts, Civil Liberties and the Administration of Justice, put it in a debate concerning federal financial support for alternative dispute resolution:

---

43. *See* COUNCIL ON THE ROLE OF COURTS, THE ROLE OF COURTS IN AMERICAN SOCIETY (1984).

44. Sander, *supra* note 2.

45. *Id.* More recently Sander has produced an extended treatment of the dispute processing perspective in the form of a law school textbook. *See* S. GOLDBERG, E. GREEN & F. SANDER, DISPUTE RESOLUTION (1985). That text pulls together and organizes a wide range of material on the disputing process, but it is more than an ordinary collection. It is animated by, and develops, a distinctive perspective on the role of courts and of non-judicial mechanisms for processing disputes.

46. These themes are explored in SMALL CLAIMS STUDY GROUP, LITTLE INJUSTICES (1972).

> The federal government is not interested in silencing a particular barking dog or solving a given family squabble; it is interested in assuring that forums exist at the State and local level to resolve these disputes so that State and local governments may preserve public order, promote harmony among citizens and guarantee access to legal justice.[47]

The American Bar Association ("ABA") has also taken a leading role in this effort because the development of responsive dispute resolution mechanisms is thought to contribute to legal legitimacy. The ABA sponsored the 1976 Pound Conference on Popular Dissatisfaction with the Administration of Justice which launched a national campaign to experiment with mediation and arbitration. Following the recommendations of the Pound Conference, the United States Department of Justice created the Office for Improvements in the Administration of Justice (OIAJ) one of whose tasks was to develop support for informal dispute resolution. Several offices of the Justice Department (National Institute of Law Enforcement and Criminal Justice as well as OIAJ) collaborated with local sponsors in the development of experimental neighborhood justice centers following national guidelines established with the help of the ABA. These pilot programs, and legislative efforts to expand and institutionalize them, drew support from the highest ranks of legal establishment including former Chief Justice Warren Burger, Attorney General Griffin Bell, as well as a host of local legal elites.[48]

At the same time, however, these efforts generated opposition from inside and outside the legal community. Supporters of legal services for the poor opposed the federal government's involvement with ADR as an effort to undermine government legal services programs.[49] Moreover, the alliance between the ABA and the Department of Justice encouraged opposition from organized consumer groups who had been working for nearly a decade to establish a national consumer protection agency and other formal processes specifically designed to redress consumer grievances. They criticized the neighborhood justice center experiments as

47. COMMITTEE ON THE JUDICIARY, DISPUTE RESOLUTION ACT REPORT, H.R. DOC. NO. 492H.2, 96th Cong. 1st Sess. (1979). *See also* C. HARRINGTON, *supra* note 13, at 101 (for an analysis of the political interests and groups who lobbied for and against federal legislation creating federally sponsored and funded ADR programs).

48. From 1977-1980, House and Senate committees held hearings on an act to institutionalize ADR. Among those testifying in favor of the legislation were Daniel Meador, Assistant U.S. Attorney General; John Cratsley, Acting Presiding Justice of Salem District Court, Commonwealth of Massachusetts; Talbot D'Alemberte, Chairman, and Professor Frank Sander, Harvard Law School, representing the ABA Special Committee on Resolution of Minor Disputes; Samuel E. Zoll, Chief Justice of District Court Department, Trial Court, Commonwealth of Massachusetts; Jeffrey L. Perlman representing the U.S. Chamber of Commerce; Lee Richardson, Acting Director U.S. Office of Consumer Affairs; as well as representatives from the OIAJ, the Better Business Bureau, and the National Home Improvement Association.

49. *See* Sarat, *Informalism, Delegalization and the Future of the American Legal Profession*, 35 STAN. L. REV. 1217 (1983); C. Harrington, *supra* note 13, at 78. According to Harrington, Ralph Nader's Public Citizen Litigation Group only reluctantly supported some aspects of the neighborhood justice concept. The Director of the Legal Services Corporation, Thomas Erhlich, was also reluctant to join a coalition of the ABA and the Department of Justice. C. HARRINGTON, *supra* note 13.

likely to evolve, like small claims courts, into collection agencies for business rather than effective forums for redressing failed market transactions. Opponents of ADR favored expanded opportunities and resources for the legal protection of a wide range of commercial, public, and private rights rather than wholesale delegalization through the creation of informal dispute resolution.

For legal elites, maintenance and protection of the legal field and the capacity of courts to protect already existing rights required active resistance to such expansionist demands. Maintaining legal legitimacy and judicial capacity required, in their view, a coordinated effort at rationalization in which asking less of courts was an essential first step. The technique of "fitting the forum to the fuss" and of devising alternatives to courts like Neighborhood Justice Centers[50] was part of an effort to develop rational mechanisms for allocating and channeling disputes into appropriate processes. Elite practitioners and academics sought to create a generalized engineering capacity for managing legal and social issues. They looked to ADR as a strategy of incremental adjustment, not radical transformation,[51] and, in so doing, they focused on the question of how disputes and dispute processing techniques could be matched up, of how an understanding of different forms of dispute processing could "be utilized so that some criteria can be devised for allocating various types of disputes to different dispute resolution processes."[52]

Here they have frequently drawn on the work of Lon Fuller.[53] In a series of well known papers, Fuller identified characteristics that differentiate various dispute resolution processes from other modes of social ordering.[54] In each work, he sought to abstract from history and con-

50. Rosenberg, *Let the Tribunal Fit the Case—Establishing Criteria for Channeling Matters into Dispute Resolution Mechanisms*, 80 F.R.D. 147, 166 (1977).

51. Sander, *supra* note 2.

52. *Id.* at 26. Those who imagine this kind of rational allocation of society's dispute resolution business employ, or would employ, several standards for making allocative decisions. Although they may not state it exactly in this fashion, their approach suggests the following standards for channeling disputes: (A) *The magnitude of the rights at issue.* Disputes involving questions of fundamental or basic rights belong in a formal judicial process Other disputes, which do not raise such issues, can be dealt with informally. (B) *Complexity.* The standard of complexity seems to be offered to justify both formal and informal processes. Thus some argue that technical complexity, for example in complex economic litigation, should be accompanied by formality; mirroring arguments that supported the establishment of small claims courts, promoters of informalism suggest that the simpler the dispute, the more appropriate informal treatment. However, some promoters of informalism suggest that very complex issues, such as those in some tort or environmental litigation or regulatory rule-making, are better handled and should be considered through informal negotiating fora. (C) *Finality.* Court judgments, so the argument goes, fail to resolve disputes where the real cause of the dispute cannot be captured in or by the legal cause of action. This is often the case in disputes arising out of ongoing personal relations. In such cases, informal dispute processing seems more appropriate. (D) *Cost.* Informalism is said to be less expensive. Disputes should be processed by the least costly alternative so long as that alternative is able to meet other salient allocation standards. *See* Sarat, *The Role of the Courts and the Logic of Court Reform*, 64 JUDICATURE 300, 305 (1981).

53. *See* COUNCIL ON THE ROLE OF COURTS, *supra* note 43; Sander, *supra* note 2.

54. Fuller, *The Forms and Limits of Adjudication*, 92 HARV. L. REV. 353 (1979) [hereinafter Fuller, *Adjudication*]; Fuller, *Mediation, Its Forms and Functions*, 44 S. CAL. L. REV. 305 (1971); Fuller, *Collective Bargaining and the Arbitrator*, 1963 WIS. L. REV. 1.

text, to see beyond variations in local practices and to define the essential form of adjudication, negotiation or mediation.[55] Like Fuller, Sander[56] suggests that dispute processing techniques can be classified into discrete and separate clusters, for example, negotiation, mediation, and adjudication, by identifying the essential attributes of the techniques in each cluster.[57] In this work, the contexts and various forms of dispute processing practice are given less attention than the effort to achieve definitional purity.

Proponents of ADR use the essential attributes of each technique or institution to deduce an understanding of its distinctive capacities and limits, an understanding of what kinds of disputes different forms of dispute processing are best equipped to handle.[58] Fixed characteristics appear, in this argument, to impose fixed limits such that disputes appropriate for one dispute processing technique may be inappropriate for another.[59] As one example, Sander argues that disputes should be channelled to and matched with, appropriate dispute processing techniques. He assumes that the nature and characteristics of disputes and disputing processing mechanisms are sufficiently stable so that each dispute can be assigned to an appropriate process. In their discussion of adjudication Sander and his co-authors announce that "our goal is to understand better what tasks courts are particularly well suited to perform and what tasks they are less well suited to perform."[60] Institu-

55. Fuller writes that his goal is to "define 'true adjudication' or adjudication as it might be if the ideals that support it were fully realized." Fuller, *Adjudication*, *supra* note 54, at 357. While there have been other attempts to define essential characteristics of dispute processing techniques, Fuller's was, and remains, the most influential. *See, e.g.*, M. SHAPIRO, COURTS (1981).

56. S. GOLDBERG, E. GREEN & F. SANDER, *supra* note 45; Sander, *supra* note 2.

57. For other similar attempts, see D. HOROWITZ, COURTS AND SOCIAL POLICY (1977); J. MARKS, E. JOHNSON & P. SZANTON, DISPUTE RESOLUTION IN AMERICA (1984); Cappelletti & Garth, *Access to Justice: The Worldwide Movement to Make Rights Effective*, in 1 ACCESS TO JUSTICE 3 (1978); Eckhoff, *The Mediator, The Judge and the Administrator in Conflict Resolution*, 10 ACTA SOCIOLOGICA 148, 158 (1967).

58. *See also* D. HOROWITZ, *supra* note 57.

59. Sander's advocacy of dispute resolution is based on his belief that given the right match of dispute and dispute processing technique, harmony can be restored, problems can be dealt with so as to produce resolutions that satisfy the disputants and are therefore likely to be final. Sander, *supra* note 2. Thus, *Dispute Resolution* talks about dispute resolution rather than dispute processing, suggesting closure and completion of the dispute. *See also* J. MARKS, E. JOHNSON & P. SZANTON, *supra* note 57; Rosenberg, *Civil Justice Research and Civil Justice Reform*, 15 LAW & SOC. REV. 473 (1980-81). This emphasis on resolution suggests an image of social life in which harmony prevails, in which conflicts are idiosyncratic and in which mediation, arbitration, adjudication and other dispute processing techniques work to put an end to such conflict. S. GOLDBERG, E. GREEN & F. SANDER, *supra* note 45. *See* Rosenberg, *supra*.

60. S. GOLDBERG, E. GREEN & F. SANDER, *supra* note 45, at 150. Sander's advocacy of a dispute processing approach emerges from and is continuous with one major effort to reconstitute and reconstruct legal thought in the aftermath of legal realism. *Compare* B. ACKERMAN, RECONSTRUCTING AMERICAN LAW (1984); Peller, *The Metaphysics of American Law*, 73 CALIF. L. REV. 1152 (1985). It is, from this perspective, an extension of the so called "legal process" approach to an apparently more disputatious world. H. Hart & A. Sacks, The Legal Process (1958) (unpublished materials). *See also* Brest, *The Substance of Process*, 42 OHIO ST. L.J. 131 (1981); Mensch, *The History of Mainstream Legal Thought*, in THE POLITICS OF LAW: A PROGRESSIVE CRITIQUE (1982); Tushnet, *Truth, Justice and the American Way: An Interpretation of Public Law Scholarship in the 70s*, 57 TEX. L. REV. 1307 (1979). For a

tional capacity problems are in this view largely problems of institutional overload.[61] In this way, the critique of adjudication becomes a defense of adjudication.

Access to Justice Proponents

Another part of the contemporary ADR movement begins with a very different critique of adjudication. It focuses on the costs and delays associated with adjudication and, in particular, on its resulting inaccessibility. For these proponents ADR is a means to increase access to justice. The access to justice group is generally thought of as progressive and motivated by a desire to help the socially disadvantaged.[62] Yet from within the legal field, practitioners and scholars turned to ADR as a half century earlier others had looked to small claims and juvenile courts to increase their market share of legal work. Calls for increased access to justice have long been associated with the professional interests of marginal practitioners and those who seek to bring the poor and dispossessed within the network of legality.

Following on the heels of the civil rights movement and the extension of the new legal rights to blacks, members of ethnic and religious minorities, women, the aged, and the handicapped, increased access to justice professed to address the needs of a broad constituency.[63] The phrase itself, "access to justice," is a rhetorical symbol of undeniable attractiveness and mobilizing power.[64] Beyond its symbolic import however, the phrase, and the political/legal movement it named, incorporated an ambivalent attitude toward, and a systemic contradiction within, liberal legalism. To increase access to justice means changing the structure and procedures of adjudication; yet, at the same time such demands reaffirm faith in law and in legal procedure, and in the justice they provide.[65]

---

more complete treatment see Sarat, *The New Formalism in Disputing and Dispute Proceeding*, 21 LAW & SOC'Y REV. 695 (1988).

61. Edwards, *Commentary. Alternative Dispute Resolution: Panacea or Anathema?* 99 HARV. L. REV. 668, 669 (1986).

62. *E.g.*, J. CARLIN, J. HOWARD & S. MESSINGER, CIVIL JUSTICE AND THE POOR: ISSUES FOR SOCIOLOGICAL RESEARCH (1967).

63. Although much legal policy and research treats persons with these status attributes as if they were socially and materially—ontologically—distinct, it is important to remind ourselves that we do not experience ourselves simply as a member of a racial, ethnic, religious, or gender category without also experiencing that status modified by one's other characteristics. Despite the too common notion that rights have been extended on the basis of particular, and favored, statuses, no one is, for example, black without also having a religious, class, and gender identity. For an extended discussion criticizing the contrary notion, that there are essential social characteristics or roles experienced unmediated or modified by other aspects of identity, see E. SPELLMAN, THE INESSENTIAL WOMAN (1988).

64. *See* Sarat, *Access to Justice*, in LAW AND THE SOCIAL SCIENCES (1987).

65. Friedman explains, however, that access to justice becomes a noticeable social problem when liberal legalism, with its insistence that law be both general and equal in its application, becomes widespread, as it seemed to be in the civil rights movement of the 1950s and 60s. Friedman, *Access to Justice: Social and Historical Context*, in 2 ACCESS TO JUSTICE (1978). Indeed, the liberal desire to equalize social relationships, or at least to ensure that the legal order treat all citizens equally, has typically provided the energy behind the "access to justice" movement.

Because legal systems habitually recognize a broader range of legal rights than they are capable of vindicating,[66] there is always a "huge latent demand" for adjudication that calls for "rethinking of the system of supply—the judicial system."[67] Rights, it is argued, are meaningless without effective institutional mechanisms for their vindication.[68] This argument presupposes[69] that the political and legal order actually intends legal rights to have significant instrumental value.[70] Legal rights are, in this view, created to alter political relationships, and to redress basic social inequities; if they fail to do so—to change the distribution of social resources—the failure must be one of implementation, not intention. Thus, the problem is a problem of institutions and institutional design. To increase access to justice means expanding dispute processing mechanisms in order to decide questions of right that would otherwise not be addressed.

Reformers have tried to increase access to justice by expanding legal representation and improving adjudicative procedures to accommodate different types of litigants and issues.[71] Reformers also seek,

> changes in the structure of courts or the creation of new courts, the use of lay persons and paraprofessionals both on the bench and in the bar, modifications in the substantive law designed to avoid disputes or to facilitate their resolution, and the use of private or informal dispute resolution mechanisms.[72]

They want to encourage the creation of new dispute processing institutions and procedures, and they imagine the judicial system supplemented, though not supplanted, by a number of different forums to which citizens might bring their disputes. The defining characteristic of these forums would be their informality,[73] speed, and low cost which

---

66. Friedman, *The Idea of Right as a Social and Legal Concept*, 27 J. Soc. Issues 189 (1971). *Cf.* Silbey & Bittner, *The Availability of Law*, 4 Law & Pol'y Q. 399 (1982).

67. Cappelletti & Garth, *supra* note 57, at 51.

68. *Cf.* O. Holmes, The Common Law (1881).

69. *E.g.*, Access to Justice (M. Cappelletti ed. 1978).

70. For a criticism of such a view, see S. Scheingold, The Politics of Rights: Lawyers, Public Policy, and Political Change (1974).

71. Access to justice reforms have occurred in what Cappelletti and Garth describe as three distinct "waves." The first wave began in the early 1960s and provided for the extension of legal aid to the poor through state subsidized and privately funded legal services. In this wave, incorporating the poor within the legal field required the legal profession to compromise one of the central tenets of its ideology—independence from the state. Since, by definition, the poor could not provide a market for legal services the state substituted for the market mechanism. As in other areas, professional self-interest overcame professional ideology.

The second wave focused upon the representation of diffuse or collective interests, especially, although not exclusively, the interests of consumers and environmentalists. The vindication of many public, collective, or diffuse rights seemed to require the relaxation of standing rules, provisions for class actions, as well as activist judiciary. *Cf.* Orren, *Standing to Sue: Interest Group Conflicts in the Federal Courts*, 70 Am. Pol. Sci. Rev. 723 (1978). This wave promoted the adaptation of adjudication to changes in both the substance and volume of demands newly voiced through expanded legal representation. The third wave incorporates the first two, but goes beyond the traditional concern with legal representation and procedure that is basic to both. Cappelletti & Garth, *supra* note 61.

72. Cappelletti & Garth, *supra* note 57, at 52.

73. There has been, of course, extensive discussion in the dispute processing litera-

collectively would mean more access to justice.

Quality Proponents

A third group of ADR proponents directed their critique of courts to issues of quality not issues of efficiency or access. This group criticized adjudication for its alleged inadequacy in addressing the substance of disputes and relationships between disputants. These advocates envisaged processes that would get at the "underlying" trouble from which disputes emerge, and they proposed dispute resolution techniques that would both restore harmony and empower disputants while responding to personal needs and to detailed understandings of their situations.

Such "ideal" resolutions required dispute processes that were forward looking, constructive and creative rather than processes that narrowed issues to fit the prescribed forms of legal argument.

> For the most part, litigation is a way of viewing the past through the eyes of the present. Perhaps justice is best done by starting with the present—with present needs and present demands—and using the past only where it reveals equitable considerations which will provide guidance in shaping a remedy. . . . We are still—in contract law, in domestic law, in landlord-tenant law, in tort law—engaged in a quest for fault, for 'who did what when' as a way of deciding how the risk should be borne and who should pay, perform or provide remedy. Yet, in domestic relations, industrial injuries, automobile accidents, we are finding that the quest for fault is time consuming, elusive and not particularly productive in terms of enabling human beings to get back on their feet and to cope with the present or chart a rational course for the future.[74]

For this third group, ADR is one method of moving dispute resolution procedures away from the alleged adversarial all-or-nothing, blame-or-guilt orientation of courts.[75] Just as centuries earlier, equity sought to reform law by expanding the range of actions and remedies, this group seeks to expand the range of relevant issues to be taken into account when disputes are processed. As a result of their ability to reach

---

ture about the distinction between formal and informal dispute processing institutions; indeed, the effort to work through these distinctions spurred the growth of the "disputes" industry. Abel says that: "institutions are informal to the extent that they are non-bureaucratic in structure and relatively undifferentiated from the larger society, minimize the use of professionals, and eschew official law in favor of substantive and procedural norms that are vague, unwritten, commonsensical, flexible, ad hoc, and particularistic." Abel, *Introduction*, in 1 THE POLITICS OF INFORMAL JUSTICE 2 (1982). As Abel acknowledges, however, this definition is more a rough sketch of potential traits of informal justice than a precise delineation of exclusive characteristics.

74. Cahn & Cahn, *What Price Justice: The Civilian Perspective Revisited*, 41 NOTRE DAME L. REV. 927, 932 (1966). The Cahns did not specifically advocate what has come to be known as ADR although they did urge the creation of "community based crisis intervention teams" employing a variety of professional skills. These suggestions, however, fed the call for alternative processes in a variety of institutional settings and social problem areas and were frequently cited in the literature recommending the adoption of ADR.

75. Danzig, *supra* note 25, at 15.

and assess all relevant issues, alternative dispute resolution procedures, it was argued, would resolve disputes by developing a consensus about future conduct rather than by assigning responsibility for events in the past. Freed from formal legal categories and procedures, informal alternatives could get at the heart of problems and actually solve them, rendering true or better justice, contributing to social harmony and stability.

Thus, for example, in place of the conventional models of the criminal process,[76] Griffiths proposed an altogether different conception, what he called the family model of criminal procedure.[77] He began by noting that whatever the variations were in conventional images of the criminal justice system, all formulations relied upon a singular ideology which pitted the individual against the community in a battle for the detection, apprehension, prosecution and punishment of offenders.[78] He wanted to radically alter the ideology of criminal adjudication—promoting reconciliation, resolution, and adjustment of differences within an environment of harmony and love. Others followed Griffiths with very concrete proposals for restructuring the courts, if not to reproduce the ideological premises of the family, then to incorporate a broader range of procedures and to achieve substantively better results.[79]

---

76. These models are described by H. PACKER, THE LIMITS OF THE CRIMINAL SANCTION (1968).

77. Griffiths, *Ideology in Criminal Procedure, or a Third "Model" of the Criminal Process*, 79 YALE L.J. 359 (1971). It should be noted that unlike many of the supporters of ADR and others whose work was used to promote the institutionalization of ADR, Griffiths was more tentative. He writes:

> I should nevertheless induce the doubter to suspend disbelief, at least temporarily, by making the proposed alternative ideology as plausible as possible. So I propose to gather some respectability by using an allusive name for it: a name, that is, that invokes a "real world" institution which occasionally inflicts punishments on offenders for their offenses but which is nonetheless built upon a fundamental assumption of harmony of interest and love—and as to which no one finds it odd, or even particularly noteworthy, that this is the case. I will, then (following Packer in using the word "model" only for convenience sake, and preferring to think of it as an ideological metaphor) offer a "Family Model" of the criminal process. I wish to emphasize, however, that this allusive reference is to our family ideology as I take it to be, not to the facts of all or particular families.

Id. at 372.

78. Griffiths notes that punishment goes on in other settings, especially families, and there punishment is neither conceived of nor executed as a battle of antagonistic interests. "A parent and child have far more to do with each other than obedience, deterrence and punishment, and any process between them will reflect the full range of their relationship and the concerns growing out of it." *Id.* at 373. If criminal courts functioned as families in adjudicating offenses and meting out punishment, Griffiths argued, we would be required to reconceptualize both the crime and the criminal from anti-social acts and persons demanding exclusion to a recognition of the variability of social behavior and the ultimate reconcilability and interconnectedness of the offender, the offense and the community. Offenses would be acknowledged to be what they are—regular not extraordinary occurrences, just as punishment is not an isolated phenomenon but part of a continuing relationship between child and parent.

These changes in the conception of offenses and offenders would also entail changes in the attitude toward, and of, public officials in the legal system. Rather than removed and disinterested, the family model presupposes a close, dependent, and caring relationship between officials and suspects, as well as fundamentally altered procedures for responding to troubles, crimes and disputes. Griffiths, *supra* note 77.

79. Danzig, for example, recommended the creation of community moots to handle

Supporters of ADR argued that adjudication frequently fails in cases involving persons with ongoing relationships and that this failure could be responded to in a new system which built upon those relationships.

> A moot might handle family disputes, some marital issues . . . juvenile delinquency, landlord-tenant relations, small torts and breaches of contract involving only community members and misdemeanors affecting only community members. The present system does not, after all, perform the job of adjudication in most of these cases. Civil proceedings are generally avoided because the parties are too ignorant, fearful, or impoverished to turn to small claims courts, legal aid, or similar institutions. Many matters which may technically be criminal violations will not be prosecuted because they are viewed by the prosecuting attorney as private and trivial matters. The criminal adjudicative model seems particularly insufficient and a system of conciliation correspondingly well advised when we know that due to institutional overcrowding and established patterns of sentencing the vast majority of misdemeanants and some felons are not likely to be imprisoned. For these defendants, the judicial process is not a screen filtering those who are innocent from those who will be directed to the corrective parts of the process. Rather, it is the corrective process; as such it fails to be more than a "Bleak House," profoundly alienating, rather than integrating.[80]

Courts, it was argued, subjected the delicacy of interdependent and ongoing relationships to a very considerable degree of overkill. As Simon Rifkind puts it, the object of judicial intervention in disputes is to bring them "to an end by determining whether the plaintiff or the defendant prevailed."[81] The judge is obligated to declare who was or was not guilty or at fault for what actions, and the judicial decision must state whether the claim originally asserted in the lawsuit was or was not valid. Such clarity about blame can be unfortunate in relationships involving trust, spontaneity, and reciprocity. Here, it was argued, adjudication has the tendency to disrupt further rather than to heal.[82]

Because, for the third group of ADR entrepreneurs, the problems

---

local disputes and disturbances, and Fisher called for the establishment of community courts to adjudicate minor criminal offenses. Danzig, *supra* note 25; Comment, *Community Courts: An Alternative to Conventional Criminal Adjudication*, 24 AM. U.L. REV. 1253 (1975). Adopting a therapeutic approach, in contrast to the traditional adversarial justice concern with responsibility and just dessert, they urged that local courts be supplemented by dispute resolution processes that emphasized integrative and conciliatory outcomes.

80. Danzig, *supra* note 25, at 44.

81. Rifkind, *supra* note 2, at 101.

82. The dynamics of interpersonal relations require a mutual acceptance of responsibility as a face-saving way out of conflict. Social practice has it that apologies should be met either with a polite acceptance or with a professed, if not sincere, sharing of guilt. *See* Wagatsuma & Rossett, *The Implications of Apology*, 20 LAW & SOC'Y REV. 461 (1986). Branding one party to a dispute as blameworthy makes reintegration and resumption of previous relationships difficult. Macaulay, *Non-Contractual Relations in Business: A Preliminary Study*, 28 AM. SOC. REV. 55 (1963). *Cf.* Yngvesson, *Re-examining Continuing Relations and the Law*, 1985 WIS. L. REV. 623. This is especially so when the label is applied authoritatively and pub-

of courts were to be found in their inability to resolve disputes fully and finally, increasing court and law enforcement capacities would not solve the problems plaguing the courts. Those problems were attributed to the distant, bureaucratic and authoritative character of courts. To remedy these structural failings, those who advocated community moots relied on emotional bonds and community networks joining judge and disputants rather than upon social distance and hierarchy; they encouraged wide ranging discussion "so that all tensions and viewpoints psychologically—if not legally—relevant to the issue were expressed."[83] Rather than emphasizing the trappings of formal authority and coercive power, moots would operate in familiar surroundings of the home and the community and employ everyday logic, norms and manner.

This critique of courts was advanced simultaneously by those trying to break out of the legal field and develop a strategy for community empowerment, and by those trying to extend the precinct of legal control by softening its allegedly rough edges. Groups like the American Friends Service Committee ("AFSC"), a private nonprofit Quaker organization, were active in the critique of adjudication described above and in promoting what they called community dispute resolution. They hoped that "community mediation centers [would] provide an avenue to strengthen and empower local communities by decentralizing social control functions and providing community residents with an enhanced sense of their ability to handle legal and political problems on their own."[84] The AFSC created the Grassroots Citizen Dispute Resolution Clearinghouse which served as a resource center for community groups seeking to organize citizen dispute resolution ("CDR") programs.[85]

---

licly, and when the adjudication of guilt or blame, juxtaposed with an original denial of responsibility, may be construed as an official finding that the denial was a lie.

The substance of a dispute, however, includes more than the relationship between the parties; it refers to facts in dispute, to issues and questions and details of the problematic events or relationships. Therefore, some of those who advocated reform because it would provide substantively better justice were concerned less with disputes between persons in ongoing relationships than with disputes where the issues were complex, technical, and apparently beyond the expertise of judges. Two kinds of litigation in particular seemed to raise calls for different forms of dispute resolution: 1) cases in which the issues were scientific or so technical that the litigation became a matter of debate between experts, and beyond the generalist expertise of many judges, and 2) cases in which the issues were so broad as well as complex that they were likely to confound any single attempt at amelioration. *See* Cavanagh & Sarat, *Thinking About Courts: Toward And Beyond A Jurisprudence of Judicial Competence*, 14 LAW & SOC'Y REV. 371 (1980).

83. Danzig, *supra* note 25, at 43.

84. Merry, *supra* note 25, at 17.

85. Although it closed within a decade for lack of funding, the CDR Clearinghouse was, during its lifetime, a national advocate for grass roots programs, that is, programs of informal dispute resolution unattached to courts, police, or prosecutorial offices. The Community Dispute Settlement Service of the Friends Suburban Project in Delaware County, Pennsylvania, just outside of Philadelphia, and the Community Association for Mediation in Pittsburgh were prominent examples of CDR, the former middle class dominated and the latter an effort to build CDR "directly into the fabric of a black neighborhood." Wahrhaftig, *An Overview of Community-Oriented Citizen Dispute Resolution Programs in the United States*, in 1 THE POLITICS OF INFORMAL JUSTICE 75, 93 (1982). The San Francisco Community Board Program, established in 1978, is another example of the promotion of informal justice as a way to strengthen neighborhoods and communities.

AFSC did not view dispute resolution as an alternative to existing processes or institutions. It was for them a constituent part of community life. The neighborhood and volunteer orientation of dispute resolution programs was, in their view, essential. "From the Clearinghouse's perspective the importance of dispute resolution is not just in providing another nicely packaged court service, but is in the potential for restoring to neighborhoods the responsibility of taking a major role in problem solving. Neighborhood responsibility is the key."[86]

This focus upon community empowerment meant that CDR programs would not easily fit with court-sponsored ADR. In fact, CDR programs would not operate where the coercive power of the state was part of the dispute situation and therefore would not accept referrals of disputes that had already been filed in courts. Moreover, court-annexed dispute resolution programs were rejected because they were organized in tandem with the institutional structure of the court system, often on a city-wide or county-wide pattern, and thus did not mesh with neighborhoods. Finally, the state-sponsored programs did not easily accommodate staffing on a part-time or totally volunteer basis as the community groups required.[87] CDR thus represented a direct and frontal challenge to programs and experiments, for example, neighborhood justice centers,[88] favored by the elite bar and its theoreticians. CDR appeared to threaten the legal profession's ability to control new developments in dispute processing and to contain them within the domain of their expertise and authority.

By the mid-1980s, the hopes of those who had joined the critique of adjudication from the community empowerment perspective had largely been dashed. The CDR Clearinghouse was closed and many community-based programs were either abandoned or taken over by courts or

86. Letter from Paul Wahrhaftig to W. Philip Mclaurin, Director, Urban Crime Prevention Program, Office of Domestic and Anti-Poverty Operations, ACTION, Washington D.C. (1979) (on file with the authors). The Clearinghouse published a quarterly, *The Mooter*, which devoted its Summer, 1979, issue to the role of volunteers in CDR.

87. Because the community empowerment focus was somewhat at odds with proliferating state ADR programs, much of the Clearinghouse's energy went into monitoring and critiquing such efforts. Wahrhaftig described the dual role of the AFSC as a resource for, and critic of, dispute resolution programs. *See* Wahrhaftig, *supra* note 86. The AFSC attempted to provide information and resources to funding recipients so that they had current information from experienced sources on community organizing, while also attempting to monitor the experience of government sponsored programs. "We will critique and analyze the problems and pitfalls that are inherent in the structure of the programs or arise under it. We hope that by focusing attention on problem areas as soon as they arise we may be able to help groups avoid pitfalls initially or at least avoid repetition."

88. There was some discussion as to whether the Neighborhood Justice Center ("NJC") established by the Justice Department in Venice, California was a "grass roots" effort. Although the three experimental centers were sometimes presented as three alternative models (Kansas City NJC was viewed as an extension of the criminal justice system, Venice California as a grass roots program, and Atlanta as a hybrid—location in the community but with strong court sponsorship) Wahrhaftig wonders "whether Venice might more properly be called a strawman." *See* Wahrhaftig, *supra* note 85, at 88. Attorney General Griffin Bell, whose strong support was instrumental in the creation of the NJCs, regarded their creation as an effort to increase access to and reduce the costs of justice. The Venice NJC was an hierarchical organization, monitored and evaluated on the basis of its contribution and relationship to the criminal justice system.

other state agencies.[89] The result within the ADR movement has been increased professionalization.[90] ADR is now firmly within the domain of the legal field and has been effectively made to service the professional projects of practicing lawyers.[91]

ADR extends the reach of the legal field, even as it is based on a critique of adjudication, through a set of complex strategies. Non-adjudicatory alternatives diminish the visible coercion and "violence" associated with the judicial process.[92] Because coercion is less extreme and less visible in these informal institutions, the reach of control can be wider, less resistance is generated, and even "trivial" problems can be subject to regulation.[93] Moreover, because informal processes appear to be less expensive—at least to begin with—they permit intervention, in one form or another, in a larger number of cases. The quantity of resources for state social control is increased by relieving formal legal institutions of some demands while nonetheless maintaining the overall capacity of those institutions.[94] Because informal processes do not require violations of law to initiate action, and do not stigmatize participants—who are respondents and complainants not defendants and victims—intervention can be earlier, covering a wider array of behaviors and attitudes, unconstrained by jurisdictional boundaries or legal categories.[95] Coercion is replaced by persuasion, threat, manipulation, but power and authority is exercised nonetheless.[96] Finally, ADR expands

89. R. HOFRICHTER, NEIGHBORHOOD JUSTICE IN CAPITALIST SOCIETY 98 (1987).

90. One need only note the growth of such organizations as the Society of Professionals in Dispute Resolution and the growth of private, for-profit providers of dispute resolution services. The promise of increased efficiency and lower costs which were associated with ADR have been used by economic entrepreneurs to market ADR for private concerns (for example businesses, insurance companies) that are regular users of court services. They argue that just as privatization promises cost/effect, market sensitive action in the regulatory or administrative arena, private justice would produce similar benefits for users of the court system. *See generally* Galanter, *Why the "Haves" Come Out Ahead: Speculations on the Limits of Legal Change*, 9 LAW & SOC'Y REV. 95, 134 (1974).

Mini-trials and rent-a-judge programs as well as mediation and arbitration services were promoted by for-profit concerns like ENDISPUTE. Businesses were prepared to buy the product and support ADR in these areas because they perceived themselves as all too often victimized by public justice and runaway juries. The result has been the creation of a two track world of ADR—the lower world of publicly-supported programs for minor criminal, neighborhood, and family disputes; the upper world of privately marketed dispute resolution services for business disputes. Merry, *supra* note 42, at 2067.

91. Y. Dezalay, *supra* note 7; R. HOFRICHTER, *supra* note 89.

92. Cover, *Violence and the Word*, 95 YALE L.J. (1986).

93. Abel, *The Contradictions of Informal Justice*, in 1 THE POLITICS OF INFORMAL JUSTICE 267, 270-71 (1982).

94. *Id.*

95. R. HOFRICHTER, *supra* note 89; Abel, *supra* note 93, at 272.

96. S. Silbey & S. Merry, Interpretive Process in Mediation and Courts (1986) (unpublished manuscript). The notion that power disappears in the absence of hierarchy seems fundamental among ADR promoters. If the direct, legally sanctioned ability to exercise or command the exercise of coercion, force, or confiscation of property is lacking, observers too often assume that power in its other forms is also absent or, if not missing, is somehow shared. *See generally* M. FOUCAULT, POWER/KNOWLEDGE (1980); S. LUKES, POWER: A RADICAL VIEW (1974); D. WRONG, POWER: ITS FORMS, BASES AND USES (1979). The attention to greater participation by disputants in the processes of dispute resolution suggests to some observers that the outcomes are therefore shaped by the parties. This argument, however, ignores the possibility that the parties may be participating in the legitimation of their own

the legal field by coopting or undermining mechanisms of dispute processing in traditional social institutions and by bringing them within the preview of law and the legal profession.[97]

III. The Disciplinary Domain: Social Science and Legal Thought

The ADR movement and its critique of adjudication also emerges out of the efforts of social scientists to find a place for themselves in the production of academic legal scholarship. The issue here is whether legal study can be made scientifically respectable, empirically rigorous and theoretical[98] or whether legitimate legal scholarship is irreducibly normative. Like the contemporary critique of institutions which has fueled the ADR movement, the modern struggle for scientifically-sound scholarship about law replays earlier struggles within the legal academy which were precipitated by the effort of legal realists to advance an instrumentalist conception of law and to ground legal policy in empirical observation.[99]

Realists saw the start of the twentieth century as a period of knowledge explosion and knowledge transformation.[100] Some saw in both the natural and emerging social sciences the triumph of rationality over tradition, inquiry over faith, and the human mind over its environ-

subjugation or control. *See* S. Silbey, On the Relationship Between State Theory and Sociolegal Research (1988) (paper presented at the 1988 Annual Meeting Law and Society Association, Vail, Colorado); S. Silbey & S. Merry, *supra*.

97. Abel, *supra* note 93. This is ironic, Abel suggests, because some impetus for the creation of alternatives derives from a nostalgia for traditional authority. *See Joint Hearings on Resolution of Minor Disputes. Before the Subcommittee on Courts, Civil Liberties and the Administration of Justice of the Committee on the Judiciary and Subcommittee on Consumer Protection and Finance of the Committee on Interstate and Foreign Commerce, House of Representatives*, 96th Cong., 1st Sess. (1979) (statement of Daniel J. Meador); Snyder, *Anthropology, Dispute Processes and Law: A Critical Introduction*, 8 Brit. J.L. & Soc'y 141 (1981). *Cf.* Silbey, *Who Speaks for the Consumer?* (Book Review), 1985 Am. B. Found. Res. J. 429. Traditional institutions do not simply wither away but are, Abel claims, actively destroyed by the growth of state, state-supported institutions and professions. *Cf.* C. Lasch, Haven in a Heartless World (1977). The institutionalization of ADR furthers the state's monopoly of social control by mobilizing additional mechanisms and processes of social regulation and further expropriating the conflicts and troubles of citizens. Paradoxically the appropriation of conflict takes place within processes which attempt to narrow the interactions, number of participants and public/justice considerations within any disputes, thus both neutralizing and privatizing conflict. Christie, *Conflicts as Property* 17 Brit. J. Criminology 1 (1977). *Cf.* Silbey, *The Consequences of Responsive Regulation*, in Regulation Enforcement (1984).

Although this analysis suggests that the expansion of state power increases oppression, it is important to remember, as Joel Handler has reminded us, that traditional institutions are not necessarily havens of freedom and solicitude, nor are they models of equality and neutrality. Recourse to law is often undertaken to get out from under the oppression of personalistic, idiosyncratic decision making.

98. *See* D. Black, The Behavior of Law (1976).

99. Legal realism was by no means, however, a unified or singular intellectual movement. At one and the same time, the label "legal realist" embraced radical skeptics and those who exhibited strong faith in science and technique. *See* A. Hunt, The Sociological Movement in Law (1978); L. Kalman, Legal Realism at Yale 1927-1960 (1986); Cohen *Transcendental Nonsense and the Functional Approach*, 35 Calif. L. Rev. 1152 (1985); Llewellyn, *A Realistic Jurisprudence—The Next Step*, 30 Colum. L. Rev. 431 (1930); Peller, *supra* note 60.

100. Reisman, *Law and Social Science: A Report on Michael and Eschsler's Casebook on Criminal Law and Administration* (Book Review), 50 Yale L.J. 636 (1941).

ment.[101] They took, as one of their many projects, the task of opening law to this explosion and transformation. Moreover, some realists argued that the law's rationality and efficacy were ultimately dependent upon an alliance with science.[102] By using the questions and methods of science to assess the consequences of legal decisions, realists claimed that an understanding of what law *could* do would help in establishing what law *should* do.[103] Thus, realism initiated a dialogue between law and social science by staking a claim for the importance of phenomenon beyond legal categories and by attacking the self-centered arrogance of legal decision makers.[104]

While realists fought, fifty years ago, to transform legal scholarship by bringing social science into the legal academy, in the contemporary period the effort to further develop and legitimate the social scientific bases of legal scholarship has been associated with attempts to advance the concept of dispute as a way of talking about law. In search of methods that would be scientific, that is independent of the subjects and contexts of study, anthropologists began, in the 1950s, to elaborate the concept of dispute as a way of understanding the role of law in society.[105] Motivated by intellectual dilemmas specific to their discipline, and by a desire to bring law within their professional study, these social scientists tried to reconstitute the subject matter of law by transforming talk about law into talk about disputes.

At first, they defined disputes as public assertions, usually through some standard procedures, of what are initially dyadic disagreements.[106] They argued that the use of this concept offers a way of developing neutral and objective tools of inquiry while overcoming static dichotomies that had characterized anthropological studies of law. Traditionally, anthropological studies had alternately focused upon either particular legal institutions or upon particular legal ideas and conceptions.[107] By focusing upon cases and disputes, researchers tried to get beyond the abstracted categories of institutional or ideational analyses and to attend

---

101. McDougal, *Fuller v. The American Legal Realists: An Intervention*, 50 YALE L.J. 827 (1941).

102. *See* Schlegel, *American Legal Realism and Empirical Social Science: The Singular Case of Underhill Moore*, 29 BUFFALO L. REV. 195 (1980).

103. Llewellyn, *Some Realism About Realism*, 44 HARV. L. REV. 1222 (1931).

104. *See* B. CARDOZO, THE NATURE OF THE JUDICIAL PROCESS, (1921); Llewellyn, *On Reading and Using the Newer Jurisprudence*, 40 COLUM. L. REV. 581 (1940); Pound, *The Theory of Judicial Decision*, 36 HARV. L. REV. 641 (1923). By pointing to the scientific impulse in realism, however, we do not want to suggest that there was only one model of empirical social science available for adoption just as we do not want to suggest that there was only one thread of realist practice. The social scientific styles within realism included a wide range of institutionalists as well as very quantitative behavioralists. *See* E. PURCELL, THE CRISIS OF DEMOCRATIC THEORY (1973).

105. The following discussion begins from an analysis of the concept of dispute presented in Merry & Silbey, *What Do Plaintiffs Want? Reexamining the Concept of Dispute*, 9 JUST. SYS. J. 15 (1984).

106. *See* Gulliver, *Dispute Settlement Without Courts*, in LAW IN CULTURE AND SOCIETY 14 (1969).

107. Moore, *Law and Anthropology*, in BIENNIAL REVIEW OF ANTHROPOLOGY (1969), *reprinted in* S. MOORE, LAW AS PROCESS 214 (1978).

to the social action which constituted legal forms—ideas and institutions. The effort was to find ways of studying law that could be truly scientific, free of socio-cultural and legal/doctrinal categories. This effort was, thus, part of a struggle for control of legal scholarship itself. In this sense their use of the concept of dispute was both an effort to legitimate social scientists' activities in the field of legal scholarship and was part of a debate within the discipline of anthropology itself.

By viewing disputes as a sequence of events, noting changes over time, anthropologists began to describe social processes dynamically. The suggested shift in the unit of analysis also promised to overcome the dichotomy in anthropology between law as prescription and law as reflection of social conditions. It did so by treating law as a "manipulable, value-laden language" available for any number of purposes.[108]

Attention to disputes emerged as part of a more general resistance to the structural functional paradigm which had dominated anthropological research, and which had been used to describe relationships among social processes and institutions, such as law and society. Structural functionalism was criticized for its ahistorical quality, and its reliance upon a consensual vision of social order which viewed conflict as a matter of failed conformity with unproblematic normative standards. Thus, during the 1950s and 1960s, research in the anthropology of law,

> however diverse in other respects, shared certain characteristics. [The studies] were mainly ahistorical, ethnographic descriptions, based on inductive empiricism and using some form of case method. All concerned a single ethnic group that was deemed to be relatively homogeneous and capable of being isolated, as a "society," for purposes of analysis. Most relied, explicitly or implicitly, on Western conceptions of law, and they considered disputes as the main index of law or its primary locus. Though conducted during the colonial period, they abstracted, by and large, from the processes of colonial domination and from the profound economic and social changes occurring during that period. They were generally functionalist in orientation and concerned with the maintenance of social order. Except for the studies by Malinowski and Gulliver, they considered law primarily as a framework rather than as a process.[109]

---

108. S. MOORE, LAW AS PROCESS 225 (1978). *Cf.* Silbey & Bittner, *supra* note 66.

109. Snyder, *supra* note 97, at 143. The dominance of this paradigm was reflected in particular in the work of Radcliffe-Brown who used the term "function" to refer to "the interconnections between social structure and the process of social life," and the term "social structure" to refer to the raw material of social life, to what might be called "social relations" and the patterns of those relations. A. RADCLIFFE-BROWN, STRUCTURE AND FUNCTION IN PRIMITIVE SOCIETY 12 (1952). Radcliffe-Brown used the term "structural form" to denote the abstracted and sociologically constructed models of societies which Levi-Strauss called "social structure." *See* C. LEVI-STRAUSS, STRUCTURAL ANTHROPOLOGY (1963); THE SOCIAL ANTHROPOLOGY OF RADCLIFFE-BROWN (A. Kuper ed. 1977). RadclifFeBrown insisted, however, that the social structures he was describing were directly observable phenomena and not abstracted models.

> The starting point was a set of living human beings involved in a series of social relationships with one another. This "social network," as he sometimes de-

Radcliffe-Brown, for example, regarded social structures as observable phenomenon which possessed a dynamic quality yet nonetheless displayed, like human beings, significant continuity over times. In structural functionalism, however, attention to continuity was joined to a concern for conformity so that the stability—equilibrium or disequilibrium—of a society could be measured by the amount of deviance in that society. "Where there is marked divergence," he wrote, "between the ideal or expected behavior and the actual conduct of many individuals, this is an indication of disequilibrium."[110] From this perspective, conflict among members of a group about the rules of behavior, or methods for formulating those rules, signify a deeper social instability. For Radcliffe-Brown the goal of structural functional analysis was, in the end, to determine how institutions, like law, maintained the equilibrium and wholeness of a society.

Within anthropology itself, some scholars claimed that this way of talking about law simply replicated the political biases of traditional legal scholarship. They looked for ways scholarship could explain, and promote, social transformation. Some looked for alternative concepts and methods for describing the place of law in that process and, in so doing, emphasized the importance of situations of trouble or cases of hitch, to use the phrase Llewellyn and Hoebel coined in *The Cheyenne Way*.[111] Trouble cases, or disputes, provided an opportunity, in this view, to link the study of norms and institutions with the study of change and evolution.

In a widely referenced survey of the literature, Laura Nader took up the cause and actively championed the concept of dispute as a way for social scientists to study law.[112] In order to place legal processes more directly within social contexts, while simultaneously achieving more reliable empirical and explanatory generalizations, Nader urged anthropologists to use the concept of dispute and make efforts at describing disputing behavior.[113] She argued that an analysis of disputes and responses to disputing was essential for understanding processes of social

---

> scribed it, and as it would be termed today, he called the "social structure." But behind the flux of everyday interactions, regularities could be established. The regular forms could thus be abstracted. Together these constituted the "structural form" of the society. This again was empirically real, since it corresponded to the stated norms and customary usages of various kinds of social relationships. Being real in this sense, the structural form could be functionally related to the actual processes of social life. In the paradigmatic case, recurrent social activities maintain the structural form, and are in turn determined by it.

THE SOCIAL ANTHROPOLOGY OF RADCLIFFE-BROWN 29 (A. Kuper ed. 1977).

Although he asserted that social structure was dynamic, "like that of the organic structure of a living body," *Id.*, Radcliffe-Brown emphasized the continuity of social structure through time. He argued that like biological organisms society experiences constant renewal and change. Nevertheless, he believed that the "general structural forms . . . remain relatively constant," and he insisted that "even in the most revolutionary changes some continuity of structure is maintained." *Id.*

110. A. RADCLIFFE-BROWN, SYSTEMS OF KINSHIP AND MARRIAGE, *reprinted in* THE SOCIAL ANTHROPOLOGY OF RADCLIFFE-BROWN 197 (A. Kuper ed. 1977).

111. K. LLEWELLYN & E. HOEBEL, THE CHEYENNE WAY (1941).

112. Nader, *The Anthropological Study of Law*, 67 AM. ANTHROPOLOGIST 3, 23 (1965).

113. *Id.*

control, but equally important for sophisticated and contextual analyses of law and courts, should they exist in a society. From this perspective, disputes are windows on society, openings in the social fabric, moments of exploration in which the collectivity is challenged, transformed, or repaired. Observing disputing processes within their social location, social scientists would witness discussion, reenactment or transformation of norms along with active competition among various interpretations of norms.[114]

Adopting the concept of "dispute," scholars moved from the analysis of law as a system of rules to the study of law as a process of handling trouble cases. With this move, however, formal definitions of law become unnecessary, theoretically pointless and sterile.[115] Emphasis was placed on the continuity of law and other social institutions and processes[116] rather than on the distinctiveness of law. Here, the realist

114. As Llewellyn and Hoebel suggest in describing the virtues of this lens—the trouble case or dispute:

> It is . . . the felt "norms" for conduct, whether or not derived from practice, which are likely to be injected into the case of breach. Per contra, it is the case of hitch or trouble that dramatizes a 'norm' or a conflict of 'norms' which may have been latent. It forces conscious attention; it forces the defining of issues. It colors the issues, too, as they are shaped, with the personalities which are in conflict, and with matters of "face," and with other flavors of the culture. It forces solution, which may be creation. It forces solution in a fashion to be remembered, perhaps in clear, ringing words. It is one more experiment toward new and clearer or more rigorous patterning both of behavior and of recognizable "norm" into that peculiarly legal something one may call a "recognized imperative."

K. Llewellyn & E. Hoebel, *supra* note 111, at 21.

115. *See* S. Roberts, Order and Dispute: An Introduction to Legal Anthropology (1979); Abel, *A Comparative Theory of Dispute Institutions in Society*, 8 Law & Soc'y Rev. 217 (1973); Snyder, *supra* note 97.

116. This move paralleled a more general shift within anthropology to a more voluntaristic, actor-centered mode of analysis. The description of societies came to focus more on actors' strategies and choices rather than rules of behavior. In order to escape the notion of society exclusively patterned by norms and rules, anthropologists followed sociologists of the social constructivist perspective and moved toward an analysis of actors operating through and by means of rules, yet constructing those rules and social orders on the basis of choices and strategies. *See, e.g.*, P. Berger & T. Luchman, The Social Consruction of Reality (1966); E. Goffman, The Presentation of Self in Everyday Life (1959). The individual was conceived as free to exercise choice within the constraints imposed by her culture and social structure, while simultaneously constructing that context through her actions and interactions. Study of disputes fit nicely here. Scholars could examine the choices which those involved in a dispute made as to the appropriate ways to handle disputes as well as the processes of giving meaning to those disputes in different dispute processing arenas. *See* Felstiner, Abel & Sarat, *The Emergence and Transformation of Disputes: Naming, Blaming, Claiming . . .*, 15 Law & Soc'y Rev. 631 (1980-81); Mather & Yngvesson, *Language, Audience and the Transformation of Dispute*, 15 Law & Soc'y Rev. 775 (1980-81); Nader, *Styles of Court Procedure: To Make the Balance*, in Law in Culture and Society (1969). *See also* B. Yngvesson, Public Nuisance, Private Crime: The Clerk, the Court and the Construction of Order in a New England Town (1987) (unpublished manuscript); S. Silbey & S. Merry, *supra* note 96; Sarat & Felstiner, *The Legal Construction of Social Relations: Vocabularies of Motive in Lawyer/Client Interaction*, 22 Law & Soc'y Rev. 737 (1988).

Snyder describes the intellectual movement as follows:

> [I]ts approach shifts the main enquiry from social organization to processes and also from groups to networks of individuals. It emphasizes the action of parties in disputes just as much as those of negotiators or adjudicators, hence it aims to map the perceptions of individual disputants and gives special attention to the cultural meanings and rationalizations of social action.

Snyder, *supra* note 133, at 145. Other scholars have also discussed the greater emphasis

tradition in legal scholarship legitimated the use of disputes as a way of studying law in action, and thus enabled social scientists outside law schools to claim an important place in the legal field.

The move to study law through the lens of trouble and disputes was part of a move to connect the discipline of legal study to more general developments in the human sciences. Within the human sciences, efforts were being made to cross restrictive disciplinary boundaries. There was active theoretical interest in the functions of a large variety of social institutions and concerted efforts to identify common variables and frames of reference. While anthropologists were adapting or resisting the structural functional paradigm, there were similar adaptations, challenges and echoes in the other social sciences, and continuing efforts to build links across the disciplines. The anthropological formulation of social action and disputing as choice-making strategies bore a close similarity to rational choice models in economics and political science, and it suggested some convergence with role analysis in sociology and psychology. It thus fit well with the desire to move in the direction of a unified social science with fundamental and common units of analysis. "Dispute" looked like it might be one of these essential elements and organizing concepts of social life. The notion of dispute and dispute processing fit well with a behavioral—rather than normative or legal—conception that could be used in a wide variety of situations. It did not carry with it connotations of cultural or institutional bias that were present in many early anthropological analyses that began with a model of law predicated on Anglo-American experience.[117]

In one sense, the development of the concept of dispute as a primary focus of social science research on law can be read as the culmination of a particular moment in the history of ideas in which the model of

---

on processes, transactions and individual choices. *See* THE DISPUTING PROCESS: LAW IN TEN SOCIETIES (L. Nader & H. Todd eds. 1978); POLITICAL ANTHROPOLOGY (M. Swartz, V. Turner & A. Tuden eds. 1966); Barth, *Models of Social Organization*, in ROYAL ANTHROPOLOGICAL INSTITUTE OF GREAT BRITAIN AND IRELAND (1963) (Occasional Paper 23); Nader & Yngvesson, *On Studying the Ethnology of Law and Its Consequences*, in HANDBOOK OF SOCIAL AND CULTURAL ANTHROPOLOGY 884 (1973); Van Velsen, *The Extended Case Method and Situational Analysis*, in THE CRAFT OF ANTHROPOLOGY (A. Epstein ed 1967).

117. S. MOORE, *supra* note 108, at 214. Van Velsen argued that faulty comparisons persisted in anthropological treatments of African legal systems, because anthropologists, with or without legal training, operated with "imperfect understanding of their own legal system, with which, explicitly or implicitly, they tend to compare African legal systems." Ethnocentrism seems to have been, in this argument, exacerbated by naivete, leading to very common myths concerning both Anglo-American and African law. Van Velsen describes these as the myth of informality of African law, and the formality, limitation by rules and procedures in Anglo-American courts. He also describes a second myth which asserts that African tribunals seek reconciliation while Anglo-American courts are preoccupied by other concerns which do not address considerations of social organization and composition. Van Velsen suggests that the myths derive from insufficient attention to the "lower" courts in Britain and the United States which are more likely parallels to the African tribunals under examination; he also questions whether scholars have actually determined that reconciliation is the outcome of the African processes. Van Velsen, *Procedural Informality, Reconciliation and False Comparisons*, in IDEAS AND PROCEDURES IN AFRICAN CUSTOMARY LAW 137 (1969). *See* Abel, *supra* note 115 (for extended argument that focus on dispute processes would provide a less ethnocentric, more culturally valid subject of study than law).

elementary particles and general theory in physical science fueled the dream of a true social science with equally fundamental, objective, and verifiable units of analysis. The dispute was for empirical legal research what "demands and support" would be for political science, what "stimulus and response" would be for behavioral psychology, what "utility" would be for neo-classical economics: a new paradigm that would advance the science of law.[118] Dispute became the prism for observing courts and their settings as well as other institutions for interpreting and responding to conflict. For socio-legal scholars, the way to study law was to carve out and construct from social reality "a particular social relationship called the dispute."[119]

The Civil Litigation Research Project, funded by the United States Department of Justice in 1978, was perhaps the largest and most ambitious attempt to use the concept of dispute to organize empirical work on law. Its ambition directed attention to the limitations as well as the possibilities of using "disputes as a link between law and society."[120] What started out as no more than "a general set of orientations"[121] had crystallized into a major perspective and direction for research. The result was to generate and encourage revisionism, criticism and questions about the status and adequacy of the dispute perspective in scholarship about law.

Questions about the utility of the dispute perspective in legal scholarship occurred first within the social science community and reflected narrow struggles for hegemony among legal scholars outside law schools. Some anthropologists argued that the focus on trouble and the management of trouble distracts attention from the far more general pattern of acquiescence and normative integration in social life.[122] They worried that the dispute perspective condemned social science to studying the tip of the iceberg and, as a result, limited the claim of social science knowledge within the legal field.

Engel argued that the legal culture of a community involves "patterns of behavior and norms that are recognized and respected among

---

118. Thus Trubek writes that,

> it seemed desirable to find a way to identify and describe conflicts which did not reach the courts, as well as to compare the performance of courts with that of other possible arrangements for resolving conflicts and protecting rights. These tasks called for a common unit of analysis, some way to compare the controversies in courts and other institutions; it was also necessary to identify potential judicial 'business' that never reached the courts. The answer to these problems was found in the dispute, and the idea of dispute processing.
>
> The dispute was conceived of as the common denominator uniting events outside our institutional machinery with those handled both by courts and by other forms of third-party dispute processing mechanisms. If similar disputes could be identified in court and in other settings, and if the impact of different institutions on such disputes and disputants were measured, the dispute focus would answer the need of functional analysis and institutional comparison.

Trubek, *Studying Courts in Context*, 15 LAW & SOC'Y REV. 485 (1981).

119. *Id.* at 498.

120. *Id.* at 494.

121. *Id.*

122. *See* Engel, *Legal Pluralism in an American Community: Perspectives on Civil Trial Court*, 1980 AM. B. FOUND. RES. J. 425.

particular groups in a community," and he suggested that the interaction between local "customary law," (that which is ordinarily done in a community and recognized as what ought to be done, what is proper and obligatory) and the formal legal system produces a synthesis which reflects the actual legal life and legal culture of the community.

> Conflicts, disputes and breaches of norm may become a part of the analysis [of legal culture] to the extent they show the systems at work or illustrate the limits of such systems or friction between them. Dispute is not the foundation of the analysis, however, nor is it logically even a necessary part of it.[123]

While he acknowledged that no system exists without some breaches and that disputes "always play some part in our broader understanding of the normative order as a whole,"[124] he warned that the focus on the breach directed attention away from the facticity of regular observance.[125]

"It is simply incorrect," Engel argues, "to assume that 'customary law' emerges from social conflict in the same sense that the common law emerges from cases and controversies."[126] The dispute perspective presents social relations as generated and sustained by relatively rare instances of conflict rather than the repetitive patterns of unstressful interaction through which expectations and obligations are created and particular patterns of order maintained. By conceiving of society and custom in the same way that law is conceived, the effort to understand legal culture begins from assumptions which end up denying analytic and theoretical independence to non-legal concepts. Upon a single unit of analysis, the dispute, researchers built an elaborate edifice to carry the burden of producing an accurate understanding of all of legal life. That was, in Engel's view, a burden that the concept could not adequately discharge.

Other socio-legal scholars criticize the dispute perspective for its boundless quality. They worry that that perspective would, if taken to

---

123. *Id.* at 432.

124. *Id.*

125. Moreover, in Engel's view, attention to disputes and breaches of social norms leads to the kind of functionalism discussed above, where courts and legal institutions become understood simply as dispute processing and dispute resolving institutions. Such a perspective offers very little insight about the most frequent and perhaps most significant activities of many civil courts which rarely involve actively contested disputes, and which routinely require the court to oversee or legitimate decisions and settlements made elsewhere. Although it is well understood that these decisions and settlements take place within the shadow of the court, a central focus on the dispute processing functions of courts obscures its role in processes in which disputing is minimal. Mnookin & Kornhauser, *Bargaining in the Shadow of the Law: The Case of Divorce*, 88 YALE L.J. 950 (1979). "Emphasizing as it does an idealized and misleading image of the adversary process in civil trial courts, dispute analysis tends to relegate the major part of the court's work to residual categories (such as 'routine processing'), which typically receive little, if any, analytic attention." Engel, *supra* note 122, at 435. Furthermore, the focus upon the dispute, and the individual case which is reproduced in the dispute paradigm, ignores the impact of the pattern of court activity for legitimation and for the creation of culture. Lempert, *Grievances and Legitimacy: The Beginnings and End of Dispute Settlement*, 15 LAW & SOC'Y REV. 707 (1980-81).

126. Engel, *supra* note 122, at 436.

its logical extreme, undermine its own scientific aspirations by moving social science research farther and farther away from the institutions of the official law. This criticism reflects a concern that the sociology of law will dissolve or will lose its claim to distinctiveness within the various social science disciplines. The battle of social scientists to achieve status within the legal field may, in this view, be won at the cost of a loss of status within the human sciences. This criticism arises as a worry over the kinds of professional and disciplinary claims that socio-legal scholars can make.

This worry is a reaction to recent developments in which researchers began to push inquiry in the direction of examining the life history and development of disputes. While earlier work took the existence of disputes for granted, more recent research emphasizes the problematic nature of dispute development and urges attention to the process through which unperceived injurious experiences become perceived as injurious, injuries ripen into grievances and claims, and become disputes.[127] This paradigm directs attention to the context and transformation of disputes while it gives much less attention to their resolution. Because the "potential for disputes is infinite" and "the possible sources of disputes . . . innumerable," dispute researchers argue that the "disputes which do arise are only a tiny proportion of those which might develop."[128] Thus, studying dispute transformation required a further broadening of inquiry, just as a generation earlier the study of dispute processing required a broadened inquiry in legal scholarship.

Those who urged attention to the dispute development process also urged a redefinition of the concept of dispute itself. They tried to move away from Gulliver's insistence on the *public* assertion of a dyadic disagreement. Miller and Sarat[129] and others[130] argued that grievances emerged from an "individual's belief that he/she is entitled to a resource which someone else may grant or deny," and that a "dispute exists when a claim based on a grievance is rejected either in whole or in part." From this perspective, Gulliver's definition seems to beg one of the more important questions about disputing: how do conflicts and differences enter a particular public arena, including the legal system?[131]

127. *E.g.*, Felstiner, Abel & Sarat, *supra* note 116; Mather & Yngvesson, *supra* note 116; Miller & Sarat, *Grievances, Claims and Disputes: Assessing the Adversary Culture*, 15 LAW & SOC'Y REV. 525 (1980-81). *Cf.* Emerson & Messinger, *The Micropolitics of Trouble*, 25 SOC. PROBS. 121 (1977).

128. Fitzgerald & Dickins, *Disputing in Legal and Nonlegal Contexts: Some Questions for Sociologists of Law*, 15 LAW & SOC'Y REV. 681, 684 (1980-81). In significant ways, this work mirrored earlier work by Emerson and Messinger on the natural history and sociological development of troubles, what they called "the micro-politics of trouble." Emerson & Messinger, *supra* note 127.

129. Miller & Sarat, *supra* note 127, at 527.

130. CONTENTION AND DISPUTE: ASPECTS OF LAW AND SOCIAL CONTROL IN MELANESIA (A. Epstein ed. 1974); Starr, *A Pre-Law Stage in Rural Turkish Disputes Negotiations*, in CROSS-EXAMINATIONS: ESSAYS IN MEMORY OF MAX GLUCKMAN (P. Gulliver ed. 1978).

131. Lempert, *supra* note 125, at 708, also emphasizes the "normative claim of entitlement" underlying disputes, while Mather and Yngvesson adopt Gulliver's definition, stressing the importance of the audience in the formation and recognition of social relationships and disputes. Mather & Yngvesson, *supra* note 116, at 776. In this view, the

Kidder summarized the disciplinary concern generated by this expanded definition of disputes:

> If we called all dyadic difficulties 'disputes,' even those private cases which Gulliver termed disagreements, then we would have to include nearly all of human interaction (within our study). One of sociology's major theoretical traditions tells us that everything social, even reality itself . . . is a product of negotiation, and that all things social should be thought of as a process of bargaining . . . . From this perspective, the most routine experiences become sessions in negotiation. Even humor and joke telling are treated as exercises in bargaining . . . . If we stretch the term 'dispute' to include all dyadic bargaining . . . we would have no way to address the issues of access to justice, alternative dispute mechanisms, or the levels of disputing in society as a social problem. Every instance of human interaction would be a candidate for dispute processing analysis. Disputing would be indistinguishable from all human interaction.[132]

Thus attention to the histories of disputes and especially the genesis of disputes aroused suspicion that the sociology of law would no longer have a subject,[133] and sociologists of law would have no particular or distinctive professional claim.

These criticisms suggest that the debate within legal scholarship and scholarship about law over the status of the concept of dispute is itself a struggle for power within the legal field. The claim that studying disputes helps avoid cultural and institutional biases associated with traditional legal scholarship can be acknowledged only so long as it is recognized that that concept carries its own biases. The search for a concept or method to free social science research on law from the interests and values of the community of observers—to use the concept of dispute as a fundamental social fact—was an illusion and a fantasy.[134]

---

conflict between two parties must be asserted publicly, that is, before a third party, for a social relationship to have reached the state of dispute. *Cf.* Abel, *supra* note 115, at 226-27; THE DISPUTING PROCESS: LAW IN TEN SOCIETIES (L. Nader & H. Todd eds. 1978).

132. Kidder, *The End of the Road? Problems in the Analysis of Disputes*, 15 LAW & SOC'Y REV. 707, 721-22 (1980-81).

133. Fitzgerald and Dickins go further and question whether the study of disputes has particular value for understanding law. According to their critique, because studying disputes commits social scientists to study virtually all social interactions, it makes the dispute itself less useful as a unit of analysis. Fitzgerald & Dickins, *supra* note 128. They wonder whether the subject will become so broad as to be unmanageable, and whether "the context is overwhelming the law." *Id.* at 702. They wonder whether the sociology of law will lose all definition and its claims to professional identity, and to participation in the recognizable universe of scholarship about law.

134. Cain and Kulczar suggest that as the concept of dispute was used in social science research on law it became clear that the aspirations to, and claims of, scientific status for that concept were both deeply political and deeply problematic. They state that "[d]ispute theorizing starts with the dispute, as legal theory starts with the law," and they point out that it begins by asserting the primacy of its object of study rather than posing it as a problem. Because "questions are posed about disputes in society, or in their social context . . . the primary task of the [dispute] theorist is to understand the dispute." Cain & Kulczar, *Thinking Disputes: An Essay on the Origins of the Dispute Industry*, 16 LAW & SOC'Y REV. 375 (1982). But in Cain and Kulczar's view the anticipated understanding of disputes is

Cain and Kulczar suggest that struggle over the concept of dispute was fought on the basis of a distinction between science and ideology.[135] They understand science as public discourse, with objects of study developed from known theories, identified logics, and recognizable research traditions. Subjects which are atheoretical, or make claims to be ahistorical, are, for them, ideological. Without a theory of social action, the significance of the object must be taken for granted and assumed, embedded in unstated suppositions and preferences about what is important, what is worth knowing, and why it is worth studying. The assertion that disputes provide the link between law and society[136] is "ideological" because it disguises, that is, fails to locate or theoretically specify, the sources, status, and implications of the object of study—the dispute. This criticism suggests that claims for the universality and comparability of disputes are themselves products of a particular, historically located and culturally specific notion of science, and a particular historically located and culturally specific struggle among academics within the legal field.[137]

This debate about the relative utility and ideological status of the concept of dispute among legal scholars is closely connected to strug-

limited precisely because the dispute, as a supposed form of social action, is appropriated without establishing connections to any theory of social action. Dispute scholars have, in this view, failed to specify what constitutes social interaction, so that dispute would be understandable as a subset of the interaction. Thus, the relationship between disputes and other forms or subsets of social action, and aggregated patterns of action in institutions such as law, remains problematic and undefined. *Id.* at 383.

135. *Id.*

136. Trubek, *supra* note 118, at 494.

137. The claim for the universality of disputes is stated succinctly by Roberts: "Disputes, both within groups and between them, are found everywhere in human society." S. ROBERTS, ORDER AND DISPUTES: AN INTRODUCTION TO LEGAL ANTHROPOLOGY (1979). *Cf.* C. WITTY, MEDIATION AND SOCIETY (1980); THE DISPUTING PROCESS: LAW IN TEN SOCIETIES (L. Nader & H. Todd eds. 1978); Nader, *supra* note 112. It is flawed, again according to Cain and Kulczar, because universality is a presumption, such as when the term is applied to some universal phenomenon for which a common meaning is implied by the application of the label; it cannot then be an empirical discovery. Cain & Kulczar, *supra* note 134. Moreover, empirical use of dispute has tended to apply the label to such a wide range of phenomena that it lacks boundaries and definition, and thus is suspect as a universal observation. The claim that the concept of dispute offers a fundamental unit for comparative social analysis is closely associated with the claim that disputes are universal social phenomena. "If disputes are everywhere in society, at all times and places . . . then it becomes possible (and for other reasons, desirable) to compare the ways in which this phenomenon is dealt with, and to explain any differences that occur." *Id.* at 381.

Furthermore, the criticisms which have challenged particular research methods, or definitions of dispute, as well as the relevance of value judgments and justice claims in the concept, necessarily raise questions which go beyond what Trubek refers to as "narrow" notions of method. Trubek, *supra* note 1, at 740. "The problem is not one of method," he writes, "in the narrow sense of surveys versus observation, but one that reaches to the nature of social research itself . . . . The strategy of defining injuries, grievances, and disputes in ways that avoid the issue of the researcher's values is not, paradoxically, value-free." Methods which attempt objectivity in the sense that they desire to be not only universal and comparative, but also free of the researcher's and the subject's valued preferences, "makes inaccessible to thought those injuries and injustices for which there is no objective referent in existing law, consensus, or the consciousness of affected individuals." Indeed, the researcher can try to access only that which is accessible to both her own consciousness and to the subject's consciousness. Any method will therefore be limited to the terminology, language, and methods recognized in those cultures. *Id.*

gles within the domain of institutions. Advancement of the concept of dispute among academics facilitated the critique of courts as well as the search for alternative dispute resolution mechanisms, yet it also facilitated a defense of the social importance of both courts and their alternatives.[138]

Although the concept of dispute was promoted as a general analytic category, the very earliest formulations of the dispute perspective connected the observation and study of disputes with an implicit recognition of the necessity or desirability of dispute resolution. Thus Nader's call for anthropologists to adopt a focus on disputing for cross cultural description also claimed that dispute settlement was a universal social function.

> How people resolve conflicting interests and how they remedy strife situations is a problem with which all societies have to

138. The concept of dispute facilitates the critique of courts as well as a defense of their social importance, in part, by individuating and depoliticizing social conflict. By adopting dispute, not law, as the major theoretical concept, researchers shifted inquiry from social organization to processes and from groups to individuals. They tried to "map the perceptions of individual disputants, and give special attention to the cultural meanings and rationalizations of social action." Snyder, *supra* note 97, at 145. In this effort to write from the bottom up, researchers concentrated on micro-studies of the management of conflict. Individual perceptions, interpretations, responses and strategies became the focus of research with little attention to systematic outcomes, no less to the structural sources or organization of these individual experiences.

Kidder suggests that by focusing on individual decisions as a way of understanding disputing behavior, scholars also adopted the "strong presumptions of equality, case discreteness, and individualism" prevalent in the anthropological literature. Kidder, *supra* note 132, at 719. In this way, researchers inadvertently replicated the conceptual and institutional biases in the methods of studying law that they were attempting to reform. The conception of individuated grievances and cases interacted with an abstracted vision of the parties and created a radically depoliticized vision of conflict. According to this critique, the concept of "dispute" reproduces a legal ideology rather than subjecting legality and legal ideology to critical inquiry.

In the small scale agricultural and hunter-gatherer societies which anthropologists study, the relative equality of the parties in any particular dispute, in terms of organizational structure (individuals, groups, status), disputing competence and social resources, is taken for granted. These assumptions prove problematic when the model is applied to advanced industrial societies, and although much of the more recent literature on disputing has paid homage to the importance of the relative power of the parties, the concepts "power" and "equality," like the concept of "dispute" itself, are used without a theoretical framework to help identify relevant indicators or aspects of power and social position. Merry, *supra* note 25. Without such a framework, allusions to power and inequality do little to challenge the individualistic assumptions of the dispute paradigm because both the disputant and the dispute are removed from the social fabric which provides definition and meaning for the participants as well as for the observer's analysis of the situation.

According to Cain and Kulczar, the dispute model suggests that "differences in power are capable of being equalized: more money, more knowledge, more organization, even more experience, may be given to the weaker party, and then the difference would disappear." Cain & Kulczar, *supra* note 134, at 380. The problem, according to this criticism, is that qualitative, experiential and cognitive differences between parties are treated quantitatively, as independent dimensions which can be manipulated, either reduced or increased and aggregated to construct equal parties—equivalent social actors. The model suggests that social equality can be reduced to quantitative measures without attention to consciousness, cognition or context. The result is a radical abstraction of social action; stripped of its situated and socially constructed meanings, the model of dispute reduces social action to behavioral phenomenon without the accompanying consciousness of others and interpretation of context which constitutes sociability and social interaction.

deal; and usually they find not one but many ways to handle grievances. In any society . . . there are various remedy agents which may be referred to when a grievance reaches a boiling point, and an understanding of all such agencies is necessary for a comprehensive analysis of social control and for a sophisticated analysis of the court system, should one exist.[139]

Dispute researchers treated disputes as social eruptions that needed to be eliminated, managed and contained. Kidder described this as the "pressure cooker model" in which "dispute processing mechanisms [serve] as relief valves preventing social catastrophe . . . . The functionalist assumption, or pressure cooker model, is that each dispute is a discrete disruption which can be rectified if given appropriate and timely treatment."[140] This bias toward dispute settlement reflects the assumption that a dispute constitutes some imbalance or upset requiring treatment or restoration.[141] From this perspective, the trajectory of disputing is "a settlement in the specific case which permits the group to return to normal."[142] Dispute researchers identified different forms of dispute resolution which would provide channels through which social eruptions might pass, with informal mechanisms of social control in the family and the neighborhood handling everyday conflicts, and more formalized complaint and grievance systems of the market and the legal system managing more serious conflicts not settled informally. The image of a funnel with dispute resolution regulating the flow of social interaction and maintaining the balance of pressure between conflict and conformity became a powerful image in the effort to institutionalize ADR.

Indeed it is the very convergence of the effort to promote a scientific study of law through the concept of dispute and the promotion of dispute resolution as a model for adjudication that precipitated the strongest opposition from within traditional legal scholarship. That reaction and opposition is elaborated by Owen Fiss in *Against Settlement*.[143] There Fiss warns that the dispute perspective and the equation of adjudication with dispute resolution are based on a fundamental misunderstanding of the nature of law as well as of judicial institutions.[144] Fiss argues that proponents of the dispute perspective "act as though courts arose to resolve quarrels between neighbors who had reached an impasse and turned to a stranger for help. Courts are seen as the institutionalization of the stranger and adjudication is viewed as the process by which the stranger exercises power."[145] This account, in his view, "trivializes" the purposes of adjudication and the nature of legal procedure.[146] In his view adjudication is not comparable in any important

139. Nader, *supra* note 112.
140. Kidder, *supra* note 132, at 718-19.
141. Nader, *supra* note 116.
142. Kidder, *supra* note 132, at 719.
143. Fiss, *supra* note 1.
144. *Id.* at 1075.
145. *Id.* at 1082.
146. *Id.* at 1085.

way to other mechanism for resolving disputes. Thus the effort to treat courts as just another dispute processing mechanisms and to develop a scheme for rationally allocating disputes among courts and other institutions makes no sense to Fiss. As he puts it, courts possess "power that has been defined and conferred by public law not by private agreement."[147] As a result, "their job is not to maximize the ends of private parties, nor simply to secure the peace, but to explicate and give force to the values embodied in authoritative texts . . . to interpret those values and to bring reality into accord with them."[148]

The dispute processing perspective is dangerous, in Fiss' view, precisely because it elevates process over substance. It portrays law as just another way of ordering private relations rather than as embodying and articulating public values, values that have determinable meanings. In his view the task of legal scholars should be to help identify those values and meanings and to encourage judges to use them in dealing with matters of public consequence. Legal scholarship is, in this view, a type of moral philosophy for which social scientists, among others, have no claim to competence.[149] Fiss' response to the dispute processing perspective embodies a claim to hegemony within the legal field as well as a claim about the distinctive nature of law. He worries that by embracing the perspective of social scientists, of those who administer courts, or of social workers, traditional legal scholars lose control of the legal product. The opportunity to articulate legal values gives way to an overemphasis on efficiency and technique[150] which diminishes the value of law and, as a result, the distinctiveness and social utility of the legal profession itself. Thus the debate about the place of the dispute processing perspective in legal scholarship is, in this view, a debate about fundamental issues confronting law and lawyers.

---

147. *Id.*

148. *See* Fiss, *The Death of Law?*, 72 CORNELL L. REV. 1 (1986).

149. *See* Fiss, *supra* note 1, at 1086. Fiss' conception of the challenges facing legal scholarship is, in turn, challenged by some, like Bruce Ackerman who suggests that lawyers should be skilled practitioners of both moral philosophy and social science. B. ACKERMAN, *supra* note 60. *See* Fiss, *supra* note 148.

150. Fiss opposes the dispute processing perspective because it encourages legal scholars and judges to regard litigated cases as annoyances or administrative inconveniences. For him the legal field is defined by the efforts of legal professionals to make judgments about the content and applicability of values like equal protection and to think about the ways those values are systematically undermined by the practices of political and social institutions. His critique is thus overtly political. As he argues, the proponents of the dispute processing perspective "begin with a certain satisfaction with the status quo . . . ." Fiss, *supra* note 1, at 1086. But, Fiss continues, "when one sees injustices that cry out for correction . . . the value of avoidance diminishes and the agony of judgment becomes a necessity. Someone has to confront the betrayals of our deepest ideals and be prepared to turn the world upside down to bring these ideals to fruition." *Id.*

Fiss worries that the dispute processing perspective represents a "capitulation to the condition of mass society." *Id.* at 1075. He believes that lawyers and legal scholars should be skeptical about the attempt to encourage diversion or settlement of cases from courts. In his view, adjudication neither mirrors inequalities in private relations nor translates those inequalities into judicial decisions; mediation, negotiation and other dispute processes, on the other hand, do nothing to counteract inequalities among or between disputants. For another view see Galanter, *supra* note 90. *See also* D. BLACK, *supra* note 98.

IV. Reconstituting the Juridical Subject: Rights, Interests and Needs

The struggle over the place of ADR in the institutional domain and the competition among legal academics and socio-legal scholars for hegemony within the theoretical domain would, in and of themselves, be enough to command the attention of those trying to assess the significance of disputing and dispute processing within the legal field. However, more is at stake than possible rearrangements in the division of society's dispute resolution labor or in the configuration of disciplinary power within legal scholarship. The combination of such institutional and disciplinary changes makes possible, and is made possible by, a reconstitution of the juridical subject.[151] Thus, Fiss' defense of law[152] is more than a defense of adjudication and of legal scholarship as the explication and critique of public values through legal doctrine; it is even more than a defense of the social authority and professional terrain of lawyers. He defends law and lawyering to promote the idea that the relationship of citizens and legal institutions is, or should be, defined by the idea of rights. He seeks to protect rights against those who would displace them as central juridical ideas. The ADR movement and the social science colonization of legal scholarship participate in, and advances, a critique of rights, a critique which in turn promotes alternative conceptions of the relationship of actors within the legal field.

In American legal theory, the juridical subject has been traditionally conceptualized as a possessor of rights, of entitlements to particular kinds of treatment by the state. The legal field has been considered the province for the vindication of claims of right, for the resolution of disputes between persons or between the collectivity and particular individuals. Moreover, the definition of rights, the articulation of the values protected by rights and the fashioning of remedies to vindicate claims of right has been largely the province of judges and of courts.[153] Although rights claims may be asserted against political authority, they are always advanced through public authority; thus, rights have a clear public aspect in the sense that they imply a willingness to make demands on the state, to use public institutions, or to appeal to collective sentiments for validation of those claims.

Contemporary rights discourse has many voices. For example, Dworkin describes rights as trumps, that is, claims that are not matters of discretion.[154] He describes two models of rights, one a "natural"

151. Foucault suggests that it is precisely the reconstitution of the subject which necessarily accompanies the development of the human sciences. M. Foucault, Discipline and Punish (1977). The reconstitution of the subject makes possible, as it compels, the development of new institutional arrangements.

152. Fiss, *supra* note 148.

153. J. Brigham, The Cult of the Court (1987); R. Nagel, Constitutional Cultures: The Mentality and Consequences of Judicial Review (1989).

154. R. Dworkin, Taking Rights Seriously (1978). In contrast, Michael Perry says that, although *one may not want to, one can dispense* with rights talk because it adds nothing to the discussion of duties, obligations and discretion. He argues that rights talk is derivative

model and the other a "constructive" model of rights. The "natural" model locates rights in an objective moral reality where rights are not created by persons or societies but rather are discovered just as we are said to discover the laws of physics. Rights, in this view, rest upon the notion of universal, perhaps eternal and immutable, principles of social action that constitute our shared human nature. The natural model of rights implies the possibility of a plan of life, a blueprint of general principles, according to which life evolves and is ordered, an underlying structure which is in fact discoverable by human reason. "Moral reasoning or philosophy" according to Dworkin's conception of natural rights, "is a process of reconstructing the fundamental principles by assembling concrete judgments in the right order, as a natural historian reconstructs the shape of the whole animal from the fragments of its bones that he has found."[155] In practical terms, this means that the role of courts and judges is to discover fragments of the natural moral order by acknowledging particular claims of right and establishing their relationship to written laws and policies. In this model, positive law or legislative mandates are entitled to obedience only so long as they record, transcribe, or fit with these general principles of natural right.[156]

The "constructive" model of rights, which Dworkin prefers, is based on a vision of moral principles more like to common law adjudication than the discovery of fundamental general principles of morality. The constructive model "treats intuitions of justice not as clues to the existence of independent principles, but rather as stipulated features of a general theory" that must be constructed through human action.[157] In this model, rights are neither pre-existing, to be discovered, nor can they be either true or false representations of some external objective moral reality. Rather, the constructive model of rights assumes that persons, and especially public officials who exercise power over others, have a responsibility to justify their actions, or the judgments on which they act, by demonstrating their place in a coherent and general program of action. The role of the judge is to read past decisions and precedents in light of present demands and to both compose and articulate a general theory. This model of rights and judging "presupposes that articulated consistency, decisions in accordance with a program that can be made public and followed until changed, is essential to any conception of justice."[158]

The constructive model neither denies not affirms the natural model of rights; instead, it is a claim for reasoned consistency, independent of any argument for the objective standing of these reasoned positions. Yet both the natural and constructive models rest in large

and thus dispensable. Perry, *Rights-Talk and the "Critique of Rights"*, 62 TEX. L. REV. 1405 (1984).

155. R. DWORKIN, *supra* note 154, at 160.

156. For an extended discussion of natural rights, see L. STRAUSS, NATURAL RIGHTS AND HISTORY (1953). *See also* H. ARKES, FIRST THINGS (1986).

157. R. DWORKIN, *supra* note 154, at 160.

158. *Id.* at 162.

part on Dworkin's modest claim for legal justice, that "it is unfair for officials to act except on the basis of a general *public* theory that will constrain them to consistency, provide a public standard for testing or debating or predicting what they do, and not allow appeals to unique intuitions that might mask prejudice or self-interest in particular cases."[159] Both models establish a special relationship between persons, conceived as rights' claimants, and particular public officials, judges, whose job it is to articulate and protect rights.

Fiss's conception of rights derives from his understanding of the function of adjudication as the process through which we give meaning to public values.[160] He describes legal debate as an effort to specify the content of those values. "Whether in the nineteenth century or twentieth century, torts or criminal law, contract or anti-trust, McCulloch v. Maryland, or Brown v. Board of Education," the function of adjudication, "has not been to resolve disputes between individuals, but rather to give meaning to our public values."[161] In this conception, rights are legal facilities used to express and specify fundamental values. "A right", Fiss writes, "is a particularized and authoritative declaration of meaning."[162] It can exist without a remedy as a standard of criticizing social practices. Remedies, however, expresses the judge's desire to give tangible, efficacious, and "fullblooded" meaning to constitutional values rather than merely to declare what is right.[163]

Fiss argues that the range of voices that participate in the process of giving meaning to constitutional values and to rights "is as broad as the public itself."[164] Nonetheless, like Dworkin, he also makes a strong argument for the special role of the judiciary in concretizing and harmonizing the public values expressed in the Constitution. He points to the structure of judicial office, and what he sees as constraints upon ideological and personal bias, that enable and encourage judges to be more rather than less objective and to "constantly strive for the true meaning of the constitutional value."[165]

Fiss stresses the judge's obligation to participate in a public dialogue by giving reasons for his decisions as that aspect of the institutional design of the office which makes the judiciary especially appropriate for articulating public values and for protecting rights.[166] The quality of the judicial process, he argues, is an indicator of the judge's authority to speak to public issues and the obligation of others

159. *Id.* at 163.

160. Fiss, *The Supreme Court 1978 Term. Foreword: The Forms of Justice*, 93 HARV. L. REV. 1 (1979).

161. *Id.* at 36.

162. *Id.* at 52.

163. *Id.* at 46.

164. *Id.* at 1-2. *See* J. BRIGHAM, *supra* note 153 (for an extended discussion of how the Supreme Court has come to monopolize discourse on the public values embodied in the Constitution and for an argument that the debate on public values and the Constitution should be a less professional and more public enterprise).

165. Fiss, *supra* note 160, at 13.

166. *Id.* at 14.

to listen. In the end, he believes, the legitimacy of the adjudication depends upon reasoned, independent, and careful attention to the process of articulating rights.

Minow elaborates a conception of rights as dialogical opportunities rather than already articulated values or the construction of judges.[167] She suggests that legal texts, and rights-talk as a common theme in those texts, help "to create communities, to establish shared discourse and to provide contexts for linking past with future, and creativity with tradition."[168] Building upon Dworkin's sense that "law's attitude is constructive," laying "principle over practice to show the best route to a better future, keeping the right faith with the past,"[169] yet rejecting his notion that rights are trumps and Fiss's notion that rights are grounded in particular meanings, Minow sees rights as "the language we use to try to persuade others to let us win this round."[170] She wishes to retain what she sees as the attractive features of rights talk in American culture, its association with notions of equality, freedom, respect for individuals; at the same time, she wants to eschew positivistic notions that assign authoritative or fixed meanings to rights "beyond current human choices."[171]

In this conception, the emphasis is on process with rights "understood as the language of a continuing process rather than the fixed rules" of that process. This imagines a community of interaction focused upon competing claims, a discourse in which decisions signify resting points "from which new claims can be made."[172] Rights, then, are markers which guarantee the opportunity to participate in this discourse. The juridical subject is, however, understood to be neither an already constituted possessor of entitlements nor a supplicant awaiting the articulation or constitution of rights by a judge. The juridical subject is, in Minow's conception, whole but incomplete, connected in an ongoing and shared process of building humane social arrangements. Minow seeks to establish the importance of rights talk while leaving open the shifting content of those rights, noting that what draws the community together is less specific claims than the notice and debate which those claims demand. "The rhetoric of rights," she says, "draws those who use it inside the community, and urges the community to pay attention to the individual claimants." At the same time as rights discourse includes participants within a shared community, it "underscores the power of the established order to respond or withhold response" to those claims.[173] In the end, Minow, like Dworkin, makes a seemingly

167. Minow, *Interpreting Rights: An Essay for Robert Cover*, 96 YALE L.J. 1860 (1987).

168. Minow, *supra* note 167, at 1865.

169. R. DWORKIN, *supra* note 154, at 413.

170. Minow, *supra* note 167, at 1876. "Rights represent articulations—public or private, formal or informal—of claims that people use to persuade others (and themselves) about how they should be treated and about what they should be granted." *Id.* at 1867.

171. *Id.* at 1877.

172. *Id.* at 1876.

173. *Id.* at 1877.

modest claim for rights, but here the claim is one of participation rather than publicly defensible coherence.

Despite the variation within rights talk, it nonetheless takes place within a terrain which, as Minow suggests, draws the participants together in a community of argument and struggle. The boundaries of that discourse are marked by the consistency, in each of these conceptions, of the association of rights with public moral debate. Each vision emphasizes the collective or public articulation of claims and responses. Variation in these formulations centers on the forms of participation and the relative position and authority of different participants in this discourse. While Dworkin and Fiss stress the role of the judge as the authoritative voice for publicly articulating values and portray the juridical subject in terms of autonomy and individuality (which is paradoxically constituted by judicial authority), Minow emphasizes the shared context and interdependence within a public discourse which is constituted by making claims as well as responding to them.

Rights talk and the conception of the juridical subject which it constitutes is, of course, the object of intense struggle within the legal field. A critique of rights and the juridical subject as a rights holder has been an important part of ADR's critique of adjudication. Some critics suggest that rights talk has gotten out of hand so that instead of functioning as the grounds for shared discourse, rights have become a source of social conflict. The proliferation of rights has been unhealthy, it is argued, because new rights have been recognized in the absence of legitimate authority. These newly created rights, so the argument goes, lack foundation in the Constitution and thus, rather than securing the "blessings" of law, weaken the foundations of all legitimate legal claims. Thus, conservatives suggest that rights consciousness and rights talk undermine the community.

From this perspective, rights are associated with litigiousness and blamed for a variety of social and institutional disorders. Critics of litigiousness in American society argue that we seek legal redress for every injury and, in so doing, allow law to invade hitherto immune areas and drastically raise the costs of professional and business life. Rights discourse is, according to this argument, just a cover for self-interested behavior which threatens to disrupt social equilibrium.[174] Critics argue

174. Although research on why people sue is scanty, there is some evidence challenging this view. It suggests that plaintiffs litigate to vindicate rights and debate social values rather than to pursue individualistic self-interest. Litigants frequently describe their actions as an attempt at social rehabilitation, claiming that they want to send a message to the government, to their neighbors, or simply to the person who injured them, saying that the offending action was wrong, has to stop, and should be publicly condemned.

> [Plaintiffs] say that money is not their prime motivation. On the contrary, they believe it often makes more sense in purely economic terms to settle before going to court. But . . . their grievances have turned into matters of principles. And many plaintiffs say they want to "send a message" to the rest of the country.

Stewart, *Seeking Justice: People Prone to Sue Have Many Reasons and Money is But One*, Wall St. J., May 20, 1986, at 1.

However, many litigants express great reluctance to take action against others whose behavior has injured them because they feel that "minding your own business" is an essen-

that too much of modern social interaction is waged by deploying rights in a game which should be, and in the past has been, played outside the legal field. The ability to overcome normative reluctance to take public action and thus the desire to vindicate rights through litigation is seen as a reflection of the decline of traditional sources of authority, indeed a transformation in the valued currencies of social life.[175]

Critics from the political left suggest that the use of rights in contemporary political environments impedes rather than promotes progressive social forces.[176] They argue that rights are incoherent, contradictory, unstable and indeterminate.[177] This critique suggests that rights are abstract and unstable because small changes in circumstances often "make it difficult to sustain the claim that a right remains implicated."[178] Tushnet, for example, maintains that "rights-talk often conceals a claim that things *ought* to be different within an argument that things *are* as the claimant contends."[179] Every situation or setting opens debate anew as to the merits of particular rights claims; there seems to be little generalizability or transferability beyond particular claims. In addition, this critique suggests that the language of rights is so open and indeterminate that competing interests can use similar language to express opposing positions.

A claim of right, this critique asserts, "falsely converts into an empty abstraction . . . real experiences that we ought to value for their own sake."[180] By describing an aspect of experience in the language of rights, we deny and subvert the complexity, ambiguity, and contradiction of social experience. The juridical subject crystallizes experience, not in an authentic form but as a set of alienating abstractions.[181] More-

---

tial ethic in modern urban life. Thus, many grievances are never articulated or acted upon. Miller & Sarat, *supra* note 127. But sometimes the circumstances seem so painful, or so unlikely to change, that plaintiffs overcome the normative reluctance "to go public" with their problems and decide to file suit. Only when talk or avoidance fails do they turn to an outside agency. And when that happens, "the parties no longer wish to settle the dispute by discussion and negotiation. At this point they conceptualize their problem as a principled grievance for which they seek an authoritative and binding solution, not as a conflict of interest in which they have limited and negotiable goals," but as a matter of right and justice. Merry & Silbey, *supra* note 105, at 154.

175. "The father, the priest, the prison warden—they've all suffered a decline in public confidence. But the federal judge has gained in stature. People file lawsuits," according to Lawrence Friedman, "because they have confidence in the legal system." L. FRIEDMAN, *supra* note 17 (quoted in Stewart, *supra* note 174).

176. Tushnet, *An Essay on Rights*, 61 TEX. L. REV. 1363 (1984).

177. *See* Singer, *The Players and the Cards*, 94 YALE L.J. 997 (1984).

178. Tushnet, *supra* note 176, at 1363.

179. *Id.* at 1371 (emphasis added).

180. *Id.* at 1364.

181. Kennedy, *Form and Substance in Private Law Adjudication*, 89 HARV. L. REV. 1685 (1976).

Marx described the alienated self as a product of the liberal state's denial to each of us of our species membership, and the institutionalization of an isolating loneliness that is then justified as human nature. The liberal state, he argued, abolished distinctions based upon birth, social rank, education, and occupation when it declared, as it did in the American Declaration of Independence or the French Rights of Man, that all men are created equal. The liberal state assured to each citizen the equal right to participate in the collective sovereignty and denied the relevance of birth, social rank, education and occupation

over, rights talk defines a sphere of allegedly individuated actions without acknowledging the social context which produces and nurtures the individual. Rights constitute the juridical subject by constructing boundaries between persons while denying the arbitrariness and violence of those boundaries. More importantly, rights discourse suggests that painful existential contradictions, the problem of being in but not totally within society, the necessity but abhorrence of others, the reliance upon sociality for meaning at the same time as we are dominated by its power, have been resolved.[182]

The entrance of disputing and dispute processes, as well as the ADR movement, into both the institutional and disciplinary domains of the legal field advances, as well as depends upon, such criticisms of rights. There is a way in which some forms of rights-talk, especially the dialogic concept of rights, as well as some of the critiques of rights, especially those which point to the alienating consequences of rights, seem

---

to that participation. However, far from denying the importance of these distinctions, Marx argued, the liberal state presupposed and institutionalized these distinctions by relegating inequalities of birth, social rank, education and occupation to protected status in the realm of civil society, liberalism creates a fundamental schism between man (in civil society) and citizen (in the state) which is naturalized in the conception of universal and fundamental human rights. The liberal state, Marx argued, derived its raison d'etre—the protection of the fundamental rights of man—by cabining the material inequality of civil society. As a consequence, Marx wrote, the citizen lived in a state organized by a set of "privatized" relationships which it claimed—through the conception of rights—were beyond the state to affect. Rights, in this conception, are the means by which participation is organized but they could not provide fundamental and "real" emancipation; here, rights are creations of the liberal state and the means of alienating the individual from his species consciousness—life in civil society.

Following this tradition, Gabel defines alienation as a "paradoxical form of reciprocity between two beings who desire authentic contact with each other and yet at the same time deny this very desire in the way they act toward one another." Gabel, *The Phenomenology of Rights-Consciousness and the Pact of the Withdrawn Selves*, 62 TEX. L. REV. 1563, 1567 (1984). He argues that individuals desire intersubjective recognition—authentic connection—but deny this desire as they confront others across a "forbidding distance." As a consequence, the individual "withdraws her own self and adopts a false self," with which she confronts and interacts in the world. Thus we live in a world in which we perpetually feel "at once unconnected to everyone else and yet anxiously committed to the pretense of connection that is manifested in the reciprocity of roles." *Id.* at 1573. Rights provide a basis for denying this dilemma. They become part of the stories we tell ourselves about how we are collectively constituted, yet remain individuals.

182. Thus, critics assert, rights-talk is fundamentally mystifying. It masks the ambiguity it reproduces, incorporating its partiality in claims of universality. More importantly, it silences opposition by encouraging people to think that so long as rights are protected, and argued about through "non-political" legal processes, that political action aimed at transforming the content of those rights is misplaced and illegitimate. Rights-consciousness mystifies because it is portrayed as the complete and total embodiment of rights as well as the process for validating rights-claims. Thus law supplants the ideals for which it is an incomplete, partial, and distorted substitute. Moreover, rights-talk tends to blind us to social problems for which no rights currently exist and to focus attention on the absence of legal remedies rather than on the organization of social problems. M. KELMAN, A GUIDE TO CRITICAL LEGAL STUDIES 275 (1987). Rights-talk has historically developed a particular tautological formulation in which rights exist only in so far as remedies exist; where there is no remedy, there is no right. *Cf.* O. HOLMES, *supra* note 68. In the absence of remedy and right, "there is no significant interest to vindicate," and the "absence of a ready legal solution becomes confused with the absence of a significant social problem; the world appears perfect . . . because our tools for further perfecting it are so dull." M. KELMAN, *supra*, at 276.

to advance ADR by pointing out the importance of attending to very basic forms of human connection and communication. Thus, one can easily imagine the heady confidence that might develop by throwing off the entire mantle and burden of rights-talk and trying to reconceptualize the nature of the juridical subject. There are indeed moments in the movement for ADR when one can detect this kind of passion for going beyond modest tinkering with new procedures by reimagining the grounds on which persons interact and relate to legal institutions.

There is also a degree to which the ADR movement fails to engage the critique of rights. ADR advances a non-rights based conception of the juridical subject, one that neither the dialogic conception of rights, nor the phenomenological critique of alienation can fully capture. Eschewing rights, ADR proponents deploy the discourse of interests and needs. They reconceptualize the person from a carrier of rights to a subject with needs and problems, and in the process hope to move the legal field from a terrain of authoritative decision making where force is deployed to an arena of distributive bargaining and therapeutic negotiation.

From Rights to Interests

Disputing and dispute processing, as portrayed in some parts of the ADR movement and by some social scientists, reconceptualize the juridical subject by emphasizing interests and preferences as the grounds on which individuals relate to legal authorities. By moving their focus from rights to a concern with interests, advocates of dispute resolution build on the work of those American legal realists, who having exposed conventional rights-talk as just so much "transcendental nonsense,"[183] tried to build a realistic jurisprudence through closer attention to interests.[184]

Although Llewellyn advocated a move from rights to interests as a move toward realism in law, he recognized that interest as a fundamental category for legal decision making would be no more objective than using rights as a fundamental category. His reasoning was straightforward: At first, legal thinkers believed that the rules of law specified the remedies which law would make available to a litigant. The rules of law were statements governing the specific ways one man might get courts to deal with another man. Later legal writers regarded this as primitive and realized that the remedies made available through law served social,

183. Cohen, *Transcendental Nonsense and the Functional Approach*, 35 COLUM. L. REV. 309 (1935).

184. Llewellyn, *supra* note 99. The methodological advice of the realists was to maintain, at all times, a healthy skepticism, a skepticism about the adequacy of legal concepts and received categories for ordering social phenomenon, and about the tendency of categories "to take on the appearance of solidity, reality and inherent value which has no foundation in experience." *Id.* Thus by urging attention to interests, Llewellyn made no claim to remove the fundamental inadequacies and ambiguities clouding conventional legal categories and reasoning; he meant only to promote a form of legal analysis that would invite discovery of those inadequacies.

not merely individual, purposes. In this move, the rules of law articulated protected purposes, claims and values which remedies were meant to realize. The move to rights, however, created fundamental and irreducible ambiguities, some of which we discussed above.

Identifying interests as a basis of law would not, Llewellyn argued, remove such ambiguity. While interests emphasized more strongly the social purposes which rights served, "we do not know what interests are."[185] With the move to interests, he argued, law achieved not greater clarity but a more complete and honest subjectivity. Nonetheless, Llewellyn believed that a focus upon interests would do better than rights in encouraging lawyers and judges to pay homage to law as,

> something manmade, something capable of criticism, of change, of reform—and capable of criticism, change and reform not only according to standards found inside the law itself . . . but also according to standards vastly more vital *outside* law itself, in the society law purports both to govern *and to serve*.[186]

Although the attribution of social interest necessarily involved value judgments, Llewellyn claimed that it nonetheless isolated these judgments from the observed phenomenon on which they rested. Attention to interests, he argued, pushed legal inquiry into a more pronounced and self-conscious attention to behavior, empirical data, facts, "the actual doings of judges and the effects of their doings on the data claimed to represent an interest."[187] Interests seemed to more forthrightly demand and empower empirical demonstration and would therefore provide the basis for a more realistic legal science.

The work of Vilhelm Aubert constructed a bridge between the realists' formulation of the role of interests in law and ADR's conception of disputes as conflicts of interests.[188] Aubert, a Norwegian sociologist of law, described two forms of conflict which he characterized as competition and dissensus. The former referred to conflicts of interest that derived from situations of scarcity in which two or more actors desired or valued the same thing. Such conflicts were resolvable, he argued, through the market or through mechanisms which compromised the demands, gains, and losses to each side. Because differences between the parties were not differences of commitment or ethics, but arose instead from competition over scarce resources, they could be resolved by mechanisms which "minimize[d] the likelihood of maximal loss" to each side. Conflicts of interest, he continued, "emphasized the similarity of the contestants, their common needs and aspirations."[189]

In contrast, conflicts of value arose not from competition but from disagreements "concerning the normative status of a social object."[190]

185. *Id.*
186. *Id.*
187. *Id.*
188. Aubert, *Competition and Dissensus: Two Types of Conflict and Conflict Resolution*, 7 J. Conflict Resolution 26 (1963).
189. *Id.* at 29.
190. *Id.*

According to Aubert there was nothing in dissensus that should lead people to attack one another; nonetheless, it is apparent that conflicts of value do often lead to serious and violent aggression.[191] Although he was skeptical that conflicts of value could be resolved or compromised in the ways conflicts of interest could, he suggested that successful conflict resolution might depend upon the "interrelations between the dissensus and the interests of the parties."[192] Furthermore, he suggested that for dissensus and conflicts of value, law and courts would provide the most appropriate mode of conflict resolution.

Aubert's analysis was cautiously framed; he noted that although there was a correspondence between the sources of conflict (interests and values) and mechanisms of conflict resolution (bargaining and law), there was no reason to assume that the source or type of conflict would fully determine the appropriate mechanism. He hypothesized that the invocation of law and judicial conflict resolution would, however, transform conflicts of interest into dissensus and conflicts of value, and suggested that the dyadic relationship between disputing parties became in the legal process a triad with the possibilities of resolution constructed out of the probable alliances between the third party and one of the disputants.[193]

Aubert's analysis laid a theoretical foundation for alternative dispute resolution. He argued that so long as conflicts of interest could be kept uncontaminated by dissensus and normative objectification through law, compromise solutions were possible. Solutions to such conflicts would necessarily involve what he called "a natural adjustment of needs"[194] because no grounds existed for differentiating better or worse, right or wrong, true or false values. Judges, in his view, lacked rational grounding for their normative decisions. Against this background, proponents of ADR have argued that law fails to take account of disputants interests. It necessarily abstracts and objectifies their situations by transforming conflicts of interest into conflicts of value which are, in the end, resolved by raw power rather than reason or truth.[195]

---

191. The classic statement of the view that disagreements of value, that is, basic fundamental moral disagreements, cannot be settled by argument was presented by Ayer. A. AYER, LANGUAGE, TRUTH, AND LOGIC 51 (1936). *Cf.* C. STEVENSON, ETHICS AND LANGUAGE (1944). The position is sometimes referred to as emotivism, suggesting that value statements are expressions of emotion and disagreement is non-cognitive.

192. Aubert, *supra* note 188, at 30.

193. Aubert wrote:

> The clash of interests is now formulated as a disagreement concerning either certain facts in the past or concerning what norms apply to the existing state of affairs or both, in a way which often makes it hard to distinguish clearly between questions of fact and questions of law. *The needs of the parties, their wishes for the future, cease to be relevant to the solution.* Whether the solution harmonizes two contrasting sets of needs and plans for the future is no longer material. *The problem has become objectified in the sense that a solution can be reached by an outsider who knows the rules of evidence and is able to perform logical manipulations within a normative structure.*

Id. at 30.

194. *Id.* at 34.

195. Aubert's analysis suggested that successful dispute resolution should respond to the parties' interests and needs, which after all was, from the perspective of legal realism, the real foundation of law, remedies and rights. Moreover, his analysis alluded to the

Aubert's work was published just as anthropological and cross cultural studies of disputing were becoming well known, at a time when social scientists were becoming more actively engaged in legal scholarship, and attention to disputes was becoming prominent in the legal field. Aubert offered an analysis which explained why forms of dispute resolution observed in small scale societies of Africa, central Asia and central America worked as they did. Mediation, negotiation, and other processes of informal dispute resolution based upon compromise and conciliation succeeded, following Aubert's analysis, because they addressed conflicts of interest without transforming them into conflicts of value or institutionalizing responses through formal law.[196]

Over the next two decades Aubert's analysis has become orthodox. Courts are, ADR promoters claim, preoccupied with rights talk, while mediation, negotiation and other forms of alternative dispute resolution encourage disputants to think in terms of interests.[197] Descriptions of the mediation process, guides for practitioners and training manuals for students repeatedly describe mediation as a process designed to eluci-

possibilities for processes of conflict resolution which might increase opportunities for autonomous decision making while limiting the scope of authoritative social control. Aubert suggested that conflict resolution ought to, by definition, "harmonize two contrasting sets of needs and plans." Modes of resolution which focused upon the conflicts of interest, eschewed concern with normative valuations, judgments of right and wrong, assignment of blame, and pronouncements of innocence would, it followed, be able to compromise differences and address the "needs and interests" of the parties. *Id.*

196. Three years after Aubert's article appeared, Torstein Eckhoff published a paper in which he elaborated the implications of Aubert's analysis, with specific reference to the roles of mediator and judge. *See* Eckhoff, *supra* note 57. Eckhoff began his paper by defining mediation as the process of "influencing the parties to come to an agreement by appealing to their own interests." The mediator, according to Eckhoff, works on in order disputants to give more weight to their common interests or less consideration to their competing interests. Although mediators do not have to promote compromise solutions, Eckhoff suggested mediators would normally do so because it added to their prestige as moderate and reasonable third parties. Eckhoff acknowledged that mediators might use threats of sanction if the parties did not seem anxious or willing to settle and mediators might also mobilize normative rules as a means of urging parties to renounce unreasonable demands. If, however, the parties acknowledged common norms but disagreed as to the particular applicability of a norm, or as to the way in which the norm might be used to resolve the current dispute, then mediation was less likely to succeed. Thus Eckhoff reiterated Aubert's observation, which he also supported by references to anthropological studies of disputing, that disagreements about norms were generally unsuitable for mediation. He also emphasized the fact that both mediators and judges needed to be seen as neutral to be effective in their roles, but nonetheless drew on different sources of authority and prestige and were therefore unlikely to be combined well in one office.

Following Aubert, Eckhoff distinguished the judge from the mediator by associating the judge with the domain of norms rather than interests. As a result he identified several important differences in the two methods of conflict resolution. The mediator is looks forward, explores a variety of possible solutions, is generally adaptable, cooperative and constructive. The judge, on the other hand, looks backward toward events already past, determins or allocats rights and responsibilities, and abandons the contest and the parties once this function was performed. The judge speaks with authority but has less of an investment in resolving disputes. *Id.*

197. Economic analysis of law constitutes the juridical subject in similar terms. Instead of interests, economic analysis speaks in terms of preferences. Disputes are understood to arise as rational utility maximizers; each pursue optimizing strategies. Appropriate resolutions facilitate the movement of resources to their most highly valued use; they ape the free market, and are, as a result, efficient. *See* M. POLINSKY, AN INTRODUCTION TO LAW AND ECONOMICS (1983).

date disputants' interests while developing options to meet those interests. For example, Patton reminds students that the overall goals of mediation remain constant despite variations in practice; those goals are "to help parties separate relationship from substance, to elucidate their interests, and to focus their attention on options that take into account both sides' interests and on independent objective standards for choosing among such options."[198]

Ury, Brett and Goldberg argue that mediation can be understood as an effort to change the frame of dispute resolution from power and rights to interests.[199] They suggest that interest based claims say "I want it;"[200] and thus framing disputes in terms of interests "tends over a series of disputes to generate the highest level of mutual satisfaction with outcomes."[201] This is because wants and interests constitute the real motivation for claims, while rights are merely justifications. "Another way of saying this" they write, "is that focusing on interests deals directly with the problem that led to the dispute in the first place in a way that focusing on rights and power cannot."[202] The juridical subject is thus constituted as a bearer of desires or preferences who is forced, when dealing with judicial institutions, to speak a "foreign language" instead of the more natural language of interests.[203]

In this analysis, disputes arise from conflicts of interest that frustrate the satisfaction of wants and desires. The disputing process can be modeled, following this approach, as a series of "dispute decisions" designed to maximize the free exchange of individuated wants, perceptions and resources.[204] Although it borrows from standard conceptions

---

198. B. Patton, A Brief Outline of the Mediation Process 2 (1982) (unpublished manuscript). *But see* Susskind & Madigan, *New Approaches to Resolving Disputes in the Public Sector*, 9 JUST. SYS. J. 179 (1984).

199. W. Ury, J. Brett & S. Goldberg, Into the Fray 2-25 (1987) (unpublished manuscript).

200. *Id.* at 2-3.

201. *Id.* at 2-20.

202. *Id.* at 2-19.

203. Contemporary promoters of ADR try to overcome what Llewellyn thought was the necessary subjectivity in the concept of "interest" by following lines of Aubert's analysis and converting interests into economic commodities which can be measured by objective criteria. *See* Llewellyn, *supra* note 99. Thus, Fisher and Ury include within their five rules of successful interest-based negotiation the need to separate the people from the problem, to focus on interests and not positions, to invent options for mutual gain, and to insist on objective criteria. Raiffa also urges mediators to help parties seek joint gains as well as "derive responsible reservation prices." Mediators are urged to develop objective standards for discussing the terms of a negotiation, for measuring the interests and demands of the parties, and for assessing compliance with settlements. *See* H. RAIFFA, THE ART AND SCIENCE OF NEGOTIATION (1982).

204. Trubek, *supra* note 118, at 496-98. Trubek describes the "interdisciplinary" model adopted by the Civil Litigation Project as follows:

> Our working theory can be described as a "modified stakes" model of dispute decision-making. We began by focusing on the decisions made by disputants. To explain these choices, we took the economic model, illustrated by Johnson (1980-81) and Gollop-Marquardt (1980-81), as a starting point and assumed that a major determinant of decision-making in a case would be the relationship between what the parties perceived to be at stake and their estimates of the costs of various dispute choices (Posner, 1977). Parties would invest in litigation and other forms of dispute processing as long as the expected gain (or loss reduction) exceeded

of economic markets, this rational-choice model of disputing adds to the usual economic variables factors describing the nature of the relationship between the parties, personal and organizational characteristics, the professional organization of legal resources, and a "series of factors related to the type of dispute itself, including areas of law, legal complexity, forum."[205] At the heart of the dispute decision model is the conception of the dispute as an arena of competitive decision making by rationally calculating individuals motivated by utility maximization.[206] The model predicts that disputants will respond enthusiastically, that is, rationally, when presented with more efficient fora in which to negotiate their interests. Thus when disputants did not turn voluntarily or in large numbers to newly created, supposedly less expensive and more efficient alternatives to the courts,[207] promoters suggested that it must be because the parties lacked sufficient knowledge or were actively discouraged from making informed and rational choices.[208] In this economic/interest model, more information and "freedom" from the pressure of legal institutions and ideology should correct for "irrational" choices.[209] Cost reduction and party satisfaction become the benchmarks of negotiated justice and ADR, objective measures of the ability of various processes to serve disputants' interests.

Moving to Needs

The image of the juridical subject in dispute processing discourse is not fully captured through the language of commodification or the appropriation of economic metaphors. The constitution of the subject in ADR is elaborated further in other descriptions of the purpose of negotiation and dispute processing. Those descriptions focus on needs and, in so doing, portray ADR not as a response to socially located and con-

---

> the cost. They would prefer the choice that offered the highest ratio of expected return to estimated expenditure. Incorporating non-monetary goals and costs, however, presented significant difficulties.

Id. at 498. *See* R. Posner, Economic Analysis of Law (2d ed. 1977); Gollop & Marquardt, *A Macroeconomic Model of Household Choice*, 15 Law & Soc'y Rev. 611 (1980-81); Johnson, *Lawyer's Choice*, 15 Law & Soc'y Rev. 567 (1980-81).

205. Trubek, *supra* note 118, at 498-99.

206. *See* Merry & Silbey, *supra* note 105 (for an extended criticism of the concept of disputing as rational choice decision making).

207. *See* C. Harrington, *supra* note 13; Harrington, *The Politics of Participation and Non-Participation in Dispute Processes*, 6 Law & Pol'y Q. 203 (1984).

208. *See* Pearson, *An Evaluation of Alternatives to Court Adjudication*, 7 Just. Sys. J. 420 (1982).

209. Although the model of disputing as a form of rational optimizing behavior drew most prominently from models associated with economic transactions, it also built upon game theory and strategic analysis which has been used in a variety of settings including international relations and labor management as well as commercial disputes. *See* Kidder, *supra* note 132, at 717. Cain and Kulczar comment upon a particular irony, however, in the use of the dispute model by liberal and moderate reformers who "end up with a more economic-determinist interpretation than any contemporary Marxist scholar would adopt." *See* Cain and Kulczar, *supra* note 134, at 381. Here, "knowledge (ideology) and organization (politics), when reduced to quantitative dimensions which are, furthermore independent of each other, become facets of an equally quantitative dimension called money (economy)." *Id.* at 380.

structed demands but rather to essential human requisites and capacities. One begins to see this movement in discussions of what are called underlying interests.[210] Interests articulated as wants, preferences, or desires, may not fully constitute a disputant's "real" interests, and successful dispute resolution must explore more fundamental, deep-seated matters.

Some proponents of ADR warn that dispute processing should not be exclusively centered upon each party's strategies for optimizing their interests.[211] In place of this limited focus third parties "can more effectively accomplish their goals by focusing on the parties' *actual objectives* and creatively attempting to *satisfy the needs of both* parties."[212] What is called "problem-solving" negotiation tries to explore disputants' needs where "adversarial negotiation" speaks only of articulated interests. Thus, Menkel-Meadow suggests that dispute resolution should be designed to meet what she calls the parties' "total set of 'real' needs . . . in both the short and long term."[213]

While Menkel-Meadow talks about disputants in terms of needs, her understanding of needs remains quite narrow. By needs, she says she means only something other, or more, than a legally justifiable claim.[214]

---

210. *See* W. Ury, J. Brett & S. Goldberg, *supra* note 199.

211. *See* Menkel-Meadow, *Toward Another View of Legal Negotiation: The Structure of Problem Solving*, 31 UCLA L. Rev. 754 (1984).

212. *Id.* at 758 (emphasis added).

213. *Id.* at 760. Menkel-Meadow offers six additional criteria for successful ADR:

> Does the solution promote the relationship the client desires with the other party? Have the parties explored all the possible solutions that might either make each better off or one party better off with no adverse consequences to the other party? Has the solution been achieved at the lowest possible transaction costs relative to the desirability of the result? Is the solution achievable or has it only raised more problems that need to be solved? Are the parties committed to the solution so it can be enforced without regret? Has the solution been achieved in a manner congruent with the client's desire to participate in and affect the negotiation? Is the solution "fair" and "just"? Have the parties considered the legitimacy of each others claims and made any adjustments they feel are humanely or morally indicated?

Id. at 760-61. She claims that her criteria, with the exception of the last, are utilitarian; that is, she argues that legal negotiations that meet these standards will produce agreements that are "more satisfactory to the parties, thus enhancing commitment to and enforcement of the agreement." *Id.* at 761.

214. Menkel-Meadow writes: "Problem solving is an orientation to negotiation which focuses on finding solutions to the parties' sets of underlying needs and objectives." She elaborates this by stating: "By 'real' problem or objective I mean that which the client wants to accomplish, not how those needs are translated into legal remedies. In disputes it is often useful to look not only at what the dispute is about," here she seems to mean legally possible or probable remedies, "but what brought the parties into a relationship in the first place." *Id.* at 794 & n. 155.

There is an interesting tension in her analysis which imagines very different grounds for negotiation than those we have conventionally institutionalized through adjudication and negotiation, new grounding in the attention to "total needs, goals and objectives"; at the same time, she seems to worry that she has bitten off too much and retreats by creating a strawperson of conventional legal negotiation. In Menkel-Meadow's analysis, adversarial negotiations use law, legal claims, and arguments, as chips to meet disputants' interests. However, she mistakes the chips that are bartered, for the goals—that is, winning the negotiation—and thus imagines the goal of adversarial negotiation to be the successful staking of a legal claim. It is against this reified version of negotiation that she can offer attention to "needs" as something distinct from legal "interests" while simultaneously de-

Despite the limitations of her analysis, it nonetheless signifies an important movement in dispute processing discourse which reconceptualizes the focus of disputes from conventional legal claims of right, beyond utilitarian demands of interest, to both relational and therapeutic understandings of need. The fundamental premise of this analysis is that disputants share certain essential human needs and that attention to those needs will reveal grounds of interdependence, reciprocity, and compatibility which are masked, if not explicitly denied, in adversarial proceedings.

The analysis of need begins with the assumption that "not all needs will be mutually exclusive."[215] By identifying underlying needs, negotiators, according to Menkel-Meadow, can identify shared purposes that would be collapsed in the specification of legal remedies and, in so doing, open up possibilities for solutions that meet both parties' needs.[216] The notion of a satisfactory resolution is not compromise between antithetical preferences. It requires, instead, penetration to the layer of shared attributes and common needs in which the juridical subject is constituted by allegedly universal and invariant human attributes.

In their effort to create effective problem solving mechanisms rather than adversarial claims adjustment systems, proponents identify particular human needs and capacities which they argue are better met by ADR.

---

nying that she is moving beyond more traditional notions of "interest." Thus Menkel-Meadow begins with a narrow reading of the literature on negotiation which explicitly speaks to meeting clients' interests, which she argues means legal interests. Menkel-Meadow then argues that meeting disputants' needs is a way of moving beyond law without stating the terrain to which she is moving— except in a negative way.

215. *Id.* at 795.

216. Menkel-Meadow's premises are justified by reference to Carol Gilligan's work on gender differences in moral reasoning. *See* C. GILLIGAN, IN A DIFFERENT VOICE (1982). Gilligan challenges the necessity and utility of hierarchical and deductive reasoning as a model of problem solving, arguing that it limits the possible solutions and denies the ambiguities, relationships, and attachments which constitute the experience of moral dilemma. She criticizes the way in which dilemmas are traditionally formulated in experiments and public discourse so that right answers demand win or lose solutions. In their place, she urges attention to different ways in which problems can be framed and analyzed to produce shared outcomes. She thus proposes what she considers a feminist conception of moral reasoning, which involves a valorization of relationships, and which demands careful attention to the reciprocal needs which bind the parties or which do not necessarily set them in perfectly opposed positions.

Menkel-Meadow concurs with Gilligan's argument that conventional models of moral reasoning narrow questions and disputes to simplistic bi-polar constructions, ignoring the wider array of contextual frames. In response she identifies five basic categories of need: economic, legal, social (relationships), psychological (feelings, including risk aversion), and ethical or moral (fairness), which more accurately map the terms of social relationships and disputes while expanding the possibilities for types of settlement and satisfaction. She calls for a careful inquiry by attorneys, and by implication, other dispute handlers, concerning the relative weights of these needs, their implications in the short and long run, as well as their manifest or latent status for parties in dispute. She does not, however, provide any suggestions for mediating among competing and incompatible needs but seems to assume that in most cases they can be worked out. She concludes that value differences may persist and keep parties at odds, but insists nonetheless that the attempt to take account of both parties' needs, "regardless of how limited the possible solutions may appear to be [are] far more likely to satisfy the parties and effectuate a more permanent agreement." Menkel-Meadow, *supra* note 211, at 808-09.

For example, both Lincoln[217] and Patton[218] suggest that cooperative styles of dispute resolution and mediation meet people's psychological needs for harmony and peace. Echoing earlier functional theories of disputing, Lincoln says that "most people don't like chaos"[219] and are frustrated by it. Thus, he argues, mediation should begin by engaging disputants in the creation and discovery of ground rules by which to manage the chaos of their dispute situation. "Ventilation" is another necessary part of mediation because it allows the people to air the "few things burning inside them" which they are usually afraid to air because people are generally "afraid to . . . ventilate anger."[220] Others argue that cooperative, problem-solving, alternative dispute resolution mechanisms are more likely to meet human needs for autonomy, integrity and dignity.[221] For these proponents, the development of ADR is part of a rethinking of our entire culture, not only the legal system but the culture of corporations and other institutions in which the social self lives and develops. This argument suggests that our dominant culture and institutions foster orientations and attitudes which work against our real human needs.[222]

New dispute resolution methods promote integrity, it is argued, because they require "enormous personal commitment and commitment to hold one's emotions and ego in check long enough to absorb all sides of a problem."[223] Individuals are invited to accept responsibility for their mistakes, without requiring anyone to suffer for misjudgments and lapses. In contrast to legal procedures which instantiate rights, and traditional negotiations which validate while distributing competitive interests, ADR relies less upon well-defined rules, standards or tactical orchestration developed in those processes, and more explicitly upon the integrity and sense of responsibility of the participants.

Unfortunately, Millhauser argues, some of the unspoken resistance to ADR also derives from "often unstated and sometimes unrecognized human needs and desires,"[224] those same needs and desires which ADR

---

217. *See* W. Lincoln, Mediation (1976).

218. *See* B. Patton, *supra* note 198.

219. W. Lincoln, *supra* note 217, at 15.

220. *Id.* at 16.

221. *See* Millhauser, *The Unspoken Resistance to Alternative Dispute Resolution*, 3 Negotiation J. 29 (1987).

222. The transformation of needs into legal claims involves, in this view, a process in which the individual becomes not merely a client but a dependent of the lawyer who provides not merely a legitimate voice in the process but an authoritative vision of social relations generally. *See* Sarat & Felstiner, *supra* note 116; Sarat & Felstiner, *Law and Strategy in the Divorce Lawyer's Office*, 20 Law & Soc'y Rev. 93 (1986). The client must rely on the lawyer for representation within the legal process and for explanations and interpretations of that process. Along with this very expected advice, however, the client also receives what is experienced as authoritative interpretation of his or her own feelings, wants, and experiences and learns from the lawyer not only what is appropriate behavior in the legal process, but how to understand and interpret other experiences and events. Given this perception of the legal system and legal professionals, ADR is advanced as part of a general strategy of personal empowerment.

223. *See* Millhauser, *supra* note 221.

224. *Id.* at 29.

would work both to satisfy and to change. "Left to their own devices and instincts today, most lawyers and clients will seek to 'win' in a traditional sense," Millhauser says.[225] Those instincts can be transformed, she believes, by recognizing more fundamental needs for trust, cooperation, and relationship. In this view, dispute processing gets to the "core" of human personality and human character; in this view, the right form of disputing processing can encourage disputants to see themselves as essentially similar beings rather than as creatures of irreconcilable rights and interests.

Others link ADR to more comprehensive theories of needs.[226] Some theories rest upon a picture of universal, ontological and generic/genetic human needs transcending observable differences of race, class, or culture, in other words, human needs that transcend variations in norms, laws, social structures and institutions.[227] They speak of dispute resolution as aiding "individuals who seek to fulfill a set of deep-seated, universal needs . . . ."[228]

Based on the work of Robert Ardry, E. O. Wilson in sociobiology, Abraham Maslow in psychology, as well as research in stimulus response behaviorism, Burton[229] and Burton and Sandole,[230] following Sites,[231] postulate nine fundamental human needs which collectively constitute human nature: a need for consistent response, a need for stimulation, a need for security, a need for recognition, a need for distributive justice, a need to appear rational, a need for meaning in response, and a need for role defense, defined as the "protection of means and tactics that

225. *Id.* at 34.

226. *See, e.g.*, J. BURTON, DEVIANCE, TERRORISM AND WAR (1979). Burton provides one of the most synthetic formulations of this type of needs-based approach to dispute resolution which he describes as a Kuhnian "paradigm shift" in the study of conflict and conflict management. *See* T. KUHN, THE STRUCTURE OF SCIENTIFIC REVOLUTIONS (1962). The shift Burton describes moves away from a model of conflict and social exchange based upon power, coercion, and zero-sum calculations, to one based upon problem-solving and "win-win" outcomes. He also moves away from institutional structural analyses which were important in interest-based dispute resolution to a social theory that places primary analytic importance upon the individual.

Avruch and Black challenge Burton's claim that his model constitutes a paradigm shift in studies of conflict. They argue that his emphasis upon individual agency and consciousness instead of social organization and institutions is simply a restatement of the debate between Freud in *Civilization and its Discontents* and Durkheim in *The Rules of the Sociological Method*. A restatement of these arguments, even an elaboration and extension of traditional arguments does not, in Avruch and Black's perspective, constitute a paradigm shift. *See* Avruch & Black, *A Generic Theory of Conflict Resolution: A Critique*, 3 NEGOTIATION J. 87 (1987).

227. This model of conflict, Burton claims, applies to all levels of social exchange—interpersonal, inter-organizational, international—and thus eschews any disciplinary-based (for example, psychological, anthropological, sociological) understandings of conflict which accept or respond to the reality of different levels of social interaction. J. BURTON, *supra* note 226.

228. Avruch & Black, *supra* note 226.

229. *See* J. BURTON, *supra* note 226, at 72-73.

230. *See* Burton & Sandole, *Generic Theory: The Basis of Conflict Resolution*, 2 NEGOTIATION J. 333 (1986).

231. *See* P. SITES, CONTROL: THE BASIS OF SOCIAL ORDER (1973).

actors develop for purposes of protecting and fulfilling needs."[232] "Conflicts," Burton and Sandole argue, "may involve . . . not a clash of basic needs as such but a clash of . . . culturally determined ways in which needs are expressed."[233] Rights talk, for example, is one such culturally determined way of expressing our essential needs. Thus the reconstitution of the juridical subject requires a confrontation with the language of rights which both artificially generates conflict and contributes to human alienation.[234] Proper techniques of conflict management do not just respond to dominant cultural motifs for expressing needs. They transform culture itself by making available "better" modes for expressing and realizing our needs.

This argument suggests that conventional models of conflict begin with erroneous assumptions about scarcity and differences between individuals and groups. As against those assumptions, Burton argues that social goods, associated with the nine basic human needs are not limited and, indeed, may increase through use and exchange.[235] Thus for example, identity, security, and responsiveness, are not, in his view, in short supply and can be increased by greater interaction and exchange. However, positional goods, those attached to specific social roles, for example leadership and prestige, may be in relatively short supply. These are not, however, truly fundamental human needs nor do they respond to basic human nature. Thus persistent conflict is, in this argument, a surface problem, one which is exacerbated through the constitution of the juridical subject in terms of rights or interests. Identification of shared needs provides a basis for the resolution of particular disputes and, more importantly, for building a more harmonious social life.[236]

---

232. Burton & Sandole, *Expanding the Debate on Generic Theory of Conflict Resolution: A Response to a Critique*, 3 NEGOTIATION J. 97 (1987).

233. Burton & Sandole, *supra* note 230, at 343.

234. It is to this type of confrontation that Fiss responds. *See* Fiss, *supra* note 1.

235. J. BURTON, *supra* note 226.

236. Burton and Sandole suggest that the juridical subject as traditionally conceived is based on untested and untheorized assumptions about order, harmony, conformity and the role of law in meeting these needs. The extensive and apparently successful movement for alternative dispute resolution, they claim, signifies a shift away from these conventional, perhaps mythical, understandings to scientifically based explorations of the specific ways in which institutions and motivations can be harmonized with human aspirations. Thus contemporary dispute resolution promises to reconceptualize the juridical subject to conform to the logic and insights of the human sciences. *See* Burton & Sandole, *supra* notes 230, 232.

Milner, Lovaas and Adler describe the prevalence of this conception of human needs in a series of rather diverse ADR programs. They find that the six mediation programs they studied vary in organizational structure and goals and the degree to which the program seeks to transform subject/authority and public/private distinctions in contemporary American society. Nonetheless, they share a common vision of conflict and human needs that transcends the differences between them. *See* N. Milner, K. Lovaas & P. Adler, The Public and the Private in Mediation: The Movement's Own Story (1987) (working paper for Program on Conflict Resolution, University of Hawaii). Milner, Lovaas and Adler argue that the program differences may be homogenized by a "myth of relationships" which conceptualizes human subjectivity in terms of the needs of the private self rather than in terms of entitlements, as in the conception of rights. "Contemporary North American mediation programs may share an overriding singularly unanimous vision of mediation as a discourse in which the language of interdependence, relationships and interests dominate." *Id.* at 26. This "relational language of mediation often stresses the need for the

The Significance of the Shift From Rights to Interests and Needs

Rights, interests and needs appear to derive from, and participate in, different epistemologies and, coincident with those alternative knowledge claims, appear to provide different rationalizations for competing sources of authority. Each vision seems to constitutes a different human subject; each constitutes its own grounds for legitimate legal and political debate and for activity within the legal field. Each, however, displays a similar set of contradictions within itself, and, in so doing, each reinforces, even as it critiques, the claims of the other. Each plays out a set of complicated relationships between and among autonomy and connectedness, self and community.

While the jurisprudence of rights, with its associated focus on courts as the proper institutional location for authoritative interpretations of those rights, has been criticized for expanding the domain of legal authority beyond reason, and for obscuring and mystifying the grounds of human interaction,[237] judgments between conflicting rights both distinguish among alternative moral claims and establish grounds for human connection. Rights arguments carve a space for legitimately generalizing an individual's preferences by saying that what is good for me may also be good for you.[238] Thus in articulating my claim, I stake a claim for you as well.

Although rights talk in its classical formulations may seem to constitute an alienating individualism, as the radical critique suggests, its voice, nonetheless, creates a recognizable way to understand social life, that is, what constitutes "we" rather than solely "me." There is a way in which rights make possible the kind of community, interaction and connection sought in the discourse of needs at the very moment that they seem to encapsulate individuality, separateness and difference. Thus, one might ask, what the movement for ADR offers in place of the contradictions of legal rights? What does the discourse of interests and needs offer as grounds for political debate and social decisions? How does it conceptualize "me" and "we"?

While the critique of rights empowers advocates of ADR, the discourses of interests and needs fail to solve the contradictions of rights talk. At first glance, the turn to interests flattens human interaction to a marketed exchange of preferences[239] while the move to needs suggests a more complex but unfortunately essentialist ground for interaction.

private self to emerge and to be expressed more freely . . . . The myth conceptualizes interactions between parties in terms of their interests rather than in terms of entitlement and obligations." *Id.* at 2. "Subscribers to this myth believe that relationships emphasizing interests rather than rights, bring us closer to ourselves and to valuable cultural tools whose existences have been threatened by modern life." *Id.* at 3. Finally, "decisions based on relationships will be implemented successfully enough to bring about important political and social change." *Id.* at 26. *Cf.* Silbey & Merry, *Mediator Settlement Strategies*, 8 LAW & POL'Y Q. 7 (1986).

237. *See* R. UNGER, POLITICS (1987).

238. *See* Minow, *supra* note 167.

239. *See* M. SANDEL, LIBERALISM AND THE LIMITS OF JUSTICE (1982).

In one vision, the alienating aspects of individual rights are extended so that the juridical subject is not simply treated for limited purposes as an individual but is thoroughly isolated into a set of behavioral responses, wants and preferences. Yet this vision cannot convincingly demonstrate that juridical subjects begin in, or aspire to, a condition of perfect competition for the maximization of those wants and preferences. As Coleman argues, it is equally compatible with the idea that human subjectivity is basically a series of preferences to assume cooperation as the original condition.[240] Thus the conception of the juridical subject in interest terms replicates the contradiction between self and other which plagues the rights conception.[241]

In the move to needs the juridical subject is provided with a more complicated, richer human character. Yet that character stands at some distance from itself and, as a result, presents an incomplete understanding of "real" needs. While we may know what we want, that very knowledge is believed to prevent us from clearly seeing or articulating our needs.[242] As a result, the juridical subject is never complete without an external reference helping to sort out the short-term expression of wants from the long-term recognition of essential needs. Self is again made possible by the mediation of other.

The move to interests makes preferences and wants the basis of the juridical subject and seems to challenge rights discourse's inherent need to generalize or join individual claims in an interactive moral engagement. Interest claims seem both individuated and irreconcilable because human wants are understood to be the constitutive elements of distinct and separate human personalities—no two are ever the same. Personality is, in this view, the unique prism of an ontological, physical individuality which generates competitive and distinct preferences as a direct product of that ontological separateness. The legal field should function in this view to maximize the realization of individual preferences by imposing the fewest possible moral constraints on the allegedly free activities of individuals. The activity of legal professionals should be as much technical or instrumental as moral or philosophical.[243]

Interest-based dispute processing while emphasizing the seemingly irreconcilable individuality of wants and preferences insists upon their compromisability. ADR proponents consider interests, preferences and wants compromisable because interests and wants are understood behaviorally. Wants and preferences are seen as responses to a bundle of ever-changing experiences and stimuli. Those responses are understood as if they were distinct from the social or moral context which gives them meaning and value; only by ignoring that context can interest-based dispute resolution deny to third-party dispute handlers any le-

240. *See* Coleman, *Competition and Cooperation*, 98 ETHICS 76 (1987).

241. *See* Kennedy, *supra* note 181.

242. *See* I. ILLICH, TOWARDS A HISTORY OF NEEDS (1977).

243. *See* B. ACKERMAN, *supra* note 60.

gitimate claim to look behind or beyond the articulated preferences of the disputants.

The focus on interest requires, even as it denies, the exploration of the basis of competing claims and the social or moral grounds which sustain them. Yet it often does not develop a language with which to deal with those issues. It is not surprising, therefore, that the written agreements produced through negotiation and mediation, agreements which articulate the compromises and "shared" interests uncovered and constructed through "creative problem solving," often read like sets of performance instructions and indicators.[244] Such agreements transform structural and normative disputes into behavioral strategies which side-step or ignore the sources of difference[245] even as they flatten the basis

244. *See* Nelken, *The Use of "Contracts" as a Social Work Technique*, in CURRENT LEGAL PROBLEMS (1987).

245. Kolb reports on the ways in which organizational ombudsmen, charged with mediating conflicts within formal organizations such as corporations and universities, pacify complainants by removing them from their situations of distress. *See* Kolb, *Corporate Ombudsmen in Organizational Conflict Resolution*, 31 J. CONFLICT RESOLUTION 673 (1987). Ombudsman routinely arrange transfers of employees from one department to another when employees report situations of conflict, harassment, inefficiency, neglect of duty and the like. The ombudsman becomes the mechanism for legitimating and facilitating exit and avoidance. *Cf.* A. HIRSCHMAN, EXIT, VOICE AND LOYALTY (1970); Felstiner, *Influences of Social Organizations on Dispute Processing*, 9 LAW & SOC'Y REV. 63 (1974). Moreover, the ombudsman's ability to act is predicated upon strict confidentiality and an explicit agreement that the ombudsman will deal only with parties who voluntarily seek the ombudsman's help. Therefore, the relevant parties and interests for the ombudsman must be limited to the situation presented to the third party. It follows that no records are kept, and no patterns of complaint can be constructed in order to respond to systemic sources of dispute. *Cf.* Abel, *supra* note 93; Silbey, *supra* note 97. Such interest focused negotiation turns all disputes into problems of behavior. Silbey and Merry describe the ways in which differences in cultural expectations about what constitutes a good person or what is required to be a neighbor, are transformed in mediation into instructions about how to behave when these disagreements prove unavoidable. Since the mediator cannot ally with one or another conception of the good wife or the good father, and the parties have not been able to agree about what is required for these roles, the solution is an agreement about what to do when disagreements become unendurable. Silbey & Merry, *supra* note 236.

The behaviorizing consequences of ADR are seen most clearly in interpersonal disputes. It has been observed repeatedly, for example, that in labor negotiation and mediation, the field of ADR with the longest and most respected history, the employment relationship has been reduced to a set of behavioral rules. Rather than a discourse about how we might organize materials and manpower to sustain and improve human life, employment and production has been turned, in Dunlop's phrase, into a "web of rules" about hours, pay and working conditions. Although it is widely reported that shortly after World War II, Walter Reuther, at the time head of the United Auto Workers, asked the management of General Motors to enter a partnership with labor to develop methods of more efficient automobile production, or at least to discuss a variety of means of organizing that production. General Motors considered those issues irrelevant to labor/management negotiations. *Cf.* H. KATZ, CHANGING GEARS (1985).

Kolb describes in great detail the ways in which labor negotiations turn the employment relationship into a set of measures and behavioral instructions. *See* D. KOLB, THE MEDIATORS (1985). She describes how negotiations are orchestrated to produce settlements by ignoring, and sometimes denying, the framework of assumptions which allows the negotiations to continue and by removing from contention the issues which cannot be transformed into commodity and behavioral exchanges. Kolb's work describes how mediators who work for a federal mediation agency organize their work—the scheduling of meetings, the appropriate topics of conversation, the dimensions of better or worse agreements—on the basis of a set of cognitive maps which define for them the meaning of labor

of connection which make them possible.

Because the constitution of the juridical subject in terms of needs seems to assert the existence and primacy of an historically developed but nonetheless essential human nature,[246] it appears rooted in a search

negotiation. The mediator's activities take place within a framework of assumptions about the relative roles and rights of capital and labor, the appropriate issues for negotiation, and the place of the state in these relationships. This ideology of free collective bargaining assumes the legitimacy of strikes in labor conflict and denies a legitimate role for government or any outsider in collective bargaining. Although these issues frame the negotiations, they are never explicitly discussed and the negotiations become a process of trading chips that never threaten to expose the lines of cleavage and disagreement. These frames, both at the industry level and the macro-sociological level, constrain both the methods and issues in negotiation, although they never surface for discussion. The history of labor negotiations thus becomes a story of the ways in which contested moral ground can be denied and excluded by effective dispute resolution.

Many proponents of interest-based negotiation deny the charge that attention to "interest" necessarily leads to disaggregation, individuated or merely behavioral responses. They argue that the negotiator must encourage the parties to explore a wide range of possible interests and must delve beneath surface preferences. As we have already seen, advocates of ADR claim that the process of dispute resolution itself encourages a readjustment of personal values and attitudes as well as behavior. But this concern to guard against the narrowing conceptions of articulated wants and preferences raises troublesome issues about the authority and legitimacy of the third-party dispute handler. At what point is this person a facilitator of communication between the parties and at what point does this facilitation become instruction and leadership? Moreover, what set of professional norms, and what social theories, govern the mediator's exploration and possible construction of underlying interests? If third parties lead disputants to places, claims, and values, that the parties had not themselves articulated or been conscious of, how can one claim that the third party lacks power? If the mediator's social and economic theories about what constitutes underlying interests shape the manner in which the dispute is understood by the parties, what is the distinction between informal dispute resolution and formal dispute resolution through law? Are third parties exercising authority and power without accountability? Are third parties practicing law without rights? Or are they possibly practicing politics without a constituency? *Cf.* Mather & Yngvesson, *supra* note 116.

The responses move in two directions. In one approach, third party mediators are advised to develop criteria of fairness and justice by which to assess the quality of negotiations and agreements; they are encouraged to develop a moral discourse about mediation. Thus in various descriptions of public issue negotiation, Susskind suggests a set of questions which third party facilitators should address to determine whether interests have really been met, to make sure they have successfully delved beneath surface claims so that the solutions achieved meet the real interests of the parties. *See* L. SUSSKIND & J. CRUIKSHANK, BREAKING THE IMPASSE: CONSENSUAL APPROACHES TO RESOLVING PUBLIC DISPUTES (1987). These questions or criteria for professional mediation of public disputes constitute, without so naming them, a jurisprudence of mediation. They lack, however, any mechanism for checking the individual mediator's performance or holding the mediator accountable for her personal assessments of fairness and justice. Moreover, the moral discourse of mediation is conceived of as a personal morality of professional mediators and as a standard for professional achievement. The second direction in which interests are pushed beyond articulated preferences and wants, side-steps the criticisms and calls for responsiveness by dispute handlers to parties' fundamental needs.

246. Ignatieff's conception of "need" points to essential elements of human subjectivity, but posits these as nonetheless historical and relative. We create needs for ourselves; "we are the only species with the capacity to create and transform our needs, the only species whose needs have a history." M. IGNATIEFF, THE NEEDS OF STRANGERS (1984). Thus the only needs which we can specify are those "absolute prerequisites for any human pursuit . . . because whatever we choose to do with our lives, we can scarcely be reconciled to ourselves and to others without them." *Id.* at 14.

> In the end, a theory of human needs has to be premised on some set of choices about what humans need in order to be human; not what they need to be happy or free, since these are subsidiary goals, but what they need in order to realize the full extent of their potential. There cannot be any eternally valid account of what

for objectivity that is absent in the analysis of wants, desires and preference. Moreover, the force of a needs claim derives in part from that perceived objectivity.[247] Although some welfare economists claim that the only thing that ultimately matters is the satisfaction of wants, proponents of needs discourse argue that something much more basic is at stake. In making such an argument, Thompson for example, suggests that the failure to meet needs implies serious harm;[248] harm cannot be defined in terms of either actual desires or well-informed wants, the grounds of utilitarian reasoning, because we can need something without knowing that we do.[249] Here again we see the external, objective perspective which informs needs discourse, a perspective which suggests the radical incompleteness of the juridical subject.[250]

Although needs discourse describes a dependent juridical subject, public discourse about needs points to much more than the basic necessities of survival. "To define human nature in terms of needs is to define what we are in terms of what we lack, to insist on the distinctive emptiness and incompleteness of humans as a species."[251] The discourse of needs portrays the human tragedy wherein the spiral of created, recreated and escalated needs render subjects impotent to meet needs of which they are aware only when they are connected to others. The lack of that connection stimulates the recognition of the need.

Needs talk in politics or dispute resolution thus generates at least two types of dependency. There is the logical, syntactical dependency which Nancy Frazer describes as "in order to" statements.[252] Needs

---

> it means to be human. All we have to go on is the historical record of what men have valued most in human life.

Id. at 15.

247. *Cf.* D. Braybrooke, Meeting Needs (1987); D. Wiggins, Needs, Values, Truth (1987).

248. *See* G. Thomson, Needs (1987).

249. Thus Thompson argues that the normative claim of need is much stronger than a claim for wants because desires are clearly not preemptory in the way that harm is. Brian Barry writes that "we tend to think that needs possess a kind of preemptory status that mere desires lack; if you say you need something you seem to be presenting a weightier claim than if you say you want it." *See* Barry, *Priorities of the Selfgovliset*, N.Y. Times, Feb. 5, 1988, Literary Supplement, at 140. Further, Wiggins provides an elaborated version of the absolute or normative claim of need: "The thought we have now arrived at is that a person needs *x* [absolutely] if and only if . . . he will be harmed if he goes without *x*." D. Wiggins, *supra* note 247, at 14. His discussion explores the ways needs are entrenched within future expectations, are substitutable, immediate and urgent, basic, etcetera.

250. The discourse of "interests" suggests no such incompleteness: No one can know my wants or preferences better than I. Thus it makes no sense to suggest that in the articulation of those preferences I am in any way dependent on others.

251. *See* M. Ignatieff, *supra* note 246, at 14.

> Rights language offers a rich vernacular for the claims an individual may make on or against the collectivity, but it is relatively impoverished as a means of expressing individual's needs for the collectivity. It can only express the human ideal of fraternity as mutual respect for rights, and it can only defend the claim to be treated with dignity in terms of our common identity as rights-bearing creatures. Yet we are more than rights-bearing creatures and there is more to respect in a person than his rights . . . . It is because money cannot buy the human gestures which confer respect, nor rights guarantee them as entitlements, that any decent society requires a public discourse about the needs of the human person.

Id. at 13.

252. *See* N. Frazer, Talking About Needs: Cultural Constructions of Political Conflict in

have a relational structure, "x needs y in order to," describing needs claims as a nested series or chains of such "in order to" statements. Thus needs, in contrast to the things needed, are "states of dependency which have as their proper object things x needed."[253] However, there is also a material and behavioral dependency which develops historically through the social and political creation of needs. Offers of help and provision of service create needs, discourage self reliance, and thus foster a sense of incompetence and dependency.[254]

But the discourse of need, even as it establishes human interdependence, creates a domain of independent authority for those who specify and service human needs.[255] By asserting the existence of shared and objective grounds for dispute resolution, the concept of need denies legitimacy to those who disagree about what is needed, or who is needy, while empowering those who work within the "uncontested" arena. By mobilizing the discourse of need, proponents of ADR remove specific areas of human interaction from political and moral argument, or what appears to be interminable and ineffective debate, and in so doing empower alleged experts. Thus needs discourse, like the discourses of rights and interests, embodies claims to both connection and separateness.

The movement from rights to interests might have exaggerated the political dimensions and inefficiencies of dispute resolution by challenging the possibility of collective or disinterested grounds for settlement of differences except through market transactions. The move to needs, however, suggests the possibility of not only disinterested but relatively unproblematic grounds for dispute resolution. When deployed by ADR advocates, needs talk is of this latter type, apolitical and distinctly technocratic.

Needs-based dispute resolution takes for granted the desire of expert helpers to meet needs, and defines the dispute as merely a technical and individual problem of correlating available means to essential needs. Disputes are no longer arenas of competition for the distribution of valued goods, or the legitimation of moral claims. Dispute resolution becomes a technocratic activity because it is defined as the creation or design of pragmatic solutions to problems. Compromise between the parties allows people to live with their problems. Here the claim is made that all problems can be solved. As such, dispute resolution is similar to many other forms of engineering in which knowledge is mobilized to achieve material and behavioral goals.[256] What technology produces, however, is not only the creation of solutions but the

---

Welfare State Societies (Feb. 3, 1988) (talk presented to Mary Ingraham Bunting Institute, Radcliffe College, Cambridge, Mass.).

253. *See* D. WIGGINS, *supra* note 247, at 16.

254. *See* I. ILLICH, *supra* note 242. *Cf.* Abel, *supra* note 93, at 283; R. TOMASIC, LAWYERS AND THE COMMUNITY 22-25 (1978).

255. *See* I. ILLICH, *supra* note 242; J. HABERMAS, TOWARD A RATIONAL SOCIETY (1970); C. LASCH, *supra* note 97.

256. *See* M. HEIDEGGER, BASIC WRITINGS (1965).

externalization of guidance, which specifies the relationship between means and ends—the solutions to problems.[257] Because technocratic problems involve control through explicit and exhaustive instructions and rules, they appear to be independent of human will; thus, technological decision making is presented by its promoters to be apolitical and uncontroversial.[258] By legitimating a conception of dispute resolution that is simultaneously independent of the articulated preferences, wants or interests of the parties, and independent of the historical context of collective wants and preferences embodied in rights, the discourse of needs enables a form of dispute resolution that also seems outside of power or authority while it nonetheless gives independence to experts who can specify the correct relationship between relatively unproblematic needs and available means.[259]

Constituting the juridical subject in terms of needs thus makes possible some of the institutional critiques of courts which we described in Part II. Judges think in terms of rights and are, as a result, not able to get to what is 'really' at issue. As a result, so the argument goes, needs are unmet; moreover, the language of rights is said to overlay and prevent the recognition of either the sources or nature of the conflict. Thus conflict continues or takes new forms.[260]

V. Conclusions

The emergence of disputing and dispute processing within the legal field takes place at several interdependent levels. At each level dispute processing involves both a competition among different professional projects and an incorporation of different professional projects within

257. What else is a computer or any machine but a set of instructions formulated for endless production? Nonetheless those instructions are specified by people whose job it is to create such formulas. *See* J. Weizenbaum, Computer Power and Human Reason (1976).

258. *See* Bittner, *Technique and the Conduct of Life*, 30 Soc. Probs. 249 (1983). Thus the discourse of "needs" imagines a dispute handler in much the same way that some varieties of liberal theory imagines judges. *See* Singer, *supra* note 177.

259. It also neutralizes and depoliticizes disputes by offering to meet needs through creative, responsive and participatory problem-solving; nonetheless the needs pursued through participatory dispute processes may not be the needs the parties articulate or desire. Thus Delgado criticizes ADR for the ways in which it denies to minority and impoverished populations the ability to make a social claim against the collectivity, to get that claim validated as legitimate for others as well as the individual complainant, and to demand a response from more than the particular respondent. *See* Delgado, *Fairness and Formality*, 1985 Wis. L. Rev. 1359. Law, Delgado argues, necessitates that others, not party to the particular dispute, nonetheless acknowledge the legitimacy of the claims of the prevailing party. By denying dispute resolution on grounds other than the particular interests of the specific parties, ADR closes the door to those who seek affirmation that they are not alone in their wants or needs. Needs-talk, like interest-negotiation, responds to the individual claimant but denies that person's desire to have her want acknowledged by the community. Moreover, Delgado argues that minority populations have particular needs for processes of dispute resolution which challenge racial and ethnic prejudice, and which empower the disadvantaged. Such groups, Delgado suggests, do not want, nor do they need, dispute resolution forums which are neutral and disinterested. Inequalities of status and power demand institutions which provide partisanship rather than unchannelled responsiveness and participation.

260. *See* Felstiner, Abel & Sarat, *supra* note 116.

the legal field. Within the domain of legal institutions, elite lawyers, access to justice reformers and community organizers compete to control the market in dispute processing just as in the domain of legal scholarship social scientists contest the hegemonic position of traditional law professors by reformulating the subject of law as disputing and dispute processing. Yet each of these contests takes place within the legal field and is fully contained within it just as each brings new professional projects within its reach. Moreover, competition within each domain is made possible by developments within the other. Theoreticians provide new weapons for combat over, and within, institutions just as that combat energizes and legitimates theoretical production. Competition and interdependence are also visible in the constitution of the juridical subject. Here the explicit rhetoric is a rhetoric of competition and displacement, yet, as we have shown, the discourses of rights, interest and needs embody similar contradictions between autonomy and connection, individuality and sociality, separateness and relationship.

Thus, to speak of the reconstitution of the juridical subject or the transition within the legal field from rights to interests and needs suggests more completeness than is attained or attainable. Rights talk is by no means displaced;[261] it is, however, transformed, and, in some ways domesticated, in the face of the discourses of interest and needs. The rights language of Dworkin,[262] Fiss[263] and Minow[264] is recognizably modern and different, perhaps less terrifying and compelling than the rights discourse of earlier eras.[265] Unalienable rights become products of a judicially-led process of textual interpretation. Rights become parts of the fabric of social life rather than constraints existing outside or prior to it. Alternatively, in other voices, rights no longer serve as guarantees against non-interference or the sanctity of an inviolable personal space;[266] they aren't guarantees that individuals can dictate or control the uses of their own persons or property. They become, instead, guarantees that when others make particular decisions regarding my person or my property I will have a claim to a judicially enforced obligation to payment for their preferred uses. This domesticated rights talk represents a discursive accommodation of significant proportions. It makes possible an uneasy pluralism of communities with the legal field.[267] No longer is rights talk a hegemonic form; no longer does the juridical subject as a possessor of rights reign supreme. At the same time, however, ADR has not been able, itself or in combination with other things, to dislodge the rights conception.

In addition, the language of rights reshapes and challenges the way

261. *See* Haskell, *The Curious Persistance of Rights Talk in the "Age of Interpretation"*, 1988 J. Am. Hist. 1.

262. *See* R. Dworkin, *supra* note 154.

263. *See* Fiss, *supra* note 1.

264. *See* Minow, *supra* note 167.

265. *See* H. Arkes, *supra* note 156.

266. *See* Calabresi & Malamed, *Property Rules, Liability Rules and Inalienability*, 85 Harv. L. Rev. 1089 (1972).

267. *See* Minow, Law Turning Outward (1987) (unpublished manuscript).

interests and needs are expressed in debates over dispute processing. The latter take on meaning only as theoretical counterweights to rights. Interests and needs become, if nothing else, alternative bases for claims of rights. Moreover, while the language of interests and needs seems at first to strengthen strains of opposition within the legal field, it serves in the end to strengthen the social position of the legal field by making it more complex and resilient, by selectively incorporating, and making accommodations with, political opponents and by extending the sphere of surveillance and control that gives the legal field its place within society. ADR by precipitating accommodations at the level of institutional practice, academic theorizing and the constitution of the juridical subject supplements rather than displaces the force of law and the social space which it occupies.

Part V
The Quality of Alternative Dispute Resolution

[14]

Evaluations of Dispute Processing: We Do Not Know What We Think and We Do Not Think What We Know

John P. Esser*

Table of Contents

Introduction

The past two decades have witnessed a growing body of empirical studies of dispute processing. A significant number of these articles form a distinct type of literature which we call "evaluations." Evaluations report assessments of existing dispute processing programs in a form which contributes to our general knowledge of dispute processing.

* Hewlett Fellow, Dispute Processing Research Program, University of Wisconsin-Madison. I am grateful to Marc Galanter, David Trubek, Cathy Meschievitz and Tom Tylerm for their critical comments on this paper. I am also indebted to the fellowship support I received from the William and Flora Hewlett Foundation through the Dispute Processing Research Program of the Institute for Legal Studies, University of Wisconsin-Madison.

Their production and distribution involve the combined effort of policy makers, dispute processing professionals, and academics. Policy makers, professionals, and academics are also the primary consumers of this literature.

Published evaluations of dispute processing programs are now so numerous that it is difficult for the average scholar, policy maker, or practitioner to locate, read or digest them all. This difficulty does not obviate the need felt by many of these potential readers to obtain a mastery of this material. Scholars of dispute resolution believe that to speak with authority as experts, they must know the state of knowledge in the field. Policy makers believe that in order to best address the problems their jurisdictions experience, they must identify those reforms which have had the greatest success. Practitioners, called on to account for the success or failure of their programs, seek models to follow when instituting evaluations of their own. For these readers, a review article and bibliography on the topic appears to be the answer. Such an article can abstract and summarize the essence of the important results reported by the literature so that these readers can obtain the information they need without having to identify, collect and review the entire literature themselves.

This article will identify, describe, and review the existing evaluations literature on dispute resolution. However, it may not provide the quick answers that some readers are looking for. Prior to reviewing the literature for its results, I will review the questions which have framed this literature and which, I argue, frame the field's interest in a literature review of the kind suggested above. This is an important first step, for the contribution which the empirical results of evaluations research makes to dispute processing knowledge, depends on the questions which the field asks of it. This article will argue that the framework of questions predominant in dispute resolution today blinds us to some of the significant findings of existing evaluations research and also arouses unreasonable expectations about what such research can find in the future. In other words, our framework can divert us from thinking about what we already know and may deceive us into believing that we know more than we actually do. It is my hope that the reader will use this paper not only to assess the results of existing research, but also to assess the framework through which she renders these results meaningful.

I. Why Must We Examine Our Frameworks Before We Examine Our Results

This preliminary section will explain and substantiate the importance of critically examining the frameworks through which policy makers, program implementors, program evaluators, and evaluation readers understand processes of dispute processing. I will make four points. First, the reporting of empirical results is framed by the conceptual perspective of the author. Second, while these frameworks facilitate our understanding of certain aspects of dispute processing, at the same time, they distract our attention from other aspects of these processes. Third, these conceptual frameworks are not specific to individual evaluators but are shared by other evaluators, policy makers, program administrators, and additional consumers of published evaluations. Fourth, by shaping our perceptions and expectations, these frameworks help shape our motivations, our actions, the strategies of reform we pursue, and the institutions we establish to achieve these reforms.[1]

All researchers are aware that dispute resolution programs, like all aspects of social life, are extremely complex phenomena. In order to describe and evaluate the success of a given program, researchers must structure their observations, measurements, and reports to highlight a few characteristics or variables which are, in the eyes of the researcher, particularly significant.[2] The reviewer of the evaluations literature faces a similar task. This body of literature presents a vast array of observations and conclusions across thousands of pages of text. In order to summarize these findings in a concise, interesting, and useful form, the reviewer must abstract those which are, to his eyes, the most important—the most essential.

While a framework of questions facilitates our understanding of a particular program or body of literature by focusing our attention on certain aspects of this complex reality, it also diverts our attention from those aspects of the program or literature which are deemed irrelevant by the framework's perspective. Measuring the time to disposition of a

---

1. The importance of interrogating the conceptual frameworks which orient socio-legal research was the central theme of the Law and Society Association's 1988 annual meeting. Calling this theme the "Archeology of Sociolegal Studies: Constructing Questions," the program committee specified six issues for discussion:

> 1. How we define the legal phenomena that are studied.
> 2. How we determine what questions are asked. How we select propositions to guide our research. In short, what questions are asked and what questions remain not asked or left unexamined.
> 3. How certain forms of data, "evidence," and arguments become persuasive in developing the knowledge base of our field and what accounts for the sources of influence.
> 4. How disciplinary orientations and/or theoretical paradigms inform and limit our perspectives on socio-legal phenomena.
> 5. How explicit and implicit ideologies, values and belief systems create assumptions, biases, and silences in our research (e.g. positivism, critical theory, feminism, ethnocentrism).
> 6. How varied purposes (e.g. policy, evaluation, litigation, basic research) affect the content of our research.

LAW AND SOCIETY ASSOCIATION, ARCHEOLOGY OF SOCIOLOGICAL STUDIES: CONSTRUCTING QUESTIONS (1988). This paper can be seen as an attempt to apply these questions to the specific field of dispute processing evaluations rather than the more general field of socio-legal research *per se*.

2. Lind and Shapard, for example, begin their evaluation of three federal court-annexed arbitration programs by explicitly stating the aim of their research: "The primary aim of the evaluation effort reported here was to determine whether these local rules produce the beneficial consequences anticipated without unacceptable adverse consequences. The anticipated benefits of the rules are that they will reduce both the time and expense of resolving certain civil cases and the burden these cases place on court resources" A. LIND & J. SHAPARD, EVALUATION OF COURT-ANNEXED ARBITRATION IN THREE FEDERAL DISTRICT COURTS 5 (1983). In this passage Lind and Shapard are telling the reader that they have decided to focus on the cost in time and money of processing certain civil cases. They have used the anticipated benefits of the rules to define this focus.

given case in an arbitration program may help systematize our knowledge concerning the speed with which this arbitration program can process cases, but this focus diverts our attention from the interactions between disputants, counsel, and arbitrator which take place within this time period and which actually cause the resolution of the case.[3] Consequently, the facilitation of our understanding comes at a cost. While our framework helps us to systematize our understanding of the data which our questions deem significant, it also diverts us from making other observations which may have as great, if not greater, significance for our knowledge of dispute processing.

While the orienting conceptual frameworks used by individual evaluators vary to some degree, they can not be entirely idiosyncratic. When seeking funding for research, when conducting an evaluation, and when writing up results, the evaluator must be concerned with the interests of her audience. For example, she must ask herself: "What is it about this dispute resolution program that my readers are interested in knowing?" Also, "How do I report it in a manner which is useful, comprehendible, and interesting to my readers?" If orienting frameworks were entirely idiosyncratic, answering such questions would be impossible. However, answering questions like these is not impossible. Despite their differences, policy makers, practitioners, and academics often share common or related goals, interests, evaluative criteria, and perspectives. It is only because of some minimal agreement over the nature of disputes and dispute processing that individuals from such diverse occupations as law, social work, and social science scholarship can perceive themselves as members of a shared field. We can expect, for example, that anyone active in the dispute processing field who is reading the results of an evaluation will immediately question the type of program being evaluated (arbitration, mediation, negotiation, and others), the type of data examined (court records, interviews, questionnaires with disputants, and others), and the measure of success or failure (cheaper, faster, more equitable, and others). This sharing of outlook constitutes, in part, the boundaries of the dispute processing field.

In establishing the importance of shared perspectives in defining the dispute resolution field, I do not mean to suggest that behind this minimal level of agreement there are not important differences. On the contrary, I accept the existence of these differences but seek to explain them as differences in conceptual perspectives rather than as differences in the perspectives of individuals. I argue that the most important differences are not differences among particular individuals' works, but rather between a small number of distinct and competing shared outlooks within the field. Consider, for example, differences over the proper term for labeling our field. Is our focus of concern "dispute res-

3. Consider the example of Lind and Shapard discussed in the previous footnote. By restricting their perspective to the analysis of the case costs in terms of time and expense to the courts, the authors have purposely decided to ignore, for example, which arbitrator techniques facilitate settlement and which do not. *Id.*

olution," "*alternative* dispute resolution" ("ADR"), or "dispute *processing*?" Such debates have more at stake then semantics: they express differences in which programs colleagues look at, differences in the criteria used in assessing program success, and differences in what it is hoped these programs will achieve. If we use "alternative dispute resolution," then we tend to focus on forums for dispute resolution outside the traditional court system.[4] If we use "dispute resolution" rather than ADR, then we tend to include the processes of pre-trial negotiation and judicial settlement which already exist in traditional institutions of adjudication. If we use "dispute processing" rather than "dispute resolution," then we tend to emphasize that the purpose or the result of the "dispute resolution" institutions is not always the resolution of disputes.[5]

Conceptual frameworks provide more than descriptions of what we find and expect to find in dispute processing programs. By framing our experience of dispute processing, they define what we perceive to be problematic with those processes, suggest reforms which promise to address these problems, and thereby suggest actions and institutions required to achieve these reforms. Consequently, in addition to providing us with an orienting perspective, conceptual frameworks provide us with strategies of policy reform and strategies for socio-legal research.

The reader should be aware that the degree and direction of causality between these various determinants of social life such as conceptual perspectives, individual motivations, strategies of policy reform, and others, is a subject of great debate. It is unclear, for example, whether the modern ADR movement originated either with reform proposals by academics suggesting that reform strategies originate with new conceptual perspectives, with court administrators experiencing an explosion of litigation which suggests that new conceptual perspectives result from institutional crises, with grass-roots demands for increased access to justice which suggests that innovations in conceptual perspectives as well as institutional reforms result from social movements, or with some other source. Most of the disputes processing literature ascribes some determination to a combination of these causes without specifying their interrelationship or individual degree of determination.[6]

In the analysis that follows, I will use a description of a prevailing conceptual framework as my point of departure. I will then go on to discuss the policy reforms, research agendas, institutional innovations, actions, and impacts suggested by such an orienting framework. The reader should not take this choice to imply that conceptual frameworks are the sole or primary determinant of individual motivations, individual actions, policy reform strategies, research strategies, or the creation and persistence of institutions. Rather, it should be understood simply as

4. Sander, *Varieties of Dispute Processing*, 70 F.R.D. 79, 111 (1976).

5. *See, e.g.*, Felstiner, *Influences of Social Organization on Dispute Processing*, 9 LAW & SOC'Y REV. 63 (1974).

6. *See* S. GOLDBERG, E. GREEN & F. SANDER, DISPUTE RESOLUTION 3-5 (1985).

my selection of one from many analytic approaches to the study of the complex field of social phenomena called "dispute processing." The selection of this point of departure over others is defined by the objectives of the paper: to identify, describe, and review a body of literature produced and published by this field.

II. THE NEW FORMALISM

The evaluations literature combines a particular perspective on dispute processing with particular methods of social science research. *The New Formalism* is the predominant conceptual perspective in the dispute processing field. It provides its adherents not only with a description of dispute processing, but also with agendas for socio-legal research and for policy reform. *Impact analysis* is a type of empirical social science investigation whose assumptions and methods are particularly well suited to New Formalism's research agenda. In this section, I will use a description of The New Formalism and of impact analysis as an analytic approach to identify, describe, review and critique evaluations of dispute processing as a component of a policy reform project.

A. *The New Formalist Perspective*

Fuller,[7] Danzig,[8] and Sander[9] are often cited as the intellectual origins of the modern disputes processing field. Implicit and explicit assumptions concerning the nature of disputes and disputes processing presented in these early works have formed an orienting conceptual framework that has been used and advanced by subsequent writings in the field. After Sarat, I call this framework "the New Formalism."[10]

Lon Fuller's work establishes the possibility of a general theory of dispute processing.[11] Fuller sought to distinguish the various "order-producing and order-restoring processes of society"[12] on the basis of their "distinguishing characteristics,"[13] "general structure,"[14] or "central qualities."[15] Fuller assumes that these central qualities determine

7. *See generally* Fuller, *The Forms and Limits of Adjudication*, 92 HARV. L. REV. 353 (1978) [hereinafter Fuller, *Adjudication*]; Fuller, *Mediation—Its Forms and Functions*, 44 S. CAL. L. REV. 305 (1971) [hereinafter Fuller, *Mediation*]; Fuller, *Collective Bargaining and The Arbitrator*, 1963 WIS. L. REV. 3 [hereinafter Fuller, *Collective Bargaining*].

8. Danzig, *Towards the Creation of a Complementary, Decentralized System of Criminal Justice*, 26 STAN. L. REV. 1 (1973).

9. Sander, *supra* note 4.

10. *See* Sarat, *The "New Formalism" in Disputing And Dispute Processing*, 21 LAW & SOC'Y REV. 695 (1988). For a similar discussion see Merry, *Disputing Without Culture*, 100 HARV. L. REV. 2057 (1987). The New Formalism is not the only perspective on disputes processing present in the current literature and Fuller, Danzig, and Sander are not its only intellectual origins. For the origins and development of another, "non-formalist" perspective on disputes processing present in the current literature, see Abel, *A Comparative Theory of Dispute Institutions in Society*, 8 LAW & SOC'Y REV. 217 (1973), and the articles found in volume 9, issues 1 and 2, of Law and Society Review.

11. *See* sources cited *supra* note 7.

12. Fuller, *Mediation*, *supra* note 7, at 327.

13. Fuller, *Adjudication*, *supra* note 7, at 357.

14. Fuller, *Mediation*, *supra* note 7, at 309.

15. *Id.* at 327.

the intrinsic limitations of the process; that is, they determine which types of social problems the process is and is not well suited to handle. Actually existing programs may vary in the degree to which they maintain the "integrity" of a pure process type and its ideal jurisdiction. A particular program may mix distinguishing properties from a variety of general process types and may be applied to social problems which it is not well suited to address. In such cases where the "integrity" of the general form is lost, the program outcomes will be characterized by "failure" and ineffectiveness.[16]

Danzig demonstrates how assumptions such as Fuller's can be used to explain the failure of governmental institutions and to recommend policy reforms to correct these failures.[17] Danzig questions why the existing American urban justice system fails in its efforts to control crime through criminal adjudication. He argues that this is not the result of a failure of adjudication *per se*, but rather of the application of adjudication to too broad a range of social problems. Hence, failures in crime control can best be addressed not by replacing adjudication but by supplementing it with complementary processes of social regulation. The proper balance of complementary processes can be identified by assuming a systems approach to society's handling of crimes and criminals.

A systems approach views the various processes which a society uses for handling social problems as forming a system. "The systematic perspective views a change in one component of the subsystem as forcing changes in the others."[18] In regard to Danzig's issue of urban criminal justice, a change in one component means changing the jurisdictional boundaries of a given procedure. "Widening or narrowing the definition of crimes increases or decreases police, court, and correction business; changes in police techniques may overburden or free the time of judges and prison staffs . . . ."[19] Problems with existing public institutions can thus be explained as the result of an unbalanced system: when adjudication is applied to too wide a range of social problems, it fails to effectively process all its cases. The resolution of these problems can be understood as changes to the system which restore balance: introducing decentralized community moots as a complementary component of the criminal justice system not only improves the system's resolution of problems which the moot takes over from traditional adjudication, but also improves the system's resolution of those problems which remain in adjudication's jurisdiction.

Sander accepts Fuller's assumption concerning the possibility of a general theory of order-restoring processes, accepts Danzig's systems approach to the diagnosis of public policy reform, and applies these assumptions to the processing of civil disputes.[20] Like Fuller, Sander as-

---

16. Fuller, *Adjudication*, *supra* note 7, at 382.
17. Danzig, *supra* note 8.
18. *Id.* at 5.
19. *Id.*
20. Sander, *supra* note 4.

pires to develop a general theory of alternative dispute processing programs. Like Danzig, he uses the principles of this theory to explain the ineffectiveness of the existing system, a burdensome judicial caseload, and to propose reforms which will produce a more effective system, by increasing use of alternatives outside the courts. Sander goes on, however, to argue that the principles of a general theory can be used as "rational criteria for allocating various types of disputes to different dispute processes."[21] That is, these principles are useful not only for program designers, such as legislators, foundations, and policy intellectuals who provide funding and authorization for programs but also for program implementors, such as administrators who run the program from day to day.[22]

Implicit in these early works of the dispute processing field are three propositions:

> 1. There are a small number of essential types of procedures for the resolution of disputes.[23] These are distinguished by their distinctive general characteristics. These characteristics make each essential process particularly well suited to resolve certain types of disputes.[24]
> 2. Every society establishes a number of dispute processing programs, each with its own distinctive jurisdictional boundaries. These programs form a system which functions effectively or ineffectively depending on the type of programs it includes, the type of jurisdictional boundaries it defines for each, and the manner in which these different programs complement one another.[25]
> 3. The ineffectiveness of an existing system of dispute processing programs can be explained and reforms which correct this ineffectiveness proposed by applying the general principles of a dispute processing theory.[26]

---

21. Sander summarizes the questions he addresses as follows:

> 1. What are the significant characteristics of various alternative dispute resolution mechanisms (such as adjudication by courts, arbitration, mediation, negotiation, and various blends of these and other devices)?
> 2. How can these characteristics be utilized so that, given the variety of disputes that presently arise, we can begin to develop some rational criteria for allocating various types of disputes to different dispute resolution processes?

Id. at 113.

22. This is the program feature which advances Danzig's concept of a complementary system to Sander's concept of a multi-door courthouse. To Danzig's complementary system Sander adds a gatekeeper which allocates cases according to rational criteria rather than depending on each citizen to make the "which process" decision herself.

23. In this paper I will use "process" and "mechanism" interchangeably to refer to essential types of dispute processing procedures. I will use "dispute processing programs" to refer to the institutionalization of a given process or mechanism in a specific concrete organization.

24. *See also* M. Cappelletti & B. Garth, Access to Justice (1978); D. Horowitz, The Courts and Social Policy (1977); J. Marks, E. Johnson & P. Szanton, Dispute Resolution in America (1984); Fine, Moukad & Taylor, *CPR Working Taxonomy of Alternative Legal Processes*, Alternatives, May 1983, at 9, Aug. 1983, at 4, Nov. 1983, at 5, Dec. 1983, at 5.

25. *See also* Abel, *supra* note 10; McGovern, *Toward a Functional Approach for Managing Complex Litigation*, 53 U. Chi. L. Rev. 440 (1986).

26. *See also* Bush, *Dispute Resolution Alternatives and the Goals of Civil Justice: Jurisdictional*

These three propositions describe the general features of disputes, dispute processing, dispute processing institutions and dispute processing systems. They constitute "the New Formalism."

B. *The New Formalism as a Vision of the Future*

As I have argued above, perspectives do more than simply frame the descriptions we have of the world around us. By defining what *does* exist, frameworks also define what *should* exist and *can* exist. They help shape one's diagnosis of what is wrong with the present as well as one's prescription for an improved future. Such is the case with the New Formalist perspective. The three propositions identified above include not only a description of the present but also a vision of the future.

Proposition one makes claims about the nature of social processes. These claims identify a field of social phenomena—dispute processing—which operates according to certain social laws. The implication is that researchers can construct a general theory concerning dispute processing by identifying the social laws which govern these phenomena. If social life indeed follows such laws, then researchers can use methods of scientific investigation to construct verifiable descriptions of the properties of various types of disputes and dispute resolution institutions, can state these properties as principles, and can interrelate these principles as a theory of dispute resolution.

Proposition one also suggests the form such a theory will have once it is constructed. It suggests that a theory of dispute resolution will have at least six variables. It assumes that there are a finite number of essential processes for the resolution of disputes (X_1, X_2, X_3, . . .). These types of disputes are distinguished by a particular combination of a finite set of process characteristics (a_1, a_2, a_3, . . .). There are also a finite number of essential types of disputes (W_1, W_2, W_3, . . .). These are distinguished by a particular combination of a finite set of dispute characteristics (b_1, b_2, b_3, . . .). For each type of dispute there is one set of outcomes which results from the application of the various general types of processes to this particular type of dispute (Y_1, Y_2, Y_3, . . .). These types of outcomes are characterized by their own set of characteristics (c_1, c_2, c_3, . . .). For each type of dispute, one outcome (Y) constitutes the most effective processing of this given type of dispute. This outcome identifies the optimum match between process type and dispute type. Each optimum match between process type and dispute type can be stated as a scientific principle.[27] These principles can then be interre-

Principles for Process Change, 1984 WIS. L. REV. 893; Priest & Klein, *The Selection of Disputes for Litigation*, 13 J. LEGAL STUD. 1 (1984).

27. In his three articles on mediation, arbitration, and adjudication, Fuller proposes a number of principles of the type described. Consider, for example, the following statements regarding mediation:

> The central quality of mediation [is] . . . its capacity to reorient the parties toward each other, not by imposing rules on them, but by helping them to achieve a new and shared perception of their relationship, a perception that will redirect their attitudes and dispositions toward one another . . . .

Fuller, *Mediation*, *supra* note 7, at 327.

lated to create a general theory of dispute processing. This archetypical theory of dispute processing is graphically represented in Chart I.

Proposition two makes claims about the nature of dispute processing institutions. These claims provide an explanation as to why some dispute processing programs succeed while others fail. The degree to which a given program is effective or ineffective depends on the degree to which the program's institutional design and jurisdictional limits correspond to those laws of social action which govern dispute processing; these laws determine the ideal "match" between process type and dispute type. Consequently, the "effectiveness" of a program is a technical question rather than a question of value. Individuals may disagree as to why an effective program is desired. But from the New Formalist perspective, these desired outcomes will all be achieved under the same set of conditions. When the design of an actual program (in terms of the technique applied and the jurisdiction of cases it is applied to) corresponds to the social laws governing dispute processing, *all* desirable program outcomes or impacts will be achieved simultaneously.

A program's "effectiveness" should be distinguished from its "efficiency." "Efficiency" is usually interpreted as meaning the achievement of a desired outcome with a minimum of time, effort, or expense. Many reformers are interested in a general theory of dispute processing because they are interested in instituting an "efficient" dispute processing system—that is, one which minimizes the cost and time required to process disputes. Within the New Formalist perspective, the most "efficient" dispute processing system is the system which has the most "effective" design—that is, the system whose existing programs and jurisdictions correspond to the principles of the general theory of dispute processing.[28]

Proposition two not only assumes the possibility of an effective dispute processing system but also suggests how the design for such a system can be obtained: namely, through social science research. If dispute processing mechanisms are things with stable attributes, capacities, and limits which are ideally suited for resolving certain types of disputes with stable attributes of their own, then the world is such that human beings can identify a rational ground for defining and orienting enlightened social policy regarding disputes processing. Scientific

> Mediation is itself subject to intrinsic limitations; I have discussed two of these: (1) it cannot generally be employed when more than two parties are involved; (2) it presupposes an intermeshing of interests of an intensity sufficient to make the parties willing to collaborate in the mediational effort

Id. at 330. In these sentences, Fuller defines the pure mechanism type "mediation" using its distinctive characteristic features. He defines two general characteristic features of disputes, and he identifies disputes which have these characteristics as those which mediation is most ideally suited to process.

28. Reformers can disagree as to whether the outcomes desired and the measures used should be limited to questions of *efficiency* (some reformers may wish to include other outcomes such as increased access to justice, increased quality of justice, and others). But they can disagree regarding desired outcomes and measures while agreeing that their various outcomes will be achieved under the same conditions: when the system is designed *effectively*.

CHART I
Outline for a General Theory of Dispute Processing as Defined by the New Formalist Perspective

Type of Dispute	Type of Mechanism						
	X_1	X_2	X_3	X_4	X_5	X_6	$X_7 \ldots X_k$
W_1	Y_1	Y_2	Y_3	Y_4	Y_5	Y_6	$Y_7 \ldots Y_k$
W_2	Y_8	Y_9	Y_{10}	Y_{11}	Y_{12}	Y_{13}	$Y_{14} \ldots Y_m$
W_3	Y_{15}	Y_{16}	Y_{17}	Y_{18}	Y_{19}	Y_{20}	$Y_{21} \ldots Y_n$
W_4	Y_{22}	Y_{23}	Y_{24}	Y_{25}	Y_{26}	Y_{27}	$Y_{28} \ldots Y_o$
W_5	Y_{29}	Y_{30}	Y_{31}	Y_{32}	Y_{33}	Y_{34}	$Y_{35} \ldots Y_p$
W_6	Y_{36}	Y_{37}	Y_{38}	Y_{39}	Y_{40}	Y_{41}	$Y_{42} \ldots Y_q$
W_7	Y_{43}	Y_{44}	Y_{45}	Y_{46}	Y_{47}	Y_{48}	$Y_{49} \ldots Y_r$
	:	:	:	:	:	:	: :
W_k	Y_a	Y_b	Y_c	Y_d	Y_e	Y_f	$Y_g \ldots Y_z$

Where:

$$X_k = a_1 + a_2 + a_3 + a_4 + \ldots a_k$$
$$W_k = b_1 + b_2 + b_3 + b_4 + \ldots b_k$$
$$Y_k = c_1 + c_2 + c_3 + c_4 + \ldots c_k$$

And Where:

X_k = Type of Mechanism
W_k = Type of Dispute
Y_k = Type of Outcome
a_k = Mechanism Characteristics
b_k = Dispute Characteristics
c_k = Outcome Characteristics

knowledge of the laws of social behavior which define the most effective fit between types of disputes and types of dispute processing institutions can provide policy makers and implementors with rational guidance in designing, employing, assessing, and adjusting the legal system so that it most effectively achieves its goals and functions. In short, the design for an effective system can be found in the general theory of dispute processing.

Proposition three makes claims regarding the responsibilities of policy makers, practitioners, and researchers and the use they must make of a general theory of dispute processing in executing these responsibilities. Implicit in these claims is a vision of the proper division of labor between these three vocations in a society which implements New Formalism's enlightened dispute processing policy. In such a society *researchers* are charged with identifying the properties of various types of dispute resolution institutions, with stating these properties as principles, and with interrelating them as a theory of dispute resolution. *Policy makers* use this knowledge to guide their construction of a balanced system of dispute resolution institutions. The theory tells them what type of mechanisms are best suited to process different types of disputes. It is then their job to make sure that each type of mechanism is available and accessible in the society. *Professional practitioners* locate and implement these programs so that they operate in the most effective manner. A theory of dispute resolution can help them in this responsibility in two ways. First, this knowledge can provide practitioners with rational criteria for assigning disputes to the most effective arena for their resolution. Second, this knowledge can provide practitioners with standards by which they can assure, through periodic evaluations, that operation of their programs optimize the efficiency and quality of their output. Should the institution fall short, these principles can be guides to adjust the institution.

C. *The New Formalism as a Social Project*

While writers such as Fuller, Danzig, and Sander anticipate a general theory of dispute resolution and a rational dispute processing system, they do not propose that these are already completed projects.[29] While they assume that disputes and dispute processing follow social laws, they do not pretend that human beings have as yet specified these laws as principles of knowledge. They think that a balanced, effective system of dispute processing institutions is possible, but they do not assume that such mechanisms have actually been established, or, if instituted, have been applied to those types of disputes for which they are most ideally suited.

29. "Nothing said in this Article," writes Danzig, "should be taken to mean that the time for looking has passed and that we are ready to leap. Though advanced with enthusiasm, recommendations based on so rudimentary a collection of observations as those presented here should be tested in practice (and doubtless modified) before it can be decided whether and how they should be put into effect on a large scale. This Article should be read only as a blueprint for experimentation." Danzig, *supra* note 8, at 12-13.

However, by juxtaposing the description of a flawed present and a perfect future, New Formalist assumptions can provide incentives to make its vision of the future a reality. If social scientists define their vocation as the accumulation of general knowledge, they will interpret the definition of a new field of phenomena as both an opportunity and demand for new research. If policy makers see it as their duty to fulfill social needs in the most effective manner possible, they will interpret the promise of a more effective dispute processing system as a call to action. If practitioners are charged with administering their programs as successfully as possible and with substantiating that success, they will find appealing the promise of a set of guidelines which insure effective program operation.

If social actors aspire to achieve New Formalism's aspirations then they adopt the framework's vision of the future as their goals for the present. Through this process, the framework's assumptions can shape the direction and style of social action. Researchers who adopt the New Formalist perspective will use it to define their research goals: to construct a general theory modeled on the archetype illustrated in Chart I. Policy makers will use it to define their policy objectives: to construct a balanced and effective system of dispute processing institutions by organizing new programs and by adjusting those that already exist. Practitioners will use its principles to fine-tune the operation of their programs: to maximize the effectiveness of their program by insuring that the program applies the right set of procedures.

Undertaking the realization of New Formalism's vision of the future as a social project raises questions of *strategy* and *method*. If such a theory is possible and its construction is accepted as a goal, by what method should one construct such a theory? Should it be deduced from principles or should it be induced from empirical experience? If an enlightened system of institutions can be designed using a general theory and fabrication of such system accepted as a social project, what strategy should be followed in constructing its institutions? Should the general theory be completed before designing and implementing programs? Or should the development of theory and the development of programs be concurrent enterprises?

While some New Formalists have relied on methods of deduction,[30] most argue that a verified theory can only be developed using a method of empirical observation and experimentation. "[T]he system presented here," writes Danzig, "is designed to move from existing knowledge, empirically derived, to a scheme of larger, more coordinated experiments, and then ultimately, to a higher level of implementation."[31] Sander concurs:

30. *See, e.g.*, D. LUBAN, THE QUALITY OF JUSTICE (1987); D. WATERMAN & M. PETERSON, MODELS OF LEGAL DECISIONMAKING: RESEARCH DESIGN AND METHODS (1981); Bush, *supra* note 26; Fuller, *Adjudication*, *supra* note 7; Fuller, *Mediation*, *supra* note 7; Fuller, *Collective Bargaining*, *supra* note 7; Priest & Klien, *supra* note 26.

31. Danzig, *supra* note 8, at 13.

> [T]here is so much we do not know. Among other things, we need better data than are presently available in many states on what is in fact going on in the courts so that we can develop some sophisticated notion of where the main trouble spots are and what types of cases are prime candidates for alternative resolution. We need more evaluation of the comparative efficacy and cost of different dispute resolution mechanisms. And we need more data on the role played by some of the key individuals in the process (e.g., lawyers) . . . .[32]

Adopting a method of empirical research has important consequences for the strategy pursued. Researchers cannot obtain the data they require without observing existing institutions. Since a variety of dispute resolution mechanisms have not been tried in practice, researchers are dependent on policy makers to institute untested experimental mechanisms.[33] Therefore, the selection of a method of empirical observation and experimentation requires a strategy which develops a general theory and a reformed system of dispute processing institutions concurrently.

This method and strategy requires the cooperation of policy makers, practitioners, and researchers. Since a complete and verified general theory does not yet exist, all three classes of actors pursue their projects with imperfect information. Policy makers must experiment with new or untried types of dispute processing mechanisms. When implementing these programs, practitioners must select among a range of unproved criteria to use for sorting cases and for evaluating program success. Researchers must use hypothetical typologies of mechanisms and dispute types when constructing, conducting, and interpreting experiments.

Given imperfect knowledge, all three classes of actors can facilitate their respective goals through cooperation and the exchange of information. Researchers cannot obtain the data they require to either induce general propositions or to test the validity of these propositions without observing existing institutions. Policy makers cannot design new institutional forms that promise improved dispute processing without theoretical suggestions from researchers or descriptions of what has already been tried by existing programs. Practitioners can neither assess the success of programs nor justify their continued funding without standards, measures, and methods of success provided by researchers.

In summary, if the New Formalist perspective is correct, if a grounded theory of dispute processing does not yet exist, and if a method of empirical experimentation and a strategy of concurrent development are the proper means to achieve an enlightened future, then policy makers, practitioners, and researchers must unite in a common project of *evaluation*. An evaluation is "an internal effort to define and

32. Sander, *supra* note 4, at 133.

33. Such programs are often "experiments" not only in the sense that they are new, but also in the sense that they are programs with limited jurisdiction for a provisional period of time.

improve operations over time while providing descriptive information to the field."[34] It combines the "internal" interests of policy makers and practitioners to assess and improve the success of their particular program with the "external" interest of researchers to construct scientific knowledge which is of general use to all programs.

D. *Impact Analysis*

Researchers who see the world in New Formalist terms can use evaluations to construct an empirically-grounded theory of dispute processing.[35] With the implementation of each new type of mechanism X_1 with jurisdiction for dispute type W_1, social scientists can observe the outcome Y_1 which this configuration produces. Once a sufficient number of experimental programs ($X_k + W_k$) have yielded a sufficient number of outcomes (Y_k), then the cross-comparison of these results should manifest discernable patterns of effective combinations of program type and dispute type.

This method requires periodic literature reviews of the existing body of evaluations.[36] These reviews summarize the data required for such a cross-comparison. The review identifies those evaluations that have been conducted, summarizes the type of programs that have been tried ($X_1 + W_1$), and reports the outcomes (Y_1) that have resulted from each program. These data can then be arranged according to the archetype in Chart I. Given sufficient data, such a chart should manifest those combinations of mechanism type and dispute type which yield the best results. These patterns of effective combinations represent a first approximation of the principals of a general theory.

However, in order for this research strategy to succeed, the data must be collected in a manner which insures its validity and be presented in a form which allows for cross-comparison. New Formalist assumptions do not specify how these conditions of validity and comparability can be achieved. While there are a number of social science methods available which claim to produce valid and comparable results, the method of choice in dispute processing evaluations has tended to be "impact analysis."[37]

34. Comment by Janis Roehl at a workshop on Identifying and Measuring the Quality of Dispute Resolution Processes and Outcomes, held at the University of Wisconsin-Madison Law School. (July 14, 1987) (quoted by Christine Harrington).

35. In this paper I use the terms "researchers," "sociologists of law," and "socio-legal scholars" interchangeably. I will also use the term "social scientists." Unless otherwise specified, when I use the term "social scientists" I mean to imply social scientists involved in the study of dispute processing.

36. "Above all . . . we need to accumulate and disseminate the presently available learning concerning promising alternative resolution mechanisms, and encourage continued experimentation and research." Sander, *supra* note 4, at 133.

37. For an explicit prescription for the use of impact analyses in dispute processing, see FEDERAL JUDICIAL CENTER ADVISORY COMMITTEE ON EXPERIMENTATION IN THE LAW, EXPERIMENTATION IN THE LAW: REPORT OF THE FEDERAL JUDICIAL CENTER ADVISORY COMMITTEE ON EXPERIMENTATION IN THE LAW (1981). The disputes processing literature uses social science methods other than impact analysis to insure the validity and comparability of measured outcomes. For the use of social psychological methods of experimentation

Impact analysis is a social science method whose assumptions are particularly compatible with the assumptions of the New Formalism. The objective of the New Formalist research strategy outlined above is to empirically assess the effectiveness with which a particular dispute program processes the particular disputes in its jurisdiction. Impact analysis is a set of procedures for assessing the impact of a set of activities on a set of objects in a manner which is comparable and valid. It insures the comparability of data by compiling it in a quantitative form. It insures the validity of the data by using collection procedures that are open to logical substantiation.

Larry Mohr has recently completed a formal presentation of impact analysis:

> Let us take the term *impact analysis* to mean determining the extent to which one set of directed human activities (X) affected the state of some objects or phenomena (Y_1 . . .) and—at least sometimes—determining why the effects were as small or large as they turned out to be. We usually think of X as being some established program and each Y as being one of the many possible outcomes of the program . . . .[38]

According to Mohr, every impact analysis has, implicitly or explicitly, a program theory. The theory predicts that a particular problem will be resolved by applying a particular treatment to a set of objects. It is expected that this treatment will result, by way of a set of intermediate causal links, in an outcome which remedies or improves the problem.

The purpose of the impact analysis is to construct a measure which assesses the degree to which the actual outcome of the treatment improves or fails to improve the problem at hand over the situation that would have resulted had the treatment not been applied. This measure thus tests whether the theory of treatment outcome is correct. Sometimes the impact analysis also includes measures of intervening causal conditions in order to substantiate the expected causal mechanism as well as the expected outcomes. These measures can test whether the explanation given by the theory of outcome is correct. Therefore, Mohr asserts that all impact studies have three major components:

> 1. *The theory* has component elements; impact analysis consists largely of making observations about these elements and relat-

see Thibaut & Holden, *Discovery and Presentation of Evidence in Adversary and Non-Adversary Proceedings*, 71 MICH. L. REV. 1129 (1973); Thibaut, Walker, LaTour & Holden, *Procedural Justice as Fairness*, 26 STAN. L. REV. 1271 (1974); Thibaut, Walker & Lind, *Adversary Presentation and Bias in Legal Decisionmaking*, 86 HARV. L. REV. 386 (1972). For the use of general random surveys, see W. BRAZIL, SETTLING CIVIL DISPUTES (1985) (judicial settlement); D. KING & K. MCEVOY, NATIONAL TECHNICAL INFORMATION SERVICE, U.S. DEP'T OF COMMERCE, A NATIONAL SURVEY OF THE COMPLAINT-HANDLING PROCEDURES USED BY CONSUMERS (1976); Brazil, *Improving Judicial Controls over the Pretrial Development of Civil Actions: Model Rules for Case Management and Sanctions*, 1981 AM. B. FOUND. RES. J. 873 (1981); Brazil, *Views From The Front Lines: Observations by Chicago Lawyers About the Civil Discovery System*, 1980 AM. B. FOUND. RES. J. 217 (1980); Brazil, *Civil Discovery: Lawyers' Views of Its Effectiveness*, 1980 AM. B. FOUND. RES. J. 787 (1980); *Special Issue on Dispute Processing and Civil Litigation*, 15 LAW & SOC'Y REV. 391 (1980-81).

38. L. MOHR, IMPACT ANALYSIS FOR PROGRAM EVALUATION 1 (1988).

> ing them to one another. The primary elements are the problem, the activities, the outcome of interest (sometimes called the objective) and the subobjectives . . . .
> 2. There must be some means for determining whether the theory is correct. Whatever means one uses can be called *the design*.
> 3. There must be *a way of quantifying the program's effectiveness*. This is accomplished through statistics . . . .[39]

In both impact analysis and the New Formalism, the goal of research is to assess the extent to which a program impacts on a set of objects. In the New Formalist study of dispute processing, an existing suboptimal match between a dispute processing mechanism and dispute type is the problem and counterfactual, the experimental dispute processing program is the treatment, the disputes that fall within the jurisdiction of the program are the objects to which the treatment is applied, and the improved performance of the program in processing the dispute is the desired outcome.

Lind and Shapard's evaluation of court-annexed arbitration in three federal district courts is a good example of the use of impact analysis in the evaluation of dispute processing programs.[40] Consider the following passages from this evaluation:

> The anticipated benefits of the rules are that they will reduce both the time and expense of resolving certain civil cases and the burden these cases place on court resources . . . .[41] We can suggest two potential functions of court-annexed arbitration and consider the consequences . . . that these functions might produce. The first potential function of the rules is that they compel subject cases to obtain an advisory verdict through an informal, trial-like proceeding. This advisory verdict might resolve the case prior to trial, either by being accepted by the parties or by serving as the basis of a post-hearing settlement. The second potential function of the rules is that they set a time limit on preparing the case for the arbitration hearing, by requiring that the hearing be held within about seven months from the time the case is filed . . . .[42] A prompt time schedule for the arbitration hearing provides a motivation for counsel to prepare their cases promptly, and the expense of attorney time spent in the arbitration hearing may motivate settlement in advance of the hearing. If the case goes to arbitration, the hearing itself may provide an excellent basis for assessing the strengths and weaknesses of the case, and the arbitrator's award may be regarded as a reliable estimate of the likely verdict at trial; both sorts of information may provide a sound foundation for negotiated settlement. This may lead to acceptance of the arbitration award, or to settlement soon after the

39. *Id.* at 2.
40. A. LIND & J. SHAPARD, *supra* note 2.
41. *Id.* at 5.
42. *Id.* at 8.

award is issued.[43]

The most obvious way in which the arbitration rules may reduce the time from filing to termination of subject cases is if all, or nearly all, cases reaching an arbitration hearing were terminated by acceptance of the arbitration award *and* if a substantial number of cases reached an arbitration hearing in less time than it would normally take to resolve them.[44]

If the rules provide a realistic and prompt time frame for the preparation of cases, or if the arbitration hearings produce reliable judgments of case value, then there is reason to hope that the rules will expedite settlement. The evaluation attempts to determine the effects of the rules on time from filing to termination by two methods: (a) direct comparison of the duration of arbitration cases with an estimate of what the duration would have been in the absence of the rule, and a survey of attorney perceptions of the effects of the rule on case duration.[45]

In this *program theory*, the *problem* is "the burden" which civil cases put on the courts. The *treatment* is (1) compulsion to attend an arbitration hearing and (2) a limit on the time period within which the hearing must take place. These treatments are applied to the *objects* "federal personal injury or contract cases involving damages of not more than $100,000." The *ultimate outcome* is to reduce the burden which civil cases place on the courts. The *outcome of interest* is to have nearly all arbitrated cases end with an arbitrated award reached in less time than a fully adjudicated trial. The *counterfactual* is the time and expense of resolving a civil case in the absence of arbitration and its time limits. The *subobjectives* include (1) early settlement, resulting from (2) an early framework for settlement, (3) acceptance of an early advisory verdict, or (4) parties experiencing the cost of attorneys time earlier in the process due to (5) attorneys preparing their cases earlier in the process. There are two *quantitative measures*. First, a measure of the average duration of arbitrated and non-arbitrated cases is used to assess the outcome of interest. Second, a measure of attorney perception regarding whether arbitration contributed to early settlement is used to assess the theory's explanation of why the outcome of interest occurred.

E. *The New Formalism as Ideal Type*

The reader should not expect to find the New Formalist perspective present in published evaluations with the conceptual purity of the description above. It will not be found in its totality within the head of any concrete individual or in the argument of any written evaluation. However, the reader will find *elements* of this perspective in most of the dispute processing literature. These New Formalist elements will be found mixed in with elements from other perspectives on dispute process-

43. *Id.* at 10.
44. *Id.* at 8-9.
45. *Id.* at 11-12.

ing.[46] In other words, my description of "the New Formalist perspective" should be understood as an *ideal type*.[47]

If the New Formalism is a sometimes present and sometimes absent set of assumptions, then it is instructive to consider at what times it is present and at what times it is absent in the body of published evaluations. My presentation above suggests that New Formalist assumptions define a project for knowledge, provide a set of procedures through which this knowledge should be pursued, provide a set of orienting concepts to be used in presenting the results of these procedures, and explain how the results from one evaluation should combine with the results of other evaluations to construct general knowledge regarding dispute processing. In short, these assumptions *promise* that if experience is digested in a particular form in the present, it will yield a definitive type of result in the future. Specifically, it will yield an empirically-grounded theory of dispute processing that can be used as a rational ground for enlightened policy-making.

Therefore, New Formalist assumptions most frequently appear in the disputes processing literature at those moments when the author needs some guidance as to which experiences will prove to be significant and as to how such experiences can be reported so as to have an impact on future work. Thus, the real impact of the New Formalist perspective can be found in *the promises it makes*. These promises impact on social action by motivating and shaping current perceptions. It encourages policy makers, practitioners, and evaluators to accord significance to certain of their experiences of experimental programs and to ignore others as insignificant. New Formalism influences the experiences that evaluators report, the manner in which these experiences are patterned, and the form in which they are presented as published evaluations. Further, these anticipations of the future explain to those who read and review published evaluations how to cross-compare and synthesize them into a body of knowledge. When one constructs or reads a literature review, New Formalist assumptions lead one to see certain results in cer-

---

46. *See, e.g.*, C. HARRINGTON, SHADOW JUSTICE (1985); Abel, *The Contradictions of Informal Justice*, in THE POLITICS OF INFORMAL JUSTICE 267 (1982); Dezalay, Negotiated Justice as Renegotiation of the Division of Tasks Within the Field of Law: The French Example, (June 15, 1987) (paper presented at the Conference on Dispute Resolution Research in Europe, Washington, D.C.); Dezalay, 'The Forum Should Fit The Fuss . . .': The Economics and Politics of Negotiated Justice: A Historical Approach (December 4, 1987) (paper presented to the Amherst Seminar, Amherst, Mass.); Mather & Yngvesson, *Language, Audience, and the Transformation of Disputes*, 15 LAW & SOC'Y REV. 775 (1980-81); Yngvesson, *Re-examining Continuing Relations and the Law*, 1985 WIS L. REV. 623.

47. According to Weber, an ideal type:

> . . . is formed by the one-sided *accentuation* of one or more points of view and by the synthesis of a great many diffuse, discrete, more or less present and occasionally absent *concrete individual* phenomena, which are arranged according to those one-sidedly emphasized viewpoints into a unified *analytical* construct. In its conceptual purity, this mental construct cannot be found empirically anywhere in reality . . . . Historical research faces the task of determining in each individual case, the extent to which this ideal-construct approximates to or diverges from reality . . . .

WEBER, THE METHODOLOGY OF THE SOCIAL SCIENCES 90 (1949) (emphasis added).

tain forms as significant and open to cross-comparison and to see other results as idiosyncratic and insignificant.

III. A New Formalist Literature Review: We Do Not Know What We Think

In this section, I will assess New Formalism's claims by constructing a review of the results collected from the research projects it has inspired. New Formalist assumptions propose that the most crucial features of an experimental program are the type of mechanism used, the type of dispute to which it is applied, and a measure of the success of the outcome this match generates. They promise that if this essential information is extracted from a sufficient number of experiments (evaluations), the pattern of results should reveal matches which achieve optimal results. Organizing the experimental results in this form should yield a general theory of dispute processing.

In the following pages, I will attempt to organize actual results from published impact studies in this manner. As the Appendix demonstrates, there are now a number of impact studies of dispute processing programs that have been completed and reported. If the premises and promises of the New Formalism are correct, then it should be possible to use these premises to organize published impact study results. If there are a sufficient number of results, organizing these results in the form of Chart I should reveal which combinations of mechanism and dispute type are effective and which are ineffective. The specification of effective combinations will constitute the postulates of a general theory.

This exercise will critically assess the New Formalist research project in three ways. First, it will assess the extent to which this research project is complete. By organizing the results reported in the form dictated by New Formalism's premises, I will show the extent to which the universe of process types, dispute types, and process/dispute matches have been tried.

Second, this exercise will make manifest some of the difficulties involved in completing the New Formalist project. The New Formalism makes certain promises about what its research project will yield at its completion. However, it does not identify the difficulties encountered in getting there nor does it give instruction on how to overcome these difficulties. In constructing a New Formalist review of impact study results, I will come across a number of the difficulties which must be addressed before the New Formalist project can be completed. As will be seen, overcoming these difficulties often requires making certain assumptions. If these assumptions are unacceptable, then completing the New Formalist research project becomes difficult.

Finally, this exercise will test the veracity of New Formalism's premises. As visions or promises of the future which orient our understanding, perspectives such as the New Formalism are rarely tested. However, since New Formalism's premises make certain predictions about patterns which should emerge in empirical results, we can test the veracity of these premises by seeing whether the pattern of outcomes they predict in fact occur in published results. In using New Formalist assumptions to organize the existing knowledge in the field of dispute processing evaluations, I am simultaneously "testing" the predictive power of these assumptions.

For this exercise, I will assume that New Formalism's premises are correct descriptions of the laws of social action. My purpose in this section is not to criticize these premises outright, but to examine the difficulties one encounters if one assumes that these premises are correct and attempts to follow through on their promises. I am also assuming the results reported by impact studies to be "facts." That is, I assume that the outcomes reported are accurate descriptions of the outcomes which "actually" occur. This means, first, that there have been no errors in measuring or reporting the outcomes and, second, that the measurement of outcomes is not subject to the particular perspective or biases of the evaluator. It is assumed that any evaluator who replicates these impact studies using acceptable scientific procedures would obtain the same results. In Section IV below I will once again relax these assumptions.

A. *The Extent of the Existing Data*

In order to organize impact study results in the manner called for by New Formalist assumptions and illustrated in Chart I, I must specify a typology of dispute resolution mechanisms (X_k), a typology of disputes (W_k), and a set of comparable measures (c_k) of program outcomes (Y_k). New Formalist assumptions presume that the correct typologies and measures are already defined by the laws of social action. Unfortunately, the dispute processing field has yet to ascertain these "true" taxonomies and measures. Consequently, evaluations of dispute processing programs must be used not only for measuring outcomes, but also for inferring typologies or for confirming theoretically-hypothesized typologies.

This lack of knowledge regarding proper typologies and measures creates an unfortunate indeterminacy in the proper interpretation of evaluation results. Assuming the principles of New Formalism are true, a more effective outcome indicates one or both of the following. First, a more effective outcome indicates that the mechanism or dispute jurisdiction being evaluated more closely approximates the characteristics of a pure type then those programs which yield less effective results. In this case, the program is effective because it maintains the integrity of the pure process or dispute type. In other words, the effective outcome indicates that in designing the program, the administrator has "happened" to apply the true typology of mechanisms or the true typology of disputes as defined by the, as yet unknown, laws of social action.

Second, a more effective outcome indicates that the correlation of mechanism and dispute type provided by the program approximates more closely an ideal match of mechanism and dispute type than those with less effective results. In this case, the program is effective because the program has applied a mechanism to its appropriate subject; the program conforms to the laws of social action which govern dispute processing.

Therefore, charting these outcomes tests two elements of existing knowledge simultaneously: the accuracy of the taxonomies and the effectiveness of the different correlations they define.[48] While this simultaneity is not desirable from the standpoint of scientific research design, it is unavoidable because in practice it is impossible to separate these effects.

Given that the "true" taxonomies are not known, which available approximations should be used in charting impact study results? There are two possibilities: the best taxonomy currently developed by dispute processing theorists or a compilation of the types actually used by the programs evaluated.

Mechanism Types (X_k)

It would seem that comparison of tested outcomes requires using a typology constructed from the mechanisms and jurisdictions actually tested. Unfortunately, a review of the existing evaluations literature reveals a wide variety of program types. Arbitration, for example, may be court-annexed or independent of the court, may have mandatory participation or be voluntary, may sanction or not sanction parties for refusing to accept the arbitrated award, may or may not have a time limit within which the hearing takes place, and so on. If programs that differ in institutional features such as these are treated as distinct types of mechanisms, then the catalogue of mechanism types quickly multiplies to a large number of types with one entry each.

However, if the premises of the New Formalism are taken seriously, then mechanism categories need not be multiplied in this manner. These premises suggest that dispute processing techniques can be classified into separate and distinct types by identifying the essential characteristics of the program. While individual arbitration programs may vary in some of their institutional features, all arbitration programs should share certain important and essential features. And it is these features which make this type of mechanism well suited to address particular classes of disputes. Therefore, one can utilize a theoretically-derived taxonomy of mechanism types where types are distinguished by important differences in their essential characteristics if the programs reported lend themselves to re-classification within such categories.

48. If I knew and used the "true" taxonomies, then charting the outcomes would only test the optimal correlations between their categories. However, since we do not yet have a verified general theory of these social laws, I must use approximations to the "actual" taxonomies. It is remotely possible that I am in fact using the "true" categories and do not know it. But since I cannot be sure, I must assume that I am using the outcomes reported by actual impact studies to test both the accuracy of the taxonomy and the efficiency of the correlation simultaneously.

In the introduction to their casebook on dispute processing, Goldberg, Green and Sander[49] identify four types of mechanisms (adjudication, arbitration, mediation, negotiation) and five "hybrids" (private judging, neutral expert fact finding, mini-trial, ombudsman, summary jury trial) on the basis of seven characteristics (voluntariness of the proceeding, binding nature of the agreement, presence and responsibilities of the third party, degree of formality of the proceeding, nature of the proceeding, and whether the proceeding is public or private). This definition of nine mechanism types (X_k) based on seven essential characteristics (a_k) is reproduced in Table I. While the programs evaluated by impact studies vary widely in design, most are labeled or characterized by the program evaluators as one of these nine mechanism types. Thus, in choosing a taxonomy of mechanisms, the two sources of such a taxonomy (theoretically-defined or practically-defined) appear compatible.

Dispute Types (W_k)

It is more difficult to select a taxonomy of dispute types. One reason for this difficulty is the lack of any concrete proposals for such a taxonomy by theorists in the field. Once again Goldberg, Green and Sander provide the best lead. While they do not propose specific categories of disputes (W_k), they do identify six characteristics for distinguishing disputes by type (b_k):

1. The relationship between the disputants (whether it is ongoing or not).
2. The nature of the dispute (whether it is polycentric, whether it involves a novel legal issue, etc.).
3. The amount at stake.
4. The speed of processing the dispute.
5. The cost of processing the dispute.
6. The power relationship between the parties (whether one disputant has significantly less bargaining strength).[50]

If researchers have been slow in constructing a taxonomy of dispute types, policy makers have been even slower in experimenting with a wide range of theoretically-significant dispute types. A review of existing impact studies reveals that evaluated programs draw their jurisdictional boundaries in two general ways. The most common characteristic for drawing jurisdictional boundaries is the jurisdictional boundary of a court ("criminal cases," "civil cases," or "minor civil cases") usually further restricted by a limit as to the amount at stake. Other programs define their jurisdictions according to the subject under dispute. Some of these subjects are defined using legal categories such as "medical malpractice" while others use non-legal categories such as "neighborhood disputes," "consumer disputes," or "employment disputes." Many evaluations specify categories within the program's broad jurisdic-

49. S. GOLDBERG, E. GREEN, & F. SANDER, *supra* note 6, at 7-10.
50. *Id.* at 10.

tions, but few measure program outcomes separately for each of these subdivisions.

Therefore, there is an unfortunate incompatibility between a theoretically-significant taxonomy of dispute jurisdictions ("dispute types") and the taxonomy of actually-existing jurisdictions. Jurisdictions actually used in evaluated programs are self-defined using only one of Goldberg, Green, and Sander's six dispute characteristics ("amount at stake"), and it is difficult if not impossible for the reviewer to code evaluated programs using their other five characteristics. Since I must depend on actually existing programs as the source of my data, I must use the jurisdictional limits defined by the authorizing rules of the programs to construct my typology of disputes.[51]

Mapping Combinations Tested

Using the single typology of mechanism types and the two typologies of dispute types, I have constructed *two* specifications of Chart I. In Chart II I have coded existing impact studies which define their dispute jurisdiction by court and case value. In Chart III I have coded existing impact studies which define their dispute jurisdiction by the substantive nature of the case. In both charts the type of mechanism is defined using Goldberg, Green, and Sander's nine-fold typology. Charts II and III illustrate those combinations of mechanism type and dispute type that have been tested and "scientifically" measured by existing evaluations. In other words, they illustrate the extent of the data presently available to the field.

These charts demonstrate that existing impact studies do not provide the field with sufficient data to construct a general theory of dispute processing as envisioned by the New Formalist perspective. At the present time, there has not been sufficient experimentation with either mechanism types or dispute types. Only two mechanisms have been the subject of more than a handful of impact studies: mediation and arbitration. Arbitration has been experimented with exclusively in civil cases. The types of cases to which arbitration has been applied have been limited mainly to those defined in terms of one general dispute characteristic: amount at stake (although this single dispute characteristic has been specified at varying amount limits). Mediation has been applied to both civil and criminal cases. In some programs, it has been applied to a single type of substantively-defined case. These studies of mediation and

51. The difficulty of integrating a taxonomy of dispute types based on jurisdictions actually used with a taxonomy based on theoretically-defined case characteristics is a major obstacle in New Formalism's research strategy. The New Formalism suggests that there are essential types of mechanisms and disputes, and that it is possible to know what these essential types are. Evaluations and literature reviews of evaluations are often written as if each new evaluation brings us one step closer to revealing the character of these essential types. But if the definition of jurisdictional limits using valuation, severity, or substantive legal types is an incorrect strategy for specifying the essential types of disputes, then the New Formalist research project is in trouble: for there is no promise that in the future experimental programs will test jurisdictions drawn using theoretically-identified case characteristics.

CHART II
A Mapping of Sources of Evaluations Data

TYPE OF DISPUTE [W]	TYPE OF MECHANISM [X] Adjudication	Arbitration	Mediation	Negotiation	Private Judging	Neutral Expert Fact-Finding	Mini-Trial	Ombudsman	Summary Jury Trial
ALL CIVIL CASES (Unspecified)									Jacoubovitch, 1982 Lambros, 1985
CIVIL CASES WITH CASE VALUES:									
Under $150,000		Lind, 1983							
Under $25,000	Seltzer, 1980	Weller, 1982a							
Under $20,000		Cerino, 1984							
Under $15,000		Hensler, 1981 Hensler, 1983 Rolph, 1984							
Under $10,000		Adler, 1983	Shuart, 1983 Shuart, 1985						
Under $6,000		Weller, 1982a Weller, 1982b							
Under $2,000		Rosenberg, 1961							
Under $1,000		Kritzer, 1983 Bartolini, 1957							
Under $800			McEwen, 1981 McEwen, 1984 Vidmar, 1987						
MINOR CIVIL (Unspecified)			Cook, 1980 Roehl, 1982 Bales, 1980						
MINOR CRIMINAL (Unspecified)			Connor, 1977 Cook, 1980 Roehl, 1982 Felstiner, 1978 Felstiner, 1980 Felstiner, 1982 Snyder, 1978 Davis, 1982						

CHART III
A Mapping of Sources of Evaluations Data

TYPE OF DISPUTE [W]	TYPE OF MECHANISM [X]								
	Adjudication	Arbitration	Mediation	Negotiation	Private Judging	Neutral Expert Fact-Finding	Mini-Trial	Ombudsman	Summary Jury Trial
Consumer				Ross, 1975 Ross, 1978		Whitford, 1974		Hanning, 1977	
Education			Singer, 1985						
Employment			Wolf, 1985						
Family			Pearson, 1981 Pearson, 1982 Pearson, 1984 Maddi, 1977 Bahr, 1981 Merry, 1985						
Medical Malpractice		Heintz, 1977							
Bodily Injury				Ross, 1970 Ross, 1975 Ross, 1978					

arbitration provide the best hope for using empirical data to make general distinctions between dispute types on the basis of dispute characteristics. There is insufficient data regarding the other seven mechanism types to draw general distinctions.

B. *Measuring Outcome: Problems of Validity and Comparability*

While Charts II and III illustrate the combinations of dispute and mechanism type for which impact studies exist, they do not actually report the results of these studies. In order to construct a general theory of dispute processing, one must report the outcomes determined by impact studies in a manner which permits cross-comparison of results. Only by measuring the effectiveness of each outcome and comparing it with the outcomes of other studies can one discern patterns of effectiveness and ineffectiveness across different combinations of mechanism and dispute type.

The New Formalism defines increased effectiveness of dispute processing as the ultimate outcome desired from experimental programs. New Formalism's archetypical general theory (summarized in Chart I) presumes that this outcome can be measured directly (as Y_k). If this can be done, then patterns of effectiveness across different combinations of mechanism and dispute type can be observed.

Unfortunately, effectiveness cannot be measured directly. In fact, it is difficult to imagine what an "effective" outcome would look like, much less how it could be measured. In practice, evaluators must always operationalize this ultimate outcome as a number of more specific outcomes of interest. A review of the existing evaluations literature shows some agreement on seven outcomes of interest. An effective dispute processing program will *minimize the cost* of processing disputes, *minimize the time* it takes to process a dispute, *maximize the permanence* of the resolution obtained, provide a dispute resolution process which is more *fair*, provide greater *party satisfaction* in the process, process disputes in a more *equitable* manner, and will insure that dispute processing and the resolutions it produces contribute to *the strengthening of community*.[52] These outcomes of interest may be thought of as the "general characteristics of outcomes" expressed as "c_k" in Chart I. These general characteristics constitute the ultimate outcome "effective system operation."[53]

While the operationalization of program effectiveness (Y_k) as seven outcomes (c_k) of interest gets us closer to a practical measure of effectiveness, it does not guarantee that different impact studies will use the same measures. Does this invalidate any cross-comparison of results?

The comparability of outcomes raises a number of issues. First, are

52. For a more complete discussion of these outcomes, see Bush, *supra* note 26, and Merry, *supra* note 10.

53. The presumption is that the counterfactual—the existing system of dispute processing institutions—does not minimize cost, speed of processing, permanence of resolution, fairness, equity, or strength of community because it is not designed to process each type of dispute using the type of mechanism most ideally suited to address it.

the various impact studies being compared testing the same outcomes of interest? Second, does the research design of each evaluation insure equal validity of results? Third, are the outcomes assessed using measures which are either the same or comparable? The three major components of impact analysis—program theory, research design, and quantitative measures of assessment—are each designed to address these three issues within a particular program evaluation. In constructing a review of various program results, one must address these same three issues as they apply to the cross-comparison of impact studies.

The Program Theory

In order to insure comparability, the various evaluations must be examined to insure that they share common or compatible program theories. I have demonstrated that program theories include a problem, a treatment (the program), an ultimate outcome (effectiveness) which is not measured, and various outcomes of interest (the objectives) which are measured. The New Formalist program for knowledge does not require that all problems, treatments, or outcomes be the same; it does require that all problems, treatments, or outcomes be subject to classification using a consistent typology of problems, treatments, and outcomes. I have established such a consistent set of typologies in the discussion above. The typology of problems is the typology of disputes (W_k); the typology of treatments is the typology of disputes processing mechanisms (X_k); and the typology of outcomes is the various measures of program effectiveness (Y_k).

Research Design

The degree to which one can place stock in the validity of particular program results depends on the validity of the procedures followed in executing the program and in collecting the data. The issue here is not whether each program uses the same set of procedures, but whether the procedures followed are equally valid. Different procedures can yield equally valid results. Further, differences in the validity of results are not necessarily barriers to the comparability of results. While variations in validity across results adds to the uncertainty of the overall pattern in effectiveness, it does not prevent the comparison of individual outcomes. Consequently, this problem is similar to the problem of specifying the types of mechanisms and the types of disputes: it adds to the uncertainty of overall results, but it does not bar one from constructing some provisional findings.

Quantified Measures

Given the specification of seven outcomes of interest, evaluation results should be compared using these outcomes. Ideally, each impact study would assess all seven outcomes of interest using a standardized quantitative measure for each outcome. The seven standardized measures for each outcome of interest would then be combined into a single measure of the program's overall effectiveness.

The operationalization of "effectiveness" into outcomes of interest coupled with the small number of typical data sources available to an evaluator produces the appearance that these seven objectives of interest can themselves be measured directly. For example, it would seem a rather straightforward exercise to measure the time savings of using a more appropriate dispute processing mechanism. Since almost all programs record the date of case filing and the date a case is resolved, average case disposition time would appear to be a relatively easy measure to obtain.[54]

In fact, it is more difficult then it appears to obtain measures of these seven outcomes which are directly comparable. Each outcome of interest is mixed with a host of other determinative forces to constitute program results. In evaluating a particular experiment, a method such as impact analysis is needed to discern each outcome of interest from other aspects of program results. A review of existing evaluations shows a variety of measures used for each outcome of interest. This suggests that there are no absolute measures of time savings, cost savings, fairness, and others, just as there are no absolute measures of effectiveness. Consequently, measures of the seven outcomes of interest are indirect and must make implicit or explicit comparisons with a counterfactual. Hence, the measures reported by impact studies are not absolute assessments of program success; rather, each impact study compares the degree to which its treatment group achieves an outcome of interest as compared to its own control group.

However, this need not be a problem in comparing results. The New Formalist perspective assumes that each of these outcomes is determined by the same underlying laws of social behavior. Therefore, an overview of various independent measures should demonstrate an overall pattern of outcomes which reveals their common determination by the same laws of social action. In fact, the variety of different measures of outcome used by the various impact studies should provide a more convincing confirmation of these underlying laws. Webb, Campbell, Schwartz and Sechrest write:

> Once a proposition has been confirmed by two or more independent measurement processes, the uncertainty of its interpretation is greatly reduced. The most persuasive evidence comes through a triangulation of measurement processes. If a proposition can survive the onslaught of a series of imperfect measures, with all their irrelevant error, confidence should be placed in it.[55]

In short, while the variety of measures produced by different studies

54. This accounts, perhaps, for the failure of many impact studies to explicitly identify their counterfactual. If an evaluator believes that he is measuring his objective of interest directly, then he feels no need to contrast this measure with a standard for comparison.

55. E. Webb, D. Campbell, R. Schwartz & L. Sechrest, Unobtrusive Measures: Normative Research in Social Science 4 (1973).

CHART IV
Specification of a Theory of Dispute Processing
as Defined by the New Formalist Perspective

	Type of Mechanism						
Type of Dispute	X_1	X_2	X_3	X_4	X_5	X_6	$X_7 \ldots X_k$
W_1	Y_1	Y_2	Y_3	Y_4	Y_5	Y_6	$Y_7 \ldots Y_k$
W_2	Y_8	Y_9	Y_{10}	Y_{11}	Y_{12}	Y_{13}	$Y_{14} \ldots Y_m$
W_3	Y_{15}	Y_{16}	Y_{17}	Y_{18}	Y_{19}	Y_{20}	$Y_{21} \ldots Y_n$
W_4	Y_{22}	Y_{23}	Y_{24}	Y_{25}	Y_{26}	Y_{27}	$Y_{28} \ldots Y_o$
W_5	Y_{29}	Y_{30}	Y_{31}	Y_{32}	Y_{33}	Y_{34}	$Y_{35} \ldots Y_p$
W_6	Y_{36}	Y_{37}	Y_{38}	Y_{39}	Y_{40}	Y_{41}	$Y_{42} \ldots Y_q$
W_7	Y_{43}	Y_{44}	Y_{45}	Y_{46}	Y_{47}	Y_{48}	$Y_{49} \ldots Y_r$
	:	:	:	:	:	:	: :
W_k	Y_a	Y_b	Y_c	Y_d	Y_e	Y_f	$Y_g \ldots Y_z$

Where:

X_k = Type of Mechanism = adjudication, arbitration, mediation, negotiation, private judging, neutral expert fact-finding, minitrial, ombudsman, and summary jury trial.

W_k = Type of Dispute = civil cases under $150,000, civil cases under $50,000, civil cases under $25,000, etc., *or* consumer disputes, education disputes, employment disputes, etc.

Y_k = Type of Outcome = more effective vis-a-vis counterfactual, less effective vis-a-vis counterfactual.

a_k = Mechanism Characteristics = voluntariness, bindingness, third party type, degree of formality, nature of proceeding, nature of outcome, private or public proceeding.

b_k = Dispute Characteristics = undefined.

c_k = Outcome Characteristics = time, cost, party satisfaction, equity, fairness, permanence, community.

CHART V
Effectiveness of Outcome Measures From Evaluations of Family Mediation Programs

EFFECTIVENESS OF OUTCOME [Y]		MEDIATION	
Outcome Characteristic	Measure of Effectiveness Characteristic	More Effective Vis-à-Vis Counterfactual	Less Effective Vis-à-Vis Counterfactual
Time	Average Disposition Time		
Cost	Average Cost per Case for the Court System	Pearson, 1981	
Cost	Average Cost per Case for the Disputants	Bahr, 1981	Pearson, 1982
Time/Cost	Court Backlog	Merry, 1985	Maddi, 1977
Party Satisfaction	Disputant and/or Counsel Satisfaction with Outcome	Pearson, 1984 Bahr, 1981	
Party Satisfaction	Disputant and/or Counsel Satisfaction with Process	Merry, 1985 Pearson, 1981, 1982, 1984	
Equity	Equity of Access Across Disputant Characteristics		Pearson, 1981
Equity	Equality of Outcome Across Disputant Characteristics	Pearson, 1981	
Fairness	Disputants and/or Counsel Perceive Program to be a Fairer Process	Merry, 1985 Pearson, 1984 Bahr, 1981	
Permanence	Longer Lasting Resolution	Merry, 1985 Pearson, 1982, 1984	
Community	Strengthens Community		

does not allow one to compare fine differences in the degree to which effectiveness is achieved, it does permit one to stand back and compare crude patterns in these reported outcomes. A rough standardization across studies can be achieved by determining in each case whether or not the application of the treatment improved the outcome of interest as compared to the counterfactual case. Reducing outcome measures to "yes or no" answers facilitates a search for patterns in outcomes. The one drawback to this approach is that it does not permit the aggregation of outcome-of-interest measures into a single measure of overall program effectiveness.

C. *Mapping Outcomes*

In attempting to organize evaluation results in the form called for by a New Formalist theory of dispute processing, I have had to accept a number of assumptions. I have accepted:

1. The three propositions which constitute the New Formalist perspective.
2. The premises of impact analysis.
3. That the essential types of dispute processing mechanisms (X_k) are the eight identified by Goldberg, Green, and Sander.
4. That the essential types of disputes (W_k) include, correspond to, or fall within (but are not necessarily exhausted by), the jurisdictional limits used by existing programs.
5. That the general characteristics of system effectiveness (c_k) assessed by existing evaluations can be summarized as cost, time, permanency, fairness, party satisfaction, equity, community.
6. That different statistical measures of the same outcome of interest can be standardized by expressing each outcome as either "improvement over its counterfactual" or "no improvement over its counterfactual."[56]

Chart IV illustrates how these assumptions give specification to the general theory of dispute processing provided in Chart I.

If these six assumptions are acceptable, then the outcomes of published impact studies can be compared by coding them onto Chart IV. Unfortunately, actually producing such a chart is difficult given the fact that the effectiveness of each program involves seven or more measures. Therefore, I have taken two steps to make my presentation of these results more manageable. First, I have only coded outcome measures for arbitration and mediation because Charts II and III show that these are the only mechanism types which have a sufficient number of data points (individual outcome measures from individual programs) to manifest any pattern of outcomes. Second, in coding these results I have eliminated differentiation of evaluations by dispute type. These two steps

56. We should also keep in mind that: (1) our categorization of types of mechanisms and types of disputes may be slightly off; and (2) the validity of various outcomes vary because the validity of the research designs used vary.

allow me to present a manageable summary of empirical measures of outcomes in Chart V.

While I cannot actually present a version of Chart IV fully coded with the outcome measures from all evaluated mediation and arbitration programs, Charts II, III, and V provide the reader with the raw materials she needs to construct such a chart herself. To construct a fully coded version of Chart IV or one of its cells, use Charts II and III to identify the evaluations that have actually tested a given combination of mechanism and dispute type. Then use Chart V to identify the measures taken by each evaluation identified.

For purposes of illustration, I will present a coding of measures for a single combination of mechanism and dispute type (a single cell in Chart III): evaluation results of programs which have applied mediation to family disputes. These evaluations of family mediation are compared in Chart VI.

With the help of Chart VI, we can use the empirical results from evaluations of family mediation to test several of the New Formalism's key assumptions. If New Formalist assumptions are correct, then it would be expected that Chart VI would demonstrate certain patterns in outcomes.

First and foremost, New Formalist assumptions predict that several programs with the same or similar mechanism and jurisdiction features should yield the same results. However, Chart VI demonstrates that this expectation is not substantiated by impact studies of family mediation. In Chart VI, we see that programs with the same general mechanism and the same general jurisdiction yield opposite results. Bahr,[57] Merry & Rocheleau[58] find a reduction in costs vis-a-vis their counterfactual while Pearson & Thoennes[59] and Maddi[60] find an increase in costs vis-a-vis their counterfactual.

Second, New Formalist assumptions predict that a given program should yield consistent results across the seven outcomes of interest. Contrary to these expectations, Chart VI demonstrates differences across measures for a given program. Pearson & Thoennes[61] find a less efficient cost vis-a-vis their counterfactual but more efficient party satisfaction vis-a-vis their counterfactual. Similar inconsistencies can be found by comparing results from impact studies evaluating other combinations of mechanism and jurisdiction type.

---

57. Bahr, *Mediation is the Answer*, 3 FAM. ADVOC. 32 (1981).

58. S. MERRY & A. ROCHELEAU, MEDIATION IN FAMILIES: A STUDY OF THE CHILDREN'S HEARINGS PROJECT (1985).

59. Pearson & Thoennes, *Mediation and Divorce: The Benefits Outweigh the Costs*, 4 FAM. ADVOC. 26 (1982).

60. Maddi, *The Effect of Conciliation Court Proceedings on Petitions for Dissolution of Marriage*, 13 J. FAM. L. 767 (1977).

61. Pearson & Thoennes, *supra* note 59.

CHART VI

Effectiveness of Outcome Measures For Arbitration and Mediation Programs

EFFECTIVENESS OF OUTCOME [Y]		ARBITRATION		MEDIATION	
Outcome Characteristic	Measure of Effectiveness Characteristic	More Effective Vis-à-Vis Counterfactual	Less Effective Vis-à-Vis Counterfactual	More Effective Vis-à-Vis Counterfactual	Less Effective Vis-à-Vis Counterfactual
Time	Average Disposition Time	Adler, 1982 Bartolini, 1957 Kritzer, 1983 Lind, 1983 Rolph, 1984 Weller, 1982	Weller, 1982	Cook, 1980 Wolf, 1985 Roehl, 1982	
Cost	Average Cost per Case for the Court System	Bartolini, 1957 Rolph, 1984	Kritzer, 1983	Fearson, 1981 Wolf, 1985	Connor, 1977 Cook, 1980 Felstiner, 1980 Felstiner, 1982
Cost	Average Cost per Case for the Disputants	Barolini, 1957 Hensler, 1981 Weller, 1982		Bahr, 1981 Shuart, 1983	Pearson, 1982 Wolf, 1985
Time/Cost	Court Backlog	Lind, 1983 Rolph, 1984 Rosenberg, 1961	Hensler, 1981 Weller, 1982	Merry, 1985 Shuart, 1983	Cook, 1980 Conner, 1977 Maddi, 1977 Roehl, 1982 Snyder, 1978
Party Satisfaction	Disputant and/or Counsel Satisfaction with outcome	Bartolini, 1957 Weller, 1980 Cerino, 1984 Lind, 1983		Bahr, 1981 Connor, 1977 Pearson, 1984 Roehl, 1982 Vidmar, 1987 Wolf, 1985	
Party Satisfaction	Disputant and/or Counsel Satisfaction with Process	Alder, 1983 Bartolini, 1957 Weller, 1982 Lind, 1983	Weller, 1982	McEwen, 1981, 1984 Merry, 1985 Pearson, 1981,1982,1984 Roehl, 1982 Wolf, 1985	Davis, 1982

CHART VI - continued

EFFECTIVENESS OF OUTCOME [Y]		ARBITRATION		MEDICATION	
Outcome Characteristic	Measure of Effectiveness Characteristic	More Effective Vis-à-Vis Counterfactual	Less Effective Vis-à-Vis Counterfactual	More Effective Vis-à-Vis Counterfactual	Less Effective Vis-à-Vis Counterfactual
Equity	Equality of Access Across Disputant Characteristics	Adler, 1983 Hensler, 1981			Pearson, 1981
Equity	Equality of Outcome Across Disputant Characteristics	Cerino, 1984	Adler, 1983 Rosenberg, 1961 Hensler, 1981 Weller, 1982	Pearson, 1981	Cook, 1980 Davis, 1982 Felstiner, 1980 Wolf, 1985
Fairness	Disputants and/or Counsel Perceive Program to be a Fairer Process	Adler, 1983 Cerino, 1984 Weller, 1982 Hensler, 1981 Weller, 1982		McEwen, 1981, 1984 Merry, 1985 Pearson, 1984 Bahr, 1981 Roehl, 1982	Wolf, 1985
Permanence	Longer Lasting Resolution or Lower Recidivism			Cook, 1980 Davis, 1982 McEwen, 1981, 1984 Merry, 1985 Pearson, 1982, 1984 Roehl, 1982 Snyder, 1978	Conner, 1977
Community	Strengthens Community				Roehl, 1982

D. *Conclusions*

Because New Formalist assumptions present themselves as descriptions of reality, we often fail to recognize that these assumptions are just that: assumptions. Further, because these assumptions call for an empirical research strategy, we often fail to recognize that *the assumptions themselves* are rarely subjected to this empirical testing.

While the inconsistency of results manifested Chart V, together with similar inconsistencies identifiable through Chart VI, do not definitively disprove the assumptions of the New Formalism,[62] such discrepancies between the pattern of results anticipated by New Formalist assumptions and the pattern of results actually found in existing impact studies highlights the importance of questioning and testing New Formalism's assumptions. We should make these claims explicit and examine their veracity before we allow them to chart our reform projects for the future.

IV. New Formalism's Blind Spots: We Do Not Think What We Know

I have argued that evaluators use the New Formalist perspective to frame their experience of particular programs and to relate the significance of these experiences to their readers. In the preceding section, I used this perspective to frame a review and synthesis of various evaluation results. In so doing, I accepted without question the truthfulness of New Formalism's assumptions. In this section, I will demonstrate that framing our experience with this perspective narrows our field of vision and blinds us to the significance of certain experiences and insights which fall outside its boundaries. In so doing, I will call into question the usefulness and the truthfulness of New Formalism's assumptions.

A. *How New Formalism Structures Program Experience*

When an evaluator or her readers adopt a New Formalist perspective, their experience of a program is framed in a particular way. This framing conforms that experience to the principle elements of impact analysis: program theory, research design, and quantified measures.

Program Theory

The dispute processing field brings together groups with different agendas: court administrators are concerned with the time and cost involved in processing cases and with the court backlogs that delays create; liberal legal practitioners are concerned that traditional adjudica-

62. They can be explained in a manner which does not challenge the perspective. From within a New Formalist perspective, inconsistencies such as those in Chart VI result because (1) existing impact studies yield invalid results because they follow poor research design; (2) an insufficient number of studies exist to discern between small but significant variations in mechanism or jurisdiction type; or (3) the measures are not properly comparable.

tion constitutes an institutional barrier to the provision of equal access to justice; professionals in mediation, arbitration, and other non-traditional dispute resolution skills seek to advance their technique, and their practice of that technique, as social reform; and other groups as well.

While the New Formalist perspective is not the source of these various interests, it does provide a framework which appears to bring these interests and strategies of action together under a common project. Because the New Formalism relies on a systems logic, it does not have to specify the values or interests which are achieved by securing a proper fit between mechanism type and dispute type. By assuming that "effective" correlations are defined by laws of social behavior, the New Formalism implicitly assumes that all values and interests are maximized when a match established between a mechanism and a dispute corresponds to the social laws governing dispute processing.[63] It can thus present itself as a framework which combines various interests without privileging any one, and presents the advancement of these interests as an objective and scientific project of enlightened reason.

However, the seven outcomes of interest which dispute processing experiments are designed to achieve are stated so abstractly that *no specific content* can be given to these terms. Rather, a variety of meanings can be read into each of these phrases and these interpretations can be changed from time to time and from place to place. Each phrase has been used to refer to a number of *different benefits* assumed to accrue to a number of *different actors* through a number of *different intervening mechanisms* or subobjectives.

Consider as an example, one of the most common goals used to rationalize dispute resolution innovations: minimized cost. The assertion that, for example, a court-annexed arbitration program can 'improve efficiency' has been interpreted to mean:

1. That the court system will experience a decreased average cost for processing filed cases due to an earlier settlement of disputes.
2. That the court system will experience a decreased average cost for processing filed cases due to the use of a less costly alternative preceding (due, perhaps, to the use of volunteer arbitrators rather than high-salaried judges).
3. That the court system will experience a decreased average cost for processing filed cases because the court system can process cases remaining in the courts in a faster or less-expensive manner.
4. That the court system will save money because arbitration

63. A muted form of New Formalism can be constructed which does not assume that all outcome characteristics are simultaneously maximized. In this form, exemplified by Bush, *supra* note 26, it is acknowledged that some outcomes of interest may be mutually incompatible with other outcomes of interest. However, this muted approach still assumes that "optimum outcomes" are possible. Rather than maximizing all outcome characteristics simultaneously, these outcomes provide the most improvement for the most outcomes possible despite some loss in a few outcomes. Note that even in this case selection of the most "effective" design remains a technical question rather than a question of values.

provides longer-lasting settlements, thereby eliminating the costs of processing future recidivism.
5. That disputants save money directly because arbitration decreases attorney fees or decreases witness fees and other trial costs.
6. That disputants save money indirectly because arbitration renders earlier settlements, thereby reducing the amount of time disputants must miss work to tend to their dispute.

Table II lists these and other advantages, interests, and mechanisms which I found through a cursory review of the literature. The purpose of this table is not to provide an exhaustive enumeration, but rather to demonstrate how quickly such a list proliferates. The reader is invited to identify advantages, interests, and mechanisms not included in Table II as a demonstration that this list is not, and cannot be, exhaustive.

By bringing together a variety of interests under its common framework, the New Formalism does not thereby guarantee that all evaluations conducted within its premises will address each of these interests. It does assume, however, that evaluations which overemphasize the examination of one set of problems can eventually be integrated with evaluations which examine other types of problems. It also assumes that once the right match between mechanism type and dispute type is found, that all interests will be simultaneously achieved. In other words, the New Formalist framework assumes that one set of interests need not be advanced at the expense of others. If one set of interests does suffer, it is due solely to ignorance (insufficient knowledge) or error (insufficient dissemination of what we know). Both can be corrected through expanded experimentation and evaluation.

Unfortunately, the evaluations themselves present evidence that the objectives of dispute processing experiments are neither consensual nor commensurate. All groups in the dispute processing field do not agree on all the objectives advanced and furthermore it is impossible to achieve all the objectives advanced simultaneously. Also, just as the seven characteristics of effective outcomes identified above may not be consensual nor commensurate, so each of these issues may serve as umbrella terms for a variety of non-consensual and contradictory outcomes. For example, Hensler, Lipson and Rolph found that court-annexed arbitration in California reduced case-processing costs to disputants while simultaneously increasing case costs to the state.[64] They also found that arbitration may cost the state more while costing the counties less. Therefore, one cannot make statements such as: "arbitration reduces costs."

Charts II, III and V provide us with a means to test the New Formalist assertion that there is an ideal correlation of types of dispute processing mechanisms to types of disputes. New Formalist assumptions suggest that a given treatment should advance all seven issues simulta-

64. D. Hensler, A. Lipson & E. Rolph, Judicial Arbitration in California: The First Year (1981).

neously. If this assumption is true, then we should find a consistent pattern of outcomes for a given program across the seven outcomes of interest. If, for example, arbitration is ideally suited to processing all civil disputes of valuation less than $10,000.00, then the evaluation testing this type of program should find improvement in cost, time, permanency of resolution, fairness, party satisfaction, equality, and improved community. In other words, the same pattern of "yes" and "no" should appear on a chart like Chart IV. However, a review of Chart VI shows this not to be the case. For almost all measures of effectiveness, experimental outcomes show both positive and negative results vis-a-vis the counterfactual. Inconsistency in outcomes even occurs within a given study.[65]

Research Design

The New Formalist perspective, through its appropriation of impact analysis, assumes that if we are able to construct a good research design for our experimental program and data analysis (before and after treatment data collection, random assignment between treatment and control group, and so on), then we can be certain that the empirical data produced are a valid description or measure of the way things are. Conversely, if we are unable to implement a good research design, then the validity of our data will be questionable.

Unfortunately, given the conditions under which adjudication and the alternatives to adjudication are implemented, a program can rarely meet the rigid demands of good research design. Program implementors have interests other than good research design in implementing programs.[66] And even where program implementors are willing to try their best to incorporate good design features like random assignment of disputes into their experimental program, the pressures and responsibilities of public institutions and the rights of individuals processed through those institutions makes it difficult to maintain the design. Several arbitration programs have attempted random selection, and in both cases, judges had to acquiesce to disputant demands that they have their right to a trial immediately (rather than follow through on their random assignment to an arbitration hearing).[67]

The consequence of the application of these rigid standards for research design to programs which are almost always either unwilling or unable to incorporate these designs is that evaluators and their readers are continually troubled by the validity of their findings. As a result,

65. *See, e.g.*, Weller, Ruhnka & Martin, *Compulsory Civil Arbitration: The Rochester Answer to Court Backlogs*, 20 JUDGES J. 3 (1982) (arbitration); R. COOK, J. ROEHL & D. SHEPPARD, NEIGHBORHOOD JUSTICE CENTERS FIELD TEST—FINAL EVALUATION REPORT (1980) (mediation).

66. *See* FEDERAL JUDICIAL CENTER ADVISORY COMMITTEE ON EXPERIMENTATION IN THE LAW, *supra* note 37.

67. *See* A. LIND & J. SHAPARD, *supra* note 2; M. ROSENBERG, PRETRIAL CONFERENCES AND EFFECTIVE JUSTICE (1964). For an example of similar pressures in experimentation with ombudsman programs, see Gwyn, *Obstacles within the Office of Economic Opportunity to the Evaluation of Experimental Ombudsmen*, 1976 PUB. ADMIN. 177, 185.

when various impact studies produce inconsistent outcomes, New Formalists are predisposed to blame these inconsistencies on the poor validity of their data rather than the usefulness of New Formalist assumptions. This makes poor research design, coupled with the small number of evaluations which have entered the professional literature, an easy scapegoat for all the shortcomings which true believers in New Formalist assumptions find between the empirical data actually accumulated and the expectations promised by the New Formalist perspective.

Quantified Measures

The New Formalist perspective *assumes* that disputes and dispute processing programs are things with essential characteristics. It therefore seeks to explain variations in outcome in terms of variations in the essential characteristics of these mechanisms and dispute types. If it finds variation within essential types or change in these objects over time, it ascribes this change to the current state of empirical evidence rather than to a fault in the assumptions.

When impact analysis is used in the service of New Formalist objectives, further limits are placed on the types of experience which are recognized as valid and legitimate assessments of outcome. Impact analysis requires assessing the extent of the divergence between the outcome of treatment and the counterfactual using a quantified measure. Therefore, non-quantifiable sources of experience are either eliminated or the time, effort, and importance given to their investigation limited.

The field of valid experience is restricted yet again when one considers the extent to which quantifiable data is actually available in the evaluation of dispute processes. Existing dispute processing programs offer limited sources for data which are subject to quantification and statistical manipulation. A review of the literature shows that the quantitative data used in dispute processing evaluations is almost exclusively derived from program records, forms designed by evaluators and filled out by program staff, and interviews with or questionnaires given to parties, lawyers, third party interveners, and program administrators. Consequently, there is a relatively small set of quantitative measures which evaluators tend to depend on in constructing, conducting, and reporting their evaluations, and which their readers tend to draw on in cross-comparing their work.

Unfortunately, while there is some consistency in measures used, there is great difference in how these measures are interpreted. Consider "average case duration" as a measure of the outcome "time saved." Some studies, such as Adler, Hensler and Nelson interpret a decrease in average case duration as a measure of successful time reduction.[68] Other studies, like Lind and Shapard, interpret a decrease in average case time as a measure of successful *cost* reduction.[69] Still other

68. J. Adler, D. Hensler & C. Nelson, Simple Justice: How Litigants Fare in the Pittsburgh Arbitration Program (1983).
69. A. Lind & J. Shapard, *supra* note 2.

studies, such as McEwen and Maiman, interpret an increase in average case duration as an increase in the judge time applied to the case, which in turn is interpreted to be a measure of successful increases in fairness because McEwen and Maiman assume that increased judge time provides a fairer hearing.[70]

In addition to variations in how measures are interpreted, there are also variations in the manner in which these measures are constructed. Even when evaluations are able to agree on the same *theoretically-defined* measure for assessing the same outcome of interest, differences in constraints force them to construct the same measure in different ways. These different ways of constructing the same "measure" often involve different types of data and different assumptions.

Compare, for example, Hensler[71] with Felstiner and Williams.[72] Both evaluations attempt to measure the general outcome "reduced costs." Both attempt to assess this goal using the same theoretically-defined measure: a comparison of the average cost of processing a case in an innovative program with the average cost of processing the case using traditional adjudication. Both find that data regarding this seemingly straightforward measure does not exist. Therefore, both research teams are forced to construct estimates using proxy data and assumptions. In each case, selecting different proxy data or going the other way on a required assumption can mean the difference between finding the program successful or unsuccessful in achieving its goal of cost savings

These differences make it highly questionable whether the findings of these two studies can be compared. This is true even if the studies are using the same measure and even if they both come up with a quantitative estimate of the "same" measure.

B. *The Return of the Repressed*

New Formalist assumptions have a powerful impact on the manner in which the evaluations literature is produced and read. Its tendency to narrow one's field of vision in the ways outlined above is powerful as well. Nevertheless, such a framework is not the only perspective which guides our experience. I have argued that the New Formalism is not the exclusive determinant of the questions, structure, strategy, or perspective of any single concrete evaluation. Despite the powerful influence which the New Formalist perspective has over how individual evaluators pattern their observations, program experiences which are not consistent with New Formalist assumptions but whose importance in determining outcomes is self-evident to the evaluator often do work their way into written evaluations. In this section I would like to examine a few of the insights reported in the evaluations literature which are often over-

70. McEwen & Maiman, *Small Claims Mediation in Maine: An Empirical Assessment*, 33 ME. LAW REV. 237 (1981).

71. D. HENSLER, A. LIPSON & E. ROLPH, *supra* note 64.

72. W. FELSTINER & L. WILLIAMS, COMMUNITY MEDIATION IN DORCHESTER, MASSACHUSETTS (1980).

looked in the search for effective correlations between disputes and mechanisms. They are overlooked because they challenge the assumptions of the New Formalist framework.

We might consider the insistent presence of these insights despite the power of New Formalism's assumptions to filter experience as "the return of the repressed." Despite New Formalism's tendency to "repress" these observations because they are not recognized as significant in relation to other observations, the determinative importance of these repressed experiences continues to impress the observer to the point where they "return." That is, they work their way into the text of an evaluation despite the fact that they violate the assumptions which frame and explain what the evaluation reports as significant.

Institutional Features

Within the New Formalist framework, certain general institutional features of programs are viewed as essential defining characteristics which distinguish which type of mechanism the program is. For example, the acceptance of a hearing with a third-party decision maker is an institutional feature which coupled with other essential characteristics defines a program as an example of arbitration. In contrast, other institutional features which are more specific to particular programs, are viewed as inessential characteristics which distinguish one arbitration program from another.

The New Formalism allows for such variations within essential types of mechanisms. While these features may affect the degree to which a given program "fits" with a particular type of dispute, the occurrence of a non-essential, "accidental" feature should not change the "fit." Otherwise, New Formalist assumptions would be violated.

Nevertheless, a review of existing evaluations finds an argument for the importance of specific process features to be one of the most recurring conclusions across studies. For example, Lind and Shapard find in their study of court-annexed arbitration that the success of the program in reducing processing time is a direct consequence of a court rule demanding that the arbitration hearing take place within a specific period of time:

> It appears that court-annexed arbitration can serve as an effective deadline for case preparation, substituting for trial not as a forum for case resolution, but as a stimulus to settlement. Questionnaires from counsel whose cases were terminated prior to arbitration support the view that the arbitration rule expedited settlement and show general endorsement of the arbitration rules.[73]

Such a rule, however, is never cited as an essential defining feature of arbitration.

If the success of an arbitration program in reducing the duration of

---

73. A. LIND & J. SHAPARD, *supra* note 2, at xiii.

a case vis-a-vis the regular adjudication process is dependent on certain institutional features which may not be present in every arbitration program, then specifying this feature must be a necessary qualification whenever the results of arbitration are discussed or compared. This directly challenges the New Formalist assumption that all institutionalizations of a given type of mechanism share essential properties which make them ideally suited to deal with particular types of disputes.

In order to preserve this assumption, New Formalism must assume that arbitration with a time limit provision and arbitration without a time limit provision are entirely different types of mechanisms. However, if we further divide Sander's eight types into a larger number of mechanism types on the basis of differences in their institutional features, then the number of permutations quickly threatens the parsimoniousness of the model. Consequently, following this path to save New Formalism's assumptions has consequences which call these assumptions into doubt.

Even more damaging to the assumptions of New Formalism are the conclusions by some studies that the importance of specific institutional features changes from program to program, place to place, and time to time. For example, Shuart, Smith and Polanet, in their study of mediation in Wayne County, Michigan, conclude that:

> A settlement mechanism must be designed to meet the needs and to utilize the resources of the jurisdiction developing a procedure . . . . The experience in Wayne County highlights those procedural aspects which should be considered in planning a settlement device: the administration and financing of the procedure, the type of settlement technique employed, the composition and selection of the valuation body, the timing of the hearing, the selection of appropriate cases, the format of the hearing, and the inclusion of the penalty. *The importance may not be in the way each of these aspects is ultimately handled, but rather that each is addressed.*[74]

This conclusion directly contradicts the most fundamental assumptions of New Formalism that specific mechanisms, disputes, and outcomes hold essential characteristics across time and space.

Dispute Characteristics

The New Formalism assumes that disputes are things that are present in every society. It therefore begins with the assumption that they exist, and goes on to question the most effective way to process them. The selection of a mechanism is a purely technical matter. Dispute processing mechanisms are tools which are more or less useful in dealing with the inevitable problem of disputes.

However, consider the conclusions emerging from some evaluations regarding the chara teristics of disputants who use the treatments tested and who win or lose in the outcomes determined by the treat-

74. Shuart, Smith & Polanet, *Settling Cases in Detroit: An Examination of Wayne County's "Mediation" Program*, 8 JUST. SYS. J. 307, 323 (1983) (emphasis added).

ments. These questions can be legitimately raised from within the New Formalist perspective. Optimal outcomes should include maximization of fairness and equality as outcomes. But addressing these questions from within New Formalism brings results that have implications more for the question of *where disputes come from* and *why they end up in experimental programs* than *how the programs treat these disputes*.

For example, Cook, Roehl and Sheppard found that there was an over-representation of low income persons in the cases processed by Neighborhood Justice Centers:

> The information gathered on disputants indicates, with the exception of individuals representing businesses, that the people who use the NJCs are generally representative of the community in terms of ethnicity. However, it appears that the NJCs attract primarily low income residents. This may be partially a reflection . . . of the characteristics of the litigants in the court system. It may also be the case that middle-and upper-income people tend to hire third party (attorneys, counselors, etc.) to resolve their disputes. On the other hand, this finding indicates that the NJCs are providing dispute resolution services to poor people, some of whom may have had less access to the justice system in the past. But if, as originally intended, the Centers are to serve a cross-section of their communities, they will have to attract more higher income citizens.[75]

Note that the lesson the evaluation draws from its quantitative results is that the goal of equality (equal access to justice) is being achieved. Further, the rationale for why low-income people are over represented in the NJCs is that this reflects who uses the court system. The interesting question here, however, is not whether the operation of the system increases access, but *for whom* is access increased and *for what* purposes. This raises the question of where disputes come from, and why one type of disputant tends to use, or be channeled, into public dispute processing agencies while other types are not. The results suggest that where disputes are taken differs by economic class. However, since the New Formalist perspective assumes that dispute types are formally the same everywhere (regardless of changes in the class of the disputants), that they occur naturally in all societies, and that they are individual objects, this perspective cannot explain why economic class is an important indicator of the dispute process utilized.

V. Conclusion

For the past two decades, the New Formalist perspective has given the dispute processing field a set of comforting explanations as to what the field is, what it should do, and how its work can contribute to a better future. However, while New Formalist assumptions have inspired useful scientific research and improved social policy making, the results of the research so inspired have not substantiated the intellectual coher-

75. R. Cook, J. Roehl & D. Sheppard, *supra* note 65, at 107.

ence which these assumptions promise and predict. New Formalist assumptions have also blinded researchers to the significance of certain data which they have collected in their research. There is a good deal of data which has impressed these researchers as significant experiences but which has not been analyzed because it violates New Formalist definitions of significance. Most importantly, New Formalist premises have blinded the dispute processing field to the political dimensions of dispute processing and dispute processing research. Therefore, as we assess the current state of empirical knowledge in the dispute processing field, it is important that we also assess the framework we are using to evaluate this knowledge.

Name Index